THE COMPLETE GUIDE TO CHOOSING

Landscape Plants

THE COMPLETE GUIDE TO CHOOSING
LANDSCAPE PLANTS

Series Concept: Robert J. Dolezal
Encyclopedia Concept: Barbara K. Dolezal
Managing Editor: Victoria Cebalo Irwin
Encyclopedia Author: Robert J. Dolezal
Photography Editor: John M. Rickard
Designer: Jerry Simon
Layout Artist: Barbara K. Dolezal
Photoshop Artist: Gerald A. Bates
Horticulturist: Peggy Henry
Photo Stylist: Peggy Henry
Proofreader: Jim Gebbie/Gebbie & Associates
Index: Dolezal & Associates

President/CEO: Michael Eleftheriou
Vice President/Editorial: Linda Ball
Vice President/Retail Sales & Marketing: Kevin Haas

Home Improvement/*Gardening*
Executive Editor: Bryan Trandem
Editorial Director: Jerri Farris
Creative Director: Tim Himsel

Created by: Dolezal & Associates,
in partnership with Creative Publishing international, Inc.

PHOTOGRAPHY & ILLUSTRATION

Principal Photography

All photographs by **John M. Rickard,** except as noted below.

Other Photography:

Gerald A. Bates: pgs. 38 (top), 40 (top), 44 (mid), 98 (bot), 99 (bot), 112 (top), 179 (mid), 187 (top), 189 (top), 190 (top), 191 (top), 198 (top), 205 (top), 211 (mid), 213 (top), 227 (top), 249 (mid) • **Carol Bruce:** pg. 184 (top) • **Tim Butler:** pgs. 3 (mid), 25 (top), 30 (top), 36 (bot), 37 (top), 40 (bot), 42 (top & bot), 43 (mid), 47 (top & mid), 48 (top & mid), 56 (bot), 57 (bot), 60 (top), 62 (mid), 96 (mid), 160 (top), 169 (top), 173, 174 (top), 181 (top), 232, 237 (mid), 285 (bot, steps 1-3) • **Kyle Chesser:** pgs. 294 (top L), 300 (top R & bot R) • **Alan Copeland:** pgs. 28 (mid), 37 (bot), 38 (mid), 44 (top), 49 (bot), 163, 164, 165, 167 (top & bot), 172 (bot), 188 (bot), 295 (steps 2-4 & 6) • **CORBIS:** © **Michael Boys,** pg. 151 (mid); © **Nigel J. Dennis,** pg. 128 (bot); ©**Hal Horwitz,** pgs. 126 (bot), 134 (mid); © **Eric and David Hosking,** pg. 270 (mid); © **Staffan Widstrand,** pg. 128 (mid) • **Cab Covay:** pg. 29 (top) • **CREATIVE PUBLISHING INTERNATIONAL:** pgs. 38 (bot), 68 (bot), 83, 100 (top) • **Doug Dealey:** pgs. 42 (mid), 85, 93 (top), 180 (mid) • **Joan de Grey:** pgs. 40 (mid), 88 (mid), 107 (mid), 123 (top), 206 (bot), 254 (top), 260 (top) • **Robert J. Dolezal:** pgs. i, 8, 124 (mid) • **ANDREW B. GAGG'S PHOTO FLORA:** pg. 159 (top) • **David Goldberg:** pgs. 110 (top), 150 (top), 237 (top), 278 (bot), 279 (mid) • **Saxon Holt:** pgs. 25 (bot), 27 (bot), 34 (top), 115 (mid), 119 (bot), 127 (mid), 213 (bot) • **HORTICULTURAL PHOTOGRAPHY:** ©**Judy White,** pgs. 95 (bot), 198 (bot), 199 (bot) • **Donna Krischan:** pgs. 72 (mid & bot), 73 (top), 76 (mid), 93 (mid), 103 (bot), 106 (bot), 111 (mid), 117 (bot), 124 (top), 127 (bot), 132 (top & mid), 136 (bot), 137 (bot), 145 (mid), 148 (mid), 150 (mid), 156 (top), 162 (top), 226 (bot), 227 (bot), 270 (top) • **FRANK LANE PICTURE AGENCY:** ©**Michael Rose,** pg. 243 (mid) • **NETHERLAND FLOWER BULB INFORMATION CENTER:** pgs. 117 (top), 121 • **NOAA: National Estuarine Research Reserve/Joan Muller:** pg. 216 (mid) • **Charles Nucci:** pgs. 167 (mid), 175 (bot) • **Jerry Pavia:** pgs. 34 (bot), 41 (top), 45 (top), 49 (mid), 51 (top), 52 (mid), 53 (top & mid), 54 (mid), 55, 56 (top), 58 (top), 60 (mid), 61(top & bot), 62 (mid), 64, 66 (mid), 67 (bot), 69 (mid), 71 (top), 72 (top), 74 (bot), 79 (bot), 80 (mid & bot), 82 (top), 84 (top), 88 (bot), 89 (bot), 90 (mid & bot), 92 (top & bot), 93 (bot), 94 (mid), 96 (bot), 98 (mid), 99 (mid), 101 (top & bot), 102 (mid), 104 (mid), 106 (top & mid), 107 (top), 108 (top), 109 (top & mid), 110 (mid), 111 (top), 113 (top & bot), 114 (top & bot), 119 (mid), 120 (top), 123 (bot), 124 (bot), 125 (mid), 126 (mid), 130 (bot), 134 (top), 137 (top), 140 (top & bot), 141 (top & bot), 146 (bot), 148 (top), 149 (mid & bot), 155, 156 (mid), 157 (bot), 158 (top & mid), 160 (mid & bot), 161 (top & bot), 162 (mid & bot), 168 (bot), 171 (mid), 184 (bot), 188 (top), 189 (mid), 192 (top & bot), 196 (mid & bot), 201 (top & bot), 202, 203, 210 (mid & bot), 211 (bot), 212 (top & mid), 214 (top), 215 (top), 217 (bot), 220 (mid & bot), 224, 225 (bot), 227 (mid), 228, 229 (mid), 230, 234, 236, 237 (bot), 239 (top), 240 (top), 242 (bot), 244 (mid & bot), 245 (top & mid), 248 (top & bot), 252 (mid), 257 (mid), 260 (bot), 261 (mid), 262 (top & mid), 264 (top), 266 (mid), 268, 269 (top), 277, 278 (top & mid) • **Pam Peirce:** pgs. 53 (bot), 75 (top), 76 (top), 251 (mid) • **Charles Slay:** pgs. 27 (mid), 31 (bot), 35 (mid), 36 (top), 43 (top), 63 (bot), 70 (top & mid), 77 (top), 80 (top), 89 (mid), 91 (bot), 95 (top & mid), 101 (mid), 111 (bot), 146 (mid), 147 (top), 181 (bot), 190 (mid), 191 (bot), 214 (bot), 222 (mid), 225 (mid), 226 (top), 239 (bot) • **Tina Smith:** pg. 199 (top) • **Brian Taylor:** pg. 183 (top) • **Yvonne Williams:** pgs. 31 (top), 34 (mid), 71 (bot), 89 (top), 194 (bot)

Cartography and Illustration:

HILDEBRAND DESIGN/Ron Hildebrand

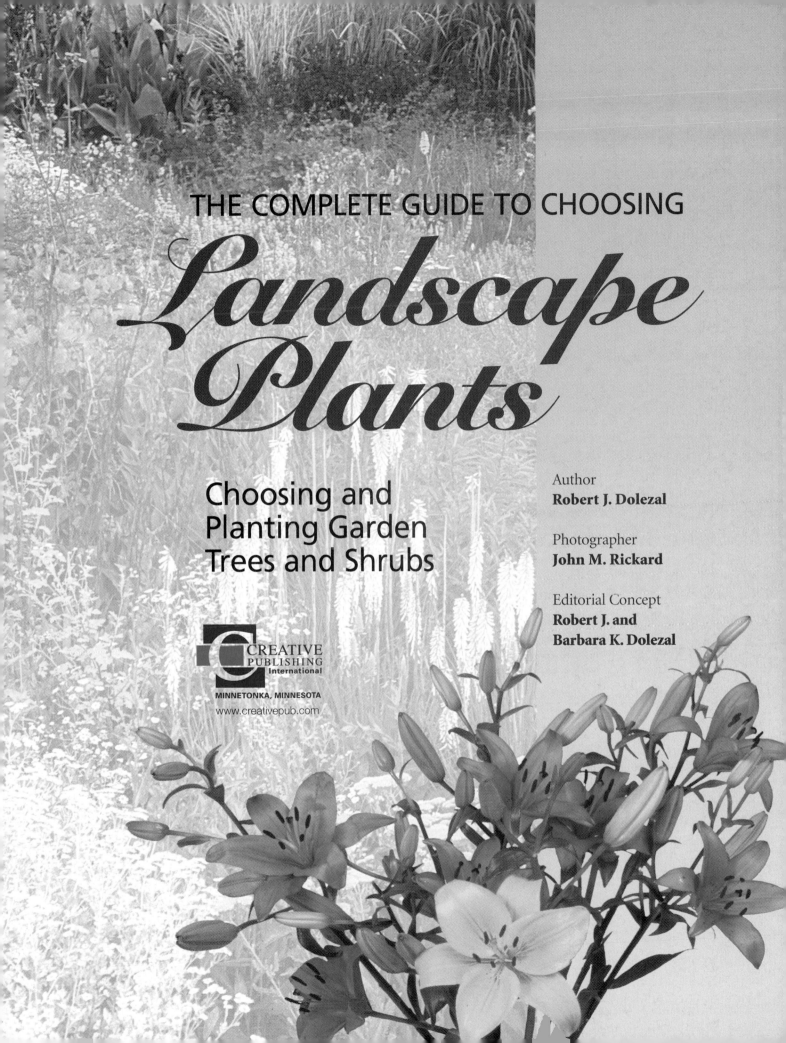

THE COMPLETE GUIDE TO CHOOSING

Landscape Plants

Choosing and Planting Garden Trees and Shrubs

Author
Robert J. Dolezal

Photographer
John M. Rickard

Editorial Concept
**Robert J. and
Barbara K. Dolezal**

CREATIVE PUBLISHING International

MINNETONKA, MINNESOTA
www.creativepub.com

THE COMPLETE GUIDE TO CHOOSING *Landscape Plants*

CONTENTS

INTRODUCTION

THE WORLD OF LANDSCAPE PLANTS is filled with beautiful species. There are flowering annuals, perennials, and bulbs that will gladden your heart and soul during every season of the year.

In springtime, blossoms can be found clothing the branches of trees and shrubs. Summer abounds with beauty, whether in the trumpets of a gladiolus or gorgeous pom-poms of a dahlia. For those to whom brilliant foliage color in autumn marks the requiem of summer, many choices fill the bill. If you seek the sculptural charm found in rosy red branches filled with swelling

buds and silhouetted against winter's snows, there are cold-tolerant, deciduous shrubs with striking character.

Turning the leaves of this book will lead you into a delectable world of plant communities, where many species share common ground and benefit one another. You'll see a garden showcase filled to the brim with hundreds of popular landscape plants, learn their needs, and select them for planting in your home's garden.

And you'll also find all the practical information you need to landscape your yard, from tips on testing your soil and planting many   species to ways of watering, fertilizing, and pruning them. You'll learn how to keep them healthy and ways to defend them from pests.

The *Complete Guide to Choosing Landscape Plants* will give you all of the information that you need, in a form that is easily accessible and understood. You'll find that this book, with its clear, colorful photographs and concise, accurate text, is a valuable companion for every aspect of landscape gardening.

Choosing Landscape Plants

Selecting Landscape Plants Starts by Knowing Your Purpose, Site, Soil, and Climate

AMONG THE GOALS OF EVERY LANDSCAPE GARDENER is to beautify their home with flowering plants, trees, and shrubs, fill their beds and borders with greenery and foliage, and add enjoyment to their daily use of the the yard beyond their walls.

Achieving these objectives can be a source of pride and accomplishment, but sometimes they also are a challenge. Plants may struggle to survive or suffer infestation by insect and animal pests, while our aesthetic efforts may fall short of the mark.

The information, landscape plants, and techniques found in the pages that follow will help you achieve all of your gardening goals, creating beautiful and flowing plant communities that thrive in your yard and climate. Using the detailed information about each plant and information gained about your site, you'll be able to select those plants that complement one another visually, as well as those that grow well together.

Matching plants to your garden has always been somewhat of a mystery, a task for experts. For the first time, you'll learn the secrets behind garden professionals' selection technique. You'll be asked three simple questions that will help you choose the right plants for your landscape, each and every time. First, you'll be asked to reflect on the purpose of your plantings and to decide the function that each species will play in your garden. Next, you'll identify the plants that can play that role in your specific setting. Then, you'll look at your site and classify it in terms of its climate, its soil, and its exposure to sunlight.

Armed with the answers to these questions, you'll be ready to select the beautiful plants that will thrive in your landscape.

The glory of summer includes Papaver orientale, *or Oriental poppy. You'll be able to choose from hundreds of colorful annual and perennial flowers as you select plants for your beds and borders using the information found in the encyclopedia of this book. You'll find six sections containing the most popular categories of landscape plants.*

PURPOSE AND FUNCTION

When you first consider plantings in your landscape, give some thought to the goals you have in mind. If you are looking to add bright seasonal color to a walkway, your choices will differ from those of someone seeking to add a tree for shade in summer. Depending on your goals, very different landscapes can result.

Landscape designers divide generalized goals into two categories: purpose and function. Purpose speaks to the results that you want your plantings to achieve, while function addresses the ways in which your effort accomplishes those goals. Take a few minutes to look at your home, its existing landscape—or potential landscapes, if you are in a newly built home—and areas that could be improved. If you are starting from scratch, try to divide your yard into functional areas such as play areas that will receive heavy traffic, screens to divide your yard from that of your neighbors or enhance your view, formal beds and borders that might contain roses or seasonal flowers, and areas of turfgrass lawn or ground covers. If you are modifying an existing landscape, gauge how well the space previously was divided. Note all existing and planned paths, natural boundaries defined by terrain or features, and fencelines, driveways, and hedges.

Next, work within each outdoor room defined by its common needs. If one of your areas will be used for leisure and entertaining, consider whether to add seating, a deck, or a barbeque as well as new shrubs and trees. Will use of your yard be seasonal or year-round? Will it be seen at night as well as day? How much time do you have to devote to the care of your garden? The answers to each question will help guide your decisions and plantings.

These mental exercises will lead your thinking to the plants that you'll need to execute your plan. How will you shade an area from hot summer sun? What plantings will conserve water? As you identify your purpose in each area, the way your plants need to function also will be defined.

(Above) Welcome spring as well as your visitors by making your entry vibrant with color. Keep the area bright as days grow warmer by replacing flowers as they fade with newly blooming species planted in similar pots.

(Right) Climbing roses drape a rustic splitrail fence, filling it with profuse, colorful clusters of blossoms. Try to imagine how different either landscape would look if the flowers were missing.

ROLE OF PLANTS IN THE LANDSCAPE

Plants can play many different roles in your landscape, depending on your needs. A low and trailing species, used for a ground cover on a sloped bank in one yard, might be planted into a wall to cloak it with green foliage in another setting. Vines may drape across an overhead shade structure, climb a trellis, or create a woven arbor. In a similar manner, trees and shrubs can become screens, hedges, a roadside planting, or a vertical accent, all depending on your needs and your site.

It's common for landscapes to include plants of many different heights. Including vertical changes in your plantings adds interest that depends on plant forms rather than flower or foliage color for its effect, and lasts throughout the year. Tall shrubs and trees often are leggy—they have sparse foliage at their base. Planting low-growing shrubs and seasonal flowers around them cloaks their trunks and completes your beds.

If color is your goal, choose plants with different bloom times. Bulbs often bloom early, sometimes before trees sprout their leaves. Flowering cherries take the torch from the bulbs, passing it to azaleas and rhododendrons. By late spring, many annual and perennial flowers begin their display—you get the idea. Plant successions to keep the flowers coming.

When you know the role the plant will play, it's much easier to make an appropriate selection from the many species available.

An allée is a roadside planting that defines a lane with trees. Here, rows of flowering cherry greet passersby with their dainty, pink, cloudlike blossoms.

(Above) A birdbath hidden in mounds of flowers makes all the difference in this vignette. The stonework adds interest and contrast to the brightly colored flowers.

(Left) Turfgrass lawns often benefit from flower borders. Here, the mounding form of bedding plants helps ease the transition from grass to shrub border and trees.

UNDERSTANDING YOUR SITE

Every landscape grows within the context of its site. Some considerations of which you should be aware are the climate—and microclimate—of your surrounding area; the sun exposure and any structures or trees that may shade the site; its terrain; the soil's composition, texture, fertility, and acid-alkaline balance; how water runs from the property and in which direction; and any structures, plantings, or improvements that already have been made.

Take a matter-of-fact look at the conditions in your yard—it's a step that is vital to your plants' long-term health. Measure your site and decide on the area or areas that you want to develop, change, or improve. A few minutes spent now making sketches and notes will save time, effort, and resources later.

Check the grade or slope of the land. Look for signs of erosion or standing water. Sometimes, boggy conditions are revealed by plants that struggle to stay healthy. If water pools on the ground after a rainstorm, consider installing drains to safely carry it away. By contrast, if water rushes downhill, terracing the site to slow its passage could help your plants and neighbors.

Determine the location of all the physical elements on the site such as structures, fences, paths, patios, and large rocks. Note any big trees—they're a treasure that may take decades to replace by new trees you plant.

With these things in mind, note the position of the sun, the direction shadows fall, the areas they cover, and whether the land slopes toward the light or away from it. We'll look at the effect of sun and climate in detail later, but it's good to make yourself aware of the site's general plan [see Garden Seasons and Climates, pg. 6]. If the site is subject to wind, note its prevailing direction and whether it affects the trees and shrubs on the site. Winds can dry delicate foliage and cause it to become windburned or drop prematurely.

Next, examine your soil. Is it loose, sandy loam rich with decayed plant matter? Is it free of rocks and debris? Does the blade of a shovel penetrate easily into it, and is water applied to it easily absorbed? If your soil meets all these conditions, you are lucky, and you soon will be able to proceed to selecting your plants and installing them. If instead, as is more likely the case, your soil lacks some of these desirable traits, now is the time for a soil test that will prescribe amendments or fertilizers that it may need [see Soil Testing, this pg.].

Most soils are mixtures of three mineral components of varied sizes—sand, silt, and clay—and humus, as well as decayed plant matter.

(Above) Electronic pH meters measure the acid-alkaline balance of soil.

(Below) A hillside site requires care in both the choice of trees and in their installation. Here, terraces were cut for each tree.

SOIL TESTING

Soil tests are important to perform when you install a new landscape or notice plants that previously were growing well starting to struggle.

The mix of mineral particles and organic matter a soil contains will govern its texture and drainage. The amount of nutrients it contains will control its fertility. The amount of nutrients available to the plants is affected by its acid-alkaline balance.

Performing a soil test is easy. You can use a home test kit or electronic test meters or have it performed by a chemist with the help of a soil laboratory [see Soil Testing, pg. 283].

All three methods are economical and reliable ways to ensure a healthy garden filled with thriving plants.

The best soils have equal parts of all four components. When soil contains too much clay, it has few beneficial microorganisms, tends to absorb water too slowly, is prone to fast runoff, and contains minimal carbon dioxide and oxygen. Soils with too much sand dry too quickly and hold few nutrients. It's possible to correct both of these conditions by adding compost or humus. This organic material retains both air and water, holds nutrients that your plants need, and is a binder between the clay particles, which clump together, or the sand, which is too loose. Additional information about soil texture and testing is found later in the book [see Soil Analysis, pg. 282].

The one item of your landscape that you're least likely to change is your site. Short of moving to a new home, you should plan to accept and enhance the site that you've inherited. So what can be done?

Improve your soil a bit at a time, starting in those areas that are protected from wind and receive good sun. Remember that landscape trees and large shrubs do best in native soil; for them, it's a matter of choosing the right species for your soil rather than changing it to fit a plant. For your other plantings, consider adding raised beds or masonry planters that you can fill with rich loam.

Install or expand existing paths to make maintenance easier and use more enjoyable. Paths should be wide enough for a garden cart, have a slip-free surface, and be durable. For low-access areas, use natural materials such as bark, cinder, pea gravel, or wood chips

If you live in an area that is arid or which experiences periods with little rain, consider installing an in-ground irrigation system on an automatic timer to reduce the time needed to water your plants [see Installing In-Ground Irrigation, pg. 295].

Structures like arbors, gazebos, pergolas, shade covers, or trellises can all add to your landscape's ambience, as can features such as fountains, garden pools, and watercourses.

If you plan to visit your garden during the evening hours, add low-voltage lighting fixtures for your paths and spotlights to showcase trees and shrubs.

The time spent analyzing your site and installing these so-called hardscape elements will be repaid many times over when they are surrounded by your new flowers, shrubs, and trees. Next, we'll look at plants' needs, including their hardiness to frost and the effect of climate and seasons on your garden.

(Below, top) Low-voltage light fixtures illuminate paths after dark and showcase plants.

(Below, middle) A small-space, urban garden is an inviting spot to install lattice panels and overhead shade structures.

(Bottom) Carefully considered plantings make this straight path more interesting. It's a good example of an unusual solution to a common situation.

GARDEN SEASONS AND CLIMATES

Plants are adaptable, sometimes to a wide range of conditions. The coldest tolerable temperature is one limit on their ability to grow in your garden. There are plants that will survive temperatures to −40°F (−40°C) or lower, while others will succumb if the thermometer drops below 50°F (10°C). Another limitation is the amount of sunlight they need for their chlorophyll to convert elemental salts into sugars.

Plants may tolerate conditions from full sun to full shade, depending on the species, or sometimes a range of light conditions. A third element is the acid-alkaline balance of their soil. The chemical makeup of soil helps some compounds to dissolve, and it speeds up or slows down the organic chemical processes in the roots and foliage of plants. Most plants prefer soils that are slightly acidic; some prefer very acidic or alkaline conditions. This is measured by their point on a scale ranging from 0 to 14, very acidic to very alkaline.

In the pages that follow, these plant preferences can help you identify communities that thrive in similar conditions, allowing you to match your site and climate to the plants that are best able to live in your yard. To use this information, it's necessary to understand your site in terms of three characteristics: *hardiness* (hardy, semi-hardy, tender), *exposure* (full sun, filtered sun, open shade, partial shade, full shade), and *pH tolerance* (very acidic, acidic, neutral, alkaline, very alkaline). Let's look at them one at a time.

Plant hardiness. Exposure to cold is a consequence of the revolution of the earth around the sun, the tilt of its axis, and our location on the earth's surface [see diagram, below]. In general, the farther one gets from the equator, the larger the area a beam of sunlight must heat—more simply said, the poles are colder than the equator, which receives the most sunlight. Summer and winter occur when rays of the sun are more or less direct. First the northern, then the southern hemisphere receives greater amounts of sunlight, divided by solstices when the tropic of Cancer, then the tropic of Capricorn line up directly with the sun. These effects cause the seasons—spring, summer, autumn, and winter.

(Right) Some plants, including this pine, are very cold tolerant. Others wilt at the first touch of frost. Knowing the hardiness for the plants in your garden will help you maintain their health and care for them effectively.

(Below) The seasons are caused by variations in sunlight falling on the earth. This results from the slight tilt of the planet, which remains constant in amount and direction as the earth circles the sun in the course of a year. As the earth orbits, it progressively exposes northern then southern regions to the sun's direct rays.

While many global and local conditions affect the climate, the lowest temperatures generally are felt in the highest latitudes, during winter. Plants that tolerate winter low temperatures down to 50°F (10°C) are termed tropicals. Those that can survive to 32°F (0°C) are subtropical or tender. Still others, able to tolerate temperatures in the subfreezing range, say to 20°F (−7°C), are called semi-hardy. And finally, the plants that tolerate deep freezing conditions below 20°F (−7°C) are hardy. Each species has its own hardiness range.

Summer in the Northern Hemisphere

Vernal Equinox

Sun

Arctic Circle

Tropic of Cancer

Equator

Autumnal Equinox

Tropic of Capricorn

Summer in the Southern Hemisphere

The minimum temperature at which the species will survive determines both its classification and its geographic distribution in its native range. For gardeners, it also defines the range of temperatures it can tolerate in a landscape. Sometimes, plant species can tolerate deep cold but fail to thrive in too-warm temperatures. For this reason, plant hardiness is expressed as a range of plant hardiness zones.

The U.S. Department of Agriculture (USDA) has mapped those zones by grouping locations around the world with similar average low winter temperatures into color-coded maps [see Plant Hardiness, this pg.].

Exposure. All green plants need sunlight to fuel their conversion of nutrients and carbon dioxide into sugars within their cells. Depending on their leaf structure and adaptation to climate, they may do best in full sun, full shade, or exposure somewhere between the two. It's little coincidence that shade-tolerant plants frequently have broad, flat leaves able to garner every bit of sunlight from their environment, or that cacti and succulents of arid, sunny locations frequently have very small leaves, drop them when a drought begins, or lack visible leaves altogether.

Most frequently, plants have a "sweet spot" of ideal sunlight conditions that they tolerate but also can survive in conditions with slightly more or less light almost equally well. This is expressed as a range such as full sun to partial shade.

pH tolerance. The chemical reactions within each plant and in its soil surroundings are governed by the temperature, moisture, and the acid-alkaline condition of the water in which nutrients are dissolved. Most plants exist in conditions with a pH of 5.0 (very acid) to 8.0 (very alkaline), although a few exceptions may be found of plants that tolerate environments with more extreme pH measurements. Alkaline-tolerant plants will fail in too-acidic soils, as will acid-tolerant plants in too-alkaline conditions. A cultural condition known as chlorosis sometimes occurs when soils become too alkaline, preventing uptake of iron, manganese, and zinc essential to plant health.

> **PLANT HARDINESS**
> A good approximation of a species' plant hardiness can be obtained by referring to the plant listings found in this book [see Encyclopedia of Landscape Plants, pgs. 23–279].
>
> To determine your plant hardiness zone, consult the zone maps [see USDA Plant Hardiness, pgs. 10–11]. Find your location on the map, then match its zone color to the legend.
>
> Keep in mind that the zones were created by measuring the average of low temperatures over several years and that unusually cold winters may cause your zone to be lower than shown. Local conditions—elevation, bodies of water, terrain differences, and wind exposure—also can affect your hardiness zone.

(Above) Arid deserts are host to many cacti, succulents, and other unique trees adapted by nature to conserve water and tolerate alkaline soils.

(Right) Tropical weather—hot and humid—frequently is the companion of shade. Plants in such locales develop broad leaves to gather light and thrive in the acidic soils from decaying plant matter littering the forest floor.

To prepare for selecting the landscape plants that will thrive in your garden, you will need information about these three characteristics for your site. Remember that your plant hardiness zone may be affected by so-called microclimate conditions that are caused by elevation, terrain, prevailing winds, or other local conditions. Seek the aid of a qualified garden expert, such as the staff of your garden center, nursery, the USDA's or a local university's extension, or your Agriculture Canada field office to assist you in determining your site's climate and soil conditions.

Landscape Plant Communities

WHAT MAKES A SHADE-DAPPLED WOODLAND GLADE different than a sunny meadow or an arid rock garden differ from a formal French *par terre* filled with carefully clipped shrubs? The answers lie in the plants each contains—communities of species with similar requirements for climate, light, and soil.

In nature, plant communities develop spontaneously. The native species of a region are adapted to its climate, regardless of how much they may differ from plants found in other climates. Species that thrive and prosper in one soil often are found together, rarely associated with plants that grow best in a different soil. Their need for light also is similar, symbiotic, and complementary.

What's new in the pages that follow are lists that divide common landscape plants into groups that grow in similar climate, light, and soil conditions.

For best results, you'll need to perform a soil test [see Soil Testing, pg. 283]. It will determine your soil's pH, or where it ranks on the acid-alkaline scale, from 0 for extreme acidity to 14 for extreme alkalinity. A soil that measures 7.0 is neutral—equally alkaline and acidic. Home test kits and electronic meters both measure pH. Next, look up your plant hardiness zone on the maps [see USDA Plant Hardiness, pg. 10–11]. Finally, check the amount of light that falls on your planting site, dividing it into one of the three primary categories: full or filtered sun, open or partial shade, or full shade. Then you'll be ready to choose your plants.

Let our plant community lists be a source of inspiration and your starting point as you select landscape plants to beautify your home and enhance the appeal of your yard.

Selecting Plants for a Landscape Is Quicker and Easier Than Ever Before, Using Our Plant Community Lists

A mossy glade with conifers, showy azaleas, and other acid-soil, moisture-loving plants, such as this garden in Seattle, Washington, is an example of a complete plant community. From soil to sky, each species interacts and assists the others that surround it. In the pages that follow, you'll find plant communities you can grow in your landscape.

USDA Plant Hardiness
North America

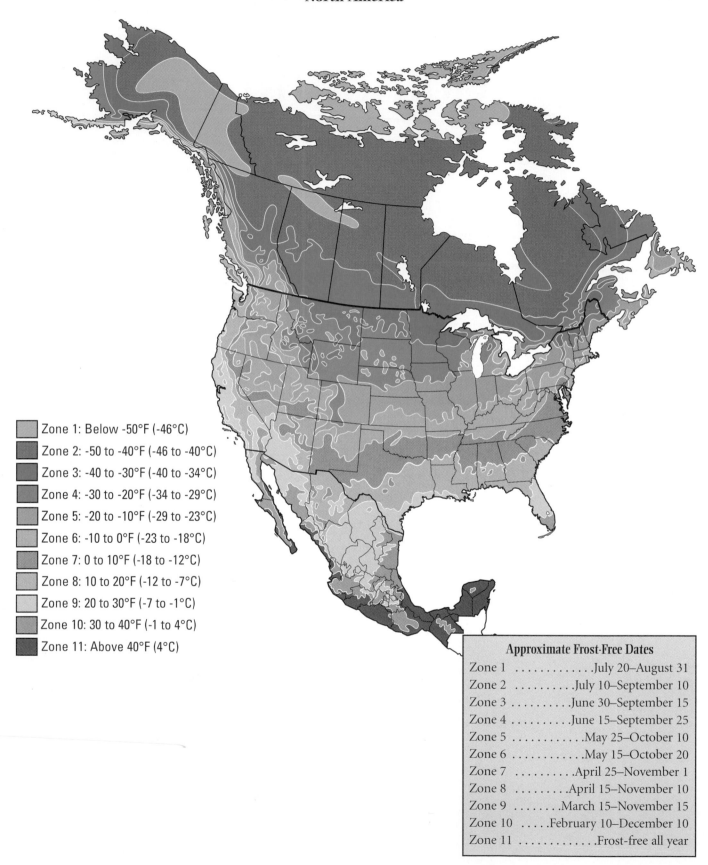

Zone 1: Below -50°F (-46°C)

Zone 2: -50 to -40°F (-46 to -40°C)

Zone 3: -40 to -30°F (-40 to -34°C)

Zone 4: -30 to -20°F (-34 to -29°C)

Zone 5: -20 to -10°F (-29 to -23°C)

Zone 6: -10 to 0°F (-23 to -18°C)

Zone 7: 0 to 10°F (-18 to -12°C)

Zone 8: 10 to 20°F (-12 to -7°C)

Zone 9: 20 to 30°F (-7 to -1°C)

Zone 10: 30 to 40°F (-1 to 4°C)

Zone 11: Above 40°F (4°C)

Approximate Frost-Free Dates	
Zone 1	July 20–August 31
Zone 2	July 10–September 10
Zone 3	June 30–September 15
Zone 4	June 15–September 25
Zone 5	May 25–October 10
Zone 6	May 15–October 20
Zone 7	April 25–November 1
Zone 8	April 15–November 10
Zone 9	March 15–November 15
Zone 10	February 10–December 10
Zone 11	Frost-free all year

USDA **Plant Hardiness**
Australia

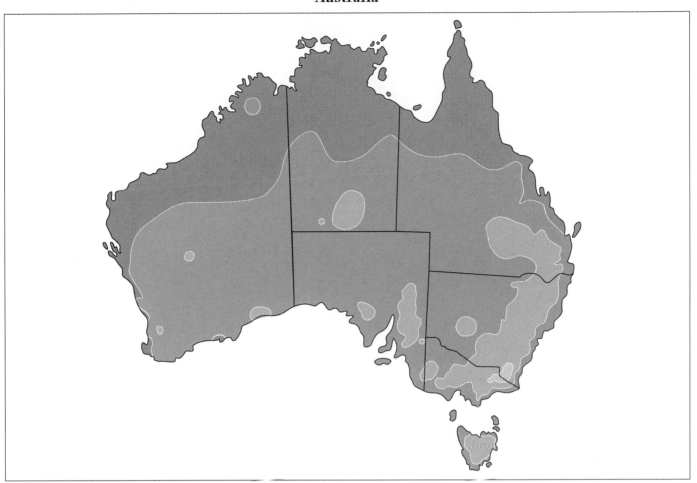

South Africa

New Zealand

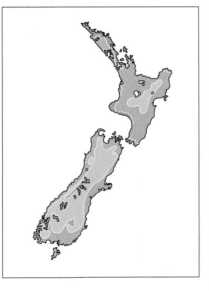

Europe

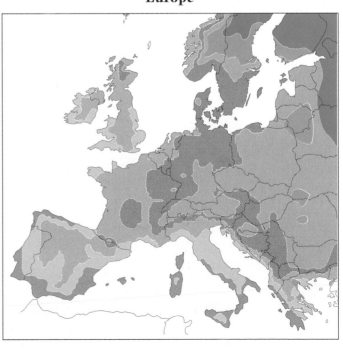

Landscape Plant Communities

Landscape Plant Community Concept and Contents Copyright ©2002, Dolezal & Associates. All Rights Reserved.

Plant Community	Full to Filtered Sun	Open to Partial Shade	Full Shade
Acidic Soils 5.0–6.0 pH Zones 1–3 **Perennial Plants**	*Acorus calamus, Acorus gramineus, Alchemilla sp., Alternanthera ficoidea, Anchusa sp., Aruncus dioicus, Asparagus setaceus, Aster sp., Astilbe sp., Caltha palustris, Chelone lyonii, Chrysanthemum sp., Cimicifuga sp., Convolvulus sabatius, Coreopsis sp., Cosmos atrosanguineus, Dionaea muscipula, Dodecatheon sp., Drosera sp., Echinops sp., Eustoma grandiflorum, Filipendula rubra, Fragaria sp., Gaillardia sp., Gaura lindheimeri, Gazania sp., Geranium maculatum, Geranium sanguineum, Gerbera jamesonii, Gunnera manicata, Hedychium sp., Helianthus sp., Hydrocotyle verticillata, Iberis sempervirens, Lewisia cotyledon, Limonium platyphyllum, Lupinus sp., Lysichiton americanum, Lysimachia nummularia, Lythrum virgatum, Macleaya sp., Melampodium leucanthum, Mentha sp., Menyanthes trifoliata, Mimulus cardinalis, Myosotis scorpioides, Nolana paradoxa, Oenanthe javanica, Paeonia hyb., Peltandra virginica, Penstemon sp., Phormium sp., Physostegia virginiana, Primula sp., Rehmannia elata, Rodgersia sp., Sagittaria latifolia, Salvia sp., Sarracenia sp., Saururus cernuus, Scrophularia auriculata, Stokesia laevis, Thalictrum sp., Tolmiea menziesii, Tradescantia virginiana, Trollius sp., Typha minima, Vinca sp., Viola sp.*	*Aconitum napellus, Alternanthera ficoidea, Anchusa sp., Aruncus dioicus, Astilbe sp., Bergenia cordifolia, Caltha palustris, Chrysanthemum sp., Cimicifuga sp., Convolvulus sabatius, Dodecatheon sp., Filipendula rubra, Geranium maculatum, Gerbera jamesonii, Gunnera manicata, Helianthus sp., Helleborus orientalis, Heuchera sanguinea, Hosta sp., Houttuynia cordata, Hydrocotyle verticillata, Lewisia cotyledon, Ligularia sp., Lysichiton americanum, Lysimachia nummularia, Meconopsis cambrica, Mentha sp., Menyanthes trifoliata, Mimulus cardinalis, Myosotis scorpioides, Oenanthe javanica, ORCHIDACEAE, Paeonia hyb., Peltandra virginica, Penstemon sp., Physostegia virginiana, Primula sp., Rehmannia elata, Rodgersia sp., Saururus cernuus, Scrophularia auriculata, Thalictrum sp., Tolmiea menziesii, Tradescantia virginiana, Trollius sp., Typha minima, Vinca sp., Viola sp.*	*Astilbe sp., Bergenia cordifolia, Helleborus orientalis, Heuchera sanguinea, Hosta sp., Houttuynia cordata, Hydrocotyle verticillata, Ligularia sp., Meconopsis cambrica, Mentha sp., Myosotis scorpioides, ORCHIDACEAE, Pulmonaria sp., Rodgersia sp., Saururus cernuus, Vinca sp.*
Grasses and Ground Covers	*Andropogon gerardii, Carex sp., Cerastium tomentosum, Juniperus horizontalis, Mentha sp., Scirpus cyperinus*	*Ajuga reptans, Carex sp., Mentha sp., Scirpus cyperinus*	*Ajuga reptans, Carex sp.*
Cacti, Ferns, and Shrubs	*Arctostaphylos sp., Berberis sp., Clethra alnifolia, Euonymus sp., Juniperus communis, Pinus mugo var. mugo, Potentilla fruticosa, Rhus sp., Sambucus sp., Viburnum sp.*	*Arctostaphylos sp., Berberis sp., Clethra alnifolia, Dennstaedtia punctilobula, Juniperus communis, Potentilla fruticosa, Rhus sp., Viburnum sp.*	*Clethra alnifolia, Dennstaedtia punctilobula*
Landscape Trees	*Acer sp., Aesculus sp., Amelanchier sp., Betula sp., Carpinus caroliniana, Elaeagnus angustifolia, Gleditsia triacanthos var. inermis, Juniperus sp., Larix sp., Picea sp., Pinus sp., Populus sp., Pseudotsuga menziesii, Quercus sp., Robinia pseudoacacia, Salix sp., Sequoiadendron giganteum, Sorbus aucuparia, Tilia sp.*	*Elaeagnus angustifolia, Pseudotsuga menziesii*	*Carpinus caroliniana*
Acidic Soils 5.0–6.0 pH Zones 4–5 **Perennial Plants**	*Acorus calamus, Alchemilla sp., Anchusa sp., Aruncus dioicus, Aster sp., Astilbe sp., Caltha palustris, Chelone lyonii, Chrysanthemum sp., Cimicifuga sp., Coreopsis sp., Echinops sp., Eustoma grandiflorum, Filipendula rubra, Fragaria sp., Gaillardia sp., Gaura lindheimeri, Geranium sanguineum, Helianthus sp., Iberis sempervirens, Lewisia cotyledon, Limonium platphyllum, Lupinus sp., Lysichiton americanum, Lysimachia nummularia, Lythrum virgatum, Macleaya sp., Melampodium leucanthum, Mentha sp., Menyanthes trifoliata, Myosotis scorpioides, Peltandra virginica, Penstemon sp., Physostegia virginiana, Rodgersia sp., Sagittaria latifolia, Salvia sp., Saururus cernuus, Scrophularia auriculata, Stokesia laevis, Thalictrum sp., Trollius sp., Typha minima, Vinca sp.*	*Aconitum napellus, Anchusa sp., Aruncus dioicus, Astilbe sp., Bergenia cordifolia, Caltha palustris, Chrysanthemum sp., Cimicifuga sp., Filipendula rubra, Helianthus sp., Helleborus orientalis, Heuchera sanguinea, Hosta sp., Lewisia cotyledon, Ligularia sp., Lysichiton americanum, Lysimachia nummularia, Mentha sp., Menyanthes trifoliata, Myosotis scorpioides, ORCHIDACEAE, Peltandra virginica, Penstemon sp., Physostegia virginiana, Rodgersia sp., Saururus cernuus, Scrophularia auriculata, Thalictrum sp., Trollius sp., Typha minima, Vinca sp.*	*Astilbe sp., Bergenia cordifolia, Helleborus orientalis, Heuchera sanguinea, Hosta sp., Ligularia sp., Mentha sp., Myosotis scorpioides, ORCHIDACEAE, Pulmonaria sp., Rodgersia sp., Saururus cernuus, Vinca sp.*
Grasses and Ground Covers	*Andropogon gerardii, Butomus umbellatus, Carex sp., Cerastium tomentosum, Glyceria maxima, Hypericum calycinum, Juniperus horizontalis, Mentha sp., Pennisetum alopecuroides, Phalaris arundinacea, Phlox stolonifera, Phragmites australis, Scirpus cyperinus, Sedum sp., Sisyrinchium sp.*	*Ajuga reptans, Carex sp., Glyceria maxima, Hypericum calycinum, Mentha sp., Pachysandra terminalis, Pennisetum alopecuroides, Phlox stolonifera, Scirpus cyperinus, Sedum sp., Sisyrinchium sp.*	*Ajuga reptans, Carex sp., Pachysandra terminalis, Phlox stolonifera*
Cacti, Ferns, and Shrubs	*Arctostaphylos sp., Aronia arbutifolia, Berberis sp., Calluna vulgaris, Chaenomeles speciosa, Clethra alnifolia, Cotinus coggygria, Echinocereus sp., Erica sp., Euonymus sp., Euphorbia sp., Exochorda racemosa, Fothergilla gardenii, Hydrangea sp., Indigofera sp., Juniperus communis, Kalmia latifolia, Kerria japonica, Ligustrum sp., Lonicera sp., Myrica pensylvanica, Paxistima sp., Pieris japonica, Pinus mugo var. mugo, Potentilla fruticosa, Rhododendron sp., Rhus sp., Sambucus sp., Spiraea × vanhouttei, Viburnum sp., Yucca filamentosa*	*Arctostaphylos sp., Aronia arbutifolia, Berberis sp., Calluna vulgaris, Clethra alnifolia, Dryopteris arguta, Euphorbia sp., Fothergilla gardenii, Hydrangea sp., Juniperus communis, Kalmia latifolia, Kerria japonica, Ligustrum sp., Lonicera sp., Mahonia aquifolium, Myrica pensylvanica, Paxistima sp., Pieris japonica, Polystichum sp., Potentilla fruticosa, Rhododendron sp., Rhus sp., Spiraea × vanhouttei, Viburnum sp.*	*Clethra alnifolia, Dennstaedtia punctilobula, Dryopteris arguta, Kalmia latifolia, Mahonia aquifolium, Polystichum sp., Rhododendron sp.*
Landscape Trees	*Abies concolor, Acer sp., Aesculus sp., Amelanchier sp., Betula sp., Catalpa bignonioides, Cercidiphyllum japonicum, Cercis canadensis, Chamaecyparis sp., Chionanthus virginicus, Cladrastis kentukea, Crataegus sp., Franklinia alatamaha, Ginkgo biloba, Gleditsia triacanthos inermis, Juniperus sp., Laburnum × watereri, Larix sp., Liriodendron tulipifera, [cont. next pg.]*	*Cornus sp., Elaeagnus angustifolia, Fagus sp., Hamamelis virginiana, Magnolia sp., Oxydendrum arboreum, Pseudotsuga menziesii*	*Alnus sp., Carpinus caroliniana*

Plant Community	Full to Filtered Sun	Open to Partial Shade	Full Shade
Acidic Soils 5.0–6.0 pH Zones 4–5 Landscape Trees	*Malus floribunda, Metasequoia glyptostroboides, Michelia doltsopa, Nyssa sylvatica, Parrotia persica, Picea sp., Pinus sp., Platanus × acerifolia, Populus sp., Prunus sp., Pyrus calleryana, Quercus sp., Robinia pseudoacacia, Salix sp., Sassafras albidum, Sequoiadendron giganteum, Sophora japonica, Sorbus aucuparia, Styrax japonicus, Taxodium distichum, Tilia sp., Tsuga canadensis, Ulmus parvifolia*		
Acidic Soils 5.0–6.0 pH Zones 6–7 Perennial Plants	*Acorus calamus, Acorus gramineus, Alchemilla sp., Anchusa sp., Aruncus dioicus, Asparagus setaceus, Aster sp., Astilbe sp., Caltha palustris, Chelone lyonii, Chrysanthemum sp., Cimicifuga sp., Convolvulus sabatius, Coreopsis sp., Cosmos atrosanguineus, Dodecatheon sp., Echinops sp., Eustoma grandiflorum, Filipendula rubra, Fragaria sp., Gaillardia sp., Gaura lindheimeri, Gazania sp., Geranium maculatum, Geranium sanguineum, Gunnera manicata, Helianthus sp., Iberis sempervirens, Lewisia cotyledon, Limonium platyphyllum, Lupinus sp., Lysichiton americanum, Lysimachia nummularia, Lythrum virgatum, Macleaya sp., Melampodium leucanthum, Mentha sp., Menyanthes trifoliata, Mimulus cardinalis, Myosotis scorpioides, Paeonia hyb., Peltandra virginica, Penstemon sp., Phormium sp., Physostegia virginiana, Primula sp., Rehmannia elata, Rodgersia sp., Sagittaria latifolia, Salvia sp., Sarracenia sp., Saururus cernuus, Scrophularia auriculata, Stokesia laevis, Thalictrum sp., Tolmiea menziesii, Tradescantia virginiana, Trollius sp., Typha minima, Vinca sp., Viola sp.*	*Aconitum napellus, Anchusa sp., Aruncus dioicus, Astilbe sp., Bergenia cordifolia, Caltha palustris, Chrysanthemum sp., Cimicifuga sp., Convolvulus sabatius, Dodecatheon sp., Filipendula rubra, Geranium maculatum, Gunnera manicata, Helianthus sp., Helleborus orientalis, Heuchera sanguinea, Hosta sp., Houttuynia cordata, Lewisia cotyledon, Ligularia sp., Lysichiton americanum, Lysimachia nummularia, Meconopsis cambrica, Mentha sp., Menyanthes trifoliata, Mimulus cardinalis, Myosotis scorpioides, ORCHIDACEAE, Paeonia hyb., Peltandra virginica, Penstemon sp., Physostegia virginiana, Primula sp., Rehmannia elata, Rodgersia sp., Saururus cernuus, Scrophularia auriculata, Thalictrum sp., Tolmiea menziesii, Tradescantia virginiana, Trollius sp., Typha minima, Vinca sp., Viola sp.*	*Astilbe sp., Bergenia cordifolia, Helleborus orientalis, Heuchera sanguinea, Hosta sp., Houttuynia cordata, Ligularia sp., Meconopsis cambrica, Mentha sp., Myosotis scorpioides, ORCHIDACEAE, Pulmonaria sp., Rodgersia sp., Saururus cernuus, Vinca sp.*
Grasses and Ground Covers	*Andropogon gerardii, Arundo donax, Butomus umbellatus, Carex sp., Cerastium tomentosum, Glyceria maxima, Hypericum calycinum, Juniperus horizontalis, Mentha sp., Pennisetum alopecuroides, Phalaris arundinacea, Phlox stolonifera, Phragmites australis, Scirpus cyperinus, Sedum sp., Sisyrinchium sp.*	*Ajuga reptans, Arundo donax, Carex sp., Glyceria maxima, Hypericum calycinum, Mentha sp., Pachysandra terminalis, Pennisetum alopecuroides, Phlox stolonifera, Scirpus cyperinus, Sedum sp., Sisyrinchium sp.*	*Ajuga reptans, Carex sp., Pachysandra terminalis, Phlox stolonifera*
Cacti, Ferns, and Shrubs	*Abelia × grandiflora, Arctostaphylos sp., Aronia arbutifolia, Aucuba japonica, Berberis sp., Buxus sp., Calluna vulgaris, Chaenomeles speciosa, Clethra alnifolia, Corylopsis sp., Cotinus coggygria, Cyathea cooperi, Deutzia sp., Echinocereus sp., Enkianthus campanulatus, Erica sp., Euonymus sp., Euphorbia sp., Exochorda racemosa, Fothergilla gardenii, Fuchsia × hybrida, Gymnocalycium saglione, Hydrangea sp., Indigofera sp., Juniperus communis, Kalmia latifolia, Kerria japonica, Kolkwitzia amabilis, Leucothoe sp., Ligustrum sp., Lonicera sp., Myrica pensylvanica, Paxistima sp., Photinia sp., Pieris japonica, Pinus mugo var. mugo, Potentilla fruticosa, Pyracantha sp., Rhododendron sp., Rhus sp., Sambucus sp., Spiraea × vanhouttei, Viburnum sp., Xylosma congestum, Yucca filamentosa*	*Arctostaphylos sp., Aronia arbutifolia, Aucuba japonica, Berberis sp., Buxus sp., Calluna vulgaris, Clethra alnifolia, Corylopsis sp., Cyrtomium falcatum, Dennstaedtia punctilobula, Deutzia sp., Dryopteris arguta, Enkianthus campanulatus, Euphorbia sp., Fothergilla gardenii, Hydrangea sp., Juniperus communis, Kalmia latifolia, Kerria japonica, Kolkwitzia amabilis, Leucothoe sp., Ligustrum sp., Lonicera sp., Mahonia aquifolium, Myrica pensylvanica, Paxistima sp., Pieris japonica, Polystichum sp., Potentilla fruticosa, Rhododendron sp., Rhus sp., Spiraea × vanhouttei, Viburnum sp., Xylosma congestum*	*Clethra alnifolia, Cyrtomium falcatum, Dennstaedtia punctilobula, Dryopteris arguta, Kalmia latifolia, Mahonia aquifolium, Polystichum sp., Rhododendron sp.*
Landscape Trees	*Abies concolor, Acer sp., Alnus sp., Amelanchier sp., Betula sp., Carpinus caroliniana, Catalpa bignonioides, Cedrus sp., Celtis sp., Chamaecyparis sp., Chilopsis linearis, Chionanthus virginicus, Citrus sp., Cornus sp., Corylus sp., Crataegus sp., Cycas sp., Elaeagnus angustifolia, Fagus sp., Franklinia alatamaha, Ginkgo biloba, Gleditsia triacanthos inermis, Grevillea sp., Hamamelis virginiana, Ilex sp., Juniperus sp., Larix sp., Leucodendron argenteum, Liriodendron tulipifera, Magnolia sp., Metasequoia glyptostroboides, Michelia doltsopa, Nyssa sylvatica, Oxydendrum arboreum, Parrotia persica, Picea sp., Pinus sp., Pistacia chinensis, Podocarpus sp., Populus sp., Pseudotsuga menziesii, Punica granatum, Quercus sp., Robinia pseudoacacia, Salix sp., Sassafras albidum, Sequoia sempervirens, Sequoiadendron giganteum, Sorbus aucuparia, Stewartia sp., Styrax japonicus, Taxodium distichum, Tilia sp., Tsuga canadensis, Ulmus parvifolia*	*Alnus sp., Carpinus caroliniana, Cornus sp., Corylus sp., Cycas sp., Elaeagnus angustifolia, Fagus sp., Grevillea sp., Halesia carolina, Hamamelis virginiana, Ilex sp., Magnolia sp., Oxydendrum arboreum, Podocarpus sp., Pseudotsuga menziesii*	*Alnus sp., Carpinus caroliniana*
Acidic Soils 5.0–6.0 pH Zones 8–9 Perennial Plants	*Acorus calamus, Acorus gramineus, Alchemilla sp., Alternanthera ficoidea, Anchusa sp., Aruncus dioicus, Asparagus setaceus, Aster sp., Astilbe sp., Caltha palustris, Chelone lyonii, Chrysanthemum sp., Cimicifuga sp., Convolvulus sabatius, Coreopsis sp., Cosmos atrosanguineus, Dionaea muscipula, Dodecatheon sp., Drosera sp., Echinops sp., Eustoma grandiflorum, Filipendula rubra, Fragaria sp., Gaillardia sp., Gaura lindheimeri, Gazania sp., Geranium maculatum, Geranium sanguineum, Gerbera jamesonii, Gunnera manicata, Hedychium sp., Helianthus sp., Hydrocotyle verticillata, Iberis sempervirens, Lewisia cotyledon, Limonium platyphyllum, Lupinus sp., Lysichiton americanum, [cont. next pg.]*	*Aconitum napellus, Alternanthera ficoidea, Anchusa sp., Aruncus dioicus, Astilbe sp., Bergenia cordifolia, Caltha palustris, Chrysanthemum sp., Cimicifuga sp., Convolvulus sabatius, Dodecatheon sp., Filipendula rubra, Geranium maculatum, Gerbera jamesonii, Gunnera manicata, Helianthus sp., Helleborus orientalis, Heuchera sanguinea, Hosta sp., Houttuynia cordata, Hydrocotyle verticillata, [cont. next pg.]*	*Astilbe sp., Bergenia cordifolia, Helleborus orientalis, Heuchera sanguinea, Hosta sp., Houttuynia cordata, Hydrocotyle verticillata, Ligularia sp., Meconopsis cambrica, [cont. next pg.]*

Plant Community	Full to Filtered Sun	Open to Partial Shade	Full Shade
Acidic Soils 5.0–6.0 pH Zones 8–9 **Perennial Plants**	*Lysimachia nummularia, Lythrum virgatum, Macleaya* sp., *Melampodium leucanthum, Mentha* sp., *Menyanthes trifoliata, Mimulus cardinalis, Myosotis scorpioides, Nolana paradoxa, Oenanthe javanica, Paeonia* hyb., *Peltandra virginica, Penstemon* sp., *Phormium* sp., *Physostegia virginiana, Primula* sp., *Rehmannia elata, Rodgersia* sp., *Sagittaria latifolia, Salvia* sp., *Sarracenia* sp., *Saururus cernuus, Scrophularia auriculata, Stokesia laevis, Thalictrum* sp., *Tolmiea menziesii, Tradescantia virginiana, Trollius* sp., *Vinca* sp., *Viola* sp.	*Lewisia cotyledon, Ligularia* sp., *Lysichiton americanum, Lysimachia nummularia, Meconopsis cambrica, Mentha* sp., *Menyanthes trifoliata, Mimulus cardinalis, Myosotis scorpioides, Oenanthe javanica,* ORCHIDACEAE, *Paeonia* hyb., *Peltandra virginica, Penstemon* sp., *Physostegia virginiana, Primula* sp., *Rehmannia elata, Rodgersia* sp., *Saururus cernuus, Scrophularia auriculata, Thalictrum* sp., *Tolmiea menziesii, Tradescantia virginiana, Trollius* sp., *Vinca* sp., *Viola* sp.	*Mentha* sp., *Myosotis scorpioides,* ORCHIDACEAE, *Pulmonaria* sp., *Rodgersia* sp., *Saururus cernuus, Vinca* sp.
Grasses and Ground Covers	*Andropogon gerardii, Arundo donax, Baumea rubingosa, Butomus umbellatus, Carex* sp., *Cerastium tomentosum, Cyperus prolifer, Glyceria maxima, Hypericum calycinum, Juniperus horizontalis, Mentha* sp., *Pennisetum alopecuroides, Phalaris arundinacea, Phlox stolonifera, Phragmites australis, Scirpus cyperinus, Sedum* sp., *Sisyrinchium* sp.	*Ajuga reptans, Arundo donax, Carex* sp., *Cyperus prolifer, Glyceria maxima, Hypericum calycinum, Mentha* sp., *Pachysandra terminalis, Pennisetum alopecuroides, Phlox stolonifera, Scirpus cyperinus, Sedum* sp., *Sisyrinchium* sp.	*Ajuga reptans, Carex* sp., *Pachysandra terminalis, Phlox stolonifera*
Cacti, Ferns, and Shrubs	*Abelia* × *grandiflora, Abutilon hybridum, Aloysia triphylla, Arctostaphylos* sp., *Aronia arbutifolia, Aucuba japonica, Berberis* sp., *Buxus* sp., *Cestrum nocturnum, Chaenomeles speciosa, Choisya ternata, Cibotium glaucum, Clethra alnifolia, Corylopsis* sp., *Cotinus coggygria, Cyathea cooperi, Davallia trichomanoides, Deutzia* sp., *Dicksonia antarctica, Echinocereus* sp., *Enkianthus campanulatus, Erica* sp., *Euonymus* sp., *Euphorbia* sp., *Exochorda racemosa, Fothergilla gardenii, Fuchsia* × *hybrida, Gymnocalycium saglione, Hydrangea* sp., *Indigofera* sp., *Juniperus communis, Kalmia latifolia, Kerria japonica, Kolkwitzia amabilis, Leonotis leonurus, Leucothoe* sp., *Ligustrum* sp., *Lonicera* sp., *Murraya paniculata, Musa* sp., *Myrica pensylvanica, Myrtus communis, Paxistima* sp., *Photinia* sp., *Pieris japonica, Pinus mugo* var. *mugo, Platycerium bifurcatum, Plumeria rubra, Potentilla fruticosa, Pyracantha* sp., *Rhododendron* sp., *Rhus* sp., *Sambucus* sp., *Schlumbergera bridgesii, Spiraea* × *vanhouttei, Strelitzia reginae, Tibouchina urvilleana, Viburnum* sp., *Xylosma congestum, Yucca filamentosa*	*Abutilon hybridum, Adiantum capillus-veneris, Arctostaphylos* sp., *Aronia arbutifolia, Asplenium nidus, Aucuba japonica, Berberis* sp., *Buxus* sp., *Camellia* sp., *Choisya ternata, Clethra alnifolia, Corylopsis* sp., *Cyrtomium falcatum, Davallia trichomanoides, Denstaedtia punctilobula, Deutzia* sp., *Dicksonia antarctica, Enkianthus campanulatus, Euphorbia* sp., *Fatsia japonica, Fothergilla gardenii, Gardenia jasminoides, Hydrangea* sp., *Juniperus communis, Kalmia latifolia, Kerria japonica, Kolkwitzia amabilis, Leucothoe* sp., *Ligustrum* sp., *Lonicera* sp., *Mahonia aquifolium, Murraya paniculata, Myrica pensylvanica, Paxistima* sp., *Pieris japonica, Platycerium bifurcatum, Polystichum* sp., *Potentilla fruticosa, Rhododendron* sp., *Rhus* sp., *Schlumbergera bridgesii, Spiraea* × *vanhouttei, Tibouchina urvilleana, Viburnum* sp., *Xylosma congestum*	*Adiantum capillus-veneris, Asplenium nidus, Clethra alnifolia, Cyrtomium falcatum, Dennstaedtia punctilobula, Dicksonia antarctica, Dryopteris arguta, Fatsia japonica, Kalmia latifolia, Mahonia aquifolium, Polystichum* sp., *Rhododendron* sp., *Schlumbergera bridgesii*
Landscape Trees	*Abies concolor, Acer* sp., *Alnus* sp., *Amelanchier* sp., *Betula* sp., *Carpinus caroliniana, Catalpa bignonioides, Cedrus* sp., *Celtis* sp., *Chamaecyparis* sp., *Chilopsis linearis, Chionanthus virginicus, Citrus* sp., *Cornus* sp., *Corylus* sp., *Crataegus* sp., *Cycas* sp., *Elaeagnus angustifolia, Fagus* sp., *Franklinia alatamaha, Ginkgo biloba, Gleditsia triacanthos inermis, Grevillea* sp., *Hamamelis virginiana, Ilex* sp., *Juniperus* sp., *Larix* sp., *Leucodendron argenteum, Liriodendron tulipifera, Magnolia* sp., *Metasequoia glyptostroboides, Michelia doltsopa, Nyssa sylvatica, Oxydendrum arboreum, Parrotia persica, Picea* sp., *Pinus* sp., *Pistacia chinensis, Podocarpus* sp., *Populus* sp., *Pseudotsuga menziesii, Punica granatum, Quercus* sp., *Robinia pseudoacacia, Salix* sp., *Sassafras albidum, Sequoia sempervirens, Sequoiadendron giganteum, Sorbus aucuparia, Stewartia* sp., *Styrax japonicus, Taxodium distichum, Tilia* sp., *Tsuga canadensis, Ulmus parvifolia*	*Pseudotsuga menziesii, Cornus* sp., *Corylus* sp., *Cycas* sp., *Elaeagnus angustifolia, Fagus* sp., *Grevillea* sp., *Halesia carolina, Hamamelis virginiana, Ilex* sp., *Magnolia* sp., *Oxydendrum arboreum, Podocarpus* sp.	*Alnus* sp., *Carpinus caroliniana*
Acidic Soils 5.0–6.0 pH Zones 10–11 **Perennial Plants**	*Acorus calamus, Acorus gramineus, Alternanthera ficoidea, Asparagus setaceus, Astilbe* sp., *Chrysanthemum* sp., *Convolvulus sabatius, Coreopsis* sp., *Cosmos atrosanguineus, Dionaea muscipula, Drosera* sp., *Fragaria* sp., *Gazania* sp., *Geranium sanguineum, Gerbera jamesonii, Gunnera manicata, Hedychium* sp., *Hydrocotyle verticillata, Iberis sempervirens, Limonium platyphyllum, Menyanthes trifoliata, Mimulus cardinalis, Myosotis scorpioides, Nolana paradoxa, Oenanthe javanica, Paeonia* hyb., *Penstemon* sp., *Phormium* sp., *Rehmannia elata, Sagittaria latifolia, Salvia* sp., *Sarracenia* sp., *Scrophularia auriculata, Stokesia laevis, Tradescantia virginiana, Vinca* sp., *Viola* sp.	*Alternanthera ficoidea, Astilbe* sp., *Chrysanthemum* sp., *Convolvulus sabatius, Gerbera jamesonii, Gunnera manicata, Hosta* sp., *Houttuynia cordata, Hydrocotyle verticillata, Ligularia* sp., *Menyanthes trifoliata, Mimulus cardinalis, Myosotis scorpioides, Oenanthe javanica,* ORCHIDACEAE, *Paeonia* hyb., *Penstemon* sp., *Rehmannia elata, Scrophularia auriculata, Tradescantia virginiana, Vinca* sp., *Viola* sp.	*Astilbe* sp., *Hosta* sp., *Houttuynia cordata, Hydrocotyle verticillata, Ligularia* sp., *Myosotis scorpioides,* ORCHIDACEAE, *Vinca* sp.
Grasses and Ground Covers	*Andropogon gerardii, Arundo donax, Baumea rubingosa, Cerastium tomentosum, Cyperus prolifer, Glyceria maxima, Hypericum calycinum, Pennisetum alopecuroides, Phalaris arundinacea, Phragmites australis, Rotala rotundifolia, Scirpus cyperinus, Sedum* sp.	*Arundo donax, Cyperus alternifolius, Cyperus prolifer, Glyceria maxima, Hypericum calycinum, Pennisetum alopecuroides, Rotala rotundifolia, Scirpus cyperinus, Sedum* sp.	(Site is challenging for most species.)
Cacti, Ferns, and Shrubs	*Abutilon hybridum, Aloysia triphylla, Aronia arbutifolia, Aucuba japonica, Cestrum nocturnum, Choisya ternata, Cibotium glaucum,* [cont. next pg.]	*Abutilon hybridum, Adiantum capillus-veneris, Aronia arbutifolia,* [cont. next pg.]	*Adiantum capillus-veneris,* [cont. next pg.]

Plant Community	Full to Filtered Sun	Open to Partial Shade	Full Shade
Acidic Soils 5.0–6.0 pH Zones 10–11 Cacti, Ferns, and Shrubs	*Cyathea cooperi, Davallia trichomanoides, Dicksonia antarctica, Echinocereus* sp., *Erica* sp., *Euonymus* sp., *Euphorbia* sp., *Fuchsia* × *hybrida, Gymnocalycium saglione, Hydrangea* sp., *Indigofera* sp., *Leonotis leonurus, Ligustrum* sp., *Murraya paniculata, Musa* sp., *Myrtus communis, Pinus mugo* var. *mugo, Platycerium bifurcatum, Plumeria rubra, Rhododendron* sp., *Sambucus* sp., *Schlumbergera bridgesii, Strelitzia reginae, Tibouchina urvilleana, Xylosma congestum, Yucca filamentosa*	*Asplenium nidus, Aucuba japonica, Camellia* sp., *Choisya ternata, Cibotium glaucum, Cyrtomium falcatum, Davallia trichomanoides, Dennstaedtia punctilobula, Dicksonia antarctica, Euphorbia* sp., *Fatsia japonica, Gardenia jasminoides, Hydrangea* sp., *Ligustrum* sp., *Murraya paniculata, Platycerium bifurcatum, Rhododendron* sp., *Schlumbergera bridgesii, Tibouchina urvilleana, Xylosma congestum*	*Asplenium nidus, Cyrtomium falcatum, Dennstaedtia punctilobula, Dicksonia antarctica, Fatsia japonica, Rhododendron* sp., *Schlumbergera bridgesii*
Landscape Trees	*Acer* sp., *Alnus* sp., *Catalpa bignonioides, Cedrus* sp., *Chilopsis linearis, Citrus* sp., *Cornus* sp., *Cycas* sp., *Grevillea* sp., *Leucodendron argenteum, Magnolia* sp., *Michelia doltsopa, Podocarpus* sp., *Punica granatum, Quercus* sp., *Robinia pseudoacacia, Salix* sp., *Sequoia sempervirens, Taxodium distichum, Ulmus parvifolia*	*Magnolia* sp., *Cornus* sp., *Cycas* sp., *Grevillea* sp., *Halesia carolina, Podocarpus* sp.	*Alnus* sp.
Neutral Soils 6.5–7.5 pH Zones 1–3 Perennial Plants	*Achillea* sp., *Acorus calamus, Adenophora* sp., *Aethionema* sp., *Agastache* sp., *Alcea rosea, Alchemilla* sp., *Anchusa* sp., *Anthemis tinctoria, Aquilegia* sp., *Aruncus dioicus, Asclepias tuberosa, Aster* sp., *Baptisia australis, Calamintha nepeta, Caltha palustris, Campanula persicifolia, Centaurea* sp., *Chelone lyonii, Cimicifuga* sp., *Delphinium* sp., *Dianthus* × *allwoodii, Dicentra* sp., *Dictamnus albus, Digitalis* sp., *Doronicum* sp., *Echinacea purpurea, Equisetum hyemale, Erigeron* sp., *Eustoma grandiflorum, Filipendula rubra, Fragaria* sp., *Gaillardia* sp., *Gaura lindheimeri, Geranium sanguineum, Geum* sp., *Helenium* hyb., *Iberis sempervirens, Lewisia cotyledon, Lobelia cardinalis, Lysimachia nummularia, Lythrum virgatum, Mertensia pulmonarioides, Nasturtium officinale, Nepeta* sp., *Papaver* sp., *Penstemon* sp., *Perovskia* sp., *Phlox paniculata, Physalis alkekengi, Physostegia virginiana, Platycodon grandiflorus, Sagittaria latifolia, Scabiosa caucasica, Senecio cineraria, Solidago* hyb., *Trollius* sp., *Typha minima, Valeriana officinalis, Verbascum* sp., *Veronica* sp., *Vinca* sp.	*Adenophora* sp., *Agastache* sp., *Anchusa* sp., *Aquilegia* sp., *Aruncus dioicus, Baptisia australis, Bergenia cordifolia, Brunnera macrophylla, Calamintha nepeta, Caltha palustris, Campanula persicifolia, Cimicifuga* sp., *Delphinium* sp., *Dicentra* sp., *Dictamnus albus, Digitalis* sp., *Echinacea purpurea, Equisetum hyemale, Erigeron* sp., *Filipendula rubra, Geum* sp., *Hosta* sp., *Lewisia cotyledon, Lysimachia nummularia, Mertensia pulmonarioides,* ORCHIDACEAE, *Papaver* sp., *Penstemon* sp., *Phlox paniculata, Physalis alkekengi, Physostegia virginiana, Platycodon grandiflorus, Scabiosa caucasica, Tiarella cordifolia, Trollius* sp., *Typha minima, Valeriana officinalis, Veronica* sp., *Vinca* sp.	*Bergenia cordifolia, Hosta* sp., ORCHIDACEAE, *Pulmonaria* sp., *Tiarella cordifolia, Vinca* sp.
Grasses and Ground Covers	*Andropogon gerardii, Armeria maritima, Campanula poscharskyana, Carex* sp., *Cerastium tomentosum, Helictotrichon sempervirens, Juniperus horizontalis, Mentha* sp., *Schizachyrium scoparium, Scirpus cyperinus, Sorghastrum avenaceum, Thymus serpyllum*	*Ajuga reptans, Carex* sp., *Mentha* sp., *Scirpus cyperinus*	*Ajuga reptans, Carex* sp.
Cacti, Ferns, and Shrubs	*Arctostaphylos* sp., *Athyrium filix-femina, Berberis* sp., *Caragana arborescens, Clethra alnifolia, Coryphantha vivipara, Euonymus* sp., *Juniperus communis, Matteuccia struthiopteris, Osmunda regalis, Pinus mugo* var. *mugo, Potentilla fruticosa, Rhus* sp., *Rosa* sp., *Sambucus* sp., *Symphoricarpos* sp., *Syringa vulgaris, Thuja occidentalis, Viburnum* sp.	*Arctostaphylos* sp., *Athyrium filix-femina, Berberis* sp., *Clethra alnifolia, Dennstaedtia punctilobula, Juniperus communis, Matteuccia struthiopteris, Potentilla fruticosa, Rhus* sp., *Syringa vulgaris, Taxus* sp., *Viburnum* sp.	*Athyrium filix-femina, Clethra alnifolia, Dennstaedtia punctilobula, Matteuccia struthiopteris, Taxus* sp.
Landscape Trees	*Acer* sp., *Aesculus* sp., *Amelanchier* sp., *Betula* sp., *Carpinus caroliniana, Elaeagnus angustifolia, Gleditsia triacanthos inermis, Juniperus* sp., *Larix* sp., *Picea* sp., *Pinus* sp., *Populus* sp., *Pseudotsuga menziesii, Quercus* sp., *Robinia pseudoacacia, Salix* sp., *Sequoiadendron giganteum, Sorbus aucuparia, Tilia* sp.	*Carpinus caroliniana, Elaeagnus angustifolia, Pseudotsuga menziesii*	*Carpinus caroliniana*
Neutral Soils 6.5–7.5 pH Zones 4–5 Perennial Plants	*Achillea* sp., *Acorus calamus, Adenophora* sp., *Aethionema* sp., *Agastache* sp., *Alcea rosea, Alchemilla* sp., *Amsonia tabernaemontana, Anchusa* sp., *Anthemis tinctoria, Aquilegia* sp., *Artemisia* sp., *Aruncus dioicus, Asclepias tuberosa, Aster* sp., *Astilbe* sp., *Astrantia major, Baptisia australis, Calamintha nepeta, Caltha palustris, Campanula persicifolia, Centaurea* sp., *Centranthus ruber, Chelone lyonii, Chrysanthemum* sp., *Cimicifuga* sp., *Coreopsis* sp., *Crambe* sp., *Delphinium* sp., *Dianthus* × *allwoodii, Dianthus caryophyllus, Dicentra* sp., *Dictamnus albus, Digitalis* sp., *Doronicum* sp., *Echinacea purpurea, Equisetum hyemale, Erigeron* sp., *Eryngium* sp., *Eustoma grandiflorum, Filipendula rubra, Fragaria* sp., *Gaillardia* sp., *Gaura lindheimeri, Geranium sanguineum, Geum* sp., *Gypsophila paniculata, Helenium* hyb., *Helianthus* sp., *Iberis sempervirens, Lewisia cotyledon, Limonium platyphyllum, Linum perenne, Lobelia cardinalis, Lupinus* sp., *Lysichiton americanum, Lysimachia nummularia, Lythrum virgatum, Macleaya* sp., *Malva alcea, Melampodium leucanthum, Melissa officinalis, Mentha* sp., *Mertensia pulmonarioides, Myosotis scorpioides, Nasturtium officinale, Nepeta* sp., *Oenothera* sp., *Papaver* sp., *Patrinia* sp., *Peltandra virginica, Penstemon* sp., *Perovskia* sp., *Phlox paniculata, Physalis alkekengi, Physostegia virginiana, Platycodon grandiflorus, Rodgersia* sp., *Sagittaria latifolia, Salvia* sp., *Saururus cernuus, Scabiosa caucasica, Scrophularia auriculata, Sempervivum tectorum, Senecio cineraria, Sidalcea* sp., *Silene californica,* [cont. next pg.]	*Adenophora* sp., *Agastache* sp., *Amsonia tabernaemontana, Anchusa* sp., *Aquilegia* sp., *Artemisia* sp., *Aruncus dioicus, Astilbe* sp., *Astrantia major, Baptisia australis, Bergenia cordifolia, Brunnera macrophylla, Calamintha nepeta, Caltha palustris, Campanula persicifolia, Chrysanthemum* sp., *Cimicifuga* sp., *Delphinium* sp., *Dicentra* sp., *Dictamnus albus, Digitalis* sp., *Echinacea purpurea, Equisetum hyemale, Erigeron* sp., *Filipendula rubra, Geum* sp., *Helianthus* sp., *Helleborus orientalis, Heuchera sanguinea, Hosta* sp., *Lewisia cotyledon, Ligularia* sp., *Lysichiton americanum, Lysimachia nummularia, Malva alcea, Mentha* sp., *Mertensia pulmonarioides, Monarda didyma, Myosotis scorpioides,* ORCHIDACEAE, *Papaver* sp., *Peltandra virginica, Penstemon* sp., *Phlox paniculata, Physalis alkekengi, Physostegia virginiana, Platycodon grandiflorus, Rodgersia* sp., *Saururus cernuus, Scabiosa caucasica,* [cont. next pg.]	*Pulmonaria* sp., *Rodgersia* sp., *Saururus cernuus, Tiarella cordifolia, Vinca* sp.

Plant Community	Full to Filtered Sun	Open to Partial Shade	Full Shade
Neutral Soils 6.5–7.5 pH Zones 4–5 **Perennial Plants**	*Solidago* hyb., *Stachys byzantina*, *Stokesia laevis*, *Thalictrum* sp., *Trollius* sp., *Typha minima*, *Valeriana officinalis*, *Verbascum* sp., *Veronica* sp., *Vinca* sp.	*Scrophularia auriculata*, *Sidalcea* sp., *Silene californica*, *Stachys byzantina*, *Thalictrum* sp., *Tiarella cordifolia*, *Trollius* sp., *Typha minima*, *Valeriana officinalis*, *Veronica* sp., *Vinca* sp.	
Grasses and Ground Covers	*Andropogon gerardii*, *Armeria maritima*, *Butomus umbellatus*, *Calamagrostis* x *acutiflora*, *Campanula poscharskyana*, *Carex* sp., *Cerastium tomentosum*, *Chamaemelum nobile*, *Delosperma cooperi*, *Deschampsia caespitosa*, *Duchensnea indica*, *Festuca glauca*, *Glyceria maxima*, *Helictotrichon sempervirens*, *Hypericum calycinum*, *Juniperus horizontalis*, *Lampranthus* sp., *Mentha* sp., *Miscanthus sinensis*, *Panicum virgatum*, *Pennisetum alopecuroides*, *Phalaris arundinacea*, *Phlox stolonifera*, *Phragmites australis*, *Potentilla tabernaemontani*, *Sagina subulata*, *Schizachyrium scoparium*, *Scirpus cyperinus*, *Sedum* sp., *Sisyrinchium* sp., *Sorghastrum avenaceum*, *Thymus serpyllum*	*Ajuga reptans*, *Calamagrostis* x *acutiflora*, *Carex* sp., *Chamaemelum nobile*, *Deschampsia caespitosa*, *Duchensnea indica*, *Galium odoratum*, *Glyceria maxima*, *Hypericum calycinum*, *Mentha* sp., *Miscanthus sinensis*, *Pachysandra terminalis*, *Pennisetum alopecuroides*, *Phlox stolonifera*, *Potentilla tabernaemontani*, *Sagina subulata*, *Scirpus cyperinus*, *Sedum* sp., *Sisyrinchium* sp.	*Ajuga reptans*, *Carex* sp., *Deschampsia caespitosa*, *Duchensnea indica*, *Galium odoratum*, *Pachysandra terminalis*, *Phlox stolonifera*
Cacti, Ferns, and Shrubs	*Aesculus parviflora*, *Arctostaphylos* sp., *Aronia arbutifolia*, *Athyrium filix-femina*, *Berberis* sp., *Calluna vulgaris*, *Calycanthus* sp., *Caragana arborescens*, *Chaenomeles speciosa*, *Clethra alnifolia*, *Coryphantha vivipara*, *Cotinus coggygria*, *Echinocereus* sp., *Euonymus* sp., *Euphorbia* sp., *Exochorda racemosa*, *Forsythia* x *intermedia*, *Fothergilla gardenii*, *Hydrangea* sp., *Indigofera* sp., *Juniperus communis*, *Kalmia latifolia*, *Kerria japonica*, *Ligustrum* sp., *Lonicera* sp., *Matteuccia struthiopteris*, *Myrica pensylvanica*, *Opuntia* sp., *Osmunda regalis*, *Paxistima* sp., *Pieris japonica*, *Pinus mugo* var. *mugo*, *Potentilla fruticosa*, *Rhododendron* sp., *Rhus* sp., *Rosa* sp., *Sambucus* sp., *Spiraea* x *vanhouttei*, *Symphoricarpos* sp., *Syringa vulgaris*, *Teucrium* x *lucidrys*, *Thuja occidentalis*, *Viburnum* sp., *Weigela* sp., *Yucca filamentosa*	*Arctostaphylos* sp., *Aronia arbutifolia*, *Athyrium filix-femina*, *Berberis* sp., *Calluna vulgaris*, *Calycanthus* sp., *Clethra alnifolia*, *Daphne* sp., *Dennstaedtia punctilobula*, *Dryopteris arguta*, *Euphorbia* sp., *Fothergilla gardenii*, *Hydrangea* sp., *Juniperus communis*, *Kalmia latifolia*, *Kerria japonica*, *Ligustrum* sp., *Lonicera* sp., *Mahonia aquifolium*, *Matteuccia struthiopteris*, *Myrica pensylvanica*, *Paxistima* sp., *Philadelphus coronarius*, *Pieris japonica*, *Polystichum* sp., *Potentilla fruticosa*, *Rhododendron* sp., *Rhus* sp., *Spiraea* x *vanhouttei*, *Syringa vulgaris*, *Taxus* sp., *Viburnum* sp., *Weigela* sp.	*Athyrium filix-femina*, *Clethra alnifolia*, *Dennstaedtia punctilobula*, *Dryopteris arguta*, *Kalmia latifolia*, *Mahonia aquifolium*, *Matteuccia struthiopteris*, *Polystichum* sp., *Rhododendron* sp., *Taxus* sp.
Landscape Trees	*Abies concolor*, *Acer* sp., *Aesculus* sp., *Alnus* sp., *Amelanchier* sp., *Betula* sp., *Carpinus caroliniana*, *Catalpa bignonioides*, *Cercidiphyllum japonicum*, *Cercis canadensis*, *Chamaecyparis* sp., *Chionanthus virginicus*, *Cladrastis kentukea*, *Cornus* sp., *Crataegus* sp., *Elaeagnus angustifolia*, *Fagus* sp., *Ginkgo biloba*, *Gleditsia triacanthos inermis*, *Hamamelis virginiana*, *Juniperus* sp., *Laburnum* x *watereri*, *Larix* sp., *Liriodendron tulipifera*, *Magnolia* sp., *Malus floribunda*, *Metasequoia glyptostroboides*, *Michelia doltsopa*, *Nyssa sylvatica*, *Oxydendrum arboreum*, *Parrotia persica*, *Picea* sp., *Pinus* sp., *Platanus* x *acerifolia*, *Populus* sp., *Prunus* sp., *Pseudotsuga menziesii*, *Pyrus calleryana*, *Quercus* sp., *Robinia pseudoacacia*, *Salix* sp., *Sassafras albidum*, *Sequoiadendron giganteum*, *Sophora japonica*, *Sorbus aucuparia*, *Styrax japonicus*, *Syringa reticulata*, *Taxodium distichum*, *Tilia* sp., *Tsuga canadensis*, *Ulmus parvifolia*	*Cercis canadensis*, *Cornus* sp., *Elaeagnus angustifolia*, *Fagus* sp., *Halesia carolina*, *Hamamelis virginiana*, *Magnolia* sp., *Oxydendrum arboreum*, *Pseudotsuga menziesii*, *Syringa reticulata*	*Cercis canadensis*, *Cornus* sp., *Elaeagnus angustifolia*, *Fagus* sp., *Halesia carolina*, *Hamamelis virginiana*, *Magnolia* sp., *Oxydendrum arboreum*, *Pseudotsuga menziesii*, *Syringa reticulata*
Neutral Soils 6.5–7.5 pH Zones 6–7 **Perennial Plants**	*Acanthus mollis*, *Achillea* sp., *Acorus* sp., *Adenophora* sp., *Aethionema* sp., *Agastache* sp., *Alcea rosea*, *Alchemilla* sp., *Amsonia tabernaemontana*, *Anchusa* sp., *Anthemis tinctoria*, *Aquilegia* sp., *Artemisia* sp., *Aruncus dioicus*, *Asclepias tuberosa*, *Asparagus setaceus*, *Aster* sp., *Astilbe* sp., *Astrantia major*, *Baptisia australis*, *Calamintha nepeta*, *Caltha palustris*, *Campanula* sp., *Centaurea* sp., *Centranthus ruber*, *Chelone lyonii*, *Chrysanthemum* sp., *Cimicifuga* sp., *Convolvulus sabatius*, *Coreopsis* sp., *Cosmos atrosanguineus*, *Crambe* sp., *Delphinium* sp., *Dianthus* x *allwoodii*, *Dianthus caryophyllus*, *Dicentra* sp., *Dictamnus albus*, *Digitalis* sp., *Dodecatheon* sp., *Doronicum* sp., *Echeveria elegans*, *Echinacea purpurea*, *Equisetum hyemale*, *Erigeron* sp., *Erodium reichardii*, *Eryngium* sp., *Eupatorium* sp., *Eustoma grandiflorum*, *Filipendula rubra*, *Fragaria* sp., *Gaillardia* sp., *Gaura lindheimeri*, *Gazania* sp., *Geranium maculatum*, *Geranium sanguineum*, *Geum* sp., *Gunnera manicata*, *Gypsophila paniculata*, *Helenium* hyb., *Helianthus* sp., *Helichrysum bracteatum*, *Iberis sempervirens*, *Lavandula* sp., *Lavatera arborea*, *Lewisia cotyledon*, *Limonium platyphyllum*, *Linum perenne*, *Lobelia cardinalis*, *Lupinus* sp., *Lysichiton americanum*, *Lysimachia nummularia*, *Lythrum virgatum*, *Macleaya* sp., *Malva alcea*, *Melampodium leucanthum*, *Melissa officinalis*, *Mentha* sp., *Mertensia pulmonarioides*, *Mimulus cardinalis*, *Myosotis scorpioides*, *Nasturtium officinale*, *Nepeta* sp., *Oenothera* sp., *Osteospermum* sp., *Paeonia* hyb., *Papaver* sp., *Patrinia* sp., *Peltandra virginica*, *Penstemon* sp., *Perovskia* sp., *Phlox paniculata*, *Phormium* sp., *Physalis alkekengi*, *Physostegia virginiana*, *Platycodon grandiflorum*, *Primula* sp., *Rehmannia elata*, *Rodgersia* sp., *Sagittaria latifolia*, *Salvia* sp., *Santolina chamaecyparissus*, *Sarracenia* sp., *Saururus cernuus*, *Saxifraga stolonifera*, *Scabiosa caucasica*, *Scaevola* sp., *Scrophularia auriculata*, *Sempervivum tectorum*, [cont. next pg.]	*Acanthus mollis*, *Adenophora* sp., *Agastache* sp., *Amsonia tabernaemontana*, *Anchusa* sp., *Aquilegia* sp., *Artemisia* sp., *Aruncus dioicus*, *Astilbe* sp., *Astrantia major*, *Baptisia australis*, *Bergenia cordifolia*, *Brunnera macrophylla*, *Calamintha nepeta*, *Caltha palustris*, *Campanula persicifolia*, *Chrysanthemum* sp., *Cimicifuga* sp., *Convolvulus sabatius*, *Delphinium* sp., *Dicentra* sp., *Dictamnus albus*, *Digitalis* sp., *Dodecatheon* sp., *Echinacea purpurea*, *Equisetum hyemale*, *Erigeron* sp., *Erodium reichardii*, *Eupatorium* sp., *Filipendula rubra*, *Geranium maculatum*, *Geum* sp., *Gunnera manicata*, *Helianthus* sp., *Helleborus orientalis*, *Heuchera sanguinea*, *Hosta* sp., *Houttuynia cordata*, *Lewisia cotyledon*, *Ligularia* sp., *Lysichiton americanum*, *Lysimachia nummularia*, *Malva alcea*, *Meconopsis cambrica*, *Mentha* sp., *Mertensia pulmonarioides*, *Mimulus cardinalis*, *Monarda didyma*, *Myosotis scorpioides*, *Omphalodes* sp., ORCHIDACEAE, *Paeonia* hyb., *Papaver* sp., *Peltandra virginica*, *Penstemon* sp., [cont. next pg.]	*Acanthus mollis*, *Astilbe* sp., *Bergenia cordifolia*, *Helleborus orientalis*, *Heuchera sanguinea*, *Hosta* sp., *Houttuynia cordata*, *Ligularia* sp., *Meconopsis cambrica*, *Mentha* sp., *Myosotis scorpioides*, *Omphalodes* sp., ORCHIDACEAE, *Pulmonaria* sp., *Rodgersia* sp., *Saururus cernuus*, *Tiarella cordifolia*, *Vinca* sp.

Plant Community	Full to Filtered Sun	Open to Partial Shade	Full Shade
Neutral Soils 6.5–7.5 pH Zones 6–7 **Perennial Plants**	*Senecio cineraria, Sidalcea* sp., *Silene californica, Solidago* hyb., *Stachys byzantina, Stokesia laevis, Thalictrum* sp., *Tolmiea menziesii, Tradescantia virginiana, Trollius* sp., *Typha minima, Valeriana officinalis, Verbascum* sp., *Veronica* sp., *Vinca* sp., *Viola* sp.	*Phlox paniculata, Physalis alkekengi, Physostegia virginiana, Platycodon grandiflorus, Primula* sp., *Rehmannia elata, Rodgersia* sp., *Saururus cernuus, Saxifraga stolonifera, Scabiosa caucasica, Scrophularia auriculata, Sidalcea* sp., *Silene californica, Stachys byzantina, Thalictrum* sp., *Tiarella cordifolia, Tolmiea menziesii, Tradescantia virginiana, Trollius* sp., *Typha minima, Valeriana officinalis, Veronica* sp., *Vinca* sp., *Viola* sp.	
Grasses and Ground Covers	*Andropogon gerardii, Armeria maritima, Arundo donax, Butomus umbellatus, Calamagrostis* × *acutiflora, Campanula poscharskyana, Carex* sp., *Cerastium tomentosum, Chamaemelum nobile, Delosperma cooperi, Deschampsia caespitosa, Duchensnea indica, Dymondia margaretae, Festuca glauca, Glyceria maxima, Helictotrichon sempervirens, Hypericum calycinum, Juniperus horizontalis, Lagurus ovatus, Lampranthus* sp., *Liriope muscari, Mentha* sp., *Miscanthus floridulus* 'Rubra', *Miscanthus sinensis, Panicum virgatum, Pennisetum alopecuroides, Phalaris arundinacea, Phlox stolonifera, Phragmites australis, Potentilla tabernaemontani, Rosmarinus officinalis prostratus, Sagina subulata, Schizachyrium scoparium, Scirpus cyperinus, Sedum* sp., *Sisyrinchium* sp., *Sorghastrum avenaceum, Thymus serpyllum*	*Ajuga reptans, Arundo donax, Calamagrostis* × *acutiflora, Carex* sp., *Chamaemelum nobile, Deschampsia caespitosa, Duchensnea indica, Galium odoratum, Glyceria maxima, Hypericum calycinum, Liriope muscari, Mentha* sp., *Miscanthus floridulus* 'Rubra', *Miscanthus sinensis, Ophiopogon japonicus, Pachysandra terminalis, Pennisetum alopecuroides, Phlox stolonifera, Potentilla tabernaemontani, Sagina subulata, Scirpus cyperinus, Sedum* sp., *Sisyrinchium* sp.	*Ajuga reptans, Carex* sp., *Deschampsia caespitosa, Duchensnea indica, Galium odoratum, Liriope muscari, Ophiopogon japonicus, Pachysandra terminalis, Phlox stolonifera*
Cacti, Ferns, and Shrubs	*Abelia* × *grandiflora, Aesculus parviflora, Arctostaphylos* sp., *Aronia arbutifolia, Athyrium filix-femina, Aucuba japonica, Berberis* sp., *Brugmansia* × *candida, Buddleia* sp., *Buxus* sp., *Calluna vulgaris, Calycanthus* sp., *Caragana arborescens, Carnegiea gigantea, Caryopteris* sp., *Chaenomeles speciosa, Cistus albidus, Clethra alnifolia, Corylopsis* sp., *Coryphantha vivipara, Cotinus coggygria, Cyathea cooperi, Deutzia* sp., *Echinocactus grusonii, Echinocereus* sp., *Enkianthus campanulatus, Euonymus* sp., *Euphorbia* sp., *Euryops pectinatus, Exochorda racemosa, Ferocactus* sp., *Forsythia* × *intermedia, Fothergilla gardenii, Fuchsia* × *hybrida, Genista* sp., *Gymnocalycium saglione, Hibiscus mutabilis, Hydrangea* sp., *Indigofera* sp., *Juniperus communis, Justicia brandegeana, Kalmia latifolia, Kerria japonica, Kolkwitzia amabilis, Lagerstroemia indica, Leucophyllum frutescens, Leucothoe* sp., *Ligustrum* sp., *Lonicera* sp., *Mammillaria bocasana, Matteuccia struthiopteris, Myrica pensylvanica, Nandina domestica, Opuntia* sp., *Osmunda regalis, Paxistima* sp., *Photinia* sp., *Pieris japonica, Pinus mugo* var. *mugo, Pittosporum tobira, Potentilla fruticosa, Pyracantha* sp., *Rhododendron* sp., *Rhus* sp., *Rosa* sp., *Sambucus* sp., *Spiraea* × *vanhouttei, Stenocereus thurberi, Symphoricarpos* sp., *Syringa vulgaris, Teucrium* × *lucidrys* hyb., *Thuja occidentalis, Viburnum* sp., *Weigela* sp., *Xylosma congestum, Yucca filamentosa*	*Arctostaphylos* sp., *Aronia arbutifolia, Athyrium filix-femina, Aucuba japonica, Berberis* sp., *Buddleia* sp., *Buxus* sp., *Calluna vulgaris, Calycanthus* sp., *Clethra alnifolia, Corylopsis* sp., *Cotoneaster divaricatus, Cyrtomium falcatum, Daphne* sp., *Dennstaedtia punctilobula, Deutzia* sp., *Dryopteris arguta, Echinocactus grusonii, Enkianthus campanulatus, Euphorbia* sp., *Fothergilla gardenii, Hydrangea* sp., *Juniperus communis, Kalmia latifolia, Kerria japonica, Kolkwitzia amabilis, Leucothoe* sp., *Ligustrum* sp., *Lonicera* sp., *Mahonia aquifolium, Mammillaria bocasana, Matteuccia struthiopteris, Myrica pensylvanica, Nandina domestica, Paxistima* sp., *Philadelphus coronarius, Pieris japonica, Polystichum* sp., *Potentilla fruticosa, Rhododendron* sp., *Rhus* sp., *Spiraea* × *vanhouttei, Syringa vulgaris, Taxus* sp., *Viburnum* sp., *Weigela* sp., *Xylosma congestum*	*Athyrium filix-femina, Clethra alnifolia, Cyrtomium falcatum, Dennstaedtia punctilobula, Dryopteris arguta, Kalmia latifolia, Mahonia aquifolium, Matteuccia struthiopteris, Polystichum* sp., *Rhododendron* sp., *Taxus* sp.
Landscape Trees	*Abies concolor, Acer* sp., *Aesculus* sp., *Albizia julibrissin, Alnus* sp., *Amelanchier* sp., *Araucaria heterophylla, Arbutus unedo, Betula* sp., *Callistemon* sp., *Carpinus caroliniana, Catalpa bignonioides, Cedrus* sp., *Celtis* sp., *Cercidiphyllum japonicum, Cercis canadensis, Chamaecyparis* sp., *Chamaerops humilis, Chilopsis linearis, Chionanthus virginicus, Cladrastis kentukea, Cornus* sp., *Corylus* sp., *Crataegus* sp., *Elaeagnus angustifolia, Eucalyptus* sp., *Fagus* sp., *Fraxinus* sp., *Ginkgo biloba, Gleditsia triacanthos* var. *inermis, Halesia carolina, Hamamelis virginiana, Ilex* sp., *Jacaranda mimosifolia, Juniperus* sp., *Laburnum* × *watereri, Larix* sp., *Laurus nobilis, Liquidambar styraciflua, Liriodendron tulipifera, Magnolia* sp., *Malus floribunda, Metasequoia glyptostroboides, Michelia doltsopa, Nyssa sylvatica, Olea europaea, Oxydendrum arboreum, Parrotia persica, Phoenix* sp., *Picea* sp., *Pinus* sp., *Pistacia chinensis, Platanus* × *acerifolia, Podocarpus* sp., *Populus* sp., *Prunus* sp., *Pseudolarix amabilis, Pseudotsuga menziesii, Psorothamnus spinosus, Pyrus calleryana, Quercus* sp., *Robinia pseudoacacia, Salix* sp., *Sassafras albidum, Schinus molle, Sequoia sempervirens, Sequoiadendron giganteum, Sophora japonica, Sorbus aucuparia, Stewartia* sp., *Styrax japonicus, Syringa reticulata, Taxodium distichum, Tilia* sp., *Tsuga canadensis, Ulmus parvifolia, Vitex agnus-castus*	*Albizia julibrissin, Alnus* sp., *Arbutus unedo, Carpinus caroliniana, Cercis canadensis, Chamaerops humilis, Cornus* sp., *Corylus* sp., *Elaeagnus angustifolia, Fagus* sp., *Halesia carolina, Hamamelis virginiana, Ilex* sp., *Liquidambar styraciflua, Magnolia* sp., *Oxydendrum arboreum, Podocarpus* sp., *Pseudotsuga menziesii, Syringa reticulata*	*Alnus* sp., *Carpinus caroliniana*
Neutral Soils 6.5–7.5 pH Zones 8–9	*Abelmoschus moschatus, Acanthus mollis, Achillea* sp., *Acorus calamus, Acorus gramineus, Adenophora* sp., *Aethionema* sp., *Agastache* sp., *Alcea rosea, Alchemilla* sp., *Aloe* sp., *Alternanthera ficoidea, Amsonia tabernaemontana, Anchusa* sp., *Anthemis tinctoria, Antirrhinum majus, Aquilegia* sp., *Arctotis venusta, Artemisia* sp., *Aruncus dioicus, Asclepias tuberosa, Asparagus setaceus,* [cont. next pg.]	*Acanthus mollis, Adenophora* sp., *Agastache* sp., *Alternanthera ficoidea, Amsonia tabernaemontana, Anchusa* sp., *Aquilegia* sp., *Artemisia* sp., *Aruncus dioicus, Astilbe* sp., *Baptisia australis,* [cont. next pg.]	*Acanthus mollis, Astilbe* sp., *Bergenia cordifolia, Browallia speciosa, Helleborus* [cont. next pg.]

Plant Community	Full to Filtered Sun	Open to Partial Shade	Full Shade
Neutral Soils 6.5–7.5 pH Zones 8–9 **Perennial Plants**	*Aster* sp., *Astilbe* sp., *Bacopa caroliniana, Baptisia australis, Begonia* × *semperflorens-cultorum, Browallia speciosa, Calamintha nepeta, Calceolaria* sp., *Calibrachoa* sp., *Caltha palustris, Campanula* sp., *Campanula persicifolia, Capsicum annuum, Centaurea* sp., *Centranthus ruber, Chelone lyonii, Chrysanthemum* sp., *Cimicifuga* sp., *Convolvulus sabatius, Coreopsis* sp., *Cosmos atrosanguineus, Crambe* sp., *Delphinium* sp., *Dianthus* × *allwoodii, Dianthus caryophyllus, Dicentra* sp., *Dictamnus albus, Digitalis* sp., *Dionaea muscipula, Dodecatheon* sp., *Doronicum* sp., *Drosera* sp., *Echeveria elegans, Echinacea purpurea, Equisetum hyemale, Erigeron* sp., *Erodium reichardii, Eryngium* sp., *Eschscholzia californica, Eupatorium* sp., *Eustoma grandiflorum, Filipendula rubra, Fragaria* sp., *Gaillardia* sp., *Gaura lindheimeri, Gazania* sp., *Geranium maculatum, Geranium sanguineum, Gerbera jamesonii, Gunnera manicata, Gypsophila paniculata, Hedychium* sp., *Helenium* hyb., *Helianthus* sp., *Helichrysum bracteatum, Hydrocotyle verticillata, Iberis sempervirens, Impatiens wallerana, Lavandula* sp., *Lavatera arborea, Lewisia cotyledon, Limonium platyphyllum, Linum perenne, Lobelia cardinalis, Lobelia erinus, Lupinus* sp., *Lysichiton americanum, Lysimachia nummularia, Lythrum virgatum, Macleaya* sp., *Malva alcea, Matthiola incana, Melampodium leucanthum, Melissa officinalis, Mentha* sp., *Mertensia pulmonarioides, Mimulus cardinalis, Myosotis scorpioides, Nasturtium officinale, Nolana paradoxa, Oenanthe javanica, Oenothera* sp., *Osteospermum* sp., *Paeonia* hyb., *Papaver* sp., *Patrinia* sp., *Pelargonium* sp., *Peltandra virginica, Penstemon* sp., *Phlox paniculata, Phormium* sp., *Physalis alkekengi, Physostegia virginiana, Platycodon grandiflorus, Primula* sp., *Rehmannia elata, Rodgersia* sp., *Sagittaria latifolia, Salvia* sp., *Santolina chamaecyparissus, Sarracenia* sp., *Saururus cernuus, Saxifraga stolonifera, Scaevola* sp., *Scrophularia auriculata, Sempervivum tectorum, Senecio cineraria, Senecio* × *hybridus, Sidalcea* sp., *Silene californica, Soleirolia soleirolii, Solidago* hyb., *Stachys byzantina, Stokesia laevis, Thalictrum* sp., *Tolmiea menziesii, Tradescantia virginiana, Trollius* sp., *Valeriana officinalis, Verbascum* sp., *Verbena* sp., *Veronica* sp., *Vinca* sp., *Viola* sp.	*Begonia* × *semperflorens-cultorum, Bergenia cordifolia, Browallia speciosa, Brunnera macrophylla, Calamintha nepeta, Caltha palustris, Campanula persicifolia, Chrysanthemum* sp., *Cimicifuga* sp., *Convolvulus sabatius, Delphinium* sp., *Dicentra* sp., *Dictamnus albus, Digitalis* sp., *Dodecatheon* sp., *Echinacea purpurea, Equisetum hyemale, Erigeron* sp., *Erodium reichardii, Eupatorium* sp., *Filipendula rubra, Geranium maculatum, Gerbera jamesonii, Gunnera manicata, Helianthus* sp., *Helleborus orientalis, Heuchera sanguinea, Hosta* sp., *Houttuynia cordata, Hydrocotyle verticillata, Impatiens wallerana, Lewisia cotyledon, Ligularia* sp., *Lysichiton americanum, Lysimachia nummularia, Malva alcea, Matthiola incana, Meconopsis cambrica, Mentha* sp., *Mertensia pulmonarioides, Mimulus cardinalis, Monarda didyma, Myosotis scorpioides, Oenanthe javanica, Omphalodes* sp., ORCHIDACEAE, *Paeonia* hyb., *Papaver* sp., *Peltandra virginica, Penstemon* sp., *Phlox paniculata, Physalis alkekengi, Physostegia virginiana, Platycodon grandiflorus, Primula* sp., *Rehmannia elata, Rodgersia* sp., *Saururus cernuus, Saxifraga stolonifera, Scrophularia auriculata, Sidalcea* sp., *Silene californica, Soleirolia soleirolii, Stachys byzantina, Thalictrum* sp., *Tiarella cordifolia, Tolmiea menziesii, Tradescantia virginiana, Trollius* sp., *Valeriana officinalis, Veronica* sp., *Vinca* sp., *Viola* sp.	*orientalis, Heuchera sanguinea, Hosta* sp., *Houttuynia cordata, Hydrocotyle verticillata, Impatiens wallerana, Ligularia* sp., *Meconopsis cambrica, Mentha* sp., *Myosotis scorpioides, Omphalodes* sp., ORCHIDACEAE, *Pulmonaria* sp., *Rodgersia* sp., *Saururus cernuus, Tiarella cordifolia, Vinca* sp.
Grasses and Ground Covers	*Andropogon gerardii, Aptenia cordifolia, Armeria maritima, Arundo donax, Baumea rubinosa, Butomus umbellatus, Calamagrostis* × *acutiflora, Carex* sp., *Cerastium tomentosum, Chamaemelum nobile, Cyperus prolifer, Delosperma cooperi, Deschampsia caespitosa, Duchensnea indica, Dymondia margaretae, Festuca glauca, Glyceria maxima, Helictotrichon sempervirens, Hypericum calycinum, Juniperus horizontalis, Lagurus ovatus, Lampranthus* sp., *Lantana montevidensis, Liriope muscari, Mentha* sp., *Miscanthus floridulus* 'Rubra', *Miscanthus sinensis, Panicum virgatum, Pennisetum alopecuroides, Phalaris arundinacea, Phlox stolonifera, Phragmites australis, Potentilla tabernaemontani, Rosmarinus officinalis prostratus, Sagina subulata, Schizachyrium scoparium, Scirpus cyperinus, Sedum* sp., *Sisyrinchium* sp., *Sorghastrum avenaceum, Thymus serpyllum*	*Ajuga reptans, Arundo donax, Calamagrostis* × *acutiflora, Carex* sp., *Chamaemelum nobile, Cyperus prolifer, Deschampsia caespitosa, Duchensnea indica, Galium odoratum, Glyceria maxima, Hypericum calycinum, Liriope muscari, Mentha* sp., *Miscanthus floridulus* 'Rubra', *Miscanthus sinensis, Ophiopogon japonicus, Pachysandra terminalis, Pennisetum alopecuroides, Phlox stolonifera, Potentilla tabernaemontani, Sagina subulata, Scirpus cyperinus, Sedum* sp., *Sisyrinchium* sp.	*Ajuga reptans, Carex* sp., *Deschampsia caespitosa, Duchensnea indica, Galium odoratum, Liriope muscari, Ophiopogon japonicus, Pachysandra terminalis, Phlox stolonifera*
Cacti, Ferns, and Shrubs	*Abelia* × *grandiflora, Abutilon hybridum, Aesculus parviflora, Agave* sp., *Aloysia triphylla, Arctostaphylos* sp., *Aronia arbutifolia, Athyrium filix-femina, Aucuba japonica, Berberis* sp., *Brugmansia* × *candida, Buddleia* sp., *Buxus* sp., *Calycanthus* sp., *Caragana arborescens, Carnegiea giganteum, Caryopteris* sp., *Cephalocereus senilis, Cereus peruvianus, Cestrum nocturnum, Chaenomeles speciosa, Choisya ternata, Cibotium glaucum, Cistus albidus, Clethra alnifolia, Cordyline fruticosa, Corylopsis* sp., *Coryphantha vivipara, Cotinus coggygria, Cyathea cooperi, Davallia trichomanoides, Deutzia* sp., *Dicksonia antarctica, Echinocactus grusonii, Echinocereus* sp., *Enkianthus campanulatus, Euonymus* sp., *Euphorbia* sp., *Euryops pectinatus, Exochorda racemosa, Ferocactus* sp., *Forsythia* × *intermedia, Fothergilla gardenii, Fuchsia* × *hybrida, Genista* sp., *Gymnocalycium saglione, Hebe* sp., *Hibiscus* sp., *Hydrangea* sp., *Indigofera* sp., *Isopogon formosus, Juniperus communis, Justicia brandegeana, Kalmia latifolia, Kerria japonica, Kolkwitzia amabilis, Lagerstroemia indica, Lantana* hyb., *Leonotis leonurus, Leucophyllum frutescens, Leucothoe* sp., *Ligustrum* sp., *Lonicera* sp., *Mammillaria bocasana, Matteuccia struthiopteris, Murraya paniculata, Musa* sp., *Myrica pensylvanica, Myrtus communis, Nandina domestica, Nerium oleander, Opuntia* sp., *Osmunda regalis, Paxistima* sp., *Photinia* sp., *Pieris japonica, Pinus mugo* var. *mugo, Pittosporum tobira, Platycerium bifurcatum, Plumeria rubra, Polygala* × *dalmaisiana, Potentilla fruticosa, Pyracantha* sp., *Rhododendron* sp., *Rhus* sp., *Rosa* sp., *Sambucus* sp., *Schlumbergera bridgesii, Spiraea* × *vanhouttei, Stenocereus thurberi, Strelitzia reginae, Symphoricarpos* sp., *Syringa vulgaris, Teucrium* × *lucidrys, Thuja occidentalis, Tibouchina urvilleana, Viburnum* sp., *Weigela* sp., *Xylosma congestum, Yucca filamentosa*	*Abutilon hybridum, Adiantum capillus-veneris, Arctostaphylos* sp., *Aronia arbutifolia, Asplenium nidus, Athyrium filix-femina, Aucuba japonica, Berberis* sp., *Buddleia* sp., *Buxus* sp., *Calycanthus* sp., *Camellia* sp., *Choisya ternata, Cibotium glaucum, Clethra alnifolia, Corylopsis* sp., *Cotoneaster divaricatus, Cyrtomium falcatum, Daphne* sp., *Davallia trichomanoides, Dennstaedtia punctilobula, Deutzia* sp., *Dicksonia antarctica, Dryopteris arguta, Echinocactus grusonii, Enkianthus campanulatus, Euphorbia* sp., *Fatsia japonica, Fothergilla gardenii, Hebe* sp., *Hibiscus* sp., *Hydrangea* sp., *Juniperus communis, Kalmia latifolia, Kerria japonica, Kolkwitzia amabilis, Leucothoe* sp., *Ligustrum* sp., *Lonicera* sp., *Mahonia aquifolium, Mammillaria bocasana, Matteuccia struthiopteris, Murraya paniculata, Myrica pensylvanica, Nandina domestica, Paxistima* sp., *Philadelphus coronarius, Pieris japonica, Platycerium bifurcatum, Polystichum* sp., *Rhododendron* sp., *Rhus* sp., *Spiraea* × *vanhouttei, Syringa vulgaris, Tibouchina urvilleana, Viburnum* sp., *Weigela* sp., *Xylosma congestum*	*Adiantum capillus-veneris, Asplenium nidus, Athyrium filix-femina, Clethra alnifolia, Cyrtomium falcatum, Dennstaedtia punctilobula, Dicksonia antarctica, Dryopteris arguta, Fatsia japonica, Kalmia latifolia, Mahonia aquifolium, Matteuccia struthiopteris, Polystichum* sp., *Rhododendron* sp., *Schlumbergera bridgesii, Taxus* sp.

Plant Community	Full to Filtered Sun	Open to Partial Shade	Full Shade
Neutral Soils 6.5–7.5 pH Zones 8–9 **Landscape Trees**	*Abies concolor, Acacia* sp., *Acer* sp., *Aesculus* sp., *Albizia julibrissin, Alnus* sp., *Amelanchier* sp., *Araucaria heterophylla, Arbutus unedo, Betula* sp., *Callistemon* sp., *Carpinus caroliniana, Catalpa bignonioides, Cedrus* sp., *Celtis* sp., *Cercidiphyllum japonicum, Cercis canadensis, Chamaecyparis* sp., *Chamaerops humilis, Chilopsis linearis, Chionanthus virginicus, Cinnamomum camphora, Citrus* sp., *Cladrastis kentukea, Cornus* sp., *Corylus* sp., *Crataegus* sp., *Cycas* sp., *Elaeagnus angustifolia, Eucalyptus* sp., *Fagus* sp., *Fraxinus* sp., *Ginkgo biloba, Gleditsia triacanthos* var. *inermis, Grevillea* sp., *Hamamelis virginiana, Hedyscepe canterburyana, Ilex* sp., *Jacaranda mimosifolia, Juniperus* sp., *Laburnum* × *watereri, Laurus nobilis, Leucodendron argenteum, Liquidambar styraciflua, Liriodendron tulipifera, Magnolia* sp., *Malus floribunda, Metasequoia glyptostroboides, Michelia doltsopa, Nyssa sylvatica, Olea europaea, Oxydendrum arboreum, Parrotia persica, Phoenix* sp., *Picea* sp., *Pinus* sp., *Pistacia chinensis, Platanus* × *acerifolia, Podocarpus* sp., *Populus* sp., *Prunus* sp., *Pseudotsuga menziesii, Psorothamnus spinosus, Punica granatum, Pyrus calleryana, Quercus* sp., *Robinia pseudoacacia, Salix* sp., *Sassafras albidum, Schinus molle, Sequoia sempervirens, Sequoiadendron giganteum, Sophora japonica, Sorbus aucuparia, Stewartia* sp., *Styrax japonicus, Syringa reticulata, Taxodium distichum, Tilia* sp., *Tsuga canadensis, Ulmus parvifolia, Vitex agnus-castus*	*Albizia julibrissin, Alnus* sp., *Arbutus unedo, Carpinus caroliniana, Cercis canadensis, Chamaerops humilis, Cornus* sp., *Corylus* sp., *Cycas* sp., *Elaeagnus angustifolia, Fagus* sp., *Grevillea* sp., *Halesia carolina, Hamamelis virginiana, Ilex* sp., *Liquidambar styraciflua, Magnolia* sp., *Oxydendrum arboreum, Podocarpus* sp., *Pseudotsuga menziesii, Syringa reticulata*	*Alnus* sp., *Carpinus caroliniana*
Neutral Soils 6.5–7.5 pH Zones 10–11 **Perennial Plants**	*Abelmoschus moschatus, Acanthus mollis, Achillea* sp., *Acorus* sp., *Agastache* sp., *Alcea rosea, Aloe* sp., *Alternanthera ficoidea, Anthemis tinctoria, Antirrhinum majus, Aquilegia* sp., *Arctotis venusta, Artemisia* sp., *Asparagus setaceus, Astilbe* sp., *Bacopa caroliniana, Begonia* × *semperflorens-cultorum, Browallia speciosa, Calamintha nepeta, Calceolaria* sp., *Calibrachoa* sp., *Campanula* sp., *Capsicum annuum, Centranthus ruber, Chrysanthemum* sp., *Convolvulus sabatius, Coreopsis* sp., *Cosmos atrosanguineus, Delphinium* sp., *Dianthus caryophyllus, Dionaea muscipula, Drosera* sp., *Echeveria elegans, Echinacea purpurea, Equisetum hyemale, Erigeron* sp., *Eschscholzia californica, Eupatorium* sp., *Fragaria* sp., *Gazania* sp., *Geranium sanguineum, Gerbera jamesonii, Gunnera manicata, Hedychium* sp., *Helichrysum bracteatum, Heliotropium arborescens, Hydrocotyle verticillata, Iberis sempervirens, Impatiens wallerana, Lavandula* sp., *Limonium platyphyllum, Linum perenne, Lobelia cardinalis, Lobelia erinus, Malva alcea, Mertensia pulmonarioides, Mimulus cardinalis, Myosotis scorpioides, Nasturtium officinale, Nolana paradoxa, Oenanthe javanica, Oenothera* sp., *Osteospermum* sp., *Paeonia* hyb., *Patrinia* sp., *Pelargonium* sp., *Penstemon* sp., *Phlox paniculata, Phormium* sp., *Physalis alkekengi, Rehmannia elata, Sagittaria latifolia, Salvia* sp., *Santolina chamaecyparissus, Sarracenia* sp., *Saxifraga stolonifera, Scaevola* sp., *Scrophularia auriculata, Sempervivum tectorum, Senecio cineraria, Senecio* × *hybridus, Sidalcea* sp., *Silene californica, Soleirolia soleirolii, Solidago* hyb., *Stachys byzantina, Stokesia laevis, Tradescantia virginiana, Valeriana officinalis, Vinca* sp., *Viola* sp.	*Acanthus mollis, Agastache* sp., *Alternanthera ficoidea, Aquilegia* sp., *Artemisia* sp., *Astilbe* sp., *Begonia* × *semperflorens-cultorum, Browallia speciosa, Brunnera macrophylla, Calamintha nepeta, Campanula persicifolia, Chrysanthemum* sp., *Convolvulus sabatius, Delphinium* sp., *Echinacea purpurea, Equisetum hyemale, Erigeron* sp., *Eupatorium* sp., *Gerbera jamesonii, Gunnera manicata, Heliotropium arborescens, Hosta* sp., *Houttuynia cordata, Hydrocotyle verticillata, Impatiens wallerana, Ligularia* sp., *Malva alcea, Mertensia pulmonarioides, Mimulus cardinalis, Myosotis scorpioides, Oenanthe javanica, Omphalodes* sp., ORCHIDACEAE, *Paeonia* hyb., *Penstemon* sp., *Phlox paniculata, Physalis alkekengi, Rehmannia elata, Saxifraga stolonifera, Scrophularia auriculata, Sidalcea* sp., *Silene californica, Soleirolia soleirolii, Stachys byzantina, Tradescantia virginiana, Valeriana officinalis, Vinca* sp., *Viola* sp.	*Acanthus mollis, Astilbe* sp., *Browallia speciosa, Hosta* sp., *Houttuynia cordata, Hydrocotyle verticillata, Impatiens wallerana, Ligularia* sp., *Myosotis scorpioides, Omphalodes* sp., ORCHIDACEAE, *Vinca* sp.
Grasses and Ground Covers	*Andropogon gerardii, Aptenia cordifolia, Armeria maritima, Arundo donax, Baumea rubignosa, Cerastium tomentosum, Chamaemelum nobile, Cyperus prolifer, Delosperma cooperi, Duchensnea indica, Dymondia margaretae, Glyceria maxima, Hypericum calycinum, Lagurus ovatus, Lampranthus* sp., *Lantana montevidensis, Liriope muscari, Miscanthus floridulus* 'Rubra', *Miscanthus sinensis, Pennisetum alopecuroides, Phalaris arundinacea, Phragmites australis, Rosmarinus officinalis prostratus, Rotala rotundifolia, Schizachyrium scoparium, Scirpus cyperinus, Sedum* sp., *Thymus serpyllum*	*Arundo donax, Chamaemelum nobile, Cyperus alternifolius, Cyperus prolifer, Duchensnea indica, Glyceria maxima, Hypericum calycinum, Liriope muscari, Miscanthus floridulus* 'Rubra', *Miscanthus sinensis, Ophiopogon japonicus, Pennisetum alopecuroides, Rotala rotundifolia, Scirpus cyperinus, Sedum* sp.	*Duchensnea indica, Liriope muscari, Ophiopogon japonicus*
Cacti, Ferns, and Shrubs	*Abutilon hybridum, Aesculus parviflora, Agave* sp., *Aloysia triphylla, Aronia arbutifolia, Athyrium filix-femina, Aucuba japonica, Brugmansia* × *candida, Buddleia* sp., *Caryopteris* sp., *Cereus peruvianus, Cestrum nocturnum, Choisya ternata, Cibotium glaucum, Cistus albidus, Cordyline fruticosa, Coryphantha vivipara, Cyathea cooperi, Davallia trichomanoides, Dicksonia antarctica, Echinocactus grusonii, Echinocereus* sp., *Euonymus* sp., *Euphorbia* sp., *Euryops pectinatus, Ferocactus* sp., *Fuchsia* × *hybrida, Gymnocalycium saglione, Hibiscus mutabilis, Hibiscus rosa-sinensis, Hydrangea* sp., *Indigofera* sp., *Isopogon formosus, Justicia brandegeana, Lagerstroemia indica, Lantana* hyb., *Leonotis leonurus, Leucophyllum frutescens, Ligustrum* sp., *Mammillaria bocasana, Murraya paniculata, Musa* sp., *Myrtus communis, Nandina domestica, Nerium oleander, Opuntia* sp., *Osmunda regalis, Pinus mugo* var. *mugo, Pittosporum tobira, Platycerium bifurcatum, Plumeria rubra, Polygala* × *dalmaisiana, Rhododendron* sp., *Rosa* sp., *Sambucus* sp., *Schlumbergera bridgesii, Stenocereus thurberi, Strelitzia reginae, Teucrium* × *lucidrys, Tibouchina urvilleana, Xylosma congestum, Yucca filamentosa*	*Abutilon hybridum, Adiantum capillus-veneris, Aronia arbutifolia, Asplenium nidus, Athyrium filix-femina, Aucuba japonica, Buddleia* sp., *Camellia* sp., *Choisya ternata, Cibotium glaucum, Cyrtomium falcatum, Davallia trichomanoides, Dennstaedtia punctilobula, Dicksonia antarctica, Echinocactus grusonii, Euphorbia* sp., *Fatsia japonica, Hibiscus rosa-sinensis, Hydrangea* sp., *Ligustrum* sp., *Mammillaria bocasana, Murraya paniculata, Nandina domestica, Platycerium bifurcatum, Rhododendron* sp., *Schlumbergera bridgesii, Tibouchina urvilleana, Xylosma congestum*	*Adiantum capillus-veneris, Asplenium nidus, Athyrium filix-femina, Cyrtomium falcatum, Dennstaedtia punctilobula, Dicksonia antarctica, Fatsia japonica, Rhododendron* sp., *Schlumbergera bridgesii*

Plant Community	Full to Filtered Sun	Open to Partial Shade	Full Shade
Neutral Soils 6.5–7.5 pH Zones 10–11 Landscape Trees	*Acacia* sp., *Acer* sp., *Albizia julibrissin*, *Alnus* sp., *Araucaria heterophylla*, *Arbutus unedo*, *Callistemon* sp., *Catalpa bignonioides*, *Cedrus* sp., *Chamaerops humilis*, *Chilopsis linearis*, *Cinnamomum camphora*, *Citrus* sp., *Cornus* sp., *Cycas* sp., *Eucalyptus* sp., *Fraxinus* sp., *Grevillea* sp., *Hedyscepe canterburyana*, *Jacaranda mimosifolia*, *Laurus nobilis*, *Leucodendron argenteum*, *Magnolia* sp., *Michelia doltsopa*, *Olea europaea*, *Phoenix* sp., *Podocarpus* sp., *Punica granatum*, *Quercus* sp., *Robinia pseudoacacia*, *Salix* sp., *Schinus molle*, *Sequoia sempervirens*, *Sophora japonica*, *Taxodium distichum*, *Ulmus parvifolia*, *Vitex agnus-castus*	*Albizia julibrissin*, *Alnus* sp., *Arbutus unedo*, *Chamaerops humilis*, *Cornus* sp., *Cycas* sp., *Grevillea* sp., *Halesia carolina*, *Magnolia* sp., *Podocarpus* sp.	*Alnus* sp.
Akaline Soils 8.0–8.5 pH Zones 1–3 Perennial Plants	*Achillea* sp., *Acorus calamus*, *Aethionema* sp., *Aruncus dioicus*, *Caltha palustris*, *Centaurea* sp., *Dianthus* × *allwoodii*, *Dicentra* sp., *Filipendula rubra*, *Fragaria* sp., *Geranium sanguineum*, *Geum* sp., *Lysimachia nummularia*, *Sagittaria latifolia*, *Scabiosa caucasica*, *Typha minima*, *Vinca* sp.	*Aruncus dioicus*, *Caltha palustris*, *Dicentra* sp., *Filipendula rubra*, *Geum* sp., *Lysimachia nummularia*, *Scabiosa caucasica*, *Typha minima*, *Vinca* sp.	*Vinca* sp.
Grasses and Ground Covers	*Armeria maritima*, *Helictotrichon sempervirens*, *Juniperus horizontalis*, *Scirpus cyperinus*	*Scirpus cyperinus*	(Site is challenging for most species.)
Cacti, Ferns, and Shrubs	*Caragana arborescens*, *Euonymus* sp., *Juniperus communis*, *Pinus mugo* var. *mugo*, *Potentilla fruticosa*, *Thuja occidentalis*	*Juniperus communis*, *Potentilla fruticosa*	(Site is challenging for most species.)
Landscape Trees	*Elaeagnus angustifolia*, *Gleditsia triacanthos* var. *inermis*, *Juniperus* sp.	*Elaeagnus angustifolia*, *Gleditsia triacanthos* var. *inermis*, *Juniperus* sp.	(Site is challenging for most species.)
Akaline Soils 8.0–8.5 pH Zones 4–5 Perennial Plants	*Achillea* sp., *Acorus calamus*, *Aethionema* sp., *Aruncus dioicus*, *Caltha palustris*, *Centaurea* sp., *Centranthus ruber*, *Dianthus* × *allwoodii*, *Dianthus caryophyllus*, *Dicentra* sp., *Filipendula rubra*, *Fragaria* sp., *Geranium sanguineum*, *Geum* sp., *Gypsophila paniculata*, *Limonium platyphyllum*, *Lysichiton americanum*, *Lysimachia nummularia*, *Myosotis scorpioides*, *Rodgersia* sp., *Sagittaria latifolia*, *Saururus cernuus*, *Scabiosa caucasica*, *Scrophularia auriculata*, *Silene californica*, *Typha minima*, *Vinca* sp.	*Aruncus dioicus*, *Caltha palustris*, *Dicentra* sp., *Filipendula rubra*, *Geum* sp., *Lysichiton americanum*, *Lysimachia nummularia*, *Myosotis scorpioides*, *Rodgersia* sp., *Saururus cernuus*, *Scabiosa caucasica*, *Scrophularia auriculata*, *Silene californica*, *Typha minima*, *Vinca* sp.	*Myosotis scorpioides*, *Rodgersia* sp., *Saururus cernuus*, *Vinca* sp.
Grasses and Ground Covers	*Armeria maritima*, *Butomus umbellatus*, *Delosperma cooperi*, *Glyceria maxima*, *Helictotrichon sempervirens*, *Juniperus horizontalis*, *Lampranthus* sp., *Phalaris arundinacea*, *Phragmites australis*, *Scirpus cyperinus*, *Sisyrinchium* sp.	*Glyceria maxima*, *Scirpus cyperinus*, *Sisyrinchium* sp.	(Site is challenging for most species.)
Cacti, Ferns, and Shrubs	*Calycanthus* sp., *Caragana arborescens*, *Cotinus coggygria*, *Euonymus* sp., *Euphorbia* sp., *Forsythia* × *intermedia*, *Juniperus communis*, *Ligustrum* sp., *Pinus mugo* var. *mugo*, *Potentilla fruticosa*, *Spiraea* × *vanhouttei*, *Teucrium* × *lucidrys*, *Thuja occidentalis*	*Calycanthus* sp., *Euphorbia* sp., *Juniperus communis*, *Ligustrum* sp., *Potentilla fruticosa*, *Spiraea* × *vanhouttei*	(Site is challenging for most species.)
Landscape Trees	*Elaeagnus angustifolia*, *Gleditsia triacanthos* var. *inermis*, *Juniperus* sp., *Laburnum* × *watereri*	*Elaeagnus angustifolia*	(Site is challenging for most species.)
Akaline Soils 8.0–8.5 pH Zones 6–7 Perennial Plants	*Achillea* sp., *Acorus* sp., *Aethionema* sp., *Aruncus dioicus*, *Caltha palustris*, *Centaurea* sp., *Centranthus ruber*, *Convolvulus sabatius*, *Cosmos atrosanguineus*, *Dianthus* × *allwoodii*, *Dianthus caryophyllus*, *Dicentra* sp., *Echeveria elegans*, *Erodium reichardii*, *Filipendula rubra*, *Fragaria* sp., *Geranium sanguineum*, *Geum* sp., *Gunnera manicata*, *Gypsophila paniculata*, *Limonium platyphyllum*, *Lysichiton americanum*, *Lysimachia nummularia*, *Mimulus cardinalis*, *Myosotis scorpioides*, *Osteospermum* sp., *Phormium* sp., *Rodgersia* sp., *Sagittaria latifolia*, *Saururus cernuus*, *Scabiosa caucasica*, *Scaevola* sp., *Scrophularia auriculata*, *Silene californica*, *Typha minima*, *Vinca* sp.	*Aruncus dioicus*, *Caltha palustris*, *Convolvulus sabatius*, *Dicentra* sp., *Erodium reichardii*, *Filipendula rubra*, *Geum* sp., *Gunnera manicata*, *Houttuynia cordata*, *Lysichiton americanum*, *Lysimachia nummularia*, *Mimulus cardinalis*, *Myosotis scorpioides*, *Rodgersia* sp., *Saururus cernuus*, *Scabiosa caucasica*, *Scrophularia auriculata*, *Silene californica*, *Typha minima*, *Vinca* sp.	*Houttuynia cordata*, *Myosotis scorpioides*, *Rodgersia* sp., *Saururus cernuus*, *Vinca* sp.
Grasses and Ground Covers	*Armeria maritima*, *Arundo donax*, *Butomus umbellatus*, *Delosperma cooperi*, *Glyceria maxima*, *Helictotrichon sempervirens*, *Juniperus horizontalis*, *Lagurus ovatus*, *Lampranthus* sp., *Phalaris arundinacea*, *Phragmites australis*, *Rosmarinus officinalis prostratus*, *Scirpus cyperinus*, *Sisyrinchium* sp.	*Arundo donax*, *Glyceria maxima*, *Scirpus cyperinus*, *Sisyrinchium* sp.	(Site is challenging for most species.)
Cacti, Ferns, and Shrubs	*Aucuba japonica*, *Calycanthus* sp., *Caragana arborescens*, *Carnegiea gigantea*, *Cistus albidus*, *Cotinus coggygria*, *Echinocactus grusonii*, *Euonymus* sp., *Euphorbia* sp., *Euryops pectinatus*, *Ferocactus* sp., *Forsythia* × *intermedia*, *Juniperus communis*, *Kolkwitzia amabilis*, *Leucophyllum frutescens*, *Ligustrum* sp., *Mammillaria bocasana*, *Pinus mugo* var. *mugo*, *Pittosporum tobira*, *Potentilla fruticosa*, *Pyracantha* sp., *Spiraea* × *vanhouttei*, *Stenocereus thurberi*, *Teucrium* × *lucidrys*, *Thuja occidentalis*	*Aucuba japonica*, *Calycanthus* sp., *Echinocactus grusonii*, *Euphorbia* sp., *Juniperus communis*, *Kolkwitzia amabilis*, *Ligustrum* sp., *Mammillaria bocasana*, *Potentilla fruticosa*, *Spiraea* × *vanhouttei*	(Site is challenging for most species.)

Plant Community	Full to Filtered Sun	Open to Partial Shade	Full Shade
Akaline Soils 8.0–8.5 pH Zones 6–7 Landscape Trees	*Albizia julibrissin, Arbutus unedo, Callistemon sp., Celtis sp., Chamaerops humilis, Corylus sp., Elaeagnus angustifolia, Fraxinus sp., Gleditsia triacanthos var. inermis, Jacaranda mimosifolia, Juniperus sp., Laburnum × watereri, Laurus nobilis, Olea europaea, Phoenix sp., Psorothamnus spinosus*	*Albizia julibrissin, Arbutus unedo, Chamaerops humilis, Corylus sp., Elaeagnus angustifolia*	(Site is challenging for most species.)
Akaline Soils 8.0–8.5 pH Zones 8–9 Perennial Plants	*Achillea sp., Acorus sp., Aethionema sp., Aloe sp., Aruncus dioicus, Calibrachoa sp., Caltha palustris, Centaurea sp., Centranthus ruber, Convolvulus sabatius, Cosmos atrosanguineus, Dianthus × allwoodii, Dianthus caryophyllus, Dicentra sp., Dionaea muscipula, Echeveria elegans, Erodium reichardii, Filipendula rubra, Fragaria sp., Geranium sanguineum, Gunnera manicata, Gypsophila paniculata, Limonium platyphyllum, Lysichiton americanum, Lysimachia nummularia, Mimulus cardinalis, Myosotis scorpioides, Osteospermum sp., Phormium sp., Rodgersia sp., Sagittaria latifolia, Saururus cernuus, Scaevola sp., Scrophularia auriculata, Silene californica, Vinca sp.*	*Aruncus dioicus, Caltha palustris, Convolvulus sabatius, Dicentra sp., Erodium reichardii, Filipendula rubra, Gunnera manicata, Houttuynia cordata, Lysichiton americanum, Lysimachia nummularia, Mimulus cardinalis, Myosotis scorpioides, Rodgersia sp., Saururus cernuus, Scrophularia auriculata, Silene californica, Vinca sp.*	*Houttuynia cordata, Myosotis scorpioides, Rodgersia sp., Saururus cernuus, Vinca sp.*
Grasses and Ground Covers	*Armeria maritima, Arundo donax, Baumea rubingosa, Butomus umbellatus, Cyperus prolifer, Delosperma cooperi, Glyceria maxima, Helictotrichon sempervirens, Juniperus horizontalis, Lagurus ovatus, Lampranthus sp., Phalaris arundinacea, Phragmites australis, Rosmarinus officinalis prostratus, Scirpus cyperinus, Sisyrinchium sp.*	*Arundo donax, Cyperus prolifer, Glyceria maxima, Scirpus cyperinus, Sisyrinchium sp.*	(Site is challenging for most species.)
Cacti, Ferns, and Shrubs	*Aucuba japonica, Calycanthus sp., Caragana arborescens, Carnegiea giganteum, Cephalocereus senilis, Cereus peruvianus, Cistus albidus, Cotinus coggygria, Echinocactus grusonii, Euonymus sp., Euphorbia sp., Euryops pectinatus, Ferocactus sp., Forsythia × intermedia, Juniperus communis, Kolkwitzia amabilis, Leucophyllum frutescens, Ligustrum sp., Mammillaria bocasana, Pinus mugo var. mugo, Pittosporum tobira, Polygala × dalmaisiana, Potentilla fruticosa, Pyracantha sp., Spiraea × vanhouttei, Stenocereus thurberi, Teucrium × lucidrys, Thuja occidentalis*	*Aucuba japonica, Calycanthus sp., Echinocactus grusonii, Euphorbia sp., Juniperus communis, Kolkwitzia amabilis, Ligustrum sp., Mammillaria bocasana, Potentilla fruticosa, Spiraea × vanhouttei*	(Site is challenging for most species.)
Landscape Trees	*Albizia julibrissin, Arbutus unedo, Callistemon sp., Celtis sp., Chamaerops humilis, Corylus sp., Elaeagnus angustifolia, Fraxinus sp., Gleditsia triacanthos var. inermis, Hedyscepe canterburyana, Jacaranda mimosifolia, Juniperus sp., Laburnum × watereri, Laurus nobilis, Olea europaea, Phoenix sp., Psorothamnus spinosus*	*Albizia julibrissin, Arbutus unedo, Chamaerops humilis, Corylus sp., Elaeagnus angustifolia*	(Site is challenging for most species.)
Akaline Soils 8.0–8.5 pH Zones 10–11 Perennial Plants	*Achillea sp., Acorus sp., Aloe sp., Calibrachoa sp., Centranthus ruber, Convolvulus sabatius, Cosmos atrosanguineus, Dianthus caryophyllus, Dionaea muscipula, Echeveria elegans, Fragaria sp., Geranium sanguineum, Gunnera manicata, Limonium platyphyllum, Mimulus cardinalis, Myosotis scorpioides, Osteospermum sp., Phormium sp., Sagittaria latifolia, Scaevola sp., Scrophularia auriculata, Silene californica, Vinca sp.*	*Convolvulus sabatius, Gunnera manicata, Houttuynia cordata, Mimulus cardinalis, Myosotis scorpioides, Scrophularia auriculata, Silene californica, Vinca sp.*	*Houttuynia cordata, Myosotis scorpioides, Vinca sp.*
Grasses and Ground Covers	*Armeria maritima, Arundo donax, Baumea rubingosa, Cyperus prolifer, Delosperma cooperi, Glyceria maxima, Lagurus ovatus, Lampranthus sp., Phalaris arundinacea, Phragmites australis, Rosmarinus officinalis prostratus, Scirpus cyperinus*	*Arundo donax, Cyperus alternifolius, Cyperus prolifer, Glyceria maxima, Scirpus cyperinus*	(Site is challenging for most species.)
Cacti, Ferns, and Shrubs	*Aucuba japonica, Cereus peruvianus, Cistus albidus, Echinocactus grusonii, Euonymus sp., Euphorbia sp., Euryops pectinatus, Ferocactus sp., Leucophyllum frutescens, Ligustrum sp., Mammillaria bocasana, Pittosporum tobira, Polygala × dalmaisiana, Stenocereus thurberi, Teucrium × lucidrys*	*Aucuba japonica, Echinocactus grusonii, Euphorbia sp., Ligustrum sp., Mammillaria bocasana*	(Site is challenging for most species.)
Landscape Trees	*Albizia julibrissin, Arbutus unedo, Callistemon sp., Chamaerops humilis, Fraxinus sp., Hedyscepe canterburyana, Jacaranda mimosifolia, Laurus nobilis, Olea europaea, Phoenix sp.*	*Albizia julibrissin, Arbutus unedo, Chamaerops humilis*	(Site is challenging for most species.)

A Note on Annuals, Tender Perennials, and Bulbs: In many areas, plants are offered as nursery starts or bedding plants, to be planted for a single season. Bulbs often are lifted after they bloom and are stored for planting the following season or simply discarded. Bedding plants have vigorous root systems at the time they are planted; bulbs bring their stored energy with them to the planting site. As a consequence, either group of plants will perform well in any reasonably well-drained soil, and they have been omitted from the Landscape Plant Commmunity lists on the preceeding pages. Complete data on the ideal plant hardiness zones, soil needs, and light requirements are given in the encyclopedia listings for each specific plant, where it can be used to plan a naturalized or self-seeding bed [see Annuals and Tender Perennials, pgs. 24–47, and Bulbs and Bulbous Plants, pgs. 116–153].

Encyclopedia of Landscape Plants

Gallery of Popular Landscape Plants for Home Gardens

Everyone's dream is a carefree garden of outstanding beauty, whether in an open meadow, a natural glade, a woodland setting, or a seaside retreat. Depending on the plants you choose and the design selected, your landscape may be cottage charming or formal, whimsical or practical.

GARDENS IN HOME LANDSCAPES ARE COMMUNITIES of plants that can include annual and perennial flowers, turf and ornamental grasses, ground covers, vines, cacti, ferns, shrubs, and trees. Choosing the right plants for your landscape is easiest when you have complete information to aid your selection.

More than a thousand landscape plant species are discussed or pictured in the pages that follow. Each was selected because of three criteria: it must be readily available in the majority of garden centers and nurseries, be commonly planted in many different settings in a variety of home landscapes and gardens, and have outstanding beauty in flowers, foliage, or habit.

The plants also were selected to ensure you would have a good selection of each plant type for most landscaping purposes, for every USDA Plant Hardiness Zone, and for a variety of site conditions ranging from sun to shade, in soils from acid to alkaline, from clay to sandy loam, from moist to dry.

You'll find that the plants that follow have been divided into convenient sections by their type, each entry alphabetized by its scientific genus and species. A plant index, found in the back of the book, lists every entry by each of its common names and its scientific name, making finding a specific plant quick and easy, whether you browse by type or specifically look it up.

Most important, complete information to describe, plant, and care for every plant accompanies its color photograph. Take a moment to look at any plant, and you will find that each of the other entries in that section contains equivalent information under their shared headings, to make locating key information a snap.

Annuals and Tender Perennials

*A*nnual plants and tender perennials are the showstoppers of every garden. From towering sunflowers to diminutive pansies, they bloom in a breathtaking array of hues, flower forms, and sizes. Some are climbing vines that cascade over an arbor, others sit demurely at the edge of a border, still others stand erect or trail from a wall.

Carefully selected, they will perform in frosty gardens or those with near-searing heat, in sun or shade. They bring seasonal color to landscapes found in the reaches of the polar arctic, and they create stunning displays in arid deserts in springtime.

Annual plants are those that, if given enough time and hospitable weather, will sprout, grow, form flowers, and develop seed in a single season, then die. A new generation grows from their seed the following year. Also found in most annual collections, including the one that follows, are tender perennial plants that would live on to grow again in mild or subtropical climates, but which frequently are planted as nursery starts in cold-winter regions and used as annual flowers for a single season in the landscape.

Annual: *Ageratum houstonianum.* ASTERACEAE (COMPOSITAE).
Common name: Flossflower (Ageratum, Pussy-Foot).
Description: Many cultivars of mounding, upright annual herbs, to 30 in. (75 cm) tall. Fuzzy, green, heart-shaped, finely toothed leaves, to 5 in. (13 cm) long. Common cultivars include *A. houstonianum* 'Album', 'Blue Blazer', 'Blue Danube', 'Blue Horizon', 'North Sea', and 'Summer Snow'.
Bloom: Many tiny, blue, pink, purple, violet, white, fuzzy flowers, to ¼ in. (6 mm) wide, in clustered heads, in early summer–autumn. Long-lasting blooms.
Plant hardiness: Self-seeding, zones 4–11.
Soil: Moist, well-drained soil. Fertility: Rich. 6.5–7.0 pH.
Planting: Start indoors in early spring, zones 2–9, transplanting after frost hazard has passed, in full sun to partial shade; sow outdoors when soil warms, zones 10–11, 6–9 in. (15–23 cm) apart.
Care: Easy. Keep moist during growth and bloom. Fertilize monthly. Deadhead spent flowers to prolong bloom. Protect from sun, heat, zones 9–11. Propagate by seed.
Features: Good choice for beds, borders, containers, edgings in cottage, formal, meadow, wildlife gardens. Good for cutting; scald stems after picking, soak in cool water before arranging. Attracts birds, butterflies. Mealybug, orthegia, whitefly and sclerotinia wilt susceptible.

Annual: *Amaranthus caudatus.* AMARANTHACEAE.
Common name: Love-Lies-Bleeding (Tassel Flower).
Description: Several cultivars of erect, branching annual herbs, 3–5 ft. (90–150 cm) tall. Alternate, smooth, medium green, oval, pointed, veined, edible leaves, to 10 in. (25 cm) long. Common cultivars include *A. caudatus* 'Green Thumb' and 'Pygmy Torch'. See also *A. tricolor,* 'Joseph's-Coat'.
Bloom: Many tiny, deep red, flute-shaped flowers, in cascading woolly, tasseled or ropelike clusters, 18–24 in. (45–60 cm) long, in summer–late autumn, forming edible seed.
Plant hardiness: Self-seeding, zones 2–10.
Soil: Damp to dry, well-drained soil. Fertility: Rich–average. 7.0–7.5 pH.
Planting: Mid- to late spring in full sun, 2 ft. (60 cm) apart, after soil warms. Avoid transplanting.
Care: Easy. Keep damp during growth and bloom; allow soil surface to dry between waterings. Fertilize monthly. Drought, heat tolerant. Propagate by seed.
Features: Good choice for accents, backgrounds, beds, fencelines, walls in cottage, meadow, natural, wildlife gardens. Good for drying, salads, grain. Pest and disease resistant.

Annual: *Amaranthus tricolor.* AMARANTHACEAE.
Common name: Joseph's-Coat (Tampala).
Description: Several cultivars of branching, upright herbs 1–4 ft. (30–120 cm) tall. Alternate, smooth, green, red, yellow, mottled and variegated, oval, pointed, edible leaves, to 4 in. (10 cm) wide and 6 in. (15 cm) long, in tiers vertically along the stalk. See also *A. caudatus,* love-lies-bleeding.
Bloom: Insignificant flowers; grown primarily for foliage.
Plant hardiness: Self-seeding, zones 2–10.
Soil: Damp to dry, well-drained soil. Fertility: Average–low. 5.5–7.0 pH.
Planting: Spring in full sun, 18 in. (45 cm) apart, after soil warms. Avoid transplanting.
Care: Easy. Keep damp during growth and bloom; allow soil surface to dry between waterings. Avoid fertilizing. Drought, heat tolerant. Stake tall cultivars. Propagate by seed.
Features: Good choice for accents, backgrounds, borders, containers, mixed plantings in cottage, formal, meadow gardens. Good for cutting, salads. Pest and disease resistant.

Annual: *Brachycome iberidifolia.* ASTERACEAE (COMPOSITAE).
Common name: Swan River Daisy.
Description: Several cultivars of branching, mounding, upright annual herbs, to 18 in. (45 cm) tall. Alternate, yellow green, feathery, divided, deeply cut leaves, to 3 in. (75 mm) long, forming a circular, radiating base. Common cultivars include *B. iberidifolia* 'Bravo', 'City Lights', 'New Amethyst', 'Splendor', and 'Summer Skies'.
Bloom: Many blue, pink, white, daisylike, fragrant flowers, to 1 in. (25 mm) wide, with yellow, buttonlike centers, in late spring–early summer. Plant in 3-week successions to prolong bloom.
Plant hardiness: Self-seeding, zones 5–10.
Soil: Moist, well-drained, sandy soil. Fertility: Rich. 6.5–7.5 pH.
Planting: Spring in full sun to partial shade, 6–12 in. (15–30 cm) apart, after frost hazard has passed. Start seed indoors 6 weeks before final frost for early blooms; transplant when soil becomes workable.
Care: Easy. Keep moist during growth and bloom. Fertilize monthly. Pinch to promote bushy growth; deadhead spent flowers to prolong bloom. Protect from sun, zones 9–11. Propagate by seed.
Features: Good choice for hanging baskets, beds, borders, containers, edgings, massed plantings in cottage, formal, rock gardens.

Annual: *Brassica oleracea.* BRASSICACEAE (CRUCIFERAE).
Common name: Ornamental Kale (Decorative Kale, Wild Cabbage).
Description: Many hybrids of low, open annual herbs, to 20 in. (50 cm) wide. Shiny or waxy, cream, green, pink, purple, red, yellow, edible leaves, to 1 ft. (30 cm) long, form wavy rosettes, sometimes with contrasting fringes or feathered edges. Best color after frost in cool seasons. Common cultivars include *B. oleracea* 'Dynasty Pink' and 'Tokyo'.
Bloom: Many tiny, cream, green, white, yellow, 4-petaled flowers, in erect, feathery plumes, in summer–autumn.
Plant hardiness: Self-seeding, zones 2–10. Frost hardy.

Soil: Moist, well-drained, sandy loam. Fertility: Rich–average. 6.5–7.5 pH.
Planting: Spring in full sun, 1–2 ft. (30–60 cm) apart, after frost hazard has passed. Start seed indoors 8–10 weeks before final frost for early blooms; transplant when soil becomes workable.
Care: Easy. Keep evenly moist. Fertilize monthly. Protect from heat to avoid bolting, zones 9–11. Propagate by seed.
Features: Good choice for accents, borders, containers, edgings in formal, small-space gardens. Good for geometric pattern plantings. Larva and caterpillar susceptible.

Annual: *Calendula officinalis.* ASTERACEAE (COMPOSITAE).
Common name: Pot Marigold.
Description: Many cultivars of upright, branching or mounding herbs, to 2 ft. (60 cm) tall. Alternate, textured, medium green, broadly oval, wavy-edged, sometimes toothed leaves, to 1½ in. (38 mm) long. Common cultivars include *C. officinalis* 'Fiesta', 'Gypsy Festival', 'Pacific Apricot', and 'Touch of Red'. Dwarf cultivars available. *Tagetes erecta*, marigold, is a related plant.
Bloom: Many showy, deep orange, light or bright yellow, round, button-shaped, double-petaled, edible flowers, to 4 in. (10 cm) wide, in spring–autumn. Repeat blooming.
Plant hardiness: Self-seeding, zones 2–10.
Soil: Moist, well-drained loam. Fertility: Rich–average. 6.5–7.5 pH.
Planting: Spring in full sun, 6–12 in. (15–30 cm) apart, after frost hazard has passed. Start seed indoors 6–8 weeks before final frost for early blooms; transplant when soil warms.
Care: Easy. Keep moist. Fertilize every 2 months. Deadhead spent flowers to prolong bloom. Stake tall cultivars. Propagate by seed.
Features: Good choice for beds, borders, containers in cottage, formal, meadow, small-space gardens. Good for cutting. Source of medicinal and culinary herb. Spider mite, whitefly susceptible.

Annual: *Callistephus chinensis.* ASTERACEAE (COMPOSITAE).
Common name: China Aster (Annual Aster).
Description: Many cultivars of erect or branching annual herbs, 8–32 in. (20–80 cm) tall. Matte, green, oval or lance-shaped, deeply toothed leaves, to 5 in. (13 cm) long. Common cultivars include *C. chinensis* 'Dwarf Queen', 'Giant Perfection', and 'Powerpuff Super Bouquet'. See also *Aster*, a related perennial plant family.
Bloom: Solitary blue, pink, purple, red, white, yellow, round, single- or double-petaled flowers, 2–5 in. (50–125 mm) wide, in early summer–first frost.
Plant hardiness: Self-seeding, zones 6–10.
Soil: Moist, well-drained soil. Fertility: Rich. 6.5–7.0 pH.
Planting: Spring in full to filtered sun, 1 ft. (30 cm) apart, after soil warms.
Care: Easy. Keep evenly moist; avoid wetting foliage. Fertilize monthly. Mulch. Deadhead spent flowers and pinch foliage to prolong bloom. Propagate by seed. Rotate plantings each year.
Features: Good choice for beds, borders, containers in cottage, formal, meadow, shade gardens. Good for cutting. Root aphid, blister beetle, leafhopper and aster wilt, aster yellows susceptible.

Annual: *Campanula medium.* CAMPANULACEAE.
Common name: Canterbury-Bells.
Description: Many cultivars of erect, upright biennial herbs, 2–3 ft. (60–90 cm) tall. Alternate, rough-textured, deep green, oval, pointed leaves, to 10 in (25 cm) long, on hairy stalks. Dwarf cultivars available. See also *Campanula* species, many closely related biennial and perennial plants.
Bloom: Many violet blue, pink, white, bell-shaped, sometimes double-petaled flowers, to 2 in. (50 mm) long and 1 in. (25 mm) wide, with reflexed petals, in tiers vertically along the stalk, in spring–early summer.
Plant hardiness: Ground hardy, zones 6–8.
Soil: Moist, well-drained soil. Fertility: Rich. 7.0–7.5 pH.
Planting: Early spring in partial shade, 1 ft. (30 cm) apart, after frost hazard has passed. Start seed indoors 6–8 weeks before final frost for early blooms; transplant when soil warms. Sow seed for flowers the following season or plant nursery containers.

Care: Moderate. Keep moist. Fertilize monthly. Deadhead spent flowers to prolong bloom. Stake tall varieties. Propagate by seed.
Features: Good choice for accents, backgrounds, borders in cottage, meadow, shade, woodland gardens. Good for cutting. Disease resistant. Spider mite and slug, snail susceptible.

Annual: *Carthamus tinctorius.* ASTERACEAE (COMPOSITAE).
Common name: Safflower (False Saffron).
Description: A few cultivars of erect, branching, narrow, spiny annual herbs, to 3 ft. (90 cm) tall and 12–18 in. (30–45 cm) wide. Alternate, shiny, textured, gray or olive green, lance-shaped, spine-toothed leaves, 2–3 in. (50–75 mm) long. Spineless cultivars available.
Bloom: Showy, solitary, golden yellow, thistlelike, thread-rayed, edible flowers, to 1½ in. (38 cm) wide, in a rosette of green, armed bracts, in summer, form edible seed.
Plant hardiness: Self-seeding, zones 2–10. Best in arid climates.
Soil: Damp, well-drained, sandy loam. Fertility: Average. 6.5–7.5 pH.
Planting: Spring in full sun, 4–6 in. (10–15 cm) apart.
Care: Easy. Keep damp; allow soil surface to dry between waterings. Fertilize every 2 months. Stake tall cultivars. Propagate by seed.
Features: Good choice for accents, backgrounds, barriers, borders, fencelines, massed plantings, walls in cottage, meadow, seaside gardens. Good for cutting, drying. Pest resistant. Fungal disease susceptible.

Annual: *Catananche caerulea.* ASTERACEAE (COMPOSITAE).
Common name: Cupid's-Dart.
Description: Several cultivars of short-lived, erect, mounding perennial herbs, to 18 in. (45 cm) tall and 1 ft. (30 cm) wide. Alternate, woolly, gray green, narrow, grasslike, somewhat toothed leaves, to 1 ft. (30 cm) long. Common cultivars include *C. caerulea* 'Alba', 'Bicolor', and 'Major'.
Bloom: Many blue violet, white, daisylike flowers, to 2 in. (50 mm) wide, with jagged-toothed petals and dark centers, in summer–autumn.
Plant hardiness: Plant as tender annual, zones 2–11; ground hardy, zones 3–8.
Soil: Damp to dry, well-drained soil; avoid winter moisture. Fertility: Average. 6.5–7.5 pH.
Planting: Spring in full sun, 1 ft. (30 cm) apart, after frost hazard has passed.
Care: Moderate. Keep damp during growth; allow soil surface to dry between waterings. Fertilize every 2 months. Propagate by division, seed.
Features: Good choice for borders, containers, edgings in cottage, formal, meadow gardens. Good for cutting, drying. Pest resistant. Fungal disease susceptible.

Annual: *Catharanthus roseus (Vinca rosea).* APOCYNACEAE.
Common name: Periwinkle (Madagascar Periwinkle).
Description: Several cultivars of erect, creeping and spreading, perennial herbs to 20 in. (50 cm) tall and 18 in. (45 cm) wide. Opposite, shiny, deep green, oval, pointed leaves, to 2 in. (50 mm) long. Common cultivars include *C. roseus* 'Little Linda', 'Parasol', 'Polka Dot', and 'Pretty in Pink'.
Bloom: Many rose pink, rose, white, simple, 5-petaled flowers with contrasting centers, to 1½ in. (38 mm) wide, in late spring–autumn.
Plant hardiness: Plant as tender annual, zones 4–8; ground hardy, zones 9–11. Self-seeding.
Soil: Moist, well-drained, sandy or loamy soil. Fertility: Rich. 6.5–7.5 pH.
Planting: Spring in full sun to partial shade, 9–12 in. (23–30 cm) apart, after soil warms. Start seed indoors 12–16 weeks before final frost for early blooms; transplant when frost hazard has passed.
Care: Very easy. Keep evenly moist. Fertilize monthly. Shear in late autumn, zones 9–11. Protect from frost. Propagate by seed.
Features: Good choice for beds, borders, containers, edgings, ground covers in arid, formal, shade, woodland gardens. Smog resistant. Disease resistant. Slug, snail susceptible.

Annual: *Celosia* species. AMARANTHACEAE.
Common name: Woolflower (Cockscomb).
Description: Nearly 60 species of mounding, dense annual or perennial herbs, 10–36 in. (25–90 cm) tall. Alternate, bright green or variegated, lance-shaped leaves, to 2 in. (50 mm) long. Dwarf cultivars available. Common cultivars include *Celosia* 'Dwarf Fairy Fountains', 'Intermediate Apricot Brandy', 'Kimono', 'New Look', 'Pink Castle', 'Prestige Scarlet', 'Tall Forest Fire Improved', and 'Toreador'.
Bloom: Many tiny, bright gold, orange, purple, red, white, yellow, woolly, yarnlike flowers form erect plumes or rounded, nodding, crestlike clusters, to 4 in. (10 cm) tall, in summer–first frost.
Plant hardiness: Self-seeding, zones 2–11. Best in hot-summer climates.
Soil: Moist, well-drained soil. Fertility: Rich–low. 6.5–7.5 pH.
Planting: Spring in full sun, 9–12 in. (23–30 cm) apart, after frost hazard has passed.
Care: Moderate. Keep moist; allow soil surface to dry between waterings. Fertilize every 2–3 months. Deadhead spent flowers to prolong bloom. Propagate by seed.
Features: Good choice for beds, borders, containers, edgings in cottage, formal, meadow, small-space gardens. Good for cutting, drying. Pest and disease resistant.

Annual: *Centaurea cyanus.* ASTERACEAE (COMPOSITAE).
Common name: Cornflower (Bachelor's-Button).
Description: Many cultivars of upright, slender annual herbs, to 2 ft. (60 cm) tall. Hairy, gray green, narrow, lance-shaped leaves, to 3 in. (75 mm) long, with gray undersides. Common cultivars include *C. cyanus* 'Alba', 'Blue Diadem', 'Jubilee Gem', and 'Polka Dot'. *C. cineraria*, dusty-miller, is a closely related perennial species prized for its silver foliage.
Bloom: Many solitary, blue, burgundy, pink, red, white, pinwheel-like flowers, to 18 in. (45 cm) wide, with narrow petals, in early summer–autumn.
Plant hardiness: Self-seeding, zones 3–9. Light frost tolerant.
Soil: Moist, well-drained soil. Fertility: Average–low. 6.5–7.0 pH. Poor soil tolerant.
Planting: Spring in full sun, 8–12 in. (20–30 cm) apart, after frost hazard has passed. Avoid transplanting. Plant successions every 2 weeks to prolong bloom.
Care: Easy. Keep evenly moist. Fertilize monthly during growth. Deadhead spent flowers to prolong bloom. Propagate by seed.
Features: Good choice for beds, borders, edgings, massed plantings in cottage, formal, meadow, small-space, wildlife gardens. Attracts birds, butterflies. Pest and disease resistant.

Annual: *Chrysanthemum frutescens (Argyranthemum frutescens).* ASTERACEAE.
Common name: Marguerite (Paris Daisy, White Marguerite).
Description: Several cultivars of bushy, woody-stemmed perennial herbs, 3–4 ft. (90–120 cm) tall. Alternate, light to bright or gray green, oval, featherlike, deeply cut, pointed leaves, 2–4 in. (50–100 mm) long. Common cultivars include *C. frutescens* 'Chryaster', 'Silver Leaf', 'Snow White', and 'White Lady'.
Bloom: Showy, white, yellow, daisylike, single-or double-petaled flowers, to 2 in. (50 mm) wide, in late spring–autumn.
Plant hardiness: Plant as tender annual, zones 4–6; ground hardy, zones 7–11.
Soil: Moist, well-drained, sandy soil. Fertility: Rich–average. 5.5–7.0 pH.
Planting: Spring in full sun, 4–5 ft. (1.2–1.5 m) apart, after frost hazard has passed.
Care: Moderate. Keep evenly moist. Fertilize every 2 months. Deadhead spent flowers and prune lightly to shape. Propagate by cuttings, seed.
Features: Good choice for beds, borders, containers, massed plantings in cottage, formal, meadow, seaside gardens. Disease resistant. Leaf miner, nematode, thrips and root gall susceptible.

Annual: *Chrysanthemum multicaule.* ASTERACEAE (COMPOSITAE).
Common name: Annual Chrysanthemum.
Description: Many cultivars of low and mat-forming, fleshy annual herbs, to 1 ft. (30 cm) tall. Smooth, bright green, oval or spoon-shaped, succulent, usually coarsely toothed or feathery leaves, to 3 in. (75 mm) long. Common cultivars include *C. multicaule* 'Autumn Glory', 'Primrose Gem', 'Rainbow Mixed', and 'Yellow Buttons'.
Bloom: Many showy, gold, yellow, daisylike flowers, to 2½ in. (63 mm) wide, with buttonlike, gold, yellow centers, in summer–autumn.
Plant hardiness: Self-seeding, zones 4–10.
Soil: Moist, well-drained soil. Fertility: Rich–average. 6.5–7.5 pH.
Planting: Spring in full sun to partial shade, 1–2 ft. (30–60 cm) apart, after frost hazard has passed. Plant successions to prolong bloom.
Care: Moderate. Keep evenly moist. Fertilize monthly. Pinch early foliage shoots to shape, again on mature plants to maintain dense foliage. Propagate by seed.
Features: Good choice for beds, containers, edgings, ground covers in cottage, formal, rock, small-space gardens. Good for cutting. Aphid, midge and rust susceptible.

Annual: *Clarkia amoena.* ONAGRACEAE.

Common name: Satin Flower (Clarkia, Farewell-to-Spring, Godetia).

Description: Several cultivars of upright or spreading annual herbs, 6–24 in. (15–60 cm) tall. Alternate, smooth, light green, lance-shaped, tapered, pointed leaves, 1½–3 in. (38–75 mm) long. Common cultivars include *C. amoena* 'Dwarf Mixed Colors', and 'Tall Mixed Colors'.

Bloom: Many showy, lavender, pink, simple, 4-petaled, cup-shaped flowers, 2–3 in. (50–75 mm) wide, often with contrasting edges and centers, in spring–early summer.

Plant hardiness: Self-seeding, zones 2–10. Best in mild-summer climates.

Soil: Moist to damp, well-drained soil. Fertility: Average. 7.0 pH. Poor soil tolerant.

Planting: Spring in full sun to partial shade, 8–10 in. (20–25 cm) apart, when soil is workable. Avoid transplanting.

Care: Easy. Keep moist during growth; allow soil surface to dry between waterings. Fertilize quarterly. Pinch foliage to encourage bushy growth. Propagate by seed.

Features: Good choice for beds, borders, edgings in cottage, meadow, rock, seaside, woodland gardens. Pest and disease resistant.

Annual: *Cleome hasslerana.* CAPPARACEAE.

Common name: Spider Flower.

Description: Many cultivars of erect, branching or shrublike annual herbs, to 5 ft. (1.5 m) tall, armed with sharp spines at leaf nodes. Smooth, light green, palmlike, divided, pointed, fragrant leaves, each with 5–7 leaflets, 2–3 in. (50–75 mm) long. Common cultivars include *C. hasslerana* 'Cherry Queen', 'Helen Campbell', 'Pink Queen', and 'Queen Mixed Colors'. *C. spinosa*, spiny spider flower, is a closely related species with similar care needs.

Bloom: Showy, purple fading to white, 4-petaled flowers with threadlike stamens, to 2½ in. (63 mm) long, in round, ball-like clusters, to 6 in. (15 cm) wide, in summer–late autumn.

Plant hardiness: Self-seeding, zones 2–11.

Soil: Moist, well-drained soil. Fertility: Rich–average. 6.0–7.0 pH.

Planting: Spring in full sun to partial shade, 18–24 in. (45–60 cm) apart; early spring in areas with long, warm summers. Start seed indoors 8–10 weeks before final frost for early blooms; transplant when soil warms.

Care: Moderate. Keep evenly moist. Fertilize every 2 months. Stake tall cultivars. Propagate by seed.

Features: Good choice for accents, backgrounds, borders in cottage, natural, wildlife gardens. Good for cutting, drying. Attracts hummingbirds. Pest and disease resistant.

Annual: *Coleus* × *hybridus (Solenostemon scutellariodes).* LAMIACEAE (LABIATAE).

Common name: Garden Coleus (Flame Nettle, Painted Leaf Plant, Painted Nettle).

Description: Many cultivars of upright, shrublike, perennial, tropical herbs, to 7 ft. (2.2 m) tall. Opposite, textured, green, orange, pink, red, white, yellow, variegated, heart- or dagger-shaped, saw-edged leaves, 3–7 in. (75–180 mm) long, often with contrasting edges, radiate from branching square stems. Common cultivars include *Coleus* 'Carefree', 'Fijis', 'Fringed Leaf', 'Rainbow Series', 'Saber', and 'Wizard'.

Bloom: Many insignificant blue, violet, nettlelike flowers; grown for colorful foliage.

Plant hardiness: Plant as tender annual, zones 2–9; ground hardy, zones 10–11.

Soil: Moist, well-drained soil. Fertility: Rich. 7.0–7.5 pH.

Planting: Spring in full sun to partial shade, 10–12 in. (25–30 cm) apart. Start seed indoors 8–10 weeks before final frost for early blooms; transplant when soil warms.

Care: Moderate. Keep evenly moist. Fertilize monthly. Pinch flower buds for best leaf development. Propagate by cuttings, seed.

Features: Good choice for accents, beds, borders, containers, edgings, massed plantings in cottage, shade, small-space gardens. Disease resistant. Aphid susceptible.

Annual: *Consolida ambigua.* RANUNCULACEAE.

Common name: Rocket Larkspur (Annual Delphinium, Rocket).

Description: Many cultivars of erect, narrow annual herbs, 1–5 ft. (30–150 cm) tall. Smooth, green, fernlike, coarsely divided, deeply toothed leaves, to 4 in. (10 cm) long. Common cultivars include *C. ambigua* 'Blue Fountains', 'Blue Heaven', 'Dwarf Blue Butterfly', and 'Pacific Giants'.

Bloom: Many showy, blue, pink, rose, violet, white, open, 7-petaled flowers, to 1½ in. (38 mm) wide, in tiers along an erect stalk, in spring–early summer, zones 8–10; summer, zones 4–7.

Plant hardiness: Self-seeding, zones 4–10.

Soil: Moist, well-drained soil. Fertility: Rich. 7.0–7.5 pH.

Planting: Spring, zones 4–7; late summer, zones 8–10, in full sun to partial shade, 8–15 in. (20–38 cm) apart. Avoid transplanting. Avoid crowding.

Care: Moderate. Keep moist. Fertilize monthly. Stake tall cultivars. Protect from wind. Propagate by seed.

Features: Good choice for beds, borders, fencelines, massed plantings in cottage, formal, shade, woodland gardens. Good for cutting, drying. Pest and disease resistant.

Annual: *Convolvulus tricolor.* CONVOLVULACEAE.

Common name: Dwarf Morning-Glory.

Description: Many cultivars of upright, spreading or trailing annual herbs, to 1 ft. (30 cm) tall and 2 ft. (60 cm) wide. Smooth, deep green, lance-shaped, pointed leaves, to 3 in. (75 mm) long. Common cultivars include *C. tricolor* 'Blue Ensign', 'Blue Flash', 'Dwarf Rainbow Flash', and 'Royal Ensign'. See also *Ipomoea* species, morning glory, a related perennial vine.

Bloom: Many mostly bright blue, pink, purple, round, open, slightly cone-shaped flowers, to 1½ in. (38 mm) wide, with white, yellow contrasts and centers, often as triplets, in spring–summer.

Plant hardiness: Self-seeding, zones 2–10.

Soil: Damp to dry, well-drained, sandy soil. Fertility: Average–low. 6.5–7.5 pH.

Planting: Spring in full sun, 1 ft. (30 cm) apart, after soil warms. Start seed indoors 6 weeks before final frost for early blooms; transplant when frost hazard has passed.

Care: Easy. Keep damp; allow soil surface to dry between waterings. Avoid fertilizing. Propagate by seed.

Features: Good choice for borders, containers, edgings, massed plantings in arid, heritage, rock, seaside gardens. Invasive. Pest and disease resistant.

Annual: *Coreopsis tinctoria.* ASTERACEAE (COMPOSITAE).

Common name: Calliopsis (Coreopsis, Tickseed).

Description: Many cultivars of upright, branching, narrow annual herbs, 18–36 in. (45–90 cm) tall. Opposite, smooth, green, divided, feathery leaves, to 6 in. (15 cm) long, with narrow, cosmoslike leaflets, to 1 in. (25 mm) long. Common cultivars include *C. tinctoria* 'Carmen', 'Double Flower', 'Mardi Gras Dwarf', 'Tall Mixed Colors', and 'Zagreb'.

Bloom: Showy, brown, gold, red, yellow, daisylike or saucer-shaped, single- or double-petaled flowers, to 2 in. (50 mm) wide, with brown, deep red centers, in spring–early autumn.

Plant hardiness: Self-seeding, zones 4–9.

Soil: Damp to dry, well-drained, sandy soil. Fertility: Average. 6.5–7.5 pH.

Planting: Spring in full sun, 6–12 in. (15–30 cm) apart, after frost hazard has passed. Plant successions to prolong bloom.

Care: Easy. Keep damp; allow soil surface to dry between waterings. Drought tolerant. Fertilize quarterly. Deadhead spent flowers to prolong bloom. Propagate by seed.

Features: Good choice for accents, beds, borders, fencelines in arid, cottage, meadow, seaside gardens. Attracts birds. Good for cutting. Pest and disease resistant.

Annual: *Cosmos bipinnatus.* ASTERACEAE (COMPOSITAE).

Common name: Cosmos.

Description: Many cultivars of upright, branching or bushy annual herbs, 7–10 ft. (2.2–3 m) tall. Shiny, yellow green, feathery, divided leaves, to 5 in. (13 cm) long, with narrow leaflets, to 1 in. (25 mm) long. Common cultivars include *C. bipinnatus* 'Candy Stripe', 'Double Crested', 'Early Sensation', 'Imperial Pink', 'Sea Shells', 'Sensation', 'Sonata', and 'Versailles'.

Bloom: Showy, pink, red, violet, flat-faced flowers, 2–3 in. (50–75 mm) wide, with bright yellow centers and scalloped petals, in summer–autumn.

Plant hardiness: Self-seeding, zones 5–11.

Soil: Damp to dry, well-drained, sandy soil. Fertility: Average–low. 7.0–7.5 pH. Best blooms in low-fertility soil.

Planting: Spring in full to filtered sun, 1 ft. (30 cm) apart, after soil warms. Avoid transplanting.

Care: Easy. Keep damp; allow soil to dry between waterings. Drought tolerant. Avoid fertilizing. Deadhead spent flowers to prolong bloom. Stake and protect from wind. Propagate by seed.

Features: Good choice for accents, backgrounds, beds, borders in arid, cottage, heritage, meadow, seaside gardens. Good for cutting. Attracts birds, butterflies. Pest and disease resistant.

Annual: *Cosmos sulphureus.* ASTERACEAE (COMPOSITAE).

Common name: Yellow Cosmos.

Description: Several cultivars of upright, branching or bushy annual herbs, 6–10 ft. (1.8–3 m) tall. Shiny, green, feathery, divided leaves, to 5 in. (13 cm) long, with narrow leaflets, to 1 in. (25 mm) long. Common cultivars include *C. sulphureus* 'Dwarf Klondike' and 'Sunny'. See also *C. bipinnatus,* cosmos.

Bloom: Showy, gold, yellow, flat-faced flowers, 2–3 in. (50–75 mm) wide, with bright yellow centers and scalloped petals, in summer–autumn.

Plant hardiness: Self-seeding, zones 5–11.

Soil: Dry, well-drained, sandy soil. Fertility: Average–low. 7.0–7.5 pH. Best blooms in low-fertility soil.

Planting: Spring in full to filtered sun, 1 ft. (30 cm) apart, after soil warms. Avoid transplanting.

Care: Easy. Keep damp; allow soil surface to dry between waterings. Drought tolerant. Avoid fertilizing. Deadhead spent flowers to promote bloom. Stake and protect from wind. Propagate by seed.

Features: Good choice for accents, backgrounds, beds, borders in cottage, heritage, meadow, seaside gardens. Attracts birds, butterflies. Good for cutting. Pest and disease resistant.

Annual: *Cuphea ignea.* LYTHRACEAE.

Common name: Cigar Flower (Firecracker Plant, Red-White-and-Blue Flower).

Description: A few cultivars of upright, branching, bushy, shrublike perennial herbs, 1–3 ft. (30–90 cm) tall. Smooth, deep green, lance-shaped, narrow, pointed leaves, to 1½ in. (38 mm) long, in whorled clusters.

Bloom: Many shiny, orange red, cigar-shaped, tubular flowers, to 1½ in. (38 mm) long, with brown tips surrounding protruding stamens, in summer–autumn.

Plant hardiness: Plant as tender annual, zones 3–9; ground hardy, zones 10–11.

Soil: Moist, well-drained, sandy loam. Fertility: Rich–average. 7.0–7.5 pH.

Planting: Start indoors in spring, zones 3–8, transplanting when frost hazard has passed, in full sun; sow outdoors when soil warms, zones 9–11, 9 in. (23 cm) apart. Start seed indoors 8–10 weeks before final frost for early blooms.

Care: Easy. Keep evenly moist. Fertilize every 2 weeks. Pinch to direct growth. Propagate by cuttings, seed.

Features: Good choice for accents, borders, containers, massed plantings in cottage, wildlife gardens. Attracts hummingbirds. Heat, humidity tolerant. Disease resistant. Spider mite susceptible.

Annual: *Dianthus barbatus.* CARYOPHYLLACEAE.

Common name: Sweet William.

Description: Many cultivars of upright, bushy biennial herbs, 1–2 ft. (30–60 cm) tall. Shiny, green, lance-shaped, narrow leaves, 1–2½ in. (25–63 mm) long. Common cultivars include *D. barbatus* 'Albus', 'Hollandia', 'Nana', and 'Rondo'.

Bloom: Many tiny, pink, purple, red, white, bicolored, saucer-shaped, sometimes fragrant flowers, to ⅓ in. (8 mm) wide, with bearded petals, form dense clusters, in summer–early autumn.

Plant hardiness: Ground hardy, zones 5–10. Self-seeding.

Soil: Moist, well-drained soil. Fertility: Rich. 7.0–7.5 pH.

Planting: Late spring in filtered sun to partial shade, 1–3 ft. (30–90 cm) apart. Sow seed for flowers the following season or plant nursery containers.

Care: Easy. Keep moist; allow soil surface to dry between waterings. Fertilize monthly; apply diluted garden lime quarterly. Propagate by seed.

Features: Good choice for beds, borders, containers, massed plantings in cottage, heritage, shade gardens. Good for cutting. Spider mite and rust, mosaic virus, fusarium wilt susceptible.

Annual: *Dianthus chinensis.* CARYOPHYLLACEAE.

Common name: Pink (China Pink).

Description: Many cultivars of short-lived, erect, mounding biennial or perennial herbs, to 2 ft. (60 cm) tall and 1 ft. (30 cm) wide. Shiny, mostly gray green, narrow, grasslike, evergreen leaves, to 2 in. (50 mm) long.

Bloom: Showy, pink, rose, white, occasionally yellow, bicolored, lacy, fragrant flowers, 1–1½ in. (25–38 mm) wide, in spring–summer.

Plant hardiness: Plant as tender annual, zones 2–7; ground hardy, zones 8–10. Self-seeding.

Soil: Damp, well-drained, sandy soil. Fertility: Rich. 7.0–8.0 pH.

Planting: Spring, after frost hazard has passed, zones 2–7; late summer or autumn, zones 8–10, in full sun, 12–15 in. (30–38 cm) apart. Sow seed for flowers the following season or plant nursery containers.

Care: Easy. Keep damp; allow soil surface to dry between waterings. Mulch lightly, zones 4–6. Propagate by cuttings, division, layering, seed.

Features: Good choice for accents, borders, containers in cottage, heritage, meadow, wildlife gardens. Attracts birds, butterflies, hummingbirds. Good for cutting. Spider mite and rust, fusarium wilt susceptible.

Annual: *Diascia barberae.* SCROPHULARIACEAE.

Common name: Twinspur.

Description: Many cultivars of erect, spreading annual herbs, to 1 ft. (30 cm) tall and 18 in. (45 cm) wide. Opposite, textured, green, oval, pointed, toothed leaves, to 1½ in. (38 mm) long, along lower portion of stalk. Common cultivars include *D. barberae* 'Blackthorn Apricot' and 'Pink Queen'.

Bloom: Many peach, pink, rose, flared flowers, to ½ in. (12 mm) wide, with twin spurs or horns protruding from back of petals, in vertical, spiking clusters, in summer–late autumn.

Plant hardiness: Self-seeding, zones 7–9.

Soil: Moist, well-drained soil. Fertility: Rich. 6.5–7.5 pH.

Planting: Spring in full sun to partial shade, 6 in. (15 cm) apart, after frost hazard has passed. Start seed indoors 6–8 weeks before final frost for early blooms; transplant when soil warms.

Care: Easy. Keep moist; allow soil surface to dry between waterings. Fertilize monthly. Prune spent stalks to promote repeat bloom. Propagate by seed.

Features: Good choice for borders, containers in cottage, rock gardens. Attracts bees. Pest and disease resistant.

Annual: *Dimorphotheca pluvialis* and hybrids. ASTERACEAE (COMPOSITAE).
Common name: Cape Marigold.
Description: Many hybrids of erect, branching annual herbs, to 16 in. (40 cm) tall. Hairy, gray green, oval, often divided leaves, 2–3½ in. (50–90 mm) long. Common cultivars include *D. pluvialis* 'Aurantica Hybrid', Glistening White', and 'Salmon Queen'.
Bloom: Many showy, orange, pink, white, yellow, daisylike flowers, to 2 in. (50 mm) wide, with powdery blue, cream, purple undersides, in early–late summer, zones 2–7; winter–early spring, zones 8–10.
Plant hardiness: Self-seeding, zones 2–10.
Soil: Damp to dry, well-drained soil. Fertility: Average. 6.5–7.5 pH.
Planting: Spring in full sun, 1 ft. (30 cm) apart, after frost hazard has passed.
Care: Easy. Keep damp; allow soil surface to dry between waterings. Fertilize annually in spring. Deadhead spent flowers to prolong bloom. Propagate by seed.
Features: Good choice for banks, borders, containers, massed plantings in cottage, meadow gardens and roadside plantings. Pest resistant. Fungal disease susceptible in moist soil.

Annual: *Erysimum cheiri* (*Cheiranthus cheiri*). BRASSICACEAE (CRUCIFERAE).
Common name: Wallflower.
Description: Many cultivars of erect, branching biennial or perennial herbs, 12–30 in. (30–75 cm) tall. Shiny, blue to bright green, lance-shaped, narrow, pointed leaves, to 3 in. (75 mm) long.
Bloom: Many apricot, cream, pink, purple, red, white, yellow, double- or 4-petaled, fragrant flowers, to 1 in. (25 mm) wide, in spiking, stocklike clusters, in spring–early summer.
Plant hardiness: Plant as tender annual, zones 3–6; ground hardy, zones 6–9. Self-seeding. Best in mild-summer, mild-winter climates.
Soil: Moist, well-drained, loamy soil. Fertility: Rich–low. pH 7.0–7.5.

Planting: Spring in partial shade, 6–12 in. (15–30 cm) apart, after frost hazard has passed. Sow seed of biennial cultivars for flowers the following season or plant nursery containers.
Care: Easy. Keep evenly moist. Fertilize quarterly. Protect from frost, heat. Propagate by seed.
Features: Good choice for beds, borders, containers, edgings, massed plantings in cottage, formal, rock, shade gardens. Good for cutting, companion to spring bulbs. Pest and disease resistant.

Annual: *Euphorbia marginata*. EUPHORBIACEAE.
Common name: Snow-on-the-Mountain (Ghostweed).
Description: Several cultivars of erect, branching annual herbs, usually 2–4 ft. (60–120 cm) tall and 1–2 ft. (30–60 cm) wide. Shiny, light green, white, variegated, broadly oval, pointed leaves, to 3 in. (75 mm) long, mostly white on top tiers becoming solid green on bottom tiers. Common cultivars include *E. marginata* 'Fireglow', 'Polychroma', 'Summer Icicle', and 'White Top'.
Bloom: Insignificant green flowers, to ½ in. (12 mm) wide, with green bracts; grown primarily for foliage.
Plant hardiness: Self-seeding, zones 2–10.

WARNING
Sap of *Euphorbia marginata* can cause skin irritation in sensitive individuals. Wear rubber gloves when cutting or pruning plants.

Soil: Moist to dry, well-drained soil. Fertility: Average–low. 6.5–7.5 pH.
Planting: Early spring in full sun to open shade, 8–12 in. (20–30 cm) apart, when soil is workable.
Care: Easy. Keep damp; allow soil surface to dry between waterings. Avoid fertilizing. Pinch to control growth. Propagate by seed.
Features: Good choice for accents, beds, borders in formal, shade, woodland gardens. Good for cutting; sear stems over flame after cutting. Pest and disease resistant.

Annual: *Exacum affine.* GENTIANACEAE.

Common name: Persian Violet.

Description: Several cultivars of branching, bushy annual or biennial herbs, to 2 ft. (60 cm) tall. Opposite, shiny, green, oval, pointed leaves, to 1½ in. (38 mm) long. Common cultivars include *E. affine* 'Atrocaeruleum'.

Bloom: Many blue violet, white, 5-petaled, fragrant flowers, to ½ in. (12 mm) wide, with bright yellow stamens in their centers, in summer–early autumn.

Plant hardiness: Plant as tender annual, zones 3–5; ground hardy, zones 6–11.

Soil: Moist, well-drained soil. Fertility: Rich. 6.5–7.5 pH.

Planting: Spring in partial shade, 6–8 in. (15–20 cm) apart, on top of soil. Start seed indoors 8 weeks before final frost for early blooms; transplant when frost hazard has passed. Sow seed of biennial cultivars for flowers the following season or plant nursery containers.

Care: Moderate. Keep moist; allow soil surface to dry between waterings. Drought tolerant when established. Fertilize every 2 weeks. Deadhead spent flowers to prolong bloom. Propagate by seed.

Features: Good choice for beds, containers, edgings in shade, small-space gardens. Good as houseplant. Aphid and fungal disease susceptible.

Annual: *Gaillardia pulchella.* ASTERACEAE (COMPOSITAE).

Common name: Blanket Flower.

Description: Many cultivars of erect, bushy annual herbs, to 3 ft. (90 cm) tall. Alternate, hairy, textured, deep gray green, lance-shaped leaves, 3–6 in. (75–150 mm) long. Common cultivars include *G. pulchella* 'Gaiety Mixed Colors', 'Indian Blanket', 'Indian Chief', 'Lorenziana', 'Red Giant', 'Red Plume', and 'Yellow Sun'.

Bloom: Showy, gold, deep red, yellow flowers, 3–4 in. (75–100 mm) wide, tipped in yellow, and with brown, deep purple, or yellow centers, in early summer–autumn.

Plant hardiness: Plant as tender annual, zones 3–4; self-seeding, zones 5–9.

Soil: Damp to dry, well-drained, sandy humus. Fertility: Average low. 6.0–7.5 pH.

Planting: Spring in full sun, 10–15 in. (25–38 cm) apart, when soil is workable.

Care: Easy. Keep damp; allow soil surface to dry between waterings. Avoid fertilizing. Deadhead spent flowers to promote bloom. Stake taller cultivars. Propagate by seed.

Features: Good choice for beds, borders in cottage, meadow, wildlife gardens. Good for cutting. Attracts birds, butterflies. Aphid and leaf spot, powdery mildew susceptible.

Annual: *Gomphrena globosa.* AMARANTHACEAE.

Common name: Globe Amaranth.

Description: Many cultivars of upright, branching annual herbs, 9–24 in. (23–60 cm) tall. Alternate, opposite, hairy, bright green, oval to lance-shaped leaves, 2–3½ in. (50–90 mm) long. Common cultivars include *G. globosa* 'Buddy', Cissy', 'Dwarf Buddy Rich', 'Nana', and 'Strawberry Fields'.

Bloom: Solitary pink, purple, red, round, cloverlike flowers, ½–1 in. (12–25 mm) wide, atop branching stems, in summer. Everlasting if dried.

Plant hardiness: Self-seeding, zones 3–11.

Soil: Damp, well-drained soil. Fertility: Average. 6.5–7.5 pH.

Planting: Spring in full sun, 9–12 in. (23–30 cm) apart. Start seed indoors 6 weeks before final frost for early blooms; transplant when frost hazard has passed.

Care: Easy. Keep damp; allow soil surface to dry between waterings. Fertilize quarterly. Propagate by seed.

Features: Good choice for beds, borders, containers, edgings in cottage, meadow, small-space gardens. Good for cutting, drying. Pest and disease resistant.

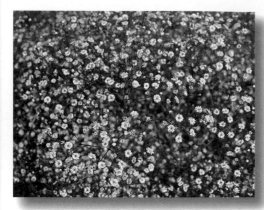

Annual: *Gypsosphila elegans.* CARYOPHYLLACEAE.

Common name: Annual Baby's-Breath.

Description: Several cultivars of open, mounding annual herbs, 8–20 in. (20–50 cm) tall. Deep green, lance-shaped, succulent leaves, 1–2 in. (25–50 mm) long. Common cultivars include *G. elegans* 'Carmina', 'Covent Garden', 'Grandiflora Alba', 'Kermesina', 'Purpurea', and 'Rosea'. See also *G. paniculata,* perennial baby's breath, a closely related species with similar care needs.

Bloom: Many pink, purple, white, 5-petaled flowers, ¼–1 in. (6–25 mm) wide, in cloudlike profusion, in late spring–summer.

Plant hardiness: Self-seeding, zones 3–9.

Soil: Damp to dry, well-drained soil. Fertility: Average–low. 7.0–8.0 pH.

Planting: Spring in full sun, 12–18 in. (30–45 cm) apart, after frost hazard has passed. Start seed indoors 4–5 weeks before final frost for early blooms; transplant when frost hazard has passed. Plant successions for continual bloom.

Care: Easy. Keep damp; allow soil surface to dry between waterings. Fertilize annually in spring. Propagate by seed.

Features: Good choice for borders, containers, fillers, foregrounds in cottage, formal, rock, small-space gardens. Good for cutting, drying. Disease resistant. Gopher and slug, snail susceptible.

Annual: *Helianthus annuus.* ASTERACEAE (COMPOSITAE).

Common name: Common Sunflower (Cut-and-Come-Again, Mirasol).

Description: Many cultivars of upright, narrow annual herbs, to 10 ft. (3 m) tall. Alternate or opposite, coarse-textured, yellow green, oval, usually coarsely toothed leaves, to 1 ft. (30 cm) long. Common cultivars include *H. annuus* 'Giganteus', 'Italian White', 'Moonshadow', 'Sunbright', and 'Sunburst'. See also *Helianthus* species, closely related perennial species with similar care needs.

Bloom: Single or double, orange yellow, round flowers, 6–12 in. (15–30 cm) wide, with dark centers, either solitary or in clusters, in summer–autumn, form edible seed.

Plant hardiness: Self-seeding, zones 4–9.

Soil: Moist, well-drained soil. Fertility: Average. 5.0–7.0 pH.

Planting: Spring in full sun to partial shade, 18–36 in. (45–90 cm) apart, after soil warms.

Care: Easy. Keep moist. Fertilize every 2 months. Stake tallest cultivars. Propagate by seed.

Features: Good choice for borders, fencelines, massed plantings. Attracts birds, butterflies. Good for cutting, seed. Stalk borer, sunflower maggot, sunflower moth larva and powdery mildew, rust susceptible.

Annual: *Helipterum roseum.* ASTERACEAE (COMPOSITAE).

Common name: Everlasting (Strawflower).

Description: Many cultivars of upright, branching herbs to 2 ft. (60 cm) tall. Alternate, green, lance-shaped, narrow leaves, to 2½ in. (63 mm) long. Common cultivars include *H. roseum* 'Accroclinium' and 'Rhodanthe'.

Bloom: Showy, solitary, rose, white, daisylike, layered flowers, to 2 in. (50 mm) wide, with papery rays, in summer–early autumn. Everlasting if dried.

Plant hardiness: Self-seeding, zones 3–10.

Soil: Damp, well-drained, sandy loam. Fertility: Rich–low. 7.0–7.5 pH.

Planting: Spring in full sun, 1 ft. (30 cm) apart, after frost hazard has passed. Start seed indoors 6 weeks before final frost for early blooms; transplant when soil warms.

Care: Easy. Keep damp; allow soil surface to dry between waterings. Drought tolerant. Fertilize quarterly. Propagate by seed.

Features: Good choice for beds, borders, containers, foregrounds in cottage, meadow, small-space gardens. Good for cutting, drying. Pest and disease resistant.

Annual: *Iberis umbellata.* BRASSICACEAE (CRUCIFERAE).

Common name: Globe Candytuft.

Description: Many cultivars of bushy, branching annual herbs, to 16 in. (40 cm) tall. Shiny, green, lance-shaped, narrow leaves, to 3½ in. (90 mm) long. Common cultivars include *I. umbellata* 'Fairy Mixed', 'Flash Mixed', and 'White Pinnacle'. See also *I. sempervirens,* candytuft, a related perennial species with similar care needs.

Bloom: Many pink, purple, red, simple, 4-petaled flowers, ¼–½ in. (6–12 mm) wide, in round, globelike clusters, to 3 in. (75 mm) wide, in late spring–autumn.

Plant hardiness: Self-seeding, zones 3–10.

Soil: Moist, well-drained soil. Fertility: Rich. 6.5–7.5 pH.

Planting: Spring in full sun, 12–15 in. (30–38 cm) apart, after frost hazard has passed. Start seed indoors 6–8 weeks before final frost for early blooms; transplant when frost hazard has passed. Plant successions for continual bloom.

Care: Easy. Keep moist; allow soil surface to dry between waterings. Fertilize monthly. Deadhead spent flowers to prolong bloom. Propagate by seed.

Features: Good choice for beds, borders, containers, massed plantings in cottage, rock gardens. Good companion for spring bulbs. Smog tolerant. Pest and disease resistant.

Annual: *Lathyrus odoratus.* FABACEAE (LEGUMINOSAE).

Common name: Sweet Pea (Vetchling).

Description: Many cultivars of bushy or vining annual herbs, to 3 ft. (90 cm) tall or to 6 ft. (1.8 m) long. Alternate, smooth, bright green, lance- or oval-shaped, paired leaves to 2 in. (50 mm) long. Common cultivars include *L. odoratus* 'Antique Factory', 'Bijou Mixed', 'Little Sweeheart', and 'Royal Family'.

Bloom: Many pink, purple, red, violet, white, pea- or snapdragon-like, fragrant flowers to 2 in. (50 mm) wide, often with mixed colors on a plant, in late spring–summer, forming pea pods in summer, to 2 in. (50 mm) long, containing pealike seed.

Plant hardiness: Self-seeding, zones 2–10.

Soil: Moist, well-drained loam. Fertility: Rich. 7.0–7.5 pH.

Planting: Early spring in full sun, 6–12 in. (15–30 cm) apart, when soil is workable.

Care: Moderate. Keep moist. Fertilize monthly. Deadhead spent flowers to prolong bloom. Stake vining cultivars. Protect from wind. Propagate by seed.

Features: Good choice for accents, arbors, edgings, fencelines, massed plantings, trellises in cottage, formal, small-space gardens. Good for cutting. Disease resistant. Slug, snail susceptible.

Annual: *Lavatera trimestris.* MALVACEAE.

Common name: Tree Mallow.

Description: Many cultivars of branching, bushy annual herbs, 3–5 ft. (90–150 cm) tall. Alternate, hairy, green, heart- or maple-shaped leaves, to 2 in. (50 mm) long. Common cultivars include *L. trimestris* 'Loveliness', 'Mont Blanc', 'Mont Rose', 'Ruby Regis', 'Silver Cup', 'Splendens', and 'Tanagra'.

Bloom: Many pink, red, white, satiny, saucer-shaped flowers, to 4 in. (10 cm) wide, in summer–late autumn.

Plant hardiness: Self-seeding, zones 2–10.

Soil: Moist to damp, well-drained soil. Fertility: Rich–average. 6.5–7.5 pH. Salt tolerant.

Planting: Early spring in full sun, 2 ft. (60 cm) apart, after frost hazard has passed. Avoid transplanting.

Care: Moderate. Keep damp; allow soil surface to dry between waterings. Fertilize monthly. Deadhead spent flowers to prolong bloom. Propagate by seed.

Features: Good choice for accents, beds, borders, fencelines in cottage, meadow, rock gardens. Pest resistant. Rust succeptible.

Annual: *Linaria maroccana.* SCROPHULARIACEAE.

Common name: Toadflax (Baby Snapdragon, Spurred Snapdragon).

Description: A few cultivars of erect, narrow annual herbs, 18–24 in. (45–60 cm) tall and 6–8 in. (15–20 cm) wide. Whorled, smooth, light to yellow green, lance-shaped, narrow leaves, to 1 in. (25 mm) long. Dwarf cultivars available. Common cultivars include *L. maroccana* 'Fairy Bouquet', 'Fairy Lights Mixed', 'Fantasy', 'Gemstones', and 'Northern Lights'. *L. purpurea* and *L. reticulata* are closely related species with similar care needs.

Bloom: Many showy, gold, pink, purple, red, tan, violet, multicolored, snapdragon-like, spurred flowers, to 1½ in. (38 mm) wide, in spiking, often triplet clusters, in summer, zones 3–7; late winter–early spring, zones 8–10.

Plant hardiness: Self-seeding, zones 3–10.

Soil: Moist, well-drained, sandy soil. Fertility: Rich–average. 6.5–7.5 pH

Planting: Spring, zones 3–7; autumn, zones 8–10, in full to filtered sun, 4–6 in. (10–15 cm) apart.

Care: Easy. Keep evenly moist until established. Drought tolerant. Fertilize every 2 months. Propagate by seed.

Features: Good choice for borders, containers, massed plantings in cottage, meadow, rock gardens. Pest and disease resistant.

Annual: *Linum grandiflorum.* LINACEAE.

Common name: Flowering Flax.

Description: Many cultivars of upright, branching, narrow annual herbs, 1–2 ft. (30–60 cm) tall. Alternate, smooth, gray green, lance-shaped leaves, to 1 in. (25 mm) long. Common cultivars include *L. grandiflorum* 'Bright Eyes', 'Diamint White', and 'Rubrum'. See also *L. perenne*, perennial flax, a closely related species.

Bloom: Many solitary, pink, red, white, simple, 5-petaled flowers, to 1¼ in. (32 mm) wide, in late spring–late summer. Flowers last one day; bloom lasts 4–6 weeks.

Plant hardiness: Self-seeding, zones 2–9.

Soil: Damp, well-drained, sandy loam. Fertility: Rich–average. 6.5–7.5 pH.

Planting: Early spring in full sun to open shade, 4 to 6 in. (10–15 cm) apart. Avoid transplanting. Plant successions to prolong bloom.

Care: Easy. Keep damp; allow soil surface to dry between waterings. Drought tolerant. Fertilize quarterly. Propagate by seed.

Features: Good choice for accents, beds, borders, foregrounds, massed plantings in cottage, meadow, rock, shade gardens. Pest and disease resistant.

Annual: *Lobularia maritima.* BRASSICACEAE (CRUCIFERAE).

Common name: Sweet Alyssum.

Description: Many cultivars of low, branching, spreading, fine-textured perennial herbs, to 1 ft. (30 cm) tall. Smooth, gray green, lance-shaped, narrow leaves, to 2 in. (50 mm) long. Common cultivars include *L. maritima* 'Carpet of Snow', 'Little Gem', 'Rosie O'Day', 'Royal Carpet', 'Violet Queen', and 'Wonderland'.

Bloom: Many tiny, pink, purple, white, simple, 4-petaled flowers, to ¼ in. (6 mm) wide, in showy, carpetlike clusters, in late spring to late autumn.

Plant hardiness: Plant as tender annual, all zones; ground hardy, zones 7–11.

Soil: Moist, well-drained soil. Fertility: Average. 6.5–7.0 pH.

Planting: Early spring in full sun to partial shade, 6 in. (15 cm) apart, when soil is workable. Start seed indoors 6–8 weeks before final frost for early blooms; transplant when frost hazard has passed.

Care: Easy. Keep moist. Avoid fertilizing. Deadhead spent flowers and shear plants to prolong bloom, promote repeat blooms. Propagate by seed.

Features: Good choice for hanging baskets, borders, containers, edgings, foregrounds in cottage, meadow, rock gardens. Disease resistant. Slug, snail susceptible.

Annual: *Lupinus texensis (L. subcarnosus).* FABACEAE (LEGUMINOSAE).

Common name: Texas Bluebonnet (Lupine).

Description: Several cultivars of upright or bushy annual and perennial herbs, 12–16 in. (30–40 cm) tall. Fuzzy, yellow green, palmlike, deeply lobed leaves, to 4 in. (10 cm) long, with lance-shaped, pointed leaflets.

Bloom: Many deep blue, cream, white, bicolored, pealike flowers, arranged on spikes, to 1 ft. (30 cm) long, in spring–summer.

Plant hardiness: Mostly hardy. Self-seeding. Plant as annual, zones 2–3; ground hardy, zones 4–10.

Soil: Damp to dry, well-drained, sandy soil. Fertility: Rich–low, depending on species. 6.0–7.0 pH.

Planting: Spring in full to filtered sun, 8–12 in. (20–30 cm) apart, after frost hazard has passed.

Care: Easy. Keep damp; allow soil surface to dry between waterings. Fertilize annually in spring. Deadhead spent flowers for autumn bloom. Protect from wind. Propagate by division, seed.

Features: Good choice for backgrounds, beds, borders, fencelines in cottage, meadow, natural, wildlife, woodland gardens. Attracts birds, hummingbirds. Disease resistant. Lupine aphid susceptible.

> **WARNING**
> All parts of *Lupinus texensis* are hazardous if eaten. Avoid planting in areas frequented by pets or children.

Annual: *Matthiola longipetala.* BRASSICACEAE (CRUCIFERAE).

Common name: Evening Stock (Evening Scented Stock, Perfume Plant).

Description: A few cultivars of erect, branching, open annual herbs, to 18 in. (45 cm) tall. Smooth, gray green, lance-shaped leaves, to 3½ in. (90 mm) long.

Bloom: Many pink, purple, yellow, horned, very fragrant flowers, to ¾ in. (19 mm) wide, in low, spiking clusters, in summer.

Plant hardiness: Plant as tender summer annual, zones 2–7, or winter annual, zones 8–11; self-seeding, zones 8–9. Best in mild-summer climates.

Soil: Moist, well-drained, sandy loam. Fertility: Rich–average. 6.5–7.5 pH.

Planting: Spring, zones 2–7, after frost hazard has passed; autumn, zones 8–11, in full sun to partial shade, 1 ft. (30 cm) apart.

Care: Easy. Keep moist; allow soil surface to dry between waterings. Avoid wetting foliage. Fertilize monthly. Stake. Protect from wind. Propagate by seed.

Features: Good choice for backgrounds, beds, borders, containers in cottage, meadow, shade gardens. Good for cutting. Pest and disease resistant.

Annual: *Mimulus × hybridus.* SCROPHULARIACEAE.

Common name: Monkey Flower.

Description: Many cultivars of short-lived, erect, mounding perennial herbs, 12–18 in. (30–45 cm) tall. Smooth, green, broadly oval, finely toothed, paired leaves, to 2 in. (50 mm) long. Common cultivars include *M. × hybridus* 'Apricot', 'Calypso', 'Velvet', and 'Viva'.

Bloom: Many brown, cream, orange, red, yellow, multicolored or solid, monkey-face-like, 5-petaled flowers, 2–2½ in. (50–63 mm) wide, with reflexed pairs of upper petals and triplets of lower petals, and with tonguelike centers, in summer–autumn except during periods of heat.

Plant hardiness: Plant as tender annual, zones 3–8; ground hardy, zones 9–11.

Soil: Moist, well-drained humus or, in water features, shoreline sites. Fertility: Rich. 6.5–7.5 pH.

Planting: Spring, zones 3–7; late winter, zones 8–11, in partial to full shade, 6 in. (15 cm) apart. Start seed indoors 10 weeks before final frost for early blooms; transplant when soil warms.

Care: Moderate. Keep moist. Fertilize monthly. Deadhead spent flowers to prolong bloom. Propagate by seed.

Features: Good choice for beds, borders, containers in rock, shade gardens and water feature shorelines. Pest and disease resistant

Annual: *Moluccella laevis.* LAMIACEAE (LABIATAE).
Common name: Bells-of-Ireland (Shellflower).
Description: Several cultivars of erect, narrow annual herbs, to 3 ft. (90 cm) tall. Opposite, smooth, green, oval to round, finely toothed leaves, to 2 in. (50 mm) long.
Bloom: Tiny, white, tubular flowers, to ¾ in. (19 mm) long, each within a showy, cup- or bell-shaped, bright green, veined calyx, to 2 in. (50 mm) wide, in whorls around an erect stalk, in summer.
Plant hardiness: Self-seeding, zones 2–10.
Soil: Moist, well-drained soil. Fertility: Rich–average. 6.5–7.5 pH
Planting: Early spring, zones 2–8; autumn, zones 9–10, in full sun, 9 in. (23 cm) apart.
Care: Easy. Keep moist; allow soil surface to dry between waterings. Fertilize monthly. Deadhead spent flowers, leaves on lower stalk. Stake. Propagate by seed.
Features: Good choice for accents, backgrounds, beds, borders in cottage, rock gardens. Good for cutting, drying. Protect from rain, wind. Pest and disease resistant.

Annual: *Myosotis sylvatica (M. alpestris).* BORAGINACEAE.
Common name: Garden Forget-Me-Not (Woodland Forget-Me-Not).
Description: Many cultivars of upright, branching annual or biennial herbs, 6–24 in. (15–60 cm) tall. Hairy or sticky, deep green, broadly lance-shaped, pointed leaves, 2–4 in. (50–100 mm) long. Common cultivars include *M. sylvatica* 'Blue Bird', 'Carmine King', 'Ultramarine', and 'Victoria Blue'.
Bloom: Many tiny, pink, purple, white flowers, ⅛–¼ in. (3–6 mm) wide, in open, ball-shaped clusters, in spring–autumn.
Plant hardiness: Ground hardy, zones 5–8. Self-seeding.
Soil: Moist, well-drained soil or, in water features, shoreline sites. Fertility: Rich–average. 6.5–7.5 pH.
Planting: Early spring in filtered sun to partial shade, 6–8 in. (15–20 cm) apart. Sow seed of biennial cultivars for flowers the following season or plant nursery containers.
Care: Easy. Keep moist. Fertilize monthly. Progagate by division, seed.
Features: Good choice for beds, borders, containers, edgings in cottage, formal, rock, shade, woodland gardens or water feature shorelines. Good companion for spring bulbs. Invasive. Disease resistant. Slug, snail susceptible.

Annual: *Nemesia strumosa* and hybrids. SCROPHULARIACEAE.
Common name: Pouch Nemesia (Bluebird).
Description: Several cultivars of erect, bushy annual herbs, 6–24 in. (15–60 cm) tall. Alternate or opposite, green, lance-shaped, toothed leaves, 2–4 in. (50–100 mm) long. Common cultivars include *N. strumosa* 'Blue Gem', 'Carnival Mixed Colors', 'Mellow Red and White', and 'National Ensign'. *N. caerulea* is a closely related perennial species with similar care needs.
Bloom: Many irregular, orange, pink, purple, white, yellow, lobed-petaled flowers, to 1 in. (25 mm) wide, with fan-shaped upper petals over liplike lower petals, in branching clusters, in late spring.
Plant hardiness: Self-seeding, zones 3–10. Best in mild-summer climates.
Soil: Moist, well-drained soil. Fertility: Rich. 6.5–7.0 pH.
Planting: Spring in full to filtered sun, 6 in. (15 cm) apart, after frost hazard has passed. Start seed indoors 8–10 weeks before final frost for early blooms; transplant when frost hazard has passed.
Care: Easy. Keep evenly moist. Fertilize monthly. Pinch growth tips to promote bushiness. Protect from heat. Propagate by seed.
Features: Good choice for hanging baskets, beds, borders, containers in cottage, heritage, rock gardens. Good for cutting. Pest and disease resistant.

Annual: *Nemophila maculata.* HYDROPHYLLACEAE.

Common name: Five-Spot.

Description: A few cultivars of low, mounding, spreading or trailing annual herbs, to 1 ft. (30 cm) tall and wide. Opposite, hairy, light green, feathery, divided leaves, to 4 in. (10 cm) long, with 5–9 leaflets. See also *N. menziesii*, baby-blue-eyes.

Bloom: Many white, striped, simple, round, cup-shaped flowers, 1½–2 in. (38–50 mm) wide, with a purple spot at the tip of each petal, in spring.

Plant hardiness: Self-seeding, zones 7–9. Best in mild-summer climates.

Soil: Moist, well-drained humus. Fertility: Rich. 6.0–7.5 pH.

Planting: Spring, zones 3–6, when soil is workable; autumn, zones 7–9, in full sun to partial shade, 9–12 in. (23–30 cm) apart.

Care: Easy. Keep evenly moist. Fertilize monthly. Protect from heat, humidity. Propagate by seed.

Features: Good choice for hanging baskets, beds, borders, containers, edgings, walls in cottage, formal, natural, rock, woodland gardens. Good companion for spring bulbs. Disease resistant. Slug, snail susceptible.

Annual: *Nemophila menziesii.* HYDROPHYLLACEAE.

Common name: Baby-Blue-Eyes.

Description: Many cultivars of low, spreading or trailing annual herbs, to 1 ft. (30 cm) tall. Opposite, smooth, feathery, divided leaves, to 2 in. (50 mm) long, with 5–9 leaflets. Common cultivars include *N. menziesii* 'Alba', 'Cramboides', 'Margarita', 'Pennie Black', and 'Snowstorm'. See also *N. maculata*, five-spot.

Bloom: Many blue, purple, violet, white, 5-petaled, saucerlike flowers, 1–1½ in. (25–38 mm) wide, in early summer–late frost.

Plant hardiness: Self-seeding, zones 2–10.

Soil: Moist, well-drained humus. Fertility: Rich–average. 6.5–7.0 pH.

Planting: Spring, zones 2–6, when soil is workable; autumn, zones 7–10, in full sun to partial shade, 9–12 in. (23–30 cm) apart.

Care: Easy. Keep evenly moist. Fertilize monthly. Mulch with leaf mold. Protect from heat, humidity. Propagate by seed.

Features: Good choice for beds, borders, containers, edgings in cottage, natural, rock gardens. Good companion for spring bulbs. Pest and disease resistant.

Annual: *Nicotiana alata.* SOLANACEAE.

Common name: Flowering Tobacco (Nicotiana).

Description: Many cultivars of erect, branching, open perennial herbs, 3–4 ft. (90–120 cm) tall. Alternate, green, broadly lance-shaped leaves, 4–6 in. (10–15 cm) long, forming a circular, radiating base. Common cultivars include *N. alata* 'Grandiflora', 'Havana Apple Blossom', 'Jasmine Tobacco', and 'Starship Series'.

Bloom: Many showy, green, pink, red, white, tubular, 5-petaled, often fragrant flowers, to 3 in. (75 mm) wide, flaring into star-shaped trumpets, in branching clusters, in early summer–early autumn.

Plant hardiness: Plant as tender annual, zones 2–8; ground hardy, zones 9–10. Self-seeding.

Soil: Moist, well-drained soil. Fertility: Moderate. 6.5–7.5 pH.

Planting: Spring in full sun to partial shade, 1–2 ft. (30–60 cm) apart, after frost hazard has passed. Start seed indoors 6–8 weeks before final frost for early blooms; transplant when frost hazard has passed.

> **WARNING**
> Foliage and sap of *Nicotiana alata* are fatally hazardous if eaten. Avoid planting in areas frequented by pets or children.

Care: Easy. Keep evenly moist. Fertilize monthly. Stake tall cultivars. Propagate by seed.

Features: Good choice for beds, borders, containers in cottage, heritage, shade, woodland gardens. Pest and disease resistant.

Annual: *Nierembergia caerulea (N. hippomanica).* SOLANACEAE.
Common name: Cupflower.
Description: Several cultivars of mounding, spreading perennial herbs, to 1 ft. (30 cm) tall and wide. Alternate, green, spoon-shaped or fernlike leaves, to ¾ in. (19 mm) long. Common cultivars include *N. caerulea* 'Mont Blanc', 'Purple Robe', and 'Violacea'.
Bloom: Many purple, violet, white, cup-shaped, 5-petaled flowers, 1–2 in. (25–50 mm) wide, with yellow throats, in summer–early autumn.
Plant hardiness: Plant as tender annual, zones 2–6; ground hardy, zones 7–10.
Soil: Moist, well-drained soil. Fertility: Rich. 6.5–7.5 pH.
Planting: Late winter to early spring in filtered sun to partial shade, 6 in. (15 cm) apart, when soil is workable. Start seed indoors 10–12 weeks before final frost for early blooms; transplant when frost hazard has passed.
Care: Easy. Keep evenly moist. Fertilize monthly. Prune or shear after blooms fade to renew, promote repeat bloom. Propagate by cuttings, division, seed.
Features: Good choice for hanging baskets, borders, containers, ground covers in natural, rock gardens. Pest and disease resistant.

Annual: *Nigella damascena.* RANUNCULACEAE.
Common name: Love-in-a-Mist (Fennel Flower, Wild Fennel).
Description: Many cultivars of erect, branching, narrow annual herbs, to 18 in. (45 cm) tall and 10 in. (25 cm) wide. Smooth, shiny, green, strand- or thread-like, divided leaves, to 2 in. (50 mm) long, with 8–12 opposed leaflets, to ¾ in. (19 mm) long.
Bloom: Many solitary, blue, pink, purple, rose, white, fluffy, very double flowers, to 1½ in. (38 mm) wide, often with layered, pointed petals surrounding green, horned, many-segmented seedpods, in spring–summer, containing edible seeds.
Plant hardiness: Self-seeding, zones 2–10.
Soil: Moist, well-drained, sandy or gravelly soil. Fertility: Rich–average. 6.5–7.5 pH.

Planting: Spring, zones 2–8, when soil is workable; spring or autumn, zones 9–10, in full sun, 1 ft. (30 cm) apart. Plant successions every 2–3 weeks to prolong bloom.
Care: Easy. Keep moist; allow soil surface to dry between waterings. Fertilize every 2 months. Deadhead to prolong blooms. Protect from heat. Propagate by seed.
Features: Good choice for beds, borders, fillers in cottage, meadow, natural gardens. Seedpods good for drying; seed good as culinary spice. Pest and disease resistant.

Annual: *Ocimum basilicum.* LAMIACEAE (LABIATAE).
Common name: Sweet Basil (Common Basil).
Description: Many cultivars of erect, bushy annual herbs, 8–24 in. (20–60 cm) tall and wide. Shiny, deeply textured, deep green, purple, often variegated with brown, oval, pointed, fragrant leaves, 3–5 in. (75–125 mm) long, sometimes with ruffled edges. Common cultivars include *O. basilicum* 'Citriodorum', 'Dark Opal', 'Minimum', and 'Purple Ruffles'.
Bloom: Insignificant, tiny, cream, purple, white flowers in spiking clusters, in summer.
Plant hardiness: Self-seeding, zones 2–11.
Soil: Moist to damp, well-drained soil. Fertility: Rich–average. 6.0–7.0 pH.
Planting: Early spring in full sun, 8–12 in. (20–30 cm) apart, when soil is workable. Start seed indoors 4–6 weeks before final frost for early foliage; transplant when soil warms. Plant successions every 2 weeks to prolong foliage display.
Care: Easy. Keep moist. Fertilize every 2 months. Mulch. Pinch back flowers to prolong foliage growth. Propagate by seed.
Features: Good choice for borders, containers, edgings in herb gardens. Foliage good as culinary spice, fresh or dried. Disease resistant. Slug, snail susceptible.

Annual: *Papaver rhoeas.* PAPAVERACEAE.

Common name: Flanders Poppy (Field Poppy, Shirley Poppy).

Description: Many cultivars of erect, branching annual herbs, to 3 ft. (90 cm) tall, with hairy stems. Shiny, hairy, bright green, divided, feathery leaves, to 6 in. (15 cm) long.

Bloom: Showy, solitary or paired, pink, purple, red, white, often bicolored, saucerlike, single- or double-petaled flowers, 2–3 in. (50–75 mm) wide, with crepe-paper-like petals, in late spring–early summer.

Plant hardiness: Plant as tender annual, zones 2–4; self-seeding, zones 5–10.

Soil: Moist to damp, well-drained, sandy soil. Fertility: Rich–average. 6.5–7.0 pH.

Planting: Early spring, zones 2–7; autumn or early spring, zones 8–10, in full sun, 1 ft. (30 cm) apart. Tolerates mild frosts. Plant successions every 3–4 weeks to prolong bloom.

Care: Easy. Keep damp; allow soil surface to dry between waterings. Fertilize every 2 months. Deadhead spent flowers to prolong bloom. Protect from wind. Propagate by seed.

Features: Good choice for beds, borders, massed plantings in cottage, meadow, natural gardens. Good for cutting; sear stems over flame after cutting. Aphid and blight susceptible.

> **WARNING**
> Seed of *Papaver rhoeas* can be hazardous if eaten. Avoid planting in areas frequented by pets or children.

Annual: *Petunia* × *hybrida.* SOLANACEAE.

Common name: Petunia (Common Garden Petunia).

Description: Many hybrid cultigens of bushy, mounding or spreading annual or perennial herbs, to 1 ft. (30 cm) tall. Sticky, deep green, oval, veined leaves, to 2 in. (50 mm) long.

Bloom: Many blue, pink, purple, red, white, sometimes bicolored or striped, open, flared, trumpetlike, 5-petaled flowers, 1–5 in. (25–125 mm) wide, often with ruffled petals, in late spring–early autumn.

Plant hardiness: Self-seeding, zones 3–10.

Soil: Moist to damp, well-drained soil. Fertility: Rich–average. 6.5–7.5 pH.

Planting: Spring in full sun to partial shade, 7–10 in. (18–25 cm) apart, after frost hazard has passed. In zones 3–8, start seed indoors 10–12 weeks before final frost for early blooms; transplant when frost hazard has passed.

Care: Easy. Keep moist until established; allow soil surface to dry between waterings. Fertilize quarterly. Protect from rain, wind. Propagate by cuttings, seed.

Features: Good choice for hanging baskets, beds, borders, containers, ground covers in cottage, formal, meadow, shade, gardens. Tobacco budworm and botrytis, smog susceptible.

Annual: *Phlox drummondii.* POLEMONIACEAE.

Common name: Annual Phlox (Drummond Phlox).

Description: Many cultivars of bushy, mounding annual herbs, to 20 in. (50 cm) tall, with hairy stems. Alternate, paired, green, lance-shaped, narrow or oval, pointed leaves, to 2 in. (50 mm) long.

Bloom: Many cream, pink, purple, red, white, star-shaped flowers, to 1 in. (25 mm) wide, in tightly grouped clusters, in summer–autumn.

Plant hardiness: Self-seeding, zones 3–10.

Soil: Moist to dry, well-drained soil. Fertility: Rich–average. 6.5–7.0 pH.

Planting: Start indoors in spring, zones 3–6, transplanting when soil warms, in full sun to partial shade; sow outdoors, zones 7–10, 10–12 in. (25–30 cm) apart.

Care: Easy. Keep evenly moist. Fertilize monthly. Pinch to promote bushiness, prolong bloom. Propagate by seed.

Features: Good choice for beds, borders, containers, edgings, ground covers in cottage, meadow, shade gardens. Attracts butterflies, hummingbirds. Phlox bug, spider mite and powdery mildew susceptible.

Annual: *Portulaca grandiflora*. PORTULACACEAE.
Common name: Moss Rose (Eleven-O'Clock, Rose Moss, Sun Plant).
Description: Many cultivars of low, spreading annual herbs, to 8 in. (20 cm) tall and 18 in. (45 cm) wide, with succulent, branching stems. Alternate, smooth, green, fleshy, needlelike leaves, to 1 in. (25 mm) long. Common cultivars include *P. grandiflora* 'Afternoon Delight', 'Cloudbeater Mix', 'Sundial', and 'Swan'.
Bloom: Many showy, orange, pink, red, white, yellow, old-fashioned-rose-like, shiny-petaled, single or double flowers, to 1 in. (25 mm) wide, in spring–late summer. Blooms close in late afternoon.
Plant hardiness: Plant as tender annual, zones 3–8; self-seeding, zones 9–11.
Soil: Damp, well-drained, sandy soil or loam. Fertility: Average–low. 6.5–7.0 pH.
Planting: Spring in full sun, 6–8 in. (15–20 cm) apart, after frost hazard has passed. Start seed indoors 4–6 weeks before final frost for early blooms; transplant when frost hazard has passed.
Care: Easy. Keep damp; allow soil surface to dry between waterings. Avoid fertilizing. Heat, sun tolerant. Propagate by cuttings, seed.
Features: Good choice for banks, beds, containers, edgings, ground covers, massed plantings, slopes in cottage, heritage, rock gardens. Pest and disease resistant.

Annual: *Pratia pedunculata (Laurentia fluviatilis)*. CAMPANULACEAE (LOBELIACEAE).
Common name: Blue-Star Creeper (Isotoma).
Description: A few cultivars of low, mounding, spreading, or trailing perennial herbs, 3–4 in. (75–100 mm) tall and to 2 ft. (60 cm) wide, with branching, rooting stems. Alternate, smooth, light to deep green, round or lance-shaped leaves, to ½ in. (12 mm) long.
Bloom: Many tiny, blue, white, star-shaped, 5-petaled flowers, to ⅝ in. (16 mm) wide, in ball-shaped clusters, in early summer.
Plant hardiness: Plant as tender annual, zones 3–7; self-seeding, zones 5–10. Ground hardy, zones 7–10.
Soil: Moist, well-drained soil. Fertility: Rich–average. 7.0–7.5 pH.
Planting: Spring in full sun to partial shade, 8–12 in. (20–30 cm) apart, after frost hazard has passed.
Care: Easy. Keep damp until established; drought tolerant thereafter. Shear after blooms fade to renew, promote repeat blooms.
Features: Good choice for hanging baskets, borders, ground covers, paths in rock gardens. Invasive. Pest and disease resistant.

Annual: *Primula malacoides*. PRIMULACEAE.
Common name: Primrose (Baby Primrose, Fairy Primrose).
Description: Many cultivars of short-lived, mounding perennial herbs, 4–18 in. (10–45 cm) tall and wide. Shiny, textured, deep green, broadly oval, finely toothed leaves, to 10 in. (25 cm) long, on fleshy stalks.
Bloom: Many showy, pink, light purple, rose, wide, saucerlike, 4-petaled flowers, to ½ in. (12 mm) wide, in spring.
Plant hardiness: Plant as tender annual, zones 2–6; ground hardy, zones 7–10. Best in mild climates.
Soil: Moist, well-drained humus. Fertility: Rich. 6.5–7.0 pH.
Planting: Spring in full sun to partial shade, 4–6 in. (10–15 cm) apart, after soil warms. Start seed indoors 8–12 weeks before final frost for early blooms; transplant when frost hazard has passed. Best from nursery-grown transplants.
Care: Easy. Keep evenly moist. Fertilize monthly. Deadhead spent flowers to prolong bloom. Protect from sun in hot-summer climates. Propagate by seed.
Features: Good choice for beds, borders, containers, edgings in cottage, formal, shade, small-space gardens. Attracts bees and butterflies. Disease resistant. Slug, snail susceptible.

Annual: *Ricinus communis.* EUPHORBIACEAE.

Common name: Castor Bean (Caster-Oil-Plant).

Description: Several widely varied, erect, branching, shrubby annual herbs, sometimes to 40 ft. (12 m) tall but seldom more than 15 ft. (4.5 m) tall in landscape use. Alternate, red purple becoming deep green, deeply lobed, finely toothed, pointed, veined leaves, to 3 ft. (90 cm) wide. Dwarf cultivars available.

Bloom: Many insignficant white flowers, in summer, form ball-shaped, hairy and spiny seedpods, to 1 in. (25 mm) wide, in autumn; grown primarily for foliage.

Plant hardiness: Plant as tender annual, zones 4–9; self-seeding, zones 5–11. Perennial-like, zones 10–11.

Soil: Moist to damp, well-drained, sandy soil. Fertility: Rich–low. 6.5–8.0 pH.

Planting: Spring, zones 4–9; winter, zones 10–11, in full sun, 4–6 ft. (1.2–1.8 m) apart.

Care: Moderate. Keep moist until established; drought tolerant thereafter. Fertilize quarterly. Pinch seedpods to prevent seed formation. Propagate by seed.

Features: Good choice for backgrounds, containers, screens in arid, meadow, natural gardens. Pest and disease resistant.

> **WARNING**
> Sap and seed of *Ricinus communis* are fatally hazardous if eaten, can cause skin irritation. Avoid planting in gardens frequented by pets or children and wear gloves when handling.

Annual: *Rudbeckia hirta.* ASTERACEAE (COMPOSITAE).

Common name: Black-Eyed Susan (Coneflower, Gloriosa Daisy).

Description: Many cultivars of tall, upright, branching, annual, biennial, or short-lived perennial herbs, 2–3 ft. (60–90 cm) tall. Textured, hairy, green, lance-shaped leaves, to 4 in. (10 cm) long.

Bloom: Showy, solitary, orange-yellow blend, daisylike flowers, 2–4 in. (50–100 mm) wide, with brown, purple, cone-shaped centers, in summer–autumn.

Plant hardiness: Planted as annual in all zones; ground hardy, zones 3–10.

Soil: Moist, well-drained soil. Fertility: Average. 6.0–7.5 pH.

Planting: Spring in full sun to partial shade, 1 ft. (30 cm) apart. Sow seed of biennial cultivars for flowers the following season or plant nursery containers.

Care: Easy. Keep moist; allow soil surface to dry between waterings. Deadhead spent flowers. Divide perennials when crowded. Propagate by cuttings, division, seed.

Features: Good choice for accents, backgrounds, borders, fencelines, massed plantings in cottage, meadow, wildlife gardens. Good for cutting. Attracts birds, butterflies. Pest and disease resistant.

Annual: *Salpiglossis sinuata.* SOLANACEAE.

Common name: Painted-Tongue (Velvet Flower).

Description: Several cultivars of upright, open perennial herbs, to 30 in. (75 cm) tall. Sticky, deep green, broadly oval, pointed, toothed leaves, to 4 in. (10 cm) long.

Bloom: Many blue, orange, pink, red, yellow, or multicolored, variegated, patterned, flared, trumpet-shaped, 5-petaled flowers, to 2 in. (50 mm) wide, in late spring–early autumn.

Plant hardiness: Plant as tender annual, zones 2–7; ground hardy, zones 8–10. Self-seeding.

Soil: Moist, well-drained soil. Fertility: Rich. 6.5–7.5 pH.

Planting: Spring in full sun, 8–12 in. (20–30 cm) apart, after soil warms. Start seed indoors 6–8 weeks before final frost for early blooms; transplant when frost hazard has passed.

Care: Easy. Keep moist; allow soil surface to dry between waterings. Fertilize monthly; avoid high-nitrogen fertilizers. Pinch to encourage branching. Stake. Propagate by seed.

Features: Good choice for backgrounds, borders, containers, massed plantings in cottage, small-space gardens. Good for cutting. Pest and disease resistant.

Annual: *Sanvitalia procumbens.* ASTERACEAE (COMPOSITAE).

Common name: Creeping Zinnia (Trailing Sanvitalia).

Description: Many cultivars of low, branching or spreading annual herbs, to 6 in. (15 cm) tall and 18 in. (45 cm) wide. Opposite, hairy, light green, broadly lance-shaped leaves, to 2½ in. (63 mm) long. Common cultivars include *S. procumbens* 'Flore-Pleno', 'Gold Braid', and 'Mandarin Orange'.

Bloom: Many solitary, orange, yellow, daisylike, single- or double-petaled flowers, ¾–1 in. (19–25 mm) wide, with large, purple brown centers, in summer–late autumn.

Plant hardiness: Self-seeding, zones 2–11

Soil: Moist to damp, well-drained soil. Fertility: Average–low. 7.0–7.5 pH.

Planting: Late spring in full sun, 6–12 in.(15–30 cm) apart, after frost hazard has passed. Avoid transplanting.

Care: Easy. Keep moist until established; allow soil surface to dry between waterings. Fertilize quarterly. Propagate by seed.

Features: Good choice for banks, hanging baskets, borders, containers, fillers, ground covers, in cottage, meadow, natural, rock gardens. Pest and disease resistant.

Annual: *Scabiosa atropurpurea (S. grandiflora).* DIPSACACEAE.

Common name: Pincushion Flower (Mourning-Bride, Sweet Scabious).

Description: Several cultivars of erect, narrow annual herbs, to 2 ft. (60 cm) tall and 1 ft. (30 cm) wide. Opposite, smooth, green, nearly fernlike, finely cut or lobed leaves, 2–3 in. (50–75 mm) long. Common cultivars include *S. atropurpurea* 'Butterfly Blue', 'Giant Imperial', 'Grandiflora', 'Nana', 'Paper Moon', 'Ping Pong', and 'Salmon Queen'. Dwarf cultivars available.

Bloom: Showy, solitary, pink, light to deep purple, rose, white flowers, to 2 in. (50 mm) wide, with irregular, ruffled, tubular or flat petals tucked around raised, cushionlike centers, in summer–autumn.

Plant hardiness: Self-seeding, zones 4–11.

Soil: Moist to damp, well-drained loam. Fertility: Rich–average. 7.0–8.0 pH.

Planting: Early spring in full sun, 1 ft. (30 cm) apart, when soil is workable.

Care: Easy. Keep moist until established; drought tolerant thereafter. Fertilize every 2 months. Deadhead spent flowers to prolong bloom. Propagate by seed.

Features: Good choice for backgrounds, beds, borders, massed plantings in cottage, formal, meadow, rock gardens. Good for cutting, drying. Pest and disease resistant.

Annual: *Schizanthus pinnatus.* SOLANACEAE.

Common name: Poor-Man's Orchid (Butterfly Flower).

Description: A few cultivars of upright, branching herbs, to 2 ft. (60 cm) tall. Alternate, green, feathery, finely cut leaves, to 5 in. (13 cm) long. Common cultivars include *S. pinnatus* 'Angel Wings', 'Excelsior', 'Grandifloris', 'Roseus', and 'Star Parade'.

Bloom: Showy, pink, purple, white, yellow, orchidlike flowers, 1–1½ in. (25–38 mm) wide, with upper, extended petals marked in intricate, contrasting patterns of bright yellow, in profuse branching clusters, in summer–early autumn.

Plant hardiness: Self-seeding, zones 3–10. Best in cool-summer climates.

Soil: Moist, well-drained, sandy loam. Fertility: Rich. 6.5–7.5 pH.

Planting: Start indoors in spring, zones 3–8, transplanting after frost hazard has passed, in full sun to partial shade; sow outdoors when soil warms, zones 9–10, 1 ft. (30 cm) apart. Plant successions every 2 weeks to prolong bloom.

Care: Easy. Keep moist. Fertilize monthly. Protect from frost, heat, wind. Propagate by seed.

Features: Good choice for beds, borders, containers in cottage, small-space gardens. Good for cutting. Pest and disease resistant.

Annual: *Tagetes erecta.* ASTERACEAE (COMPOSITAE).
Common name: Marigold (African Marigold, Aztec Marigold).
Description: Many cultivars of mounding, bushy annual herbs, to 3 ft. (90 cm) tall. Opposite, smooth, deep green, feathery, deeply lobed, toothed, fragrant leaves, to 3 in. (75 mm) long.
Bloom: Many showy, cream, gold, white, yellow, round, wavy-fringed flowers, to 2½ in. (63 mm) wide, in summer–autumn.
Plant hardiness: Self-seeding, zones 3–10.
Soil: Moist, well-drained soil. Fertility: Average. 6.5–7.0 pH.
Planting: Spring in full sun, 8–16 in. (20–40 cm) apart, after frost hazard has passed. Start seed indoors 6–8 weeks before final frost for early blooms; transplant when frost hazard has passed.
Care: Easy. Keep evenly moist. Fertilize monthly. Deadhead spent flowers to prolong bloom. Propagate by seed.
Features: Good choice for beds, borders, containers in cottage, formal, small-space, wildlife gardens. Attracts birds, butterflies. Aphid, leafhopper and powdery mildew susceptible.

Annual: *Thymophylla tenuiloba (Dyssodia tenuiloba).* ASTERACEAE (COMPOSITAE).
Common name: Dahlberg Daisy (Golden-Fleece).
Description: Many cultivars of short-lived, mounding or spreading perennial herbs, to 1 ft. (30 cm) tall and 18 in. (45 cm) wide. Opposite becoming alternate, deep green, feathery, divided, fragrant leaves, to 3 in. (75 mm) long, with 7–11 lance-shaped, hairy leaflets, to ¾ in. (19 mm) long.
Bloom: Many showy, bright yellow, daisylike flowers, to 1 in. (25 mm) wide, with button-like, gold, yellow centers, in summer–autumn.
Plant hardiness: Plant as tender annual, zones 2–7; ground hardy, zones 8–11.
Soil: Damp, well-drained, sandy soil. Fertility: Average. 6.5–7.5 pH.
Planting: Spring, zones 2–7; autumn, zones 8–11, in full sun, 9–12 in. (23–30 cm) apart, after soil warms. Start seed indoors 10–12 weeks before final frost for early blooms; transplant when frost hazard has passed.
Care: Easy. Keep damp; allow soil surface to dry between waterings. Fertilize quarterly. Deadhead spent flowers to prolong bloom. Propagate by seed.
Features: Good choice for accents, borders, containers, massed plantings in cottage, formal, small-space, wildlife gardens. Good for cutting. Attracts butterflies. Pest and disease resistant.

Annual: *Tithonia rotundifolia.* ASTERACEAE (COMPOSITAE).
Common name: Mexican Sunflower.
Description: Several cultivars of erect, narrow annual herbs to 6 ft. (1.8 m) tall, 3–4 ft. (90–120 cm) wide. Alternate, shiny, deep green, oval, 3-lobed leaves, to 1 ft. (30 cm) long. Common cultivars include *T. rotundifolia* 'Aztec Sun', 'Goldfinger', 'Sundance', and 'Torch'.
Bloom: Many showy, bright gold, orange, yellow, round, daisylike flowers, to 3 in. (75 mm) wide, in branching clusters, in summer–autumn.
Plant hardiness: Plant as tender annual, zones 3–11; self-seeding, zones 9–10. Best in hot-summer climates.
Soil: Moist to damp, well-drained soil. Fertility: Average–low. 6.5–7.5 pH.
Planting: Spring in full sun, 2 ft. (60 cm) apart, after frost hazard has passed. Start seed indoors 6–8 weeks before final frost for early blooms; transplant when frost hazard has passed.
Care: Easy. Keep moist until established; drought tolerant thereafter. Avoid fertilizing. Stake. Propagate by seed.
Features: Good choice for accents, backgrounds, screens in arid, meadow, wildlife gardens. Good for cutting; sear stems to close before placing in arrangement. Attracts birds, butterflies, hummingbirds. Heat tolerant. Pest and disease resistant.

Annual: *Torenia fournieri.* SCROPHULARIACEAE.
Common name: Wishbone Flower (Blue Torenia, Bluewings).
Description: A few cultivars of branching, tropical annual herbs, to 1 ft. (30 cm) tall and wide. Opposite, textured, deep to blue green, broadly oval, toothed leaves, to 2 in. (50 mm) long.
Bloom: Showy, purple, violet, white, irregular, 5-petaled flowers, to 1¼ in. (32 mm) wide, each with a yellow, oval petal highlight or other patterned contrasts, in summer–late autumn.
Plant hardiness: Plant as tender annual, zones 3–8; self-seeding, zones 4–11.
Soil: Moist, well-drained humus. Fertility: Rich. 6.5–7.5 pH.
Planting: Spring in partial to full shade, 6–8 in. (15–20 cm) apart, after frost hazard has passed. Start seed indoors 6–8 weeks before final frost for early blooms; transplant when frost hazard has passed.
Care: Moderate. Keep evenly moist. Fertilize monthly. Pinch foliage buds to promote bushy growth. Propagate by seed.
Features: Good choice for accents, hanging baskets, borders, containers, edgings in rock, shade, tropical gardens. Pest and disease resistant.

Annual: *Tropaeolum majus.* TROPAEOLACEAE.
Common name: Garden Nasturtium (Common Nasturtium).
Description: Many cultivars of climbing, mounding, or trailing, succulent annual herbs, to 3 ft. (90 cm) tall and wide. Shiny, deep green, round, parasol-shaped leaves, to 3 in. (75 mm) wide. Common cultivars include *T. majus* 'Alaska', 'Double Dwarf Jewel', 'Empress of India', and 'Whirlybird'.
Bloom: Many orange, pink, red, white, yellow, multicolored, deep-throated, edible, fragrant flowers, to 2½ in. (63 mm) wide, in summer–autumn. Double-flowered and dwarf cultivars available.
Plant hardiness: Self-seeding, zones 6–10.
Soil: Moist, well-drained, sandy soil. Fertility: Rich–low. 6.5–7.0 pH.
Planting: Spring in full to filtered sun, 8–12 in. (20–30 cm) apart, after frost hazard has passed.
Care: Easy. Keep evenly moist. Avoid fertilizing. Deadhead spent flowers to prolong bloom. Stake tall cultivars. Propagate by seed.
Features: Good choice for hanging baskets, borders, containers, edgings in cottage, formal, small-space gardens. Attracts birds, butterflies, hummingbirds. Invasive. Aphid, leaf miner and fusarium wilt susceptible.

Annual: *Viola cornuta.* VIOLACEAE.
Common name: Viola (Horned Violet, Tufted Pansy).
Description: Several cultivars of short-lived, mounding perennial herbs, to 1 ft. (30 cm) tall. Shiny, medium green, oval leaves, to 1 in. (25 mm) long, with scalloped edges. Common cultivars include *V. cornuta* 'Bluebird', 'Columbine', 'Cuty', 'Sorbet', 'Whiskers', and 'Yesterday, Today and Tomorrow'.
Bloom: Many purple, white, multicolored, pansylike, spurred flowers, to 1½ in. (38 mm) wide, in late spring–autumn.
Plant hardiness: Plant as tender annual, zones 2–5; ground hardy, zones 3–9.
Soil: Moist, well-drained loam. Fertility: Rich–average. 6.5–7.5 pH.
Planting: Late spring in full sun to partial shade, 4–6 in. (10–15 cm) apart, after soil warms. Start seed indoors 10–12 weeks before final frost for early blooms; transplant after frost hazard has passed.
Care: Easy. Keep evenly moist. Fertilize every 2 months. Deadhead spent flowers to prolong bloom. Propagate by division, seed.
Features: Good choice for hanging baskets, beds, borders, containers, edgings in cottage, formal, rock, shade, woodland gardens. Good for cutting, companion to follow spring bulbs. Slug, snail, violet sawfly larva and anthracnose susceptible.

Annual: *Viola* × *wittrockiana.* VIOLACEAE.

Common name: Pansy (Garden Pansy, Heartsease, Ladies-Delight).

Description: Many hybrid cultivars of upright, mounding annual or short-lived perennial herbs, 6–9 in. (15–23 cm) tall. Shiny, deep green, oval to heart-shaped leaves, to 2 in. (50 mm) long, with scalloped edges.

Bloom: Many showy, blue, brown, burgundy, light and deep purple, red, white, yellow, irregular, 5-petaled flowers, 2–5 in. (50–125 mm) wide, with striking, facelike appearances due to contrasting petal markings, in early spring–late autumn or early winter.

Plant hardiness: Plant as tender annual, zones 2–7; ground hardy, zones 3–9. Best bloom in cool-summer climates.

Soil: Moist, well-drained loam. Fertility: Rich–average. 6.5–7.5 pH.

Planting: Late spring in full sun to partial shade, 6–8 in. (15–20 cm) apart, after soil warms. Start seed indoors 10–12 weeks before final frost for early blooms; transplant when soil warms.

Care: Easy. Keep moist. Fertilize monthly. Deadhead spent flowers. Propagate by division, seed.

Features: Good choice for hanging baskets, beds, borders, containers, massed plantings in cottage, formal, rock, shade, woodland gardens. Good for cutting, companion for spring bulbs. Slug, snail, violet sawfly larva and anthracnose susceptible.

Annual: *Zinnia angustifolia.* ASTERACEAE (COMPOSITAE).

Common name: Narrow-Leaved Zinnia.

Description: Several cultivars of erect, dense annual herbs, to 15 in. (38 cm) tall and wide. Opposite, smooth, lance-shaped, narrow, pointed leaves, 2½–3 in. (63–75 mm) long. Common cultivars include *Z. angustifolia* 'Classic', 'Crystal White', and 'White Star'.

Bloom: Many showy, orange, white, yellow, round, daisylike, open flowers, to 1½ in. (38 mm) wide, with green-veined undersides, and with cone-shaped, gold, orange centers, in summer–late autumn.

Plant hardiness: Plant as tender annual, zones 2–7; self-seeding, zones 8–11.

Soil: Moist, well-drained humus. Fertility: Rich. 6.0–7.0 pH.

Planting: Spring in full sun, 6–8 in. (15–20 cm) apart, after soil warms.

Care: Easy. Keep evenly moist. Fertilize monthly. Deadhead spent flowers to prolong bloom. Propagate by seed.

Features: Good choice for accents, beds, borders, containers, edgings, massed plantings in cottage, meadow, natural, wildlife gardens. Good for cutting. Japanese beetle, borer, slug, snail and powdery mildew susceptible.

Annual: *Zinnia elegans* and hybrids. ASTERACEAE (COMPOSITAE).

Common name: Garden Zinnia (Common Zinnia, Youth-and-Old-Age).

Description: Many hybrid cultivars of bushy annual herbs, 1–4 ft. (30–120 cm) tall. Opposite, textured, green, lance-shaped or oval, pointed leaves, to 5 in. (13 cm) long.

Bloom: Many green, orange, pink, purple, red, yellow, round, double, quilled, or crested flowers, 1–7 in. (25–180 mm) wide, in summer–autumn.

Plant hardiness: Self-seeding, zones 4–11.

Soil: Moist, well-drained soil. Fertility: Rich–average. 7.0–7.5 pH.

Planting: Spring in full sun, 6–12 in. (15–30 cm) apart, after soil warms.

Care: Easy. Keep moist; avoid overhead watering of foliage to prevent fungal disease. Fertilize quarterly. Deadhead spent flowers to prolong bloom. Propagate by seed.

Features: Good choice for accents, beds, borders, containers, edgings in cottage, formal, meadow, natural, wildlife gardens. Good for cutting. Attracts birds, butterflies, hummingbirds. Japanese beetle, borer, slug, snail and powdery mildew susceptible.

Perennial Plants

Many gardeners admire perennials as the stars of their garden. They bloom in every color, size, and shape, from the blue sentinels of delphinium to the bold statement of a red-hot poker. Perennials put on a show of garden flowers and foliage that becomes more lush and beautiful with each passing year.

Horticulturists classify as perennial those plants with fibrous roots that grow and bloom for more than two years, while annuals grow, bloom, set seed, and die in a single season, and biennials complete their life cycle in two years. Perennials differ from shrubs such as azalea, which also grow and bloom repeatedly, because the shrubs have woody stems.

Some annuals, biennials, bulbs, and shrubs perform virtually the same as perennials in the landscape or garden. For this reason, the following collection of plants includes some that otherwise would fit into those categories. Both they and the many true perennials listed here are worthy of consideration as you select long-lasting additions that will beautify your garden and contribute to its interest.

Perennial: *Abelmoschus moschatus (Hibiscus moschatus)*. MALVACEAE.

Common name: Silk Flower (Musk Mallow, Rose Mallow, Swamp Hibiscus).

Description: Several cultivars of bushy, semi-evergreen perennial herbs, usually to 2 ft. (60 cm) tall and wide; zones 9–11, to 6 ft. (1.8 m) tall and wide. Textured, deep green, deeply cut and toothed leaves, to 18 in. (45 cm) long at base, smaller at branch ends. Evergreen, zones 8–10. Close relative of okra.

Bloom: Many pink, red, white, hibiscus-like, 5-petaled flowers, 3–5 in. (75–125 mm) wide, in summer.

Plant hardiness: Tender. Plant as annual, zones 3–8; ground hardy, zones 9–11.

Soil: Moist, well-drained soil. Fertility: Rich–average. 6.5–7.5 pH.

Planting: Spring in full to filtered sun, 12–18 in. (30–45 cm) apart, after soil warms.

Care: Easy. Keep evenly moist. Fertilize monthly spring–autumn. Mulch. Protect from frost. Propagate by seed.

Features: Good choice for accents, beds, borders, massed plantings in bog, cottage, natural, wildlife gardens. Good for cutting, drying. Attracts birds, butterflies. Pest resistant. Powdery mildew, stem rot susceptible.

Perennial: *Acanthus mollis*. ACANTHACEAE.

Common name: Bear's-Breech (Artist's Acanthus).

Description: Several cultivars of mounding, spreading, deciduous perennial herbs, to 3 ft. (90 cm) tall and wide. Shiny, soft-textured, deep green, oval, 5- and 7-lobed, pointed, deeply cut and toothed leaves, to 30 in. (75 cm) long, form a circular, radiating base.

Bloom: Many pink, purple, white, tubular flowers, to 2 in. (50 mm) long, beneath green bracts, on multiple tall, stout spikes, to 5 ft. (1.5 m) tall, with leaflike bracts between the flowers, in summer.

Plant hardiness: Tender. Plant as annual, zones 3–6; ground hardy, zones 7–10. *A. mollis* 'Latifolius' is ground hardy, zones 7–8.

Soil: Moist, well-drained loam. Fertility: Average. 6.5 7.5 pH.

Planting: Spring in full sun to full shade, 3 ft. (90 cm) apart.

Care: Easy. Keep evenly moist. Fertilize annually in spring. Protect from frost. Propagate by division, seed.

Features: Good choice for accents, backgrounds, fencelines in shade, woodland gardens. Good for cutting. Disease resistant. Snail, slug susceptible.

Perennial: *Achillea* species. ASTERACEAE (COMPOSITAE).

Common name: Yarrow.

Description: Almost 100 species of erect, open, semi-deciduous perennial herbs, 6–54 in. (15–135 cm) tall, 12–18 in. (30–45 cm) wide. Soft-textured, gray green, green, silver, finely cut, often toothed, fragrant leaves, to 8 in. (20 cm) long. Evergreen, zones 9–10. Common cultivars include *A. millefolium* 'Christel', 'Martina', and 'Orange Queen'.

Bloom: Many pink, red, white, yellow flowers, in flat clusters, 3–5 in. (75–125 mm) wide, in spring or continually blooming, depending on species and zone.

Plant hardiness: Hardy. Zones 3–10.

Soil: Dry, well-drained soil. Fertility: Average–low. 6.5–8.0 pH.

Planting: Spring, zones 3–8; autumn, zones 9–10, in full sun, 1–2 ft. (30–60 cm) apart.

Care: Easy. Keep moist until established; drought tolerant thereafter. Fertilize annually in spring. Stake tall cultivars. Propagate by cuttings, division.

Features: Good choice for accents, beds, borders, massed plantings in cottage, natural, wildlife, woodland gardens. Good for cutting, drying. Attracts birds, butterflies. Pest resistant. Powdery mildew, stem rot susceptible.

Perennial: *Aconitum napellus.* RANUNCULACEAE.
Common name: Garden Monkshood (Aconite, Helmet Flower).
Description: Many cultivars of erect, narrow, deciduous perennial herbs, 3–4 ft. (90–120 cm) tall. Hairy, deep green, 3-lobed, deeply toothed leaves, 2–4 in. (50–100 mm) wide. *A. carmichaelii* and *A. henryi* are closely related species with similar care needs.
Bloom: Many blue, violet, helmet-shaped flowers, 1–2 in. (25–50 mm) wide, with visorlike extensions, form dense spiking clusters, to 1 ft. (30 cm) tall, in late summer–autumn.
Plant hardiness: Hardy. Zones 2–9. Best in cold-winter climates.
Soil: Moist, well-drained soil. Fertility: Rich. 5.0–6.0 pH.
Planting: Autumn in partial shade, 18 in. (45 cm) apart.
Care: Easy. Keep moist; allow soil surface to dry between waterings. Mulch the first winter in coldest regions. Stake taller plants. Propagate by division, seed.
Features: Good choice for backgrounds, beds, borders in country, natural, woodland gardens. Good for cutting. Source of the medical drug aconite, a pain reliever. Pest and disease resistant.

> **WARNING**
> All parts of *Aconitum napellus* are fatally toxic if eaten. Avoid planting in any area frequented by pets or children.

Perennial: *Acorus calamus.* ARACEAE.
Common name: Sweet Flag.
Description: Several cultivars of upright and arching, rhizomatous, deciduous, aquatic perennial herbs, to 6 ft. (1.8 m) tall and wide. Smooth, bright green, striped, or variegated, long, narrow, iris- or grasslike, ribbed, fragrant leaves, to 5 ft. (1.5 m) long. See also *A. gramineus,* Japanese sweet flag, a closely related species with similar care needs.
Bloom: Insignificant greenish brown flowers when rooted in water; flower stalk is shorter than leaves.
Plant hardiness: Hardy. Zones 3–10.
Soil: Very moist, well-drained humus or, in water features, shallow-depth marginal or shoreline sites. Fertility: Rich. 6.0–8.0 pH.
Planting: Spring in full sun, 3 ft. (90 cm) apart, or submerged to 6 in. (15 cm).
Care: Easy. Keep evenly moist. Fertilize annually in spring. Divide when crowded. Propagate by division, seed.
Features: Good choice for accents, borders in boggy soil or water features. Rhizome is a source of the medicinal extract, calamus. Pest and disease resistant.

Perennial: *Acorus gramineus.* ARACEAE.
Common name: Japanese Sweet Flag (Dwarf Sweet Flag, Grassy-Leaved Sweet Flag).
Description: Many cultivars of mounding, rhizomatous, semi-evergreen perennial herbs, to 18 in. (45 cm) tall and wide. Shiny, gold, green, variegated, narrow, straplike, grasslike, fragrant leaves, to 1 ft. (30 cm) long and ½ in. (12 mm) wide, in low-growing, fan-shaped, grasslike tufts. *A. gramineus* 'Oboruzuki' and 'Ogon' are golden-leaved varieties; 'Variegatus', with green leaves striped with white edges, grows more slowly.
Bloom: Insignificant flowers; grown primarily for foliage.
Plant hardiness: Semi-hardy. Zones 6–10.
Soil: Evenly moist humus or, in water features, shallow-depth marginal or shoreline sites. Fertility: Rich. 6.0–8.0 pH.
Planting: Spring in full to filtered sun, 1 ft. (30 cm) apart, or submerged to 10 in. (25 cm).
Care: Easy. Keep evenly moist. Fertilize annually in spring. Divide when crowded. Propagate by division, seed.
Features: Good choice for accents, borders, ground covers in boggy soil, shade gardens, or water features. Pest and disease resistant.

Perennial: *Adenophora* species. CAMPANULACEAE (LOBELIACEAE).

Common name: Ladybells.

Description: Up to 40 species of erect, narrow, deciduous perennial herbs, 2–3 ft. (60–90 cm) tall. Opposite, softly hairy, deep green, lance-shaped, finely cut leaves, to 3 in. (75 mm) long. Commonly cultivated species include *A. bulleyana, A. confusa, A. liliifolia,* and *A. triphylla.* See also *Campanula* species, a close relative.

Bloom: Showy, blue, white, bellflower-like, nodding, tubular, flared flowers, to 1 in. (25 mm) long, usually in twins or triplets, in summer–autumn, depending on species.

Plant hardiness: Hardy. Zones 3–9.

Soil: Damp, well-drained soil. Fertility: Rich–average. 6.5–7.5 pH.

Planting: Spring in full sun to partial shade, 18–24 in. (45–60 cm) apart.

Care: Easy. Keep damp; allow soil surface to dry between waterings. Fertilize monthly during growth. Avoid division or transplanting. Propagate by seed.

Features: Good choice for borders, containers, edgings in country, natural, wildlife, woodland gardens. Attracts butterflies, hummingbirds. Pest and disease resistant.

Perennial: *Aethionema* species. BRASSICACEAE (CRUCIFERAE).

Common name: Stone Cress.

Description: Over 30 species of dense, erect, rounded, shrubby annual or perennial herbs, to 10 in. (25 cm) tall and wide. Powdery, blue gray, deep green, wide, oval, pointed leaves, to 1 in. (25 mm) long. Commonly cultivated species include *A. arabicum; A. grandiflorum,* Persian stone cress; *A. iberideum; A. saxiatile; A. schistosum;* and *A. stylosum.*

Bloom: Many pink, rose, white, yellow, 4-petaled flowers, to ½ in. (12 mm) wide, form dense, rounded, terminal clusters, to 4 in. (10 cm) wide, in late spring–summer.

Plant hardiness: Hardy. Zones 3–9. Best in cold-winter climates. *A. × warleyense,* Warley rose, a hybrid of *A. grandiflorum,* is best in zones 7–9.

Soil: Damp to dry, well-drained soil. Fertility: Average–low. 7.0–8.0 pH.

Planting: Spring in full sun, 1 ft. (30 cm) apart.

Care: Easy. Keep damp until established; drought tolerant thereafter. Avoid fertilizing. Mulch. Deadhead spent flowers to prolong bloom. Propagate by division, seed.

Features: Good choice for borders, containers, edgings, massed plantings in country, meadow, natural, rock gardens. Pest and disease resistant.

Perennial: *Agastache* species and hybrids. LAMIACEAE (LABIATAE).

Common name: Hyssop (Giant Hyssop, Hummingbird Mint).

Description: About 30 species of branching, mounding, upright perennial herbs, 2–4 ft. (60–120 cm) tall. Opposite, light green, oval, pointed, finely toothed, veined, fragrant leaves, to 3 in. (75 mm) long. Commonly cultivated species include *A. barberi* and *A. foeniculum,* anise hyssop. Most popular cultivars are hybrids, selected for bloom color, habit, or size.

Bloom: Many blue, orange, pink, red, mintlike, edible flowers, to ¼ in. (6 mm) wide, form conical spikes, to 6 in. (15 cm) tall, in summer.

Plant hardiness: Hardy or semi-hardy. Zones 3–11.

Soil: Damp, well-drained, sandy soil. Fertility: Rich–average. 6.5–7.5 pH.

Planting: Spring in full to filtered sun, 1 ft. (30 cm) apart, after soil warms.

Care: Easy. Keep moist; allow soil surface to dry between waterings. Fertilize annually in spring. Deadhead spent flowers to prolong bloom. Propagate by division, seed.

Features: Good choice for backgrounds, borders, edgings, fencelines in arid, country, natural, rock, wildlife gardens. Attracts bees, hummingbirds. Pest and disease resistant.

Perennial: *Alcea rosea (Althaea rosea)*. MALVACEAE.

Common name: Hollyhock.

Description: Upright, narrow biennial herb, to 9 ft. (2.7 m) tall. Textured, green, round leaves, 6–8 in. (15–20 cm) wide, forming a circular, radiating base. Widely available cultivars include *A. rosea* 'Chater's Double', a double-flowered perennial; dwarf forms; and several with first-year blooms.

Bloom: Showy, maroon, pink, red, white, yellow, saucer-shaped flowers, to 4 in. (10 cm) wide, opening upward along the stalk, in summer–autumn.

Plant hardiness: Hardy. Zones 2–10.

Soil: Moist, well-drained soil. Fertility: Average. 7.0–7.5 pH.

Planting: Spring for annual-performing cultivars; late summer for biennial-performing cultivars in full sun to partial shade; 1 ft. (30 cm) apart.

Care: Easy. Keep evenly moist. Stake. Protect from wind. Cut stalks after flowers fade. Transplant second-season seedlings in spring. Propagate by division, seed.

Features: Good choice for accents, backgrounds, beds in cottage, formal, natural, wildlife gardens. Attracts birds, hummingbirds. Slug, snail and rust susceptible.

Perennial: *Alchemilla* species. ROSACEAE.

Common name: Lady's-Mantle.

Description: Nearly 200 species of mostly low, spreading, deciduous annual or perennial herbs, 6–24 in. (15–60 cm) tall, with runnerlike stolons. Soft-textured, light green, sometimes silver-fringed, round or heart-shaped, deeply lobed leaves, 2–5 in. (50–125 mm) wide. Most commonly cultivated is *A. mollis*.

Bloom: Many tiny, green, yellow flowers, in terminal branching clusters, to 2–3 in. (50–75 mm) wide, in summer.

Plant hardiness: Hardy. Zones 3–9. Best in cool climates.

Soil: Moist, well-drained loam. Fertility: Average. 6.0–7.0 pH.

Planting: Spring in full to filtered sun, 12–18 in. (30–45 cm) apart, depending on species.

Care: Easy. Keep evenly moist. Fertilize monthly during growth. Protect from heat. Propagate by division, runners, seed.

Features: Good choice for accents, edgings, foregrounds, ground covers in shade, woodland gardens. Good for cutting. Pest and disease resistant.

Perennial: *Aloe* species. LILIACEAE.

Common name: Aloe.

Description: Between 200 and 250 species of long-lived succulent perennials, shrubs, trees, 6–144 in. (15–360 cm) tall. Powdery, blue green, gray green, long, tapering, fleshy leaves, some armed with sharp, spiny edges, in mostly stemless rosettes, some climbing and branchlike. Among the many cultivated species are *A. arborescens*, candelabra aloe; *A. aristata*, torch plant; *A. distans*, jewelled aloe; and *A. nobilis*, golden-toothed aloe.

Bloom: Many cream, orange, red, yellow, tubular flowers, 1–8 in. (25–200 mm) long, on tall, branching spikes, to 6 ft. (1.8 m) long, intermittently in spring–autumn, only in warm-summer climates.

Plant hardiness: Tender. Zones 9–10.

Soil: Dry, well-drained, sandy soil. Fertility: Average. 7.0–8.0 pH.

Planting: Spring in full sun, 1–10 ft. (30–305 cm) apart, depending on species.

Care: Easy. Water deeply during growth; reduce or withhold water during dormancy. Protect from frost. Propagate by cuttings, offsets, suckers.

Features: Good choice for accents, containers, edgings, rocky slopes in arid, rock gardens. *A. vera*, medicinal aloe, is a source of topical skin-irritation salves. Pest and disease resistant.

Perennial: *Alternanthera ficoidea.* AMARANTHACEAE.

Common name: Parrotleaf (Alligator Weed, Joseph's-Coat, Joyweed).

Description: Several cultivars of fast-growing, low, trailing, perennial herbs, 6–15 in. (15–38 cm) tall. Shiny, green, orange, pink, red, white, variegated, oval, pointed leaves, 2–3 in. (50–75 mm) long, color-splashed and deeply veined, on creeping stems. Common cultivars include *A. ficoidea* 'Amoena', with orange, red veins; 'Bettzickiana', with red, yellow, variegated leaves; and 'Versicolor', with round, copper red leaves.

Bloom: Insignificant cream, white flowers; grown primarily for foliage.

Plant hardiness: Tender. Plant as annual, zones 3–7; ground hardy, zones 8–11. Color best in warm climates.

Soil: Moist, well-drained humus or, in water features, shoreline sites. Fertility: Rich. 6.0–7.5 pH.

Planting: Spring in full sun to partial shade, 4–10 in. (10–25 cm) apart, after frost hazard has passed.

Care: Easy. Keep evenly moist until established. Fertilize monthly. Pinch, shear foliage to control growth, prevent bloom. Propagate by cuttings, division, seed.

Features: Good choice for beds, borders, ground covers, massed plantings in formal, natural gardens and water feature shorelines. Good for tropical effects. Pest and disease resistant. Salt susceptible.

Perennial: *Amsonia tabernaemontana.* APOCYNACEAE.

Common name: Bluestar.

Description: Several varieties and cultivars of slow-growing, long-lived, erect, slender, shrublike, deciduous herbs, to 42 in. (1.1 m) tall, 18–24 in. (45–60 cm) wide. Matte, bright green, lance-shaped, willowlike leaves, to 9 in. (23 cm) long, turning yellow in autumn.

Bloom: Many gray blue, steel gray, star-shaped flowers, to ¾ in. (19 mm) wide, with light blue centers, in drumsticklike, terminal clusters, to 6 in. (15 cm) wide, in late spring–early summer.

Plant hardiness: Hardy. Zones 4–9.

Soil: Damp, well-drained soil. Fertility: Rich–average. 6.5–7.0 pH.

Planting: Spring, zones 4–7; autumn, zones 8–9, in full sun to partial shade, 6–9 in. (15–23 cm) apart.

Care: Easy. Keep damp until established; allow soil surface to dry between waterings. Drought tolerant thereafter. Fertilize monthly during growth. Propagate by cuttings, division, seed.

Features: Good choice for borders in natural, wildlife gardens. Good for cutting. Attracts butterflies, hummingbirds. Pest and disease resistant.

Perennial: *Anchusa* species. BORAGINACEAE.

Common name: Bugloss (Alkanet, Cape Forget-Me-Not).

Description: About 35 species of erect or spreading annual and perennial herbs, 3–5 ft. (90–150 cm) tall. Alternate, hairy, textured, deep green, oval, pointed leaves, 3–4 in. (75–100 mm) long. Commonly cultivated species include *A. azurea, A. capensis,* and *A. officinalis.*

Bloom: Many bright blue, violet, white, forget-me-not-like, 5-petaled flowers, ½ in. (12 mm) wide, in drooping, terminal clusters, to 6 in. (15 cm) wide, in summer.

Plant hardiness: Zones 3–8, depending on species.

Soil: Moist, well-drained soil. Fertility: Average–low. 6.0–7.5 pH.

Planting: Spring in full sun to partial shade, 18–30 in. (45–75 cm) apart.

Care: Easy. Keep damp; allow soil surface to dry between waterings. Avoid fertilizing. Stake tall species. Protect from wind. Propagate by cuttings, seed.

Features: Good choice for backgrounds, borders, fencelines in formal, natural, woodland gardens. Good for cutting. Leafhopper and crown rot susceptible.

Perennial: *Anthemis tinctoria.* ASTERACEAE (COMPOSITAE).

Common name: Golden Marguerite.

Description: Several cultivars of short-lived, rounded, shrublike, deciduous biennial and perennial herbs, 2–3 ft. (60–90 cm) tall and wide. Smooth, light green, fernlike, deeply cut, fragrant leaves, to 3 in. (75 mm) long, with felt gray undersides. Evergreen in warm climates.

Bloom: Single gold, orange, white, yellow, daisylike, multirayed, upturned flowers, 1½–2 in. (38–50 mm) wide, with wide yellow centers, in profuse masses in summer–early autumn.

Plant hardiness: Semi-hardy. Zones 3–10. Self-seeding, zones 8–10.

Soil: Damp to dry, well-drained soil. Fertility: Low. 6.5–7.0 pH. Avoid heavy, moist, clayey soil.

Planting: Late spring or early summer in full sun, 15–18 in. (38–45 cm) apart, after soil warms.

Care: Easy. Keep damp; allow soil surface to dry between waterings. Avoid fertilizing. Deadhead spent flowers to prolong blooms. Propagate by cuttings, division, seed.

Features: Good choice for borders in cottage, natural gardens. Good for cutting. Flowers yield yellow dye. Disease resistant. Aphid susceptible.

Perennial: *Antirrhinum majus.* SCROPHULARIACEAE.

Common name: Snapdragon (Garden Snapdragon).

Description: Upright, climbing, vining perennial herb, to 3 ft. (90 cm) tall. Shiny, medium green, lance-shaped leaves, to 3 in. (75 mm) long. Many cultivars are available, including azalea-like, bell-flowered, double-flowered, and dwarf forms.

Bloom: Many orange, pink, red, white, yellow, bicolored, 2-lipped or sometimes double flowers, to 2 in. (50 mm) long, in spring–early summer.

Plant hardiness: Semi-hardy. Plant as annual, zones 3–7; ground hardy, zones 8–11.

Soil: Moist, well-drained humus. Fertility: Rich. 6.5–7.0 pH.

Planting: Spring in full to filtered sun, 4–6 in. (10–15 cm) apart, when soil is workable.

Care: Easy. Keep moist; avoid overhead watering of foliage to prevent rust. Pinch stem tips when plant reaches 2–4 in. (50–100 mm) tall to promote bushiness and flowering. Propagate by seed.

Features: Good choice for beds, edgings, fencelines, trellises in cottage, formal, meadow, wildlife gardens. Good for cutting. Attracts birds, butterflies, hummingbirds. Aphid, leaf miner, whitefly and rust susceptible.

Perennial: *Aquilegia caerulea.* RANUNCULACEAE.

Common name: Rocky Mountain Columbine.

Description: Several cultivars of graceful, upright, open perennials, 18–36 in. (45–90 cm) tall. Fine-textured, light silvery green, feathery, double-divided leaves, to 8 in. (20 cm) wide, in 2–3-leaflet groups, each to 3 in. (75 mm) long. Common cultivars include *A. caerulea* 'Alba', 'Citrina', and 'Rosea'. *A. vulgaris* is a closely related species with similar care needs.

Bloom: Showy, blue, white, rose, yellow, bicolored, cup-and-saucer-shaped flowers, 1½–2 in. (38–50 mm) wide and to 2 in. (50 mm) long, with trailing, feathery spurs, in early summer.

Plant hardiness: Hardy. Zones 3–10.

Soil: Moist, very well-drained, sandy humus. Fertility: Rich–average. 6.5–7.5 pH.

Planting: Spring in full sun to partial shade, 1–2 ft. (30–60 cm) apart, after soil warms.

Care: Easy. Keep moist during active growth; reduce watering after flowers fade. Fertilize semi-monthly during growth; dilute liquid fertilizer to half its recommended rate. Propagate by division, seed.

Features: Good choice for borders, containers, massed plantings in natural, wildlife, woodland gardens. Attracts bees, birds, butterflies, hummingbirds. Aphid, leaf miner and powdery mildew, rust, wilt disease susceptible.

Perennial: *Aquilegia formosa.* RANUNCULACEAE.

Common name: Western Columbine.

Description: Many cultivars of graceful, upright, open perennials, 2–3 ft. (60–90 cm) tall. Fine-textured, light silvery green, feathery leaves, to 3 in. (75 mm) long, in 2–3 lobed groups, to 8 in. (20 cm) wide. Common cultivars include *A. formosa* 'Nana', 'Rubra Plena'.

Bloom: Showy, blue, pink, white, yellow, bicolored, cup-and-saucer-shaped flowers, 1–2½ in. (25–63 mm) wide and to 6 in. (15 cm) long, with trailing, feathery spurs, in early summer.

Plant hardiness: Hardy. Zones 3–10.

Soil: Moist, very well-drained, sandy humus. Fertility: Rich–average. 6.5–7.5 pH.

Planting: Spring in sun to partial shade, 1–2 ft. (30–60 cm) apart, after soil warms.

Care: Easy. Keep moist during active growth; reduce watering after flowers fade. Fertilize semi-monthly during growth; dilute liquid fertilizer to half its recommended rate. Propagate by division, seed.

Features: Good choice for borders, containers, massed plantings in natural, wildlife, woodland gardens. Attracts bees, birds, butterflies, hummingbirds. Aphid, leaf miner and powdery mildew, rust, wilt disease susceptible.

Perennial: *Arctotis venusta (A. stoechadifolia)* and hybrids. ASTERACEAE.

Common name: African Daisy.

Description: Many cultivars and hybrids of erect, branching or mounding, deciduous perennial herbs, to 2 ft. (60 cm) tall. Hairy, textured, gray green, green, lobed leaves, 3–4 in. (75–100 mm) long. See also *Dimorphotheca pluvialis*.

Bloom: Single cream, pink, purple, red, white, yellow, daisylike, many-petaled flowers, 2–3 in. (50–75 mm) wide, in late spring–summer. Best blooms on first-year plants.

Plant hardiness: Tender. Plant as annual, zones 2–7; ground hardy, zones 8–10. Best in cool, coastal areas.

Soil: Moist, well-drained, sandy soil. Fertility: Rich. 6.5–7.5 pH.

Planting: Spring, zones 2–7, when soil warms; autumn, zones 8–10, in full sun, 6–12 in. (15–30 cm) apart.

Care: Easy. Keep damp; allow soil surface to dry between waterings. Fertilize monthly. Deadhead spent flowers to promote new buds. Protect from heat. Propagate by cuttings, division, seed.

Features: Good choice for beds, borders, containers in cottage, natural, woodland gardens. Good for cutting. Pest and disease resistant.

Perennial: *Artemisia* species and hybrids. ASTERACEAE (COMPOSITAE).

Common name: Sagebrush (Angel's-Hair, Old-Man, Southernwood, Wormwood).

Description: About 200 species and many hybrids of bushy, mounding, shrublike annual, biennial, and perennial herbs, 1–4 ft. (30–120 cm) tall. Powdery, gray, green, silver, white, lacy or feathery, sometimes rosemary-like, often deeply cut, fragrant leaves, to 4 in. (10 cm) long. Commonly cultivated species include *A. abrotanum, A. absinthium,* and *A. tridentata.*

Bloom: Insignificant yellow flowers; grown primarily for foliage.

Plant hardiness: Hardy. Plant as annual, zones 2–4; ground hardy, zones 5–10.

Soil: Damp, well-drained loam. Fertility: Average–low. 6.5–7.5 pH.

Planting: Spring in full sun to partial shade, 12–15 in. (30–38 cm) apart.

Care: Easy. Keep damp; allow soil to dry between waterings. Avoid wetting foliage. Drought tolerant. Fertilize annually in spring. Prune woody stems in spring to promote bushiness. Propagate by cuttings, division, seed.

Features: Good choice for beds, containers, ground covers, massed plantings in arid, formal, rock gardens. Good in hanging baskets. Pest and disease resistant.

Perennial: *Aruncus dioicus (A. sylvester).* ROSACEAE.
Common name: Goatsbeard.
Description: Several cultivars of mounding, deciduous perennial herbs, to 6 ft. (1.8 m) tall, 4 ft. (1.2 m) wide. Deeply textured, deep green, oval, divided leaves, to 1 ft. (30 cm) long, with coarsely toothed, oval leaflets, on radiating stalks.
Bloom: Many tiny, cream, white flowers, in plumelike, sometimes nodding, terminal clusters, to 18 in. (45 cm) long, in late spring–early summer.
Plant hardiness: Hardy. Zones 3–9.
Soil: Moist, well-drained, sandy loam or, in water features, shoreline sites. Fertility: Rich. 6.0–8.0 pH.
Planting: Spring in full sun to partial shade, 18–24 in. (45–60 cm) apart.
Care: Easy. Keep evenly moist. Fertilize annually in spring. Propagate by division, seed.
Features: Good choice for beds, borders, nooks in shade, woodland gardens and water feature shorelines. Good for drying. Pest and disease resistant.

Perennial: *Asclepias tuberosa.* ASCLEPIADACEAE.
Common name: Milkweed (Butterfly Weed, Indian Paintbrush).
Description: Several cultivars of upright and branching, hairy-stalked perennial herbs, 2–3 ft. (60–90 cm) tall, 12–18 in. (30–45 cm) wide. Smooth, green, lance-shaped leaves, to 4½ in. (11 cm) long, in spirals or clusters.
Bloom: Many showy, orange, red, yellow, starlike flowers, to ⅓ in. (8 mm) wide, with light-colored centers, in broad, flat, mounding clusters, in summer, form beanlike pods bearing thread-covered seed, in autumn.
Plant hardiness: Hardy. Zones 3–9.
Soil: Dry, well-drained soil. Fertility: Low. 6.5–7.0 pH.
Planting: Early spring, zones 3–6, after frost hazard has passed; autumn, zones 7–9, in full sun, 12–18 in. (30–45 cm) apart.
Care: Easy. Water when soil is thoroughly dry. Drought tolerant. Avoid fertilizing. Propagate by division, seed.
Features: Good choice for accents, beds, borders, containers in natural, meadow, wildlife gardens. Good for cutting. Attracts birds, butterflies, hummingbirds. Somewhat invasive. Pest and disease resistant.

Perennial: *Asparagus setaceus (A. plumosus).* LILIACEAE.
Common name: Asparagus Fern (Lace Fern).
Description: Slow-growing, branching, vining, evergreen perennial shrub, to 4 ft. (1.2 m) wide. Shiny, green, feathery, fernlike foliage, to 6 in. (15 cm) long, in delicate sprays on wirelike, thorny stems. *A. setaceus* 'Nanus' is a dwarf cultivar. Emerald fern, *A. densiflorus* 'Sprengeri', is a commonly cultivated relative.
Bloom: Inconspicuous flowers; grown for lacy foliage. Forms purple, berrylike fruit.
Plant hardiness: Tender. Zones 7–11.
Soil: Damp, well-drained humus. Fertility: Rich. 6.0–7.0 pH.
Planting: Spring in full to filtered sun, 3 ft. (90 cm) apart, after soil warms.
Care: Easy. Water when soil surface dries; water sparingly in winter. Fertilize monthly in spring; dilute liquid fertilizer to half its recommended rate. Prune sparingly. Propagate by cuttings, division, seed.
Features: Good choice for hanging baskets, beds, borders, containers in shade, woodland gardens. Good for cutting. Pest resistant. Fungal disease susceptible.

ASTER

Nearly 625 species of rarely annual or biennial, but mostly perennial herbs are included in the *Aster* genus. All have composite, daisylike flowers with showy rays surrounding a disk made up of many tiny flowers. Most are rhizomatous or fibrous-rooted, and they are native to every continent except Antarctica.

Cultivated species range in height from 4–6 in. (10–15 cm) tall for ground covers to more than 6 ft. (1.8 m) for tall plants with shrublike habits. While the solitary or clustered flowers vary in size, most are 1–2½ in. (25–63 mm) wide, and blue, pink, purple, red, and white comprise a nearly complete spectrum of appealing colors.

Most asters are sturdy, fast-growing plants. While generally pest and disease resistant, they're susceptible to powdery mildew. Use them in wildlife gardens where their bright blooms and abundant seed will attract both birds and butterflies. Many cultivars are self-seeding or will multiply freely.

Asters flower in summer to autumn in a long-lasting display that makes them right for cutting and arranging. Choose from the popular species listed at right.

A. alpinus, alpine aster
A. amellus, Italian aster
A. bellidiastrum, Michael aster
A. cordifolius, blue wood aster
A. divaricatus, white wood aster
A. dumosus, bushy aster
A. ericoides, heath aster
A. grandiflorus, great aster
A. laevis, smooth aster
A. macrophyllus, big-leaved aster
A. novae-angliae, New England aster
A. novi-belgii, Michaelmas daisy
A. patens, late purple aster
A. spectabilis, seaside aster
A. tataricus, Tatarian aster

Asters are the right choice for landscape gardens, whether you are seeking a colorful accent, a background for a mixed-perennial border, or a massed planting. They perform well in containers, planters, and pots in small-space gardens such as decks, balconies, and patios.

Plant asters in early spring in full to filtered sun. They are tolerant of sun and heat once they become established, as long as they receive regular waterings to keep their soil evenly moist. They perform best in loose, well-drained soil and loam containing equal parts of sand and humus.

For best flowering, feed them with nitrogen liquid fertilizer every month as they sprout and grow. Reduce your fertilizer applications after flower buds form to avoid too much foliage at the expense of flowers. As flowers fade, pinch them off to encourage new buds to form.

Perennial asters will thrive in the garden—some species and hybrids are invasive if planted adjacent to turf or flower beds. The central plants in a group will fade over time as they lose vigor and their offspring compete for nutrients. Renew your plantings in late autumn or early spring by dividing the roots, discarding the central plants, and replanting the young offshoots in the bed's center.

Asters are the right choice for heritage gardens, whether formal or informal. Their reputation for reliable color is well deserved, and for generations, they have been a featured part of most flower gardens.

Perennial: *Aster* species. ASTERACEAE (COMPOSITAE).

Common name: Aster.

Description: Over 600 species of bushy, upright, sometimes shrublike, deciduous, mostly perennial herbs, to 4–60 in. (10–150 cm) tall and wide, with tall flower stalks. Hairy, deep green, lance-shaped leaves, 3–5 in. (75–125 mm) long.

Bloom: Showy, blue, pink, purple, red, white, daisylike flowers, to 2½ in. (63 mm) wide, in late summer–autumn.

Plant hardiness: Hardy. Zones 2–9.

Soil: Moist, well-drained, sandy soil. Fertility: Rich–average. 6.0–7.0 pH.

Planting: Spring in full to filtered sun, 3–4 ft. (90–120 cm) apart, when frost hazard has passed and soil is workable.

Care: Easy. Keep evenly moist. Fertilize monthly during growth. Deadhead spent flowers to prolong bloom. Divide when crowded. Propagate by cuttings, division.

Features: Good choice for accents, backgrounds, containers, massed plantings in cottage, formal, natural, wildlife gardens and water feature margins. Good for cutting. Attracts birds, butterflies. Very invasive. Aphid and mildew, aster yellows susceptible.

Perennial: *Astilbe* species. SAXIFRAGACEAE.

Common name: Astilbe (False Spiraea, Meadow Sweet).

Description: About 14 species of prostrate, mounding, deciduous perennial herbs, 8–36 in. (20–90 cm) tall, 1–2 ft. (30–60 cm) wide. Shiny, copper, pink becoming deep green, neatly formed, feathery, fernlike, finely divided, toothed leaves, to 3 in. (75 mm) long. Most nursery plants are *A.* × *arendsii* hybrids.

Bloom: Many tiny, pink, deep red, white, tiny flowers form dramatic, fluffy plumes, to 1 ft. (30 cm) tall, above plant foliage on narrow, stiff stalks, in summer.

Plant hardiness: Semi-hardy. Zones 4–10. Best in zones 7–10.

Soil: Moist, well-drained, sandy humus or, in water features, shoreline sites. Fertility: Rich–average. 5.5–7.0 pH.

Planting: Spring in full sun to full shade, 1–2 ft. (30–60 cm) apart.

Care: Easy–moderate. Keep moist. Fertilize annually in spring. Mulch. Shear to ground in late winter. Propagate by division, seed.

Features: Good choice for borders, containers, ground covers in cottage, shade gardens and water feature shorelines. Good for cutting, drying. Leave dried flower spikes on plants through winter for ornamental effect. Japanese beetle, slug, snail and powdery mildew susceptible.

Perennial: *Astrantia major.* APIACEAE (UMBELLIFERAE).

Common name: Masterwort.

Description: Several cultivars of mounding, deciduous perennial herbs, 2–3 ft. (60–90 cm) tall. Textured, light green, sometimes variegated, palm-shaped, 5-lobed leaves, to 1 ft. (30 cm) wide.

Bloom: Showy, creamy white, pink- or purple-centered flowers, tinged pink by a collar of purple leafy bracts below true petals, in clusters, 2–3 in. (50–75 mm) wide, in late spring.

Plant hardiness: Zones 5–7.

Soil: Moist, well-drained soil or, in water features, shoreline sites. Fertility: Average. 6.5–7.0 pH.

Planting: Early spring, zones 5–6; autumn, zone 7, in full sun to partial shade, 18 in. (45 cm) apart.

Care: Easy. Keep evenly moist. Mulch. Propagate by division, seed.

Features: Good choice for backgrounds, borders, screens in natural, woodland gardens and water feature shorelines. Good for cutting, drying. Pest and disease resistant.

Perennial: *Bacopa caroliniana (B. amplexicaulis).* SCROPHULARIACEAE.

Common name: Lemon Hyssop (Water Hyssop).

Description: Several cultivars of succulent, evergreen, aquatic perennial herbs, to 2 ft. (60 cm) tall. Opposite, shiny, delicate pale green, oval, fragrant leaves, ½–1 in. (12–25 mm) long. *Sutera cordata*, bacopa or little stars, is a close relative with a trailing habit suited to damp garden soil in shady sites.

Bloom: Many, single, blue, white, star-shaped, terminal flowers, to ½ in. (12 mm) wide, in summer.

Plant hardiness: Tender. Zones 9–11.

Soil: Evenly moist, well-drained humus or, in water features, shallow-depth marginal or shoreline sites. Fertility: Average. 6.5–7.0 pH.

Planting: Spring in full sun to partial shade, 1–2 ft. (30–60 cm) apart, in boggy soil or submerged to 6 in. (15 cm).

Care: Easy. Keep evenly moist. Fertilize monthly during growth. Mulch. Pinch to control growth. Propagate by cuttings.

Features: Good choice for banks, ground covers, edges in rock, shade, tropical gardens or water feature margins, shorelines. Pest and disease resistant.

Perennial: *Baptisia australis.* FABACEAE (LEGUMINOSAE).

Common name: False Indigo (Blue False Indigo, Wild Indigo).

Description: Several cultivars of upright, clump-forming, deciduous perennial herbs, 2–6 ft. (60–180 cm) tall. Matte, blue green, oval leaves, 2½ in. (63 mm) long, in 3-leaflet groups. *B. alba,* white false indigo; *B. leucantha,* prairie false indigo; and *B. tinctoria,* wild indigo, are closely related plants with similar care needs.

Bloom: Many blue, pealike flowers, to 1 in. (25 mm) wide, in long terminal racemes, in early summer, form beanlike pods bearing seed, in autumn.

Plant hardiness: Hardy. Zones 3–9.

Soil: Damp to dry, well-drained loam. Fertility: Average–low. 6.5–7.0 pH.

Planting: Spring, zones 3–7; autumn, zones 8–9, in full or filtered sun to partial shade, 2–3 ft. (60–90 cm) apart.

Care: Easy. Keep damp until established; water when soil surface dries. Drought tolerant thereafter. Avoid fertilizing. Stake in windy areas. Propagate by division, seed.

Features: Good choice for backgrounds, borders, massed plantings, screens in cottage, meadow gardens. Good for cutting. Deer, pest, and disease resistant.

Perennial: *Begonia* × *semperflorens-cultorum* hybrids. BEGONIACEAE.

Common name: Bedding Begonia (Wax Begonia).

Description: Many cultivars of fast-growing, bushy, upright, succulent, fibrous-rooted, half-hardy perennial herbs, 8–12 in. (20–30 cm) tall. Smooth, shiny, bronze, green, red, white, variegated leaves, to 1 in. (25 mm) wide. *B. coccinea,* angel wing begonia, is a close relative with many attractive cultivars.

Bloom: Waxy, pink, red, white single flowers, to 1 in. (25 mm) wide, in spring–autumn.

Plant hardiness: Tender. Plant as annual, zones 2–7; ground-hardy, zones 8–10.

Soil: Moist, well-drained humus. Fertility: Rich. 6.5–7.5 pH.

Planting: Spring in filtered sun to partial shade, 8–10 in. (20–25 cm) apart.

Care: Easy. Keep evenly moist. Fertilize monthly spring–autumn. Mulch. Pinch to promote fullness. Protect from frost. Propagate by cuttings, seed.

Features: Good choice for hanging baskets, beds, borders, containers, foregrounds, window boxes in formal, shade gardens. Mealybug, whitefly and leaf spot susceptible.

Perennial: *Bergenia cordifolia.* SAXIFRAGACEAE.

Common name: Heartleaf Bergenia.

Description: Several cultivars of open and spreading, rhizomatous, semi-evergreen perennial herbs, to 18 in. (45 cm) tall. Hairy, shiny, red becoming green, heart-shaped or round, wavy-edged leaves, 6–10 in. (15–25 cm) wide, in basal rosettes. Creeping rootstock forms slowly expanding colonies. *B. ciliata,* winter begonia; *B. crassifolia,* leather bergenia; *B. purpurascens,* purple-leaved bergenia; and *B. stracheyi,* Strachey bergenia, are closely related species with similar care needs.

Bloom: Showy, deep pink, pink, purple, red, white, nodding, 5-petaled flowers, ¾ in. (19 mm) wide, in clusters, to 16 in. (40 cm) tall, in early spring.

Plant hardiness: Hardy. Zones 3–8.

Soil: Moist, well-drained soil. Fertility: Average–low. 6.0–7.5 pH.

Planting: Spring in partial to full shade, 1 ft. (30 cm) apart.

Care: Easy. Keep moist until established; drought tolerant thereafter. Fertilize quarterly during growth. Propagate by division, seed.

Features: Good choice for borders, edgings, ground covers in natural, shade, woodland gardens. Very cold tolerant. Nematode, slug susceptible.

Perennial: *Browallia speciosa.* SOLANACEAE.

Common name: Bush Violet (Amethyst Flower, Lovely Browallia).

Description: Many cultivars of mounding, rounded, shrublike deciduous perennial herbs, to 2 ft. (60 cm) tall. Hairy, light green, narrow, oval, pointed leaves, to 2½ in. (63 mm) long. Common cultivars include *B. speciosa* 'Blue Bells', 'Heavenly Blue', 'Jingle Bells', 'Major', and 'Starlight'. *B. americana (B. elata),* amethyst browallia, is a closely related annual species with branching habit and similar care needs.

Bloom: Many bright blue, violet, white, petunia-like, 5-petaled flowers, to 2 in. (50 mm) wide, with contrasting white centers, in late spring–summer.

Plant hardiness: Tender. Plant as tender annual, zones 4–8; ground hardy, zones 9–11. Best in hot, humid climates.

Soil: Moist, well-drained soil. Fertility: Rich. 6.5–7.5 pH.

Planting: Spring, after soil warms, zones 4–9; autumn, zones 10–11, in partial to full shade, 1 ft. (30 cm) apart. Tolerates full sun if soil is cooled by mulch and frequent watering.

Care: Easy. Keep damp. Mist foliage occasionally. Avoid fertilizing. Pinch growth buds to encourage bushiness. Propagate by cuttings, seed.

Features: Good choice for hanging baskets, beds, borders, containers, window boxes in country, shade gardens. Good for cutting. Pest and disease resistant.

Perennial: *Brunnera macrophylla.* BORAGINACEAE.

Common name: Siberian Bugloss (Heartleaf Brunnera).

Description: Several cultivars of bushy, low, deciduous perennial herbs, 18–24 in. (45–60 cm) tall, 12–18 in. (30–45 cm) wide. Alternate, hairy, deep green, variegated, heart-shaped leaves, to 4 in. (10 cm) wide, 6–8 in. (15–20 cm) long.

Bloom: Many tiny, blue, delicate flowers, to ¼ in. (6 mm) wide, with contrasting yellow centers, in open, branching clusters on wiry, slightly hairy stems, to 6 in. (15 cm) tall, in spring–summer.

Plant hardiness: Hardy. Zones 3–10.

Soil: Moist, well-drained humus. Fertility: Rich. 6.5–7.0 pH.

Planting: Autumn in partial shade, to 1 ft. (30 cm) apart.

Care: Easy. Keep moist; allow soil surface to dry between waterings. Fertilize annually in spring. Mulch. Propagate by cuttings, division, seed.

Features: Good choice for borders, edgings, fill, ground covers in shade, woodland gardens. Self-sows. Pest and disease resistant.

Perennial: *Calamintha nepeta (C. nepetoides).* LAMIACEAE (LABIATAE).

Common name: Calamint (Calamint Savory).

Description: Several cultivars of low, mounding, rhizomatous, deciduous perennial herbs, to 2 ft. (60 cm) tall. Opposite, deep gray green, oval, pointed, finely toothed, very fragrant leaves, to ¾ in. (19 mm) long. *C. grandiflora* and *C. sylvatica* are closely related species with similar care needs.

Bloom: Many lavender, white, 2-part flowers, to ¾ in. (19 mm) long, bearing prominent stamens, in showy clusters, in summer.

Plant hardiness: Semi-hardy. Zones 3–10.

Soil: Moist, well-drained loam. Fertility: Average. 6.5–7.0 pH.

Planting: Spring in full sun to partial shade, 15–18 in. (38–45 cm) apart.

Care: Moderate. Keep moist. Fertilize quarterly during growth. Mulch heavily in winter in zones 3–6. Pinch, shear to control growth. Propagate by cuttings, division.

Features: Good choice for hanging baskets, beds, borders, containers, entries, ground covers in natural, small-space, woodland gardens. Foliage is good for fragrance, herbal tea. Attracts bees. Invasive. Pest and disease resistant.

Perennial: *Calceolaria* species and hybrids. SCROPHULARIACEAE.
Common name: Slipper Flower (Pocketbook Plant, Slipperwort).
Description: About 500 species of branching, shrublike, deciduous perennial herbs, 6–72 in. (15–180 cm) tall, depending on species and cultivar. Heavily textured, deep green, oval, pointed, toothed leaves, to 3 in. (75 mm) long. Common cultivars include *C. herbeohybrida,* florist's calceolaria; and *C. integrifolia,* a landscape plant.
Bloom: Many bronze, maroon, pink, red, yellow, pouchlike flowers, ½–1 in. (12–25 mm) long, often with green or purple markings, in open clusters, in spring–early summer.
Plant hardiness: Tender. Plant as annual, zones 2–7; ground-hardy, zones 8–10.
Soil: Moist, well-drained soil. Fertility: Rich–average. 7.0 pH.
Planting: Spring in full to filtered sun, 6–12 in. (15–30 cm) apart, after frost hazard has passed. Start seed indoors 12 weeks before final frost, zones 2–7, transplant to garden when soil warms.
Care: Moderate. Keep damp; allow soil surface to dry between waterings. Fertilize monthly. Propagate by cuttings, seed.
Features: Good choice for hanging baskets, beds, borders, containers in country, shade, woodland gardens. Spider mite susceptible.

Perennial: *Calibrachoa* species. SOLANACEAE.
Common name: Million Bells.
Description: Several cultivars of low and trailing or mounding, deciduous perennial herbs, to 2 ft. (60 cm) tall. Textured, deep green, oval, pointed, toothed leaves, to 1 in. (25 mm) long, on narrow, flexible stems. Closely related to *Petunia* × *hybrida,* petunia.
Bloom: Many showy, blue, pink, purple, red, violet, petunia-like flowers, to 1 in. (25 mm) wide, in summer.
Plant hardiness: Tender. Plant as annual, zones 4–7; ground-hardy, zones 8–10.
Soil: Moist, well-drained humus. Fertility: Rich–average. 6.5–8.0 pH. Best in low-clay soils.
Planting: Spring in full to filtered sun, 18 in. (45 cm) apart, after soil warms.
Care: Moderate. Keep damp; allow soil surface to dry between waterings. Fertilize monthly. Self-cleaning; avoid deadheading. Pinch to direct growth. Propagate by cuttings, seed.
Features: Good choice for beds, borders, containers in formal, country gardens. Pest resistant. Fungal disease susceptible.

Perennial: *Caltha palustris.* RANUNCULACEAE.
Common name: Marsh Marigold (Cowslip, Kingcup, Meadow-Bright).
Description: Several cultivars of fleshy and succulent, deciduous perennial herbs, 1–3 ft. (30–90 cm) tall, 1–2 ft. (30–60 cm) wide. Textured and veined becoming leathery, bright green, round to heart-shaped, deeply toothed leaves, to 7 in. (18 cm) wide. Plants become dormant in summer.
Bloom: Single yellow, buttercup-like, 5-petaled flowers, to 2 in. (50 mm) wide, on long, flexible stems in early spring.
Plant hardiness: Hardy. Zones 3–8.

> **WARNING**
> All parts of *Caltha palustris* may cause skin irritation in sensitive individuals. Wear rubber gloves when handling or pruning plants.

Soil: Wet, well-drained soil or, in water features, shoreline or shallow-depth marginal sites. Fertility: Rich. 6.0–8.0 pH.
Planting: Late summer in full sun to partial shade, 1–2 ft. (30–60 cm) apart, in boggy soil or submerged to 6 in. (15 cm).
Care: Easy. Keep evenly moist. Fertilize quarterly during growth. Mulch. Propagate by division, seed.
Features: Good choice for borders in bog, shade, woodland gardens and water feature margins, shorelines. May self-sow. Pest and disease resistant.

CAMPANULA (BELLFLOWER)

More than 300 species of perennial, biennial, or annual herbs are included in the *Campanula* genus. All have showy, bell- or cup-shaped flowers arranged vertically in alternating or whorled tiers along a spiking stalk. They are native to the northern hemisphere, with many Mediterranean and Eurasian species.

Cultivated species range in height from 6–36 in. (15–90 cm) tall. While the clustered flowers vary, most are less than 1½ in. (38 mm) or less in width and colored in shades of blue, purple, violet, and white. They bloom reliably from spring to autumn if spent stalks are deadheaded.

Most bellflowers are fast-growing plants. They are susceptible to spider mites and harbor both slugs and snails. Although mostly disease resistant, they are susceptible to aster yellows, a viral infection. Use them in a variety of landscape settings, choosing the smallest species for accents, borders, and edgings in rock and small-space gardens. Those with sprawling habits are good ground covers in cottage and natural gardens, while tall-habit species make good backgrounds. Choose from the commonly cultivated species listed at right.

C. alliariaefolia, spurred bellflower
C. americana, tall bellflower
C. aucheri, Aucher bellflower
C. barbara, bearded bellflower
C. boboniensis, Russian bellflower
C. carpatica, Carpathian bellflower
C. drabifolia, Greek bellflower
C. glomerata, clustered bellflower
C. isophylla, trailing Italian bellflower
C. lactiflora, milky bellflower
C. latifolia, great bellflower
C. medium, Canterbury bells
C. poscharskyana, Serbian bellflower
C. rapunculoides, creeping bellflower
C. trachelium, Coventry bells

Bellflowers are colorful companions that brighten the garden, whether as a low ground cover for banks, trailing on walls, spiking from baskets, containers, and pots, or planted in the middle of beds or backgrounds of borders. Start annual species 6–8 weeks before the last frost in cold-winter climates and transplant them into the garden when the soil warms, or plant biennial and perennial species outdoors in autumn.

Bellflowers perform best in sites with full or lightly filtered sun, those with at least 5–6 hours per day. They perform best in evenly damp, loose, well-drained humus. Always water them at their base.

For best flowering, feed them at the beginning of the season when they are planted or as new foliage emerges. Their flowers open vertically from bottom to top of the stalk, each lasting several days. As the flowers fade, pinch them off for best display, then deadhead the spent stalk to encourage branches to form.

Annual species should be replanted each year, while biennial and perennial plants perform best when transplanted from nursery-container starts. Some biennial cultivars bloom in the first season.

Campanula—especially Canterbury bells and Coventry bells—are heritage favorites with centuries of cultivation. Because many of the species hail from Mediterranean Italy, Greece, and Turkey, they also are good choices for natural and rock gardens. Bellflowers are destined to become personal favorites as the beauty of their graceful spires transforms low beds into towers of blooms, and slopes into fields of color.

Perennial: *Campanula* species. CAMPANULACEAE.
Common name: Bellflower.
Description: More than 300 species of mostly low, slender, leafy annual, biennial, or perennial herbs, 6–36 in. (15–90 cm) tall. Shiny or textured, green, spear-shaped leaves, 4–8 in. (10–20 cm) long, with central flower stalks, forming a circular, radiating base. Evergreen, zones 9–10. Closely related species with similar care needs have spreading, trailing, or upright habits.
Bloom: Many blue, purple, violet, white, cup-shaped flowers, to 1½ in. (38 mm) wide, in spring–autumn.
Plant hardiness: Plant as tender annual or mulch heavily, zones 3–5; ground hardy, zones 6–10.
Soil: Damp, well-drained humus. Fertility: Average. 6.5–7.0 pH.
Planting: Spring in full to filtered sun, 12–18 in. (30–45 cm) apart, after frost hazard has passed.
Care: Easy. Keep moist. Fertilize annually in spring. Deadhead spent flowers. Divide when crowded to maintain vigor. Propagate by cuttings, division, seed.
Features: Good choice for accents, beds, borders, fencelines, ground covers, walls in cottage, rock, wildlife gardens. Good for cutting. Attracts birds, hummingbirds. Spider mite, slug, snail and aster yellows susceptible.

Perennial: *Campanula persicifolia.* CAMPANULACEAE.
Common name: Willow Bellflower (Peach-Bells).
Description: Several cultivars of upright, narrow, dense perennial herbs, 2–3 ft. (60–90 cm) tall and about 1 ft. (30 cm) wide. Smooth, bright green, peach, narrow, lance-shaped leaves, 4–8 in. (10–20 cm) long. Evergreen, zones 9–10.
Bloom: Many blue, purple, white, cupped, dainty flowers, to 1½ in. (38 mm) wide, in loose sprays on slender, wiry stems, 2–3 ft. (60–90 cm) tall, in late spring–autumn.
Plant hardiness: Hardy. Zones 3–10.
Soil: Moist, well-drained humus. Fertility: Rich–average. 6.5–7.0 pH.
Planting: Spring in full sun to partial shade, 12–18 in. (30–45 cm) apart.
Care: Easy. Keep moist. Fertilize monthly. Divide when crowded to maintain vigor. Propagate by cuttings, division, seed.
Features: Good choice for backgrounds, beds, borders, edgings in rock, shade, wildlife, woodland gardens. Good for cutting. Attracts birds, hummingbirds. Slug, snail and aster yellows susceptible.

Perennial: *Capsicum annuum.* SOLANACEAE.
Common name: Ornamental Pepper (Christmas Pepper).
Description: Many cultivars of branching, shrublike, deciduous perennial herbs, 1–4 ft. (30–120 cm) tall. Shiny, light to deep green, oval, pointed leaves, to 3 in. (75 mm) long. Common cultivars include *C. annuum* 'Fiesta', 'Holiday Cheer', 'Red Missile', 'Treasure Red'. Closely related to edible peppers.
Bloom: Many white flowers, to ½ in. (12 mm) wide, with yellow centers, in summer, followed by pink, purple, red, yellow, seed-filled, edible fruit, in late summer–late autumn.
Plant hardiness: Plant as tender annual, zones 3–8; ground hardy, zones 9–11.
Soil: Moist, loamy, well-drained soil. Fertility: Rich. 6.5–7.0 pH.
Planting: Spring in full sun, 6–12 in. (15–30 cm) apart, after soil warms.
Care: Easy. Keep moist; allow soil surface to dry between waterings. Fertilize monthly during growth. Propagate by seed.
Features: Good choice for accents, borders, containers in arid, rock gardens or as an indoor plant in a warm, sunny location. Disease resistant. Aphid, cutworm, weevil, whitefly susceptible.

Perennial: *Centaurea* species. ASTERACEAE (COMPOSITAE).
Common name: Knapweed (Dusty-Miller).
Description: Nearly 500 species of bushy, rounded, deciduous annual, biennial, and perennial herbs, 1–5 ft. (30–150 cm) tall. Fuzzy, gray green, often silver, needlelike, often deeply cut leaves, to 1 ft. (30 cm) long, with gray, white undersides. Commonly cultivated species include *C. americana*, basket flower; *C. cineraria*; *C. gymnocarpa*; and *C. montana*, mountain bluet. *C. moschata*, sweet-sultan, is a related annual species. See also *C. cyanus*, cornflower.
Bloom: Many blue, lavender, pink, yellow, fringed, tubular, thistlelike, tufted flowers, 2–3 in. (50–75 mm) wide, either single or clustered, in spring–summer. Silver-leaved species are grown primarily for foliage.
Plant hardiness: Hardy. Zones 3–9.
Soil: Moist, well-drained loam. Fertility: Average. 6.5–8.0 pH.
Planting: Early spring, after frost hazard has passed, zones 3–7; autumn, zones 8–9, in full to filtered sun, 1–2 ft. (30–60 cm) apart.
Care: Easy. Keep moist; allow soil surface to dry between waterings. Fertilize annually in spring. Stake taller species. Propagate by division, seed.
Features: Good choice for accents, backgrounds, beds, borders in arid, formal, rock gardens. Good for cutting. Disease resistant. Aphid susceptible.

Perennial: *Centranthus ruber (Valeriana rubra).* VALERIANACEAE.
Common name: Red Valerian (Jupiter's-Beard).
Description: Several cultivars of bushy, rounded, deciduous perennial herbs, to 3 ft. (90 cm) tall. Opposite, shiny, blue green, green, oval, pointed leaves, to 4 in. (10 cm) long. *C. calcitrapa,* annual valerian; and *C. macrosiphon,* spur valerian, are closely related species with similar care needs.
Bloom: Many blue, pink, red, white, tubular, flared flowers, ½–1½ in. (12–38 mm) wide, in terminal clusters, to 3 in. (75 mm) wide, in spring–summer.
Plant hardiness: Hardy. Zones 4–11.
Soil: Moist, well-drained loam. Fertility: Average–low. 6.5–8.0 pH. Color best in alkaline soils.
Planting: Spring in full sun, 2–3 ft. (60–90 cm) apart, when soil is workable.
Care: Easy. Keep moist until established; drought tolerant thereafter. Avoid fertilizing. Deadhead spent flowers to prevent self-seeding. Propagate by division, seed.
Features: Good choice for accents, backgrounds, beds, borders, massed plantings in arid, meadow, natural, rock gardens. Invasive, self-seeding. Pest and disease resistant.

Perennial: *Chelone lyonii.* SCROPHULARIACEAE.
Common name: Turtlehead (Balmony, Snakehead).
Description: Many cultivars and horticultural varieties of erect, narrow, deciduous perennial herbs, to 4 ft. (1.2 m) tall and 2 ft. (60 cm) wide. Opposite, textured, deep green, broadly oval, pointed, toothed leaves, 4–7 in. (10–18 cm) long.
Bloom: Many pink, purple, rose, tubular, narrow, 2-lipped flowers, to 1 in. (25 mm) long, in spiking clusters, 6–8 in. (15–20 cm) long, on narrow, woody stems, in summer–autumn.
Plant hardiness: Hardy. Zones 3–9.
Soil: Moist, well-drained humus. Fertility: Average–low. 6.0–7.5 pH.
Planting: Spring in full to filtered sun, 12–18 in. (30–45 cm) apart, or submerged to 2 in. (50 mm).
Care: Easy–moderate. Keep evenly moist. Fertilize semi-monthly during growth. Mulch. Pinch to control, direct growth. Propagate by division, seed.
Features: Good choice for backgrounds, borders in bog, natural, shade, woodland gardens and shorelines. Pest and disease resistant.

Perennial: *Chrysanthemum* species. ASTERACEAE (COMPOSITAE).
Common name: Chrysanthemum.
Description: Over 150 species and many cultivars of semi-evergreen annual, perennial herbs, 1–5 ft. (30–150 cm) tall, 18–24 in. (45–60 cm) wide, with habits ranging from bushy and compact to tall and upright, depending on species. Leathery or shiny, deep green to silver, narrow or broadly oval, deeply cut leaves, to 3 in. (75 mm) long, often with white or gray undersides. See also *C. maximum,* Shasta daisy; and *C.* x *morifolium,* florist's chrysanthemum.
Bloom: Showy, lilac, pink, red, white, mostly double-petaled, fragrant flowers, 1–6 in. (25–150 mm) wide, either single or clustered, in summer–autumn. Blooms are highly varied.
Plant hardiness: Hardy. Zones 6–10.
Soil: Moist, well-drained humus. Fertility: Rich. 6.0–7.0 pH.
Planting: Spring in full sun to partial shade, 18 in. (45 cm) apart.
Care: Easy. Keep evenly moist. Fertilize monthly during growth; withhold fertilizer after blooms fade. Mulch, zones 6–8. Pinch buds and foliage of tall cultivars to promote bushiness and large flowers. Shear after frost. Propagate by cuttings, division, seed.
Features: Good choice for borders, containers in formal, small-space gardens or as an indoor plant in a warm, sunny location. Good for cutting. Aphid, borer, slug, snail and gall susceptible.

Perennial: *Chrysanthemum maximum (C. × superbum).* ASTERACEAE (COMPOSITAE).
Common name: Shasta Daisy.
Description: Many hybrid cultivars of upright, mounding, deciduous perennial herbs, 2–3 ft. (60–90 cm) tall. Leathery to shiny, textured, deep green, oval to lance-shaped, coarsely toothed leaves, to 1 ft. (30 cm) long. Dwarf cultivars available.
Bloom: Mostly showy, cream, white, sometimes double, fringed, frilly, or quilled flowers, 2–6 in. (50–150 mm) wide, with gold centers, in late spring–autumn. Common cultivars include plants with classic, double, or unusual flower forms.
Plant hardiness: Hardy. Zones 4–10.
Soil: Moist to damp, well-drained soil. Fertility: Rich–average. 7.0 pH.
Planting: Spring in full sun to partial shade, 2 ft. (60 cm) apart.
Care: Easy. Keep moist until established; drought tolerant thereafter. Fertilize annually in spring. Stake tall cultivars. Protect from heat. Propagate by division, seed.
Features: Good choice for accents, backgrounds, beds, borders in cottage, natural gardens. Good for cutting. Long blooming. Nematode, slug, snail and gall susceptible.

Perennial: *Chrysanthemum × morifolium.* ASTERACEAE (COMPOSITAE).
Common name: Florist's Chrysanthemum.
Description: Thousands of varied hybrid cultivars of upright, mounding, deciduous perennial herbs, 1–6 ft. (30–180 cm) tall. Leathery, textured, gray green, thick, oval to lance-shaped, coarsely toothed, fragrant leaves, to 1 ft. (30 cm) long, with gray undersides. Dwarf cultivars available.
Bloom: Showy, bronze, cream, lavender, orange, pink, purple, white, multi-colored flowers, 2–6 in. (50–150 mm) wide, some with contrasting centers, in summer–autumn. Common cultivars include such flower forms as anemone-like, dahlialike, pompon, quilled, reflexed, single, spiderlike, and spooned, with many variations.

Plant hardiness: Hardy. Zones 4–10.
Soil: Moist to damp, well-drained soil. Fertility: Rich–average. 7.0 pH.
Planting: Spring in full sun to partial shade, 2–4 ft. (60–120 cm) apart, depending on hybrid.
Care: Easy. Keep moist; allow soil surface to dry between waterings. Fertilize monthly during growth. Stake tall cultivars. Protect from heat. Propagate by division, seed.
Features: Good choice for accents, backgrounds, beds, borders in cottage, natural gardens. Good for cutting. Long blooming. Disease resistant. Aphid, borer, slug, snail susceptible.

Perennial: *Cimicifuga* species. RANUNCULACEAE.
Common name: Bugbane (Rattletop, Snakeroot).
Description: About 15 species of narrow, upright, deciduous perennial herbs, 30–96 in. (75–240 cm) tall, 2 ft. (60 cm) wide. Shiny, deep green, coarsely fern-like, deeply toothed, veined leaves, to 10 in. (25 cm) long, divided into leaflets 1–3 in. (25–75 mm) long. Commonly cultivated species include *C. americana, C. dahurica, C. japonica, C. racemosa,* and *C. rubifolia.*
Bloom: Many cream, white, small, bristly, horned, fragrant flowers, in slender, wandlike spikes, to 4 ft. (1.2 m) tall, in summer–early autumn.
Plant hardiness: Hardy. Zones 3–9.
Soil : Moist, well-drained humus. Fertility: Rich. 6.0–6.5 pH.
Planting: Early spring in filtered sun to partial shade, 2 ft. (60 cm) apart, when soil is workable and after frost hazard has passed.
Care: Easy. Keep moist. Fertilize monthly. Pinch to promote bushiness. Propagate by division, seed.
Features: Good choice for backgrounds, beds, borders in cottage, woodland gardens. Pest and disease resistant.

Perennial: *Convolvulus sabatius (C. mauritanicus).* CONVOLVULACEAE.
Common name: Ground Morning Glory (Bindweed).
Description: Several cultivars of open, spreading or trailing, evergreen perennial herbs, to 3 ft. (90 cm) tall. Soft-haired, gray green, round to oval leaves, to 1½ in. (38 mm) long. See also *Ipomoea* species, morning glory vine.
Bloom: Many blue, pink, purple, open, bell-shaped flowers, 1–2 in. (25–50 mm) wide, with blue or violet centers, in clusters of 1–6 blooms, in late spring–summer. Blooms open in early morning, closing when skies become overcast or evening falls.
Plant hardiness: Semi-hardy. Self-seeding. Zones 7–10.
Soil: Damp to dry, well-drained, sandy loam. Fertility: Average. 6.0–8.0 pH.
Planting: Spring in full sun to partial shade, 3 ft. (90 cm) apart.
Care: Easy. Keep moist until established; drought tolerant thereafter. Shear in late winter or early spring to prevent woody stems. Propagate by cuttings, division, seed.
Features: Good choice for hanging baskets, containers, fencelines, ground covers, edgings in natural, cottage, rock gardens. Invasive. Pest and disease resistant.

Perennial: *Coreopsis* species. ASTERACEAE (COMPOSITAE).
Common name: Tickseed (Coreopsis).
Description: Over 100 species of narrow, upright, annual or perennial herbs, 6–36 in. (15–90 cm) tall, 1 ft. (30 cm) wide. Shiny, deep green, long, straplike, toothed or lobed leaves, to 3 in. (75 mm) long.
Bloom: Many brownish orange or yellow, rose, bicolored, daisylike flowers, to 3 in. (75 mm) wide, with contrasting centers, in summer–autumn.
Plant hardiness: Hardy. Self-seeding. Zones 4–10.
Soil: Damp, well-drained soil. Fertility: Rich–low. 5.0–6.0 pH.
Planting: Spring, after soil warms, zones 4–8; autumn, zones 9–10, in full sun, 1 ft. (30 cm) apart.
Care: Very easy. Keep damp; allow soil surface to dry between waterings. Fertilize annually in spring. Deadhead spent flowers. Propagate by cuttings, division, seed.
Features: Good choice for borders, edgings, foregrounds in cottage, formal, meadow, natural, wildlife gardens. Good for cutting. Attracts birds, butterflies. Chewing insects and leaf spot, powdery mildew, rust susceptible.

Perennial: *Coreopsis verticillata.* ASTERACEAE (COMPOSITAE).
Common name: Threadleaf Coreopsis.
Description: Several cultivars of bunching, upright, perennial herbs, 2–3 ft. (60–90 cm) tall. Shiny, deep green, narrow, threadlike, finely cut, finely toothed leaves, to 2 in. (50 mm) long. Dwarf cultivars available
Bloom: Many gold, bright yellow, daisylike flowers, to 2 in. (50 mm) wide, with yellow centers, in summer–autumn.
Plant hardiness: Hardy. Self-seeding. Zones 4–10.
Soil: Damp, well-drained soil. Fertility: Average–low. 6.5–7.5 pH.
Planting: Spring, after soil warms, zones 4–8; autumn, zones 9–10, in full to filtered sun, 1 ft. (30 cm) apart.
Care: Very easy. Keep damp; allow soil surface to dry between waterings. Drought tolerant when established. Fertilize annually in spring. Deadhead spent flowers. Propagate by cuttings, division, seed.
Features: Good choice for borders, edgings, foregrounds, massed plantings in cottage, formal, meadow, natural, wildlife gardens. Good for cutting. Attracts birds, butterflies. Chewing insects and leaf spot, powdery mildew, rust susceptible.

Perennial: *Cosmos atrosanguineus.* ASTERACEAE (COMPOSITAE).
Common name: Black Cosmos (Chocolate Cosmos).
Description: Several cultivars of branching, upright, tuberous, deciduous perennial herbs, 2–8 ft. (60–240 cm) tall. Opposite, bright green leaves, to 6 in. (15 cm) long, finely cut into 5–7 threadlike segments. See also *C. bipinnatus* and *C. sulphureus,* closely related annuals.
Bloom: Many brown, chocolate, brownish red, daisylike, fragrant flowers, to 2 in. (50 mm) wide, with yellow centers, on wiry, terminal stems, in summer–autumn. Unique chocolate, vanilla-like scent.
Plant hardiness: Semi-hardy. Plant as annual bulb, zones 4–6; ground hardy, zones 7–10.
Soil: Damp, well-drained, sandy soil. Fertility: Rich. 5.0–8.0 pH.
Planting: Spring in full sun, 18 in. (45 cm) apart, after soil warms.
Care: Easy. Keep moist; allow soil surface to dry between waterings. Drought tolerant when established. Fertilize annually during active growth. Mulch. Deadhead spent flowers. Propagate by cuttings, division, seed. Lift, store as for *Dahlia* species in cold-winter climates.
Features: Good choice for accents, backgrounds, containers, foregrounds in cottage, formal, woodland gardens. Good for cutting. Aphid, red spider mite susceptible.

Perennial: *Crambe* species. BRASSICACEAE (CRUCIFERAE).
Common name: Colewort (Sea Kale).
Description: About 20 species of mounding, sometimes narrow, deciduous annual or perennial herbs, 3–7 ft. (90–215 cm) tall. Smooth, blue green, fleshy, divided, deeply cut and lobed, wavy-edged leaves, to 3 ft. (90 cm) long. Commonly cultivated species include *C. cordifolia,* colewort; *C. hispanica;* and *C. maritima,* sea kale. Dormant after bloom.
Bloom: Many fragrant, cream, green, white, round, 4-petaled flowers, ¼–½ in. (6–12 mm) wide, in profuse, branching clusters, in summer.
Plant hardiness: Hardy. Zones 4–9.
Soil: Moist, well-drained, sandy soil. Fertility: Rich. 6.5–7.5 pH.
Planting: Spring in full to filtered sun, 18–24 in. (45–60 cm) apart.
Care: Easy. Keep evenly moist. Fertilize monthly. Shear after blooms fade. Propagate by seed.
Features: Good choice for accents, early color in cottage, natural gardens. Disease resistant. Cabbage looper susceptible.

Perennial: *Delphinium* species. RANUNCULACEAE.
Common name: Larkspur (Delphinium).
Description: More than 300 species of usually upright, narrow, annual, biennial, and perennial herbs, 1–8 ft. (30–240 cm) tall, 18–36 in. (45–90 cm) wide. Textured, deep green, fanlike, coarsely lobed, deeply toothed leaves, to 8 in. (20 cm) wide. Dwarf cultivars available.
Bloom: Mostly blue or purple, sometimes cream, pink, white, or bicolored, starlike flowers, to 3 in. (75 mm) wide, with black, gold, or white centers, in summer.
Plant hardiness: Hardy. Zones 3–10.
Soil: Moist, well-drained, sandy soil. Fertility: Rich. 6.5–7.0 pH. Best in low-clay soils.
Planting: Spring in full sun to partial shade, 18–36 in. (45–90 cm) apart, when soil is workable.

> **WARNING**
> Foliage, stems, and leaves of *Delphinium* species are toxic if eaten. Avoid planting in areas frequented by pets or children.

Care: Easy–moderate. Keep evenly moist. Fertilize monthly in early and late season. Mulch. Deadhead spent blossoms for repeat blooming. Stake taller cultivars. Protect from wind. Propagate by cuttings, division, seed.
Features: Good choice for backgrounds, beds, edgings in cottage, formal, shade, wildlife, woodland gardens. Good for cutting. Attracts birds, hummingbirds. Aphid, slug, snail and fungal disease susceptible.

Perennial: *Dianthus* × *allwoodii* hybrids *(D. 'Allwoodii')*. CARYOPHYLLACEAE.

Common name: Cottage Pink (Allwood Pink).

Description: Many hybrids of low, spreading, evergreen perennial herbs, 8–16 in. (20–40 cm) tall, 2–3 ft. (60–90 cm) wide. Shiny, blue gray, narrow leaves, to 2 in. (50 mm) long, in tufted, matlike colonies. *D. caryophyllus* and *D. plumarius* are closely related parent species with similar care needs.

Bloom: Showy, crimson, pink, rose, white, very fragrant flowers, ½–1 in. (12–25 mm) wide, in pairs, in spring–summer.

Plant hardiness: Hardy. Zones 3–9.

Soil: Damp, well-drained humus. Fertility: Rich. 7.0–8.5 pH.

Planting: Spring in full sun, 12–18 in. (30–45 cm) apart, after frost hazard has passed.

Care: Easy. Keep damp; allow soil surface to dry between waterings. Drought tolerant when established. Mulch lightly to protect from cold, zones 4–6. Pinch to control growth. Deadhead spent flowers to prolong bloom. Propagate by cuttings, division, layering, seed.

Features: Good choice for accents, borders, containers, edgings, foregrounds in cottage, formal, wildlife gardens. Good for cutting. Attracts birds, butterflies, hummingbirds. Rust, fusarium wilt susceptible.

Perennial: *Dianthus caryophyllus*. CARYOPHYLLACEAE.

Common name: Carnation (Border Carnation, Florist's Carnation, Pink).

Description: Many cultivars and hybrids of either compact and low or bushy and erect, semi-evergreen perennial herbs, to 1 ft. (30 cm) tall, 12–15 in. (30–38 cm) wide. Shiny, mostly gray green, narrow, grasslike evergreen leaves, to 2 in. (50 mm) long.

Bloom: Showy, pink, rose, white, occasionally yellow, bicolored, lacy, fragrant flowers, 1–1½ in. (25–38 mm) wide, in spring–summer.

Plant hardiness: Hardy. Zones 4–10.

Soil: Damp, well-drained, sandy soil. Fertility: Rich. 7.0–8.0 pH.

Planting: Spring in full sun, 12–15 in. (30–38 cm) apart, after frost hazard has passed.

Care: Easy. Keep damp; allow soil surface to dry between waterings. Mulch lightly to protect from cold, zones 4–6. Propagate by cuttings, division, layering, seed.

Features: Good choice for accents, borders, containers, edgings, foregrounds in cottage, formal, wildlife gardens. Good for cutting. Attracts birds, butterflies, hummingbirds. Rust, fusarium wilt susceptible.

Perennial: *Dicentra* species. FUMARIACEAE.

Common name: Bleeding-Heart.

Description: About 19 species of erect, arching, rhizomatous or tuberous, deciduous perennial herbs, 12–30 in. (30–75 cm) tall, 3 ft. (90 cm) wide. Feathery, gray green, dense, heart-shaped, deeply cut and toothed foliage, to 6 in. (15 cm) long. Commonly cultivated species include *D. cucullaria*, Dutchman's-breeches; *D. formosa*, western bleeding heart; and *D. spectabilis*, common bleeding heart.

Bloom: Showy, pink, purple, red, white, heart-shaped flowers, to 1½ in. (38 mm) long, in nodding, horizontal, linear sprays, in spring–early summer.

Plant hardiness: Hardy. Zones 3–9. Best in cold-winter climates.

Soil: Damp, well-drained humus. Fertility: Rich. 7.0–8.0 pH.

Planting: Early spring in filtered sun to open shade, 3 ft. (90 cm) apart, when the soil is workable and after frost hazard has passed.

Care: Easy. Keep moist during growth until established; allow soil surface to dry between waterings. Fertilize annually in spring. Mulch, zones 8–9. Protect from wind. Propagate by division, seed.

Features: Good choice for accents, backgrounds, borders, edgings in cottage, heritage, shade, woodland gardens. Stem rot, vascular wilt susceptible.

Perennial: *Dictamnus albus.* RUTACEAE.

Common name: Gas Plant (Burning Bush, Dittany, Fraxinella).

Description: Several cultivars of erect, mounding, deciduous perennial herbs, 30–36 in. (75–90 cm) tall, 3–6 ft. (90–180 cm) wide. Alternate, shiny, textured, deep green, dense, oval, toothed, fragrant leaves, to 3 in. (75 mm) long.

Bloom: Showy, rose pink, purple, white flowers, 1 in. (25 mm) long, with prominent pistils, in loose, erect spikes, to 1 ft. (30 cm) tall, in late spring–summer, form star-shaped pods bearing seed, in autumn.

Plant hardiness: Hardy. Zones 3–8.

Soil: Moist, well-drained humus. Fertility: Rich. 6.5–7.5 pH.

Planting: Spring in full sun to partial shade, 3 ft. (90 cm) apart.

Care: Easy. Keep moist; allow soil to dry between waterings. Drought tolerant. Fertilize quarterly. Propagate by division, seed.

> **WARNING**
> All parts of *Dictamnus albus* can cause severe digestive upset if eaten. Avoid planting in areas frequented by pets or children.

Features: Good choice for backgrounds, beds, borders in cottage, shade, woodland gardens. Foliage and seedpods contain a flammable oil. Pest and disease resistant.

Perennial: *Digitalis* species. SCROPHULARIACEAE.

Common name: Foxglove.

Description: About 19 species of upright, slender, biennial or perennial herbs, 2–5 ft. (60–150 cm) tall. Hairy, gray green, oval or lance-shaped, pointed leaves, to 8 in. (20 cm) long, forming a circular, radiating base.

> **WARNING**
> Foliage and seed of *Digitalis* species can be hazardous if eaten. Avoid planting in areas frequented by pets or children.

Bloom: Large, showy, pink, purple, white, yellow, nodding, bell-shaped flowers, 2 in. (50 mm) long, with marked or spotted, brown, pink, purple, white, yellow centers, in summer.

Plant hardiness: Plant as annual; ground-hardy, zones 2–9.

Soil: Moist, well-drained humus. Fertility: Rich. 6.5–7.0 pH. Supplement with leaf mold.

Planting: Spring, zones 2–7; autumn, zones 8–9, in filtered sun to partial shade, 15–18 in. (38–45 cm) apart.

Care: Easy. Keep moist. Fertilize annually in spring. Deadhead spent stalks . Mulch, zones 2–5. Propagate by division, seed.

Features: Good choice for accents, backgrounds, fencelines in cottage, shade, wildlife, woodland gardens. Attracts birds, hummingbirds. Japanese beetle and leaf spot susceptible.

Perennial: *Digitalis grandiflora (D. ambigua).* SCROPHULARIACEAE.

Common name: Yellow Foxglove.

Description: Several cultivars of erect, narrow, deciduous biennial or perennial herbs, 2–3 ft. (60–90 cm) tall. Opposite, hairy, deep green, oval to lance-shaped leaves, to 8 in. (20 cm) long, alternate upward in a conical or pyramidal spike.

Bloom: Tiers of creamy yellow, flutelike, nodding flowers, 1–2 in. (25–50 mm) long, speckled with brown spots, in summer.

Plant hardiness: Hardy. Self-seeding. Zones 4–9.

Soil: Moist, well-drained humus. Fertility: Rich. 6.5–7.0 pH.

Planting: Autumn in partial shade, 15–18 in. (38–45 cm) apart.

Care: Easy. Keep moist. Fertilize monthly. Propagate by seed.

> **WARNING**
> Foliage and seed of *Digitalis grandiflora* can be hazardous if eaten. Avoid planting in areas frequented by pets or children.

Features: Good choice for backgrounds, beds, borders in cottage, shade, woodland gardens. Good for cutting. Foliage yields digitalis, a medical extract. Pest resistant. Leaf spot susceptible.

Perennial: *Dionaea muscipula.* DROSERACEAE.
Common name: Venus's-Flytrap.
Description: Single species of low, spreading, carnivorous, short-lived, deciduous perennial herbs, to 14 in. (36 cm) tall, 8 in. (20 cm) wide. Specialized, light green stems bear bright pink, hinged, fly-trapping lobes, to 5 in. (13 cm) long, forming a circular, radiating base. Each trap, fringed with guard hairs, bears 3 trigger hairs that cause the trap to close around visiting insects drawn to color and sweet nectar fragrance. Semi-dormant in winter.
Bloom: With sufficient protein from captured prey, produces white flowers, to ¾ in. (19 mm) wide, in late spring–early summer.
Plant hardiness: Tender. Zones 8–10. Best in cool, humid climates or terrariums.
Soil: Moist, well-drained sphagnum moss mixed with sand. Fertility: Average. 6.0–8.0 pH.
Planting: Spring in full sun, 10 in. (25 cm) apart.
Care: Challenging. Keep constantly moist; reduce water when plant growth slows. Tolerates temperatures just above freezing. Pinch new flowers and spent traps to stimulate new trap growth. Propagate by seed.
Features: Good choice for water feature margins, natural boggy soil in natural gardens and in indoor terrariums. Good for children. Slug, snail and botrytis susceptible.

Perennial: *Dodecatheon* species. PRIMULACEAE.
Common name: Shooting-Star (American Cowslip).
Description: About 14 species of erect, mounding, sometimes bulbous or rhizomatous perennial herbs, 8–18 in. (20–45 cm) tall. Smooth, light green, oval or lance-shaped, often toothed leaves, to 5 in. (13 cm) long, forming a circular, radiating base. Dormant after flowers fade.
Bloom: Showy, lavender, pink, purple, white, yellow, nodding, shooting-star-like, 5-petaled flowers, to 1½ in. (38 mm) long, in sparse or numeous, radiating clusters, on leafless, erect, scapose flower stalks, in spring.
Plant hardiness: Semi-hardy. Zones 7–9.
Soil: Moist, well-drained, sandy humus. Fertility: Rich. 6.0–7.5 pH.
Planting: Spring in full sun to partial shade, 6–12 in. (15–30 cm) apart, after soil warms.
Care: Challenging. Keep evenly moist during growth; avoid watering while dormant. Fertilize monthly until flower stalk forms. Mulch in summer. Propagate by bulbils, division, seed.
Features: Good choice for accents in natural, woodland gardens. Plant nursery stock or seed. Pest and disease resistant.

Perennial: *Doronicum* species. ASTERACEAE (COMPOSITAE).
Common name: Leopard's-Bane.
Description: About 30 species of low, mounding, rhizomatous, deciduous perennial herbs, to 2 ft. (60 cm) tall. Smooth, deep green, heart-shaped to round, toothed or lobed leaves, to 3 in. (75 mm) long, forming a circular, radiating base. Semi-dormant in summer. Commonly cultivated species include *D. cordatum*, Caucasian leopard's bane; and *D. grandiflorum*.
Bloom: Showy, gold, yellow, daisylike, sometimes double-petaled flowers, to 2 in. (50 mm) wide, on long stems, in spring.
Plant hardiness: Hardy. Zones 3–9. Best in cool-summer climates.
Soil: Moist, well-drained loam. Fertility: Rich. 6.5–7.5 pH.
Planting: Spring in full to filtered sun, 1–2 ft. (30–60 cm) apart.
Care: Easy. Keep evenly moist until blooms fade; reduce water thereafter. Fertilize in spring. Mulch. Deadhead after foliage withers. Protect from heat. Propagate by division, seed.
Features: Good choice for accents, borders, beds, containers in cottage, natural, woodland gardens. Good for cutting. Pest and disease resistant.

Perennial: *Drosera* species. DROSERACEAE.

Common name: Sundew (Daily-Dew).

Description: About 100 species of semi-erect, low or climbing, carnivorous, rhizomatous, deciduous annual and perennial herbs. Medium green, red, lobed leaves, 2–4 in. (50–100 mm) long, forming a circular, radiating base, have sticky, insect-trapping hairs above rounded, succulent ends. Semi-dormant in autumn, winter.

Bloom: Small, pink, purple, white, yellow blossoms, to ½ in. (12 mm) wide, on a slender stalk, in summer.

Plant hardiness: Tender. Zones 8–10.

Soil: Wet, well-drained sphagnum moss and sand. Fertility: Low. 6.0–7.0 pH. *D. intermedia* and *D. linearis* tolerate alkaline conditions, to 8.0 pH.

Planting: Spring in full sun, 1 ft. (30 cm) apart.

Care: Moderate. Keep evenly moist until blooms fade; reduce water thereafter. Avoid wetting foliage. Fertilize in spring. Mulch. Protect from heat. Propagate by cuttings, seed.

Features: Good choice for water feature margins, natural boggy soil in natural gardens and in indoor terrariums. Good for children. Pest and disease resistant.

Perennial: *Echeveria elegans.* CRASSULACEAE.

Common name: Hen-and-Chickens (Mexican-Gem).

Description: Many cultivars of slow-growing, flat and compact, succulent perennial herbs, to 3 in. (75 mm) high and 4 in. (10 cm) wide, with thick, short, strawberry-like, basal runners bearing miniature plants. Smooth, silver gray to green and red-tinged, fleshy, brittle, petal-like, pointed leaves, 1½–2½ in. (38–63 mm) long, in rosettes.

Bloom: Many showy, pink, yellow, bell-shaped, nodding flowers, to ½ in. (12 mm) long, in clusters on medium spikes, in spring–summer.

Plant hardiness: Tender. Zones 7–10.

Soil: Damp to dry, well-drained, sandy soil. Fertility: Average. 6.5–8.0 pH.

Planting: Spring in full sun, 6–8 in. (15–20 cm) apart.

Care: Easy. Water only after soil completely dries; avoid wetting foliage. Fertilize monthly during growth; dilute liquid fertilizer to half its recommended rate. Propagate by offsets.

Features: Good choice for borders, containers, edgings in natural, rock, seaside gardens. Pest resistant. Fungal disease susceptible.

Perennial: *Echinacea purpurea.* ASTERACEAE (COMPOSITAE).

Common name: Purple Coneflower.

Description: Many cultivars of erect, spreading, upright, deciduous perennial herbs, 2–4 ft. (60–120 cm) tall and wide. Alternate, textured, green, oval to bladelike leaves, 4–8 in. (10–20 cm) long. Common cultivars include *E. purpurea* 'Bright Star', 'Robert Bloom', and 'White Lustre'.

Bloom: Showy, pink, purple, red, white, flat or drooping flowers, 3–6 in. (75–150 mm) wide, with dark, button- or conelike centers, on tall stalks, in late summer, form abundant seed, in autumn.

Plant hardiness: Hardy. Zones 3–10.

Soil: Damp to dry, well-drained soil. Fertility: Average. 6.5–7.5 pH.

Planting: Spring in full sun to partial shade, 18–24 in. (45–60 cm) apart, after soil warms.

Care: Easy. Keep moist until established; allow soil surface to dry between waterings. Drought tolerant. Fertilize quarterly. Mulch. Propagate by division, seed.

Features: Good choice for backgrounds, borders in cottage, meadow, natural, wildlife gardens. Good for windy sites. Attracts birds, butterflies. Japanese beetle, mite and southern blight, downy and powdery mildew, rust susceptible.

Perennial: *Echinops* species. ASTERACEAE (COMPOSITAE).
Common name: Globe Thistle.
Description: About 100 species of spreading, upright, biennial and perennial herbs, 3–4 ft. (90–120 cm) tall, 18–24 in. (45–60 cm) wide. Spiny, hairy, coarse-textured, deep green, thistle-like, toothed leaves, to 1 ft. (30 cm) long, usually with white undersides.
Bloom: Spiny, blue, white, globe-shaped flowers, in dense armored clusters, 2–3 in. (50–75 mm) wide, in summer–autumn.
Plant hardiness: Hardy. Zones 3–9.
Soil: Damp, well-drained, sandy soil. Fertility: Rich–average. 5.0–6.0 pH.
Planting: Spring in full to filtered sun, 18–24 in. (45–60 cm) apart, when soil is workable.
Care: Easy–moderate. Keep moist until established; allow soil surface to dry between waterings. Drought tolerant. Fertilize annually in spring. Stake in rich soil. Thin regularly. Propagate by cuttings, division, seed.
Features: Good choice for accents, backgrounds in natural, rock, wildlife, woodland gardens. Good for cutting, drying. Attracts birds, butterflies. Pest and disease resistant.

Perennial: *Equisetum hyemale.* EQUISETACEAE.
Common name: Horsetail (Scouring Rush).
Description: Several cultivars of bunching, erect, primitive, stoloniferous, rushlike perennial herbs, 2–4 ft. (60–120 cm) tall, related to ferns. Leafless, jointed, hollow green stems bear spiky cones in summer–autumn. *E. variegatum,* variegated horsetail, is a close relative that bears radiating, tuftlike protrusions from its main stems and has similar care needs.
Bloom: Grown for foliage; produces spores rather than seed.
Plant hardiness: Hardy. Zones 3–11.
Soil: Damp, well-drained, sandy soil or, in water features, shoreline or shallow marginal sites. Fertility: Average. 6.5–7.5 pH.
Planting: Spring in full sun to partial shade, 2 ft. (60 cm) apart, or submerged to 6 in. (15 cm). Plant in buried containers to prevent spread.
Care: Easy. Keep evenly moist. Avoid fertilizing. Remove dead stalks and stems. Protect from heat, wind. Propagate by division, offsets.
Features: Good choice for accents, backgrounds in natural, woodland gardens and water feature margins, shorelines. Invasive. Pest and disease resistant.

Perennial: *Erigeron* species. ASTERACEAE. (COMPOSITAE).
Common name: Fleabane.
Description: Nearly 200 species of branching, bushy, upright, deciduous, annual, biennial, but mostly perennial herbs, to 2 ft. (60 cm) tall. Alternate, blue green, green, yellow green, narrow, lance-shaped, pointed leaves, 2–4 in. (50–100 mm) long. *E. speciosus,* Oregon fleabane, is the most commonly cultivated species.
Bloom: Showy, pink, purple, white, yellow, asterlike, single or semi-double flowers, 1½–2 in. (38–50 mm) wide, with threadlike petals and yellow centers, often in branching clusters, in spring–autumn.
Plant hardiness: Hardy. Zones 3–10.
Soil: Moist, well-drained, sandy soil. Fertility: Average–low. 6.5–7.5 pH.
Planting: Early–midspring in full sun to partial shade, 18 in. (45 cm) apart.
Care: Easy. Keep moist until established; allow soil surface to dry between waterings. Drought tolerant. Fertilize annually in spring. Deadhead spent flowers to prolong bloom. Propagate by cuttings, division, seed.
Features: Good choice for beds, borders, edgings, fencelines in meadow, natural, rock, seaside, wildlife, woodland gardens. Attracts butterflies. Heat tolerant. Pest and disease resistant.

Perennial: *Erodium reichardii (E. chamaedryoides).* GERANIACEAE.

Common name: Alpine Geranium (Crane's-Bill, Heron's-Bill, Sea Holly).

Description: Several cultivars of low, spreading or trailing, deciduous perennial herbs, to 4 in. (10 cm) tall. Shiny, textured, deep green, oval, pointed, wavy-edged leaves, ⅜ in. (9 mm) long. *E. reichardii* 'Album' is most commonly cultivated.

Bloom: Many pink, white, yellow, simple, round-petaled flowers, ½ in. (12 mm) wide, with contrasting-veined petals, in spring–autumn.

Plant hardiness: Semi-hardy. Self-seeding. Zones 7–9.

Soil: Damp to dry, well-drained, sandy soil. Fertility: Average–low. 6.5–8.0 pH.

Planting: Spring in full sun to partial shade, 1 ft. (30 cm) apart.

Care: Easy. Keep moist until established; drought tolerant thereafter. Fertilize annually in spring. Shear in autumn to renew growth. Propagate by division, seed.

Features: Good choice for borders, edgings, ground covers in natural, rock, seaside gardens. Invasive in mild climates. Pest and disease resistant.

Perennial: *Eryngium* species. APIACEAE (UMBELLIFERAE).

Common name: Sea Holly (Rattlesnake-Master, Sea Holm).

Description: Nearly 200 species of bushy, erect, deciduous perennial herbs, 1–6 ft. (30–180 cm) tall. Fleshy, hairy, green, pointed, 3-lobed, deeply cut leaves, to 2 in. (50 mm) long, with gray, white undersides, armed with sharp spines, and forming a circular, radiating base. Commonly cultivated species include *E. giganteum*, Miss Willmott's ghost; *E. maritimum*, Sea Holly; and *E. yuccifolium*, rattlesnake-master.

Bloom: Showy, light blue, yellow green, white, thistlelike flowers, 1–2 in. (25–50 mm) wide, on tall, thick stems above leaflike, spiny bracts, in summer.

Plant hardiness: Hardy. Self-seeding. Zones 4–9.

Soil: Moist to dry, well drained, sandy soil. Fertility: Average–low. 6.5–7.5 pH.

Planting: Spring in full sun, 1 ft. (30 cm) apart.

Care: Easy. Keep moist until established; drought tolerant thereafter. Fertilize annually in spring. Avoid transplanting. Propagate by division, seed.

Features: Good choice for accents, barriers, borders, edgings in meadow, natural, rock, seaside gardens. Good for cutting, drying. Invasive. Disease resistant. Slug, snail susceptible.

Perennial: *Eschscholzia californica.* PAPAVERACEAE.

Common name: California Poppy.

Description: Several hybrids, cultivars of mounding, deciduous perennial herbs, 6–24 in. (15–60 cm) tall. Matte, blue green, gray green, finely cut, deeply lobed, feathery leaves, to 4 in. (10 cm) long. Common cultivars with varied color blooms include *E. californica* 'Alba', 'Aurantiaca', 'Ballerina', 'Compacta', 'Crocea', 'Dali', 'Monarch Art Shades', 'Rosea', and 'Thai Silk'. *E. caespitosa* and *E. mexicana* are related annual species with similar care needs.

Bloom: Showy, gold, red, yellow, variegated, cup-shaped, poppylike, 4-petaled flowers, to 2½ in. (63 mm) wide, on tall, flexible stems, in spring–summer. Flowers open at dawn, close at sunset.

Plant hardiness: Tender. Self-seeding. Plant as annual, zones 3–7; ground hardy, zones 8–10.

Soil: Damp to dry, well-drained, sandy soil. Fertility: Average–low. 7.0–7.5 pH.

Planting: Spring in full sun, 6–8 in. (15–20 cm) apart.

Care: Easy. Keep moist until established; drought tolerant thereafter. Avoid fertilizing. Avoid transplanting. Deadhead spent flowers to promote new buds. Pinch to control growth. Propagate by seed.

Features: Good choice for accents, beds, borders, edgings in arid, cottage, meadow, natural, rock, seaside, wildflower, wildlife gardens. Attracts birds. Pest and disease resistant.

Perennial: *Eupatorium coelestinum.* ASTERACEAE (COMPOSITAE).
Common name: Mist Flower (Boneset, Hardy Ageratum).
Description: Several cultivars of mounding, shrublike, rhizomatous, deciduous perennial herbs, to 3 ft. (90 cm) tall. Opposite or clustered, sometimes hairy, light green, triangular to oval, toothed, coarse leaves, to 3 in. (75 mm) long. See also *E. purpureum,* Joe-Pye weed, a related species.
Bloom: Showy, blue, purple, violet, white, yellow, open, flat- or dome-shaped, fluffy, tubular, fuzzy flowers, ½ in. (12 mm) wide, in dense clusters, in summer–autumn.
Plant hardiness: Semi-hardy. Plant as annual, zones 3–5; ground hardy, zones 6–10.
Soil: Moist, well-drained, sandy loam. Fertility: Average. 6.5–7.5 pH.
Planting: Spring in full sun to partial shade, 1 ft. (30 cm) apart.
Care: Easy. Keep moist until established; allow soil surface to dry between waterings. Pinch to shape. Propagate by cuttings, division, seed.
Features: Good choice for accents, borders, edgings, fencelines in meadow, natural, rock, wildlife gardens. Attracts birds. Disease resistant. Aphid susceptible.

Perennial: *Eupatorium purpureum.* ASTERACEAE (COMPOSITAE).
Common name: Joe-Pye Weed (Green-Stemmed Joe-Pye Weed).
Description: Several cultivars of mounding, shrublike, rhizomatous, deciduous perennial herbs, to 10 ft. (3 m) tall. Opposite or clustered, sometimes hairy, light green, triangular to oval, toothed, coarse leaves, to 4 in. (10 cm) long. See also *E. coelestinum,* mist flower. *E. fistulosum,* hollow Joe-Pye weed; *E. greggii; E. hyssopifolium,* thoroughwort; *E. maculatum,* smokeweed; *E. perfoliatum,* boneset; and *E. rugosum,* white snakeroot, are related species with similar care needs.
Bloom: Showy, pink, purple, white, yellow, open, flat- or dome-shaped, fluffy, tubular, fuzzy flowers, ½ in. (12 mm) wide, in dense clusters, in autumn.
Plant hardiness: Semi-hardy. Plant as annual, zones 3–5; ground hardy, zones 6–10.
Soil: Moist, well-drained, sandy loam. Fertility: Average. 6.5–7.5 pH.
Planting: Spring in full sun to partial shade, 4–6 ft. (1.2–1.8 m) apart.
Care: Easy. Keep moist until established; allow soil surface to dry between waterings. Prune to shape. Deadhead spent flowers. Propagate by cuttings, division, seed.
Features: Good choice for accents, barriers, fencelines in meadow, natural, rock, wildlife gardens. Attracts birds. Invasive. Pest and disease resistant.

Perennial: *Eustoma grandiflorum (Lisianthus russellianus).* GENTIANACEAE.
Common name: Prairie Gentian (Lisanthus, Texas Bluebell, Tulip Gentian).
Description: Several cultivars of mounding, deciduous annual or biennnial herbs, to 3 ft. (90 cm) tall. Opposite, powdery, textured, gray green, oval to lance-shaped leaves, to 3 in. (75 mm) long, with gray undersides. Dwarf cultivars available.
Bloom: Showy, blue, cream, pink, purple, red, white, swirled-trumpet-shaped, deep-throated, single- or double-petaled flowers, to 3 in. (75 mm) wide, in summer.
Plant hardiness: Hardy. Zones 3–9.
Soil: Moist, well-drained humus. Fertility: Rich. 6.0–7.0 pH.
Planting: Spring in full to filtered sun, 3 ft. (90 cm) apart, when soil warms.
Care: Moderate. Keep moist until established; allow soil surface to dry between waterings. Deadhead spent flowers to prolong bloom. Propagate by seed.
Features: Good choice for beds, borders, containers in cottage, formal gardens. Good for cutting. Pest and disease resistant.

Perennial: *Filipendula rubra.* ROSACEAE.

Common name: Queen-of-the-Prairie (Meadowsweet).

Description: Several cultivars of erect, upright, narrow, deciduous perennial herbs, to 8 ft. (2.4 m) tall, 2–4 ft. (60–120 cm) wide. Smooth, light green, deeply cut and toothed, feathery, fernlike leaves, 4–8 in. (10–20 cm) wide. Dwarf cultivars available.

Bloom: Many tiny, pink, purple, deep red, white flowers, in plumed, branching clusters, 4–6 in. (10–15 cm) wide, in summer–autumn.

Plant hardiness: Hardy. Zones 3–9.

Soil: Moist to wet, well-drained humus. Fertility: Rich. 6.0–8.0 pH. Best in cool climates.

Planting: Spring in full sun to partial shade, 1–3 ft. (30–90 cm) apart, depending on cultivar.

Care: Moderate. Keep evenly moist. Fertilize monthly. Mulch. Propagate by division, seed.

Features: Good choice for backgrounds, fencelines in cottage, natural, woodland gardens and water feature margins. Pest resistant. Powdery mildew susceptible.

Perennial: *Fragaria* species. ROSACEAE.

Common name: Ornamental Strawberry (Beach Strawberry, Fraise du Bois, Woodland Strawberry).

Description: About 12 species of low, spreading, stoloniferous, evergreen perennial herbs, to 8 in. (20 cm) tall, 2 ft. (60 cm) wide. Leathery, deep green, oval, toothed leaves, to 5 in. (13 cm) wide, with 3-lobed leaflets, to 2 in. (50 mm) long, turning red in autumn. Spread by wiry runners bearing rooting offset plants.

Bloom: Many pink, red, white, 5-petaled flowers, to 1 in. (25 mm) wide, with yellow centers, in spring, form edible or inedible, pulpy, fruitlike pseudo-berries covered with seedlike achenes, in summer.

Plant hardiness: Hardy. Zones 3–10.

Soil: Moist, well-drained, sandy soil. Fertility: Rich–average. 6.0–8.0 pH.

Planting: Early spring in full sun, 12–30 in. (30–75 cm) apart, depending on cultivar.

Care: Moderate. Keep evenly moist. Fertilize at planting and monthly thereafter. Protect from frost. Propagate by division, offsets, runners, seed.

Features: Good choice for accents, banks, ground covers, massed plantings in natural, wildlife, woodland gardens. Attracts birds, butterflies. Pest and disease resistant.

Perennial: *Gaillardia* species. ASTERACEAE (COMPOSITAE).

Common name: Blanket Flower.

Description: About 14 species and many hybrids of bushy, upright, deciduous annual, biennial, or perennial herbs, 2–3 ft. (60–90 cm) tall. Alternate, hairy, textured, deep gray green, lance-shaped leaves, 3–6 in. (75–150 mm) long.

Bloom: Showy, gold, deep red tipped in yellow, or yellow flowers, 3–4 in. (75–100 mm) wide, with brown, deep purple, or yellow centers, in early summer–autumn.

Plant hardiness: Hardy. Self-seeding. Zones 3–9.

Soil: Damp to dry, well-drained, sandy humus. Fertility: Average–low. 6.0–7.5 pH.

Planting: Early spring in full sun, 10–15 in. (25–38 cm) apart, when soil is workable.

Care: Easy. Keep damp; allow soil surface to dry between waterings. Avoid fertilizing. Deadhead spent flowers to prolong bloom. Stake taller cultivars. Prune roots in summer. Divide when crowded. Propagate by cuttings, division, seed.

Features: Good choice for banks, beds, borders, hillsides in cottage, formal, meadow, wildlife gardens. Good for cutting. Attracts birds, butterflies. Aphid and leaf spot, powdery mildew susceptible.

Perennial: *Gaura lindheimeri.* ONAGRACEAE.
Common name: White Gaura.
Description: Several cultivars of erect deciduous perennial herbs, to 4 ft. (1.2 m) tall. Alternate, textured, light green, lance-shaped leaves, 1–3½ in. (25–90 mm) long. Common cultivars include *G. lindheimeri* 'Corrie's Gold' and 'Siskiyou Pink'. *G. coccinea* and *G. odorata* are related species with similar care needs.
Bloom: Many gold, pink, white becoming pink, 4-petaled flowers, to 1 in. (25 mm) long, arranged vertically on tall, branching spikes, in late spring–autumn.
Plant hardiness: Hardy. Self-seeding. Zones 3–9.
Soil: Damp to dry, well-drained, sandy humus. Fertility: Average–low. 6.0–7.5 pH.
Planting: Early spring in full to filtered sun, 18–32 in. (45–80 cm) apart.
Care: Easy. Keep damp; allow soil surface to dry between waterings. Drought tolerant. Fertilize quarterly. Deadhead spent flowers, dried stalks to force new flower stalks, prevent self-seeding. Propagate by seed.
Features: Good choice for accents, beds, borders in cottage, meadow, wildlife, woodland gardens and water feature margins. Good for cutting. Attracts hummingbirds. Heat tolerant. Pest and disease resistant.

Perennial: *Gazania* species and hybrids. ASTERACEAE (COMPOSITAE).
Common name: Treasure Flower (Gazania).
Description: About 16 species of rounded and shrublike or trailing, rhizomatous, evergreen, mostly perennial herbs, 10–18 in. (25–45 cm) tall, 1 ft. (30 cm) wide. Fuzzy, deep or silver green, narrow, lance-shaped, wavy-edged leaves, to 4 in. (10 cm) long, with silky white undersides, forming a circular, radiating base. Most commonly cultivated is *G. rigens*.
Bloom: Solitary bronze, copper, orange, pink, red, white, yellow, and variegated, daisylike flowers, 2–4 in. (50–100 mm) wide, with yellow or dark centers, on erect stems, in late spring–summer. Flowers open at dawn, close at sunset.
Plant hardiness: Tender. Plant as annual, zones 3–6; ground hardy, zones 7–10. *G. linearis* is semi-hardy, zones 5–10.
Soil: Damp to dry, well-drained, sandy soil. Fertility: Average. 5.5–7.0 pH.
Planting: Spring in full to filtered sun, 18 in. (45 cm) apart.
Care: Easy. Keep damp until established; allow soil surface to dry between waterings. Drought tolerant. Fertilize quarterly. Deadhead spent flowers. Propagate by seed.
Features: Good choice for accents, beds, containers, hillsides, massed plantings in formal, meadow, seaside, wildlife gardens. Attracts birds. Heat, wind tolerant. Disease resistant. Slug, snail susceptible.

Perennial: *Geranium maculatum.* GERANIACEAE.
Common name: Wild Geranium (Spotted Cranesbill, Wild Cranesbill).
Description: Several cultivars and hybrids of rounded, shrublike, deciduous or semi-evergreen perennial herbs, 1–2 ft. (30–60 cm) tall and wide. Textured, deep green, round, pointed, 3-, 5-, or 7-lobed leaves, to 5 in. (13 cm) wide, turning red in autumn. *G. sanguineum*, bloody cranesbill, is a closely related species with similar care needs.
Bloom: Solitary pink, violet, white, 5-petaled, open flowers, 1–1½ in. (25–38 mm) wide, often with cupped, white centers, on erect stems, in spring–summer.
Plant hardiness: Semi-hardy. Plant as annual, zones 3–5; ground hardy, zones 6–8. Best in cool-summer climates.
Soil: Moist, well-drained loam. Fertility: Rich. 6.0–7.0 pH.
Planting: Spring in open to partial shade, 10–15 in. (25–38 cm) apart.
Care: Easy. Keep damp until established. Fertilize monthly. Deadhead spent flowers. Propagate by division, seed.
Features: Good choice for accents, hanging baskets, borders, edgings, foregrounds in cottage, natural, rock, wildflower, woodland gardens. Invasive. Pest and disease resistant.

Perennial: *Geranium sanguineum.* GERANIACEAE.

Common name: Cranesbill (Bloody Cranesbill).

Description: Many cultivars of mounding, spreading, rhizomatous, deciduous perennial herbs, 6–18 in. (15–45 cm) tall, 2 ft. (60 cm) wide. Smooth, bright to deep green, maplelike, 5- or 7-lobed, finely cut leaves, to 2 in. (50 mm) long, turning bright red in autumn. *G. maculatum,* wild cranesbill, is a closely related species with similar care needs. See also *Pelargonium × hortorum,* florist's geranium.

Bloom: Solitary pink, purple, red, white, 5-petaled flowers, 1–2 in. (25–50 mm) wide, sometimes with contrasting veins, in late spring–summer.

Plant hardiness: Hardy. Zones 3–10.

Soil: Moist, well-drained soil. Fertility: Average. 6.0–8.0 pH.

Planting: Spring in full to filtered sun, 1 ft. (30 cm) apart, after soil warms.

Care: Easy–moderate. Keep damp until established; allow soil surface to dry between waterings. Fertilize annually in spring. Deadhead spent flowers to promote new buds. Propagate by division, seed.

Features: Good choice for accents, borders, edgings, filler, foregrounds, ground covers in cottage, natural, rock, wildflower, woodland gardens. Pest and disease resistant.

Perennial: *Gerbera jamesonii.* ASTERACEAE (COMPOSITAE).

Common name: Transvaal Daisy.

Description: Many cultivars and hybrids of mounding, arching, deciduous perennial herbs, 12–18 in. (30–45 cm) tall. Hairy, gray green, lance-shaped, pointed, lobed leaves, to 10 in. (25 cm) long, with pale, woolly undersides.

Bloom: Single or double, orange red, daisylike flowers, 2–5 in. (50–125 mm) wide, with pale red, yellow centers, in summer–autumn. Hybrids bear many other colors, including cream, pink, purple, white, yellow, and multicolored.

Plant hardiness: Tender. Plant as annual, zones 3–7; ground hardy, zones 8–11.

Soil: Moist, well-drained humus. Fertility: Rich. 6.0–7.0 pH.

Planting: Spring in full sun to partial shade, 6–12 in. (15–30 cm) apart, after soil warms.

Care: Easy. Keep moist until established; allow soil to dry between waterings. Drought tolerant. Fertilize quarterly. Deadhead spent flowers to promote new buds. Propagate by cuttings, division, seed.

Features: Good choice for accents, containers, ground covers in cottage, meadow, seaside gardens. Mulch. Good for cutting. Slug, snail and fungal disease susceptible.

Perennial: *Geum* species. ROSACEAE.

Common name: Avens.

Description: Over 50 species and many hybrids of long-lived, mounding, semi-evergreen perennial herbs, 1–2 ft. (30–60 cm) tall, 12–18 in. (30–45 cm) wide. Smooth, deep green, divided, irregular and wavy-edged, veined, toothed leaves, 2–4 in. (50–100 mm) long. Commonly cultivated species include *G. coccineum,* with orange, red flowers; *G. rivale,* Indian chocolate; and *G. triflorum,* prairie smoke.

Bloom: Single, semi-double, or double, orange, bright red, yellow, roselike flowers, on tall branching stems, in late spring–summer.

Plant hardiness: Hardy. Zones 3–7. Best in cold-winter, cool-summer climates.

Soil: Moist, well-drained humus. Fertility: Rich. 7.0–8.0 pH.

Planting: Spring in full sun to partial shade, 12–18 in. (30–45 cm) apart, after soil warms.

Care: Easy. Keep moist. Fertilize monthly during growth. Mulch. Propagate by division, seed.

Features: Good choice for accents, island beds, edgings in shade, rock, woodland gardens. Good for cutting. Downy mildew susceptible.

Perennial: *Gunnera manicata.* GUNNERACEAE.
Common name: Giant Ornamental Rhubarb.
Description: Several species and cultivars of subtropical, deciduous perennial herbs, 5–9 ft. (1.5–2.7 m) tall and wide. Rough-textured, deep or yellow green, cupped, lobed, toothed leaves, to 5 ft. (1.5 m) wide, with prickly spined undersides, on spiny, rhubarblike, fleshy stalks.
Bloom: Russet green, coblike, conical flower heads, 1–3 ft. (30–90 cm) tall, in summer.
Plant hardiness: Tender. Zones 7–10. Best in cool-summer climates.
Soil: Moist, well-drained humus or, in water features, shoreline sites. Fertility: Rich. 6.0–8.0 pH.
Planting: Spring in filtered sun to partial shade, 8 ft. (2.4 m) apart, after soil warms.
Care: Easy. Keep evenly moist. Fertilize monthly during growth. Mulch. Protect from wind. Propagate by division, seed.
Features: Good choice for accents, backgrounds, barriers, screens in shade, woodland gardens and water feature margins, shorelines. Avoid pathway or access plantings due to thorny stalks. Pest and disease resistant.

Perennial: *Gypsophila paniculata.* CARYOPHYLLACEAE.
Common name: Baby's-Breath.
Description: Several cultivars of branching, mounding, upright, wide, rhizomatous, deciduous perennial herbs, to 3 ft. (90 cm) tall and wide. Smooth, gray green, green, graceful, lance-shaped, finely toothed leaves, to 3 in. (75 mm) long. Common cultivars include *G. paniculata* 'Bristol Fairy', 'Perfecta'.
Bloom: Profuse pink, white, semi-double flowers, 1/16–1/8 in. (1.5–3 mm) wide, in single or multibranched, dense clusters, in summer.
Plant hardiness: Hardy. Zones 4–9.
Soil: Moist, well-drained soil. Fertility: Average–low. 7.0–8.0 pH.
Planting: Early spring in full sun, 24–30 in. (60–75 cm) apart.
Care: Easy. Keep moist until established; allow soil surface to dry between waterings. Fertilize annually in spring. Stake. Avoid transplanting. Propagate by cuttings, division, seed.
Features: Good choice for accents, borders, edgings, fencelines in cottage, rock, rose gardens. Good for cutting, drying. Disease resistant. Leafhopper, slug, snail susceptible.

Perennial: *Hedychium* species. ZINGIBERACEAE.
Common name: Ginger Lily (Garland Lily).
Description: Nearly 50 species of arching or erect, upright, rhizomatous, semi-evergreen, tropical perennial herbs, 3–7 ft. (90–215 cm) tall and wide. Opposite, shiny, deep green, yellow green, oval, pointed, veined leaves, to 2 ft. (60 cm) long. Commonly cultivated species include *H. coccineum,* red ginger lily; *H. coronarium,* butterfly lily; *H. flavescens,* yellow ginger. See also *Zingiber officinalis,* true ginger, a bulbous plant.
Bloom: Very showy, pink, red, white, yellow, tubular, very fragrant flowers, 2–3 in. (50–75 mm) long, with leafy basal bracts, in tall, spiking clusters, to 1 ft. (30 cm) high, in summer–autumn.
Plant hardiness: Semi-hardy. Zones 8–11. Best in tropical climates.
Soil: Wet, well-drained humus or, in water features, shoreline, marginal sites. Fertility: Rich. 6.0–7.0 pH.
Planting: Spring in full sun, 4–6 ft. (1.2–1.8 m) apart, or submerged to 5 in. (13 cm).
Care: Moderate. Keep evenly moist; mist foliage. Fertilize monthly during active growth. Mulch. Propagate by division.
Features: Good choice for accents, borders, containers, fencelines in seaside, shade, tropical gardens and water feature shorelines and margins. Good for cutting, Hawaiian leis. Pest and disease resistant.

Perennial: *Helenium* hybrids *(H. autumnale)*. ASTERACEAE (COMPOSITAE).

Common name: Sneezeweed.

Description: Over 40 species and many hybrids of erect, upright, deciduous, sometimes annual but mostly perennial herbs, 2–5 ft. (60–150 cm) tall. Alternate, opposite, shiny, light or yellow green, willowlike, lance-shaped, pointed, finely toothed leaves, to 4 in. (10 cm) long.

Bloom: Showy, bronze, brown, copper, orange, red, yellow, multicolored, daisylike, sometimes reflexed-petaled flowers, 2–3 in. (50–75 mm) wide, with brown or yellow centers, in tall terminal clusters, to 5 ft. (1.5 m) high, in late summer–autumn.

Plant hardiness: Hardy. Zones 3–9. Best in warm-summer climates

Soil: Moist, well-drained soil. Fertility: Rich. 6.5–7.5 pH.

Planting: Spring in full sun, 8–16 in. (20–40 cm) apart, after soil warms.

Care: Easy. Keep moist until established; drought tolerant thereafter. Fertilize annually in spring. Stake. Propagate by cutting, division, seed.

Features: Good choice for accents, backgrounds, beds, borders, fencelines in cottage, meadow, natural gardens. Good for cutting. Pest and disease resistant.

Perennial: *Helianthus* species. ASTERACEAE (COMPOSITAE).

Common name: Sunflower.

Description: About 150 species of upright, narrow or bushy, deciduous annual and perennial herbs, 3–7 ft. (90–215 cm) tall, 18–24 in. (45–60 cm) wide. Alternate or opposite, hairy, textured, yellow green or green, usually coarsely toothed leaves. See also *H. annuus*, annual sunflower.

Bloom: Showy, single or double, yellow, round flowers, 3–12 in. (75–305 mm) wide, with broad, black, brown, gray centers, as single or clustered blossoms, in summer–autumn.

Plant hardiness: Hardy. Zones 4–8.

Soil: Moist, well-drained soil. Fertility: Average. 5.0–7.0 pH.

Planting: Spring in full sun to partial shade, 18–36 in. (45–90 cm) apart, after soil warms.

Care: Easy. Keep moist. Fertilize semi-monthly. Stake tallest cultivars. Propagate by division, seed.

Features: Good choice for borders, containers, massed plantings in cottage, meadow, vegetable, wildlife gardens. Good for cutting. Attracts birds, butterflies. Stalk borer, sunflower maggot, sunflower moth larvae and powdery mildew, rust susceptible.

Perennial: *Helichrysum bracteatum*. ASTERACEAE (COMPOSITAE).

Common name: Strawflower (Everlasting, Immortelle).

Description: Many cultivars of upright, narrow, shrublike, deciduous perennial herbs, 2–3 ft. (60–90 cm) tall, 1 ft. (30 cm) wide. Velvety or smooth, deep or yellow green, lance-shaped, pointed leaves, 4–5 in. (10–13 cm) long.

Bloom: Showy, single or double, orange, pink, red, white, yellow, round, papery, flowerlike bracts, 3–12 in. (75–305 mm) wide, surround broad, black, brown, gray centers bearing tiny true flowers, as single or clustered blossoms, in summer–early autumn.

Plant hardiness: Semi-hardy. Plant as annual, zones 3–6; ground-hardy, zones 7–11.

Soil: Damp, well-drained soil. Fertility: Rich–low. 7.0–7.5 pH.

Planting: Spring in full sun, 1–2 ft. (30–60 cm) apart, after soil warms.

Care: Easy. Keep moist until established; drought tolerant thereafter. Fertilize semi-monthly. Stake tallest cultivars. Propagate by seed.

Features: Good choice for beds, borders, containers, massed plantings in cottage, formal, meadow, wildlife gardens. Good for cutting, drying. Attracts birds. Pest and disease resistant.

Perennial: *Heliotropium arborescens.* BORAGINACEAE.

Common name: Common Heliotrope (Cherry-Pie).

Description: Many cultivars of erect, narrow, shrublike, evergreen perennial herbs, 2–4 ft. (60–120 cm) tall. Shiny, textured, deep green, purple-tinged, oval, pointed leaves, to 3 in. (75 mm) long, with prominent veins.

Bloom: Profuse, 5-petaled, fragrant flowers, to ¼ in. (6 mm) wide, in broad, mounding or branched clusters, to 5 in. (13 cm) wide, in summer.

Plant hardiness: Tender. Plant as annual, 3–9; ground hardy, zones 10–11.

Soil: Moist, well-drained soil. Fertility: Rich. 6.5–7.5 pH.

Planting: Spring in filtered sun to partial shade, 12–16 in. (30–40 cm) apart, after soil warms.

Care: Easy–moderate. Keep evenly moist. Fertilize monthly. Mulch during winter. Propagate by cuttings, layering, seed.

Features: Good choice for accents, beds, borders, containers in cottage, natural, shade, woodland gardens. Pest and disease resistant.

Perennial: *Helleborus orientalis.* RANUNCULACEAE.

Common name: Lenten Rose (Hellebore).

Description: Several cultivars and many hybrids of erect, mounding, rhizomatous, semi-evergreen perennial herbs, 12–18 in. (30–45 cm) tall. Shiny, deep green, hand-shaped, deeply lobed and toothed or scalloped leaves, to 16 in. (40 cm) wide, forming a circular, radiating base.

> **WARNING**
> Roots of *Helleborus orientalis* are extremely hazardous if eaten. Avoid planting in areas frequented by pets and children.

Bloom: Showy, cream, green, lavender, pink, white, cup- or bell-shaped flowers, to 3 in. (75 mm) wide, with dark centers, nodding on a pendulous stalk, in late winter–spring.

Plant hardiness: Hardy. Zones 4–9.

Soil: Moist, well-drained humus. Fertility: Rich. 6.0–7.0 pH.

Planting: Early spring in partial to full shade, 18–24 in. (45–60 cm) apart, when soil is workable.

Care: Moderate–challenging. Keep moist. Fertilize monthly. Mulch in summer and winter. Propagate by division, seed.

Features: Good choice for beds, borders, containers in cottage, shade, woodland gardens. Good beneath trees. Pest resistant. Leaf spot susceptible.

Perennial: *Heuchera sanguinea.* SAXIFRAGACEAE.

Common name: Coralbells (Alumroot).

Description: Bushy perennial herb, 1–2 ft. (30–60 cm) tall and wide, with tall flower stems above foliage. Hairy, textured, dark green or silver-patterned, round to heart-shaped, 5–9-lobed, evergreen leaves, to 2 in. (50 mm) long.

Bloom: Many tiny, chartreuse, pink, red, white, nodding, bell-shaped flowers, 2–4 in. (50–100 mm) wide, in clusters, in summer–autumn.

Plant hardiness: Hardy. Zones 4–9.

Soil: Moist, well-drained humus. Fertility: Rich. 6.0–7.0 pH.

Planting: Early spring, zones 4–6 after frost hazard has passed; autumn, zones 7–9, in partial to full shade, 9–15 in. (23–38 cm) apart.

Care: Easy. Keep evenly moist. Fertilize annually in spring. Mulch in winter. Propagate by division, seed.

Features: Good choice for borders, edgings, foregrounds, paths in cottage, woodland gardens. Attracts birds, hummingbirds. Mealy bug, nematode, root weevil and stem rot susceptible.

HOSTA (PLANTAIN LILY)

More than 40 species of rhizomatous perennial herbs compose the *Hosta* genus. Among shade plants renowned for their foliage, hostas reign supreme. Their glossy, veined, often variegated leaves and mounding habit make them an ideal ground cover for shade and woodland gardens, especially in cold-winter climates where they are treasured for their rapid spring growth and cold tolerance. They mostly are native to China, Japan, and Korea.

Hosta species are 8–36 in. (20–90 cm) tall and up to 5 ft. (1.5 m) wide. Their showy flowers are 1–1½ in. (25–38 mm) long, bell- or flute-shaped, and colored cream, pink, or white.

Many hostas are prone to slug and snail damage; a single mollusk can strip a plant of its foliage in an evening. They also are crown rot susceptible in cool, moist climates when water is allowed to stand on their foliage.

Hostas flower in summer. Besides a welcome floral display in shade gardens, where their pale blossoms fairly glow in the dim light, they also are excellent when cut. Choose from the popular species and hybrids listed at right.

Plantain Lily Species:

H. decorata, blunt plantain lily

H. elata, giant hosta

H. fortunei, fortune lily

H. lancifolia, narrow-leaved hosta

H. plantaginea, fragrant plantain lily

H. sieboldiana, Siebold plantain lily

H. undulata, wavy-leaved plantain lily

H. ventricosa, blue plantain lily

H. venusta, dwarf plantain lily

Hybrid Plantain Lilies:

'Blue Umbrellas'

'Francee'

'Frances Williams'

'Gold Standard'

'Patriot'

Hostas bring cool, green, lush growth—nearly tropical in feel—to shady, woodland gardens where other plants grow leggy and lose their vigor. They are diverse plants, in size, color, and foliage texture. Most create clumplike mounds while others sprout luxurious foliage waist or chest high. They are a perfect foil to azaleas, ferns, and rhododendrons in a forest understory, and are at their best in the shade of tall deciduous trees.

Plant hostas in spring in partial to full shade. Give them regular waterings at their roots to keep their soil evenly moist and avoid wetting their foliage. They will perform best in moist, well-drained humus and prefer acidic to neutral soil conditions.

While most are grown for their striking foliage, they also produce beautiful flowers. For best results, feed them with nitrogen liquid fertilizer every two months as they sprout and grow. Reduce fertilizer applications after the flowers fade to help them slow their growth and store nutrients in their roots for autumn and winter. Pinch or prune spent flower stalks.

Hostas sometimes can be invasive in landscapes and gardens if conditions for their growth are ideal. Divide plant colonies when they become overcrowded or the central plants in a group begin to lose their vigor. Shear your plantings in late autumn, divide their rhizomes in spring, and renew your bed by discarding and replanting the center with young offshoots from the perimeter.

Perennial: *Hosta* species and hybrids. LILIACEAE.

Common name: Plantain Lily (Daylily, Hosta).

Description: About 40 species and thousands of hybrid cultivars of mounding, spreading, rhizomatous, semi-evergreen perennial herbs, 8–36 in. (20–90 cm) tall and to 5 ft. (1.5 m) wide. Shiny or smooth, gold, green, white, variegated or fringed, overlapping, oval or round, heart- or lance-shaped, often scallop-edged, pointed leaves, 6–12 in. (15–30 cm) long, forming a circular, overlapping base. Commonly cultivated species include *H. fortunei; H. plantaginea,* fragrant plantain lily; *H. sieboldiana;* and *H. ventricosa,* blue plantain lily.

Bloom: Showy, cream, pink, white, often nodding, lilylike, tubular, fragrant flowers, to 1½ in. (38 mm) long, in drooping clusters on tall, fleshy or woody stalks, in summer.

Plant hardiness: Hardy. Zones 2–10.

Soil: Moist, well-drained humus. Fertility: Rich–low. 5.5–7.0 pH.

Planting: Spring in partial to full shade, 1–3 ft. (30–90 cm) apart.

Care: Very easy. Keep evenly moist. Fertilize regularly. Mulch young plants in winter. Shear in autumn. Propagate by division.

Features: Good choice for beds, borders, ground covers in shade, woodland gardens. Good for color foliage. Slug, snail and crown rot susceptible.

Perennial: *Houttuynia cordata.* SAURURACEAE.
Common name: Chameleon.
Description: Several cultivars of low, spreading, stoloniferous, rhizomatous, deciduous perennial herbs, 1–2 ft. (30–60 cm) tall. Shiny, gold, green, purple, red, white, variegated, spotted, or fringed, ivylike, heart-shaped, pointed, fragrant leaves, 2–3 in. (50–75 mm) long, on red leaf stalks, often in circular rosettes.
Bloom: Insignificant cream, white, dogwoodlike, bractlike-petaled pseudoflowers, to ½ in. (12 mm) wide, surround tiny yellow flowers, forming clusters, to 2 in. (50 mm) wide, in summer.
Plant hardiness: Hardy. Plant as annual, zones 3–5; ground hardy, zones 6–10.
Soil: Moist, well-drained, sandy soil or, in water features, shallow-depth marginal sites. Fertility: Average. 6.0–8.0 pH.
Planting: Spring in partial to full shade, 1–3 ft. (30–90 cm) apart, or submerged 2–4 in. (50–100 mm).
Care: Very easy. Keep evenly moist. Fertilize annually in spring. Propagate by cuttings, division, offsets, seed.
Features: Good choice for borders, containers, ground covers in shade, woodland gardens and water feature margins. Invasive. Pest and disease resistant.

Perennial: *Hydrocotyle verticillata.* UMBELLIFERAE.
Common name: Water Pennywort.
Description: Several cultivars of low, spreading or trailing, mostly aquatic, deciduous perennial herbs, 2–6 in. (50–150 mm) tall, 1–5 ft. (30–150 cm) wide. Shiny or hairy, green, nasturtium-like, oval leaves, 2 in. (50 mm) wide.
Bloom: Many simple, cream, green, white, often overlapping flowers, to ½ in. (12 mm) wide, in late summer.
Plant hardiness: Tender. Plant as annual, zones 3–8; ground hardy, zones 9–10.
Soil: Wet to moist, well-drained, sandy soil or, in water features, shallow-depth marginal or shoreline sites. Fertility: Average. 6.0–7.0 pH.
Planting: Spring in full sun to full shade, 4 in. (10 cm) apart, or submerged 1 in. (25 mm).
Care: Very easy. Keep evenly moist. Fertilize annually in spring. Propagate by cuttings, division, layering, seed.
Features: Good choice for edgings, ground covers in shade, woodland gardens, boggy soil, and water feature margins. Invasive. Pest and disease resistant.

Perennial: *Iberis sempervirens.* BRASSICACEAE (CRUCIFERAE).
Common name: Candytuft.
Description: Many cultivars of compact, low, spreading or shrublike, deciduous perennial herbs, 8–12 in. (20–30 cm) tall, 16–36 in. (40–90 cm) wide. Shiny, deep green, narrow, oval, pointed leaves, to 1½ in. (38 mm) long. Common cultivars include *I. sempervirens* 'Kingwood', 'Nana', 'Pure Snow', and 'Superba', with varied habits and flower forms.
Bloom: Showy, white, 4-petaled flowers, to ⅝ in. (16 mm) wide, in round or flat clusters, to 4 in. (10 cm) wide, in early spring–summer. *I. sempervirens* 'Autumn Snow' reblooms in autumn.
Plant hardiness: Hardy. Zones 3–10.
Soil: Moist, well-drained humus. Fertility: Rich. 6.0–7.0 pH.
Planting: Spring in full to filtered sun, 6–12 in. (15–30 cm) apart.
Care: Very easy. Keep evenly moist. Fertilize monthly. Deadhead, pinch to promote new buds, keep plants compact. Propagate by cuttings, division, seed.
Features: Good choice for accents, borders, containers, edgings in cottage, formal, rock gardens. Good for cutting. Heirloom flowering plant. Disease resistant. Slug, snail susceptible.

IMPATIENS (BALSAM)

Nearly 500 species of mostly succulent, annual or perennial herbs and subshrubs make up the *Impatiens* genus. They are highly varied in habit, with alternate or opposite, mostly oval, finely toothed leaves and showy, round, five-petaled flowers borne at the junctions of their leaves with their stems. Most balsams are native to tropical and subtropical Africa and Asia.

Balsam species usually have low, mounding habits, 8–24 in. (20–60 cm) tall. Their flowers are brown, cream, orange, pink, purple, red, tan, white, 1–2 in. (25–50 mm) long, and sometimes patterned or edged in contrasting colors. They bloom reliably in showy displays from summer to autumn.

Impatiens are easy to grow, needing little more than regular watering when their soil surface dries and occasional fertilizing to bloom in profuse beauty. While they sometimes are susceptible to aphids, they generally are pest and disease resistant.

Balsam is at its best in shady beds and borders. Keep the plants bushy, dense, and compact by pinching new leaves and spent flowers, and by removing broken stems and damaged foliage. The most popular species and hybrids include those listed at right.

Balsam Species:

I. balfourii

I. balsamina, balsam

I. capensis, snapweed

I. glandulifera

I. pallida, pale snapweed

I. sodenii

I. wallerana, busy lizzy

New Guinea Hybrid Balsam:

'Celebration'

'Java'

'Paradise'

'Pure Beauty'

'Spectra'

'Variegata'

Balsams or impatiens, are reliable, colorful, flowering, shade-tolerant perennials that have a place in every garden. They also are known by the common name snapweed due to the explosive habit of their ripe seedpods, dry capsules that can open suddenly and loudly when brushed, broadcasting tiny seed some distance from the parent plant.

Plant balsam in spring in filtered sun to full shade. They perform best in moist, well-drained, sandy loam with average acid-alkaline balance. Keep their soil moist during active growth, but allow its surface to dry between waterings.

For best results, feed them monthly with nitrogen liquid fertilizer. Pinch or prune spent flowers to encourage new flower bud formation, and renew the planting by shearing when blooms have faded. Propagate new plants by taking stem cuttings in spring before buds form, dipping them in rooting hormone, and heeling them into a moist mixture of sand and perlite. Because balsam self-seeds freely, new plants also can be propagated by transplanting volunteers to your beds when they reach about 4 in. (10 cm) in height.

Balsam is a good container plant. Choose hanging baskets or pots or set containers on a low garden wall or raised step and allow the plant to trail down in a cascade of showy flowers. Remember that plants in containers need regular waterings to grow normally and produce their flowers, and that containers tend to dry and overheat more readily than does garden soil.

You'll find balsam is a beautiful contribution to your beds and borders, especially those in shade gardens.

Perennial: *Impatiens wallerana (I. holstii)*. BALSAMINACEAE.

Common name: Balsam (Busy Lizzie, Impatiens, Jewelweed, Snapweed, Sultana).

Description: Many cultivars of compact, low, spreading, succulent, deciduous perennial herbs, 8–24 in. (20–60 cm) tall. Shiny, deep green, narrow, oval, pointed leaves, to 1½–4 in. (38–100 mm) long. Common cultivars include *I. wallerana* 'Accent Star', 'Mega', 'Nana', 'Stardust', and 'Super Elfin', with varied habits and flower forms.

Bloom: Many brown, cream, orange, pink, purple, red, tan, white, variegated or fringed, 5-petaled flowers, 1–2 in. (25–50 mm) wide, in summer–early autumn.

Plant hardiness: Tender. Self-seeding. Plant as annual, zones 3–8; ground hardy, zones 9–11.

Soil: Moist, well-drained, sandy loam. Fertility: Rich. 6.5–7.5 pH.

Planting: Spring in filtered sun to full shade, 10–12 in. (25–30 cm) apart.

Care: Very easy. Keep moist; allow soil surface to dry between waterings. Fertilize monthly. Deadhead, pinch, shear to promote new buds, dense growth. Propagate by cuttings, seed.

Features: Good choice for accents, hanging baskets, beds, borders, containers, edgings, massed plantings in cottage, formal, small-space, rock gardens. Disease resistant. Aphid susceptible.

LAVANDULA (LAVENDER)

About 20 species of woody perennial herbs and shrubs are included in the *Lavandula* genus. They are fast-growing plants that are planted as annuals in USDA Plant Hardiness Zones beyond their natural range, but perform best where they are ground hardy, in zones 7–10. Their woolly, narrow, gray or gray green leaves and mounding habit make them good for accents and borders in country gardens, especially those classic-style cottage gardens found in England, France, Italy, and Spain. They are native to the Azores, the Mediterranean, the Middle East, and sub-Himalaya Asia.

Lavender ranges in height from 1–4 ft. (30–120 cm) tall and as much as 5 ft. (1.5 m) wide. Its long-lasting, showy flowers are tassel-like clusters, 3–10 in. (75–250 mm) long, in blue, lavender, pink, purple, or white, borne throughout the summer.

Lavender is remarkably resistant to most pests and diseases, and does best in arid, hot climates with low humidity.

Lavender flowers are very fragrant, and they are a good choice for cutting, drying, and for making sachets. Choose one or more of the popular species, hybrids, and cultivars listed at right.

Lavender Species and Hybrids:

L. × *allardii*

L. angustifolia, English lavender

L. canariensis, Canary Island lavender

L. dentata, French lavender

L. × *heterophylla*, sweet lavender

L. × *intermedia*, lavandin

L. lanata, woolly lavender

L. latifolia, broad-leaved lavender

L. multifida, fern-leaved lavender

L. stoechas, Spanish lavender

Lavender Cultivars:

'French Gray', French lavender

'Leucantha', Spanish lavender

'Nana', dwarf English lavender

'Wings of Night', Spanish lavender

Summer in Provence, Iberia, and Tuscany becomes complete with a stroll through fragrant fields of lavender humming with the sounds of bees collecting pollen and nectar. Bring the essence of the Mediterranean to your own backyard by planting one or more species of lavender. They are excellent plants to anchor a bed or border, line a fence or wall, and create a visual accent among foliage shrubs. Most lavenders create dome-shaped mounds that range from low herbs to shrublike bushes. They are heat and sun tolerant, ideal in an exposed garden in a hot, dry climate.

Plant lavenders in spring in full sun, once the soil has warmed. Water them at their roots to keep their soil damp, allowing the soil surface to dry out between waterings. They do best in damp to dry, well-drained, sandy soil and prefer average acid-alkaline balance.

For best results, limit your fertilizing unless they begin to lose vigor, suffer disease or insect damage, or yellow. Shear spent flower stalks from the plants to promote a new sequence of buds and blooms.

Lavender colonies slowly expand at their margins. Divide them to maintain size and shape their growth. Renew the colony after several years by pruning it severely in autumn, removing side shoots and leaving about a dozen stems at the plant's center, each cut to a height of about 1 ft. (30 cm). Water thoroughly after pruning and every week for several months until new foliage sprouts to fill out the bare branches.

Perennial: *Lavandula* species. LAMIACEAE (LABIATAE).

Common name: Lavender.

Description: About 20 species and many hybrid cultivars of dense, upright, semi-evergreen perennial herbs and shrubs, 1–4 ft. (30–120 cm) tall. Woolly, gray to gray green, needlelike leaves, to 2 in. (50 mm) long. Commonly cultivated species include *L. angustifolia*, English lavender; *L. dentata*, French lavender; *L.* × *heterophylla*, sweet lavender; and *L. stoechas*, Spanish lavender.

Bloom: Many tiny, blue, pink, purple, fragrant flowers, in dense, plumelike clusters, to 10 in. (25 cm) long, in summer.

Plant hardiness: Semi-hardy. Plant as annual, zones 5–6; ground hardy, zones 7–10.

Soil: Damp to dry, well-drained soil. Fertility: Average–low. 6.5–7.5 pH.

Planting: Spring in full sun, 12–18 in. (30–45 cm) apart, after frost hazard has passed.

Care: Easy. Keep damp; allow soil surface to dry between waterings. Avoid fertilizing. Mulch in winter, zones 7–8. Prune after bloom to shape. Propagate by cuttings, division.

Features: Good choice for accents, borders, containers, hedges in cottage, country, natural, rock gardens. Good for cutting, drying. Pest and disease resistant.

Perennial: *Lavatera arborea.* MALVACEAE.

Common name: Perennial Tree Mallow.

Description: Several cultivars of upright, treelike, deciduous biennial shrubs, 3–10 ft. (90–305 cm) tall, 6 ft. (1.8 m) wide. Soft-textured, green, round, 5-, 7-, or 9-lobed leaves, 3–9 in. (75–230 mm) in diameter, on hairy, gray stems. *L assurgentiflora,* malva rose; and *L. maritima* are closely related, shrublike species with similar care needs. See also *L. trimestris,* annual tree mallow.

Bloom: Showy, pink, purple, hollyhock-like, cup-shaped, 5-petaled flowers, to 3 in. (75 mm) wide, as single blossoms or loose clusters, in summer.

Plant hardiness: Hardy. Zones 6–9.

Soil: Moist, well-drained, sandy soil. Fertility: Average. 6.5–7.5 pH.

Planting: Spring in full sun, 3–6 ft. (90–180 cm) apart.

Care: Easy. Keep moist until established; allow soil surface to dry between waterings. Drought tolerant. Fertilize annually in spring. Mulch. Deadhead spent flowers to promote new buds. Propagate by seed.

Features: Good choice for accents, hedges, screens in cottage, meadow, natural gardens. Pest and disease resistant.

Perennial: *Lewisia cotyledon.* PORTULACACEAE.

Common name: Broadleaved Lewisia (Bitterroot).

Description: Several cultivars of mounding, evergreen perennial herbs, to 1 ft. (30 cm) tall. Soft-textured, fleshy, green, narrow, oval, sometimes scallop-edged leaves, to 3 in. (75 mm) wide. *L rediva,* bitterroot, is a closely related species with similar care needs.

Bloom: Showy, pink, white, red-striped, star-shaped, open, 9-petaled flowers, to 1 in. (25 mm) wide, in loose clusters on fleshy stalks, to 10 in. (25 cm) tall, in early spring–summer.

Plant hardiness: Hardy. Zones 3–9.

Soil: Damp to dry, very well-drained, sandy soil. Fertility: Average–low. 6.0–7.0 pH.

Planting: Spring in full sun to partial shade, 1 ft. (30 cm) apart.

Care: Challenging. Keep moist until established; allow soil surface to dry between waterings. Drought tolerant. Avoid fertilizing. Propagate by division, seed.

Features: Good choice for accents, containers in natural, rock, woodland gardens. Good for color. Pest and disease resistant.

Perennial: *Ligularia* species and hybrids. ASTERACEAE (COMPOSITAE).

Common name: Golden-Ray.

Description: Nearly 150 mounding, rounded, deciduous perennial herbs, 2–6 ft. (60–180 cm) tall. Textured, deep green, variegated, round, heart-shaped, veined leaves, 12–18 in. (30–45 cm) long and wide. Commonly cultivated species include *L. dentata,* big-leaved golden-ray; *L. stenocephala (L. przewalskii);* and *L. wilsoniana.*

Bloom: Showy, orange, white, yellow, daisylike, many-rayed flowers, 1–4 in. (25–100 mm) wide, with buttonlike, brown, yellow centers, in loose clusters or tall spikes, in summer.

Plant hardiness: Hardy. Zones 4–10.

Soil: Wet to moist, well-drained humus or, in water features, shallow-depth marginal or shoreline sites. Fertility: Rich. 5.5–7.0 pH.

Planting: Early spring in partial to full shade, 3–4 ft. (90–120 cm) apart.

Care: Easy. Keep evenly moist. Fertilize monthly. Remove spent flower stalks. Protect from heat. Propagate by division, seed.

Features: Good choice for accents, edgings in natural, woodland gardens and water feature shorelines. Good for cutting. Disease resistant. Slug, snail susceptible.

Perennial: *Limonium platyphyllum (L. latifolium).* PLUMBAGINACEAE.
Common name: Statice (Sea Lavender).
Description: Many cultivars of bushy, spreading, shrublike, woody, deciduous perennial herbs, to 30 in. (75 cm) tall and 3 ft. (90 cm) wide. Hairy, textured, deep green, oblong to elliptical, sword-shaped leaves, to 10 in. (25 cm) long.
Bloom: Tiny, blue, lavender, white, lacy flowers with blue violet centers, in cloudlike, pyramidal, loosely branched, upright clusters, to 6 in. (15 cm) wide, in spring–summer.
Plant hardiness: Hardy. Plant as annual, zones 3–4; ground hardy, zones 5–11.
Soil: Moist, well-drained, sandy soil or, in water features, shallow-depth marginal or shoreline sites. Fertility: Average–low. 6.0–8.0 pH. Salt tolerant.
Planting: Early spring in full sun, 18 in. (45 cm) apart, after soil warms.
Care: Moderate–challenging. Keep evenly moist until established; drought tolerant thereafter. Fertilize annually in spring. Stake, protect from wind. Propagate by division, seed.
Features: Good choice for beds, borders, edgings in cottage, wildlife gardens and water feature margins. Good for cutting, drying. Attracts birds, butterflies. Pest and disease resistant.

Perennial: *Linum perenne.* LINACEAE.
Common name: Perennial Flax.
Description: Many cultivars of short-lived, branching, open, upright, graceful deciduous perennial herbs, 18–24 in. (45–60 cm) tall. Alternate, gray or blue green, narrow, lance-shaped leaves, 1–1½ in. (25–38 mm) long, on long, hairy, branched stems. *L. flavum,* golden flax, is a related species with similar care needs. See also *L. grandiflorum,* annual flax.
Bloom: Many bright blue, white, open, 5-petaled flowers, 1–1¾ in. (25–44 mm) wide, with white, yellow centers, in spring–summer. Flowers last one day.
Plant hardiness: Hardy. Self-seeding. Zones 4–10.
Soil: Moist, well-drained, sandy soil. Fertility: Average–low. 6.5–7.5 pH.
Planting: Spring or summer in full sun, 18 in. (45 cm) apart, after soil warms.
Care: Easy–moderate. Keep evenly moist until established; drought tolerant thereafter. Fertilize monthly. Mulch in winter. Propagate by cuttings, division, seed.
Features: Good choice for accents, beds, borders, foregrounds, massed plantings in cottage, natural, rock gardens. Good for cutting. Pest and disease resistant.

Perennial: *Lobelia cardinalis.* CAMPANULACEAE (LOBELIACEAE).
Common name: Cardinal Flower (Indian Pink).
Description: Many hybrids and cultivars of upright, narrow, deciduous perennial herbs, 2–4 ft. (60–120 cm) tall, 1 ft. (30 cm) wide. Shiny, medium to deep green, oval to lance-shaped, finely toothed leaves, to 4 in. (10 cm) long. See also *L. erinus,* edging lobelia.
Bloom: Many mostly deep red, sometimes pink, white, spirelike, 5-petaled flowers, 1–1½ in. (25–38 mm) wide, with drooping, honeysuckle-like bracts and prominent anthers, in showy, spiking clusters, in late summer–autumn.
Plant hardiness: Hardy. Self-seeding. Zones 2–10.
Soil: Moist, well-drained humus or, in water features, shallow-depth marginal or shoreline sites. Fertility: Rich. 6.5–7.5 pH.
Planting: Spring in full to filtered sun, 1 ft. (30 cm) apart, after frost hazard has passed.
Care: Moderate–challenging. Keep evenly moist. Fertilize annually in spring. Mulch. Propagate by cuttings, division, seed.
Features: Good choice for backgrounds, beds, borders, edgings in cottage, natural, woodland gardens and water feature shorelines. Pest and disease resistant.

Perennial: *Lobelia erinus.* CAMPANULACEAE (LOBELIACEAE).
Common name: Edging Lobelia (Indian Pink).
Description: Many cultivars of low, spreading or trailing, deciduous perennial herbs, to 9 in. (23 cm) tall. Shiny, deep green, gold-tinged, oval or lance- to needle-shaped leaves, ½–1 in. (12–25 mm) long. *L. siphilitica,* great lobelia, is a related species with similar care needs.
Bloom: Many blue, pink, purple, white, open, 5-petaled flowers, to ¾ in. (19 mm) wide, with white, yellow centers, in early summer–autumn.
Plant hardiness: Tender. Self-seeding. Plant as annual, zones 3–8; ground hardy, zones 9–10.
Soil: Moist, well-drained humus. Fertility: Rich. 6.5–7.5 pH.
Planting: Spring in full to filtered sun, 1 ft. (30 cm) apart, after frost hazard has passed.
Care: Easy. Keep moist; allow soil surface to dry between waterings. Fertilize monthly. Mulch. Protect from heat. Propagate by seed.
Features: Good choice for accents, hanging baskets, beds, borders, containers, edgings, ledges in cottage, formal gardens. Pest and disease resistant.

Perennial: *Lupinus* species and hybrids. FABACEAE (LEGUMINOSAE).
Common name: Lupine.
Description: About 200 species and many hybrids of upright or bushy annual and perennial herbs, 3–5 ft. (90–150 cm) tall. Fuzzy, yellow green, palmlike, deeply lobed leaves, to 4 in. (10 cm) long. Common cultivars include *L.* x 'Russel Hybrids' and 'New Generation', to 4 ft. (1.2 m) tall, with profuse, showy blooms. Dwarf cultivars available.
Bloom: Many blue, cream, orange, pink, purple, red, white, yellow, bicolored, pealike flowers, arranged on spikes, to 2 ft. (60 cm) long, in spring–summer.
Plant hardiness: Hardy. Self-seeding. Plant as annual, zones 2–3; ground hardy, zones 4–9.
Soil: Damp to dry, well-drained, sandy soil. Fertility: Rich–low, depending on species. 6.0–7.0 pH.
Planting: Spring in full to filtered sun, 2–3 ft. (60–90 cm) apart, after soil warms.
Care: Easy. Keep damp; allow soil surface to dry between waterings. Fertilize annually in spring. Deadhead spent blossoms for autumn bloom. Protect from wind. Propagate by division, seed.
Features: Good choice for backgrounds, beds, borders, fencelines in cottage, meadow, natural, wildlife, woodland gardens. Attracts birds, hummingbirds. Disease resistant. Lupine aphid susceptible.

Perennial: *Lysichiton americanum.* ARACEAE.
Common name: Skunk Cabbage.
Description: Several cultivars of low, spreading, rhizomatous, deciduous perennial herbs, 3–6 ft. (90–180 cm) tall. Shiny, deep green, broadly oval, pointed leaves, to 5 ft. (1.5 m) wide, unfurl after bloom, bearing a slight musky odor.
Bloom: Showy, yellow, flowerlike spathes, to 8 in. (20 cm) tall, enclose a white, yellow, coblike spadix with tiny greenish flowers, in late winter–early spring.
Plant hardiness: Semi-hardy. Zones 5–9. Best in cool, moist climates.
Soil: Wet to damp, well-drained humus or, in water features, shallow-depth marginal or shore-line sites. Fertility: Rich. 6.0–8.0 pH.
Planting: Spring in full sun to partial shade, 4 ft. (1.2 m) apart, or submerged to 6 in. (15 cm). Plant 2–3-year-old plants; those grown from seed may take 6 years to bloom.
Care: Easy. Keep evenly moist. Fertilize monthly until blooms fade. Propagate by division, seed.
Features: Good choice for accents, backgrounds in bog, natural, woodland gardens or water feature margins and shorelines. Pest and disease resistant.

Perennial: *Lysimachia nummularia.* PRIMULACEAE.

Common name: Moneywort (Creeping Charlie, Creeping Jenny, Loosestrife).

Description: Several cultivars of mounding or trailing, deciduous perennial herbs, 3–10 in. (75–250 mm) tall, with stems to 20 in. (50 cm) long. Opposite, shiny, light green, round and coinlike or pointed leaves, to 1 in. (25 mm) wide. Cultivars include *L. nummularia* 'Aurea', with pale gold leaves, deepening to lime green in shade.

Bloom: Many, single gold, yellow, cup-shaped flowers, to 1 in. (25 mm) wide, on short stalks from junction of leaves and stem, in summer.

Plant hardiness: Hardy. Zones 3–8. Best in cool, moist climates.

Soil: Moist, well-drained humus or, in water features, shallow-depth marginal or shoreline sites. Fertility: Rich. 6.0–8.0 pH.

Planting: Summer in full sun to partial shade, 9–18 in. (23–45 cm) apart, or submerged to 1 in. (25 mm).

Care: Easy. Keep evenly moist. Fertilize monthly. Propagate by division.

Features: Good choice for accents, backgrounds in bog, natural, woodland gardens or water feature margins and shorelines. Pest and disease resistant.

Perennial: *Lythrum virgatum* and hybrids. LYTHRACEAE.

Common name: Purple Loosestrife.

Description: Several cultivars of erect, tall, deciduous perennial herbs, to 3 ft. (90 cm) tall. Alternate or opposite, fuzzy, light green, narrow, lance-shaped, pointed leaves, to 4 in. (10 cm) long, forming a circular, radiating base. Common hybrids include *L. virgatum* 'Dropmore Purple', 'Morden Pink', and 'Morden Rose'. Prohibited plant in some governmental jurisdictions.

Bloom: Showy, pink, purple, red, star-shaped, 6-petaled flowers, ½–¾ in. (12–19 mm) wide, in tall, cone-shaped, spiking clusters, to 5 ft. (1.5 m) tall, in summer–autumn.

Plant hardiness: Hardy. Zones 3–9. Best in cool, moist climates.

Soil: Moist, well-drained humus. Fertility: Rich. 5.5–7.0 pH.

Planting: Summer in full sun, 2 ft. (60 cm) apart.

Care: Easy. Keep evenly moist. Fertilize monthly. Mulch. Stake. Propagate by division.

Features: Good choice for accents, backgrounds, fencelines, walls in cottage, formal, meadow, natural gardens. Very invasive. Pest and disease resistant.

Perennial: *Macleaya* species *(Bocconia* species). PAPAVERACEAE.

Common name: Plume Poppy.

Description: Two species of erect, tall, loosely shrublike, stoloniferous, deciduous perennial herbs, to 5 ft. (1.5 m) tall and wide. Shiny, deep green, round, deeply lobed, upturned leaves, to 8 in. (20 cm) long, on stiff leaf stalks radiating from a tall central spike. Commonly cultivated species include *M. cordata*, plume poppy; and *M. microcarpa*.

Bloom: Many tiny, cream, pink, tan, white, frothlike flowers, in dense terminal clusters, to 8 in. (20 cm) long, in late spring–summer.

Plant hardiness: Hardy. Zones 4–9.

Soil: Moist, well-drained humus. Fertility: Rich–average. 6.0–7.0 pH.

Planting: Spring in full to filtered sun, 5 ft. (1.5 m) apart, after soil warms.

Care: Easy. Keep evenly moist. Fertilize monthly. Mulch. Stake. Propagate by division, suckers.

Features: Good choice for accents, backgrounds, fencelines, screens, walls in cottage, natural gardens. Good for tropical effects. Invasive. Pest and disease resistant.

Perennial: *Malva alcea.* MALVACEAE.
Common name: Hollyhock Mallow.
Description: Several cultivars of short-lived, erect, branching, bushy or narrow, deciduous perennial herbs, 3–4 ft. (90–120 cm) tall. Textured, green, round, feathery, deeply cut and lobed leaves, to 5 in. (13 cm) long.
Bloom: Showy, gold, pink, white, open, 4-petaled flowers, 1–2 in. (25–50 mm) wide, in late spring–early autumn.
Plant hardiness: Hardy. Self-seeding. Zones 4–10. Best in warm-summer climates.
Soil: Damp to dry, well-drained soil. Fertility: Average. 7.0–7.5 pH.
Planting: Spring in filtered sun to partial shade, 1–2 ft. (30–60 cm) apart, after soil warms.
Care: Easy. Keep moist until established; allow soil surface to dry between waterings. Fertilize monthly. Stake. Propagate by division, seed.
Features: Good choice for accents, backgrounds, borders, edgings, fencelines in cottage, formal, meadow, natural gardens. Disease resistant. Aphid, root borer susceptible.

Perennial: *Matthiola incana.* BRASSICACEAE (CRUCIFERAE).
Common name: Stock (Gillyflower, Imperial Stock).
Description: Many cultivars of erect, narrow, deciduous biennial or perennial herbs, to 30 in. (75 cm) tall. Alternate or opposite, smooth, blue or gray green, narrow, oval becoming lance-shaped leaves, to 4 in. (10 cm) long. Common cultivars include *M. incana* 'Cinderella', 'Legacy', 'Mammoth', and 'Midget'. Dwarf cultivars available.
Bloom: Showy, blue, cream, pink, purple, red, yellow, single- or double-petaled, fragrant flowers, to 1 in. (25 mm) wide, in tall spikes, in spring–summer, depending on cultivar.
Plant hardiness: Semi-hardy. Self-seeding. Plant as annual, zones 2–7; ground hardy, zones 8–9. Best in cool-summer climates.
Soil: Moist, well-drained, sandy loam. Fertility: Rich–average. 6.5–7.5 pH.
Planting: Spring, zones 2–7, after frost hazard has passed; autumn, zones 8–9, in full sun to partial shade, 1 ft. (30 cm) apart.
Care: Easy. Keep moist; allow soil surface to dry between waterings. Avoid wetting foliage. Fertilize monthly. Stake or cage. Protect from wind. Propagate by seed.
Features: Good choice for beds, borders, backgrounds, containers in cottage, meadow, shade gardens. Good for cutting. Pest and disease resistant.

Perennial: *Meconopsis cambrica.* PAPAVERACEAE.
Common name: Welsh Poppy.
Description: Several cultivars of erect, branching, deciduous perennial herbs, to 2 ft. (60 cm) tall. Hairy, deep green, feathery, pointed, coarsely toothed leaves, to 4 in. (10 cm) long, forming mounds 1 ft. (30 cm) wide.
Bloom: Showy, orange, yellow, flat- or cup-faced, 4-petaled, papery flowers, 2–3 in. (50–75 mm) wide, branching from slender stems, in late spring–early autumn.
Plant hardiness: Semi-hardy. Self-seeding. Plant as annual, zones 2–5; ground hardy, zones 6–8.
Soil: Moist, well-drained humus. Fertility: Rich. 6.0–7.0 pH.
Planting: Early spring, zones 2–6; autumn, zones 7–8, in partial to full shade, 12–18 in. (30–45 cm) apart.
Care: Challenging. Keep evenly moist. Fertilize monthly until blooms fade. Protect from heat, wind. Propagate by seed.
Features: Good choice for beds, borders, containers, foregrounds in cottage, rock, shade, woodland gardens. Good for cutting. Pest and disease resistant.

Perennial: *Melampodium leucanthum.* ASTERACEAE (COMPOSITAE).
Common name: Blackfoot Daisy.
Description: Several cultivars of short-lived, dense, low, mounding, semi-evergreen perennial herbs, 6–12 in. (15–30 cm) tall, with deep taproots. Alternate or opposite, smooth, gray green, oval, pointed leaves, 2–3 in. (50–75 mm) long. *M. divaricatum* is a related species with yellow-rayed flowers and similar care needs.
Bloom: Many white-rayed, daisylike, flat-faced, fragrant flowers, ½–1 in. (12–25 mm) wide, with yellow centers and purple veins on their undersides, in late spring–autumn or, in mild-winter climates, year-round.
Plant hardiness: Hardy. Self-seeding. Zones 4–9.
Soil: Damp to dry, well-drained, sandy soil. Fertility: Average–low. 5.5–6.5 pH.
Planting: Spring in full sun, 1–2 ft. (30–60 cm) apart.
Care: Easy. Keep damp; allow soil surface to dry between waterings. Drought tolerant. Fertilize annually in spring. Prune to shape in autumn. Avoid transplanting. Propagate by seed.
Features: Good choice for banks, beds, borders, massed plantings in cottage, meadow, rock gardens. Pest and disease resistant.

Perennial: *Melissa officinalis.* LAMIACEAE (LABIATAE).
Common name: Lemon Balm (Balm, Bee Balm, Sweet Balm).
Description: Several cultivars of erect, mounding, open, upright, deciduous perennial herbs, to 2 ft. (60 cm) tall and 18 in. (45 cm) wide. Textured, green, yellow, variegated, oval or heart-shaped, pointed, coarsely toothed, veined, fragrant leaves, 1–3 in. (25–75 mm) long. Common cultivars include *M. officinalis* 'Aurea', with gold leaves; and 'Variegata', with green and gold variegated leaves.
Bloom: Insignificant white flowers in summer; grown primarily for foliage.
Plant hardiness: Hardy. Self-seeding. Zones 4–9.
Soil: Moist, well-drained soil. Fertility: Rich–average. 6.5–7.5 pH.
Planting: Spring in full to filtered sun, 18 in. (45 cm) apart.
Care: Easy. Keep moist; allow soil surface to dry between waterings. Drought tolerant. Fertilize quarterly. Shear in autumn. Propagate by cuttings, division, seed.
Features: Good choice for banks, borders, containers, ground covers in herb, natural, woodland gardens. Good for sachets, lemon-flavored cooking herb. Invasive. Disease resistant. Whitefly susceptible.

Perennial: *Mentha aquatica.* LAMIACEAE (LABIATAE).
Common name: Water Mint.
Description: Several cultivars of erect, spreading, stoloniferous, deciduous perennial herbs, to 3 ft. (90 cm) tall. Alternate or opposite, fuzzy, textured, mint green, oval, pointed, toothed, fragrant leaves, 1–2 in. (25–50 mm) long, with light undersides.
Bloom: Many tiny, lilac blue, fragrant flowers, in plumelike heads, to 1 in. (25 mm) wide and 2 in. (50 mm) tall, in late summer–early autumn.
Plant hardiness: Semi-hardy. Zones 6–9.
Soil: Moist, dense soil or, in water features, shallow-depth marginal or shoreline sites. Fertility: Average. 6.0–8.0 pH.
Planting: Spring in full sun to partial shade, 1 ft. (30 cm) apart, or submerged to 6 in. (15 cm).
Care: Easy. Keep evenly moist. Fertilize annually in spring. Pinch foliage buds to keep compact. Propagate by cuttings, division, seed.
Features: Good choice for banks, containers, ground covers in natural, wildlife, woodland gardens and water feature margins, shorelines. Mint-flavored cooking, salad herb. Attracts bees, butterflies. Very invasive; plant in buried or submerged containers. Pest and disease resistant.

Perennial: *Mentha suaveolens (M. rotundifolia).* LAMIACEAE (LABIATAE).

Common name: Apple Mint.

Description: Several cultivars of erect, mounding or trailing, stoloniferous, deciduous perennial herbs, to 3 ft. (90 cm) tall. Alternate or opposite, hairy, textured, bright or gray green, sometimes white, variegated, oval, pointed, fine-toothed, fragrant leaves, 1–4 in. (25–100 mm) long, with gray undersides.

Bloom: Insignificant, purple-tinged, white, fragrant flowers, in summer; grown primarily for foliage.

Plant hardiness: Semi-hardy. Zones 5–9.

Soil: Moist, well-drained loam. Fertility: Rich–average. 6.5–7.5 pH.

Planting: Spring in full sun to full shade, 3 ft. (90 cm) apart.

Care: Easy. Keep evenly moist. Fertilize annually in spring. Pinch foliage to keep compact. Propagate by cuttings, division, seed.

Features: Good choice for beds, borders, containers, ground covers in cottage, natural, shade, woodland gardens. Pineapple-flavored cooking garnish, herb. Mildly invasive. Attracts bees. Pest and disease resistant.

Perennial: *Menyanthes trifoliata.* GENTIANACEAE (MENYANTHACEAE).

Common name: Marsh Trefoil (Bogbean).

Description: Several cultivars of low, creeping or trailing, rhizomatous, deciduous aquatic perennial herbs, to 8 in. (20 cm) tall. Textured, bright green, oval, pointed leaves, to 4 in. (10 cm) long, in triplets on long red stems.

Bloom: Many pink becoming white, fringed, bearded flowers, in long, branching clusters, in late spring.

Plant hardiness: Hardy. Zones 3–10.

Soil: Wet, peaty soil or, in water features, shallow-depth marginal or shoreline sites. Fertility: Average. 5.0–6.0 pH.

Planting: Spring in full sun to partial shade, 16 in. (40 cm) apart, or submerged to 6 in. (15 cm).

Care: Easy. Keep evenly moist. Fertilize annually in spring. Pinch foliage to control growth. Propagate by cuttings, division, seed.

Features: Good choice for containers, edges in bog, natural, shade, woodland gardens and water feature margins, shorelines. Very invasive; plant in buried or submerged containers. Pest and disease resistant.

Perennial: *Mertensia pulmonarioides (M virginica).* BORAGINACEAE.

Common name: Virginia Bluebells (Bluebells, Cowslip).

Description: Several cultivars of erect, upright, tuberous or rhizomatous, deciduous perennial herbs, 1–3 ft. (30–90 cm) tall, 1 ft. (30 cm) wide. Alternate, smooth, blue green, oval or lance-shaped, pointed leaves, 3–7 in. (75–180 mm) long, forming a circular, radiating base from a central stem. Semi-dormant after bloom. *M. ciliata,* mountain bluebells, is a compact, closely related species with similar care needs.

Bloom: Many pink becoming blue, drooping or nodding, bell- or trumpet-shaped, deep-throated flowers, to 1 in. (25 mm) long, in nodding clusters, in early spring.

Plant hardiness: Hardy. Zones 3–10.

Soil: Moist, well-drained humus. Fertility: Rich. 6.5–7.0 pH.

Planting: Autumn in full sun to partial shade, 1 ft. (30 cm) apart, or spring, after frost hazard has passed and soil is workable.

Care: Easy. Keep moist during growth; reduce watering when dormant. Propagate by division, seed.

Features: Good choice for accents, borders in cottage, natural, shade, woodland gardens. Attracts bees. Pest resistant. Fungal disease susceptible.

Perennial: *Mimulus cardinalis.* SCROPHULARIACEAE.

Common name: Scarlet Monkey Flower.

Description: Several cultivars of upright, branching, deciduous perennial herbs, to 4 ft. (1.2 m) tall. Opposite, sticky, textured, light green, oval, pointed, toothed leaves, to 4½ in. (11 cm) long. *M. × hibridus,* hybrid monkey flower, includes many hybrids with similar care needs.

Bloom: Many orange, scarlet, yellow, tubular or trumpet-shaped, 2-lipped flowers, to 2 in. (50 mm) wide, in late spring–autumn

Plant hardiness: Semi-hardy. Plant as annual, zones 2–5; ground hardy, zones 6–11.

Soil: Wet to moist, well-drained humus or, in water features, shallow-depth marginal or shoreline sites. Fertility: Rich. 6.0–8.0 pH.

Planting: Spring in full sun to partial shade, 2 ft. (60 cm) apart, after soil warms.

Care: Easy. Keep evenly moist. Fertilize monthly. Prune roots to control growth. Protect from wind. Propagate by cuttings, division, seed.

Features: Good choice for accents, edgings in natural, shade, wildlife, woodland gardens and water feature shorelines. Attracts hummingbirds. Pest and disease resistant.

Perennial: *Monarda didyma.* LAMIACEAE (LABIATAE).

Common name: Bee Balm (Oswego Tea).

Description: Several cultivars of upright, bushy or mounding, deciduous perennial herbs, to 4 ft. (1.2 m) tall. Textured, mint green, oval to lance-shaped, toothed, fragrant leaves, 3–6 in. (75–150 mm) long, with downy undersides. *M. fistulosa,* wild bergamot, is a closely related species with light pink or lavender flowers and similar care needs.

Bloom: Showy, pink, red, white, single- or double-whorled, fluffy, tubular, lipped, irregular flowers, to 2 in. (50 mm) long, with papery bracts, on erect, woody stems, in summer.

Plant hardiness: Hardy. Zones 4–9. Best in cold-winter climates.

Soil: Moist, well-drained humus. Fertility: Average. 6.5–7.0 pH.

Planting: Spring in partial shade, 2 ft. (60 cm) apart, after soil warms.

Care: Easy. Keep evenly moist during active growth. Avoid fertilizing. Propagate by division, seed.

Features: Good choice for backgrounds, borders, massed plantings in meadow, natural, wildlife, woodland gardens. Attracts bees, birds, butterflies, hummingbirds. Powdery mildew, rust susceptible.

Perennial: *Myosotis scorpioides.* BORAGINACEAE.

Common name: Perennial Forget-Me-Not (Water Forget-Me-Not).

Description: Many cultivars of low, mounding, stoloniferous, rhizomatous, deciduous perennial herbs, 1–3 ft. (30–90 cm) tall. Shiny, bright green, oval to lance-shaped, ribbed leaves, to 2 in. (50 mm) long. Dwarf cultivars available. See also *M. sylvatica,* garden forget-me-not.

Bloom: Many blue, open flowers, ¼–½ in. (6–12 mm) wide, with central eyes of pink, white, yellow, in clusters to 2 in. (50 mm) wide, in early summer.

Plant hardiness: Hardy. Self-seeding. Plant as annual, zones 2–4; ground hardy, zones 5–10.

Soil: Wet to moist, clayey soil or, in water features, shallow-depth marginal or shoreline sites. Fertility: Average. 6.0–8.0 pH.

Planting: Late spring in full sun to full shade, 1–2 ft. (30–60 cm) apart.

Care: Easy. Keep evenly moist. Fertilize monthly until flower buds form. Propagate by cuttings, division, seed.

Features: Good choice for accents, beds, borders, edgings, foregrounds, ground covers in natural, shade, woodland gardens or water feature shorelines. Invasive. Deer, pest, and disease resistant.

Perennial: *Nasturtium officinale.* BRASSICACEAE (CRUCIFERAE).

Common name: Watercress.

Description: Several cultivars of branching, creeping, trailing, evergreen perennial herbs, 8–30 in. (20–75 cm) long or wide. Shiny, bright green, round, divided leaves, 6 in. (15 cm) wide, with 3–11 fleshy leaflets, to 1 in. (25 mm) wide. *Tropaeolum majus,* garden nasturtium, is an unrelated, annual plant with differing care needs.

Bloom: Many tiny, white, 4-petaled flowers, ¼–½ in. (6–12 mm) wide, in clusters to 1 in. (25 mm) long, in spring–autumn.

Plant hardiness: Hardy. Zones 3–11.

Soil: Wet to moist humus or, in water features, shallow-depth marginal sites. Fertility: Average. 7.0–7.5 pH.

Planting: Early spring in full to filtered sun, 6 in. (15 cm) apart, or submerged to depth of crown.

Care: Easy. Keep evenly moist. Sensitive to water pollution. Fertilize monthly until flower buds form; use organic fertilizers and avoid herbicides and pesticides if grown for food. Propagate by cuttings, division, seed.

Features: Good choice for accents, containers, edgings, ground covers in bog, natural, shade, woodland, vegetable gardens or water feature margins. Salad green with sharp, peppery flavor. Invasive. Pest and disease resistant.

Perennial: *Nepeta* species and hybrids. LAMIACEAE (LABIATAE).

Common name: Catmint.

Description: About 250 species of open, mounding or spreading, mintlike, stoloniferous, deciduous annual or perennial herbs, 1–3 ft. (30–90 cm) tall. Opposite, textured, gray green, oval or triangular, fragrant leaves, to 2 in. (50 mm) long. Commonly cultivated species include *N. cataria,* catnip; *N.* × *faassenii,* blue catmint; and *N. sibirica,* Siberian catnip.

Bloom: Many tiny, blue, lavender, white flowers, to ¼ in. (6 mm) long, with pale purple spots, in tall, spiking clusters, in spring–summer.

Plant hardiness: Hardy. Self-seeding. Zones 3–7. Best in cold-winter climates.

Soil: Moist, well-drained loam. Fertility: Average. 6.5–7.5 pH.

Planting: Early spring in full sun, 6 in. (15 cm) apart.

Care: Very easy. Keep moist; allow soil surface to dry between waterings. Fertilize monthly. Shear. Propagate by division, seed.

Features: Good choice for beds, containers, ground covers in natural gardens. Invasive. Disease resistant. Leafhopper susceptible.

Perennial: *Nolana paradoxa.* NOLANACEAE.

Common name: Dark Blue Nolana (Chilean Bellflower).

Description: Several cultivars of low, spreading or trailing, fleshy, deciduous perennial herbs, 6–8 in. (15–20 cm) tall. Hairy, green, oval or lance-shaped leaves, to 2 in. (50 mm) long, on long leaf stems. *N. acuminata,* with yellow-centered flowers, and *N. humifusa,* with smaller flowers, are closely related species with similar care needs.

Bloom: Showy, deep blue, petunia-like, deep-throated flowers, to 2 in. (50 mm) wide, with cream, white, light yellow, spotted throats, in summer.

Plant hardiness: Semi-hardy. Plant as annual, zones 2–8; ground hardy, zones 9–11.

Soil: Moist, well-drained, sandy soil. Fertility: Average. 6.0–7.0 pH.

Planting: Spring in full to filtered sun, 12–18 in. (30–45 cm) apart, after soil warms.

Care: Easy. Keep moist; allow soil surface to dry between waterings. Fertilize monthly. Propagate by seed.

Features: Good choice for hanging baskets, beds, containers, edgings in cottage, formal gardens. Pest and disease resistant.

Perennial: *Oenanthe javanica.* APIACEAE (UMBELLIFERAE).
Common name: Water Parsley (Flamingo Celery, Japanese Watercress).
Description: A few cultivars of low, spreading or arching, fleshy, tuberous, deciduous perennial herbs, to 14 in. (36 cm) tall, 3 ft. (90 cm) wide. Smooth, green, pink, white, variegated, parsleylike, coarsely cut, deeply toothed, fragrant leaves, to 4 in. (10 cm) long, on nodding stems. Semi-dormant in winter.
Bloom: Many tiny, cream, white, fragrant flowers, to ⅛ in. (3 mm) wide, in flat, spreading, umbrella-shaped clusters, on slender, hollow, erect stems, in summer.
Plant hardiness: Tender. Plant as annual, zones 2–8; ground hardy, zones 9–11.
Soil: Wet to moist, well-drained, sandy soil or, in water features, shallow-depth marginal or shoreline sites. Fertility: Average. 6.0–7.0 pH.
Planting: Spring in full sun to partial shade, 9 in. (23 cm) apart.
Care: Easy. Keep evenly moist. Fertilize semi-weekly. Propagate by cuttings, division.
Features: Good choice for edgings in bog, shade, vegetable gardens and water feature shorelines. Invasive. Salad green, cooking vegetable similar to celery. Pest and disease resistant.

Perennial: *Oenothera* species. ONAGRACEAE.
Common name: Evening Primrose (Sundrops).
Description: About 80 species of erect, spreading, often rhizomatous, deciduous annual, biennial, but mostly perennial herbs, 6–24 in. (15–60 cm) tall, 2 ft. (60 cm) wide. Hairy or fuzzy, gray green or green, lance-shaped, pointed, lobed or toothed, scallop-edged leaves, 3–4 in. (75–100 mm) long, in radiating, feathery clusters. *O. fruticosa* blooms in daytime; *O. caespitosa* and *O. speciosa* bloom at night.
Bloom: Showy, pink, white, yellow, broad, saucer-shaped, 4-petaled, very fragrant flowers, to 5 in. (13 cm) wide, sometimes with contrasting centers, in late spring–summer.
Plant hardiness: Hardy. Zones 4–11. Best in hot-summer climates.
Soil: Damp to dry, well-drained, sandy soil. Fertility: Average–low. 6.5–7.5 pH.
Planting: Late spring–early summer in full sun, 18–24 in. (45–60 cm) apart.
Care: Very easy. Keep damp; allow soil surface to dry between waterings. Drought tolerant. Fertilize annually in spring. Propagate by division, seed.
Features: Good choice for backgrounds, fencelines, paths in cottage, evening, fragrance gardens. Good for cutting. Pest resistant. Fungal disease susceptible.

Perennial: *Omphalodes* species. BORAGINACEAE.
Common name: Navelwort (Blue-Eyed Mary, Creeping Forget-Me-Not, Navelseed).
Description: About 24 species of low, mounding, spreading or trailing, semi-evergreen annual or perennial herbs, 6–18 in. (15–45 cm) tall, 2–3 ft. (60–90 cm) wide. Alternate, smooth or finely hairy, deep green, oval, pointed leaves, 3–4 in. (75–100 mm) long. Commonly cultivated species include *O. cappadocica*, *O. nitida*, and *O. verna*. *Myosotis scorpioides* and *M. sylvatica*, which *Omphalodes* resemble, are members of a related genus.
Bloom: Many blue, white, open, 5-petaled flowers, to ½ in. (12 mm) wide, in branching sprays, in spring.
Plant hardiness: Semi-hardy. Plant as annual, zones 2–5; ground hardy, zones 6–10.
Soil: Moist, well-drained soil. Fertility: Average. 6.5–7.5 pH.
Planting: Early spring in partial to full shade, 1 ft. (30 cm) apart.
Care: Very easy. Keep moist; allow soil surface to dry between waterings. Fertilize monthly. Propagate by division, seed.
Features: Good choice for accents, ground covers, massed plantings in meadow, natural, woodland gardens. Deer, pest, and disease resistant.

ORCHIDACEAE (ORCHID)

With nearly 800 genera and as many as 30,000 species, the ORCHIDACEAE family of mostly epiphytic perennial herbs is arguably the largest of the plant families. While many are tropical, they also are native in subtropical, temperate, and even polar climates They are native to every continent except Antarctica.

Orchids range in height from tiny ground-hugging species as small as 4 in. (10 cm), to arboreal climbing vines as tall as 50 ft. (15 m). They are treasured for their enduring, often showy flowers, in most of the pastel shades plus white, variegated, or striped, borne year-round or in summer and autumn.

While they are subject to diseases that infect and soften their roots, most cultivated species are pest free and easy to rear in containers. They are at their best in mild to warm, humid climates.

Choose cultivars for your landscape from the popularly cultivated orchid genera and hybrids listed at right.

Orchids have a place in the outdoor landscape in subtropical climates as well as when used as container plants for seasonal outdoor display. Add a tropical flair to your patio, deck, or balcony with orchids once frost hazard has passed, or dress a water feature or deciduous tree with hanging baskets of orchids. Most orchids create fountain-shaped sprays of strap- or sword-shaped foliage. They are best in moist, shady garden sites.

Plant orchids in autumn in partial to full shade. A few species grow best in soil; most should be planted in a fast-draining medium of bark chips. Water the bark until it is saturated, then allow it to drain. Avoid standing water around their roots. They do best in damp conditions and prefer acidic liquid fertilizers. Replace their soil or planting medium annually in summer after flowers fade.

Orchid Species:

O. *agineta*
O. *bletilla*
O. *brassia*
O. *cattleya*
O. *cymbidium*
O. *dendrobium*
O. *epidendrum*
O. *oncidium*
O. *paphipedilum*
O. *phalaenopsis*
O. *pleione*
O. *vanda*

Orchid Hybrids:

O. × *epicattleya*
O. × *odontonia*

Fertilize every two weeks as you water, diluting the fertilizer to half its package-recommended strength.

Orchids produce numerous offset plants; divide them carefully at their base, then repot them into a container until they become established.

Perennial: ORCHIDACEAE.

Common name: Orchid Family.

Description: With 17,000–30,000 species of mounding, spreading, trailing, or vining, epiphytic or terrestrial, often rhizomatous, tuberous, or pseudobulbous, deciduous or evergreen perennial herbs, usually 4–42 in. (10–107 cm) tall, wide, or long but sometimes to 50 ft. (15 m) long, orchid is the largest and most varied plant family. Mostly shiny or smooth, light green, sword-shaped, pointed leaves, 3–24 in. (75–610 mm) long, forming an alternate or circular, radiating base, or extending from vines in opposite pairs. Semi-dormant in winter. Among the more than 80 cultivated genera and hybrids are plants from the genera *Agineta, Bletilla, Brassia, Cattleya, Cymbidium, Dendrobium,* × *Epicattleya, Epidendrum, Laelia, Liparis,* × *Odontonia, Oncidium, Orchis, Pathiopedilum, Phalaenopsis, Pleione, Spiranthes, Vanda,* and *Vanilla.*

Bloom: Many showy or inconspicuous, blue, green, pink, purple, red, tan, white, yellow, irregular, often hairy, lipped or lobed, deep-throated flowers, ¼–6 in. (6–150 mm) wide, in arching sprays, to 3 ft. (90 cm) tall, or basal clusters, year-round or in summer–autumn.

Plant hardiness: Hardy, semi-hardy, or tender, depending on species. Zones 3–11. Most cultivated species are tropical or subtropical, zones 8–11.

Soil: Moist to damp, well-drained bark chips, bark rafts, or humus, depending on species, or, in water features, shoreline sites. Fertility: Rich–low. 6.0–7.0 pH. Special orchid soil and growing mediums are available.

Planting: Autumn in partial to full shade, 1–4 ft. (30–120 cm) apart.

Care: Easy–moderate. Keep moist; allow growing medium to dry between waterings. Reduce water during dormancy. Mist foliage. Fertilize bimonthly; dilute liquid fertilizer to half its recommended strength. Temperature requirements vary by species. Protect tender species from frost or move indoors in winter. Propagate by division, seed.

Features: Good choice for accents, backgrounds, hanging baskets, beds, containers, tree planters in natural, woodland gardens or water feature margins. Good for tropical effects. Slug, snail and fungal disease susceptible.

Perennial: *Osteospermum* species and hybrids. ASTERACEAE (COMPOSITAE).
Common name: African Daisy (Freeway Daisy).
Description: More than 70 species of mounding or trailing, stoloniferous, semi-evergreen annual or perennial herbs, usually 6–12 in. (15–30 cm) tall. Alternate, smooth, deep green, lance-shaped, often toothed leaves, 2–4 in. (50–100 mm) long.
Bloom: Many showy, intensely blue, pink, purple, white, yellow, daisylike, open flowers, 2–3 in. (50–75 mm) wide, with dark centers and contrasting ray undersides, in late spring–early autumn to year-round, depending on climate.
Plant hardiness: Semi-hardy. Plant as annual, zones 3–6 and desert climates; ground hardy, zones 7–10.
Soil: Moist, well-drained humus. Fertility: Average–low. 6.5–8.0 pH.
Planting: Spring in full sun, 18 in. (45 cm) apart, or as winter annual in desert climates.
Care: Easy. Keep damp; allow soil surface to dry between waterings. Drought tolerant. Fertilize annually. Remove spent plants in colony centers. Deadhead spent flowers to prolong bloom. Shear in autumn. Propagate by division, seed.
Features: Good choice for accents, borders, containers, ground covers, paths, walls in arid, meadow, rock, seaside gardens. Good for geometric color plantings. Slug, snail susceptible.

Perennial: *Paeonia* hybrids. PAEONIACEAE.
Common name: Peony.
Description: More than 30 species of rounded, shrublike, sometimes rhizomatous or tuberous, deciduous perennial herbs, 18–60 in. (45–150 cm) tall, to 6 ft. (1.8 m) in tree species. Hairy, shiny, or textured, green, deeply lobed leaves, 3–6 in. (75–150 mm) long.
Bloom: Showy, cream, pink, purple, white, yellow, single to double, papery, often fragrant flowers, 2–10 in. (50–250 mm) wide, often with contrasting centers, in spring–summer.
Plant hardiness: Semi-hardy. Plant as annual, zones 3–6; ground hardy, zones 7–10.
Soil: Moist, well-drained loam. Fertility: Rich. 5.5–6.5 pH.
Planting: Late summer–autumn in full sun to partial shade, 2–4 ft. (60–120 cm) apart.
Care: Very easy. Keep moist. Fertilize annually in spring. Mulch in winter. Stake tall cultivars. Protect from heat. Propagate by division.
Features: Good choice for accents, backgrounds, borders, paths in cottage, heritage, formal gardens. Good for cutting. Ant, slug, snail and botrytis, phytophthora blight susceptible.

Perennial: *Papaver nudicaule.* PAPAVERACEAE.
Common name: Iceland Poppy.
Description: Many cultivars of mounding, deciduous perennial herbs, to 1 ft. (30 cm) tall. Hairy, blue or gray green, feathery, deeply lobed and cut leaves, 3–4 in. (75–100 mm) long, forming a circular, radiating base.
Bloom: Showy, single or double, cream, orange, pink, white, yellow, papery, cup-shaped, fragrant flowers, 2–3 in. (50–75 mm) wide, with blending or contrasting, darker or lighter centers, on long, wiry stems, in early spring–early summer.
Plant hardiness: Hardy. Zones 3–9. Best in cold-winter climates.
Soil: Moist, well-drained loam. Fertility: Average. 6.5–7.0 pH.
Planting: Early spring in full to filtered sun, 1 ft. (30 cm) apart, when soil is workable.
Care: Easy. Keep evenly moist. Fertilize monthly. Deadhead spent flowers to prolong bloom. Protect from heat. Propagate by seed.

> **WARNING**
> Foliage and seeds of *Papaver nudicaule* are hazardous if eaten. Avoid planting in gardens frequented by pets or children.

Features: Good choice for accents, beds, borders, paths in cottage, formal, meadow, natural gardens. Good for cutting; sear cut stems. Pest and disease resistant.

Perennial: *Papaver orientale.* PAPAVERACEAE.
Common name: Oriental Poppy.
Description: Many cultivars of mounding, deciduous perennial herbs, 2–4 ft. (60–120 cm) tall, 3 ft. (90 cm) wide. Hairy, green, feathery, deeply cut, toothed leaves, 10–12 in. (25–30 cm) long, forming a circular, radiating base.
Bloom: Very showy, single or double, cream, orange, pink, red, white, crepe-paper-like, cup-shaped, frilly flowers, 4–6 in. (10–15 cm) wide, with black, silky centers, on wiry stems, in summer–autumn.
Plant hardiness: Hardy. Zones 3–7. Best in cold-winter climates.
Soil: Moist, well-drained to heavy loam. Fertility: Rich–average. 6.5–7.5 pH.
Planting: Autumn in full sun to partial shade, 15–20 in. (38–50 cm) apart.
Care: Easy–moderate. Keep moist; allow soil surface to dry between waterings. Fertilize annually in spring. Mulch in first winter. Protect from heat. Propagate by division, seed.
Features: Good choice for accents, beds, borders in cottage, meadow, natural gardens. Good for cutting; sear cut stems. Aphid, northern root-knot nematode and bacterial blight, downy mildew susceptible.

> **WARNING**
> Foliage and seeds of *Papaver orientale* are hazardous if eaten. Avoid planting in gardens frequented by pets or children.

Perennial: *Patrinia* species. VALERIANACEAE.
Common name: Patrinia (Golden-Lace).
Description: About 15 species of erect, branching, rhizomatous or stoloniferous perennial herbs, 2–5 ft. (60–150 cm) tall. Opposite, smooth or textured, deep green, divided or whole, deeply lobed and cut, toothed leaves, 3–6 in. (75–150 mm) long, often forming a circular, radiating base.
Bloom: Many tiny, white, yellow, sometimes spurred flowers, ⅛–¼ in. (3–6 mm) wide, in profuse, branching clusters, in late summer–autumn.
Plant hardiness: Hardy. Self-seeding. Zones 5–10.
Soil: Moist, well-drained soil. Fertility: Rich. 6.5–7.5 pH.
Planting: Spring in full to filtered sun, 3 ft. (90 cm) apart, after soil warms.
Care: Easy. Keep evenly moist. Fertilize monthly during growth. Deadhead spent flowers to prolong bloom. Stake tall cultivars. Propagate by division, seed.
Features: Good choice for backgrounds, borders in meadow, rock, wildlife gardens. Attracts birds. Pest and disease resistant.

Perennial: *Pelargonium* species and *P. × hortorum.* GERANIACEAE.
Common name: Florist's Geranium.
Description: About 280 species, many hybrids of mounding annual or perennial herbs and shrubs, to 4 ft. (1.2 m) tall. Hairy, textured, mid- to gray green or variegated, round, lobed, or ivylike leaves, to 5 in. (13 cm) wide.
Bloom: Many orange, pink, purple, red, white, star-, saucer-, or butterfly-shaped, 5-petaled, fragrant flowers, to 4 in. (10 cm) wide, in clusters, in spring–summer; some are repeat bloomers.
Plant hardiness: Tender. Plant as annual, zones 3–7; ground hardy, zones 8–10.
Soil: Moist, well-drained soil. Fertility: Average. 7.0–7.5 pH.
Planting: Spring in full sun, 1 ft. (30 cm) apart, after soil warms.
Care: Easy. Keep damp; allow soil surface to dry between waterings. Fertilize monthly during growth with complete, low-nitrogen fertilizer. Deadhead spent flowers to prolong bloom. Cut to ground in autumn after frost, zones 8–10; store containers indoors, zones 3–7. Propagate by cuttings, division, seed.
Features: Good choice for hanging baskets, beds, containers, massed plantings in cottage, formal, rock, wildlife gardens. Attracts bees, birds, butterflies, hummingbirds. Aphid, spider mite, whitefly and mildew susceptible.

Perennial: *Pelargonium peltatum.* GERANIACEAE.
Common name: Trailing Geranium (Ivy Geranium, Storksbill Geranium).
Description: Many cultivars of climbing or trailing, fleshy, evergreen perennial herbs, to 3 ft. (90 cm) tall or long. Shiny, green, sometimes red- or white-fringed, maple-like, lobed leaves, to 3 in. (75 mm) wide, on trailing stems. Plants of the genus *Geranium,* cranebill, are closely related.
Bloom: Many pink, red, white, star-shaped, single- or double-petaled, fragrant flowers, ½–2 in. (12–50 mm) wide, in round clusters on long stalks, in summer–autumn.
Plant hardiness: Semi-hardy. Plant as annual, zones 3–7; ground hardy, zones 8–10.
Soil: Moist, well-drained soil. Fertility: Average. 7.0–7.5 pH.
Planting: Spring, zones 3–8; autumn, zones 9–10, in full sun, 15 in. (38 cm) apart.
Care: Easy. Keep moist. Water after soil dries; avoid wetting foliage. Fertilize monthly during growth. Deadhead spent flowers. Pinch growth tips to promote bushiness. Propagate by cuttings, seed.
Features: Good choice for hanging baskets, beds, borders in cottage, formal gardens. Aphid, spider mite and slug, snail susceptible.

Perennial: *Peltandra virginica.* ARACEAE.
Common name: Arrow Arum (Tuckahoe, Virginian Wake-Robin).

> **W A R N I N G**
> All parts of *Peltandra virginica* cause skin and mouth irritation, and digestive upset if eaten. Avoid planting in gardens frequented by pets or children.

Description: Several cultivars of erect, vase-shaped, rhizomatous, deciduous perennial herbs, to 3 ft. (90 cm) tall, 2 ft. (60 cm) wide. Shiny, bright or deep green, broadly oval leaves, to 15 in. (38 cm) long, 4–8 in. (10–20 cm) wide.
Bloom: Single cream-edged, green, white, narrow flowers, to 8 in. (20 cm) long, with yellow centers, in spring–summer, forming green turning red, berrylike fruit in autumn.
Plant hardiness: Hardy. Zones 5–9.
Soil: Moist, well-drained loam or, in water features, shallow-depth marginal or shoreline sites. Fertility: Rich. 6.0–7.0 pH.
Planting: Spring in full sun to partial shade, 3 ft. (90 cm) apart, or submerged to 6 in. (15 cm).

Care: Easy. Keep evenly moist. Fertilize monthly. Propagate by division, seed.
Features: Good choice for accents, borders, containers, screens in bog, woodland gardens or water feature margins, shorelines. Pest and disease resistant.

Perennial: *Penstemon* species. SCROPHULARIACEAE.
Common name: Beard-Tongue.
Description: About 250 species of upright or rounded, deciduous perennial herbs or woody shrubs, 2–3 ft. (60–90 cm) tall. Opposite, mostly shiny, green, lance-shaped leaves, 2–4 in. (50–100 mm) long, in whorls.
Bloom: Many pink, purple, red, white, bicolored with white, tubular or trumpet-shaped, flared flowers, 1–1½ in. (25–38 mm) long, with delicately spotted, hairy throats and lower lips, in spring–summer.
Plant hardiness: Hardy. Zones 3–10, depending on species.
Soil: Damp, very well-drained, sandy soil. Fertility: Average. 5.5–6.5 pH.
Planting: Spring in full sun to partial shade, 12–18 in. (30–45 cm) apart, after soil warms.
Care: Easy. Keep damp; allow soil surface to dry between waterings. Drought tolerant. Fertilize monthly during active growth. Deadhead spent flowers to prolong bloom. Protect from standing water, heat. Propagate by cuttings, division, seed.
Features: Good choice for beds, borders, edgings, fencelines, paths in cottage, meadow, rock, wildlife, woodland gardens. Attracts birds, hummingbirds. Pest and disease resistant.

Perennial: *Perovskia* species. LAMIACEAE (LABIATAE).

Common name: Russian Sage.

Description: About 7 species of erect, branching, spreading, woody-stalked, stoloniferous, deciduous perennial herbs, 3–4 ft. (90–120 cm) tall. Opposite, soft-textured, silver gray, oval, pointed, deeply cut, fine-toothed leaves, 1½–2 in. (38–50 mm) long.

Bloom: Many tiny, blue, lavender, pink, fragrant flowers, in erect, conical, feathery clusters, 1–4 in. (25–100 mm) long, in late spring–summer.

Plant hardiness: Hardy. Zones 3–7. Best in cold-winter, hot-summer climates.

Soil: Moist, well-drained loam. Fertility: Average. 6.5–7.5 pH.

Planting: Spring in full sun, 2–3 ft. (60–90 cm) apart.

Care: Easy. Keep moist until established. Very drought tolerant. Fertilize annually in spring. Deadhead spent flowers to prolong bloom. Propagate by cuttings, seed.

Features: Good choice for accents, borders, filler, massed plantings in cottage, meadow, rock gardens. Invasive. Pest and disease resistant.

Perennial: *Phlox paniculata.* POLEMONIACEAE.

Common name: Garden Phlox (Perennial Phlox).

Description: Several cultivars of erect, mounding or bunching, deciduous perennial herbs, 2–6 ft. (60–180 cm) tall and wide. Smooth, deep green, narrow, oval to lance-shaped, pointed, veined leaves, 3–6 in. (75–150 mm) long.

Bloom: Profuse lavender, pink, red, white, 5-petaled, fragrant flowers, to 1 in. (25 mm) wide, in round or cone-shaped clusters, 10–14 in. (25–36 cm) wide, in spring–summer.

Plant hardiness: Hardy. Zones 3–10.

Soil: Moist, well-drained soil or, in water features, shoreline sites. Fertility: Rich. 6.5–7.5 pH.

Planting: Spring in full sun to partial shade, 18 in. (45 cm) apart.

Care: Moderate. Keep moist. Fertilize monthly. Pinch to promote branched, bushy growth. Mulch. Stake. Propagate by cuttings, division, seed.

Features: Good choice for accents, borders, containers in cottage, formal, natural, shade gardens or water feature shorelines. Spider mite and powdery mildew, rust susceptible.

Perennial: *Phormium* species and hybrids. AGAVACEAE.

Common name: New Zealand Flax (Fiber Lily, Flax Lily).

Description: Members of a 2-species genus of fast-growing, bunching, evergreen herbs, 7–15 ft. (2.2–4.5 m) tall and wide. Shiny, variegated or striped, narrow, sword-shaped, pointed, stiff leaves, 3–5 ft. (90–150 cm) long. Commonly cultivated species include *P. cookianum,* fountain flax; and *P. tenax,* New Zealand flax, together with many named hybrid cultivars, including *P.* × 'Apricot Queen', 'Dazzler', 'Gold Sword', 'Maori Maiden', 'Red Heart', and 'Sundowner'.

Bloom: Showy, dull red, yellow, tubular, 6-petaled flowers, 1½–2 in. (38–50 mm) wide, in branching clusters, in spring–early summer.

Plant hardiness: Semi-hardy. Zones 7–11.

Soil: Moist to damp, well-drained, sandy humus. Fertility: Rich–low. 6.0–8.0 pH. Moderate to very salt tolerant.

Planting: Spring in full to filtered sun, 4–8 ft. (1.2–2.4 m) apart.

Care: Easy. Keep damp; allow soil surface to dry between waterings. Fertilize semi-monthly in spring–autumn. Deadhead spent flower stalks. Prune to remove broken, spent leaves at base of plant, maintain shape. Protect from freezing. Propagate by division, offsets, seed.

Features: Good choice for accents, backgrounds, banks, barriers, windbreaks in arid, seaside, Xeriscape gardens. Good companion to cacti, succulents. Frost accentuates foliage coloration. Pest resistant. Crown rot susceptible.

Perennial: *Physalis alkekengi.* SOLANACEAE.

Common name: Chinese-Lantern Plant (Japanese-Lantern, Strawberry Tomato, Winter Cherry).

Description: Many cultivars of short-lived, erect, open, rhizomatous perennial herbs, to 2 ft. (60 cm) tall and wide, with shiny, green, oval, 3-lobed, pointed leaves, 2–4 in. (50–100 mm) long. See also *Abutilon hybridum*, Chinese-lantern, an unrelated shrub species.

Bloom: Tiny, white, star-shaped flowers, in summer, form showy, nodding, pink, red, lantern-shaped, papery seed husks, to 2 in. (50 mm) long, containing edible, round, berrylike fruit in autumn. Grown primarily as an ornamental.

Plant hardiness: Hardy. Self-seeding. Zones 2–10. Best in cold-winter climates.

Soil: Moist to damp, well-drained soil. Fertility: Average. 6.5–7.5 pH.

Planting: Spring in full sun to partial shade, 1–2 ft. (30–60 cm) apart.

Care: Easy. Keep evenly moist. Fertilize quarterly. Propagate by cuttings, division, seed.

Features: Good choice for accents, containers, edgings, paths in cottage, formal, shade, woodland gardens. Good for cutting, drying, making preserves. Invasive. Pest and disease resistant.

Perennial: *Physostegia virginiana.* LAMIACEAE (LABIATAE).

Common name: Obedience Plant (False Dragonhead).

Description: Several cultivars of erect, upright, narrow, rhizomatous, deciduous perennial herbs, to 4 ft. (1.2 m) tall. Opposite, green-and-white variegated, lance-shaped, pointed, toothed leaves to 5 in. (13 cm) long.

Bloom: Showy, pink, rose, white, irregular, opened-mouthed, cone-shaped, snapdragon-like flowers, to 1 in. (25 mm) long, with rose purple centers, in dense clusters on tapering spikes, 10–12 in. (25–30 cm) tall, in early spring–early summer.

Plant hardiness: Hardy. Zones 2–9.

Soil: Moist, well-drained loam. Fertility: Rich. 6.0–6.5 pH.

Planting: Spring, zones 2–7; autumn, zones 8–9, in full sun to partial shade, 1–2 ft. (30–60 cm) apart.

Care: Very easy. Keep moist. Fertilize monthly. Pinch to keep compact. Stake. Propagate by division, seed.

Features: Good choice for backgrounds, beds, borders, containers, fencelines in cottage, formal, natural, shade, woodland gardens. Good for cutting. Invasive. Pest and disease resistant.

Perennial: *Platycodon grandiflorus.* CAMPANULACEAE (LOBELIACEAE).

Common name: Balloon Flower.

Description: Single species of long-lived, upright, bunching, deciduous perennial herbs, 18–30 in. (45–75 cm) tall. Smooth, green, oval, pointed, coarsely toothed leaves, 1–3 in. (25–75 mm) long, with blue green undersides, forming a circular, radiating base. Dwarf cultivars available. Plants of the genus *Campanula*, bellflower, are closely related.

Bloom: Showy, deep to pale blue, pink, white, single-petaled, bellflower-like, cup-shaped or 5-pointed-star-shaped, open flowers, 2–3 in. (50–75 mm) wide, in clusters on slender branching stalks, in summer–early autumn.

Plant hardiness: Hardy. Zones 3–9.

Soil: Moist, well-drained, sandy loam. Fertility: Rich. 7.0–7.5 pH.

Planting: Spring in full sun to partial shade, 12–18 in. (30–45 cm) apart. Best in shade.

Care: Easy. Keep moist. Fertilize monthly. Deadhead spent flowers to promote new buds. Propagate by division, seed.

Features: Good choice for beds, borders, fencelines in cottage, natural, shade, woodland gardens. Gopher, nematode and southern blight susceptible.

Perennial: *Primula japonica.* PRIMULACEAE.
Common name: Japanese Primrose.
Description: Many cultivars of erect, mounding, deciduous perennial herbs, 6–30 in. (15–75 cm) tall, 6–12 in. (15–30 cm) wide. Smooth or textured, pale green, round or oval leaves, 7–9 in. (18–23 cm) wide, forming a circular, radiating base.
Bloom: Showy, pink, red, white, open, deep-throated flowers, to 1 in. (25 mm) wide, in whorled clusters surrounding tall, fleshy or woody stalks, in spring–early summer.
Plant hardiness: Semi-hardy. Self-seeding. Plant as annual, zones 3–5; ground hardy, zones 6–8. Best in cool-summer climates.
Soil: Moist, well-drained, sandy loam or, in water features, shoreline sites. Fertility: Average–low. 6.0–6.5 pH.
Planting: Spring in full sun to partial shade, 6–12 in. (15–30 cm) apart.
Care: Easy. Keep moist; allow soil surface to dry between waterings. Fertilize monthly. Deadhead spent flowers to promote new buds. Protect from heat. Propagate by division, seed.
Features: Good choice for borders, edgings, ground covers in natural, shade, woodland gardens and water feature shorelines. Disease resistant. Slug, snail susceptible.

Perennial: *Primula* × *polyantha, P. vulgaris,* and hybrids. PRIMULACEAE.
Common name: English Primrose.
Description: Many hybrid cultivars of low, mounding, semi-evergreen perennial herbs, 6–9 in. (15–23 cm) tall, 6–15 in. (15–38 cm) wide. Shiny, deeply textured, bright green, paddle-shaped, toothed leaves, to 10 in. (25 cm) long, forming a circular, radiating base.
Bloom: Showy, blue, purple, red, white, yellow, open, deep throated flowers, 1½–2 in. (38–50 mm) wide, with contrasting, often yellow centers, singly or in dense clusters, in early spring–early summer.
Plant hardiness: Semi-hardy. Plant as annual, zones 2–5; ground hardy, zones 6–8.
Soil: Moist, well-drained humus. Fertility: Rich. 6.0–7.5 pH.
Planting: Spring, zones 2–6; autumn, zones 7–8, in full sun to partial shade, 6–15 in. (15–38 cm) apart.
Care: Easy. Keep moist; allow soil to dry between waterings. Fertilize monthly. Mulch in winter. Deadhead spent flowers to promote new buds. Propagate by division, seed.
Features: Good choice for accents, hanging baskets, beds, borders, containers, massed plantings in cottage, formal, rock gardens. Nematode, slug, snail and bacterial leaf spot, fungus leaf spot, root rot susceptible.

Perennial: *Pulmonaria* species. BORAGINACEAE.
Common name: Lungwort (Bethlehem Sage).
Description: About 12 species of low, mounding, spreading, hairy, rhizomatous, deciduous perennial herbs, 6–18 in. (15–45 cm) tall and wide. Smooth, deep green, silver variegated, broad, oval, pointed leaves, 3–6 in. (75–150 mm) long. Commonly cultivated species include *P. angustifolia, P. longifolia,* and *P saccharata,* Bethlehem or Jerusalem sage.
Bloom: Showy, blue, purple, red violet, bell-shaped, upturned, deep-throated flowers, ¾–1 in. (19–25 mm) wide, in spring.
Plant hardiness: Hardy. Zones 2–9.
Soil: Moist, well-drained humus. Fertility: Rich. 6.0–7.0 pH.
Planting: Spring or autumn in open to full shade, 8–12 in. (20–30 cm) apart.
Care: Easy. Keep evenly moist. Fertilize monthly. Mulch in winter. Propagate by division.
Features: Good choice for beds, borders, containers, ground covers, massed plantings in cottage, shade, woodland gardens. Disease resistant. Slug, snail susceptible.

Perennial: *Rehmannia elata (R. angulata).* GESNERIACEAE (SCROPHULARIACEAE).

Common name: Chinese Foxglove.

Description: Several cultivars of erect, hairy, fibrous-rooted, deciduous perennial herbs, to 3 ft. (90 cm) tall. Textured, green, broad, oval, pointed, lobed, toothed leaves, to 10 in. (25 cm) long, with prominent veins.

Bloom: Showy, purple, red, rose, funnel-shaped, tubular, deep-throated flowers, to 3 in. (75 mm) wide, on upright, hollyhock-like spikes, in spring–summer.

Plant hardiness: Semi-hardy. Zones 7–10.

Soil: Moist, well-drained humus. Fertility: Rich. 6.0–7.0 pH.

Planting: Spring in full sun to partial shade, 8–12 in. (20–30 cm) apart.

Care: Easy. Keep moist; allow soil surface to dry between waterings. Fertilize monthly. Mulch in winter. Propagate by cuttings, division, seed.

Features: Good choice for accents, borders, fencelines, paths in cottage, meadow, shade, woodland gardens. Good for cutting. Disease resistant. Aphid susceptible.

Perennial: *Rodgersia* species. SAXIFRAGACEAE.

Common name: Rodgersia.

Description: About 5 species of mounding, arching, rhizomatous, deciduous perennial herbs, 3–6 ft. (90–180 cm) tall, depending on species. Shiny, coarsely textured, deep green turning bronze leaves, to 2 ft. (60 cm) wide, divided into 5–9-lobed, finely toothed leaflets, to 10 in. (25 cm) long, with prominent veins. Commonly cultivated species include *R. aesculifolia,* fingerleaf rodgersia; *R. pinnata,* featherleaf rodgersia; *R. podophylla,* bronzeleaf rodgersia; and *R. tabularis,* shieldleaf rodgersia.

Bloom: Profuse tiny, pink, rose, white, plumelike flowers, in multiple branching clusters, to 1 ft. (30 cm) tall and wide, in late spring–summer.

Plant hardiness: Hardy. Zones 4–9.

Soil: Moist, well-drained humus or, in water features, shoreline sites. Fertility: Rich. 6.0–8.0 pH.

Planting: Spring in full sun to full shade, 30 in. (75 cm) apart.

Care: Easy. Keep evenly moist. Fertilize monthly. Mulch. Protect from heat, wind. Propagate by division, seed.

Features: Good choice for accents, massed plantings in cottage, rock, shade, woodland gardens or water feature shorelines. Pest and disease resistant.

Perennial: *Sagittaria latifolia.* ALISIMATACEAE.

Common name: Arrowhead (Duck Potato).

Description: Several cultivars of upright, spreading, tuberous, deciduous perennial herbs, 2–4 ft. (60–120 cm) tall. Shiny, deep green, triangular, arrowhead-shaped leaves, to 20 in. (50 cm) wide, on fleshy, arching stalks, forming a circular, radiating base. Edible.

Bloom: Showy, bright white, open, 5-petaled flowers, to 1½ in. (38 mm) wide, in whorled clusters, to 6 in. (15 cm) long, in late summer.

Plant hardiness: Hardy. Zones 3–11.

Soil: Wet to moist, well-drained humus or, in water features, shallow-depth marginal or shoreline sites. Fertility: Average. 6.0–8.0 pH.

Planting: Spring in full to filtered sun, 1 ft. (30 cm) apart, or submerged to 6 in. (15 cm).

Care: Easy. Keep evenly moist. Fertilize annually in spring. Propagate by division.

Features: Good choice for accents, edges in bog, natural, shade, woodland gardens or water feature margins. Disease resistant. Water lily aphid susceptible.

SALVIA (SAGE)

More than 900 species of highly varied, herbaceous perennials—all are closely related to mint—make up the *Salvia* genus. They are square-stemmed plants, with opposite, textured, mostly oval or lance-shaped, finely toothed leaves and showy, tubular, two-lipped flowers in dense or sparse, spiking clusters that stand above the foliage. Sages are found in rocky, dry conditions throughout most of the world.

Sages range from low-growing, nearly prostrate plants, 3–4 in. (75–100 mm) tall, to shrubs as tall as 8 ft. (2.4 m). Their bright flowers are blue, orange, pink, purple, red, white, and yellow, ¼–2 in. (6–50 mm) long, and sometimes whorled in contrasting colors at their edges. They bloom continuously from spring to autumn.

While they are susceptible to scale and whiteflies as well as leaf spot and rust, frequent inspection and treatment will give good results in most gardens.

Sages are best in full-sun locations. Keep the plants dense and compact by regularly pinching new leaves and spent flowers. The most popular species and hybrids include those listed at right.

Sage is more than a cooking herb—it's also a delightful, fragrant, colorful landscape perennial ideally suited to a sunny site. Choose sage for banks, planters atop fences and walls, borders, and formal beds, where their bright, contrasting colors can be used to create fanciful or formal geometric designs.

Plant sage in spring in full sun sites with at least 6 hours of sun exposure daily. They are best in damp, well-drained soil with average acid-alkaline balance. Keep their soil moist during active growth, allowing its surface to dry between waterings.

They need little fertilizer in most soils. Pinch or prune spent flowers to encourage new flower buds to form, and renew the plantings by shearing or replanting when blooms have faded; many popular species are annuals.

Propagate perennial plants by taking stem cuttings or dividing their roots. Because sage self-seeds freely, new plants also can be transplanted when volunteers reach about 4 in. (10 cm) in height.

Sages are bright and colorful. They are the right choice to give long-lasting color throughout the entire garden season. Sage also is a good choice for overplanting spring bulbs after their blooms fade or for an edging foreground in a shrub border.

Popular Sage Species:

- *S. africana-lutea*, beach sage
- *S. argentea*, silver sage
- *S. azurea*, blue sage
- *S. canariensis*, Canary Island sage
- *S. chamaedryoides*, germander sage
- *S. coccinea*, tropical sage
- *S. dolomitica*, dolomite sage
- *S. dorisiana*, fruit-scented sage
- *S. dorrii*, desert sage
- *S. elegans*, pineapple sage
- *S. farinacea*, mealycup sage
- *S. greggii*, autumn sage
- *S. guaranitica*, anise-scented sage
- *S. involucrata*, rose-leaved sage
- *S. leucantha*, Mexican bush sage
- *S. lyrata*, lyre-leaved sage
- *S. officinalis*, garden sage
- *S. patens*, gentian salvia
- *S. pratensis*, meadow sage
- *S. sclarea*, clary sage
- *S. splendens*, scarlet sage
- *S.* × *superba*
- *S. viridis*, Joseph sage

Perennial: *Salvia* species, hybrids, and cultivars. LAMIACEAE (LABIATAE).

Common name: Sage (Ramona).

Description: Over 900 species and many cultivars of annual, biennial, or perennial herbs and shrubs, with widely varied habits and usually fragrant, edible foliage. Cultivated perennial species include *S. apiana*, white sage; *S. argentea*, silver sage; *S. azurea* and *S. clevelandii*, blue sage; *S. coccinea*, scarlet sage; *S. farinacea*, mealy-cup sage; *S. greggii*, autumn sage; *S. lavandulafolia*, Spanish sage; *S. officinalis*, garden sage; *S. regla*, mountain sage; *S. spathacea*, hummingbird sage; and *S. splendens*, scarlet sage.

Bloom: Varied showy to inconspicuous, blue, orange, pink, purple, red, white, yellow, 2-lipped, hooded flowers, in spring–autumn, depending on species.

Plant hardiness: Hardy. Zones 4–10.

Soil: Damp, well-drained soil. Fertility: Average–low. 6.0–7.5 pH.

Planting: Spring in full sun, 10–24 in. (25–60 cm) apart, depending on species, when soil is workable.

Care: Easy. Keep moist until established; drought tolerant thereafter. Fertilize annually in spring. Mulch, zones 4–6. Pinch to control, promote dense growth. Propagate by cuttings, division, seed.

Features: Good choice for borders, edgings, mixed plantings in cottage, formal, herb, small-space, wildlife gardens. Attracts bees, birds, butterflies, hummingbirds. Disease resistant. Scale, whitefly and leaf spot, rust susceptible.

Perennial: *Santolina chamaecyparissus (S. incana).* ASTERACEAE (COMPOSITAE).
Common name: Lavender Cotton.
Description: Several cultivars of wide, mounding, branching, evergreen perennial shrubs, to 2 ft. (60 cm) tall. Powdery, coarsely textured, silver gray, feathery, lobed, finely cut, fragrant leaves, to 1¼ in. (32 mm) long.
Bloom: Many yellow, round-headed, fragrant flowers, to ¾ in. (19 mm) wide, in summer.
Plant hardiness: Semi-hardy. Plant as annual, zones 4–6; ground hardy, zones 7–10.
Soil: Damp, well-drained soil. Fertility: Average–low. 6.5–7.5 pH.
Planting: Spring in full sun, 3 ft. (90 cm) apart.
Care: Easy. Keep moist until established; drought tolerant thereafter. Fertilize annually in spring. Deadhead spent flowers. Pinch, prune, shear to promote bushy growth. Protect from frost. Propagate by cuttings.
Features: Good choice for banks, borders, edgings, ground covers in arid, coastal, cottage, wildlife gardens. Attracts bees, butterflies. Fire retardant. Deer resistant.

Perennial: *Sarracenia* species and hybrids. SARRACENIACEAE.
Common name: Pitcher Plant.
Description: Eight species and many hybrids of erect, rhizomatous, carnivorous perennial herbs, 5–25 in. (13–63 cm) tall, depending on species. Unique, shiny, green, red-spotted or striped, pitcherlike, tubular leaves, 2–4 ft. (60–120 cm) tall, each with a keel- or winglike vertical rib and terminal cap, stand erect or sprawl in a circular, radiating base.
Bloom: Showy, coral, green, pink, red, greenish yellow, nodding, caplike, 5-petaled flowers, 2–4 in. (50–100 mm) wide, on tall, fleshy stalks, in late spring–summer.
Plant hardiness: Hardy or semi-hardy. Plant as annual, zones 4–6; ground hardy, zones 7–10. *S. purpurea,* common pitcher plant, is hardy to zone 3.
Soil: Wet to moist, mixed sand and peat or, in water features, shallow-depth marginal or shoreline sites. Fertility: Average. 5.5–6.5 pH.
Planting: Spring in full to filtered sun, 1 ft. (30 cm) apart, or submerged to 1 in. (25 mm).
Care: Challenging. Keep evenly moist; avoid wetting foliage. Deadhead spent leaves. Shear in autumn. Protect tender species from frost. Propagate by division, seed.
Features: Good choice for accents, edgings in bog, natural gardens and water feature shorelines. Good for children. Attracts insects. Endangered in wild; plant only cultivated specimens. Pest and disease resistant.

Perennial: *Saururus cernuus.* SAURURACEAE.
Common name: Lizard's-Tail (Swamp Lily, Water-Dragon).
Description: Several cultivars of mounding, creeping, rhizomatous, deciduous perennial herbs, 40–60 in. (1–1.5 m) long. Fragrant, fuzzy becoming smooth, bright green, heart-shaped, pointed, veined leaves, to 6 in. (15 cm) long, on red stems.
Bloom: Showy, creamy white, pipe-cleaner-like, waxy, fragrant flowers, 4–6 in. (10–15 cm) long, in tail-like spikes curling at their tips, in summer.
Plant hardiness: Hardy. Zones 4–9.
Soil: Wet to moist loam or, in water features, shallow-depth marginal or shoreline sites. Fertility: Average. 6.0–8.0 pH.
Planting: Spring in full sun to full shade, 8 in. (20 cm) apart, or submerged 2–6 in. (50–150 mm).
Care: Easy. Keep moist to wet. Propagate by cuttings, division, seed.
Features: Good choice for accents, edgings, massed plantings in bog, natural, shade, woodland gardens and water feature margins. Pest and disease resistant.

Perennial: *Saxifraga stolonifera (S. sarmentosa).* SAXIFRAGACEAE.

Common name: Strawberry Geranium (Beefsteak Geranium, Mother-of-Thousands).

Description: Several cultivars of creeping, stoloniferous, deciduous perennial herbs, to 2 ft. (60 cm) tall. Shiny, textured, deep green, silver variegated, round, pointed, veined leaves, to 4 in. (10 cm) wide, with reddish pink undersides, forming a circular, radiating base.

Bloom: Many white, irregular flowers, to 1 in. (25 mm) wide, in tall, branching clusters on wiry stems, in late summer–autumn.

Plant hardiness: Tender. Zones 7–10.

Soil: Moist, well-drained loam. Fertility: Rich–average. 7.0–7.5 pH.

Planting: Spring in filtered sun to partial shade, 8–10 in. (20–25 cm) apart.

Care: Moderate. Keep moist; allow soil surface to dry between waterings. Fertilize monthly during growth. Protect from frost. Propagate by division, runners, seed.

Features: Good choice for accents, hanging baskets, borders, containers, edgings, ground covers in cottage, formal, natural gardens. Invasive. Disease resistant. Mealybug susceptible.

Perennial: *Scabiosa caucasica.* DIPSACACEAE.

Common name: Pincushion Flower.

Description: Several cultivars of mounding or spreading, semi-evergreen perennial herbs, 18–30 in. (45–75 cm) tall, 12–18 in. (30–45 cm) wide. Opposite, smooth, medium green, finely cut or narrow, toothed, leaves, to 5 in. (13 cm) long.

Bloom: Many showy, blue, pink, purple, red, white, ball-shaped, often fringed flowers, 2–3 in. (50–75 mm) wide, with circular, pincushion-like gray centers, on flexible, narrow stalks, in summer.

Plant hardiness: Hardy. Zones 3–7. Best in humid climates.

Soil: Moist, well-drained, sandy loam. Fertility: Rich. 7.0–8.0 pH.

Planting: Spring in full sun to partial shade, 12–15 in. (30–38 cm) apart.

Care: Moderate. Keep moist; allow soil surface to dry between waterings. Fertilize monthly. Mulch in summer, winter. Protect from frost. Propagate by division.

Features: Good choice for accents, borders, edgings, ground covers in cottage, formal, shade gardens. Good for cutting. Pest resistant. Mildew, root rot susceptible.

Perennial: *Scaevola* species and hybrids. GOODENIACEAE.

Common name: Scaevola (Beach Naupaka).

Description: Several hybrids and cultivars of variously erect or low and spreading or trailing, semi-evergreen or evergreen perennial herbs and shrubs, to 6 in. (15 cm) tall in prostrate species, 5 ft. (1.5 m) tall in shrub species. Fleshy, smooth, green, pink, oval, rounded leaves, 1–6 in. (25–150 mm) long, depending on species, on fleshy stems. Common cultivars include *S. aemula,* Australian scaevola; *S. taccada,* beach naupaka, and *S.* x 'Mauve Clusters'.

Bloom: Many showy, blue, pink, purple, white, open, flat-faced flowers, 1–3 in. (25–75 mm) wide, in summer.

Plant hardiness: Tender. Zones 7–11.

Soil: Damp to dry, well-drained, sandy soil. Fertility: Average. 6.5–8.0 pH.

Planting: Spring in full sun, 18–24 in. (45–60 cm) apart for prostrate species, 6 ft. (1.8 m) apart for shrub species.

Care: Easy. Keep moist until established; allow soil surface to dry between waterings. Drought, salt, wind tolerant. Fertilize annually in spring. Protect from frost. Propagate by cuttings, division, seed.

Features: Good choice for accents, hanging baskets, containers, ground covers, paths in arid, natural, seaside gardens. Slug, snail and fungal disease susceptible.

Perennial: *Scrophularia auriculata.* SCROPHULARIACEAE.
Common name: Water Figwort (Water Betony).
Description: Several cultivars of erect, shrublike, evergreen perennial herbs, 2–3 ft. (60–90 cm) tall. Textured, green, sometimes cream-edged, oval or lance-shaped, pointed, curving, very fragrant leaves, 2–10 in. (50–250 mm) long.
Bloom: Many greenish purple, upturned, pitcher-shaped, 2-lipped flowers, ½–¾ in. (12–19 mm) long, in summer–early autumn. Grown primarily for foliage.
Plant hardiness: Semi-hardy. Self-seeding. Zones 5–10.
Soil: Moist, well-drained soil or, in water features, shallow-depth marginal or shoreline sites. Fertility: Average. 6.0–8.0 pH.
Planting: Autumn–spring in full sun to partial shade, 18–24 in. (45–60 cm) apart, or submerged to 3 in (75 mm).
Care: Easy. Keep evenly moist. Fertilize annually in spring. Mulch. Propagate by cuttings, seed.
Features: Good choice for accents, hanging baskets, containers, ground covers in bog, natural, shade, woodland gardens and water feature shorelines. Good for cutting. Attracts bees. Slug, snail and fungal disease susceptible.

Perennial: *Sempervivum tectorum.* CRASSULACEAE.
Common name: Hen-and-Chickens.
Description: Many cultivars of low, mounding, hairy, succulent, evergreen perennial herbs, to 1 ft. (30 cm) tall, in clusters to 2 ft. (60 cm) wide. Fleshy, smooth, gray green, red-tipped, pointed, curving leaves, 2–4 in. (50–100 mm) long, armed with sharp tip spines, forming a circular, radiating base.

> **WARNING**
> Sap of *Sempervivum tectorum* causes skin and eye irritation. Wear gloves when cutting or pruning.

Bloom: Many red, purple flowers, 1–1½ in. (25–38 mm) wide, in branching clusters on fibrous, wiry stems, to 2 ft. (60 cm) tall, in summer.
Plant hardiness: Semi-hardy. Zones 5–10.
Soil: Moist, well-drained, sandy soil. Fertility: Low. 6.5–7.5 pH.
Planting: Spring or autumn in full sun, 6–9 in. (15–23 cm) apart.
Care: Easy. Keep damp; allow soil surface to dry between waterings. Drought tolerant. Avoid fertilizing. Propagate by cuttings, seed.
Features: Good choice for borders, containers, ground covers in rock, seaside, Xeriscape gardens. Fungal disease susceptible.

Perennial: *Senecio cineraria.* ASTERACEAE (COMPOSITAE).
Common name: Silver Groundsel (Dusty-Miller).
Description: Many cultivars of dense, semi-erect, mounding, shrublike, evergreen perennial herbs, to 2 ft. (60 cm) tall. Woolly, gray green to silvery white, stiff, lacelike, blunt-lobed, fragrant leaves, 2–6 in. (50–150 mm) long. Many other plants of varying genera bear the common name dusty-miller.
Bloom: Many pale to bright yellow, round, multirayed flowers, ½ in. (12 mm) wide, in round, branching clusters on stiff, short stems, to 18 in. (45 cm) tall, in late spring–early autumn. Grown primarily for foliage.
Plant hardiness: Hardy. Zones 3–10.
Soil: Moist, well-drained soil. Fertility: Rich. 6.5–7.5 pH.
Planting: Spring in full sun, 1 ft. (30 cm) apart, after frost hazard has passed.
Care: Easy. Keep damp; allow soil surface to dry between waterings. Fertilize monthly. Propagate by cuttings, division, seed.
Features: Good choice for accents, beds, borders, containers, geometric plantings in cottage, formal, rock gardens. Aphid, mealybug, thrips and powdery mildew suceptible.

Perennial: *Senecio* × *hybridus.* ASTERACEAE (COMPOSITAE).

Common name: Florist's Cineraria.

Description: Many cultivars of mounding or branching, evergreen perennial herbs, 1–3 ft. (30–90 cm) tall. Gray green to light green, heart-shaped, coarsely cut, fragrant leaves, 3–5 in. (75–125 mm) long. Sometimes mislabeled as *Cineraria stellata.*

Bloom: Many blue, pink, purple, red, violet, white, multicolored, round, flat, open, scalloped flowers, 3–5 in. (75–125 mm) wide, often with contrasting or white centers, in spring–early summer.

Plant hardiness: Tender. Self-seeding. Plant as annual, zones 3–7; ground hardy, zones 8–10. Best in mild, cool-summer climates.

Soil: Moist, well-drained soil. Fertility: Rich. 6.5–7.5 pH.

Planting: Spring in full to filtered sun, 8–10 in. (20–25 cm) apart, after soil warms.

Care: Easy. Keep damp; allow soil surface to dry between waterings. Fertilize monthly. Pinch to promote bushiness. Protect from frost. Propagate by cuttings, division, seed.

Features: Good choice for accents, beds, borders, containers, massed plantings in cottage, formal, small-space gardens. Disease resistant. Aphid, mealybug, leaf miner, spider mite, slug, snail succeptible.

Perennial: *Sidalcea* species and hybrids. MALVACEAE.

Common name: Mallow (Checkerbloom, Checkermallow, Prairie Mallow).

Description: About 20 species of erect or spreading, hollyhock-like, fibrous or rhizomatous, deciduous annual or perennial herbs, 2–4 ft. (60–120 cm) tall. Textured, deep green, round, lobed leaves, 3–8 in. (75–200 mm) long.

Bloom: Many pale to deep pink, purple, round, 5-petaled, scalloped flowers, ¾–2 in. (19–50 mm) wide, in whorled spiking clusters, in early summer, depending on species.

Plant hardiness: Hardy. Zones 4–10.

Soil: Wet to moist, well-drained loam. Fertility: Rich–average. 6.5–7.5 pH.

Planting: Spring, zones 4–7; autumn, zones 8–10, in full sun to partial shade, 18–24 in. (45–60 cm) apart.

Care: Easy. Keep moist; allow soil surface to dry between waterings. Drought tolerant. Fertilize quarterly. Stake. Propagate by division, seed.

Features: Good choice for accents, borders, massed plantings in cottage, meadow, natural gardens. Disease resistant. Aphid suceptible.

Perennial: *Silene californica.* CARYOPHYLLACEAE.

Common name: California Indian Pink (Wild Campion).

Description: Several cultivars of erect, branching, deciduous perennial herbs, 2–4 ft. (60–120 cm) tall. Textured, deep or gray green, narrow, oval, pointed, wavy-edged leaves, 3–4 in. (75–100 mm) long. *S. coeli-rosa,* viscaria; *S. shafta,* moss campion; and *S. virginica,* fire-pink catchfly, are closely related species with similar care needs.

Bloom: Showy, scarlet red, irregular, many-petaled, hairy, fringed flowers 1½ in. (38 mm) wide, in sparse to full clusters on stiff stalks, in late spring.

Plant hardiness: Hardy. Plant as annual, zones 2–4; ground hardy, zones 5–10.

Soil: Damp to dry, well-drained, sandy soil. Fertility: Average. 6.5–8.0 pH.

Planting: Spring in full sun to partial shade, 6–8 in. (15–20 cm) apart.

Care: Easy. Keep damp; allow soil surface to dry between waterings. Drought tolerant. Fertilize annually in spring. Propagate by cuttings, division, seed.

Features: Good choice for accents, banks, beds, borders in cottage, meadow, natural, seaside, wildlife gardens. Attracts bees, butterflies, hummingbirds. Pest and disease resistant.

Perennial: *Soleirolia soleirolii (Helxine soleirolii)*. URTICACEAE.
Common name: Baby's-Tears (Angel's-Tears, Corsican Carpet Plant).
Description: Several cultivars of low, creeping, evergreen perennial herbs, to 5 in. (13 cm) tall. Shiny, bright green, round, sometimes heart-shaped leaves, ¼ in. (6 mm) wide, on short stems that root with soil contact.
Bloom: Insignificant flowers; grown for foliage.
Plant hardiness: Tender. Plant as annual, zones 3–7; ground hardy, zones 8–10. Best in mild, cool-summer climates.
Soil: Moist, well-drained humus. Fertility: Rich–average. 6.5–7.5 pH.
Planting: Spring in full sun to partial shade, 8–10 in. (20–25 cm) apart, after frost hazard has passed.
Care: Easy. Keep evenly moist. Fertilize quarterly. Propagate by cuttings, division.
Features: Good choice for ground covers, paths in cottage, small-space, woodland gardens and indoor terrariums. Invasive. Disease resistant. Slug, snail succeptible.

Perennial: *Solidago* hybrids. ASTERACEAE (COMPOSITAE).
Common name: Goldenrod.
Description: Many hybrids of upright, rhizomatous perennial herbs, to 3 ft. (90 cm) tall. Hairy or shiny, green, narrow, lance-shaped, often toothed leaves, to 6 in. (15 cm) long. *Solidago* species cultivars have similar care needs.
Bloom: Showy, tiny, cream, white, bright yellow, hairy flowers, in tall, feathery plume-like clusters, to 10 in. (25 cm) long, in summer–autumn.
Plant hardiness: Hardy. Zones 2–10.
Soil: Damp, well-drained, sandy soil. Fertility: Average–low. 6.5–7.5 pH.
Planting: Spring in full to filtered sun, 18–24 in. (45–60 cm) apart, after soil warms.
Care: Easy. Keep damp; allow soil surface to dry between waterings. Drought tolerant. Fertilize annually in spring. Stake tall cultivars. Propagate by division, seed.
Features: Good choice for backgrounds, beds in cottage, meadow, natural, wildlife, woodland gardens. Invasive, zones 7–10. Attracts birds, butterflies. Reputation for causing allergic reactions in susceptible individuals is undeserved. Pest and disease resistant.

Perennial: *Stachys byzantina*. LAMIACEAE (LABIATAE).
Common name: Lamb's-Ears (Woolly Betony).
Description: Several cultivars of low, mounding or spreading, stoloniferous, perennial herbs, 1–3 ft. (30–90 cm) tall. Fuzzy or velvety, gray green to silvery white, lamb's-ear-shaped leaves, 4–6 in. (10–15 cm) long. *S. macrantha*, big betony, is a closely related species with similar care needs. *S. albotomentosa* and *S. coccinea* are closely related, tender species.
Bloom: Many tiny, pink, purple, tubular, flared-lipped or cottony, hairy flowers, ½–1 in. (12–25 mm) wide, in dense clusters on tall, wiry stalks, in late spring–early autumn. Some cultivars are non-flowering foliage plants.
Plant hardiness: Hardy. Zones 4–10. Best in cool, low-humidity climates.
Soil: Damp, well-drained, sandy soil. Fertility: Average–low. 6.5–7.5 pH.
Planting: Early spring in full sun to partial shade, 10–18 in. (25–45 cm) apart.
Care: Moderate. Keep damp; allow soil surface to dry between waterings. Avoid wetting foliage. Drought tolerant. Fertilize annually in spring. Deadhead flower stalks before or after bloom. Protect from heat, rain. Propagate by division, seed.
Features: Good choice for accents, borders, containers, contrasting foliage, edgings, ground covers, paths in cottage, formal, seaside, woodland gardens. Attracts bees. Salt tolerant. Pest, disease, and oak root fungus resistant.

Perennial: *Stokesia laevis.* ASTERACEAE (COMPOSITAE).

Common name: Stokes' Aster.

Description: Several cultivars of erect, branching, deciduous perennial herbs, 18–24 in. (45–60 cm) tall. Smooth, deep green, lance-shaped, pointed, often finely toothed leaves, 2–8 in. (50–200 mm) long, forming a circular, radiating base.

Bloom: Showy, blue, lavender, pink, white, irregular, fringed, hairy-centered flowers, 2–5 in. (50–125 mm) wide, in early summer–midautumn.

Plant hardiness: Hardy. Zones 5–10. Best in hot-summer climates.

Soil: Moist to damp, well-drained soil. Fertility: Average. 5.5–7.5 pH.

Planting: Early spring in full sun, 12–15 in. (30–38 cm) apart.

Care: Easy. Keep damp; allow soil surface to dry between waterings. Drought, heat tolerant. Fertilize annually in spring. Deadhead spent flowers to prolong bloom. Propagate by cuttings, division, seed.

Features: Good choice for accents, borders, containers, edgings in arid, cottage, formal, meadow gardens. Good for cutting. Pest and disease resistant.

Perennial: *Thalictrum* species. RANUNCULACEAE.

Common name: Meadow Rue.

Description: About 100 species of mostly erect, bushy or sprawling, open, deciduous perennial herbs, variously to 8 ft. (2.4 m) tall or low-growing, 8–18 in. (20–45 cm) tall. Shiny, textured, deep green, deeply cut and lobed, divided, pointed, veined leaves, to 6 in. (15 cm) long, in feathery leaflets, to 2 in. (50 mm) wide. Cultivated species include *T. aquilegifolium, T. dasycarpum, T. delavayi,* and *T. polygamum.*

Bloom: Many cream, pink, purple, violet, yellow, hairy flowers, in multiple, round, powderpuff-like clusters, to 2 in. (50 mm) wide, on erect, branching stems, in spring.

Plant hardiness: Hardy. Zones 4–9.

Soil: Moist, well-drained soil. Fertility: Rich. 6.0–7.0 pH.

Planting: Spring in filtered sun to partial shade, 12–16 in. (30–40 cm) apart.

Care: Easy. Keep moist. Fertilize monthly. Stake to support. Protect from wind, heat. Propagate by division, seed.

Features: Good choice for beds, borders, containers, foregrounds, fencelines in meadow, natural, shade, woodland gardens. Pest and disease resistant.

Perennial: *Tiarella cordifolia.* SAXIFRAGACEAE.

Common name: Foamflower.

Description: Several cultivars of low, mounding, rhizomatous, evergreen perennial herbs, 6–12 in. (15–30 cm) tall. Downy, textured, deep green, triangular to heart-shaped, toothed, lobed, strongly veined leaves, to 4 in. (10 cm) long, forming a circular, radiating base and turning red, yellow in autumn. *T trifoliata* var. *unifoliata,* sugar-scoop, is a closely related species.

Bloom: Many tiny, pink, white, tubular flowers, in tall, cone-shaped, spiking clusters, 2–5 in. (50–125 mm) tall, in spring–early summer.

Plant hardiness: Hardy. Zones 3–9.

Soil: Moist, well-drained humus. Fertility: Rich. 6.5–7.5 pH.

Planting: Early autumn in partial to full shade, 12–18 in. (30–45 cm) apart, after heat moderates.

Care: Easy. Keep damp during active growth; limit watering in winter. Fertilize monthly. Propagate by division, seed.

Features: Good choice for borders, containers, ground covers in natural, rock, woodland gardens. Pest and disease resistant.

Perennial: *Tolmiea menziesii.* SAXIFRAGACEAE.
Common name: Pickaback Plant (Mother-of-Thousands, Piggyback Plant).
Description: Several cultivars of mounding or trailing, rhizomatous, evergreen perennial herbs, to 1 ft. (30 cm) tall. Hairy, textured, light green or variegated, heart-shaped, pointed, lobed, toothed, veined leaves, to 4 in. (10 cm) wide, on dangling stems. Reproduces vegetatively by growing young plants at leaf-stalk junctions.
Bloom: Insignificant red, tan, tubular flowers, to ⅜ in. (9 mm) long; grown primarily for foliage.
Plant hardiness: Tender. Zones 7–9.
Soil: Moist, well-drained humus. Fertility: Rich. 6.0–7.0 pH.
Planting: Spring in open to partial shade, 1 ft. (30 cm) apart, after frost hazard has passed and soil is workable.
Care: Easy. Keep evenly moist; reduce watering in winter. Fertilize monthly during growth. Pinch growth tips to control growth. Propagate by division, layering.
Features: Good choice for hanging baskets, borders, containers, ground covers in indoor, natural, rock, shade, woodland gardens. Good houseplant. Disease resistant. Mealybug, spider mite, whitefly susceptible.

Perennial: *Tradescantia virginiana.* COMMELINACEAE.
Common name: Virginia Spiderwort (Common Spiderwort, Widow's-Tears).
Description: A few cultivars of erect, bunching, deciduous perennial herbs, 1–3 ft. (30–90 cm) tall. Smooth, deep green, grasslike, arching and folded, pointed leaves, to 1 ft. (30 cm) long. *T. fluminensis,* wandering Jew, is a related houseplant species.
Bloom: Showy, blue, pink, purple, white, open, 3-petaled flowers, to 1 in. (25 mm) wide, in late spring–early summer, in dense, rounded clusters of single-day blooms.
Plant hardiness: Semi-hardy. Self-seeding. Plant as annual, zones 3–6; ground hardy, zones 7–11.
Soil: Moist, well-drained humus. Fertility: Rich–average. 6.0–7.0 pH.
Planting: Spring in full sun to partial shade, 1–2 ft. (30–60 cm) apart, when soil warms.
Care: Easy. Keep moist; allow soil surface to dry between waterings. Fertilize annually in spring. Propagate by cuttings, division, seed.
Features: Good choice for hanging baskets, borders, containers, ground covers in natural, rock, shade, woodland gardens. Invasive. Pest and disease resistant.

Perennial: *Trollius chinensis (T. ledebourii)* and hybrids. RANUNCULACEAE.
Common name: Chinese Globeflower.
Description: Several cultivars of erect, mounding, open, fibrous, deciduous perennial herbs, 2–3 ft. (60–90 cm) tall. Shiny, deep green, pointed, lobed, cut, finely toothed, veined leaves, to 3 in. (75 mm) long. See also *T. europaeus,* globeflower.
Bloom: Showy, orange, yellow, cup-shaped, open flowers, to 2 in. (50 mm) wide, in late spring–early summer.
Plant hardiness: Hardy. Zones 3–9. Best in cool-summer climates.
Soil: Moist, well-drained humus or, in water features, shoreline sites. Fertility: Rich–average. 6.0–7.0 pH.
Planting: Late summer in full sun to partial shade, 1 ft. (30 cm) apart, after heat has moderated.
Care: Easy. Keep evenly moist. Fertilize monthly. Deadhead spent flowers to prolong bloom. Propagate by division, seed.
Features: Good choice for accents, beds, borders, massed plantings in bog, natural, rock, shade, woodland gardens or water feature shorelines. Good for cutting. Pest and disease resistant.

Perennial: *Trollius europaeus* and hybrids. RANUNCULACEAE.
Common name: Globeflower.
Description: Several cultivars of erect, mounding, open, fibrous, deciduous perennial herbs, 18–24 in. (45–60 cm) tall, 18 in. (45 cm) wide. Shiny, green, pointed, 3–5 lobed, finely toothed leaves, to 3 in. (75 mm) long, with pale gray green undersides. See also *T. chinensis,* Chinese globeflower, a closely related species with similar care needs.
Bloom: Many yellow, green yellow, round, ball-shaped flowers, 1–2 in. (25–50 mm) wide, in late spring–early summer.
Plant hardiness: Hardy. Self-seeding. Zones 3–7. Best in cool-summer climates.
Soil: Moist, well-drained humus or, in water features, shoreline sites. Fertility: Rich. 5.5–7.0 pH.
Planting: Spring or autumn in full sun to partial shade, 18 in. (45 cm) apart.
Care: Easy. Keep evenly moist. Fertilize monthly. Mulch. Deadhead spent flowers to prolong bloom. Propagate by division, seed.
Features: Good choice for accents, beds, borders in bog, natural, shade, woodland gardens or water feature shorelines. Good for cutting. Disease resistant. Aphid susceptible.

Perennial: *Typha minima.* TYPHACEAE.
Common name: Miniature Cattail.
Description: Several cultivars of erect, stoloniferous, deciduous perennial herbs, to 15 in. (38 cm) tall. Shiny, light green, straplike, pointed, vertically veined leaves, to 1 ft. (30 cm) long. *T. latifolia,* common cattail, is a taller, closely related species with similar care needs.
Bloom: Diminutive, sausage-shaped catkins, 3–5 in. (75–125 mm) long, on reedlike spikes, in late summer–autumn.
Plant hardiness: Hardy. Self-seeding. Zones 3–6.
Soil: Wet to moist, well-drained humus or, in water features, shallow or deep marginal sites. Fertility: Rich. 6.0–8.0 pH.
Planting: Spring in full sun to partial shade, 1 ft. (30 cm) apart, or submerged 6–8 in. (15–20 cm).
Care: Easy. Keep evenly moist. Fertilize monthly. Propagate by division, seed.

Features: Good choice for accents, borders in bog, natural, shade, small-space, woodland gardens or water feature margins. Good for cutting, drying. Invasive; plant in buried or submerged containers. Pest and disease resistant.

Perennial: *Valeriana officinalis.* VALERIANACEAE.
Common name: Common Valerian (Garden Heliotrope).
Description: Many cultivars of erect, upright, rhizomatous, deciduous perennial herbs, 42–60 in. (1.1–1.5 m) tall. Textured, light green, lacelike, deeply cut and divided, toothed, fragrant leaves, 18–24 in. (45–60 cm) long, with 7–10 paired leaflets. Common cultivars include *V. officinalis* 'Alba', 'Coccinea', and 'Rubra', with white, scarlet, and red flowers, respectively.
Bloom: Many lavender, pink, red, scarlet, white, funnel-shaped, very fragrant flowers, ⅛–¼ in. (3–6 mm) wide, in flat, rounded clusters atop tall stems, in late spring–summer.
Plant hardiness: Hardy. Self-seeding. Zones 3–10.
Soil: Moist, well-drained loam. Fertility: Rich–average. 6.5–7.5 pH.
Planting: Spring in full sun to partial shade, 2–3 ft. (60–90 cm) apart.
Care: Easy. Keep damp; allow soil surface to dry between waterings. Drought tolerant. Fertilize monthly. Mulch. Propagate by division, seed.
Features: Good choice for accents, containers, massed plantings in arid, meadow, woodland gardens. Good for cutting. Attracts bees, household cats. Invasive. Pest and disease resistant.

Perennial: *Verbascum* species and hybrids. SCROPHULARIACEAE.
Common name: Mullein.
Description: About 250 species of erect, mounding, hairy, deciduous sometimes annual or perennial, but mostly biennial herbs, 4–7 ft. (1.2–2.2 m) tall. Fuzzy, gray, gray green, silver, bluntly rounded, paddle-shaped leaves, 10–18 in. (25–45 cm) long, forming a circular, radiating base. Commonly cultivated species include *V. blattaria*, *V. chaixii*, and *V. phoeniceum*.
Bloom: Showy, white, sometimes red, bright or lemon yellow, trumpet-shaped, fragrant flowers, to 1 in. (25 mm) wide, often with contrasting throats, in summer, in tall, spiking clusters.
Plant hardiness: Mostly hardy; some tender species. Self-seeding. Zones 3–9. Best in hot, arid climates.
Soil: Damp to dry, well-drained, sandy soil. Fertility: Average. 6.5–7.5 pH.
Planting: Spring in full sun, 12–16 in. (30–40 cm) apart.
Care: Easy. Keep moist; allow soil surface to dry between waterings. Drought tolerant. Fertilize annually in spring. Propagate by cuttings, division, seed.
Features: Good choice for accents in arid, meadow, seaside gardens. Good for cutting. Attracts hummingbirds. Invasive. Pest and disease resistant.

Perennial: *Verbena* species and hybrids. VERBENACEAE.
Common name: Verbena (Vervain).
Description: About 200 species and many hybrids of upright or low and spreading annual and perennial herbs or shrubs, 8–18 in. (20–45 cm) tall. Opposite, hairy, deep green, oval, bluntly toothed leaves, to 4 in. (10 cm) long. Cultivated species include *V. bracteata*, *V. canadensis*, *V. hastata*, and *V. rigida*.
Bloom: Many pink, purple, red, white, yellow, broad, flat flowers, ½ in. (12 mm) wide, in clusters on wiry stems, in late spring–autumn.
Plant hardiness: Tender. Plant as annual, zones 3–7; ground hardy, zones 8–9.
Soil: Moist, well-drained soil. Fertility: Rich–average. 6.5–7.0 pH.
Planting: Spring in full sun, 1–2 ft. (30–60 cm) apart, depending on variety, after frost hazard has passed.

Care: Easy. Keep moist; avoid wetting foliage. Fertilize semi-monthly. Propagate by cuttings, division.
Features: Good choice for accents, beds, borders, containers, edgings, ground covers in cottage, meadow, natural, wildlife gardens. Attracts birds, butterflies, hummingbirds. Invasive, zones 8–9. Budworm, verbena leaf miner, verbena yellow woolly-bear caterpillar and powdery mildew susceptible.

Perennial: *Veronica* species and hybrids. SCROPHULARIACEAE.
Common name: Speedwell (Brooklime).
Description: About 250 species and many hybrids of erect or low, bushy, deciduous annual or perennial herbs, 1–4 ft. (30–120 cm) tall, 12–18 in. (30–45 cm) wide. Textured, light or gray green, lance-shaped, pointed leaves, to 2 in. (50 mm) long. Cultivated species include *V. beccabunga*, *V. chamaedrys*, and *V. officinalis*.
Bloom: Many tiny, blue, pink, white, tubular, lipped flowers, in tall, spiking, conical clusters, to 2 ft. (60 cm) tall, in late spring–summer.
Plant hardiness: Hardy. Zones 3–8.
Soil: Moist, well-drained loam. Fertility: Average–low. 6.5–7.5 pH.
Planting: Spring or autumn in full sun to partial shade, 1–2 ft. (30–60 cm) apart.
Care: Moderate. Keep moist; allow soil surface to dry between waterings. Fertilize annually in spring. Stake tall cultivars. Propagate by cuttings, division, seed.
Features: Good choice for accents, beds, borders, containers, fencelines in cottage, formal, heritage, meadow, natural gardens. Pest resistant. Downy mildew, leaf spot susceptible.

Perennial: *Vinca* species. APOCYNACEAE.

Common name: Periwinkle.

Description: More than 10 species and many cultivars of low, bushy, mounding, or trailing, evergreen perennial subshrubs, 6–24 in. (15–60 cm) tall, 1–3 ft. (30–90 cm) wide. Opposite, shiny, deep green, oval or lance-shaped, pointed leaves, to 2 in. (50 mm) long. *Catharanthus roseus*, Madagascar periwinkle, is a closely related species with similar care needs.

Bloom: Many blue, purple, white, 5-petaled flowers, 1–2 in. (25–50 mm) wide, in early spring.

Plant hardiness: Tender or hardy, depending on species. *V. major*, zones 8-11; *V. minor*, zones 3–11. Best in cool-summer climates.

Soil: Moist to dry, well-drained soil. Fertility: Average–low. 6.0–8.0 pH.

Planting: Spring in full sun to full shade, 18–24 in. (45–60 cm) apart.

Care: Easy. Keep moist until established; drought tolerant thereafter. Fertilize annually in spring. Shear in autumn. Propagate by cuttings, division.

Features: Good choice for banks, borders, containers, ground covers in natural, woodland gardens. Invasive. Disease resistant. Slug, snail susceptible.

Perennial: *Viola odorata* and hybrids. VIOLACEAE.

Common name: Sweet Violet (English Violet, Florist's Violet).

Description: Many cultivars of low, mounding, tufted, deciduous perennial herbs, 8–24 in. (20–60 cm) tall. Shiny, deep green, round or kidney-shaped, finely toothed leaves, 1–2 in. (25–50 mm) long, on short leaf stems.

Bloom: Many blue, lavender, purple, violet, white, sometimes double-petaled, 5-petaled, fragrant flowers, ½–⅞ in. (12–22 mm) wide, with short spurs, in early spring.

Plant hardiness: Hardy. Self-seeding. Plant as annual, zones, 2–5; ground hardy, zones 6–10. Best in cool climates.

Soil: Moist, well-drained loam. Fertility: Rich. 5.5–6.5 pH.

Planting: Spring, zones 2–5; late summer, zones 6–10, in filtered sun to partial shade, 8–12 in. (20–30 cm) apart.

Care: Easy. Keep evenly moist. Fertilize monthly. Protect from heat. Deadhead spent flowers. Propagate by division, offsets, runners, seed.

Features: Good choice for borders, containers, edgings, ground covers in cottage, seaside, small-space, woodland gardens. Good for cutting. Invasive. Disease resistant. Spider mite susceptible.

Perennial: *Viola tricolor* and hybrids. VIOLACEAE.

Common name: Johnny-Jump-Up (Field Pansy, Miniature Pansy).

Description: Many cultivars of short-lived, low, mounding, tufted, deciduous perennial herbs, 6–12 in. (15–30 cm) tall. Shiny or matte, green, oval or lance-shaped, pointed, deeply lobed leaves, 1–2 in. (25–50 mm) long.

Bloom: Many apricot, blue, lavender, orange, pink, purple, red, white, yellow, multicolored, rounded, flat-faced, 5-petaled flowers, ½–⅞ in. (12–22 mm) wide, with overlapping petals, in early spring–summer, zones 2–8; winter–spring, zones 9–10.

Plant hardiness: Semi-hardy. Self-seeding. Plant as annual, zones 2–6; ground hardy, zones 7–10.

Soil: Moist, well-drained soil. Fertility: Rich–average. 6.5–7.5 pH.

Planting: Spring, zones 2–8; autumn, zones 9–10, in full sun to partial shade, 4–8 in. (10–20 cm) apart, when soil is workable.

Care: Easy. Keep evenly moist. Fertilize monthly. Mulch. Deadhead spent blossoms to promote new buds. Protect from heat. Propagate by division, offsets, runners, seed.

Features: Good choice for borders, containers, edgings, ground covers in cottage, meadow, small-space, woodland gardens. Disease resistant. Slug, snail susceptible.

Bulbs and Bulbous Plants

Gardeners who choose bulbs to plant in their landscape gardens or containers usually include one or more of everyone's longtime favorites such as crocus, daffodil, dahlia, daylily, hyacinth, gladiolus, iris, lily, or tulip. Besides these popular types, there are scores of other beautiful and fascinating bulbs.

When you admire bulbs that you see in a private or public garden, compare them to the photographs found here and use the information provided to decide how to use them to beautify your garden. The bulbous plants featured here include true bulbs, corms, rhizomes, and tubers, plus those with tuberous roots. The soil needs for each bulb are described in detail, and each is classified as a spring-, summer-, autumn-, or winter-planting type, with its season of bloom given separately to help you plan your landscape and get your bulbs off to a great start.

Bulb: *Achimenes* species. GESNERIACEAE.

Common name: Orchid Pansy (Mother's-Tears, Nut Orchid).

Description: Summer rhizome. Deciduous. About 26 species. Stands 1–2 ft. (30–60 cm) tall, often trailing. Oval, toothed, short, textured, hairy, olive green leaves, often with burgundy undersides.

Bloom: Summer–autumn. Blue, orange, pink, purple, red, white, yellow. Multiple flute-shaped flowers, 1–2 in. (25–50 mm) long.

Plant hardiness: Zones 4–11; ground hardy, zones 9–11.

Soil: Well-drained humus. Fertility: Rich. 6.0–7.5 pH.

Planting: Late spring–early summer in partial shade. Protect from summer heat. Space 6–10 in. (15–25 cm) apart, 1 in. (25 mm) deep. In containers, space 1–2 in. (25–50 mm) apart.

Care: Easy. Keep moist spring–summer. Fertilize during growth; dilute fertilizer to half the recommended rate. Mulch. Stake or allow to trail. Propagate by division.

Storage: Dark, 50–60°F (10–16°C), in porous container of dampened peat moss.

Features: Good choice for hanging baskets, beds, borders, containers, edgings in cottage, formal gardens. Deer, rodent resistant. Spider mite, thrips susceptible.

Bulb: *Agapanthus africanus* and hybrids *(A. umbellatus).* AMARYLLIDACEAE.

Common name: Lily-of-the-Nile (Harriet's Flower).

Description: Summer rhizome. Deciduous or evergreen, depending on species. Stands 12–18 in. (30–45 cm) tall. Swordlike, arching, midlength, thick, shiny, succulent, green leaves.

Bloom: Summer. Blue, purple, white. Multiple flared, tube-shaped flowers form dense, spherical clusters, to 8 in. (20 cm) wide.

Plant hardiness: Zones 6–11; ground hardy, zones 7–11.

Soil: Moist to damp, well-drained soil. Fertility: Average. 5.5–6.5 pH.

Planting: Spring–autumn in full sun to partial shade. Space 1–2 ft. (30–60 cm) apart, slightly below soil level.

Care: Easy. Keep moist during growth. Fertilize during growth. Mulch, zones 6–8. Propagate by division in autumn, seed in spring.

Storage: In-ground. Protect from frost.

Features: Good choice for beds, borders, containers, mass plantings in cottage, woodland gardens. Good for cutting. Deer susceptible.

Bulb: *Allium* species. LILIACEAE.

Common name: Ornamental Onion (Allium).

Description: Summer bulb. Deciduous. About 700 species. Stands 6–60 in. (15–150 cm) tall. Narrow or broad, usually hollow, midlength gray green leaves.

Bloom: Spring–summer. Blue, pink, red, violet, white, yellow. Multiple star-shaped, often fragrant flowers, ¼–1 in. (6–25 mm) wide, form compact or loose clusters, 1–6 in. (25–150 mm) wide, on tall, leafless stems, bearing seed and bulbils.

Plant hardiness: Zones 3–10; ground hardy, zones 4–8.

Soil: Moist to damp, well-drained humus. Fertility: Average. 6.0–7.0 pH.

Planting: Autumn in full sun to partial shade. Space 4–12 in. (10–30 cm) apart, 2–8 in. (50–200 mm) deep, depending on species.

Care: Easy. Keep moist winter–spring. Fertilize in spring. Deadhead flowers. Mulch, zones 3–5. Propagate by bulbils, division, offsets in autumn, seed in spring.

Storage: Dark, 50–60°F (10–16°C), in net bag or open basket of dry peat moss.

Features: Good choice for accents, borders, containers, edgings in cottage, formal, meadow, natural, rock, woodland gardens. Good for drying. Naturalizes. Deer, rodent and disease, pest resistant.

Bulb: *Alstroemeria* species. LILIACEAE.
Common name: Lily-of-the-Incas (Peruvian Lily).
Description: Summer rhizome or tuberous root. Deciduous. About 50 species. Stands 18–48 in. (45–120 cm) tall. Lance-shaped, short green leaves on stems.
Bloom: Late spring–summer. Purple, red, white, yellow, bicolored. Multiple flared, trumpet-shaped, often fragrant, long-lasting flowers, to 2 in. (50 mm) wide, in radiating clusters.
Plant hardiness: Zones 7–10; ground hardy, zones 8–10.
Soil: Very moist, well-drained soil. Fertility: Rich. 6.0–7.0 pH.
Planting: Spring in full sun to partial shade. Space 1 ft. (30 cm) apart, 6–8 in. (15–20 cm) deep.
Care: Moderate. Keep very moist during growth. Fertilize during growth. Mulch. Lift, zone 7. Propagate by division, seed in early spring or autumn. Use care: roots are brittle.
Storage: Dark, 50–60°F (10–16°C), in net bag or open basket of dry peat moss. Lift greenhouse container plants.
Features: Good choice for beds, borders, containers in casual gardens. Good for cutting; gently pull flower stems from rhizome. Naturalizes. Deer, rodent susceptible.

Bulb: *Amaryllis belladonna*. AMARYLLIDACEAE.
Common name: True Amaryllis (Belladonna Lily, Naked-Lady).
Description: Summer bulb. Deciduous. Stands 2–3 ft. (60–90 cm) tall. Straplike, midlength, dull green leaves, in clumps, appear after blooms.
Bloom: Late summer–early autumn. Pink, red, white. Multiple flared, trumpet-shaped, fragrant flowers, 3–4 in. (75–100 mm) wide, on a tall, reddish stalk.
Plant hardiness: Zones 6–11; ground hardy, zones 8–11.
Soil: Moist to damp, well-drained humus. Fertility: Rich. 6.0–6.5 pH.
Planting: Late spring–early summer in full sun. Space 8–12 in. (20–30 cm) apart, at soil level. In containers, slightly above soil level.
Care: Moderate. Keep moist midsummer–early spring. Fertilize until buds form. Propagate by offsets. Divide only when crowded.
Storage: Dark, 55–70°F (13–21°C), in net bag or open basket of dry peat moss.
Features: Good choice for beds, borders, containers in cottage, indoor, tropical gardens. Good for cutting. Deer, rodent resistant.

Bulb: *Anemone* species and hybrids. RANUNCULACEAE.
Common name: Windflower (Lily-of-the-Field).
Description: Spring rhizome or tuberous root. Deciduous. About 120 species. Stands 2–36 in. (50–900 mm) tall. Feathery, deeply toothed, small green leaves. Commonly cultivated species include *A. blanda*, *A. coronaria*, *A.* × *fulgens*, *A.* × *hybrida*, *A. nemorosa*, and *A. sylvestris*.
Bloom: Late winter–spring. Blue, pink, purple, red, white. Solitary daisy- or poppylike flowers, to 3 in. (75 mm) wide, with distinct centers and fleshy stems.
Plant hardiness: Zones 3–10, depending on species; ground hardy, zones 6–8.
Soil: Moist to damp, well-drained humus. Fertility: Rich. 6.0–7.5 pH, depending on species.
Planting: Autumn in full sun to partial shade, zones 8–10; spring, zones 3–7. Space 4–12 in. (10–30 cm) apart, 1–2 in. (25–50 mm) deep.
Care: Easy. Keep moist autumn–spring, dry in summer. Fertilize monthly during growth. Mulch, zones 3–6. Propagate by division, seed.
Storage: Rhizomes: dark, 40–50°F (4–10°C), in porous container of dampened peat moss; tuberous roots: dark, 50–70°F (10–21°C), in open basket of dry peat moss.
Features: Good choice for beds, containers, edgings, mixed plantings in meadow, natural, woodland gardens. Good for cutting. Deer, rodent susceptible.

Bulb: *Anigozanthos* species and hybrids. HAEMODORACEAE.

Common name: Kangaroo-Paw.

Description: Spring rhizome. Deciduous. About 10 species. Stands 18–48 in. (45–120 cm) tall. Straplike, midlength green leaves. Commonly cultivated species include *A. flavidus* and *A. manglesii*, as well as many hybrid cultivars.

Bloom: Winter–spring. Green, orange, pink, red, yellow. Multiple narrow, cylinder-shaped flowers, ¾–3 in. (19–75 mm) long, atop long stalks.

Plant hardiness: Zones 8–11; ground hardy, zones 9–11.

Soil: Moist, well-drained soil. Fertility: Rich. 6.0–6.5 pH.

Planting: Spring or early autumn in full sun. Space 2 ft. (60 cm) apart, at soil level.

Care: Moderate. Keep moist spring–autumn. Fertilize until buds form. Deadhead flowers. Remove withered foliage. Propagate by division in spring.

Storage: Dark, 50–60°F (10–16°C), in net bag or open basket of dry peat moss.

Features: Good choice for backgrounds, beds, borders, containers in arid, rock gardens and greenhouses. Good for cutting. Attracts bees, hummingbirds. Deer and slug, snail susceptible.

Bulb: *Arisaema triphyllum.* ARACEAE.

Common name: Jack-in-the-Pulpit.

Description: Spring tuber. Deciduous. Stands to 2 ft. (60 cm) tall. Oval, midlength, glossy green leaves in triplets on long stems. Subspecies and cultivars include *A. triphyllum* subsp. *stewardsonii*, *A. triphyllum* subsp. *triphyllum*, and *A. triphyllum* 'Zebrinum'. *A. sikokianum*, *A. speciosum*, and *A. tortuosum* are closely related species with similar care needs.

Bloom: Spring–early summer. Brown, green, purple, with lighter veins. Solitary spiral spathe with narrow leaflike form protects clublike, green, purple central spadix.

Plant hardiness: Zones 4–9; ground hardy, zones 5–9.

Soil: Very moist, well-drained soil. Fertility: Rich–average. 5.5–6.5 pH.

Planting: Autumn in partial to full shade. Space 10–12 in. (25–30 cm) apart, 3–4 in. (75–100 mm) deep.

Care: Moderate. Keep very moist spring–autumn. Fertilize monthly during growth. Mulch. Propagate by offsets, seed.

Storage: Dark, 50–60°F (10–16°C), in net bag or open basket of dry peat moss.

Features: Good choice for beds, borders, containers in indoor, woodland gardens. Deer, rodent resistant.

Bulb: *Aristea ecklonii.* IRIDACEAE.

Common name: Aristea.

Description: Summer rhizome. Deciduous. Stands to 2 ft. (60 cm) tall. Straplike, shiny green leaves, to 2 ft. (60 cm) long, in basal rosettes. *A. ecklonii* 'Sonja', with larger blooms, is a commonly cultivated cultivar.

Bloom: Late spring–early autumn. Blue, blue violet. Multiple simple, 6-petaled flowers, ¾–1 in. (19–25 mm) wide, on branching sprays.

Plant hardiness: Zones 4–9; ground hardy, zones 7–9.

Soil: Moist, well-drained soil. Fertility: Average. 6.0–7.0 pH.

Planting: Autumn in full sun to partial shade. Space 10–12 in. (25–30 cm) apart, 2–3 in. (50–75 mm) deep.

Care: Easy. Keep moist during growth. Fertilize in spring. Deadhead after bloom. Propagate by division, seed.

Storage: In-ground.

Features: Good choice for beds, borders, containers, mixed plantings in woodland gardens. Invasive, self-sowing. Disease and pest resistant.

Bulb: *Arum italicum.* ARACEAE.

Common name: Lords-and-Ladies.

Description: Spring tuber. Deciduous. Stands 12–18 in. (30–45 cm) tall. Elongated, heart-shaped green leaves with variegated patterns.

Bloom: Spring. Green, purple, white, yellow. Solitary, nearly spiral spathe with narrow leaflike form protects central spadix, to 8 in. (20 cm) tall, which forms attractive orange, red berries. Resembles jack-in-the-pulpit; both are members of ARACEAE family. A related species, *A. maculatum,* with black spotted foliage, is commonly cultivated.

Plant hardiness: Zones 5–10; ground hardy, zones 6–10, depending on species.

Soil: Moist, well-drained soil. Fertility: Rich–average. 6.5–7.5 pH.

Planting: Autumn in partial to full shade. Space 1 ft. (30 cm) apart, 4 in. (10 cm) deep.

Care: Easy. Keep moist spring–summer. Fertilize in spring. Mulch. Protect from wind. Propagate by division in late summer–early autumn.

Storage: Dark, 50–60°F (10–16°C), in net bag or open basket of dry peat moss.

Features: Good choice for beds, borders in indoor, woodland gardens and water feature shorelines. Good for cutting. Deer, rodent and disease resistant.

> **WARNING**
> Fruit of *Arum italicum* is hazardous if eaten. Avoid planting in areas frequented by pets or children.

Bulb: *Asparagus densiflorus.* LILIACEAE.

Common name: Asparagus Fern (Ornamental Asparagus).

Description: Semi-tropical tuber. Semi-evergreen. Stands 18–24 in. (45–60 cm) tall. Shiny, bright to deep green, needlelike, leafy branches, to 2 in. (50 mm) long, form fernlike foliage on branchlets. Common cultivars include *A. densiflorus* 'Myeri' and 'Sprengeri'.

Bloom: Spring. White. Small, star-shaped, fragrant flowers form shiny, red, berrylike fruit.

Plant hardiness: Zones 9–11.

Soil: Moist, well-drained soil. Fertility: Rich–average. 6.5–7.0 pH.

Planting: Spring in full sun to partial shade. Space 2–3 ft. (60–90 cm) apart, 6–8 in. (15–20 cm) deep.

Care: Easy. Keep moist spring–autumn. Fertilize in spring. Mulch. Propagate by division in autumn.

Storage: In-ground. Protect from frost.

Features: Good choice for hanging baskets, beds, borders in arid gardens. Spider mite susceptible.

Bulb: *Babiana* species. IRIDACEAE.

Common name: Baboon Flower.

Description: Spring or summer corm, depending on species. Deciduous. About 61 species. Stands 6–12 in. (15–30 cm) tall. Straplike, short, hairy green leaves.

Bloom: Late spring–early summer. Blue, purple, red, violet, white, yellow. Multiple upright, star-shaped, often fragrant flowers 1–2 in. (25–50 mm) wide.

Plant hardiness: Zones 8–10; ground hardy, zones 9–10.

Soil: Moist, well-drained, sandy loam. Fertility: Average. 6.0–6.5 pH.

Planting: Autumn in full sun to partial shade, zones 9–10; spring, zone 8. Space 2–6 in. (50–150 mm) apart, 2–6 in. (50–150 mm) deep, depending on species. In containers, space 1 in. (25 mm) apart, 1 in. (25 mm) deep.

Care: Moderate. Keep moist autumn–early summer. Fertilize until buds form. Remove withered foliage. Protect from wind. Propagate by bulbils, seed. Divide only when crowded.

Storage: Dark, 50–60°F (10–16°C), in porous container of dampened peat moss.

Features: Good choice for accents, beds, borders, containers, drifts, edgings in cottage, meadow, natural, rock, shade gardens. Naturalizes. Pest and disease resistant.

BEGONIA

Over 1,000 wild species of the *Begonia* genus native to tropical and subtropical regions throughout the world have yielded many hybrid cultivars treasured for their distinctive flowers or unusual foliage. Most are native to Central and South America. All are summer blooming, perennial plants. Begonias are drought, heat, and smog tolerant plants that thrive in filtered sunlight and tolerate full sun in most climates.

While a few are woody shrubs, most begonias are bulbous plants with fibrous, rhizomatous, or tuberous roots and are tender; begonias generally are planted as annuals and reared indoors in USDA Plant Hardiness Zones 4–7, where they are lifted after bloom and stored for spring replanting. They also are good houseplants for use indoors. Gardeners may choose from nearly 400 commonly grown species, varieties, and cultivars.

The American Begonia Society, Inc., has divided begonias horticulturally into three broad, large groups by their rootstock type, each subdivided for exhibition and show classes based on specific flower characteristics.

Fibrous-Rooted Begonias
Wax *(Semperflorens)* Begonias
Cane and Angel-Winged Begonias
Hirsute (Hairy) Begonias
Rhizomatous-Rooted Begonias
Rex *(Rex-Cultorum)* Begonias
Other Rhizomatous Begonias
Tuberous-Rooted Begonias
Tuberous *(Tuberhybrida)* Begonias
Hardy Begonias
Multiflora Begonias

Because begonias are so varied in their growth habits, it's possible to choose from tall, upright plants with bamboolike, jointed canes, mounding varieties, and trailing forms. All can be grown during season in the garden provided that they are given protection from unseasonable frosts and heavy precipitation; many cultivars are grown indoors as colorful foliage or flowering plants. Pots may be moved outdoors during the summer months to brighten balconies, decks, and patios.

Plant begonias in spring, after the soil temperature has warmed and all hazard of frost has passed. Remember, when you water tuberous plants, avoid pooling water on the soil over the tuber; they are subject to fungal disease when soil conditions are overly moist and water stands in their concave crown. Water all begonias at the soil to avoid wetting foliage. Protect the plants from wind, as many cultivars have delicate, brittle foliage. Fertilize them monthly during active growth with liquid organic fertilizer diluted to one-half the package-recommended rate.

When autumn days begin, with reduced daylight, many begonias will begin a period of semi-dormancy. In cold-winter climates, cease watering for about 2 weeks, then lift the tubers and store them in a net bag or an open basket of dry peat moss with good air circulation. For fibrous- and rhizomatous-rooted varieties, limit watering, then cut the foliage back to the main stalk before lifting. Place them in damp peat moss or wood chips until spring, checking them occasionally to add moisture and remove any that have developed fungal disease or that have withered.

Bulb: *Begonia grandis.* BEGONIACEAE.
Common name: Hardy Begonia.
Description: Summer tuber. Deciduous. Stands 18–36 in. (45–90 cm) tall. Wing-shaped, short, bronze green leaves with red-tinted veins.
Bloom: Midsummer–autumn. Pink, white. Many drooping, fragrant flowers, 1–1 1/2 in. (25–38 mm) wide, in clusters.
Plant hardiness: Zones 6–9; ground hardy, zones 7–9.
Soil: Moist, well-drained soil. Fertility: Rich. 6.0–6.5 pH.
Planting: Spring in partial shade, zones 6–8; autumn, zone 9. Space 8–10 in. (20–25 cm) apart, 4 in. (10 cm) deep. In containers, space 3–4 in. (75–100 mm) apart, 1/4 in. (6 mm) deep.
Care: Easy. Keep moist spring–autumn. Fertilize monthly during growth. Pinch early foliage buds to promote bloom. Propagate by cutting tubers into sections, each with an eye, or by cuttings.
Storage: Dark, 50–60°F (10–16°C), in net bag or open basket of dry peat moss.
Features: Good choice for beds, borders, ground covers, mixed plantings in formal gardens and landscapes. Deer, rodent and slug, snail susceptible.

Bulb: *Begonia masoniana.* BEGONIACEAE.
Common name: Iron-Cross Begonia.
Description: Summer rhizome. Deciduous. Stands 1 ft. (30 cm) tall and 2 ft. (60 cm) wide. Rounded, toothed, deeply textured, hairy, fleshy green leaves, 6–12 in. (15–30 cm) long, with distinctive deep brown, iron-cross-shaped central markings, on fuzzy leaf stalks.
Bloom: Insignificant flowers; grown for foliage.
Plant hardiness: Zones 6–11.
Soil: Damp, well-drained soil. Fertility: Rich. 5.5–6.5 pH.
Planting: Spring in partial shade, zones 6–8; autumn, zone 9–11. Space 12–16 in. (30–40 cm) apart, 4 in. (10 cm) deep. In containers, space 3–4 in. (75–100 mm) apart, ¼ in. (6 mm) deep.
Care: Moderate. Water only when soil surface dries; water sparingly in winter. Fertilize bimonthly spring–summer. Prune sparingly. Pinch growth tips to promote fullness. Propagate by cuttings, division. Divide when crowded.
Storage: Dark, 50–60°F (10–16°C), in net bag or open basket of dry peat moss.
Features: Good choice for hanging baskets, containers in shade gardens. Good as houseplant. Powdery mildew susceptible.

Bulb: *Begonia* × *rex-cultorum* hybrids. BEGONIACEAE.
Common name: Rex Begonia.
Description: Summer rhizome. Deciduous. Stands 6–12 in. (15–30 cm) tall and 1–3 ft. (30–90 cm) wide. Heart-shaped, toothed, textured, brown, green, pink, white, yellow, always colorfully variegated leaves, 6–12 in. (15–30 cm) long, on fuzzy leaf stalks. King or painted-leaf begonia, *B. rex*, the progenitor of its many hybrids, is rarely found in cultivation as a pure species.
Bloom: Insignificant flowers; grown for foliage.
Plant hardiness: Zones 6–11.
Soil: Damp, well-drained soil. Fertility: Rich. 5.5–6.5 pH.
Planting: Spring in partial shade, zones 6–8; autumn, zone 9–11. Space 12–16 in. (30–40 cm) apart, 4 in. (10 cm) deep. In containers, space 3–4 in. (75–100 mm) apart, ¼ in. (6 mm) deep.

Care: Moderate–challenging. Water only when soil surface dries; water sparingly in winter. Fertilize bimonthly spring–summer. Prune sparingly. Pinch growth tips to promote fullness. Propagate by cuttings, division. Divide when very crowded.
Storage: Dark, 50–60°F (10–16°C), in net bag or open basket of dry peat moss.
Features: Good choice for hanging baskets, containers. Good for color. Powdery mildew susceptible.

Bulb: *Begonia* × *tuberhybrida.* BEGONIACEAE.
Common name: Tuberous Begonia.
Description: Summer or autumn tuber, depending on hybrid. Deciduous. Stands or trails 1–3 ft. (30–90 cm) tall or long. Wing-shaped, short, bronze green leaves with reddish veins.
Bloom: Summer–autumn. Orange, pink, purple, red, white, yellow, variegated. Multiple open single, double, or very double, sometimes fringed or ruffled, often fragrant flowers to 8 in. (20 cm) wide. Available in erect or cascading forms.
Plant hardiness: Zones 4–11; ground hardy, zones 7–11.
Soil: Moist, well-drained soil. Fertility: Rich. 5.5–6.5 pH.
Planting: Spring in partial shade. Space 6–12 in. (15–30 cm) apart, at soil level.
Care: Moderate. Keep moist spring–autumn. Fertilize monthly year-round. Mulch, zones 4–8. Protect from frost, zones 4–6; heat, zones 10–11. Propagate by cutting tubers into sections, each with an eye.
Storage: Dark, 40–50°F (4–10°C), in net bag or open basket of dry peat moss.
Features: Good choice for hanging baskets, beds, borders, containers in indoor gardens and landscapes. Deer, rodent and slug, snail susceptible.

Bulb: *Belamcanda chinensis*. IRIDACEAE.

Common name: Blackberry Lily (Leopard Flower).

Description: Summer rhizome. Deciduous. Stands 2–4 ft. (60–120 cm) tall. Narrow, swordlike, upright or arching, long green leaves.

Bloom: Late summer–early autumn. Orange speckled with red. Multiple open, star-shaped flowers, 2–3 in. (50–75 mm) wide, form black, berrylike, clustered seed in autumn.

Plant hardiness: Zones 5–10; ground hardy, zones 8–10.

Soil: Moist, well-drained, sandy loam. Fertility: Rich–average. 6.5–7.0 pH.

Planting: Spring in full sun to partial shade. Space 10–12 in. (25–30 cm) apart, slightly below soil level.

Care: Easy. Keep moist during growth. Fertilize until buds form. Propagate by division in autumn, seed in spring. Best left undisturbed.

Storage: Dark, 50–60°F (10–16°C), in porous container of dampened peat moss.

Features: Good choice for borders in cottage gardens and landscapes. Dry berries for arrangements. Deer, rodent resistant. Mosaic virus susceptible.

Bulb: *Caladium* × *hortulanum* (*C. bicolor*). ARACEAE.

Common name: Fancy-Leaved Caladium (Elephant's-Ear).

Description: Summer tuber. Deciduous. Stands 1–3 ft. (30–90 cm) tall. Broad, heart-shaped, short to long, light green leaves, 2–18 in. (50–450 mm) long, depending on hybrid, with pink, red, and white variegated patterns. Common cultivars include *C.* × *hortulanum* 'Ace of Hearts', 'Fire Chief', 'Little Miss Muffet', 'Red Flash', and 'White Queen'.

Bloom: Insignificant flowers; grown for foliage.

Plant hardiness: Zones 8–11; ground hardy, zones 9–11.

Soil: Moist, well-drained soil. Fertility: Rich. 5.5–6.5 pH.

Planting: Late spring in partial to full shade. Space 1 ft. (30 cm) apart, 1–3 in. (25–75 mm) deep.

Care: Moderate. Keep moist spring–autumn. Allow soil to dry when leaves wither. Fertilize until buds form. Protect from wind. Propagate by offsets.

Storage: Dark, 50–60°F (10–16°C), in net bag or open basket of dry peat moss.

Features: Good choice for borders, containers, edgings, mixed plantings in shade, tropical gardens. Good with annual and perennial flowers. Deer, rodent resistant.

Bulb: *Calochortus* species. LILIACEAE.

Common name: Mariposa Lily (Fairy-Lantern, Star Tulip).

Description: Spring bulb. Deciduous. About 60 species. Stands to 30 in. (75 cm) tall. Oval to lance-shaped, short to midlength green leaves. Commonly cultivated species include *C. albus*, fairy-lantern; *C. amabilis*, golden globe tulip; *C. kennedyi*, desert mariposa; *C. nuttallii*, sego lily; and *C. venustus*, white mariposa.

Bloom: Late spring–early summer. Pink, purple, red, white, yellow. Upright or nodding, cup-shaped or globelike flowers, 1–2 in. (25–50 mm) long, sometimes with hairy or spidery bracts.

Plant hardiness: Zones 5–10; ground hardy, zones 5–8.

Soil: Moist, well-drained loam. Fertility: Average. 5.5–6.5 pH, depending on species.

Planting: Autumn in full sun to partial shade. Space 12–18 in. (30–45 cm) apart, 3–5 in. (75–125 mm) deep. In containers, space 1 in. (25 mm) apart, 2–3 in. (50–75 mm) deep.

Care: Moderate–challenging. Keep moist spring–early summer. Fertilize first year in spring. Deadhead flowers and withered stalks. Mulch. Lift in hot, moist-summer areas. Propagate by offsets, seed.

Storage: Dark, 60°F (16°C), in net bag or open basket of dry peat moss or sand.

Features: Good choice for accents, containers in rock gardens. Good for cutting. Deer, rodent susceptible.

Bulb: *Camassia* species. LILIACEAE.

Common name: Camass.

Description: Spring bulb. Deciduous. About 5 species. Stands 30–48 in. (75–120 cm) tall. Narrow, straplike, long green leaves.

Bloom: Late spring. Blue, purple, white. Multiple star-shaped, sometimes lightly fragrant flowers, 1–2 in. (25–50 mm) wide, in tiers vertically along stalk.

Plant hardiness: Zones 3–9; ground hardy, zones 5–9.

Soil: Moist, well-drained humus. Fertility: Rich–average. 6.0–6.5 pH.

Planting: Early autumn in full sun to partial shade. Space 6–10 in. (15–25 cm) apart, 4–6 in. (10–15 cm) deep.

Care: Easy. Keep moist spring–summer. Fertilize in spring. Propagate by division, seed. Best left undisturbed.

Storage: Dark, 50–60°F (10–16°C), in porous container of dampened peat moss.

Features: Good choice for beds, borders, ground covers, mixed plantings in meadow, woodland gardens and water features. Good for cutting. Naturalizes. Deer, rodent susceptible.

> **W A R N I N G**
> All parts of *Camassia* species are hazardous if eaten. Avoid planting in areas frequented by children or pets.

Bulb: *Canna* species and hybrids. CANNACEAE.

Common name: Canna. (Indian-Shot).

Description: Summer rhizome. Semi-evergreen. About 9 species and many hybrids. Stands 4–16 ft. (1.2–4.9 m) tall. Showy, large, long, wide, bronze, green, purple, red, white, yellow leaves with variegated patterns, sometimes fringed.

Bloom: Summer–autumn. Orange, pink, red, white, yellow, bicolor. Multiple clustered, terminal, repeat-blooming flowers to 6 in. (15 cm) wide.

Plant hardiness: Zones 3–11; ground hardy, zones 7–11.

Soil: Moist, well-drained soil. Fertility: Rich. 6.0–7.0 pH.

Planting: Autumn in full sun, zones 7–11; spring, zones 3–6. Space 1–2 ft. (30–60 cm) apart, slightly below soil level.

Care: Easy. Keep moist spring–early autumn. Fertilize until buds form. Deadhead flowers. Mulch. Protect from frost, zones 3–6. Propagate by division.

Storage: Dark, 50–60°F (10–16°C), in net bag or open basket of dry peat moss.

Features: Good choice for accents, borders, containers in tropical gardens and landscapes. Attracts hummingbirds. Slug, snail susceptible.

Bulb: *Chionodoxa* species. LILIACEAE.

Common name: Glory-of-the-Snow.

Description: Spring bulb. Deciduous. About 6 species. Stands 3–6 in. (75–150 mm) tall. Narrow, straight, short, deep green leaves. Commonly cultivated species include *C. luciliae*, glory-of-the-snow; and *C. sardensis*.

Bloom: Early spring–summer. Blue, pink, white, with white centers. Multiple 6-pointed, star-shaped flowers, to 1 in. (25 mm) wide, in tiers of 6 to 10 flowers ascending vertically along stalk.

Plant hardiness: Zones 3–8; ground hardy, zones 5–8.

Soil: Moist, well-drained soil. Fertility: Average. 6.0–7.0 pH.

Planting: Autumn in full sun to partial shade. Space 2 in. (50 mm) apart, 4 in. (10 cm) deep.

Care: Easy. Keep moist autumn–spring, damp in summer. Fertilize until buds form. Mulch, zones 7–8. Protect from frost. Propagate by division, offsets, seed. Divide only when crowded.

Storage: Dark, 50–60°F (10–16°C), in net bag or open basket of dry peat moss.

Features: Good choice for borders, containers, massed plantings in cottage, meadow, rock, woodland gardens. Naturalizes. Endangered species.

Bulb: *Clivia* species. AMARYLLIDACEAE.
Common name: Woodlily (Bush Lily).
Description: Spring tuberous root. Evergreen. About 4 species. Stands to 2 ft. (60 cm) tall. Straplike, arching, long, deep green leaves. Commonly cultivated species include *C. caulescens*, *C. miniata*, and *C. nobilis*.
Bloom: Late winter–spring. Mostly orange with yellow centers, sometimes deep red, yellow. Multiple flared, trumpet-shaped flowers, to 2 in. (50 mm) wide, in round, branching clusters, on a stout, fleshy stalk, to 18 in. (45 cm) tall.
Plant hardiness: Zones 9–11; ground hardy, zones 9–11.
Soil: Moist, well-drained soil. Fertility: Average. 6.5–7.0 pH.
Planting: Autumn or spring in partial to full shade. Space 6–12 in. (15–30 cm) apart, slightly below soil level. Space mature transplants 12–16 in. (30–40 cm) apart. In containers sized at least 2 in. (50 mm) wider than root, one to a container.
Care: Easy. Keep moist. Drought tolerant. Fertilize in summer. Mulch. Propagate by division, offsets, seed.
Storage: Indirect light, 40–60°F (4–16°C), in pot of dry to slightly damp soil.
Features: Good choice for beds, borders, containers, massed plantings in woodland gardens. Popular houseplant. Pest and disease resistant.

Bulb: *Colchicum autumnale.* LILIACEAE.
Common name: Meadow Saffron (Autumn Crocus, Fall Crocus, Mysteria, Wonder Bulb).
Description: Autumn corm. Deciduous. Stands 4–12 in. (10–30 cm) tall. Straplike, midlength green leaves in spring after blooms. Common cultivars include *C. autumnale* 'Alboplenum', 'Album', 'Plenum', 'Pleniflorum', 'The Giant', and 'Waterlily'.
Bloom: Late summer–early autumn. Purple, rose, white, yellow. Multiple flared, crocuslike, single- or double-petaled flowers, to 4 in. (10 cm) wide.
Plant hardiness: Zones 4–9; ground hardy, zones 7–9.
Soil: Moist, well-drained soil. Fertility: Average. 5.5–6.5 pH.
Planting: Summer in full sun. Space 6–8 in. (15–20 cm) apart, 3–4 in. (75–100 mm) deep.

Care: Easy. Keep moist autumn–spring. Fertilize during growth. Mulch, zones 4–5. Propagate by division, cormels in summer. Divide only when crowded.
Storage: Dark, 40–50°F (4–10°C), in net bag or open basket of dry peat moss.
Features: Good choice for borders in woodland gardens. Naturalizes. Deer, rodent resistant.

Bulb: *Colocasia esculenta.* ARACEAE.
Common name: Elephant's-Ear (Taro).
Description: Summer tuber. Evergreen. Stands 3–7 ft. (90–215 cm) tall. Exotic, broad, heart-shaped, long, velvety, blue green leaves, often with contrasting veins.
Bloom: Insignificant flowers; grown for foliage.
Plant hardiness: Zones 8–11; ground hardy, zones 8–11.
Soil: Very moist, well-drained soil. Fertility: Rich. 5.5–6.5 pH.
Planting: Late spring in partial shade. Space 2 ft. (60 cm) apart, 2–3 in. (50–75 mm) deep.

> **WARNING**
> Foliage and roots of *Colocasia esculenta* are hazardous if eaten. Avoid planting in areas frequented by children or pets.

Care: Moderate. Keep very moist spring–summer. Fertilize monthly. Mulch. Propagate by offsets.
Storage: Dark, 50–60°F (10–16°C), in net bag or open basket of dry peat moss.
Features: Good choice for accents, beds, borders in tropical gardens and landscapes. Deer, rodent resistant.

Bulb: *Convallaria majalis.* LILIACEAE.
Common name: Lily-of-the-Valley (Muget).
Description: Spring rhizome. Deciduous. Stands to 8 in. (20 cm) tall. Broad, midlength, light to deep green leaves, sometimes variegated.
Bloom: Spring. Pink, white. Multiple nodding, bell-shaped, fragrant flowers, ¼–½ in. (6–12 mm) wide, in clusters of up to 20 per stem, form red, berrylike fruit in autumn.
Plant hardiness: Zones 2–9; ground hardy, zones 2–7.
Soil: Moist to damp, well-drained soil. Fertility: Rich–average. 5.5–6.5 pH.
Planting: Autumn or early spring in partial to full shade. Space 1–2 ft. (30–60 cm) apart, 1½–3 in. (38–75 mm) deep.
Care: Moderate. Keep moist year-round. Mulch. Propagate by division, pips; start pips 4–6 in. (10–15 cm) apart, transplant to garden in autumn.
Storage: Dark, 40–50°F (4–10°C), in porous container of dampened peat moss.
Features: Good choice for containers, ground covers in cottage, woodland gardens. Good for cutting. Naturalizes. Deer, rodent resistant. Mealybug susceptible.

Bulb: *Corydalis* species. FUMARIACEAE.
Common name: Fumaria (Fumewort).
Description: Spring rhizome or tuber. Deciduous. About 300 species. Stands 6–12 in. (15–30 cm) tall. Fernlike, midlength, blue green leaves. Commonly cultivated species include *C. aurea, C. bulbosa, C. cheilanthifolia, C. flexuosa, C. flavula, C. lutea, C. nobilis,* and *C. solida.*
Bloom: Spring. Blue, pink, purple, red, white, yellow. Multiple nodding, tubelike flowers, ½–1 in. (12–25 mm) long, in clusters.
Plant hardiness: Zones 4–8; ground hardy, zones 6–8.
Soil: Moist, well-drained, sandy loam. Fertility: Average. 6.0–8.0 pH.
Planting: Autumn in partial to full shade; spring for transplants. Space 3–6 in. (75–150 mm) apart, 2–4 in. (50–100 mm) deep.
Care: Easy. Keep moist in spring. Fertilize in spring. Mulch. Protect from heat. Propagate by division, seed.
Storage: Dark, 50–60°F (10–16°C), in porous container of dampened peat moss.
Features: Good choice for beds, borders in rock, shade, woodland gardens. Naturalizes, self-seeds. Deer and pest resistant.

Bulb: *Crinum americanum.* LILIACEAE.
Common name: Southern Swamp Lily.
Description: Spring bulb. Deciduous. Stands to 4 ft. (1.2 m) tall. Swordlike, arching, long green leaves. *C. Asiaticum,* spider lily; *C.* x *amarcrinum;* and *C. bulbispermum,* long-necked crinum, are closely related species with similar care needs.
Bloom: Spring–summer. Pink, white. Multiple flared, trumpet-shaped, star-petaled, fragrant flowers, 4–5 in. (10–13 cm) long, atop tall stalks.
Plant hardiness: Zones 7–11; ground hardy, zones 8–11.
Soil: Very moist soil or, in water features, marginal sites. Fertility: Rich–average. 5.5–6.5 pH.
Planting: Autumn in full sun, zones 9–11; spring, zones 7–8. Space 18 in. (45 cm) apart, with neck slightly above soil level or, in water features, submerged to 6 in. (15 cm) deep.
Care: Easy. Keep very moist. Fertilize during growth. Mulch, zones 8–9. Protect from frost. Propagate by offsets, seed.
Storage: Dark, 50–60°F (10–16°C), in porous container of dampened peat moss.
Features: Good choice for accents, beds, borders, containers in meadow, water, woodland gardens or water feature margins. Deer, rodent resistant.

Bulb: *Crocosmia* x *crocosmiiflora*. IRIDACEAE.
Common name: Montebretia.
Description: Summer corm. Deciduous. Many hybrids. Stands to 4 ft. (1.2 m) tall. Swordlike, long green leaves.
Bloom: Summer. Orange, red, yellow. Multiple funnel-shaped flowers, 1½–2 in. (38–50 mm) wide, with widely flared petals, in tiers ascending vertically along one side of multiple angled, branching spikes.
Plant hardiness: Zones 6–11; ground hardy, zones 8–10.
Soil: Moist, well-drained soil. Fertility: Average. 5.5–6.5 pH.
Planting: Spring in partial shade. Space 4–6 in. (10–15 cm) apart, 2–4 in. (50–100 mm) deep.
Care: Easy. Keep moist spring–autumn. Drought tolerant. Fertilize in spring. Mulch, zones 6–7. Propagate by division, offsets, seed.
Storage: Dark, 50–60°F (10–16°C), in net bag or open basket of dry peat moss.
Features: Good choice for accents, beds, borders, containers, drifts, edgings, mixed plantings in cottage, formal, meadow gardens and landscapes. Attracts bees, hummingbirds. Naturalizes. Invasive zones 9–10. Disease resistant. Slug, snail susceptible.

Bulb: *Crocus longiflorus*. IRIDACEAE.
Common name: Longflower Crocus.
Description: Summer corm. Deciduous. Stands 4–6 in. (10–15 cm) tall. Grasslike, shiny, long green leaves.
Bloom: Autumn. Lilac, striped, variegated, with yellow throats. Multiple cup-shaped flowers, 3–5½ in. (75–140 mm) wide, with flared petals.
Plant hardiness: Zones 5–10; ground hardy, zones 8–10.
Soil: Moist, well-drained humus. Fertility: Rich–average. 6.5–7.5 pH.
Planting: Spring in partial shade. Space 4–6 in. (10–15 cm) apart, 3 in. (75 mm) deep.
Care: Easy. Keep moist spring–autumn. Drought tolerant. Fertilize in spring. Mulch, zones 5–6. Propagate by offsets, seed.
Storage: Dark, 50–60°F (10–16°C), in net bag or open basket of dry peat moss.
Features: Good choice for beds, borders, containers, drifts, edgings, mixed plantings, turfgrass in cottage, meadow, rock gardens and landscapes.

Bulb: *Crocus* species. IRIDACEAE.
Common name: Spring Crocus.
Description: Spring or autumn corm, depending on species. Deciduous. About 80 species. Stands 3–6 in. (75–150 mm) tall. Grasslike, short, deep green leaves.
Bloom: Autumn or late winter–early spring, depending on species. Purple, white, yellow, striped. Solitary cup-shaped, sometimes fragrant flowers, 1½–3 in. (38–75 mm) long, appear stemless.
Plant hardiness: Zones 3–10; ground hardy, zones 4–8.
Soil: Moist, well-drained soil. Fertility: Average. 5.0–6.5 pH.
Planting: Autumn in full sun to partial shade. Space 1–3 in. (25–75 mm) apart, 3–5 in. (75–125 mm) deep.
Care: Easy. Keep moist winter–spring. Fertilize when shoots appear. Mulch, zones 9–10. Propagate by division in autumn. Transplant container plants to garden in second year. Divide only when crowded.
Storage: Dark, 40–50°F (4–10°C), in net bag or open basket of dry peat moss.
Features: Good choice for beds, containers, edgings, massed plantings in cottage, meadow, woodland gardens. Naturalizes. Deer, rodent susceptible.

Bulb: *Cyclamen persicum.* PRIMULACEAE.

Common name: Florist's Cyclamen (Persian Violet).

Description: Spring tuber. Deciduous. Stands to 8 in. (20 cm) tall. Heart-shaped, mostly finely toothed, short green leaves, often marbled or veined with contrasting colors. *C. cilicium*, *C. coum*, *C. hederifolium*, and *C. purpurascens* are closely related species with similar care needs and different flower forms.

Bloom: Winter–spring. Pink, purple, red, white. Multiple shooting-star-shaped, often fragrant flowers to 2 in. (50 mm) long.

Plant hardiness: Zones 9–11; ground hardy, zones 9–10.

Soil: Moist, well-drained soil. Fertility: Rich. 6.0–6.5 pH.

Planting: Autumn in partial to full shade. Space transplants 4–6 in. (10–15 cm) apart, slightly above soil level.

Care: Easy. Keep moist autumn–spring. Fertilize monthly during growth; dilute fertilizer to half the recommended rate. Mulch. Propagate by division, seed. Best left undisturbed.

Storage: Dark, 60–70°F (16–21°C), in pot of dry to slightly damp soil.

Features: Good choice for beds, borders, containers, drifts in indoor, rock, shade, wildflower, woodland gardens. Good garden gift. Naturalizes.

Bulb: *Cyrtanthus elatus (C. purpurea, Vallota speciosa).* AMARYLLIDACEAE.

Common name: Scarborough Lily.

Description: Spring, summer, or autumn bulb. Evergreen. Stands 3 ft. (90 cm) tall. Straplike, long green leaves.

Bloom: Summer–autumn. Scarlet, sometimes pink, white. Multiple flared, 6-petaled, trumpet-shaped, often fragrant flowers 3–4 in. (75–100 mm) wide.

Plant hardiness: Zones 9–11; ground hardy, zones 9–11.

Soil: Moist, well-drained soil. Fertility: Rich. 6.0–6.8 pH.

Planting: Spring in full sun. Space 6–12 in. (15–30 cm) apart, at soil level. In 6-in. (15-cm) container, plant single bulb with its top ⅓ above soil.

Care: Moderate. Keep moist through bloom, dry when dormant. Fertilize until buds form. Protect from heat. Propagate by offsets in summer. Divide only when crowded.

Storage: Dark, 55–65°F (13–18°C), in net bag or open basket of dry peat moss.

Features: Good choice for accents, beds, containers in indoor, cottage, patio, small-space, woodland gardens. Popular houseplant. Pest and disease resistant.

Bulb: *Cyrtanthus* species. AMARYLLIDACEAE.

Common name: Fire Lily (Miniature Amaryllis).

Description: Summer bulb. Deciduous or evergreen. About 45 species. Stands to 18 in. (45 cm) tall. Straplike, arching, long green leaves. Commonly cultivated species include *C. angustifolius*, *C. mackenii*, *C. ochroleucus*, and *C. sanguineus*. See also Scarborough lily, *C. elatus*.

Bloom: Summer. Pink, red, white, yellow. Multiple flared, trumpet-shaped, amaryllis-like, fragrant flowers 1–1½ in. (25–38 mm) long.

Plant hardiness: Zones 7–11; ground hardy, zones 9–11.

Soil: Damp, well-drained humus. Fertility: Rich. 6.2–6.8 pH.

Planting: Spring in full sun to partial shade. Space 6–12 in. (15–30 cm) apart, with neck at soil level.

Care: Easy. Keep damp spring–summer; avoid overwatering. Reduce watering after bloom. Fertilize until buds form. Protect from frost, zones 7–9. Propagate by division, offsets, seed.

Storage: Dark, 55–65°F (13–18°C), in net bag or open basket of dry peat moss.

Features: Good choice for beds, borders, containers in cottage, indoor gardens and landscapes. Good for cutting.

DAHLIA

The roughly 27 wild species of the *Dahlia* genus native to Mexico and Central and northern South America have yielded more than 20,000 hybrid cultivars in a wide range of colors, forms, and sizes. There are flowers ranging from 2–12 in. (50–305 mm) wide in every color except blue, bedding dahlias as short as 16 in. (40 cm), and bushes as tall as 8 ft. (2.4 m). All are summer bloomers, have tuberous roots, and are tender; dahlias are planted as annuals in USDA Plant Hardiness Zones 4–8, or are lifted after bloom and stored for spring replanting.

Dahlias were a mainstay of heritage gardens at the turn of the 20th century. Their popularity has surged recently as many gardeners rediscovered them. The most popular cultivars stem from hybrids of *D. coccinea* and *D. pinnata (D. rosea)*.

Classification of dahlias is an active sport, and the current listing of official categories may be obtained from the American Dahlia Society. Dahlias are usually divided for award purposes into 15 commonly recognized groups.

1. Single Dahlia
2. Anemone Dahlia
3. Colarette Dahlia
4. Peony Dahlia
5. Formal Decorative Dahlia
6. Informal Decorative Dahlia
7. Orchid-Flowering Dahlia
8. Ball Dahlia
9. Pompon Dahlia
10. Incurved Cactus Dahlia
11. Straight Cactus Dahlia
12. Semi-Cactus Dahlia
13. Miscellaneous Dahlia
14. Fimbriated Dahlia
15. Waterlily or Nymphaea-Flowered Dahlia

Dahlias are long-lasting, summer-blooming flowers that frequently extend their showy bloom into autumn. They usually are planted in spring as soon as soil temperatures have warmed, after several weeks with minimum nighttime air temperatures above 60°F (16°C). For USDA Plant Hardiness Zones 9–11, plant in autumn and allow the tuberous roots to remain in the garden through the winter. In other regions, lift them after their blooms fade in autumn, divide and store them through the winter in a net bag or open basket of dry peat moss, and replant them in spring.

Divide your dahlias in spring only when your plantings have become overcrowded.

Choose dahlia cultivars according to your planned use. Small varieties, to 2 ft. (60 cm) tall, are best used as bedding plants, borders, and edgings. Massed plantings of taller forms, to 8 ft. (2.4 m) tall, make an eye-catching landscape feature suitable for island beds, fenced gardens, or raised beds separated by winding paths. *D. imperialis*, tree dahlia, is a perennial, multistemmed, treelike form, 10–20 ft. (3–6 m) tall, well-suited for planting as an accent or in backgrounds and borders that will showcase its showy blossoms.

Plant dahlias in rich humus, 4–6 in. (10–15 cm) deep, depending on cultivar, spacing them to allow good air circulation and staking tall cultivars to support them.

Bulb: *Dahlia* hybrids. ASTERACEAE (COMPOSITAE).

Common name: Dahlia.

Description: Summer tuberous root. Deciduous. Stands to 15 ft. (4.5 m) tall. Swirl of 2 or 3 simple, medium-toothed, short to midlength, deep green leaves.

Bloom: Summer–autumn. Bronze, orange, pink, purple, red, white, yellow, bi- or multicolored. Multiple flowers, to 1 ft. (30 cm) wide, with single or layered petals, in widely varied forms from simple or pompon to cactuslike.

Plant hardiness: Zones 4–11; ground hardy, zones 9–11.

Soil: Moist, well-drained soil. Fertility: Rich. 6.5–7.0 pH.

Planting: Autumn in full sun, zones 9–11; spring, zones 4–8. Space 2–3 ft. (60–90 cm) apart, 6 in. (15 cm) deep. Space dwarf hybrids 10–12 in. (25–30 cm) apart, 4–5 in. (10–13 cm) deep.

Care: Moderate. Keep moist summer–autumn; allow soil surface to dry between waterings. Fertilize at planting, then monthly until buds form. Mulch. Pinch foliage buds when 1 ft. (30 cm) tall to promote fullness. Lift, zones 4–7. Protect from frost, wind. Stake to support. Propagate by division in spring.

Storage: Dark, 50–60°F (10–16°C), in net bag or open basket of dry peat moss.

Features: Good choice for accents, beds, borders, in cottage gardens and landscapes. Good for cutting. Deer, rodent and slug, snail susceptible.

Bulb: *Dicentra cucullaria.* FUMARIACEAE.
Common name: Dutchman's-Breeches.
Description: Spring tuber. Deciduous. Stands to 10 in. (25 cm) tall. Feathery, deeply toothed, short, light blue green leaves form a midheight bush. *D. chrysantha,* golden eardrops; *D. eximia,* fringed bleeding heart; *D. formosa,* western bleeding heart; and *D. spectabilis,* common bleeding heart, are closely related species with similar care needs.
Bloom: Spring–summer. Pink, white, often tipped in cream yellow. Multiple unique, nodding, pantaloon-shaped flowers, to 2 in. (50 mm) long, in branching clusters.
Plant hardiness: Zones 3–10; ground hardy, zones 4–9.
Soil: Moist, well-drained humus. Fertility: Rich. 5.5–6.5 pH.
Planting: Autumn in partial shade. Space 12–18 in. (30–45 cm) apart, 1–2 in. (25–50 mm) deep.
Care: Moderate. Keep moist during growth. Fertilize until buds form. Remove withered foliage. Mulch. Protect from heat. Propagate by division in autumn, seed in spring.
Storage: Dark, 50–70°F (10–21°C), in net bag or open basket of dry peat moss.
Features: Good choice for beds, borders in natural, rock gardens. Self-seeds. Disease resistant.

Bulb: *Epipactis gigantea.* ORCHIDACEAE.
Common name: Stream Orchid
Description: Summer pseudobulb. Deciduous. Stands to 3 ft. (90 cm) tall. Lance-shaped, deep green leaves, to 8 in. (20 cm) long.
Bloom: Summer. Pink, rose, with contrasting veins. Multiple nodding, orchid-like flowers, to 1 in. (25 mm) long, in long, trailing spikes.
Plant hardiness: Zones 9–10.
Soil: Moist, well-drained sand and humus or, in water features, shoreline sites. Fertility: Rich. 6.0–6.5 pH.
Planting: Spring in full sun. Space 2–3 ft. (60–90 cm) apart, 4–6 in. (10–15 cm) deep. Plant in buried containers to establish and maintain rich soil needs.
Care: Moderate. Keep evenly moist. Fertilize until buds form. Remove withered foliage. Mulch. Protect from heat. Propagate by cuttings, division, seed.
Storage: In-ground. Maintain year-round.
Features: Good choice for accents, beds, borders in natural, rock gardens and water feature shorelines. Disease resistant.

Bulb: *Eranthis hyemalis.* RANUNCULACEAE.
Common name: Winter Aconite.
Description: Spring tuber. Deciduous. Stands 2–6 in. (50–150 mm) tall. Radiating, saucerlike, short, bright green leaves. A related species, *E. cilicica,* bears reddish-tinged new foliage and larger blooms. *E. cilicica, E. pinnatifida,* and *E.* × *tubergenii* are closely related species with similar care needs.
Bloom: Late winter–spring. Yellow. Cheerful, bright, cup-shaped, waxy flowers, 1–1½ in. (25–38 mm) wide, with collarlike foliage beneath.
Plant hardiness: Zones 3–8; ground hardy, zones 5–8.
Soil: Moist, well-drained humus. Fertility: Rich–average. 6.0–6.5 pH.
Planting: Early autumn in full sun to partial shade. Space 2½–3 in. (63–75 mm) apart, 2 in. (50 mm) deep.
Care: Easy. Keep moist year-round; reduce watering after bloom. Fertilize in winter when growth first appears. Mulch. Protect from heat. Propagate by division, seed.
Storage: Dark, 40–50°F (4–10°C), in porous container of dampened peat moss.
Features: Good choice for borders, containers, edgings, mixed plantings in natural, rock, shade, woodland gardens and landscapes. Naturalizes. Deer, rodent resistant.

Bulb: *Erythronium* species. LILIACEAE.
Common name: Dog-Tooth Violet (Trout Lily).
Description: Spring corm. Deciduous. About 25 species. Stands 4–24 in. (10–60 cm) tall. Two tongue-shaped, short to midlength green leaves, often mottled with brown, purple, or white.
Bloom: Spring. Pink, purple, rose, white, yellow, sometimes with color contrasts. Solitary to many nodding, star-shaped flowers, to 2 in. (50 mm) wide.
Plant hardiness: Zones 3–9; ground hardy, zones 5–9.
Soil: Moist, well-drained soil. Fertility: Rich. 5.0–6.5 pH.
Planting: Early autumn in open to partial shade, zones 5–9; spring, zones 3–4. Space 6–8 in. (15–20 cm) apart, 3–4 in. (75–100 mm) deep.
Care: Moderate–challenging. Keep moist in spring. Fertilize annually in spring. Mulch. Propagate by division, seed. Best left undisturbed.
Storage: Dark, 50–60°F (10–16°C), in porous container of dampened peat moss.
Features: Good choice for beds, borders, drifts, edgings, mixed plantings in rock, shade, woodland gardens. Naturalizes, self-seeds.

Bulb: *Eucomis* species. LILIACEAE.
Common name: Pineapple Lily.
Description: Summer bulb. Deciduous. About 15 species. Stands 12–30 in. (30–75 cm) tall. Straplike, midlength green leaves, sometimes speckled with purple and often with ruffled edges.
Bloom: Summer. Greenish white, yellow, often edged in purple. Multiple star-shaped, sometimes fragrant flowers, ½–1¼ in. (12–32 mm) long, in snug tiers along stalk, form pineapple-like foliage clusters above flowers.
Plant hardiness: Zones 6–11; ground hardy, zones 9–11.
Soil: Moist, well-drained soil. Fertility: Rich. 6.0–6.5 pH.
Planting: Spring in partial shade. Space 6–8 in. (15–20 cm) apart, slightly below soil level.
Care: Easy. Keep moist spring–autumn. Fertilize during growth. Mulch. Protect from heat, zones 10–11. Propagate by offsets, seed. Divide when crowded.
Storage: Dark, 55–65°F (13–18°C), in net bag or open basket of dry peat moss.
Features: Good choice for beds, borders, containers in shade, woodland gardens. Good for cutting. Deer, rodent susceptible.

Bulb: *Freesia* species and hybrids. IRIDACEAE.
Common name: Freesia.
Description: Summer corm. Deciduous. About 19 species, many hybrids. Stands to 18 in. (45 cm) tall. Grasslike, midlength, bright green leaves, in fans.
Bloom: Spring, zones 7–10; summer, zones 4–6. Blue, orange, pink, purple, red, white, yellow. Multiple flared, sometimes double, trumpet-shaped, fragrant flowers, to 2 in. (50 mm) long, in branching, linear clusters.
Plant hardiness: Zones 4–10; ground hardy, zones 9–10.
Soil: Moist, well-drained soil. Fertility: Rich–average. 6.5–7.5 pH.
Planting: Autumn in full sun, zones 9–10; spring, zones 4–8. Space 3–4 in. (75–100 mm) apart, 1–2 in. (25–50 mm) deep. Best planted annually as new stock, zones 4–8.
Care: Moderate. Keep moist autumn–spring. Fertilize until buds form; dilute fertilizer to half the recommended rate. Deadhead. Mulch. Protect from wind. Stake to support. Propagate by offsets, seed.
Storage: Dark, 50–60°F (10–16°C), in net bag or open basket of dry peat moss.
Features: Good choice for beds, borders, containers in cottage, indoor gardens and landscapes. Good for cutting. Naturalizes.

Bulb: *Fritillaria meleagris.* LILIACEAE.
Common name: Fritillary (Checkered Lily).
Description: Spring bulb. Deciduous. Stands 16 in. (40 cm) tall. Radiating, grasslike, midlength green leaves. Close relative of crown imperial, *F. imperialis,* with bare stalks, radiating flowers, and leafy crown.
Bloom: Spring. Brown, pink, purple, violet, white, with variegated geometric patterns. Multiple nodding, bell-shaped, musk-fragrant flowers, 2–2¹/₂ in. (50–63 mm) long, in clusters.
Plant hardiness: Zones 2–9; ground hardy, zones 4–7.
Soil: Moist, well-drained, sandy loam. Fertility: Average. 6.0–7.5 pH.
Planting: Autumn in full sun to partial shade, zones 4–9; spring, zones 2–3. Space 6–8 in. (15–20 cm) apart, 4–8 in. (10–20 cm) deep.
Care: Easy–moderate. Keep moist spring–summer. Fertilize in spring. Mulch, zones 8–9. Protect from heat. Propagate by offsets. Best left undisturbed.
Storage: Dark, 40–50°F (4–10°C), in net bag or open basket of dry peat moss.
Features: Good choice for accents, beds, borders in meadow, woodland gardens and landscapes. Deer, rodent resistant.

Bulb: *Galanthus* species. AMARYLLIDACEAE.
Common name: Snowdrop.
Description: Spring bulb. Deciduous. More than 15 species. Stands 6–12 in. (15–30 cm) tall. Narrow, short to midlength, bright green leaves in groups of 2 or 3. Commonly cultivated species include *G. elwesii,* giant snowdrop; and *G. nivalis,* common snowdrop.
Bloom: Late winter–early spring. White. Solitary nodding, drop-shaped flowers 1–2 in. (25–50 mm) wide.
Plant hardiness: Zones 2–10; ground hardy, zones 4–7.
Soil: Moist, well-drained humus. Fertility: Rich–average. 6.0–6.5 pH.
Planting: Autumn in filtered sun to partial shade. Space 4–6 in. (10–15 cm) apart, 3–4 in. (75–100 mm) deep.
Care: Easy. Keep moist autumn–spring. Fertilize in spring. Mulch. Propagate by division when dormant.
Storage: Dark, 40–50°F (4–10°C), in net bag or open basket of dry peat moss.

Features: Good choice for beds, borders, containers, edgings, mixed plantings, turfgrass in meadow, rock, woodland gardens. Naturalizes. Deer, rodent resistant.

Bulb: *Galtonia candicans.* LILIACEAE.
Common name: Summer Hyacinth.
Description: Summer bulb. Deciduous. Stands 2–4 ft. (60–120 cm) tall, to 10 in. (25 cm) wide. Straplike, long green leaves.
Bloom: Late summer–autumn. Green white, white. Nodding, bell-shaped, fragrant flowers to 1¹/₂ in. (38 mm) long, in tiers ascending vertically along a tall stalk.
Plant hardiness: Zones 6–10; ground hardy, zones 8–10.
Soil: Moist, well-drained humus. Fertility: Rich–average. 5.5–6.5 pH.
Planting: Autumn in full sun to partial shade, zones 9–10; spring, zones 6–8. Space 8–12 in. (20–30 cm) apart, 6 in. (15 cm) deep.
Care: Easy–moderate. Keep moist in spring, dry in summer. Fertilize during growth. Mulch, zones 6–8. Propagate by offsets, seed.
Storage: Dark, 50–60°F (10–16°C), in net bag or open basket of dry peat moss.
Features: Good choice for accents, backgrounds, beds, borders, containers, mixed plantings in cottage, natural, woodland gardens and landscapes. Good for cutting. Deer, rodent and pest resistant. Slug, snail susceptible.

GLADIOLUS

The *Gladiolus* genus includes between 250 and 300 species—few in cultivation—plus many thousands of hybrids and cultivars, all closely related to *Iris* and mostly native to the Mediterranean region of Europe, Africa, and the Middle East. All are spring- and summer-blooming, semi-hardy or tender corms, planted in spring, lifted during autumn, divided, and stored for replanting in USDA Plant Hardiness Zones 3–6 or planted during autumn and allowed to overwinter beneath protective mulch in zones 7–11, where they are hardy. Most commonly available cultivars are hybrid grandiflora gladiolus.

Gladiolus have spear-shaped, stiff leaves and trumpet-shaped, tubular, flaring flowers arranged vertically in spiking clusters, which appear from late spring to autumn, opening upwards along the spike.

As the most popular summer bulbs, they have a special place in the landscape garden. In addition to the large hybrid cultivars, several gladiolus groupings based on flower form and individual cultivated species exist. These include those listed above, at right.

Gladiolus are easily recognized in the landscape: prior to flowering, they are tall, statuesque plants with sword-shaped, deep green leaves. Beginning in late spring, a tall, canelike flower spike emerges from the center of the plant. Over several days, the flowers open from the bottom to the top of the spike, forming an exquisite, clustered, frequently frilled cascade in a mix of blends, colors, patterns, and stripes.

1. Baby or Miniature Gladiolus
2. Abyssinian Sword Lily
   (*G. callianthus*)
3. Butterfly Gladiolus
4. Byzantine Gladiolus
   (*G. communis* var. *byzantinum*)
5. Primrose Hybrid Gladiolus
6. Grecian Gladiolus
   (*G. illyricus*)

Plant gladiolus in beds or borders where they will be the central focus, or use them as edgings along fences, paths, or structures. When your needs call for using them in containers, choose large pots to allow them ample soil; regardless of use, plant in locations where they will receive at least 6 hours of full sunlight each day, except in zones 10–11, where the sun should be filtered.

They perform best in deep, well-drained, sandy soils containing ample humus. Soils should be kept moist throughout the entire time of sprouting, growth, and bud development, but the soil should be allowed to dry after their blooms fade.

When blooms dwindle, deadhead the spikes while allowing the foliage to remain until it begins to dry. Cut the foliage back to the corm and lift or mulch over them, depending on climate. Store lifted bulbs in a net bag or open basket filled with dry peat moss.

Gladiolus are treasured for cut-flower arrangements. For best results, water plants thoroughly the evening before cutting. Prune young flower stalks with partially opened blossoms using clean, sharp bypass hand shears, and immediately immerse the cut end in a bucket of cold water. After all of the flowers have been harvested, cut their stems again under water to avoid air pockets in the cut stem.

Bulb: *Gladiolus* species. IRIDACEAE.

Common name: Gladiolus (Corn Flag, Sword Lily).

Description: Summer corm. Deciduous. About 300 species, many hybrids. Stands 1–6 ft. (30–180 cm) tall. Narrow, swordlike, midlength to long green leaves.

Bloom: Spring, zones 7–11; summer, zones 3–6. Orange, pink, purple, red, white, yellow, multi-colored, striped. Multiple upturned, flared, trumpet-shaped, often fragrant flowers, 1–8 in. (25–200 mm) wide, in tiers along one side of stalk. Blooms open from bottom to top.

Plant hardiness: Zones 3–11; ground hardy, zones 7–11.

Soil: Moist, well-drained, sandy loam. Fertility: Rich–average. 6.0–6.5 pH.

Planting: Spring–early summer in full sun, zones 3–8; year-round, zones 9–11. Space 4–6 in. (10–15 cm) apart, 4–6 in. (10–15 cm) deep.

Care: Easy. Keep moist during growth; reduce watering after blooms fade. Fertilize until buds form. Mulch. Propagate by cormels, seed.

Storage: Dark, 50–60°F (10–16°C), in net bag or open basket of dry peat moss.

Features: Good choice for beds, borders, containers in cottage, rock gardens and landscapes. Good for cutting. Deer, rodent and thrips susceptible.

Bulb: *Gloriosa superba.* LILIACEAE.
Common name: Gloriosa Lily (Climbing Lily).
Description: Summer tuber. Deciduous. Stands to 8 ft. (2.4 m) tall. Oval, pointed, short to midlength green leaves on climbing vine.
Bloom: Spring–autumn. Orange, red, yellow, often edged in green, red, white, yellow. Many shooting-star-shaped flowers, 2–3 in. (50–75 mm) long, often with frilly, fully reflexed petals.
Plant hardiness: Zones 7–11; ground hardy, zones 9–11.
Soil: Moist, well-drained soil. Fertility: Rich. 6.0–6.5 pH.
Planting: Late spring–summer in full sun. Space 1–2 ft. (30–60 cm) apart, 2 in. (50 mm) deep.
Care: Moderate. Keep moist spring–summer. Fertilize during growth. Protect from wind. Stake to support. Propagate by division, offsets.
Storage: Dark, 60–70°F (16–21°C), in net bag or open basket of dry peat moss.
Features: Good choice for containers, fencelines, lattices, trellises in tropical gardens. Good for cutting. Deer, rodent susceptible.

Bulb: *Habranthus* species. AMARYLLIDACEAE.
Common name: Habranthus (Rain Lily).
Description: Summer bulb. Tropical evergreen. About 10 species. Stands to 9 in. (23 cm) tall. Narrow, straplike, arching, midlength to long green leaves. Commonly cultivated species include *H. brachyandrus, H. robustus,* and *H. tubispathus (H. andersonii).*
Bloom: Summer; may bloom again in autumn. Copper, pink, purple, red, white, yellow. Solitary or multiple flared, trumpet-shaped flowers, to 3 in. (75 mm) wide.
Plant hardiness: Zones 8–11; ground hardy, zones 10–11.
Soil: Moist, well-drained soil. Fertility: Average. 6.0–7.0 pH.
Planting: Spring in full sun to partial shade. Space 3–6 in. (75–150 mm) apart, 1–2 in. (25–50 mm) deep.
Care: Moderate. Keep moist in late spring, dry after bloom. In zones 9–11, resume watering after 4 weeks for repeat bloom. Fertilize during growth. Mulch. Propagate by offsets, seed.
Storage: Dark, 40–50°F (4–10°C), in net bag or open basket of dry peat moss.
Features: Good choice for accents, beds, borders, containers, edgings in cottage, patio, rock gardens and landscapes.

Bulb: *Heliconia bihai (H. humilis).* HELICONIACEAE.
Common name: Lobster-Claw (False Bird-of-Paradise).
Description: Summer rhizome. Evergreen. Stands to 4 ft. (1.2 m) tall. Spoonlike, long, mid- to deep green leaves. *H. angusta, H. brasiliensis, H. psittacorum, H. rostrata, H. schiedeana,* and *H. wagnerana* are closely related species with similar care needs.
Bloom: Summer–autumn. Orange, red, yellow. Multiple lobster-claw-like flowers, 5–10 in. (13–25 cm) long, in tiers vertically atop stalk.
Plant hardiness: Zones 10–11; ground hardy, zones 10–11.
Soil: Moist, well-drained, sandy loam. Fertility: Rich. 6.0–6.5 pH.
Planting: Spring–autumn in partial shade. Space 3 ft. (90 cm) apart, as deep as the soil level in the nursery container.
Care: Moderate. Keep moist spring–autumn. Fertilize monthly during growth. Protect from wind. Propagate by division.
Storage: In-ground. Maintain year-round.
Features: Good choice for accents, borders, bouquets, containers in tropical gardens and greenhouses. Good for cutting. Pest and disease resistant.

HEMEROCALLIS (DAYLILY)

The genus *Hemerocallis* comprises more than 15 species, all native to Europe and Asia. These close lily relatives now number several thousand cultivars. All are summer or autumn bloomers and have fleshy, tuberlike, fibrous roots. Many will survive reliably in USDA Plant Hardiness Zones 3–7 when protected by a layer of mulch from freeze-thaw cycles that otherwise would damage their roots.

Daylilies adapt well to most soil conditions and do best in sites with full to filtered sun. They also are good container plants, and they can serve many different landscape purposes: banks, beds, borders, ground covers, massed and mixed plantings.

A daylily's clustered, often fragrant blooms are carried on upright stalks above its sword-shaped, arching leaves. The lilylike flowers open sequentially along the stalk from bottom to top over a period of 3–4 weeks, with each blossom lasting a single day.

While the hybrid cultivars change from season to season, the listing above, at right, gives several choices in each color tested by the All-American Daylily Selection Council.

Daylilies, named for the combined Greek words, "day + beautiful", and with a history dating back to the Old Testament, are increasingly popular flowers for summer bloom in the home landscape. Species daylilies have yielded to many named hybrid cultivars with larger flowers in a greater range of colors than their parent plants. They have retained, however, their characteristic trait of flowering for a single day. Beginning in late spring, a flower spike emerges from the center of the plant. For several weeks, trumpetlike flowers in shades of orange, pink, purple, and yellow open in the morning then close at night, gradually working from the bottom to the top of the spike.

Plant them in moist, well-drained soil in a site with either full sun, or with sun for at least 5 hours each day. They do best in average soil that is acidic and are good companions for planting with other sun- and acid-craving plants.

When blooms dwindle, deadhead the spikes to induce a new flower spike to form. Cut the foliage back to the ground in autumn and mulch, or lift the roots and store them indoors for the winter in a porous container filled with damp peat moss, in a cool, dark spot.

Daylilies are best planted in multiple groups of 3 or 5 plants and in offset rows that slowly fill to create flowing drifts of colorful flowers.

Yellow or Gold:
'Bitsy' (2002*)
'Happy Returns'
'Lady Florence'
'Miss Victoria'
'Starstruck' (1998*)
'Yellow Landscape Supreme'

Orange:
'Gertrude Condon'
'Lady Lucille'
'Lady Melanie'
'Leebea Orange Crush' (2002*)
'Leprechauns Wealth'
'Rocket City'

Pink:
'Judith' (2002*)
'Lady Georgia'
'Lady Rose'
'Lullaby Baby' (2002*)
'Miss Tinkerbell'
'Strawberry Candy'

Red:
'Lady Scarlet'
'Little Joy'
'Pardon Me'

Bicolored:
'Black Eyed Stella' (1994*)
'Lady Eva'
'Radiant Greeting'

*All-American Daylily Selection

Bulb: *Hemerocallis* species. LILIACEAE.

Common name: Daylily.

Description: Summer tuberous root. Deciduous or evergreen. About 15 species. Stands to 6 ft. (1.8 m) tall. Narrow, swordlike, arching green leaves.

Bloom: Late spring–autumn. Orange, pink, purple, yellow. Multiple flared, trumpet-shaped, sometimes fragrant flowers, to 6 in. (15 cm) wide, in clusters.

Plant hardiness: Zones 3–10; ground hardy, zones 3–10.

Soil: Moist, well-drained soil. Fertility: Average–low. 5.0–7.0 pH.

Planting: Spring in full sun to partial shade, zones 3–6; autumn, zones 7–10. Space 15–24 in. (38–60 cm) apart, slightly below soil level.

Care: Easy. Keep moist spring–summer. Avoid fertilizing. Mulch. Propagate by dividing root sections, each with a growth point.

Storage: Dark, 40–50°F (4–10°C), in porous container of dampened peat moss.

Features: Good choice for beds, borders in cottage gardens and landscapes. Disease, pest resistant. Deer, rodent susceptible.

Bulb: *Hippeastrum* hybrids. AMARYLLIDACEAE.

Common name: Florist's Amaryllis.

Description: Tropical bulb. Deciduous or evergreen. About 80 species. Stands 8–24 in. (20–60 cm) tall. Broad, straplike, arching, midlength green leaves.

Bloom: Winter–spring indoors, spring–summer outdoors. Orange, pink, red, white. One to 5 usually flared, trumpet-shaped, occasionally fragrant flowers, 5–10 in. (13–25 cm) wide, on a tall single or double stalk.

Plant hardiness: Zones 7–11; ground hardy, zones 9–10.

Soil: Moist, well-drained soil. Fertility: Rich. 6.0–6.5 pH.

Planting: Autumn–winter in full sun. Space 1–2 ft. (30–60 cm) apart, slightly above soil level. In containers sized at least 2 in. (50 mm) wider than bulb, one bulb to a container, or several in very large containers.

Care: Easy. Keep moist early spring–autumn; avoid overwatering. Fertilize bimonthly until buds form. Deadhead flowers and withered stalks. Mulch. Propagate by offsets, seed. Allow bulbs to dry, cure for 1 month after lifting.

Storage: If deciduous, dark, 50–60°F (10–16°C), in net bag or open basket of dry peat moss; if evergreen, in porous container of dampened peat moss.

Features: Good choice for beds, containers in indoor, tropical gardens. Good for cutting, garden gifts. Deer, rodent susceptible.

Bulb: *Hyacinthoides* species (*Endymion* species, *Scilla* species). LILIACEAE.

Common name: Wood Hyacinth (English Bluebell, Spanish Bluebell).

Description: Spring bulb. Deciduous. About 4 species. Stands 20 in. (50 cm) tall. Narrow, arching, long green leaves.

Bloom: Spring. Blue, pink, rose, white. Multiple bell-shaped, fragrant flowers, ¾ in. (19 mm) long, in tiers vertically along a single stalk.

Plant hardiness: Zones 4–9; ground hardy, zones 5–9.

Soil: Moist to damp, well-drained soil. Fertility: Rich. 6.0–7.0 pH.

Planting: Autumn in full sun to partial shade. Space 4–6 in. (10–15 cm) apart, 3–5 in. (75–125 mm) deep.

Care: Moderate. Keep moist winter–spring, damp in summer. Fertilize until buds form. Mulch, zones 4–6. Propagate by division, offsets. Divide only when crowded.

Storage: Dark, 40–50°F (4–10°C), in net bag or open basket of dry peat moss.

Features: Good choice for drifts, mixed plantings in cottage, woodland gardens. Good for cutting. Naturalizes. Deer, rodent resistant.

Bulb: *Hyacinthus orientalis.* LILIACEAE.

Common name: Hyacinth (Garden Hyacinth).

Description: Spring bulb. Deciduous. Stands to 1 ft. (30 cm) tall. Straplike, curved-edged, midlength green leaves.

Bloom: Spring. Apricot, blue, orange, pink, purple, red, white, yellow. Multiple flared, trumpet-shaped, fragrant flowers, to 1 in. (25 mm) wide, in snug tiers vertically along the stalk, form cone-shaped plumes.

Plant hardiness: Zones 4–11; ground hardy, zones 6–9.

Soil: Moist, well-drained, sandy loam. Fertility: Rich. 5.0–6.5 pH.

Planting: Autumn in full sun to partial shade. Protect from sun in hot climates. Space 6–8 in. (15–20 cm) apart, 5–8 in. (13–20 cm) deep.

Care: Easy. Keep moist in spring. Fertilize until buds form. Mulch. Lift after bloom, zones 4–5 and 8–11. Propagate by offsets.

Storage: Dark, 40–50°F (4–10°C), in net bag or open basket of dry peat moss.

Features: Good choice for beds, borders, containers in cottage, indoor, woodland gardens. Naturalizes, depending on cultivar. Deer, rodent resistant.

Bulb: *Hymenocallis* species. AMARYLLIDACEAE.

Common name: Spider Lily (Crown-Beauty, Sea Daffodil).

Description: Summer bulb. Deciduous. More than 30 species. Stands 10–36 in. (25–90 cm) tall. Mostly straplike, long green leaves. Commonly cultivated species include *H. caroliniana*, inland spider plant; *H. narcissiflora (Ismene calathina)*, spider-lily; and *H. speciosa*, winter-spice.

Bloom: Summer. Ivory, white. Graceful, morning-glory-like, fragrant flowers, to 6 in. (15 cm) wide, with long, thin petal tendrils.

Plant hardiness: Zones 6–10; ground hardy, zones 8–10.

Soil: Moist, well-drained, sandy loam. Fertility: Rich–average. 6.0–6.5 pH.

Planting: Spring in full sun. Space 6–18 in. (15–45 cm) apart, depending on species, slightly above soil level.

Care: Easy. Keep moist spring–summer. Fertilize during growth. Mulch, zones 6–8. Protect from wind. Propagate by division, offsets, seed.

Storage: Dark, 60–70°F (16–21°C), in net bag or open basket of dry peat moss.

Features: Good choice for beds, borders, containers in indoor, tropical, water gardens. Good for cutting. Deer, rodent resistant.

Bulb: *Hypoxis* species. HYPOXIDACEAE.

Common name: Star Grass.

Description: Spring cormlike rhizome. Evergreen. About 150 species. Stands to 1 ft. (30 cm) tall. Narrow, grasslike, midlength green leaves. Commonly cultivated species include *H. hirsuta*, *H. hygrometrica*, and *H. leptocarpa*.

Bloom: Spring–summer. White, yellow. Solitary or multiple star-shaped flowers, to 1 in. (25 mm) wide, float amid narrow, chivelike leaves.

Plant hardiness: Zones 4–10; ground hardy, zones 6–10, depending on species.

Soil: Damp, well-drained soil. Fertility: Average. 4.0–5.0 pH.

Planting: Autumn in full sun, spring for transplants. Space 6–8 in. (15–20 cm) apart, 4 in. (10 cm) deep.

Care: Moderate–challenging. Keep damp; allow soil to dry between waterings. Drought tolerant. Fertilize occasionally during growth; dilute fertilizer to half the recommended rate. Propagate by division, offsets, seed.

Storage: Dark, 40–50°F (4–10°C), in net bag or open basket of dry peat moss.

Features: Good choice for beds, containers, edgings, mixed plantings in meadow, natural, woodland gardens.

Bulb: *Ipheion uniflorum (Brodiaea uniflora, Triteleia uniflora)*. LILIACEAE.

Common name: Spring Starflower (Star Grass).

Description: Spring bulb. Deciduous. Stands 6–8 in. (15–20 cm) tall. Flat, straplike, midlength, thin green leaves, with onionlike scent. Cultivars include *I. uniflorum* 'Album', 'Rolf Fiedler', 'Violaceum', and 'Wisley Blue', with varied growth habits, bloom sizes, and flower colors.

Bloom: Early spring. Blue, white, variegated. Simple star-shaped, often fragrant flowers to 1½ in. (38 mm) wide.

Plant hardiness: Zones 6–10; ground hardy, zones 6–9.

Soil: Moist, well-drained soil. Fertility: Average. 6.0–7.0 pH.

Planting: Autumn in full sun to partial shade. Space 2–4 in. (50–100 mm) apart, 2 in. (50 mm) deep.

Care: Easy. Keep moist autumn–spring. Fertilize during growth until established. Propagate by division, offsets. Divide when crowded.

Storage: Dark, 40–50°F (4–10°C), in net bag or open basket of dry peat moss.

Features: Good choice for borders, containers, drifts, edgings, massed plantings in meadow, natural, rock, woodland gardens. Naturalizes. Deer, rodent resistant.

IRIS

Over 200 species and countless hybrid cultivars make up the genus *Iris,* mostly native to the northern temperate zone. They are related to perennial plants of more than 60 other genera with bulbous, cormous, or rhizomatous roots.

All irises have grasslike or swordlike, deep green leaves, many in flat and fan-shaped, opposite habits. They bloom in late spring–early summer. While many species and cultivars are hardy, others are semi-hardy or tender.

The distinctive, often fleur-de-lis-shaped flowers comprise drooping outer sepals or falls, inner upright petals or standards, and narrow, central petals called style-branches.

The horticultural classification of iris is complex and has been subject to many changes over time. A current listing of official categories may be obtained from the American Iris Society.

In general, irises separate into the rhizomes, subgenus *Iris;* the true bulbs, subgenera *Xiphium* or *Scorpiris;* and a single-species subgenus with pseudo-rhizomatous roots, *Nepalenses.* The first two of these divisions contain most popular cultivated irises.

Plant rhizomatous irises in late summer or autumn, bulbous irises in autumn. A sunny spot is best, but most tolerate filtered, partial sun. Most irises perform best in moist, well-drained, humus-rich soil, and some are semi-aquatic plants that grow well in wet soil.

Rhizomatous Iris:
Bearded Iris (*I.* x *germanica*)
Crested Iris (*I. confusa, I. cristata, I. japonica, I. tectorum, I. wattii*)
Beardless Iris: Japanese (*I. ensata*); Louisiana (*I. brevicaulis, I. fulva, I. giganticaerulea, I. hexagona, I. pseudacorus*); Pacific (*I. douglasiana, I. innominata, I. versicolor*); Siberian (*I. sanguinea, I. siberica*); and Spuria (*I. chrysographes, I. clarkei, I. delavayi, I. dykesii, I. forrestii, I. wilsonii*)

Bulb Iris:
Reticulata Iris (*I. danfordiae, I. histrio, I. histrioides, I. reticulata*)
Juno Iris (*I. albomarginata, I. aucheri, I. bucharica, I. caucasica, I. fosterana*)
Dutch and Spanish Iris (*I.* x *tigitana, I. xiphium*)
English Iris (*I. latifolia, I. xiphiodes*)

In USDA Plant Hardiness Zones 4–9, most iris cultivars may be left in the ground until their plantings become crowded. They should be divided by cutting the rhizomes or separating offsets in late summer. Gardeners in cold-winter climates should lift irises in autumn, storing them in a net bag filled with dry peat moss until spring arrives, the soil warms, and they can be removed from storage and replanted.

Use irises for edgings, foreground plantings in beds and borders, and featured massed plantings, or plant them in pots and along the shorelines of water features.

Irises, especially flag irises, make excellent cut flowers. Water the plants well the evening before, and choose partially opened spikes. Immerse the cut stems in cool water immediately after cutting, then trim them again underwater prior to arranging.

Dozens of new cultivars are produced each year, in addition to heritage plants and garden favorites. It's best to try a small planting of 10 to 20 rhizomes in a single spot—to gauge how they will perform in your garden and climate or microclimate—before replacing reliable plants grown in prior seasons.

Bulb: *Iris cristata.* IRIDACEAE.
Common name: Crested Iris.
Description: Spring rhizome. Deciduous. Stands 8–10 in. (20–25 cm) tall. Narrow, flat, straplike, midlength, light green leaves.
Bloom: Spring. Lilac blue, white with yellow. Graceful 3-segment falls surround inner petals and raised, crestlike, sometimes hairy centers in fragrant flowers, to 2½ in. (63 mm) wide.
Plant hardiness: Zones 4–9.
Soil: Moist, well-drained humus. Fertility: Rich–average. 6.0–7.0 pH.
Planting: Autumn in open to partial shade. Space 6–12 in. (15–30 cm) apart, 2 in. (50 mm) deep, necks slightly above soil level.
Care: Easy. Keep moist autumn–spring. Fertilize during growth until established. Propagate by division, seed. Divide when crowded.
Storage: Dark, 40–50°F (4–10°C), in net bag or open basket of dry peat moss.
Features: Good choice for borders, containers, drifts, edgings, ground covers, slopes in meadow, natural, rock, woodland gardens. Slug, snail susceptible.

Bulb: *Iris reticulata.* IRIDACEAE.
Common name: Reticulated Iris.
Description: Spring bulb. Deciduous. Stands 18 in. (45 cm) tall. Flat, straplike, midlength, thin blue green leaves, to 6 in. (15 cm) long, appear after blooms fade.
Bloom: Early spring. Blue, lavender, purple, white, often with orange, yellow markings. Violet-scented flowers to 3 in. (75 mm) wide.
Plant hardiness: Zones 3–8.
Soil: Moist, well-drained humus. Fertility: Rich–average. 6.5–7.5 pH.
Planting: Autumn in full sun. Space 2–3 in. (50–75 mm) apart, 2–3 in. (50–75 mm) deep.
Care: Easy. Keep moist autumn–late spring; reduce watering in summer. Fertilize during growth until established. Propagate by division, seed. Divide when crowded.
Storage: Dark, 40–50°F (4–10°C), in net bag or open basket of dry peat moss.
Features: Good choice for borders, containers, drifts, edgings, ground covers, slopes in meadow, natural, rock, woodland gardens. Snail, slug susceptible.

WARNING
Sap of *Iris versicolor* causes skin irritation in sensitive individuals. Always wear gloves when you handle or prune bulbs.

Bulb: *Iris versicolor.* IRIDACEAE.
Common name: Blue Flag Iris (Wild Iris).
Description: Summer rhizome. Deciduous. Stands to 30 in. (75 cm) tall. Narrow, strap- or swordlike, upright or arching, long midgreen leaves.
Bloom: Summer. Blue, lavender, white. Solitary or multiple fleur-de-lis-shaped flowers, to 3 in. (75 mm) wide, with upright petals, form drooping beardless falls.
Plant hardiness: Zones 2–9; ground hardy, zones 4–7.

Soil: Moist soil or, in water features, marginal sites. Fertility: Average. 6.0–7.0 pH.
Planting: Autumn in full sun to partial shade. Space 1–2 ft. (30–60 cm) apart, 2–3 in. (50–75 mm) deep or, in water features, submerged to 6 in. (15 cm) deep.
Care: Easy. Keep moist year-round. Fertilize annually in spring. Mulch. Propagate by division in midsummer.
Storage: Dark, 40–50°F (4–10°C), in net bag or open basket of dry peat moss.
Features: Good choice for edgings, foregrounds, massed plantings, water margins in rock, shade gardens and water features. Good for cutting. Deer, rodent and iris borer susceptible.

Bulb: *Iris* × *germanica* hybrids. IRIDACEAE.
Common name: German Bearded Iris.
Description: Summer rhizome. Deciduous. Thousands of hybrids. Stands to 30 in. (75 cm) tall. Narrow, strap- or swordlike, upright or arching, long midgreen leaves.
Bloom: Summer or repeat blooming in spring and autumn, depending on hybrid. Nearly all colors, bicolored, blends. Multiple fleur-de-lis-shaped flowers, to 3 in. (75 mm) wide, with 3 upright and 3 nodding petals bearing drooping bearded falls, on succulent stalks.
Plant hardiness: Zones 4–10; ground hardy, zones 6–10.
Soil: Moist, well-drained humus. Fertility: Average. 6.0–7.0 pH.
Planting: Autumn in full sun to partial shade, zones 8–10; late summer, zones 4–7. Space 1–2 ft. (30–60 cm) apart, 2–4 in. (50–100 mm) deep, or cluster odd number of plants 6 in. (15 cm) apart for massed color.
Care: Easy. Keep moist during growth; reduce watering after flower stalks dry. Fertilize in spring. Mulch. Propagate by division in summer, seed in spring.
Storage: Dark, 40–50°F (4–10°C), in net bag or open basket of dry peat moss.
Features: Good choice for edgings, foregrounds, massed plantings in shade gardens. Good for cutting. Deer, rodent and iris borer susceptible.

Bulb: *Ixia* species and hybrids. IRIDACEAE.

Common name: Corn Lily.

Description: Spring corm. Deciduous. About 30 species. Stands 6–36 in. (15–90 cm) tall. Grasslike, short to long, bright green leaves. Hybrids of *I. maculata* are among the most commonly available *Ixia* cultivars.

Bloom: Late spring–summer. Orange, pink, red, white, yellow. Multiple open, 6-petaled, sometimes fragrant flowers, ½–1½ in. (12–38 mm) wide, with dark, contrasting centers, in dense spikes.

Plant hardiness: Zones 4–10; ground hardy, zones 7–9.

Soil: Moist, well-drained soil. Fertility: Average. 6.5–7.0 pH.

Planting: Autumn in full sun, zones 9–10; spring, zones 4–8. Space 3–4 in. (75–100 mm) apart, 2–3 in. (50–75 mm) deep.

Care: Easy. Keep soil moist during growth. Fertilize until buds form. Mulch, zones 7–8. Lift, zones 4–6. Propagate by cormels in autumn, seed in spring.

Storage: Dark, 50–60°F (10–16°C), in porous container of dampened peat moss or in pot of dry soil.

Features: Good choice for beds, borders, containers, drifts, mixed plantings in cottage, natural, small-space gardens and landscapes. Good for cutting. Naturalizes.

Bulb: *Kniphofia uvaria*. LILIACEAE.

Common name: Torch Lily (Red-Hot-Poker).

Description: Summer rhizome. Deciduous or semi-evergreen, depending on climate. Stands to 4 ft. (1.2 m) tall. Broad, grasslike, long, gray green leaves.

Bloom: Summer. Orange, red, turning yellow as blooms age. Many drooping, tube-shaped flowers, 1 in. (25 mm) long, in tiers vertically atop fleshy stalk, form flamelike clusters, 4–6 in. (10–15 cm) long.

Plant hardiness: Zones 5–10; ground hardy, zones 8–10.

Soil: Moist, well-drained, sandy loam. Fertility: Average–low. 5.5–6.5 pH.

Planting: Spring in full sun. Space 18 in. (45 cm) apart, barely covered.

Care: Moderate. Keep moist spring–early summer, dry late summer–autumn. Fertilize in spring. Mulch. Protect from frost, zones 5–7. Propagate by division, offsets, seed in early spring.

Storage: Dark, 40–50°F (4–10°C), in net bag or open basket of dry peat moss.

Features: Good choice for mixed plantings in tropical gardens. Good for cutting. Attracts hummingbirds. Evergreen in warm-winter climates.

Bulb: *Kohleria* hybrids. GESNERIACEAE.

Common name: Tree Gloxinia (Isoloma).

Description: Summer rhizome. Deciduous. Stands 1–3 ft. (30–90 cm) tall. Oval, finely toothed, short, velvety, deep gray green leaves, often with brown, purple, red undersides, and sometimes in a whorled pattern.

Bloom: Summer. Pink, red, yellow, often bicolored. Nodding, flared, tube-shaped flowers, 1–2 in. (25–50 mm) long, with round, bulbous petals.

Plant hardiness: Zones 8–11; ground hardy, zones 10–11.

Soil: Moist, well-drained, sandy loam. Fertility: Rich. 6.0–7.0 pH.

Planting: Spring in partial shade. Space 8–12 in. (20–30 cm) apart, 1–2 in. (25–50 mm) deep.

Care: Moderate. Keep moist spring–autumn. Fertilize monthly during growth. Mulch. Propagate by cuttings, division, seed. Prefers humid climates.

Storage: Dark, 50–60°F (10–16°C), in net bag or open basket of dry peat moss.

Features: Good choice for accents, beds, borders, containers in tropical gardens, landscapes, and greenhouses. Pest and disease resistant.

Bulb: *Lachenalia* species. LILIACEAE.
Common name: Cape Cowslip (Leopard Lily).
Description: Spring bulb. Deciduous. About 90 species. Stands 6–16 in. (15–40 cm) tall. Straplike, paired, short to midlength green, sometimes spotted, leaves.
Bloom: Late winter–early spring. Blue, pink, red, white, yellow, often edged in green, red, purple. Multiple cylinder-shaped flowers, to 1½ in. (38 mm) long, in tiers vertically along a single stalk.
Plant hardiness: Zones 8–10; ground hardy, zones 9–10.
Soil: Moist, well-drained, sandy loam. Fertility: Rich. 6.0–6.5 pH.
Planting: Autumn in full sun, zones 9–10; spring, zone 8. Space 4–6 in. (10–15 cm) apart, 2–3 in. (50–75 mm) deep.
Care: Easy. Keep moist autumn–spring. Fertilize until buds form. Deadhead flowers. Protect from frost, zone 8; sun in hot climates. Propagate by bulbils, seed. Prolong bloom by moving containers to a cool location at night.
Storage: Dark, 50–60°F (10–16°C), in net bag or open basket of dry peat moss.
Features: Good choice for beds, borders, containers, rock gardens. Popular houseplant. Good for cutting. Slug, snail susceptible.

Bulb: *Leucojum* species. AMARYLLIDACEAE.
Common name: Snowflake.
Description: Spring, summer, or autumn bulb. Deciduous. About 9 species. Stands to 16 in. (40 cm) tall. Straplike, midlength, thin green leaves.
Bloom: Spring, autumn, depending on species. White, with green, red, yellow tints. Dainty, nodding, bell-shaped flowers, ½–1 in. (12–25 mm) long, with spring green highlights.
Plant hardiness: Zones 3–11. Ground hardiness varies by species.
Soil: Moist to damp, well-drained soil, depending on species. Fertility: Average. 6.0–6.5 pH.
Planting: Autumn in full to filtered sun. Follow grower directions for each species. Space 4 in. (10 cm) apart, 4 in. (10 cm) deep.

Care: Easy. Keep moist autumn–late spring, dry in summer. Fertilize annually in spring. Mulch. Propagate by bulblets, division. Best left undisturbed.
Storage: Dark, 40–60°F (4–16°C), in net bag or open basket of dry peat moss.
Features: Good choice for beds, borders in meadow, natural, woodland gardens and water feature margins. Naturalizes. Deer, rodent resistant. *L. aestivum* blooms in spring; *L. autumnale*, summer–autumn; *L. vernum*, late winter–early spring.

Bulb: *Liatris* species. ASTERACEAE (COMPOSITAE).
Common name: Blazing-Star (Gay-Feather).
Description: Summer corm, rhizome. Deciduous. About 35 species. Stands 2–5 ft. (60–150 cm) tall. Needlelike, linear, short, hairy green leaves in tiers on a columnar spike. Common cultivars include *Liatris* 'Floristan White', 'Kobold', and 'Silvertips', with flowers of various colors.
Bloom: Late summer–autumn. Purple, white. Multiple tiny, flowerlike bracts in a feathery plume, 1 ft. (30 cm) long, in tiers along stalk. Showy blooms open from top to bottom.
Plant hardiness: Zones 3–10; ground hardy, zones 4–9, depending on species.
Soil: Moist, well-drained soil. Fertility: Average. 6.0–7.5 pH.
Planting: Spring in full sun. Space 6–8 in. (15–20 cm) apart, 1 in. (25 mm) deep.
Care: Easy. Keep moist spring–summer. Fertilize until buds form. Deadhead withered stalks. Mulch, zones 3–4. Stake to support. Propagate by cormels, division in autumn, seed in spring.
Storage: Dark, 50–60°F (10–16°C), in porous container of dampened peat moss.
Features: Good choice for beds, borders, mixed plantings in meadow, natural gardens. Attracts butterflies. Deer, rodent resistant.

LILIUM (LILY)

Nearly 100 species and thousands of hybrid members of the *Lilium* genus, all native to the northern temperate zone, are sensuous, sumptuous stars of cottage gardens and formal floral arrangements. Their showy flowers can be found along mountain trails and country roadsides as well as in carefully maintained gardens. All are summer bloomers; most are true bulbs lacking tunicate sheaths and with open scales. They are highly varied in appearance and growth habit.

Lilies first became popular in North American gardens beginning in the 1930s when mass cultivation by growers first produced reliable stocks.

While lilies are generally hardy, it's best to protect them with a heavy layer of mulch in USDA Plant Hardiness Zones 6–7 if they overwinter in the garden; all lilies benefit from mulching during the summer to keep the bulbs cool and moist while their foliage and flowers are in full or filtered sun.

The North American Lily Society classifies lilies in nine divisions, but most commonly planted cultivars comprise just four informal categories.

Popular Asiatic hybrids bloom in early summer, their open flowers facing up, down, or outward. Aurelian hybrids stem from the Asiatic hybrids but bloom in midsummer with fragrant, bowl-shaped or fluted flowers. Highly fragrant Oriental hybrids produce huge, bowl-shaped blossoms to 10 in. (25 cm) wide from late summer to early autumn. Species lilies vary in habit, flower form, and bloom season. Colors run the gamut of copper, pinks, reds, whites, and yellows, even bicolored, with stripes, bands, and speckles sometimes adding to their allure.

1. Asiatic Hybrid Lilies
2. Aurelian Hybrid Lilies
3. Oriental Hybrid Lilies
4. Species Lilies

Lily flowers can be shaped like trumpets, shallow bowls, funnels, or cups, sometimes with as many as 20 or 30 blossoms on a stem. Many have petals that curve back gracefully to reveal large red, brown, or golden anthers loaded with pollen on long green filaments.

Plant most lilies in the autumn; in zones 9 and 10, place the bulbs in the vegetable keeper of a refrigerator for 4–6 weeks prior to planting unless your bulbs have been prechilled. The planting soil should be deep, well-drained, and loose. Sandy loam mixed with humus is best; supplement it with organic matter, if needed. Lilies thrive when their tops are in the sun, while their roots are kept cool by the shade cast from shrubs or bushy perennials. Lilies in exposed sites should be heavily mulched during summer to keep their roots cool. Give them regular waterings to keep the soil moist.

Plant lilies in borders or containers, or group them as garden accents. They also are excellent cut flowers. Deadhead spent blooms, leaving as much stem as possible—the foliage provides energy to developing offsets and the parent bulb.

Force lilies by chilling their bulbs, then planting in a deep pot filled with soil, covering the bulbs. Water, then place the container in a warm, well-lit location.

Bulb: *Lilium* species and hybrids. LILIACEAE.
Common name: Lily.
Description: Summer bulb. Deciduous. About 100 species, many hybrids. Stands 2–6 ft. (60–180 cm) tall. Lance-shaped, midlength, shiny, bright green leaves.
Bloom: Summer. Orange, purple, red, white, yellow, often speckled with contrasts. Solitary or multiple trumpet- or star-shaped, often fragrant flowers, 4–10 in. (10–25 cm) wide, usually with prominent stamens and often with reflexed petals.
Plant hardiness: Zones 3–10; ground hardy, zones 6–10.
Soil: Moist, well-drained soil. Fertility: Rich. 6.0–6.5 pH.
Planting: Autumn or early spring in full sun to partial shade. Space 6–12 in. (15–30 cm) apart, 6–12 in. (15–30 cm) deep, depending on species.
Care: Easy. Keep moist in summer; water plant at base. Fertilize during growth. Deadhead flowers. Mulch in summer. Propagate by bulbils, offsets in autumn.
Storage: Dark, 40–50°F (4–10°C), in net bag or open basket of dry peat moss.
Features: Good choice for accents, backgrounds, borders, containers in cottage gardens and landscapes. Good for cutting. Naturalizes. Deer, rodent and leaf fungus, lily-mosaic virus susceptible.

Bulb: *Lycoris* species. AMARYLLIDACEAE.
Common name: Naked Lily (Magic Lily, Spider Lily).
Description: Autumn bulb. Deciduous. About 11 species. Stands to 2 ft. (60 cm) tall. Narrow, straplike, midlength green leaves usually appear after bloom.
Bloom: Late summer–autumn. Pink, red, white, yellow. Flared, trumpetlike, sometimes fragrant flowers, to 3 in. (75 mm) long, with extended stamens.
Plant hardiness: Zones 4–11, depending on species or cultivar; ground hardy, zones 7–10.
Soil: Moist, well-drained, sandy loam. Fertility: Average. 6.0–7.0 pH.
Planting: Late summer in full sun. Space 6–8 in. (15–20 cm) apart, slightly below soil level.
Care: Moderate–challenging. Keep moist autumn–spring, dry in summer. Fertilize during growth. Propagate by offsets, seed. Best left undisturbed. Reliable blooms require summer heat.
Storage: Dark, 50–60°F (10–16°C), in net bag or open basket of dry peat moss.
Features: Good choice for borders, containers, mixed plantings in meadow, rock gardens. Plant with ornamental grasses, ferns to provide foliage backdrop. *L. radiata* naturalizes. Deer, rodent resistant.

Bulb: *Mirabilis jalapa.* NYCTAGINACEAE.
Common name: Four O'Clock (Marvel of Peru).
Description: Summer tuber. Deciduous. Stands to 3 ft. (90 cm) tall. Alternate lance-shaped green leaves, 2–5 in. (50–125 mm) long. Common cultivars include *M. jalapa* 'Jingles', 'Teatime'. *M. longiflora* is a closely related species with similar care needs.
Bloom: Late summer. Pink, red, white, yellow, variegated. Many flute-shaped, fringed, fragrant flowers, to 2 in. (50 mm) wide, opening in late afternoon.
Plant hardiness: Zones 3–7, as annual; ground hardy, zones 8–11.
Soil: Damp to dry, well-drained, sandy soil. Fertility: Rich–average. 6.5–7.0 pH. Tolerates poor soil.
Planting: Spring in full sun to partial shade, after soil warms. Space 1–2 ft. (30–60 cm) apart, 2–3 in. (50–75 mm) deep.
Care: Easy. Keep moist during active growth. Fertilize annually in spring. Propagate by cuttings or by cutting tubers into sections, each with an eye.
Storage: Dark, 50–60°F (10–16°C), in net bag or open basket of dry peat moss.
Features: Good choice for accents, beds, borders, edgings, hedges in patios, poolside gardens and water features. Attracts hummingbirds. Smog and disease, pest resistant.

Bulb: *Muscari* species. LILIACEAE.
Common name: Grape Hyacinth.
Description: Spring bulb. Deciduous. About 40 species. Stands 4–12 in. (10–30 cm) tall. Straplike, short to midlength green leaves. Commonly cultivated species include *M. armeniacum*, *M. azureum*, *M. comosum*, *M. latifolium*, and *M. neglectum*.
Bloom: Early spring. Blue, purple, white. Multiple tube-shaped, fragrant flowers, to ¼ in. (6 mm) long, in tiers ascending along stalk, form a cone-shaped cluster.
Plant hardiness: Zones 3–11; ground hardy, zones 5–9.
Soil: Moist, well-drained, sandy loam. Fertility: Average. 6.0–7.0 pH.
Planting: Autumn in full sun to partial shade. Space 4–6 in. (10–15 cm) apart, 2–3 in. (50–75 mm) deep.
Care: Easy. Keep moist in spring, dry in summer. Fertilize until buds form. Mulch. Propagate by offsets, seed.
Storage: Dark, 40–50°F (4–10°C), in net bag or open basket of dry peat moss.
Features: Good choice for beds, borders, containers, drifts, edgings, massed plantings, mixed plantings in indoor, meadow, rock, woodland gardens. Good for cutting. Naturalizes. Deer, rodent resistant.

NARCISSUS (DAFFODIL)

After tulips, members of the 26-species *Narcissus* genus are the second-most commonly planted spring bulbs. Many thousands of hybrid cultivars have been registered in a staggering variety of growth habits, flower forms, and colors. All are members of the wide and diverse AMARYLLIDACEAE family. Most *Narcissus* species are native to the temperate regions of Europe and North Africa.

In common usage, daffodils have large blooms as compared to the often-clustered and smaller-flowered narcissus. *N. jonquilla*, jonquil, is another popular narcissus species. All narcissus are true, tunicate bulbs with tissue-paper-like outer coverings to protect them from moisture loss.

Most daffodils and narcissus are carefree plants—hardy, easily divided, and simple to propagate. Horticulturally, *Narcissus* are divided into three subgenera—*Ajax, Corbularia,* and *Narcissus*—and six horticultural sections—*Ganymedes, Hermione, Jonquilleae, Narcissus, Serotini,* and × *Queltia*—as well as into the 12 more commonly recognized divisions listed at right.

i.	Trumpet Narcissus
ii.	Large-Cupped Narcissus
iii.	Small-Cupped Narcissus
iv.	Double Narcissus
v.	Triandrus Narcissus
vi.	Cyclamineus Narcissus
vii.	Jonquilla Narcissus
viii.	Tazetta Narcissus
ix.	Poeticus Narcissus
x.	Species and Wild-Hybrid Narcissus
xi.	Split-Corona Narcissus
xii.	Other Narcissus

The divisions use such criteria as flower number, size, proportion, petal or corona arrangement, and color to distinguish between the many narcissus cultivars available, and they are used to create groups in flower competitions for award categories. Classification terminology and registration of cultivar names is governed by the American Daffodil Society in the United States and by the Royal Horticultural Society in Britain.

Daffodil, narcissus, and jonquil usually are planted in autumn as soil temperatures cool, remain in the ground over the winter, and bloom in the spring. They can be planted in a variety of garden sites, including beds and borders, or naturalized beneath grass or as part of a rock garden. They also are popular container plants grown for outdoor landscape and houseplant use.

Plant narcissus in moist to damp, well-drained, sandy loam mixed with peat moss to increase its acidity. They perform best in full sun, filtered sun beneath deciduous trees, and in open shade. Choose those cultivars that suit your needs for time of bloom as well as their appearance and color. Dwarf and unusual-flowered cultivars of many color combinations have been developed by growers.

Narcissus blooms last longest when they are planted in partially sunny locations with cool temperatures. Even indoor pots should be kept outdoors in a sunny, cool location until the buds begin to open. Massed plantings of narcissus in open landscapes and those allowed to naturalize in turfgrass are especially attractive, as are accents, borders, edgings, and pathside plantings in the landscape, and group plantings in pots at an entry or stairway.

Bulb: *Narcissus* species. AMARYLLIDACEAE.
Common name: Daffodil.
Description: Spring bulb. Deciduous. About 26 species, many hybrids. Stands 4–24 in. (10–60 cm) tall. Narrow, flat, straplike, light to deep green leaves.
Bloom: Late winter–early spring. Cream, orange, peach, pink, red, white, yellow, bicolored. Solitary or clustered trumpet-shaped, sometimes fragrant flowers, ½–2 in. (12–50 mm) wide, with short to long, smooth or ruffled crowns, surrounded by single or double, sometimes frilly petals.
Plant hardiness: Zones 3–9; ground hardy, zones 4–9.
Soil: Moist to damp, well-drained soil. Fertility: Rich–average. 5.5–6.5 pH.
Planting: Autumn in full sun to partial shade. Space 3–5 in. (75–125 mm) apart, 5–8 in. (13–20 cm) deep.
Care: Easy. Keep moist winter–spring. Fertilize until buds form. Propagate by division, offsets in autumn. Divide only when crowded.
Storage: Dark, 40–50°F (4–10°C), in net bag or open basket of dry peat moss.
Features: Good choice for hanging baskets, beds, borders, containers, drifts, massed plantings, slopes in cottage, meadow, natural, shade, woodland gardens. Good for cutting. Naturalizes. Deer, rodent resistant. Narcissus bulb fly susceptible; discard infested bulbs.

Bulb: *Nerine* species. AMARYLLIDACEAE.
Common name: Nerine (Guernsey Lily).
Description: Autumn bulb. Deciduous or semi-evergreen. About 30 species. Stands to 3 ft. (90 cm) tall. Straplike, midlength, deep green leaves.
Bloom: Autumn. Pink, red, white. Multiple wide-flared flowers, 2–3 in. (50–75 mm) wide, with curved petal tips, form ruffled clusters atop long stalks.
Plant hardiness: Zones 8–11; ground hardy, zones 8–11.
Soil: Moist, well-drained, sandy loam. Fertility: Average. 6.0–7.0 pH.
Planting: Late summer–autumn in full sun. Space 10–12 in. (25–30 cm) apart, slightly above soil level.
Care: Easy. Keep moist autumn–spring; allow deciduous varieties to dry in summer. Fertilize during growth. Mulch. Propagate by offsets. Best left undisturbed.
Storage: Dark, 50–60°F (10–16°C), in net bag or open basket of dry peat moss.
Features: Good choice for accents, backgrounds, beds, containers in cottage, indoor, small-space gardens and greenhouses. Good for cutting. Long-lasting flowers. Deer, rodent resistant.

WARNING
The bulb and foliage of *Ornithogalum* are hazardous if eaten. Avoid planting in gardens frequented by pets and children.

Bulb: *Ornithogalum* species. LILIACEAE.
Common name: Star-of-Bethlehem (Chincherinchee).
Description: Spring or summer bulb, depending on species. Deciduous. About 80 species. Stands 1–3 ft. (30–90 cm) tall. Straplike, arching, shiny green leaves.
Bloom: Spring or summer. Orange, green white, white, yellow. Multiple 6-petaled, star-shaped, often fragrant flowers, 2–5 in. (50–125 mm) wide, in tiers ascending vertically atop stalks.
Plant hardiness: Zones 4–10; ground hardy, zones 4–10, depending on species.
Soil: Moist, well-drained soil. Fertility: Rich. 6.0–7.0 pH.
Planting: Autumn in full sun to partial shade. Space 6–8 in. (15–20 cm) apart, 3–5 in. (75–125 mm) deep.
Care: Easy. Keep moist autumn–spring. Fertilize during growth. Mulch, zones 4–8. Propagate by offsets, seed.
Storage: Dark, 50–60°F (10–16°C), in net bag or open basket of dry peat moss.
Features: Good choice for beds, borders, containers in woodland gardens. Good for cutting. Naturalizes. Deer, rodent resistant.

Bulb: *Oxalis* species. OXALIDACEAE.
Common name: Wood Sorrel.
Description: Spring bulb, tuber, or rhizome, depending on species. Deciduous. More than 800 species. Stands 4–20 in. (10–50 cm) tall. Tufted, compact, or spreading. Cloverlike, small, gray green, green, red leaves, closing at night.
Bloom: Winter–summer. Pink, rose, white, yellow, often with contrasts at center. Solitary or multiple open or funnel-shaped flowers to 1 in. (25 mm) wide.
Plant hardiness: Zones 6–9; ground hardy, zones 7–9.
Soil: Moist, well-drained soil. Fertility: Rich–average. 6.5–7.5 pH.
Planting: Late summer–autumn in full sun to partial shade. Space 2 in. (50 mm) apart, 1–4 in. (25–100 mm) deep.
Care: Easy. Keep moist spring–summer. Fertilize only at planting. Mulch, zones 6–8. Propagate by division, offsets, seed in autumn.
Storage: Dark, 50–60°F (10–16°C), in net bag or open basket of dry peat moss.
Features: Good choice for containers, ground covers in indoor, small-space, woodland gardens. Tuberous and rhizomatous species are very invasive; plant in containers. Use only bulb species in garden soil plantings. Deer, rodent resistant.

Bulb: *Polianthes tuberosa.* AGAVACEAE.

Common name: Tuberose.

Description: Summer rhizome. Deciduous. Stands to 42 in. (1.1 m) tall. Narrow, grasslike, long green leaves.

Bloom: Summer–autumn. White. Multiple wide-flared, single or double, tube-shaped, very fragrant flowers, to 2½ in. (63 mm) wide, in tiers ascending and surrounding top of stalk.

Plant hardiness: Zones 8–11; ground hardy, zones 9–11.

Soil: Moist, well-drained humus. Fertility: Rich. **6.0–6.5** pH.

Planting: Spring in full sun. Space 6–8 in. (15–20 cm) apart, 2–3 in. (50–75 mm) deep. Best planted annually as new stock in cold-winter climates.

Care: Moderate–challenging. Keep moist spring–midautumn. Fertilize monthly during growth with acidic fertilizer. Propagate by division, offsets, seed.

Storage: Dark, 50–60°F (10–16°C), in net bag or open basket of dry peat moss.

Features: Good choice for accents, beds, borders, mixed plantings in cottage, meadow, small-space gardens. Good for cutting. Naturalizes freely. Fragrance used in perfumes. Deer, rodent resistant. Aphid susceptible.

Bulb: *Polygonatum* species. LILIACEAE.

Common name: Solomon's-Seal.

Description: Spring rhizome. Deciduous. Stands 2–4 ft. (60–120 cm) tall, 18–36 in. (45–90 cm) wide. Alternate, blue green to deep green leaves, to 7 in. (18 cm) long. Graceful, arching to erect. False Solomon's-seal, *Smilacina racemosa,* is a closely related species with similar appearance and care needs.

Bloom: Spring. Green white. Solitary or clustered nodding, bell-shaped flowers, ½ in. (12 mm) long, in 2 rows on arching stems, form black, berrylike fruit.

Plant hardiness: Zones 3–9.

Soil: Moist, well-drained loam. Fertility: Rich. 5.0–6.0 pH.

Planting: Autumn in partial to full shade. Space 18–36 in. (45–90 cm) apart, 2–3 in. (50–75 mm) deep.

Care: Easy–moderate. Keep evenly moist. Fertilize monthly during growth with acidic fertilizer. Mulch during summer. Propagate by division.

Storage: Dark, 40–50°F (4–10°C), in net bag or open basket of dry peat moss.

Features: Good choice for beds, borders, containers in natural, shade gardens. Use foliage in arrangements.

Bulb: *Puschkinia scilloides.* LILIACEAE.

Common name: Striped Squill.

Description: Spring bulb. Deciduous. Stands to 6 in. (15 cm) tall. Straplike, midlength, thin, deep green leaves.

Bloom: Late winter–spring. Blue white, white. Multiple nodding, partly flared, star-shaped flowers, ½ in. (12 mm) long, in dense clusters atop stalk.

Plant hardiness: Zones 3–10; ground hardy, zones 4–8.

Soil: Moist, well-drained, sandy loam. Fertility: Average. 6.0–7.5 pH.

Planting: Autumn in partial shade. Space 2–3 in. (50–75 mm) apart, 2–4 in. (50–100 mm) deep.

Care: Easy. Keep moist in spring, dry after bloom. Fertilize in spring. Mulch. Protect from heat. Propagate by offsets when dormant.

Storage: Dark, 40–50°F (4–10°C), in net bag or open basket of dry peat moss.

Features: Good choice for borders, containers, drifts, edgings in meadow, natural, woodland gardens and landscapes. Naturalizes. Deer, rodent resistant.

Bulb: *Ranunculus* species. RANUNCULACEAE.
Common name: Buttercup.
Description: Summer tuberous root, some suited to aquatic environments. Deciduous. About 250 species. Stands 1–2 ft. (30–60 cm) tall. Fernlike, deeply toothed, midlength, deep green leaves, thinly spaced. See also *R. asiaticus,* Persian buttercup.
Bloom: Spring–summer, depending on zone. Orange, white, yellow. Solitary round, single-petaled, cup-shaped, upright flowers, to ¾ in. (19 mm) wide, atop long stems.
Plant hardiness: Zones 3–11; ground hardy, zones 8–9.
Soil: Moist, well-drained sandy loam. Fertility: Average. 6.0–7.0 pH.
Planting: Spring in partial to full shade, zones 3–7; autumn, zones 8–11. Spacing depends on species. Soak tubers for 24 hours before planting.
Care: Easy. Keep moist autumn–early spring. Keep damp late spring–summer. Fertilize in spring. Mulch, zones 4–8. Propagate by division.
Storage: Dark, 50–60°F (10–16°C), in net bag or open basket of dry peat moss.
Features: Good choice for beds, borders, containers, drifts, ground covers in cottage, rock, shade, woodland gardens and water features. Good for cutting. Deer, rodent resistant. Slug, snail susceptible.

Bulb: *Ranunculus asiaticus* and hybrids. RANUNCULACEAE.
Common name: Persian Buttercup (Florist's Ranunculus).
Description: Spring tuberous root. Deciduous. Stands 18 in. (45 cm) tall. Fernlike, deeply toothed, midlength, deep green leaves, thinly spaced.
Bloom: Early spring–summer, depending on zone. Orange, pink, purple, red, white, yellow. Multiple round, single or tightly layered, camellia-like flowers, 1½ in. (38 mm) wide, atop long stems.
Plant hardiness: Zones 4–11; ground hardy, zones 8–9.
Soil: Moist, well-drained, sandy loam. Fertility: Average–low. 5.5–6.0 pH.
Planting: Autumn in full to filtered sun, zones 8–11; spring, zones 4–7. Space 4–6 in. (10–15 cm) apart, 1–2 in. (25–50 mm) deep. Soak tubers for 24 hours before planting.
Care: Easy. Keep moist autumn–early spring. Keep damp late spring–summer. Fertilize in spring. Mulch, zones 4–8. Propagate by division.
Storage: Dark, 50–60°F (10–16°C), in net bag or open basket of dry peat moss.
Features: Good choice for beds, borders, containers, drifts in cottage, rock gardens. Good for cutting. Deer, rodent resistant. Slug, snail susceptible.

Bulb: *Romneya coulteri.* PAPAVERACEAE.
Common name: Matilija Poppy (Sunny-Side-Up).
Description: Summer rhizome. Deciduous. Stands to 8 ft. (2.4 m) tall. Smooth, oak-leaf-shaped, deeply toothed, midlength, hairy, gray green leaves, to 4 in. (10 cm) long, in triplets along stalk.
Bloom: Late spring–summer. White with large, bright yellow centers. Very showy, terminal, upright, open, cup-shaped, ruffled, crepelike flowers, to 8 in. (20 cm) wide.
Plant hardiness: Zones 7–11.
Soil: Moist, well-drained soil. Fertility: Average–low. 6.0–7.5 pH.
Planting: Autumn in full sun. Space 3–5 ft. (90–150 cm) apart, 4–6 in. (10–15 cm) deep for root divisions, 1–2 in. (25–50 mm) deep for scarified seed.
Care: Moderate. Keep moist winter–spring; reduce watering summer–autumn. Drought tolerant when established. Fertilize in spring. Propagate by division, seed, suckers.
Storage: In-ground. Protect from frost.
Features: Good choice for accents, backgrounds in arid, natural, rock gardens. Pest resistant. Fungal disease susceptible.

Bulb: *Scadoxus* species (*Haemanthus* species). AMARYLLIDACEAE.

Common name: Blood Lily.

Description: Spring bulb. Deciduous. About 9 species. Stands 1–2 ft. (30–60 cm) tall. Broad, long, bright green leaves.

Bloom: Spring–summer. Coral, red, white. Multiple brushlike flowers, 1 in. (25 mm) wide and long, in clusters to 9 in. (23 cm) wide, form berrylike fruit.

Plant hardiness: Zones 8–11; ground hardy, zones 9–11.

Soil: Moist, well-drained soil. Fertility: Rich. 5.5–6.5 pH.

Planting: Spring in full sun to partial shade. Space 1 ft. (30 cm) apart, at soil level. Choose container with ample space for root growth.

Care: Moderate. Keep moist spring–summer. Fertilize until buds form. Protect from frost, zone 8. Propagate by offsets in spring.

Storage: Best left undisturbed. If lifted, dark, 50–60°F (10–16°C), in net bag or open basket of dry peat moss.

Features: Good choice for beds, containers in patio gardens and landscapes. Good for cutting. Rodent, slug, snail and mosaic virus susceptible.

Bulb: *Scilla* species. LILIACEAE.

Common name: Squill.

Description: Spring bulb. Deciduous. About 90 species. Stands 4–18 in. (10–45 cm) tall. Straplike, short to long green leaves.

Bloom: Early spring. Blue, pink, purple, white. Multiple star-shaped flowers, to 1 in. (25 mm) wide, form tiers along a single stalk or tight clusters atop foliage, depending on species.

Plant hardiness: Zones 3–11; ground hardy, zones 4–8, depending on species.

Soil: Moist, well-drained humus. Fertility: Rich. 6.0–7.0 pH.

Planting: Autumn in full sun to partial shade, depending on species. Space 4–6 in. (10–15 cm) apart, 4 in. (10 cm) deep.

Care: Easy. Keep moist autumn–summer. Fertilize monthly during growth. Mulch. Propagate by offsets, seed.

Storage: Dark, 40–50°F (4–10°C), in net bag or open basket of dry peat moss.

Features: Good choice for borders, containers, edgings, massed plantings, paths in formal, small-space, woodland gardens. Good for cutting. Naturalizes.

Bulb: *Sinningia speciosa* hybrids (*Gloxinia speciosa*). GESNERIACEAE.

Common name: Florist's Gloxinia.

Description: Tropical tuber. Deciduous. Stands to 1 ft. (30 cm) tall. Oblong, finely toothed, midlength, hairy green leaves, often with reddish undersides.

Bloom: Year-round indoors, summer outdoors. Blue, orange, pink, purple, red, white, yellow, often banded or speckled with contrasts. One to 2 nodding, funnel-shaped, sometimes ruffled flowers to 5 in. (13 cm) wide.

Plant hardiness: Zones 10–11; ground hardy, zones 10–11.

Soil: Moist, well-drained humus. Fertility: Rich. 6.0–6.5 pH.

Planting: Early summer in partial shade, outdoors; year-round, indoors. Space 1 ft. (30 cm) apart, 1 in. (25 mm) deep. In containers sized at least 2 in. (50 mm) wider than tuber, one to a container.

Care: Easy. Keep moist during growth. Fertilize monthly during growth. Mulch. Protect from rain, wind. Propagate by cuttings, division, seed.

Storage: Dark, 60°F (16°C), in net bag or open basket of dry peat moss or pot of barely damp soil.

Features: Good choice for beds, borders, containers in indoor, tropical gardens. Popular houseplant. Good garden gift.

Bulb: *Sparaxis* species. IRIDACEAE.

Common name: Wandflower (Harlequin Flower).

Description: Summer corm. Deciduous. About 6 species. Stands to 2 ft. (60 cm) tall. Narrow, swordlike, arching, light green leaves. Commonly cultivated species include *S. grandiflora*, *S. pillansii*, and *S. tricolor*. See also *Ixia* species and hybrids, closely releated plants.

Bloom: Spring–early summer. Orange, pink, purple, red, white, yellow, bicolored. Multiple cup- or star-shaped flowers, to 2 in. (50 mm) wide, with flared petals and contrasting centers.

Plant hardiness: Zones 4–10; ground hardy, zones 7–10.

Soil: Moist, well-drained, sandy loam. Fertility: Average. 6.0–7.0 pH.

Planting: Autumn in full sun, zones 8–10; spring, zones 4–7. Space 3–4 in. (75–100 mm) apart, 2–4 in. (50–100 mm) deep. Best planted annually as new stock, zones 5–7.

Care: Easy. Keep moist autumn–spring. Fertilize monthly during growth. Mulch, zones 4–7. Propagate by cormels, offsets, seed.

Storage: Dark, 50–60°F (10–16°C), in net bag or open basket of dry peat moss.

Features: Good choice for accents, beds, borders, containers, foregrounds, mixed plantings in cottage gardens and landscapes. Good for cutting. Naturalizes. Deer, rodent susceptible.

Bulb: *Sternbergia lutea*. AMARYLLIDACEAE.

Common name: Winter Daffodil (Lily-of-the-Field).

Description: Autumn bulb. Deciduous. Stands to 1 ft. (30 cm) tall. Narrow, straplike, midlength green leaves. Common cultivars include *S. lutea* 'Major'.

Bloom: Autumn. Bright yellow. Solitary, freesialike, glossy flowers, 1½ in. (38 mm) long, form berrylike seed.

Plant hardiness: Zones 6–9; ground hardy, zones 7–9.

Soil: Moist, well-drained soil. Fertility: Rich–average. 6.5–7.5 pH.

Planting: Late summer in full sun. Space 4–6 in. (10–15 cm) apart, 4–6 in. (10–15 cm) deep. In containers, space 2–3 in. (50–75 mm) apart.

Care: Easy. Keep moist autumn–spring, dry in summer. Fertilize during growth. Mulch, zones 6–7. Propagate by division, offsets, seed.

Storage: Dark, 40–50°F (4–10°C), in net bag or open basket of dry peat moss.

Features: Good choice for accents, beds, borders, containers, edgings in meadow, natural, rock gardens. Deer, rodent resistant. Spider mite susceptible.

Bulb: *Tricyrtis hirta*. LILIACEAE.

Common name: Toad Lily.

Description: Summer rhizome. Deciduous. Stands 2–3 ft. (60–90 cm) tall. Alternate, broad, oval, upright, arching, hairy, light green or variegated leaves. Common cultivars include *T. hirta* 'Miyazaki', with pink, white flowers bearing red spots; 'Miyazaki Gold', with yellow-edged leaves; and 'Variegata', with white-variegated leaves. *T. formosana (T. stolonifera)* is a closely related species with similar care needs.

Bloom: Summer–autumn. Yellow, purple, white with distinctive spots. Solitary or clustered orchidlike flowers, to 1 in. (25 mm) wide.

Plant hardiness: Zones 4–10; ground hardy, zones 8–10.

Soil: Moist, well-drained humus or, in water features, shoreline sites. Fertility: Rich. 5.0–6.0 pH.

Planting: Spring in partial shade. Space 18–24 in. (45–60 cm) apart, 4 in. (10 cm) deep.

Care: Moderate. Keep moist. Fertilize monthly during growth with acidic fertilizer. Mulch. Propagate by division, seed.

Storage: Dark, 50–60°F (10–16°C), in net bag or open basket of dry peat moss.

Features: Good choice for accents, hanging baskets, containers, entrances, paths, tree planters in shade, tropical, woodland gardens and water feature shorelines. Good for cutting. Disease resistant. Slug, snail susceptible.

Bulb: *Tigridia pavonia.* IRIDACEAE.
Common name: Tiger Flower (Mexican Shell Flower, One-Day Lily, Shell Flower).
Description: Summer corm. Deciduous. Stands to 3 ft. (90 cm) tall. Swordlike, vertically ribbed, narrow, stiff green leaves, to 18 in. (45 cm) long.
Bloom: Summer–autumn. Orange, pink, purple, red, white, yellow. Cup-shaped or open, tripetaled, nearly triangular flowers, to 3 in. (75 mm) wide, with inset, curved, inner petals and speckled, contrasting-colored centers. Succession of blooms, each lasting a single day.
Plant hardiness: Zones 4–11; ground hardy, zones 7–9.
Soil: Moist, well-drained soil. Fertility: Average. 6.0–7.0 pH.
Planting: Late spring in full sun, zones 4–6, for bloom following season; autumn, zones 7–11. Space 4–6 in. (10–15 cm) apart, 2–3 in. (50–75 mm) deep.
Care: Moderate. Keep moist spring–summer. Fertilize during growth. Mulch, zones 4–8. Lift, zones 4–6. Protect from heat, frost. Propagate by cormlets, offsets, seed.
Storage: Dark, 50–60°F (10–16°C), in net bag or open basket of dry peat moss.
Features: Good choice for beds, borders, containers, mixed plantings in tropical gardens and landscapes. Deer, rodent and spider mite susceptible.

Bulb: *Trillium grandiflorum.* LILIACEAE.
Common name: Snow Trillium.
Description: Spring rhizome. Deciduous. Stands 12–18 in. (30–45 cm) tall. Oval or heart-shaped, smooth, deep green, veined leaves, to 6 in. (15 cm) long, in distinctive triads on a single stem. See also *Trillium* species, wake-robin.
Bloom: Spring. White becoming rose or purple. Single or double, 3-part flowers, 2–3 in. (50–75 mm) wide.
Plant hardiness: Zones 5–9.
Soil: Moist, well-drained humus. Fertility: Rich. 6.5–7.0 pH.
Planting: Spring in partial shade. Space 5 in. (13 cm) apart, 4 in. (10 cm) deep.
Care: Easy. Keep evenly moist. Fertilize annually in spring. Mulch. Propagate by division, seed.
Storage: In-ground. Protect from freeze-thaw cycles.
Features: Good choice for beds, borders, ground covers in natural, rock, shade, woodland gardens. Good for massed plantings with ferns. Disease and pest resistant.

Bulb: *Trillium* species. LILIACEAE.
Common name: Wake-Robin (Trillium).
Description: Spring rhizome. Deciduous. About 30 species. Stands 6–20 in. (15–50 cm) tall. Oval, short to midlength green leaves divided in whorled groups of 3 leaflets. Commonly cultivated species include *T. chloropetalum (T. sessile), T. erectum,* and *T. ovatum.* See also *T. grandiflorum,* snow trillium.
Bloom: Spring. Purple, white, yellow. Solitary flowers, 2–3 in. (50–75 mm) wide, usually with 3 sharp-pointed petals.
Plant hardiness: Zones 2–9; ground hardy, zones 4–8.
Soil: Moist, well-drained humus. Fertility: Rich. 6.0–7.0 pH.
Planting: Autumn in partial to full shade. Space 6–12 in. (15–30 cm) apart, 4 in. (10 cm) deep.
Care: Moderate. Keep evenly moist year-round. Fertilize annually in spring. Mulch. Propagate by division, seed.
Storage: Dark, 40–50°F (4–10°C), in porous container of dampened peat moss.
Features: Good choice for accents, borders, drifts, edgings, mounds in natural, rock, shade, woodland gardens. Pest and disease resistant. Deer, rodent susceptible.

Bulb: *Tritonia* species. IRIDACEAE.

Common name: Flame Freesia.

Description: Spring bulb. Deciduous. About 50 species. Stands to 18 in. (45 cm) tall. Straplike, arching, midlength to long, green leaves. Commonly cultivated species include *T. crocata*, saffron tritonia; *T. hyalina;* and *T. rubrolucens.*

Bloom: Early summer–autumn. Orange, pink, red, white, yellow. Multiple cup-shaped flowers 1–2 in. (25–50 mm) wide.

Plant hardiness: Zones 7–10; ground hardy, zones 9–10.

Soil: Moist, well-drained soil. Fertility: Rich–average. 6.0–7.0 pH, depending on species.

Planting: Autumn in full sun, zones 9–10; spring, zones 7–8. Space 6–10 in. (15–25 cm) apart, 3–4 in. (75–100 mm) deep.

Care: Easy. Keep moist autumn–early summer, dry in summer. Fertilize monthly during growth. Mulch. Propagate by division.

Storage: Dark, 40–50°F (4–10°C), in net bag or open basket of dry peat moss.

Features: Good choice for beds, borders, containers in indoor, tropical gardens and landscapes. Good for cutting. Naturalizes. Deer, rodent susceptible.

Bulb: *Tropaeolum tuberosum.* TROPAEOLACEAE.

Common name: Bitter Indian Nasturtium (Tuber Nasturtium).

Description: Summer tuber. Deciduous. Stands to 15 ft. (4.5 m) tall. Rounded, deeply lobed, short green leaves. *T. peregrinum*, canary-bird vine, is a closely related species with similar care needs. See also *T. majus,* garden nasturtium, an annual species.

Bloom: Spring–summer. Orange, purple, red, yellow, sometimes speckled, striped with contrasts. Nodding, fuchsialike flowers, to 1 in. (25 mm) long.

Plant hardiness: Zones 8–11; ground hardy, zones 9–11.

Soil: Moist, well-drained, sandy loam. Fertility: Average. 5.5–7.0 pH.

Planting: Autumn in full sun, zones 9–11; spring, zone 8. Space 3–5 ft. (90–150 cm) apart, 1–2 in. (25–50 mm) deep.

Care: Moderate. Keep moist during growth. Fertilize during growth. Propagate by division, seed.

Storage: Dark, 50–60°F (10–16°C), in net bag or open basket of dry peat moss.

Features: Good choice for fencelines, lattices, trellises, walls in cottage gardens and landscapes. Attracts bees. Pest and disease resistant.

Bulb: *Tulbaghia violacea.* AMARYLLIDACEAE.

Common name: Society Garlic.

Description: Summer bulb. Evergreen. Stands to 30 in. (75 cm) tall. Swordlike, midlength, thin, gray green leaves. Cultivars include *T. violacea* 'Silver Lace', 'Tricolor', and 'Variegata', with colorful leaf variegations.

Bloom: Late spring–summer. Lavender, white. Multiple flared, tube-shaped, star-flared, fragrant flowers, ¾–1 in. (19–25 mm) long, in clusters atop tall, narrow stems.

Plant hardiness: Zones 8–11; ground hardy, zones 9–11.

Soil: Moist to damp, well-drained, sandy loam. Fertility: Average. 6.5–7.5 pH.

Planting: Spring in full sun. Space 12–18 in. (30–45 cm) apart, 2 in. (50 mm) deep.

Care: Easy. Keep moist spring–autumn. Allow soil to dry between waterings. Drought tolerant when established. Fertilize during growth; dilute fertilizer to half the recommended rate. Mulch. Protect from frost, zones 8–9. Propagate by division, offsets, seed. Divide only when crowded.

Storage: Dark, 50–60°F (10–16°C), in net bag or open basket of dry peat moss.

Features: Good choice for accents, beds, borders, containers, edgings in meadow gardens and landscapes. Good for cutting. Deer, rodent resistant.

TULIPA (TULIP)

Members of the diverse *Tulipa* genus are the most popular of all spring bulbs, and more than 100,000 hybrid cultivars have been registered. Tulips are closely related to lilies, but are true bulbs with tunicates, or loose, papery shells that help them retain moisture. Most tulips are native to southern Europe and the Middle East, though many species also are found throughout Asia's temperate zones.

Many tulips offered for home gardens are either hybrids or one of the 15 or so common species tulips suitable for naturalizing in lawn, turf, or beneath a leafy bower of deciduous trees.

Growers offer early, midseason, and late tulips with a wide variety of growth habits, flower forms, and colors.

All species and hybrid tulips comprise horticultural groupings and divisions based on their flower type; for classification purposes, they first are grouped as botanical (species) or hybrid cultivars, then classified into one of 15 major divisions by the Royal Bulb Growers' Association, Netherlands.

Tulips grow in every color and hue except a true blue, have simple or exceedingly complex flowers, may have fringes or scalloped petals, and can serve many different garden and cut-flower purposes. They look best when grouped in massed plantings, allowed to naturalize and fill an area, or used as a border in the landscape.

Early Tulips
9–16 in. (23–40 cm)
  I.   Single Early Tulips
  II. Double Early Tulips
Mid-Season Tulips
16–26 in. (40–65 cm)
  III. Triumph Tulips
  IV. Darwin Hybrid Tulips
Late-Season Tulips
16–36 in. (40–90 cm)
  V.   Single Late Tulips
        (Darwin and Cottage)
  VI.   Lily-Flowered Tulips
  VII. Fringed Tulips
  VIII. Veridiflora Tulips
  IX.   Rembrandt Tulips
  X.   Parrot Tulips
  XI.   Double Late Tulips
        (Peony-Flowered)
Species Tulips
(size varies)
  XII. Kaufmanniana Tulips
  XIII. Fosterana Tulips
  XIV. Greigii Tulips
  XV.   Other Species Tulips

Plant tulips in autumn in USDA Plant Hardiness Zones 4–8 or winter, zones 9–10, in a site with full sun to partial shade. For best performance, soil for tulips should be moist, well-drained, sandy, and acidic humus. Space bulbs as recommended for the cultivar and plant them 5–8 in. (13–20 cm) deep, or about three times their height. They may be planted beneath a cover of turf or a perennial plant or ground cover.

Tulips also make excellent indoor plants when forced—planted into containers and chilled, then reared to bloom early in the season. Forced tulips provide color in winter.

Cut-flower arrangements that feature tulips also are popular in spring. Cut the stems twice: the first cut frees the stem from the plant, and the second, made underwater before arranging, eliminates any air trapped in the cut, helping to assure that the flowers in your arrangement or bouquet will last.

Bulb: *Tulipa* species. LILIACEAE.
Common name: Tulip.
Description: Spring bulb. Deciduous. Up to 100 species, many hybrids and cultivars. Stands 5–24 in. (13–60 cm) tall. Broad to straplike, light to deep green leaves, sometimes patterned with stripes or mottled.
Bloom: Spring. All colors except blue; bi- and multicolored. Solitary single or double, egg-shaped, sometimes fragrant flowers, to 4 in. (10 cm) wide, with rounded or pointed, smooth or fringed petals.
Plant hardiness: Zones 4–10; ground hardy, zones 4–7.
Soil: Moist, well-drained soil. Fertility: Rich–average. 5.5–6.5 pH.
Planting: Autumn–winter in full sun to partial shade. Space 2–4 in. (50–100 mm) apart, 5–8 in. (13–20 cm) deep, depending on species.
Care: Easy. Keep moist winter–spring. Fertilize bimonthly in spring. Mulch, zones 8–10. Protect from wind. Propagate by offsets in late summer–autumn. Divide only when crowded. Transplant container plants to garden in second year.
Storage: Dark, 40–50°F (4–10°C), in net bag or open basket of dry peat moss.
Features: Good choice for accents, beds, borders, containers, massed plantings in cottage, formal, woodland gardens. Good for cutting. Most species tulips and some hybrids naturalize. Deer, rodent and aphid susceptible.

Bulb: *Zantedeschia* species. ARACEAE.

Common name: Common Calla Lily (Arum Lily, Florist's Calla Lily, Garden Calla).

Description: Spring rhizome. Deciduous. About 6 species. Stands 1–4 ft. (30–120 cm) tall. Elongated, heart-shaped, midlength, shiny, deep green leaves, sometimes patterned with white speckles.

Bloom: Summer–autumn. Pink, red, white, yellow. Solitary petal-like spiral spathes form elegant flowers, 4½–10 in. (11–25 cm) long.

Plant hardiness: Zones 8–10; ground hardy, zones 8–10.

Soil: Damp, well-drained soil or, in water features, a shallow marginal or shoreline site. Fertility: Rich. 6.0–7.0 pH.

Planting: Early autumn in full to filtered sun. Space 1 ft. (30 cm) apart, 4 in. (10 cm) deep.

Care: Easy. Keep evenly damp year-round. Fertilize bimonthly during growth. Mulch. Propagate by division, offsets, seed.

Storage: Dark, 50–60°F (10–16°C), in net bag or open basket of dry peat moss.

Features: Good choice for borders, containers in indoor gardens and landscapes or water feature margins and shorelines. Good for cutting. Deer, rodent resistant. Spider mite susceptible.

Bulb: *Zephyranthes* species. AMARYLLIDACEAE.

Common name: Zephyr Lily (Fairy Lily).

Description: Summer bulb. Deciduous or semi-evergreen, depending on species. About 40 species. Stands to 1 ft. (30 cm) tall. Grasslike, arching, gray green leaves, 4–24 in. (10–60 cm) long.

Bloom: Summer–autumn. Pink, red, white, yellow. Solitary simple or lilylike flowers, 2–4 in. (50–100 mm) wide, with long, narrow, radiating, flared, oval petals. Some species are night blooming.

Plant hardiness: Zones 7–11; ground hardy, zones 7–11.

Soil: Moist, well-drained soil. Fertility: Average. 6.0–7.0 pH.

Planting: Spring in full sun. Space 4 in. (10 cm) apart, 2–4 in. (50–100 mm) deep.

Care: Easy. Keep moist during growth. Withhold water for one month following bloom; resume watering for repeat bloom. Fertilize during growth. Mulch, zones 7–8. Propagate by offsets, seed.

Storage: Dark, 50–60°F (10–16°C), in net bag or open basket of dry peat moss.

Features: Good choice for accents, beds, containers, edgings, mixed plantings in meadow, natural, rock gardens. Naturalizes, zones 9–11. Deer, rodent and pest, disease resistant.

Bulb: *Zingiber officinale* hybrids. ZINGIBERACEAE.

Common name: True Ginger.

Description: Summer rhizome. Deciduous or evergreen. Stands to 20 in. (50 cm) tall. Lance-shaped, midlength green leaves in tiers along stalk.

Bloom: Summer. Orange, pink, white, yellow, sometimes banded or edged with contrasts. Multiple trumpet-shaped, sometimes orchidlike flowers in upright or drooping spikes.

Plant hardiness: Zones 8–11; ground hardy, zones 9–11.

Soil: Moist, well-drained soil. Fertility: Rich–average. 6.0–6.5 pH.

Planting: Spring in open shade. Space 6–12 in. (15–30 cm) apart, 2–4 in. (50–100 mm) deep.

Care: Moderate. Keep moist during growth. Fertilize during growth. Mulch. Protect from frost, zones 8–9. Propagate by division in spring.

Storage: Dark, 60–65°F (16–18°C), in net bag or open basket of dry peat moss.

Features: Good choice for beds, borders, margins, massed plantings in tropical, woodland gardens, landscapes, and water features. Source of the cooking spice treasured for many dishes in Asian cuisine.

Ornamental Grasses, Turfgrasses, Ground Covers, and Vines

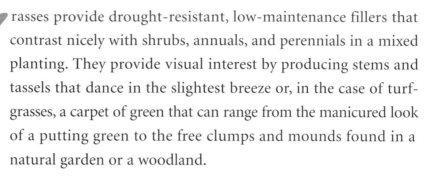

Grasses provide drought-resistant, low-maintenance fillers that contrast nicely with shrubs, annuals, and perennials in a mixed planting. They provide visual interest by producing stems and tassels that dance in the slightest breeze or, in the case of turf-grasses, a carpet of green that can range from the manicured look of a putting green to the free clumps and mounds found in a natural garden or a woodland.

Besides grasses, choices for carpeting your landscape with greenery include various broad-leaved ground covers. They are a good choice when conditions are too shady for turf or when you wish to conserve water—many species are ideal in Xeriscape settings. Many ground covers also provide pleasing foliage texture that helps to soften a border surrounding a turfgrass lawn.

What should you do when the issue is a vertical space? Choose a climbing or twining vine to fill a wall, cling to a trellis, or drape over an arbor. Many vines produce beautiful flowers and fill their space with color, while others have lovely textures that play with shadows and light, adding depth to your plantings.

All four choices can be found in the pages that follow.

ORNAMENTAL GRASSES

Ornamental grass: *Andropogon gerardii.* POACEAE (GRAMINEAE).

Common name: Big Bluestem (Beard Grass, Turkeyfoot).

Description: Several cultivars of erect, clumping perennial grasses, 3–7 ft. (90–215 cm) tall and 2–3 ft. (60–90 cm) wide. Blue green, flat, narrow leaf sheaths, to ⅜ in. (9 mm) wide, on usually soft, hairy stalks, turning gold, red in autumn. *A. hallii,* sand bluestem, is a closely related species with similar care needs

Spray/Seed: Many red, purple, whorled florets, to ⅛ in. (3 mm) long, in 3–6-branched clusters, 3–4 in. (75–100 mm) long, atop a grassy stem, in late spring–summer.

Plant hardiness: Hardy. Zones 3–10.

Soil: Moist to dry, well-drained loam. Fertility: Rich–average. 6.0–7.5 pH.

Planting: Spring in full to filtered sun, 18–24 in. (45–60 cm) apart.

Care: Easy. Keep moist during active growth. Fertilize annually in spring. Shear in spring before growth begins. Propagate by division, seed.

Features: Good choice for accents, massed plantings, screens in meadow, natural, prairie, seashore, wildlife gardens. Attracts birds. Pest and disease resistant.

Ornamental grass: *Arundo donax* varieties. POACEAE (GRAMINEAE).

Common name: Giant Reed (Carrizo, Variegated Mediterranean Rush).

Description: Several cultivars of upright, clumping, rhizomatous, deciduous perennial grasses, 6–30 ft. (1.8–9 m) tall and 3–4 ft. (90–120 cm) wide. Green, purple, yellow, or variegated, striped, flat, broadly spear-shaped leaf sheaths, to 2 ft. (60 cm) long and 2½ in. (63 mm) wide, on tall, bamboolike, reedy stalks. Common varieties include *A. donax* var. *variegata* and var. *versicolor.*

Spray/Seed: Blooms rare; red becoming white, plumelike clusters, to 2 ft. (60 cm) long, comprising florets, feathery bracts, and seed, in summer.

Plant hardiness: Tender. Zones 6–11.

Soil: Moist to wet, well-drained humus or, in water features, shoreline sites. Fertility: Rich. 6.0–8.0 pH.

Planting: Spring in full sun to partial shade, 9 ft. (2.7 m) apart.

Care: Easy. Keep evenly moist. Fertilize quarterly. Shear in autumn. Protect from wind. Propagate by division, seed.

Features: Good choice for containers, fencelines, screens, windbreaks in meadow, open, prairie, wetland gardens and water feature shorelines. Good for drying. Invasive. Pest and disease resistant.

Ornamental grass: *Baumea rubingosa* 'Variegata' (CYPERACEAE).

Common name: Variegated Rush.

Description: A few cultivars of erect, clumping, rhizomatous, evergreen, perennial grasses, 1–2 ft. (30–60 cm) tall and 1 ft. (30 cm) wide. Shiny, green, yellow, striped, round, flattened, swordlike leaf sheaths, to 2 ft. (60 cm) long, extend from basal stalks.

Spray/Seed: Inconspicuous, tiny, brown, tightly clustered seed, in summer.

Plant hardiness: Semi-hardy. Zones 8–11.

Soil: Moist, well-drained, sandy loam or, in water features, submerged marginal or shoreline sites. Fertility: Average. 6.0–8.0 pH.

Planting: Spring in full sun, 1 ft. (30 cm) apart, or submerged 1–4 in. (25–100 mm) deep in a container.

Care: Easy. Keep evenly moist. Fertilize annually in spring. Shear in late autumn. Propagate by division.

Features: Good choice for accents, containers, edgings in small-space, wetland, woodland gardens and water feature margins and shorelines. Good for mixed plantings with ferns. Pest and disease resistant.

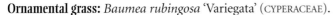

Ornamental grass: *Butomus umbellatus.* BUTOMACEAE.
Common name: Flowering Rush (Grassy Rush, Water Gladiolus).
Description: A few cultivars of a single-species genus of fast-growing, rushlike, rhizomatous, herbaceous, deciduous, aquatic perennial grasses, to 5 ft. (1.5 m) tall and 4 ft. (1.2 m) wide. Textured, deep green, narrow, cattail-like, veined leaf sheaths, to 4 ft. (1.2 m) long.
Bloom/Seed: Many showy, rose, white, 5-petaled flowers, to 1 in. (25 mm) wide, with deep red centers, in radiating, branched clusters, to 6 in. (15 cm) wide, atop long, stiff, pithy stalks, in summer, form segmented fruit containing seed, in autumn.
Plant hardiness: Hardy. Zones 4–9.
Soil: Moist to wet, well-drained, sandy loam or, in water features, shallow marginal or shoreline sites. Fertility: Average. 6.0–8.0 pH.
Planting: Spring in full to filtered sun, 4 ft. (1.2 m) apart, or submerged to 10 in. (25 cm) deep.
Care: Easy. Keep evenly moist. Fertilize annually in spring. Propagate by division.

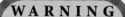

WARNING
Leaves of *Butomus umbellatus* are sharp-edged and can cause cuts and abrasions. Wear leather gloves when handling.

Features: Good for accents, borders in natural, woodland gardens or water feature margins and shorelines. Pest and disease resistant.

Ornamental grass: *Calamagrostis* × *acutiflora.* POACEAE (GRAMINEAE).
Common name: Feather Reed Grass.
Description: Several cultivars of fast-growing, erect, clumping, herbaceous perennial grasses, 4–7 ft. (1.2–2.2 m) tall and 6–12 in. (15–30 cm) wide. Textured, bright green or variegated, arching, narrow, spear-shaped, veined leaf sheaths, to 3 ft. (90 cm) long, on round, stiff, grasslike stalks, turning brown, red in autumn.
Spray/Seed: Green, purple turning gold, plumelike clusters, to 1 ft. (30 cm) long, as florets, feathery bracts, and seed, on slender, stiff stems, to 6 ft. (1.8 m) long, in spring–autumn.
Plant hardiness: Hardy. Zones 4–9. Best in cool-summer, mild-winter climates.
Soil: Moist, well-drained soil. Fertility: Average. 6.5–7.5 pH.
Planting: Spring in full sun to partial shade, 1–2 ft. (30–60 cm) apart.
Care: Easy. Keep damp; allow soil surface to dry between waterings. Fertilize annually in spring. Shear in spring before growth begins. Propagate by seed.
Features: Good choice for accents, borders, containers, walls, windbreaks in cottage, meadow gardens. Good for drying. Pest and disease resistant.

Ornamental grass: *Carex* species. CYPERACEAE.
Common name: Sedge.
Description: About 2,000 species of highly varied, fast-growing, clumping or matting, grasslike, rhizomatous perennial sedges, mostly 1–5 ft. (30–150 cm) tall. Shiny, green, red, white, often variegated and striped, narrow, spear-shaped leaves, 6–60 in. (15–150 cm) long. Commonly cultivated species include *C. buchananii, C. flacca, C. morrowii* var. *expallida,* and *C. testacea.*
Bloom/Seed: Inconspicuous, tiny, green, purple, white, yellow flowers on tall, wiry spikes, 1–5 ft. (30–150 cm) tall, in summer.
Plant hardiness: Hardy. Zones 3–9. Best in cool-summer, humid climates.
Soil: Moist to wet, well-drained soil or, in water features, shallow marginal sites. Fertility: Average. 6.0–7.5 pH.
Planting: Spring for divisions; autumn for seed, in full sun to full shade. Space as recommended for species.
Care: Easy. Keep evenly moist or damp, depending on species. Fertilize annually in spring. Propagate by division, seed.
Features: Good choice for banks, containers, edgings, ground covers in natural, wetland, wildlife, woodland gardens and water feature margins. Good for drying. Attracts birds. Invasive. Pest and disease resistant.

Ornamental grass: *Cyperus alternifolius.* CYPERACEAE.

Common name: Umbrella Plant (Umbrella Flatsedge, Umbrella Palm).

Description: Several cultivars of fast-growing, erect, woody, grasslike, rhizomatous, tropical perennial sedges, 2–4 ft. (60–120 cm) tall and to 2 ft. (60 cm) wide. Smooth, brown, purple leaf sheaths, to 6 in. (15 cm) long, on erect, shiny, deep green, tall, narrow leaf stalks, to 4 ft. (1.2 m) long, triangular when cut, with 12–20 palmlike, deep green or variegated, arching, branching, narrow terminal bracts, 4–12 in. (10–30 cm) long. Dwarf cultivars available.

Bloom/Seed: Many tiny, brown, green flowers, in dry, nodulelike clusters, in summer.

Plant hardiness: Tender. Zones 10–11. Self-seeding.

Soil: Moist to wet, well-drained humus or, in water features, shallow marginal or shoreline sites. Fertility: Rich. 6.0–8.0 pH.

Planting: Spring in partial shade, 3 ft. (90 cm) apart, or submerged 2–4 in. (50–100 mm) deep.

Care: Moderate. Keep evenly moist. Fertilize monthly. Renew colonies by dividing, discarding central plants. Protect from frost. Propagate by division, seed.

Features: Good choice for accents, containers, edgings in tropical, wetland, woodland gardens and water feature margins and shorelines. Good as houseplant. Invasive. Attracts birds. Pest and disease resistant.

Ornamental grass: *Cyperus prolifer (C. isocladus).* CYPERACEAE.

Common name: Dwarf Papyrus (Bulrush, Paper Plant).

Description: Several dwarf cultivars of fast-growing, erect, woody, grasslike, rhizomatous perennial sedges, to 18 in. (45 cm) tall and wide. Smooth, brown leaf sheaths, to 4 in. (10 cm) long, with erect, shiny, blue green, tall, narrow, pith-filled leaf stalks, to 18 in. (45 cm) long, with palmlike, deep green, arching, branching, narrow, terminal bracts, to 4 in. (10 cm) long.

Spray/Seed: Many tiny, green yellow turning brown flowers, in showy, branching, feathery, nodding, plumelike clusters, to 6 in. (15 cm) long, in summer, form lens-shaped seed in autumn.

Plant hardiness: Tender. Zones 8–11.

Soil: Moist to wet, well-drained humus or, in water features, shallow marginal or shore-line sites. Fertility: Average. 6.0–8.0 pH.

Planting: Spring in full sun to partial shade, 1 ft. (30 cm) apart, or submerged 2–4 in. (50–100 mm) deep.

Care: Easy. Keep evenly moist. Fertilize quarterly. Protect from frost. Propagate by division, seed.

Features: Good choice for accents, containers, edgings in Chinese, Japanese, tropical, wetland, woodland gardens and water feature margins and shorelines. Invasive. Attracts birds. Pest and disease resistant.

Ornamental grass: *Deschampsia caespitosa.* POACEAE (GRAMINEAE).

Common name: Tufted Hair Grass.

Description: Many cultivars of fast-growing, erect, clumping, herbaceous perennial grasses, 3–4 ft. (90–120 cm) tall and 2 ft. (60 cm) wide. Smooth, deep green, narrow, spear-shaped leaf sheaths, 18–24 in. (45–60 cm) long, on erect, shiny, deep green leaf stalks, 6–10 in. (15–25 cm) long.

Spray/Seed: Bronze, gold, green becoming yellow, white, tufted clusters, to 6 in. (15 cm) long, comprising florets, feathery bracts, and seed, on slender, stiff stems, to 4 ft. (1.2 m) long, in late spring–summer.

Plant hardiness: Hardy. Zones 4–9. Self-seeding. Best in cool-summer climates.

Soil: Moist, well-drained soil. Fertility: Rich. 6.5–7.0 pH.

Planting: Spring in full sun to full shade, 2–3 ft. (60–90 cm) apart.

Care: Easy. Keep evenly moist. Fertilize monthly. Shear in spring. Propagate by seed.

Features: Good choice for accents, borders, ground covers, massed plantings in cottage, meadow, wetland, woodland gardens. Invasive. Pest and disease resistant.

Ornamental grass: *Festuca glauca (F. ovina* var. *glauca).* POACEAE (GRAMINEAE).
Common name: Blue Fescue (Sheep Fescue).
Description: Many cultivars and horticultural varieties of fast-growing, mounding, clumping, herbaceous perennial grasses, 4–24 in. (10–60 cm) tall, 6–18 in. (15–45 cm) wide. Shiny, blue green, wiry, very narrow, needle-shaped leaf sheaths, to 1 ft. (30 cm) long. Common cultivars include *F. glauca* 'Blausilber', 'Elijah Blue', 'Siskiyou Blue', and 'Vaginata'. Dwarf cultivars available.
Spray/Seed: Inconspicuous, tiny, silver becoming tan flowers, in dangling clusters, in spring–summer; grown primarily for foliage.
Plant hardiness: Hardy. Zones 4–9.
Soil: Moist to damp, well-drained, sandy loam. Fertility: Average–low. 6.5–7.5 pH.
Planting: Spring in full sun, 6–15 in. (15–38 cm) apart.
Care: Easy. Keep damp; allow soil surface to dry between waterings. Drought tolerant. Avoid fertilizing. Deadhead spent flowers after bloom. Shear in winter. Propagate by division, seed.
Features: Good choice for banks, borders, edgings, ground covers, massed plantings in cottage, meadow, natural, seaside, Xeriscape gardens. Pest and disease resistant.

Ornamental grass: *Glyceria maxima* 'Variegata'. POACEAE (GRAMINEAE).
Common name: Variegated Manna Grass.
Description: Cultivar of fast-growing, spreading, stoloniferous, deciduous perennial grass, 2–3 ft. (60–90 cm) tall and 2 ft. (60 cm) wide. Shiny, pink becoming cream, green, white, variegated and striped, narrow, arching leaf sheaths, to 3 ft. (90 cm) long, on short, basal leaf stalks, to 2 in. (50 mm) long.
Spray/Seed: Inconspicuous cream, purple-tinged flowers, in summer; grown primarily for foliage.
Plant hardiness: Hardy. Zones 5–10.
Soil: Wet, clayey humus or, in water features, deeply submerged marginal sites. Fertility: Rich. 6.0–8.0 pH.
Planting: Spring in full sun to partial shade, 15 in. (38 cm) apart, or submerged 6–8 in. (15–20 cm) deep in a container.
Care: Easy. Keep evenly wet. Fertilize every 2 months. Shear in winter; remove solid green leaf sheaths to maintain variegated form. Propagate by division, stolons, seed.
Features: Good choice for accents, banks, borders, filler in natural, wetland gardens and water feature margins. Invasive. Pest and disease resistant.

Ornamental grass: *Helictotrichon sempervirens (Avena sempervirens).* POACEAE (GRAMINEAE).
Common name: Blue Oat Grass.
Description: Several cultivars of fast-growing, erect, tufted, fountain-shaped, herbaceous, semi-evergreen perennial grasses, to 5 ft. (1.5 m) tall and 2–3 ft. (60–90 cm) wide. Smooth, gray, blue green, narrow, spear-shaped, arching leaf sheaths, to 2 ft. (60 cm) long, on short, basal leaf stalks, to 6 in. (15 cm) long.
Spray/Seed: Many tiny, cream, yellow tufted clusters, to 6 in. (15 cm) long, comprising florets, feathery bracts, and seed, on slender, stiff stems, to 5 ft. (1.5 m) long, in spring.
Plant hardiness: Hardy. Zones 3–9.
Soil: Moist, well-drained, sandy soil. Fertility: Rich–average. 7.0–8.0 pH.
Planting: Spring in full sun, 18–24 in. (45–60 cm) apart.
Care: Easy. Keep moist; allow soil surface to dry between waterings. Drought tolerant. Fertilize every 2 months. Remove old, broken leafstalks. Propagate by division, seed.
Features: Good choice for accents, borders, filler, massed plantings in meadow, natural, rock, Xeriscape gardens. Pest and disease resistant.

Ornamental grass: *Lagurus ovatus.* POACEAE (GRAMINEAE).

Common name: Hare's-Tail Grass (Rabbit-Tail Grass).

Description: Several cultivars of fast-growing, branching, narrow, herbaceous annual grasses, to 1 ft. (30 cm) tall and 8 in. (20 cm) wide. Woolly, thick, flat, spear-shaped leaf sheaths, 6–8 in. (15–20 cm) long, on short leaf stalks, 1–3 in. (25–75 mm) long.

Spray/Seed: Tan becoming white, yellow, woolly spiking clusters, to 1¼ in. (32 mm) long, comprising awns, glumes, lemmas, and seed, on narrow, wiry stems, to 10 in. (25 cm) long, in summer.

Plant hardiness: Plant as tender annual, zones 3–6; self-seeding, zones 7–10.

Soil: Moist, well-drained soil. Fertility: Average. 7.0–8.0 pH.

Planting: Spring in full sun, 3–4 in. (75–100 mm) apart.

Care: Easy. Keep evenly moist until sprays form; limit watering thereafter. Drought tolerant. Propagate by seed.

Features: Good for borders, edgings, massed plantings in cottage, meadow, natural, wildlife gardens. Good for cutting, drying. Attracts birds. Pest and disease resistant.

Ornamental grass: *Miscanthus floridulus* 'Rubra' *(Imperata cylindrica).* POACEAE (GRAMINEAE).

Common name: Japanese Blood Grass.

Description: Cultivar of fast-growing, erect, clumping, herbaceous perennial grasses, 1–2 ft. (30–60 cm) tall and wide. Shiny, pale green turning red, narrow, spear-shaped leaf sheaths, to 2 ft. (60 cm) long, on short, branching leaf stalks, to 6 in. (15 cm) long.

Spray/Seed: Inconspicuous white clusters, comprising florets, feathery bracts, and seed, on slender, stiff stems, in late summer; grown primarily for foliage.

Plant hardiness: Hardy. Zones 7–10.

Soil: Moist, well-drained soil or, in water features, shoreline sites. Fertility: Rich–average. 6.5–7.5 pH.

Planting: Spring in full sun to partial shade, 1–2 ft. (30–60 cm) apart.

Care: Easy. Keep moist; allow soil surface to dry between waterings. Fertilize every 2 months. Shear in spring before growth begins. Propagate by division.

Features: Good choice for accents, borders, edgings, massed plantings in meadow, natural, rock, small-space gardens and water feature shorelines. Pest and disease resistant.

Ornamental grass: *Miscanthus sinensis.* POACEAE (GRAMINEAE).

Common name: Eulalia Grass (Japanese Silver Grass).

Description: Many cultivars and horticultural varieties of fast-growing, erect, clumping, herbaceous perennial grasses, 4–6 ft. (1.2–1.8 m) tall and 3–4 ft. (90–120 cm) wide. Shiny, pale green turning deep green, pink, yellow, or variegated, narrow, spear-shaped leaf sheaths, 2–3 ft. (60–90 cm) long, on short, branching leaf stalks, to 8 in. (20 cm) long, turning bronze, red in autumn.

Spray/Seed: Showy, bronze, copper, pink becoming cream, silver, white, plumelike clusters, to 1 ft. (30 cm) long, comprising florets, feathery bracts, and seed, on narrow, stiff stems, to 7 ft. (2.2 m) tall, in late summer–autumn, persisting into winter.

Plant hardiness: Hardy. Zones 5–10.

Soil: Moist to damp, well-drained soil. Fertility: Average. 6.5–7.5 pH.

Planting: Spring in full sun to partial shade, 5–6 ft. (1.5–1.8 m) apart.

Care: Easy. Keep moist; allow soil surface to dry between waterings. Fertilize every 2 months. Shear in spring before growth begins. Propagate by division, seed.

Features: Good choice for accents, backgrounds, screens, windbreaks in meadow, natural, rock gardens. Pest and disease resistant.

Ornamental grass: *Ophiopogon japonicus.* LILIACEAE.
Common name: Mondo Grass (Dwarf Lilyturf).
Description: Several cultivars of slow-growing, long-lived, clumping, mounding, grasslike, stolnoniferous, tuberous, evergreen perennial herbs, to 6 in. (15 cm) tall and wide. Shiny, deep green, narrow, spear-shaped, arching foliage, to 6 in. (15 cm) long. Member of the lily genus.
Bloom/Seed: Many tiny, lavender, pink, white, nodding, bell-shaped flowers, to ¼ in. (6 mm) wide, in spiking, open clusters on stiff, wiry stems, to 5 in. (13 cm) long, in summer, form round, purple, berrylike fruit, to ⅓ in. (8 mm) wide, in autumn.
Plant hardiness: Hardy. Zones 7–11.
Soil: Moist, well-drained soil. Fertility: Rich–average. 6.5–7.0 pH.
Planting: Spring in partial to full shade, 6–12 in. (15–30 cm) apart.
Care: Easy. Keep evenly moist. Fertilize every 2 months, spring–autumn. Shear in spring before growth begins. Propagate by division, seed, stolons.
Features: Good choice for banks, borders, edgings, ground covers, paths in natural, shade, woodland gardens. Invasive. Disease resistant. Slug, snail susceptible.

Ornamental grass: *Panicum virgatum.* POACEAE (GRAMINEAE).
Common name: Switch-Grass.
Description: Several cultivars of fast-growing, clumping, rhizomatous perennial grasses, sometimes to 10 ft. (3 m) tall but seldom more than 7 ft. (2.2 m) tall in landscape use. Smooth, deep green or gray green, erect, narrow, spear-shaped leaf sheaths, to 4 ft. (1.2 m) long, on erect, shiny, deep green leaf stalks, 1–2 ft. (30–60 cm) long, turning brown, red, yellow in autumn.
Spray/Seed: Showy, bronze, pink fading to brown, cream, white, erect, branching, open sprays, to 20 in. (50 cm) long, in summer–autumn, persisting into winter.
Plant hardiness: Hardy. Zones 4–9.
Soil: Moist to damp, well-drained soil. Fertility: Rich–average. 6.5–7.5 pH. Salt tolerant.
Planting: Late winter–early spring in full to filtered sun, 2–3 ft. (60–90 cm) apart.
Care: Easy. Keep damp; allow soil surface to dry between waterings. Drought tolerant. Fertilize quarterly. Shear in spring before growth begins. Propagate by division, seed.
Features: Good choice for accents, backgrounds, ground covers, screens, windbreaks in meadow, natural, seaside gardens. Good for drying. Pest and disease resistant.

Ornamental grass: *Pennisetum alopecuroides.* POACEAE (GRAMINEAE).
Common name: Fountain Grass (Chinese Pennisetum).
Description: Several cultivars of fast-growing, clumping, mounding, herbaceous perennial grasses, 2–4 ft. (60–120 cm) tall and 3–4 ft. (90–120 cm) wide. Shiny, bright green, arching, narrow, spear-shaped leaf sheaths, to 5 ft. (1.5 m) long, on shiny, green leaf stalks, 12–16 in. (30–40 cm) long, turning yellow in autumn, brown in winter.
Spray/Seed: Showy, pink fading to cream, yellow, erect, bristly, plumelike clusters, 4–6 in. (10–15 cm) long, in summer–autumn.
Plant hardiness: Hardy. Plant as tender annual, zones 3–4; ground hardy, zones 5–11. Self-seeding. Best in hot-summer climates.
Soil: Moist, well-drained soil. Fertility: Average. 6.0–7.0 pH.
Planting: Early spring in full sun to partial shade, 1–3 ft. (30–90 cm) apart.
Care: Easy. Keep moist. Drought tolerant when established. Fertilize annually in spring. Shear in spring before growth begins. Propagate by division, seed.
Features: Good choice for accents, borders, containers, fencelines, massed plantings, screens in cottage, meadow, natural gardens. Good for drying. Pest and disease resistant.

Ornamental Grass: *Phalaris arundinacea.* POACEAE (GRAMINEAE).
Common name: Ribbon Grass (Gardener's-Garters, Reed Canary Grass).
Description: Several cultivars and subspecies of long-lived, erect, upright, rhizomatous perennial grasses, 3–5 ft. (90–150 cm) tall and 2 ft. (60 cm) wide. Opposite, shiny, gray green, ribbonlike, pointed leaf sheaths, to 7 in. (18 cm) long, with pink, white, yellow stripes, on shiny, green leaf stalks, to 4 in. (10 cm) long.
Spray/Seed: Inconspicuous purple, white becoming tan, feathery florets, to ⅛ in. (3 mm) wide, in clusters comprising bracts and seed, to 6 in. (15 cm) long, in summer–autumn.
Plant hardiness: Hardy. Zones 4–10.
Soil: Moist, well-drained soil or, in water features, shoreline sites. Fertility: Average. 6.0–8.0 pH.
Planting: Spring in full sun, 2 ft. (60 cm) apart.
Care: Easy. Keep damp. Very drought tolerant. Avoid fertilizing. Shear in autumn or spring. Propagate by division, seed.
Features: Good choice for accents, containers, fencelines, turf substitute in meadow, rock, Xeriscape gardens and water feature shorelines. Very invasive; plant in buried containers. Pest and disease resistant.

Ornamental grass: *Phragmites australis.* POACEAE (GRAMINEAE).
Common name: Common Reed (Carrizo).
Description: Several cultivars of slow- to medium-growing, erect, stoloniferous, rhizomatous, deciduous perennial reeds, 15–20 ft. (4.5–6 m) tall and 4–5 ft. (1.2–1.5 m) wide. Opposite, shiny, bright green or variegated, broad, lance-shaped, pointed leaf sheaths, to 2 ft. (60 cm) long, on shiny, green, bamboolike leaf stalks, to 20 ft. (6 m) tall, turning gold, yellow in autumn. Dwarf cultivars available.
Spray/Seed: Showy, purple, tan, white, terminal, plumed, branching clusters, to 1 ft. (30 cm) long, comprising florets, feathery bracts, and seed, in late summer.
Plant hardiness: Hardy. Zones 5–11.
Soil: Moist, well-drained soil or, in water features, shallow-depth marginal or shoreline sites. Fertility: Average. 6.0–8.0 pH.
Planting: Spring in full sun, 4 ft. (1.2 m) apart, or submerged 6–8 in. (15–20 cm) deep.
Care: Easy. Keep evenly moist. Fertilize annually in spring. Prune to control growth. Propagate by division, stolons.
Features: Good choice for screens, windbreaks in natural, wetland, wildlife gardens. Good for cutting, drying, latticework. Attracts birds. Very invasive; plant in buried containers. Pest and disease resistant.

Ornamental grass: *Schizachyrium scoparium.* POACEAE (GRAMINEAE).
Common name: Little Bluestem Grass (Broom Beard Grass, Wire Grass).
Description: Many cultivars of slow-growing, erect, clumping, tufted, herbaceous perennial grasses, to 5 ft. (1.5 m) tall and 2–3 ft. (60–90 cm) wide. Smooth, blue green, green, purple, narrow, spear-shaped, pointed leaf sheaths, to 5 ft. (1.5 m) tall, on shiny, green, jointed leaf stalks, to 2 ft. (60 cm) long, turning orange, purple, red in autumn, persisting into winter.
Spray/Seed: Purple, red turning white, loose, open clusters, to 6 in. (15 cm) long, comprising florets, feathery bracts, and seed, in late summer–autumn.
Plant hardiness: Hardy. Zones 3–10.
Soil: Moist to dry, well-drained soil. Fertility: Average. 6.5–7.5 pH.
Planting: Spring in full sun, 1 ft. (30 cm) apart.
Care: Easy. Keep damp; allow soil to dry between waterings. Drought tolerant. Fertilize annually in spring. Shear in spring before growth begins. Propagate by seed.
Features: Good choice for borders, containers, massed plantings in meadow, natural, prairie, wildlife gardens. Attracts birds. Pest and disease resistant.

Ornamental grass: *Scirpus cyperinus (Isolepis cyperinus).* CYPERACEAE.
Common name: Woolgrass Bulrush.
Description: Several cultivars of slow-growing, erect, clumping, stoloniferous, herbaceous perennial sedges, 3–5 ft. (90–150 cm) tall and 1–2 ft. (30–60 cm) wide. Smooth, green, sterile and fertile, closed leaf sheaths, to 5 ft. (1.5 m) long, triangular when cut, with 4–12 palmlike, deep green or variegated, arching, branching, narrow, terminal bracts, 1–3 ft. (30–90 cm) long.
Spray/Seed: Many tiny, green turning brown flowers, in woolly, spike- or tassel-like clusters on branched, terminal stalks, to 2 in. (50 mm) long, in summer, form brown, ribbed fruit containing seed, to ⅛ in. (3 mm) long, in autumn.
Plant hardiness: Hardy. Zones 3–11.
Soil: Moist to wet, well-drained soil. Fertility: Low. 6.0–8.0 pH.
Planting: Spring in full sun to partial shade, 2 ft. (60 cm) apart, or submerged to 4 in. (10 cm) deep in a container.
Care: Easy. Keep evenly moist. Avoid fertilizing. Shear in spring before growth begins. Divide when crowded. Propagate by division, seed, suckers.
Features: Good choice for accents, borders, edgings in wetland, wildlife gardens. Attracts birds. Very invasive; plant in buried containers. Pest and disease resistant.

Ornamental grass: *Sisyrinchium* species. IRIDACEAE.
Common name: Blue-Eyed Grass.
Description: About 75 species of slow-growing, erect, clumping, rarely rhizomatous, deciduous perennial herbs, 1–3 ft. (30–90 cm) tall and wide. Shiny, green, blue green, arching, narrow, grasslike, pointed leaves, to 1 ft. (30 cm) long. Member of the Iris genus.
Bloom/Fruit: Many blue, purple, white, yellow, multicolored, star-shaped, rounded, 6-petaled flowers, to ½ in. (12 mm) long, in erect, branching, open clusters, to 6 in. (15 cm) long, on narrow, stiff stalks, in spring, form divided capsulelike fruit, in summer.
Plant hardiness: Hardy. Zones 5–8. Best in mild-winter climates.
Soil: Moist, well-drained soil or, in water features, shoreline sites. Fertility: Average. 6.0–8.0 pH.
Planting: Spring or autumn in full sun to partial shade, 6 in. (15 cm) apart.
Care: Easy. Keep evenly moist. Fertilize annually in spring. Shear in winter. Divide when crowded. Protect from hard freezes. Propagate by division, seed.
Features: Good choice for accents, ground covers, massed plantings in meadow, seaside, wetland, woodland gardens and water feature shorelines. Good for mixed plantings. Pest and disease resistant.

Ornamental grass: *Sorghastrum avenaceum (S. nutans).* POACEAE (GRAMINEAE).
Common name: Wood Grass (Indian Grass).
Description: Several cultivars of fast-growing, erect, bunching, rhizomatous perennial grasses, 2–5 ft. (60–150 cm) tall and 1–3 ft. (30–90 cm) wide. Shiny, green, very narrow, spear-shaped leaf sheaths, 2–3 ft. (60–90 cm) long, on erect, shiny, green leaf stalks, 8–16 in. (20–40 cm) long, turning orange, yellow in autumn.
Spray/Seed: White, yellow becoming red brown, branching, spikelike clusters, to 1 ft. (30 cm) long, comprising florets, chafflike bracts, and seed, on stiff, erect, narrow stems, to 4 ft. (1.2 m) tall, in late summer, persisting to early winter.
Plant hardiness: Hardy. Zones 3–9. Self-seeding. Best in hot-summer climates.
Soil: Moist to dry, well-drained soil. Fertility: Average. 6.5–7.5 pH.
Planting: Spring in full sun, 1 ft. (30 cm) apart.
Care: Easy. Keep damp; allow soil surface to dry between waterings. Drought tolerant. Shear in spring before growth begins. Propagate by division, seed.
Features: Good choice for accents, backgrounds, borders, massed plantings in arid, meadow, natural, wildlife gardens. Attracts birds. Invasive in moist soil. Pest and disease resistant.

TURFGRASSES

Turfgrass: *Agrostis stolonifera (A. palustris).* POACEAE (GRAMINEAE).
Common name: Creeping Bent Grass.
Description: Several cultivars of very fine-textured, slow-growing, deep green, narrow-leaved, stoloniferous, evergreen perennial turfgrasses, to 20 in. (50 cm) tall when uncut, usually mown ¼–½ in. (6–12 mm) tall for lawn use. Commonly available cultivars include *A. stolonifera* 'Congressional', 'Emerald', 'Old Orchard', 'Penncross', and 'Seaside'.
Season: Cool-season grass. Growth in spring, repeating in early autumn.
Plant hardiness: Hardy. Zones 4–8. Best in cold-winter, mild-summer climates.
Soil: Moist, well-drained, sandy loam. Fertility: Rich. 6.5–7.5 pH.
Planting: Spring in full to filtered sun, from seed, sod, sprigs. Space sprigs 4–6 in. (10–15 cm) apart.
Care: Challenging. Keep evenly moist. Mow frequently to maintain height with reel mower fitted with a sharp, fine-cutting blade. Apply ¼–½ lb. (112–225 g) of nitrogen fertilizer per 1,000 sq. ft. (93 m²) monthly during active growth. Dethatch, top dress in spring before growth begins. Tolerates some heat.
Features: Good choice for lawn bowling, croquet and tennis courts, and for putting greens. Pest resistant. Fungal disease susceptible.

Turfgrass: *Buchloe dactyloides.* POACEAE (GRAMINEAE).
Common name: Buffalo Grass.
Description: Several cultivars of a single-species genus of fine-textured, slow-growing, gray green, narrow-leaved, curly-edged, stoloniferous, evergreen perennial turfgrasses, to 8 in. (20 cm) tall when uncut, usually mown ½–2½ in. (12–63 mm) tall for lawn use. Forms dense sod, 2–4 in. (50–100 mm) deep.
Season: Warm-season grass. Growth in late spring–summer; dormant autumn–spring.
Plant hardiness: Hardy. Zones 4–8. Best in arid climates.
Soil: Moist to damp, dense, clayey soil. Fertility: Average–low. 7.0–8.5 pH. Salt tolerant.

Planting: Spring in full sun, from plugs, seed, sod. Space plugs 3–4 ft. (90–120 cm) apart.
Care: Easy. Keep moist until established; reduce watering thereafter. Mow 2–3 times per season to maintain height with reel or rotary mower. Apply 1–2 lb. (450–900 g) of nitrogen fertilizer per 1,000 sq. ft. (93 m²) at beginning of growth. Overseed in winter with annual ryegrass. Drought, heat tolerant.
Features: Good choice for lawns, playgrounds, turf paths. Good for Xeriscape lawns. Invasive. Pest and disease resistant.

Turfgrass: *Cynodon dactylon* hybrids. POACEAE (GRAMINEAE).
Common name: Hybrid Bermuda Grass (Scutch Grass).
Description: Many hybrid cultivars of medium- to fine-textured, fast-growing, bright green, narrow-leaved, stoloniferous or rhizomatous, evergreen perennial turf-grassses, to 16 in. (40 cm) tall when uncut, usually mown ½–1 in. (12–25 mm) tall for lawn use.
Season: Warm-season grass. Growth in spring–autumn; dormant in winter.
Plant hardiness: Hardy. Zones 6–10. Best in hot, arid or subtropical climates.
Soil: Moist, well-drained, sandy soil. Fertility: Rich–average. 5.5–7.0 pH.
Planting: Spring in full sun, from plugs, sod, sprigs. Space plugs 2 ft. (60 cm) apart, sprigs 6–8 in. (15–20 cm) apart.
Care: Moderate. Keep moist until established; water when soil dries thereafter. Mow frequently to maintain height with reel or rotary mower. Apply ½–1 lb. (225–450 g) of nitrogen fertilizer per 1,000 sq. ft. (93 m²) monthly during active growth and to restore after yellowing, wear. Overseed in winter with annual ryegrass. Dethatch in spring before growth begins. Drought, heat tolerant.
Features: Good choice for lawns, playgrounds, turf paths. Invasive. Very pest and disease resistant.

Turfgrass: *Eremochloa ophiuroides.* POACEAE (GRAMINEAE).
Common name: Centipede Grass (Lazy-Man's Grass).
Description: A few cultivars of coarse-textured, slow-growing, light green, narrow-leaved, stoloniferous, evergreen perennial turfgrasses, to 4 in. (10 cm) tall when uncut, usually mown 1–2 in. (25–50 mm) tall for lawn use. Common cultivars include *E. ophiuroides* 'Centennial', 'Lone Star', and 'Oklawn'.
Season: Warm-season grass. Growth in spring–autumn; dormant in winter.
Plant hardiness: Semi-hardy. Zones 7–11. Best in humid, subtropical climates.
Soil: Moist, well-drained, sandy soil. Fertility: Low. 4.5–6.0 pH.
Planting: Spring in full to filtered sun, from plugs, seed, sod. Space plugs 2 ft. (60 cm) apart.
Care: Easy–moderate. Keep evenly moist. Mow to maintain height with reel or rotary mower. Apply ¼ lb. (112 g) of nitrogen fertilizer per 1,000 sq. ft. (93 m^2) monthly during active growth. Dethatch in autumn after dormancy begins. Overseed in winter with annual ryegrass.
Features: Good choice for low-maintance lawns, low-traffic plantings. Chinch bug resistant. Mole cricket, leafhopper, nematode and chlorosis susceptible.

Turfgrass: *Festuca arundinacea* hybrids. POACEAE (GRAMINEAE).
Common name: Dwarf Fescue (Dwarf Hybrid Tall Fescue).
Description: Many dwarf hybrid cultivars of very fine-textured, slow-growing, deep green to blue green, clumping, evergreen perennial turfgrasses, 1–2 ft. (30–60 cm) tall when uncut, usually mown 1–1½ in. (25–38 mm) tall for lawn use. Common cultivars include *F. arundinacea* 'Austin', 'Balexis', 'Bonsai', 'Marathon', 'Phoenix', and 'Tomahawk'.
Season: Cool-season grass. Growth in spring, repeating in early autumn.
Plant hardiness: Hardy. Zones 3–9. Best in warm-summer, mild-winter climates.
Soil: Moist to damp, well-drained soil. Fertility: Average. 5.5–7.5 pH.
Planting: Spring in full sun to full shade, from seed, sod.
Care: Easy. Keep damp; allow soil surface to dry between waterings. Drought tolerant. Mow to maintain height with reel or rotary mower. Apply ¼–½ lb. (112–225 g) of nitrogen fertilizer per 1,000 sq. ft. (93 m^2) monthly during active growth. Dethatch in spring before growth begins. Heat tolerant.
Features: Good choice for lawns, high-traffic plantings, playgrounds, shade. Pest and disease resistant.

Turfgrass: *Festuca arundinacea* hybrids. POACEAE (GRAMINEAE).
Common name: Tall Fescue.
Description: Many hybrid cultivars of medium-textured, slow-growing, medium to deep green, clumping, evergreen perennial turfgrasses, to 4 ft. (1.2 m) tall when uncut, usually mown 1½–2 in. (38–50 mm) tall for lawn use. Common cultivars include *F. arundinacea* 'Apache', 'Bonanza', 'Rebel', 'Tempo', and 'Trident'.
Season: Cool-season grass. Growth in spring, repeating in early autumn.
Plant hardiness: Hardy. Zones 2–7. Best in cold-winter, mild-summer climates.
Soil: Moist to damp, well-drained soil. Fertility: Average. 6.0–7.5 pH.
Planting: Spring in full sun to full shade, from seed, sod.
Care: Easy. Keep damp by watering deeply; allow soil to dry between waterings. Drought tolerant. Mow to maintain height with reel or rotary mower. Apply ¼–½ lb. (112–225 g) of nitrogen fertilizer per 1,000 sq. ft. (93 m^2) monthly during active growth; avoid overfertilizing. Dethatch in spring before growth begins. Heat tolerant.
Features: Good choice for banks, erosion control, lawns, high-traffic plantings, playgrounds, shade. Blends of tall fescue with other turfgrasses are commonly available. Pest and disease resistant.

Turfgrass: *Festuca longifolia.* POACEAE (GRAMINEAE).

Common name: Hard Fescue.

Description: A few cultivars of very fine-textured, slow-growing, gray green to deep green, bunching, needle-leaved, evergreen perennial turfgrasses, 12–18 in. (30–45 cm) tall when uncut, usually mown 1½–2½ in. (38–63 mm) tall for lawn use. Common cultivars include *F. longifolia* 'Aurora', 'Spartan', and 'Tournament'.

Season: Cool-season grass. Growth in spring, repeating in early autumn.

Plant hardiness: Hardy. Zones 3–9. Best in cold-winter, mild-summer climates.

Soil: Moist to dry, well-drained soil. Fertility: Average. 6.5–7.0 pH.

Planting: Spring in full sun to full shade, from seed.

Care: Easy. Keep damp; allow soil surface to dry between waterings. Drought tolerant. Mow monthly to maintain height with reel or rotary mower. Apply ¼–½ lb. (112–225 g) of nitrogen fertilizer per 1,000 sq. ft. (93 m²) monthly during active growth; avoid overfertilizing. Dethatch in spring before growth begins. Heat tolerant.

Features: Good choice for banks, roadsides, shade, slopes in low-traffic, Xeriscape plantings. Very pest and disease resistant.

Turfgrass: *Festuca rubra* var. *commutata.* POACEAE (GRAMINEAE).

Common name: Chewing Fescue.

Description: Several cultivars of fine-textured, slow-growing, green, creeping, needle-leaved, evergreen perennial turfgrasses, to 3 ft. (90 cm) tall when uncut, usually mown 1–2½ in. (25–63 mm) tall for lawn use. Common cultivars include *F. rubra* 'Banner', 'Jamestown', and 'Victory'.

Season: Cool-season grass. Growth in spring, repeating in early autumn.

Plant hardiness: Hardy. Zones 2–7. Best in humid, cool-summer climates.

Soil: Moist to dry, well-drained soil. Fertility: Average. 6.0–7.0 pH.

Planting: Spring in full sun to full shade, from seed.

Care: Easy. Keep damp; allow soil surface to dry between waterings. Drought tolerant. Mow monthly to maintain height with reel or rotary mower. Apply

1–2 lb. (450–900 g) of nitrogen fertilizer per 1,000 sq. ft. (93 m²) monthly during active growth; avoid overfertilizing. Dethatch in spring before growth begins. Heat tolerant.

Features: Good choice for banks, roadsides, shade, low-traffic, Xeriscape plantings. Pest and disease resistant.

Turfgrass: *Festuca rubra rubra.* POACEAE (GRAMINEAE).

Common name: Creeping Red Fescue.

Description: Several cultivars of fine-textured, slow-growing, medium to deep green, creeping, needle-leaved, evergreen perennial turfgrasses, to 3 ft. (90 cm) tall when uncut, usually mown 1½–2½ in. (38–63 mm) tall for lawn use. Lower leaf sheaths tinged purple, red. Common cultivars include *F. rubra* 'Boreal', 'Flyer', 'Pennlawn', and 'Shademaster'.

Season: Cool-season grass. Growth in spring, repeating in early autumn.

Plant hardiness: Hardy. Zones 2–7. Best in humid, cool-summer climates.

Soil: Moist to dry, well-drained soil. Fertility: Average. 6.5–7.0 pH.

Planting: Spring in full sun to full shade, from seed.

Care: Easy. Keep damp; allow soil surface to dry between waterings. Somewhat drought tolerant. Mow monthly to maintain height with reel or rotary mower. Apply ¼–½ lb. (112–225 g) of nitrogen fertilizer per 1,000 sq. ft. (93 m²) monthly during active growth; avoid overfertilizing. Dethatch in spring before growth begins.

Features: Good choice for banks, fillers, roadsides, shade, low-traffic plantings. Good for meadow plantings. Pest and disease resistant.

Turfgrass: *Lolium multiflorum.* POACEAE (GRAMINEAE).
Common name: Annual Ryegrass (Darnel, Italian Ryegrass).
Description: A few cultivars of coarse-textured, fast-growing, green, narrow-leaved, clumping, annual turfgrasses, to 3 ft. (90 cm) tall when uncut, usually mown 1½–2 in. (38–50 mm) tall for lawn use. Used primarily for overseeding dormant, warm-season grasses during winter and early spring.
Season: Cool-season grass. Growth in spring–summer; late autumn–spring in mild-winter climates when used for overseeding.
Plant hardiness: Plant as annual; self-seeding, zones 4–8.
Soil: Moist to damp, loose to dense soil. Fertility: Average–low. 6.0–7.0 pH.
Planting: Spring or autumn in full sun, from seed.
Care: Easy. Keep evenly moist. Mow frequently to maintain height with a reel or rotary mower. Apply ¼–½ lb. (112–225 g) of nitrogen fertilizer per 1,000 sq. ft. (93 m²) monthly during active growth.
Features: Good choice for banks, erosion control, overseeding, temporary filler, seasonal lawn plantings. Pest and disease resistant.

Turfgrass: *Lolium perenne.* POACEAE (GRAMINEAE).
Common name: Perennial Ryegrass.
Description: A few cultivars of fine- to medium-textured, fast-growing, bright green, narrow-leaved, clumping, short-lived, evergreen perennial turfgrasses, to 2 ft. (60 cm) tall when uncut, usually mown 1½–2 in. (38–50 mm) tall for lawn use. Substitute for *L. multiflorum,* annual ryegrass, for overseeding dormant, warm-season grasses during winter and early spring. Common cultivars include *L. perenne* 'All Star', 'Derby', 'Fiesta', 'Pennant', and 'Regal'.
Season: Cool-season grass. Growth in spring–summer; late autumn–spring in mild-winter climates when used for overseeding.
Plant hardiness: Hardy. Zones 4–8. Best in cool-summer climates.
Soil: Moist, loose to dense soil. Fertility: Average–low. 6.5–7.5 pH.
Planting: Spring or autumn in full sun, from seed, sod.

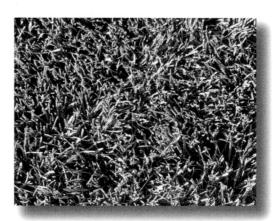

Care: Easy. Keep evenly moist. Mow frequently to maintain height with a reel or rotary mower. Apply ¼–½ lb. (112–225 g) of nitrogen fertilizer per 1,000 sq. ft. (93 m²) monthly during active growth. Dethatch, top dress, and reseed annually.
Features: Good choice for banks, erosion control, high-traffic plantings, playgrounds, overseeding, temporary filler, seasonal lawn plantings. Pest and disease resistant.

Turfgrass: *Paspalum notatum.* POACEAE (GRAMINEAE).
Common name: Bahia Grass.
Description: Several cultivars of very coarse-textured, fast-growing, bright green, broad-leaved, jointed, stoloniferous, rhizomatous, evergreen perennial turfgrasses, to 18 in. (45 cm) tall when uncut, usually mown 2–3 in. (50–75 mm) tall for lawn use. Common cultivars include *P. notatum* 'Argentine' and 'Pensacola'.
Season: Warm-season grass. Growth in spring–autumn; semi-dormant in winter.
Plant hardiness: Semi-hardy. Zones 7–11. Best in humid, subtropical climates.
Soil: Moist, well-drained, sandy soil. Fertility: Average–low. 5.0–6.5 pH.
Planting: Spring in full sun, from seed, sod.
Care: Moderate. Keep evenly moist. Mow frequently to maintain height with a sharp rotary mower. Apply ½ lb. (225 g) of nitrogen fertilizer per 1,000 sq. ft. (93 m²) monthly during active growth. Dethatch, reseed in winter.
Features: Good choice for tropical, subtropical lawns, seaside gardens. Invasive. Mole cricket, leafhopper, army worm and brown patch, chlorosis, dollar spot susceptible.

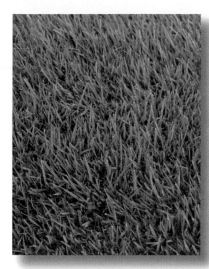

Turfgrass: *Poa pratensis.* POACEAE (GRAMINEAE).
Common name: Kentucky Bluegrass.
Description: Many cultivars of medium- to fine-textured, medium-growing, blue to deep green, narrow-leaved, clumping, rhizomatous, evergreen perennial turfgrasses, to 42 in. (1.1 m) tall when uncut, usually mown 1½–2½ in. (38–63 mm) tall for lawn use. Common cultivars include *P. pratensis* 'America', 'Challenger', 'Columbia', 'Eclipse', 'Nugget', and 'Vantage'.
Season: Cool-season grass. Growth in spring, repeating in early autumn; enters dormancy in sustained heat.
Plant hardiness: Hardy. Zones 2–7. Best in cold-winter, warm-summer climates.
Soil: Moist, well-drained loam. Fertility: Rich. 6.0–7.5 pH.
Planting: Spring in full to filtered sun, from seed, sod. Plant blends for best performance.
Care: Easy–moderate. Keep moist; allow soil surface to dry between waterings. Mow to maintain height with a reel or rotary mower. Apply ½–1 lb. (225–450 g) of nitrogen fertilizer per 1,000 sq. ft. (93 m²) monthly during active growth. Dethatch semi-annually.
Features: Good choice for lawns, high-traffic plantings, playgrounds, roadsides. Pest and disease resistant.

Turfgrass: *Stenotaphrum secundatum.* POACEAE (GRAMINEAE).
Common name: St. Augustine Grass.
Description: A few cultivars of very coarse-textured, fast-growing, green to deep green, broad-leaved, creeping, stoloniferous, tropical perennial turfgrasses, to 14 in. (36 cm) tall when uncut, usually mown 1½–2 in. (38–50 mm) tall for lawn use. Common cultivars include *S. secundatum* 'Floratum', 'Seville', and 'Sunclipse'.
Season: Warm-season grass. Growth in spring–autumn; dormant in winter.
Plant hardiness: Tender. Zones 8–11. Best in tropical climates.
Soil: Moist, well-drained, sandy soil. Fertility: Average. 6.0–8.0 pH.
Planting: Spring in full sun to full shade, from plugs, sod, sprigs. Space plugs 12–16 in. (30–40 cm) apart, sprigs 4 in. (10 cm) apart.
Care: Moderate. Keep evenly moist. Mow frequently to maintain height with a sharp rotary mower. Apply ½–1 lb. (225–450 g) of nitrogen fertilizer per 1,000 sq. ft. (93 m²) monthly during active growth. Dethatch in winter. Heat tolerant.
Features: Good choice for tropical, subtropical lawns; seaside, shade gardens. Invasive. Chinch bug, nematode, sod webworm, army worm and chlorosis, St. Augustine decline (SAD) virus susceptible.

Turfgrass: *Zoysia* species. POACEAE (GRAMINEAE).
Common name: Zoysia Grass.
Description: Three species and cultivars of fine-textured, slow-growing, blue green or deep green, narrow-leaved, creeping, stoloniferous, rhizomatous, evergreen perennial turfgrasses, to 6 in. (15 cm) tall when uncut, usually mown 1–2 in. (25–50 mm) tall for lawn use. Common species include *Z. japonica, Z. matrella,* and *Z. tenuifolia.*
Season: Warm-season grass. Growth in spring–autumn; dormant in winter.
Plant hardiness: Hardy. Zones 6–9. Best in arid, subtropical climates.
Soil: Moist to damp, well-drained, sandy soil. Fertility: Average–low. 6.0–7.5 pH.
Planting: Spring in full to filtered sun, from plugs, sod, sprigs. Space plugs 1 ft. (30 cm) apart, sprigs 4–6 in. (10–15 cm) apart.
Care: Moderate. Keep damp; allow soil surface to dry between waterings. Drought tolerant. Mow to maintain height with a reel or rotary mower. Apply ¼–½ lb. (112–225 g) of nitrogen fertilizer per 1,000 sq. ft. (93 m²) monthly during active growth. Dethatch annually in autumn when dormancy begins. Overseed in winter with annual ryegrass. Tolerates heat.
Features: Good choice for banks, high-traffic plantings, playgrounds, Xeriscapes. Disease resistant. Billbug susceptible.

GROUND COVERS

Ground cover: *Ajuga reptans.* LAMIACEAE (LABIATAE).
Common name: Carpet Bugleweed (Ajuga).
Description: Many cultivars of fast-growing, prostrate, spreading, stoloniferous, deciduous perennial herbs, 4–12 in. (10–30 cm) tall and 18–24 in. (45–60 cm) wide. Opposite, shiny, textured, bronze, deep green, pink, white, variegated, broadly oval, rounded, curly leaves, to 4 in. (10 cm) long, turning bronze, purple, red in autumn.
Bloom: Many tiny, blue, pink, purple, white, tubular, 2-lipped flowers, to ⅓ in. (8 mm) long, in whorled, spikelike clusters, to 6 in. (15 cm) long, in late spring–early summer.
Plant hardiness: Hardy. Zones 3–9.
Soil: Moist, well-drained humus. Fertility: Rich–average. 6.0–7.0 pH.
Planting: Spring in partial to full shade, 6–18 in. (15–45 cm) apart, after soil warms.
Care: Easy. Keep moist; allow soil surface to dry between waterings. Fertilize quarterly. Shear in spring before growth begins; repeat after blooms fade. Propagate by division.
Features: Good choice for banks, hanging baskets, borders, containers, paths in cottage, natural, shade, rock, woodland gardens. Leaves good for tea. Invasive. Slug, snail and leaf burn, fungal disease, crown rot susceptible.

Ground cover: *Aptenia cordifolia (Mesembryanthemum cordifolium).* AIZOACEAE.
Common name: Candy Apple (Baby Sun Rose).
Description: Several cultivars of short-lived, medium-growing, prostrate, spreading, evergreen perennial succulents, to 10 in. (25 cm) tall and 4 ft. (1.2 m) wide. Opposite, shiny, fleshy, green becoming gray green, sometimes variegated or cream-edged, broadly oval or heart-shaped leaves, to 1 in. (25 mm) long.
Bloom: Many showy, purple, red, cup-shaped flowers, to 1 in. (25 mm) wide, often in twins or triplets, in spring–summer.
Plant hardiness: Tender. Zones 8–11. Best in arid, mild-winter climates.
Soil: Damp to dry, well-drained, sandy soil. Fertility: Average. 6.5–7.5 pH.
Planting: Spring in full to filtered sun, 2 ft. (60 cm) apart, after soil warms.
Care: Easy. Keep damp; allow soil to dry between waterings. Drought tolerant. Fertilize annually in spring. Pinch to shape, control growth. Propagate by cuttings, seed.
Features: Good choice for banks, hanging baskets, borders, containers, paths, walls in arid, rock, Xeriscape gardens. Slug, snail and fungal disease susceptible.

Ground cover: *Armeria maritima.* PLUMBAGINACEAE.
Common name: Thrift (Common Thrift, Sea Pink).
Description: Many cultivars and horticultural varieties of highly varied, slow-growing, mounding or clumping, evergreen perennial herbs, to 6 in. (15 cm) tall and 1 ft. (30 cm) wide. Shiny, blue green, very narrow, needlelike leaves, 4–6 in. (10–15 cm) long. Common cultivars include *A. maritima* 'Alba', 'Bee's Ruby', 'Bloodstone', 'Cotton Tail', 'Laucheana', and 'Rubrifolia'.
Bloom: Many tiny, white, pink, purple, red flowers, to ⅛ in. (3 mm) wide, in showy, ball-shaped clusters, to ¾ in. (19 mm) wide, on erect, narrow, wiry stems rising above the foliage, 10–12 in. (25–30 cm) tall, in spring–summer.
Plant hardiness: Hardy. Zones 3–10. Self-seeding. Best in arid, mild-winter climates.
Soil: Damp to dry, well-drained, sandy soil. Fertility: Average. 6.5–8.0 pH. Salt tolerant.
Planting: Spring in full sun, 1 ft. (30 cm) apart, after soil warms.
Care: Easy. Keep damp; allow soil to dry between waterings. Drought, heat tolerant. Fertilize annually in spring. Renew colonies by dividing, discarding central plants. Propagate by cuttings, division, seed.
Features: Good choice for accents, borders, containers, edgings in cottage, rock, seaside, Xeriscape gardens. Good for cutting, drying. Pest and disease resistant.

Ground cover: *Campanula poscharskyana.* CAMPANULACEAE.

Common name: Serbian Bellflower.

Description: Several cultivars of fast-growing, prostrate, creeping, spreading, or trailing perennial herbs, to 1 ft. (30 cm) tall and 3–4 ft. (90–120 cm) wide. Smooth, textured, green, blue green, heart- or kidney-shaped, veined leaves, to 1½ in. (38 mm) long, on jointed stems, to 2 ft. (60 cm) long.

Bloom: Many pale, lavender blue, bell- or star-shaped flowers, ½–1 in. (12–25 mm) wide, often with pale blue, deep-throated centers, in late spring–autumn.

Plant hardiness: Hardy. Zones 3–7.

Soil: Damp, well-drained humus. Fertility: Average. 6.5–7.0 pH.

Planting: Spring in full to filtered sun, 12–18 in. (30–45 cm) apart, after frost hazard has passed.

Care: Easy. Keep moist. Fertilize annually in spring. Deadhead spent flowers. Propagate by cuttings, division, seed.

Features: Good choice for accents, beds, borders, walls in cottage, rock, wildlife gardens. Attracts birds, hummingbirds. Spider mite, slug, snail and aster yellows susceptible.

Ground cover: *Cerastium tomentosum.* CARYOPHYLLACEAE.

Common name: Snow-in-Summer.

Description: A few cultivars of short-lived, medium-growing, prostrate, mat-forming perennial herbs, 4–8 in. (10–20 cm) tall and 3 ft. (90 cm) wide. Opposite, woolly, gray, silver, white, lance-shaped, pointed leaves, to 1 in. (25 mm) long.

Bloom: Many tiny, bright white, divided- and 5-petaled flowers, to ½ in. (12 mm) wide, on erect, branching stems, to 1 ft. (30 cm) long, in late spring–early summer.

Plant hardiness: Hardy. Zones 1–10.

Soil: Moist to damp, well-drained, sandy loam. Fertility: Average–low. 6.0–7.0 pH.

Planting: Spring in full to filtered sun, 18 in. (45 cm) apart, when soil is workable.

Care: Easy. Keep damp; allow soil surface to dry between waterings. Drought tolerant. Fertilize annually in spring. Shear after bloom. Renew colonies by dividing, discarding central plants. Propagate by cuttings, division, seed.

Features: Good choice for accents, banks, containers, edgings, paths in cottage, meadow, rock, Xeriscape gardens. Good companion for spring bulbs. Pest and disease resistant.

Ground cover: *Chamaemelum nobile (Anthemis nobilis).* ASTERACEAE (COMPOSITAE).

Common name: Garden Chamomile (Chamomile, Roman Chamomile).

Description: Several cultivars of long-lived, slow-growing, creeping and mounding, branching perennial herbs, to 1 ft. (30 cm) tall and 18 in. (45 cm) wide. Alternate, hairy, bright green, feathery, twice-divided, finely cut, fragrant leaves, to 2 in. (50 mm) long. *Matricaria recutita,* sweet false chamomile, a related species with similar care needs, is the source of herbs used to make chamomile tea.

Bloom: Many showy, white-petaled, daisy- or buttonlike flowers, to 1 in. (25 mm) wide, with bright gold, yellow centers, in late summer–late autumn.

Plant hardiness: Hardy. Zones 4–10. Best in mild-summer climates.

Soil: Moist to damp, well-drained soil. Fertility: Rich–average. 6.5–7.5 pH.

Planting: Spring in full sun to partial shade, 4–8 in. (10–20 cm) apart, after soil warms.

Care: Easy. Keep damp; allow soil surface to dry between waterings. Drought tolerant. Fertilize every 2 months. Shear or mow mounding cultivars after bloom. Propagate by division, seed.

Features: Good choice for banks, lawn alternatives, paths, high-traffic plantings in cottage, meadow, Xeriscape gardens. Good for cutting. Pest and disease resistant.

Ground cover: *Delosperma cooperi.* AIZOACEAE.
Common name: Purple Ice Plant.
Description: Several cultivars of long-lived, slow-growing, prostrate, branching, evergreen, perennial succulent shrubs, 4–8 in. (10–20 cm) high and 18 in. (45 cm) wide. Opposite, bristly, green, gray green, tubular, fleshy, flattened, pointed leaves, to 2½ in. (63 mm) long, with rows of tiny bumps, turning red in autumn.
Bloom: Many showy, single, bright to deep purple, rose, many-petaled, open flowers, to 2 in. (50 mm) wide, with gold centers, in summer.
Plant hardiness: Semi-hardy. Zones 5–10.
Soil: Damp to dry, well-drained, sandy soil. Fertility: Average–low. 7.0–8.0 pH. Salt tolerant.
Planting: Spring in full to filtered sun, 10–12 in. (25–30 cm) apart, after soil warms.
Care: Easy. Keep damp; allow soil to dry completely between waterings. Very drought, heat tolerant. Propagate by cuttings, seed.
Features: Good choice for banks, containers, erosion control in arid, seaside, small-space, Xeriscape gardens. Disease resistant. Slug, snail susceptible.

Ground cover: *Duchesnea indica.* ROSACEAE.
Common name: Indian Mock Strawberry (Mock Strawberry).
Description: Several cultivars of long-lived, fast-growing, prostrate, branching, evergreen perennial herbs, 3–6 in. (75–150 mm) high and 3 ft. (90 cm) wide, with root-bearing runners. Shiny, blue green, strawberry-like, divided, oval, coarsely toothed leaves, with triplet leaflets, to 1 in. (25 mm) long, turning red, yellow in autumn, and with downy, light green undersides.
Bloom: Many showy, yellow, 5-petaled, open-faced flowers, ½–1 in. (12–25 mm) wide, in summer, forming round, red, mealy, strawberry-like, edible but unpalatable fruit, to ½ in. (12 mm) wide, in late summer–autumn.
Plant hardiness: Hardy. Zones 4–11.
Soil: Moist to damp, well-drained soil. Fertility: Average–low. 6.5–7.0 pH.
Planting: Spring in filtered sun to full shade, 12–18 in. (30–45 cm) apart, when soil is workable.
Care: Easy. Keep damp; allow soil surface to dry between waterings. Drought tolerant. Fertilize annually in spring. Renew colonies by dividing, discarding central plants. Propagate by division, offsets, runners, seed.
Features: Good choice for banks, hanging baskets, containers, erosion control in arid, cottage, natural, seaside, small-space, Xeriscape gardens. Invasive. Pest and disease resistant.

Ground cover: *Dymondia margaretae.* ASTERACEAE (COMPOSITAE).
Common name: Dymondia.
Description: A few cultivars of slow-growing, prostrate, branching, semi-evergreen perennial herbs, to 4 in. (10 cm) tall and 12–18 in. (30–45 cm) wide, with numerous offsets. Hairy, deep green, gray green, lance-shaped, shallow-lobed, wavy-edged leaves, 2–3 in. (50–75 mm) long, with downy, gray undersides.
Bloom: Many inconspicuous, gold, yellow, daisylike, open-faced flowers, 1–1½ in. (25–38 mm) wide, on short stalks, in summer.
Plant hardiness: Semi-hardy. Zones 7–10.
Soil: Moist to damp, well-drained loam. Fertility: Average. 6.5–7.5 pH.
Planting: Spring in full to filtered sun, 8–12 in. (20–30 cm) apart, after soil warms.
Care: Easy. Keep damp; allow soil surface to dry between waterings. Drought tolerant. Fertilize annually in spring. Shear in spring before growth begins. Renew colonies by dividing, discarding central plants. Propagate by cuttings, division, offsets, seed.
Features: Good choice for banks, paths, walls in meadow, natural, Xeriscape gardens. Pest and disease resistant.

Ground cover: *Galium odoratum (Asperula odorata).* RUBIACEAE.

Common name: Sweet Woodruff.

Description: Several cultivars of long-lived, fast-growing, prostrate, creeping, spreading perennial herbs, to 6 in. (15 cm) tall and 3–4 ft. (90–120 cm) or more wide. Smooth, bright green, lance-shaped, pointed, very finely toothed, fragrant leaves, to 1½ in. (38 mm) long, armed with bristles on the leaf tips, in dense, whorled clusters along low, woody stems.

Bloom: Many tiny, white, star-shaped, 4-petaled, open-faced flowers, to ¼ in. (6 mm) wide, in branching, open clusters, to 1½ in. (38 mm) wide, in late spring–summer.

Plant hardiness: Hardy. Zones 4–9. Self-seeding.

Soil: Damp to dry, well-drained loam. Fertility: Rich–average. 7.0–7.5 pH.

Planting: Spring in partial to full shade, 1 ft. (30 cm) apart.

Care: Easy. Keep damp; allow soil surface to dry between waterings. Avoid fertilizing to control growth. Propagate by division, seed.

Features: Good choice for accents, mixed-shrub plantings in natural, shade gardens. Good for cutting, drying. Good companion to azalea, rhododendron. Invasive; plant in buried containers. Pest and disease resistant.

Ground cover: *Hypericum calycinum.* HYPERICACEAE.

Common name: Aaron's Beard (Creeping St.-John's-Wort, Goldflower).

Description: Several cultivars of long-lived, fast-growing, prostrate, spreading, stoloniferous, evergreen perennial shrubs, to 18 in. (45 cm) tall and 18–24 in. (45–60 cm) wide. Opposite, smooth, green, lance-shaped, pointed leaves, to 4 in. (10 cm) long, with pale green, veined undersides.

Bloom: Many showy, gold, yellow, 5-petaled, open, round flowers, to 2 in. (50 mm) wide, with feathery centers of erect stamens, in summer.

Plant hardiness: Hardy. Zones 5–10.

Soil: Damp to dry, well-drained or clayey soil. Fertility: Average–low. 6.0–7.0 pH.

Planting: Spring in full sun to partial shade, 9–12 in. (23–30 cm) apart.

Care: Easy. Keep damp; allow soil surface to dry between waterings. Drought tolerant. Avoid fertilizing. Shear in spring before growth begins; repeat after bloom. Propagate by cuttings, division, seed, suckers.

Features: Good choice for banks, erosion control, understory plantings in rock, woodland, Xeriscape gardens. Invasive. Pest and disease resistant.

Ground cover: *Juniperus horizontalis.* CUPRESSACEAE.

Common name: Creeping Juniper.

Description: Many cultivars of long-lived, fast-growing, prostrate, coniferous evergreen trees, 6–12 in. (15–30 cm) tall and 6–10 ft. (1.8–3 m) wide, with woody, spreading branches. Shiny, mostly blue green, sometimes bronze, yellow, scaly, fragrant foliage with overlapped plates, and with reddish brown, furrowed bark.

Blooms/Cones: Yellow, catkinlike, male cones and light blue, aromatic, pulpy, berrylike female cones appear in spring, ripening in autumn.

Plant hardiness: Hardy. Zones 2–9.

Soil: Damp, well-drained loam. Fertility: Average. 6.0–8.0 pH.

Planting: Spring in full to filtered sun, 3–5 ft. (90–150 cm) apart.

Care: Easy. Allow soil surface to dry between waterings. Fertilize annually in spring until established. Shear new foliage in spring to train, control growth. Propagate by cuttings, grafting, seed.

Features: Good choice for banks, barriers, containers, erosion control, fencelines, understory plantings in natural, open, woodland gardens. Aphid, borer, spider mite and juniper blight susceptible.

Ground cover: *Lampranthus* species. AIZOACEAE.
Common name: Ice Plant.
Description: About 160 species of slow-growing, mostly prostrate, spreading, ever-green perennial succulents, 3–24 in. (75–610 mm) high and 1–3 ft. (30–90 cm) wide. Opposite, smooth or shiny, blue green, gray green, fleshy, tubular and often 3-sided, curved, pointed leaves, ¾–1½ in. (19–38 mm) long, turning bronze or red in autumn.
Bloom: Many showy, usually single, vivid orange, pink, purple, red, rose, white, yellow, many-petaled flowers, ½–2½ in. (12–63 mm) wide, often with broad, fuzzy centers, in winter, spring, summer, or autumn, depending on species and climate.
Plant hardiness: Tender. Zones 4–11.
Soil: Damp to dry, sandy soil. Fertility: Average–low. 7.0–8.0 pH. Salt tolerant.
Planting: Spring in full sun, 18–24 in. (45–60 cm) apart, after soil warms.
Care: Easy. Keep damp; allow soil to dry between waterings. Drought, heat tolerant. Fertilize annually in spring. Prune spent seed capsules, old leaves to maintain height, dense growth. Propagate by cuttings, seed.
Features: Good choice for banks, hanging baskets, containers, erosion control, massed plantings in arid, meadow, seaside gardens. Attracts bees. Disease resistant. Slug, snail susceptible.

Ground cover: *Lantana montevidensis* and hybrids. VERBENACEAE.
Common name: Trailing Lantana (Polecat Geranium, Weeping Lantana).
Description: Several cultivars and hybrids of fast-growing, low, spreading and trailing, woody, evergreen shrubs, to 2 ft. (60 cm) tall and 3–5 ft. (90–150 cm) wide or long. Opposite or whorled, deeply textured, deep green, often rugosa-rose-like, broadly oval, coarsely toothed, veined, fragrant leaves, to 1 in. (25 mm) long, often tinged purple, red.
Bloom: Many tiny, lilac, pink, purple, rose, 4-petaled, tubular flowers, in dense, ball-shaped clusters, 1–2 in. (25–50 mm) wide, in spring–autumn.
Plant hardiness: Tender. Plant as tender annual, zones 3–7; ground hardy, zones 8–11.
Soil: Damp, well-drained humus. Fertility: Average. 6.5–7.0 pH.
Planting: Spring in full sun, 18 in. (45 cm) apart, when soil warms.
Care: Easy. Keep damp; allow soil surface to dry between waterings. Drought tolerant. Fertilize quarterly. Prune in spring before growth begins, after blooms drop. Protect from hard frost. Propagate by cuttings, seed.
Features: Good choice for banks, hanging baskets, containers, erosion control, foregrounds, hedges in cottage, meadow, natural, seaside, small-space gardens. Mealybug, orthezia and mildew susceptible.

Ground cover: *Liriope muscari.* LILIACEAE.
Common name: Big Blue Lilyturf.
Description: Several cultivars of medium-growing, clumping, tufted, tuberous, evergreen perennial herbs, 18–24 in (45–60 cm) tall and wide. Shiny, deep green or variegated, spear- or strap-shaped, pointed leaves, to 2 ft. (60 cm) long, in fountain-shaped, tufted clusters. Common cultivars include *L. muscari* 'Grandiflora', 'Majestic', 'Munroe White', and 'Variegata'.
Bloom: Many tiny, purple, violet, white, grape-hyacinth-like flowers, in spiking, whorled clusters, 6–10 in. (15–25 cm) tall, in late summer–early autumn.
Plant hardiness: Semi-hardy. Zones 6–11.
Soil: Moist, well-drained humus or, in water features, shoreline sites. Fertility: Average. 6.5–7.0 pH.
Planting: Spring in filtered sun to full shade, 8–12 in. (20–30 cm) apart.
Care: Easy. Keep evenly moist. Fertilize annually in spring. Deadhead spent leaves. Propagate by division.
Features: Good choice for banks, borders, edgings in cottage, formal, shade, small-space gardens or water feature shorelines. Good for cutting. Disease resistant. Slug, snail susceptible.

Ground cover: *Mentha* species and hybrids. LAMIACEAE (LABIATAE).
Common name: Mint.
Description: About 25 species and many hybrid cultivars of fast-growing, erect or prostrate, creeping or mat-forming, stoloniferous, evergreen or deciduous perennial herbs, 1–3 ft. (30–90 cm) tall and 3–4 ft. (90–120 cm) wide. Mostly opposite, deeply textured, deep green or variegated, oval to lance-shaped, toothed or smooth, very fragrant leaves, 1–4 in. (25–100 mm) long. Commonly cultivated species include *M. × piperita,* peppermint; *M. pulegium,* pennyroyal; *M. requienii,* creme-de-menthe plant; *M. spicata,* spearmint; and *M. suaveolens,* apple mint.
Bloom: Many tiny, pink, purple, white, tubular, 2-lipped flowers, in branching, pyramid-shaped spiking clusters, in summer–autumn.
Plant hardiness: Hardy. Zones 2–9.
Soil: Moist, well-drained, sandy soil or, in water features, shoreline sites. Fertility: Average. 5.5–7.0 pH.
Planting: Spring in full sun to partial shade, 3 ft. (90 cm) apart, when soil is workable.
Care: Easy. Keep evenly moist. Fertilize quarterly. Shear in spring before growth begins. Renew colonies by dividing, discarding central plants. Propagate by cuttings, division, runners, stolons.
Features: Good choice for containers, edgings, massed plantings in bog, country, herb, natural, wildlife gardens and water feature shorelines. Many species good as culinary flavoring. Very invasive; plant in buried containers. Pest and disease resistant.

Ground cover: *Pachysandra terminalis.* BUXACEAE.
Common name: Japanese Spurge.
Description: Several cultivars of medium-growing, prostrate, creeping, woody, stoloniferous, semi-evergreen perennial herbs, to 1 ft. (30 cm) tall and 2 ft. (60 cm) wide. Whorled, shiny, deep green or variegated, lance-shaped, toothed, veined leaves, 2–4 in. (50–100 mm) long. Common cultivars include *P. terminalis* 'Cut Leaf', 'Green Carpet', 'Green Sheen', and 'Variegata'.
Bloom: Insignificant greenish white flowers, in spikelike clusters, to 2 in. (50 mm) tall, in late spring.
Plant hardiness: Hardy. Zones 4–9. Best in mild-summer climates.
Soil: Moist, well-drained humus. Fertility: Rich. 6.0–7.0 pH.
Planting: Spring in partial to full shade, 6–12 in. (15–30 cm) apart, when soil is workable.
Care: Easy. Keep evenly moist. Fertilize quarterly. Mulch. Shear, thin in spring before growth begins. Propagate by cuttings, division.

Features: Good choice for borders, edgings, massed plantings beneath trees in shade, woodland gardens. Invasive. Deer resistant. Euonymus scale, leaf roller and leaf blight canker, rhizoctonia root rot susceptible.

Ground cover: *Phlox stolonifera.* POLEMONIACEAE.
Common name: Creeping Phlox
Description: A few cultivars of slow-growing, hairy, prostrate, creeping or mounding, stoloniferous, evergreen perennial herbs, 6–12 in. (15–30 cm) tall and to 2 ft. (60 cm) wide. Opposite, hairy, deep green, broadly oval to lance-shaped, pointed leaves, to 4 in. (10 cm) long. Common cultivars include *P. stolonifera* 'Blue Ridge', 'Grandiflora', 'Lavender Lady', 'Rosea', and 'Violacea'.
Bloom: Many solitary, blue, lavender, pink, purple, violet, white, 5-petaled, open, blunt flowers, to 1 in. (25 mm) wide, on branched stems, in spring.
Plant hardiness: Hardy. Zones 4–9.
Soil: Moist, well-drained humus. Fertility: Rich. 5.5–7.5 pH.
Planting: Spring in filtered sun to full shade, 1–2 ft. (30–60 cm) apart.
Care: Easy. Keep evenly moist. Fertilize monthly. Shear in spring, divide before growth begins to renew. Propagate by division.
Features: Good choice for accents, edgings, massed plantings beneath trees, walls in rock, shade, woodland gardens. Spider mite and powdery mildew susceptible.

Ground cover: *Potentilla tabernaemontani (P. neumanniana).* ROSACEAE.
Common name: Spring Cinquefoil.
Description: A few cultivars of fast-growing, prostrate, mat-forming, perennial herbs, 3–6 in. (75–150 mm) tall and to 40 in. (1 m) wide, with rooting stems. Alternate, smooth, bright green, palmlike, divided leaves, with 5 oval, deeply toothed leaflets, to ¾ in. (19 mm) long. *P. atrosanguinea, P. nepalensis,* and *P. recta* are closely related species with similar care needs.
Bloom: A few showy, gold, yellow, saucer-shaped, 4-petaled, open flowers, to ⅝ in. (16 mm) wide, in spring–summer.
Plant hardiness: Hardy. Zones 5–9.
Soil: Moist to damp, well-drained soil. Fertility: Average. 6.5–7.0 pH.
Planting: Spring in full sun to partial shade, 10 in. (25 cm) apart, when frost hazard has passed.
Care: Easy. Keep damp; allow soil surface to dry between waterings. Fertilize quarterly. Shear or mow in spring before growth begins. Propagate by division, seed.
Features: Good choice for borders, edgings, hedges, low-traffic paths, massed plantings in natural, rock, shade, wildlife, woodland gardens. Attracts butterflies. Invasive; separate from turfgrass with masonry edgings. Pest and disease resistant.

Ground cover: *Rosmarinus officinalis prostratus.* LAMIACEAE (LABIATAE).
Common name: Dwarf Rosemary.
Description: Many cultivars of fast-growing, low and spreading or trailing, evergreen shrubs, to 2 ft. (60 cm) tall and 6–8 ft. (1.8–2.4 m) wide. Shiny, leathery, deep or olive green, needlelike, very fragrant leaves, to 1½ in. (38 mm) long.
Bloom: Many tiny, light blue, violet flowers, in erect, spiking clusters, to 4 in. (10 cm) long, in summer–autumn.
Plant hardiness: Tender. Plant as annual, zones 5–6; ground hardy, zones 7–11.
Soil: Damp to dry, well-drained soil. Fertility: Low. 7.0–8.0 pH. Salt tolerant.
Planting: Spring in full sun, 2–3 ft. (60–90 cm) apart, after soil warms.
Care: Easy. Keep damp; allow soil surface to dry between waterings. Avoid fertilizing. Prune, shear to shape growth. Renew colonies by dividing, discarding central plants. Propagate by cuttings, seed.
Features: Good choice for hanging baskets, beds, borders, containers, edgings, massed plantings, walls in cottage, formal, meadow gardens. Good as culinary spice, topiary. Pest and disease resistant.

Ground cover: *Rotala rotundifolia.* LYTHRACEAE.
Common name: Pink Sprite.
Description: Several cultivars of low, clumping or mounding, deciduous perennial herbs, to 4 in. (10 cm) tall and 2 ft. (60 cm) wide. Opposite, shiny, bright becoming deep green, egg-shaped leaves, to ½ in. (12 mm) wide, with pale white to red undersides.
Bloom: Many insignificant, tiny, pink, violet flowers, in erect, cone-shaped spiking clusters, to 1 in. (25 mm) tall, in summer–autumn.
Plant hardiness: Tender. Plant as annual, zones 4–9; ground hardy, zones 10–11.
Soil: Moist to wet, well-drained humus or, in water features, shallow marginal or shoreline sites. Fertility: Average. 6.0–7.0 pH.
Planting: Spring in full sun to partial shade, 1 ft. (30 cm) apart, or submerged 6–12 in. (15–30 cm) deep.
Care: Easy. Keep evenly moist. Fertilize every 2 months. Pinch, prune to direct growth.
Features: Good choice for borders, containers, foregrounds, massed plantings in bog, woodland gardens and water feature margins and shorelines. Pest and disease resistant.

Ground cover: *Sagina subulata.* CARYOPHYLLACEAE.

Common name: Irish Moss (Corsican Pearlwort, Scotch Moss).

Description: Several cultivars of slow-growing, prostrate, mat-forming, evergreen perennial herbs, to 5 in. (13 cm) tall and 6–8 in. (15–20 cm) wide, with rooting stems. Opposite, shiny, golden or deep green, mosslike, bristly, pointed leaves, to ¼ in. (6 mm) long. *Arenaria verna (A.* var. *caespitosa),* also called Irish moss, is a related species with similar habit and care needs.

Bloom: Profuse, single, tiny, white, 5-petaled flowers, ½–¾ in. (12–19 mm) wide, with yellow centers, in summer.

Plant hardiness: Hardy. Zones 4–9. Self-seeding. Best in mild-summer climates.

Soil: Moist, well-drained humus. Fertility: Rich. 6.5–7.5 pH.

Planting: Spring in full sun to partial shade, 6 in. (15 cm) apart, when soil warms.

Care: Easy. Keep evenly moist. Fertilize quarterly. Divide to avoid mounding. Propagate by division.

Features: Good choice for borders, low-traffic paths, walls in cottage, natural, rock gardens. Good for bonsai, plantings between paving stones. Invasive. Disease resistant. Cutworm, slug, snail susceptible.

Ground cover: *Sedum* species. CRASSULACEAE.

Common name: Stonecrop (Orpine).

Description: About 600 species of slow-growing, prostrate, evergreen, perennial succulent herbs, 3–12 in. (75–305 mm) tall and to 1 ft. (30 cm) wide. Alternate, smooth, fleshy, bright blue or red green, overlapping, rounded leaves, to 3 in. (75 mm) long, often with bronze, red edges, in low rosette-shaped clusters.

Bloom: Profuse, tiny, mostly white, yellow, sometimes pink, purple, red, 5-petaled flowers, in clusters to 2 in. (50 mm) wide, in spring–autumn, depending on species.

Plant hardiness: Hardy. Zones 2–11, depending on species; most are hardy, zones 4–10.

Soil: Damp to dry, well-drained, sandy soil. Fertility: Average–low. 6.0–7.5 pH.

Planting: Spring in full sun to partial shade, 1–2 ft. (30–60 cm) apart, after soil warms.

Care: Easy. Keep damp; allow soil to dry completely between waterings. Avoid fertilizing. Renew colonies by dividing, discarding central plants. Propagate by cuttings, division, seed.

Features: Good choice for accents, borders, containers, edgings, massed plantings in arid, natural, seaside, small-space gardens. Attracts butterflies. Pest and disease resistant.

Ground cover: *Thymus serpyllum (T. praecox* subs. *arcticus).* LAMIACEAE (LABIATAE).

Common name: Creeping Thyme (Mother-of-Thyme).

Description: Many cultivars of fast-growing, prostrate, mat-forming, evergreen perennial herbs, 3–6 in. (75–150 mm) high and to 3 ft. (90 cm) wide, with rooting stems. Opposite, smooth, deep or gray green, round or oval, fragrant leaves, to ½ in. (12 mm) long.

Bloom: Many tiny, pink, purple, 2-lipped flowers, 3⁄16–¼ in. (5–6 mm) wide, in summer–early autumn.

Plant hardiness: Hardy. Zones 3–10.

Soil: Damp, well-drained, sandy soil. Fertility: Average–low. 6.5–7.5 pH.

Planting: Spring in full to filtered sun, 1–2 ft. (30–60 cm) apart, after soil warms.

Care: Easy. Keep damp; allow soil surface to dry between waterings. Avoid fertilizing. Pinch to control growth; shear in spring before growth begins. Propagate by cuttings, division.

Features: Good choice for edgings, low-traffic paths, massed plantings in arid, natural, seaside gardens. Attracts bees. Disease resistant. Slug, snail susceptible.

VINES

Vine: *Ampelopsis brevipendunculata.* VITACEAE.

Common name: Porcelain Berry.

Description: Many cultivars and horticultural varieties of fast-growing, climbing, woody, deciduous vines, 25–30 ft. (7.5–9 m) long, with forked stem tendrils. Alternate, textured, bright green or variegated, broadly oval, 3–5-lobed, coarsely toothed leaves, to 5 in. (13 cm) long, turning red in autumn.

Bloom: Insignificant flowers in summer form showy, porcelain-like, round, light green becoming blue, green, pink, purple berries, to ¼ in. (6 mm) wide, in tight, branching clusters, in late summer–autumn. Blooms on new wood.

Plant hardiness: Hardy. Zones 5–10.

Soil: Moist to dry, well-drained soil. Fertility: Average–low. 6.0–7.5 pH.

Planting: Spring in full sun to full shade, 10 ft. (3 m) apart, after soil warms.

Care: Easy. Keep damp; allow soil surface to dry between waterings. Fertilize annually in spring. Provide sturdy support. Prune in late autumn to thin, direct growth. Propagate by cuttings, layering, seed.

Features: Good choice for arbors, fences, slopes, walls in cottage, shade, woodland gardens. Attracts birds. Pest and disease resistant.

Vine: *Bougainvillea* species, cultivars, and hybrids. NYCTAGINACEAE.

Common name: Bougainvillea.

> **WARNING**
> Spines of *Bougainvillea* species are sharp and cause punctures and cuts. Wear gloves when pruning or tying vines.

Description: About 14 species and many hybrid cultivars of medium-growing, shrubby, vining, woody, evergreen shrubs, 20–30 ft. (6–9 m) long, armed with sharp, thorny spines. Alternate, smooth, deep green, oval, folded, pointed leaves, to 2½ in. (63 mm) long.

Bloom: Many insignificant flowers, surrounded by showy, vivid, crimson, pink, purple, orange, yellow, paper-thin, petal-like, bracts, to 3 in. (75 mm) wide, in spring–autumn.

Plant hardiness: Tender; semi-hardy when established. Zones 7–11.

Soil: Moist to dry, well-drained soil. Fertility: Average. 6.5–7.5 pH.

Planting: Spring in full to filtered sun, 4–5 ft. (1.2–1.5 m) apart, after frost hazard has passed and soil warms.

Care: Moderate. Keep damp; drought tolerant when established. Fertilize quarterly. Tie to sturdy supports. Prune in early spring before growth begins to thin, direct growth. Protect from frost. Propagate by cuttings.

Features: Good choice for arbors, trellises in seaside, tropical gardens. Attracts birds, hummingbirds. Pest and disease resistant.

Vine: *Campsis radicans.* BIGNONIACEAE.

Common name: Trumpet Vine (Trumpet Creeper).

Description: Many cultivars and horticultural varieties of fast-growing, climbing, vining, woody, deciduous vine, 30–40 ft. (9–12 m) long, with aerial rootlets. Opposite, shiny, green, divided, 9–11-lobed leaves, with textured, oval, toothed, veined leaflets, to 2½ in. (63 mm) long.

Bloom: Many showy, orange, scarlet, trumpet-shaped, flared flowers, to 3 in. (75 mm) long, in branching clusters, in summer.

Plant hardiness: Hardy. Zones 5–10.

Soil: Damp, well-drained soil. Fertility: Average. 6.5–7.0 pH.

Planting: Spring in full to filtered sun, 4–6 ft. (1.2–1.8 m) apart.

Care: Moderate. Keep damp; allow soil surface to dry between waterings. Fertilize quarterly. Tie to supports. Pinch, thin, prune in spring to control growth. Renew by cutting to soil. Propagate by cuttings, layering, seed.

> **WARNING**
> Foliage and flowers of *Campsis radicans* may cause skin irritation in sensitive individuals. Wear gloves when pruning or tying vines.

Features: Good choice for arbors, fences, trellises, walls in cottage, formal, wildlife gardens. Attracts birds, hummingbirds. Pest and disease resistant.

Vine: *Clematis* species and hybrids. RANUNCULACEAE.

Common name: Clematis.

Description: More than 200 species and many hybrids of fast- to slow-growing, mostly vining, deciduous vines, to 20 ft. (6 m) long, with clinging leafstalks. Opposite, smooth or velvety, deep green, divided leaves, with oval or heart-shaped, veined leaflets, 2–3 in. (50–75 mm) long.

Bloom: Many showy, blue, gray, pink, purple, rose, silver, white, yellow, open, rounded, often reflexed, broad sepals, 2–10 in. (50–250 mm) wide, surrounding insignificant true flowers, in branching clusters. Bloom season varies by species: spring, summer, autumn, or twice-flowering.

Plant hardiness: Hardy. Zones 2–10, depending on species; most are hardy, zones 7–10.

Soil: Moist, well-drained, sandy loam. Fertility: Rich–average. 7.0–8.0 pH.

Planting: Spring in full sun to partial shade, 12–18 in. (30–45 cm) apart, after soil warms.

Care: Moderate. Keep evenly moist. Fertilize every 2 months. Tie to supports. Prune only spent flower stems after bloom. Propagate by cuttings, seed.

Features: Good choice for accents, arbors, containers, fences, trellises, tree trunks, walls in cottage, heritage, shade, woodland gardens. Good for drying. Clematis borer and leaf spot susceptible.

> **WARNING**
> Foliage and flowers of *Clematis* species may cause digestive upset if eaten. Avoid planting in areas frequented by pets and children.

Vine: *Euonymus fortunei (E. fortunei* var. *radicans).* CELASTRACEAE.

Common name: Winter Creeper.

Description: Many cultivars and horticultural varieties of fast-growing, climbing, spreading, or vining, evergreen shrubs, 5–20 ft. (1.5–6 m) tall and to 20 ft. (6 m) wide, with stem rootlets. Usually opposite, yellow, light becoming deep green, sometimes variegated, oval leaves, 2–3 in. (50–75 mm) long, with scalloped edges, turning purple, yellow in autumn.

Bloom: Insignificant green, pink, white flowers in spring; grown for foliage.

Plant hardiness: Hardy. Zones 5–9.

Soil: Moist to damp, well-drained soil. Fertility: Rich–low. 6.5–8.0 pH.

Planting: Spring in full sun to partial shade, 8–10 ft. (2.4–3 m) apart.

Care: Easy. Keep damp; allow soil surface to dry between waterings. Fertilize annually in spring. Tie to sturdy supports. Prune in early spring before growth begins to shape, direct growth. Propagate by cuttings, grafting, layering, seed.

Features: Good choice for fences, walls in shade, woodland gardens. Euonymus scale and crown gall susceptible.

Vine: *Hedera* species. ARALIACEAE.

Common name: Ivy.

Description: About 5 species and many cultivars of fast-growing, climbing and spreading, woody, evergreen vines, 25–50 ft. (7.5–15 m) long, with stem rootlets. Shiny, leathery, deep green or variegated, heart-shaped, deeply lobed juvenile becoming oval, pointed adult leaves, 2–8 in. (50–200 mm) long.

Bloom: Insignificant green, white flowers in summer; grown for foliage.

Plant hardiness: Hardy. Zones 5–10.

Soil: Moist to dry, well-drained humus. Fertility: Average. 6.0–7.5 pH.

Planting: Spring in full to filtered sun, 5 ft. (1.5 m) apart.

Care: Easy–moderate. Keep damp; allow soil to dry between waterings. Drought tolerant. Fertilize every 2 months in spring, summer. Train onto supports. Prune to control, direct growth. Shear to promote dense foliage. Propagate by cuttings, grafting, seed; may revert.

Features: Good choice for fences, ground covers, trellises, walls in cottage, formal, woodland gardens. Good for erosion control, topiary. Aphid, mealybug, scale, slug, snail and leaf spot susceptible; may harbor rodents.

Vine: *Ipomoea* species. CONVOLVULACEAE.

Common name: Morning Glory.

Description: About 500 species of fast-growing, vining, twining, sometimes annual, mostly perennial vines, 6–15 ft. (1.8–4.5 m) long. Alternate, smooth, green to deep green, heart-shaped or 3-lobed leaves, 3–8 in. (75–200 mm) long. Commonly cultivated species include *I. alba, I. quamoclit,* and *I. tricolor.*

Bloom: Many single, showy, blue, red, white, variegated, funnel-shaped flowers, 2–6 in. (50–150 mm) wide, in summer. Flowers open in morning, lasting one day.

Plant hardiness: Hardy. Zones 3–10, depending on species; most are hardy, zones 8–10. Self-seeding.

Soil: Moist to damp, well-drained soil. Fertility: Rich–average. 6.5–7.5 pH.

Planting: Spring in full sun to partial shade, 3–5 ft. (90–150 cm) apart.

Care: Easy. Keep damp; allow soil surface to dry between waterings. Fertilize quarterly. Tie to supports. Propagate by seed.

Features: Good choice for arbors, banks, screens, trellises in cottage, meadow, tropical gardens. Good for cutting, seasonal shade. Invasive, depending on species. Disease resistant. Aphid, tortoise beetle, cutworm, sweet potato weevil susceptible.

Vine: *Jasminum* species. OLEACEAE.

Common name: Jasmine (Jessamine).

Description: About 200 species of medium-growing, climbing, rambling, vining, woody, deciduous or evergreen shrubs, to 20 ft. (6 m) long. Alternate or opposite, smooth, deep green, divided leaves, with 3–7 heart-shaped or oval, pointed, usually finely toothed, folded leaflets, 2–3 in. (50–75 mm) long. See also *Trachelospermum jasminoides,* star jasmine, an unrelated species.

Bloom: Many showy, sometimes fragrant, pink, rose, white, yellow, pinwheel- or star-shaped flowers, ½–2 in. (12–50 mm) wide, in spring, summer, or autumn, depending on species.

Plant hardiness: Hardy, semi-hardy, or tender, depending on species. Zones 4–11; most are hardy, zones 8–11.

Soil: Moist to dry, well-drained soil. Fertility: Rich–average. 6.5–8.0 pH.

Planting: Spring in full to filtered sun, 6–10 ft. (1.8–3 m) apart.

Care: Moderate. Keep damp; allow soil surface to dry between waterings. Fertilize quarterly. Tie to supports. Prune to control, direct growth after bloom. Propagate by cuttings, layering, seed.

Features: Good choice for arbors, banks, fences, trellises, walls in cottage, rock, tropical, woodland gardens. Good for cutting. Attracts bees, birds. Pest and disease resistant.

Vine: *Mandevilla* x *amabilis* hybrids. APOCYNACEAE.

Common name: Mandevilla.

Description: Many hybrid cultivars of fast-growing, climbing, twining, woody, evergreen shrubs, 15–20 ft. (4.5–6 m) long. Opposite or whorled, shiny, deep green, oval, pointed, wavy-edged leaves, 4–8 in. (10–20 cm) long. Common cultivars include *M.* x *amabilis* 'Alice du Pont', 'Rita Marie Green', and 'Summer Snow'.

Bloom: Many showy, pink, red, white, bicolored, deep-throated, round, 5-petaled flowers, 3–4 in. (75–100 mm) wide, in loose clusters, in late spring–autumn.

Plant hardiness: Tender. Plant as annual, zones 4–7; ground hardy, zones 8–11. Best in hot-summer climates.

Soil: Moist, well-drained, sandy soil mixed with humus. Fertility: Rich. 6.5–7.5 pH.

Planting: Spring in full sun, 2–3 ft. (60–90 cm) apart.

Care: Easy. Keep evenly moist; drought tolerant when established. Fertilize monthly. Tie to supports. Pinch, prune to direct growth. Propagate by cuttings.

Features: Good choice for arbors, fences, pillars, trellises, walls in arid, tropical gardens. Good for cutting. Attracts birds, butterflies, hummingbirds. Disease resistant. Mealybug, spider mite, whitefly susceptible.

Vine: *Passiflora* species and hybrids. PASSIFLORACEAE.
Common name: Passion Vine (Passionflower).
Description: About 400 species and a few hybrid cultivars of fast-growing, climbing, woody, evergreen vines, 25–30 ft. (7.5–9 m) long, with stem tendrils. Alternate, smooth, deep green, oval or lance-shaped, often rounded, veined leaves, 3–6 in. (75–150 mm) long. Common species include *P. caerulea* and *P. laurifolia.*
Bloom: Many showy, fragrant, blue, lavender, pink, purple, violet, white, round, double, overlapping-petaled flowers, 3–5 in. (75–125 mm) wide, with crownlike, hairy, radiating, green, pink, yellow centers, in summer–autumn, form edible or inedible round fruit. Flowers of some species last one day.
Plant hardiness: Tender. Zones 7–11, depending on species; most hardy, zones 9–11.
Soil: Moist to damp, well-drained soil. Fertility: Rich. 5.5–7.0 pH.
Planting: Spring in full to filtered sun, 8–10 ft. (2.4–3 m) apart.
Care: Moderate. Keep evenly moist. Fertilize monthly. Provide sturdy support. Prune, thin in early spring before growth begins. Protect from wind. Propagate by cuttings, seed.
Features: Good choice for arbors, banks, fences, trellises, walls in arid, seaside, tropical gardens. Good for cutting; a drop of melted wax in flower center prevents closing after cutting. Attracts butterflies. Invasive. Disease resistant. Nematode susceptible.

Vine: *Philodendron bipinnatifidum (P. selloum).* ARACEAE.
Common name: Philodendron.
Description: A few cultivars of erect, treelike, vining, epiphytic, evergreen tropical herbs, to 15 ft. (4.5 m) long, with aerial roots. Shiny, bright becoming deep green, reflexed, heart-shaped, deeply cut and lobed, toothed leaves, to 3 ft. (90 cm) or longer, on stiff, pithy leafstalks.
Bloom: Rare, on mature plants, a purple cowl-like spadix, 8–12 in. (20–30 cm) long, white inside, surrounding a fleshy, green, segmented spathe, on a short flowering stalk, in summer. Grown primarily for foliage.
Plant hardiness: Tender. Zones 10–11.
Soil: Moist, well-drained humus or, in water features, shoreline sites. Fertility: Rich. 6.0–7.0 pH.
Planting: Spring in full sun to partial shade, 6–8 ft. (1.8–2.4 m) apart.
Care: Moderate. Keep evenly moist. Fertilize monthly. Tie to sturdy support. Deadhead spent leaves. Root or prune aerial roots. Protect from wind. Propagate by cuttings.
Features: Good choice for accents, banks, walls in tropical gardens and water feature shorelines. Good as houseplant. Pest and disease resistant.

Vine: *Solanum rantonnetii. (Lycianthes rantonnetii).* SOLANACEAE.
Common name: Blue Potato Bush (Paraguay Nightshade).
Description: A few cultivars of fast-growing, bushy, vining or erect, semi-evergreen or deciduous shrubs, 8–10 ft. (2.4–3 m) tall and wide, or 12–15 ft. (3.7–4.5 m) long. Alternate, smooth, bright to deep green, oval, pointed, wavy-edged leaves, 3–4 in. (75–100 mm) long.
Bloom: Many showy, blue, purple, violet, white, round, 5-petaled, open-faced flowers, ½–1 in. (12–25 mm) wide, with bright yellow centers, in branching clusters, in spring–autumn, zones 7–9; year-round, zones 10–11.
Plant hardiness: Semi-hardy. Zones 7–11.
Soil: Moist to damp, well-drained, sandy soil. Fertility: Rich–average. 5.5–7.0 pH.
Planting: Spring in full sun to partial shade, 5–7 ft. (1.5–2.2 m) apart.
Care: Easy. Keep damp; allow soil surface to dry between waterings. Fertilize quarterly. Tie to supports. Prune severely in winter. Propagate by cuttings.
Features: Good choice for accents, banks, fences, walls in informal, meadow, shade, woodland gardens. Pest and disease resistant.

Vine: *Tecoma capensis (Tecomaria capensis).* BIGNONIACEAE.

Common name: Cape Honeysuckle.

Description: A few cultivars of fast-growing, climbing, semi-evergreen tropical shrubs, to 8 ft. (2.4 m) tall and wide, or 30 ft. (9 m) long. Shiny, bright or deep green, palmlike, 5–9-lobed leaves with oval, cut leaflets, to 2 in. (50 mm) long. Common cultivars include *T. capensis* 'Aurea', 'Buff Gold', 'Lutea'. *T. × alata, T. garrocha,* and *T. stans* are closely related species with similar care needs.

Bloom: Many showy, gold, yellow, trumpet-shaped, fringed flowers, to 2 in. (50 mm) long, in erect, fountain-shaped clusters, in autumn–spring.

Plant hardiness: Semi-hardy. Zones 7–11.

Soil: Damp, well-drained, sandy soil. Fertility: Rich. 6.0–7.0 pH. Salt tolerant.

Planting: Spring in full to filtered sun, 4–5 ft. (1.2–1.5 m) apart.

Care: Easy. Keep evenly moist. Fertilize monthly. Pinch, prune to control growth, shape. Propagate by cuttings, seed.

Features: Good choice for banks, espaliers, hedges, trellises in cottage, formal, seaside gardens. Attracts hummingbirds. Pest and disease resistant.

Vine: *Thunbergia alata.* ACANTHACEAE.

Common name: Black-Eyed Susan Vine (Canary-Flower Vine, Clock Vine).

Description: Many cultivars and horticultural varieties of fast-growing, short-lived, climbing or trailing, twining, perennial herbs, to 10 ft. (3 m) long. Opposite, textured, deep green, triangular, pointed, veined leaves, to 3 in. (75 mm) long. Common cultivars include *T. alata* 'Alba', 'Angel Wings', 'Bakerii', 'Susie Mix', and 'T. Gregorii'. *T. erecta, T. grandiflora,* and *T. mysorensis* are closely related species with similar care needs. See also *T. gregorii,* orange clock vine, a closely related species.

Bloom: Many showy, gold, orange, white, yellow, tubular, flared flowers, to 1½ in. (38 mm) wide, with purple throats and partially divided, rounded petals, in summer.

Plant hardiness: Semi-hardy. Plant as annual, zones 3–6; ground hardy, zones 7–10.

Soil: Moist, well-drained, sandy loam. Fertility: Rich. 6.5–7.5 pH.

Planting: Spring in full sun to partial shade, 1 ft. (30 cm) apart, after soil warms.

Care: Easy. Keep evenly moist. Fertilize monthly. Tie to supports. Shear in autumn. Propagate by cuttings, layering, seed.

Features: Good choice for hanging baskets, containers, fences, trellises in cottage, formal, shade, woodland gardens. Attracts butterflies, hummingbirds. Pest and disease resistant.

Vine: *Thunbergia gregorii (T. gibsonii).* ACANTHACEAE.

Common name: Orange Clock Vine.

Description: A few cultivars of fast-growing, long-lived, climbing, twining, perennial herbs, to 6 ft. (1.8 m) long. Opposite, textured, gray green, triangular, pointed, toothed, veined leaves, to 3 in. (75 mm) long. See also *T. alata,* black-eyed susan vine, a closely related species.

Bloom: Many showy, single, bright orange, tubular, flared flowers, to 2 in. (50 mm) wide, with deep, orange throats and blunt petals, on long, hairy stems, in summer, zones 3–8; year-round, zones 9–11.

Plant hardiness: Tender. Plant as tender annual, zones 3–7; ground hardy, zones 8–11.

Soil: Moist, well-drained, sandy loam. Fertility: Rich. 6.5–7.5 pH.

Planting: Spring in full to filtered sun, 6 ft. (1.8 m) apart, after soil warms.

Care: Easy. Keep evenly moist. Fertilize monthly. Tie or train onto supports. Pinch to control growth. Shear in autumn to renew. Propagate by cuttings, layering, seed.

Features: Good choice for hanging baskets, containers, fences, trellises, walls in cottage, informal, meadow, tropical gardens. Attracts butterflies, hummingbirds. Pest and disease resistant.

Vine: *Trachelospermum jasminoides (Rhynchospermum jasminoides).* APOCYNACEAE.
Common name: Star Jasmine (Confederate Jasmine, Maile Haole).
Description: Many cultivars of medium-growing, low, climbing, twining, evergreen vines, to 30 ft. (9 m) long, with branch holdfast roots. Opposite, shiny, light becoming deep green or variegated, oval, pointed leaves, to 4 in. (10 cm) long.
Bloom: Many showy, very fragrant, white, star-shaped, whorled and reflexed, pointed flowers, to 1 in. (25 mm) wide, in dense, branching clusters, in spring–summer, form seedpods, to 7 in. (18 cm) long, containing a row of hairy seed, in autumn.
Plant hardiness: Tender. Zones 8–11.
Soil: Moist to damp, well-drained, sandy soil. Fertility: Average. 6.5–7.5 pH.
Planting: Spring in full to filtered sun, 4–6 ft. (1.2–1.8 m) apart, after soil warms.
Care: Easy. Keep damp; allow soil surface to dry between waterings. Drought resistant. Fertilize quarterly. Provide sturdy support. Prune in late autumn to thin, direct growth, remove spent branches. Propagate by cuttings.
Features: Good choice for banks, beds, containers, edgings, ground covers, trellises, walls in arid, cottage, fragrance, seaside, tropical, woodland gardens. Good for cutting. Attracts bees. Pest and disease resistant.

Vine: *Vitis* species. VITACEAE.
Common name: Grape.
Description: Over 20 species of medium-growing, climbing, twining, woody, deciduous vines or shrubs, with simple or forked tendrils and papery, shedding, brown bark. Textured, light green, round, deeply cut, lobed, pointed leaves, to 6 in. (15 cm) wide, turning purple, red in autumn. Commonly cultivated species include *V. coignetiae, V. labrusca, V. rotundifolia,* and *V. vinifera.*
Bloom: Insignificant tiny, green flowers, to $\frac{1}{16}$ in. (1.5 mm) wide, in spring, forming berrylike, pulpy, edible or inedible grapes, to 1 in. (25 mm) wide, in clusters, in autumn.
Plant hardiness: Hardy. Zones 5–10, depending on species; most are hardy, zones 8–11.
Soil: Damp to dry, well-drained, sandy soil. Fertility: Average. 6.5–7.5 pH.
Planting: Spring or autumn in full sun to partial shade, 6–10 ft. (1.8–3 m) apart.
Care: Easy. Keep damp; allow soil surface to dry between waterings. Fertilize annually in spring. Provide sturdy supports. Prune in winter to control growth, increase fruit size. Propagate by cuttings, grafting, seed.
Features: Good choice for accents, arbors, containers, espaliers, trellises in cottage, formal, heritage, meadow, wildlife gardens. Good for seasonal shade. Attracts birds. Leafhopper, leaf roller and fungal disease susceptible.

Vine: *Wisteria* species. FABACEAE (LEGUMINOSAE)
Common name: Wistaria (Wisteria).
Description: About 10 species of fast-growing, climbing, twining, woody deciduous tropical lianas or vines, to 100 ft. (30 m) or longer. Alternate, soft, green, feathery, divided leaves, with 9–19 leaflets, to 3 in. (75 mm) long, turning yellow in autumn.
Bloom: Many showy, often fragrant, blue, lilac, white, pealike flowers, to ¾ in. (19 mm) long, in grapelike, dangling clusters, 6–48 in. (15–120 cm) long, in summer, forming dry, beanlike pods in autumn. Commonly cultivated species include *W. floribunda* and *W. sinensis.*
Plant hardiness: Semi-hardy. Zones 5–10.
Soil: Damp, well-drained soil. Fertility: Average–low. 6.0–7.0 pH.
Planting: Spring in full sun, 8–10 ft. (2.4–3 m) apart, after soil warms.
Care: Easy. Keep damp; allow soil surface to dry between waterings. Avoid fertilizing. Provide sturdy supports. Pinch, prune to train, shape, control growth. Protect from frost until established. Propagate by cuttings, division, grafting, seed.
Features: Good choice for accents, fences, trellises, walls in cottage, formal, heritage gardens. Good for seasonal shade. Invasive, heavy. Pest and disease resistant.

Cacti, Ferns, and Shrubs

*S*hrubs—both flowering and foliage plants—are the finishing touches we apply to home landscapes. Generally larger and more durable than perennial plants yet smaller than trees, they fill the midground and borders around our homes, line pathways and fencelines, create interesting textures with their foliage and fragrances with their flowers, and anchor our plantings from the soil's surface to eye level.

In arid-climate gardens and in those exposed to drying seaside winds, cacti fill a similar role to shrubs; in moist, shade-filled glens and in the shadows of structures, your palette of low-light plants grows to include ferns, epiphytes, and tree ferns.

When planning for shrubs in the landscape, remember that the blooms on most flowering shrubs are seasonal, lasting at most for several weeks or perhaps a month. You can extend this time

of bloom by selecting plants that flower in sequence, and you can add color in other ways. Some deciduous shrubs have distinctive foliage color when their new leaves emerge, others have variegated leaves, and many turn brilliant colors in autumn. Some shrubs even become colorful in winter by virtue of their brightly colored bark or berries.

Consider all your shrub's foliage and form as you plan your shrub plantings, and vary heights by arranging shrubs, cacti, and ferns from low to tall in stature.

As your awareness grows of the possibilities available for these essential foundation plants, match your choices to your yard's character and your home's design as well as your garden's climate, soil, and exposure.

CACTI

Cactus: *Carnegiea gigantea.* CACTACEAE.
Common name: Saguaro.
Description: Single species of slow-growing, long-lived, erect, columnar, often branching, ribbed cacti, to 60 ft. (18 m) tall, armed with gray brown, awl- or needle-shaped spines. Protected, endangered species; plant only nursery-cultivated specimens.
Blooms/Fruit: Showy, cream, white, funnel-shaped, single-petaled flowers, to 5 in. (13 cm) long, opening at night and persisting until following day, in late spring on mature plants, form broadly oval, red, pulpy, edible fruit, to 3 in. (75 mm) wide, in autumn.
Plant hardiness: Zones 7–8. Semi-hardy. Best in Sonoran desert climates featuring monsoon summer and winter rains.
Soil: Damp to dry, well-drained, sandy soil. Fertility: Average–low. 7.0–8.0 pH.
Planting: Full sun. Space 10–15 ft. (3–4.5 m) apart.
Care: Moderate–challenging. Water deeply in summer, late autumn; withhold all water in spring, early autumn, winter. Drought tolerant. Fertilize annually in summer. Propagate by cuttings, offsets, seed.
Features: Good choice for accents in arid gardens and landscapes. Disease resistant. Burrowing owl-, woodpecker-damage susceptible. Spines can be hazardous; avoid planting in gardens frequented by pets and children.

Cactus: *Cephalocereus senilis.* CACTACEAE.
Common name: Old-Man Cactus.
Description: Several cultivars of slow-growing, long-lived, erect, columnar, ribbed cacti, sometimes to 50 ft. (15 m) tall but seldom more than 15 ft. (4.5 m) tall in landscape use, armed with yellow spines, to 2 in. (50 mm) long, clothed in woolly, gray, hairlike bristles, to 1 ft. (30 cm) long.
Blooms/Fruit: Showy, rose pink, tubular, flared flowers, to 2 in. (50 mm) long, opening at night, in spring on mature plants, form pear-shaped, rose red fruit in summer.
Plant hardiness: Zones 8–9. Semi-hardy. Best in arid desert climates.
Soil: Damp to dry, well-drained, sandy soil. Fertility: Average–low. 6.5–8.0 pH.
Planting: Full to filtered sun. Space 4–5 ft. (1.2–1.5 m) apart.
Care: Easy. Withhold all water until ribs become prominent, then water deeply. Drought tolerant. Fertilize annually in autumn. Protect from frost. Propagate by offsets, seed.
Features: Good choice for accents, borders, containers in arid gardens. Pest and disease resistant. Spines can be hazardous; avoid planting in areas frequented by pets and children.

Cactus: *Cereus peruvianus (C. uruguayanus).* CACTACEAE.
Common name: Apple Cactus (Giant-Club, Peru Cereus, Peruvian Apple).
Description: A few cultivars of slow-growing, long-lived, branching and shrubby or tree-like, irregularly ribbed cacti, to 10 ft. (3 m) tall and 15 ft. (4.5 m) wide, armed with needlelike spines in radiating clusters, ¾–2 in. (19–50 mm) long.
Blooms/Fruit: Showy, white, tubular, flared flowers, to 6 in. (15 cm) long and 4–5 in. (10–13 cm) wide, opening at night, in late spring–early summer, form broadly oval, pink becoming red, applelike fruit in summer.
Plant hardiness: Zones 8–11. Tender. Best in arid, mild-winter climates.
Soil: Damp to dry, well-drained, sandy soil. Fertility: Average. 7.0–8.0 pH.
Planting: Full to filtered sun. Space 7–10 ft. (2.2–3 m) apart.
Care: Easy. Water deeply; allow soil to dry completely between waterings. Drought tolerant. Fertilize annually in summer. Propagate by cuttings, seed.
Features: Good choice for accents, barriers, containers, fencelines in arid gardens and landscapes. Pest and disease resistant. Spines can be hazardous; avoid planting in gardens frequented by pets and children.

Cactus: *Coryphantha vivipara (Mammillaria vivipara).* CACTACEAE.
Common name: Fox-Tail Cactus (Beehive Cactus).
Description: Several horticultural varieties of slow-growing, ball-shaped becoming erect and oblong, knobby cacti, to 6 in. (15 cm) tall, armed with white or red, black-tipped, needlelike spines in flat, radiating clusters, to ⅝ in. (16 mm) long, surrounding erect, central spines, to 1 in. (25 mm) long.
Blooms/Fruit: Showy, yellow green, pink, purple, open, double-petaled flowers, to 2 in. (50 mm) wide, in early summer, form red, ball-shaped fruit, to 1 in. (25 mm) wide, in winter.
Plant hardiness: Zones 3–11. Hardy. Best in arid, cold-winter climates.
Soil: Damp to dry, well-drained, sandy soil. Fertility: Average. 6.5–7.5 pH.
Planting: Full sun. Space 6–12 in. (15–30 cm) apart.
Care: Easy. Keep damp; allow soil to dry completely between waterings and throughout winter. Fertilize annually in summer. Propagate by offsets, seed.
Features: Good choice for borders, containers, edgings, foregrounds in arid, natural, small-space gardens. Good as houseplant. Pest resistant. Fungal disease susceptible. Spines can be hazardous; avoid planting in gardens frequented by pets and children.

Cactus: *Echinocactus grusonii.* CACTACEAE.
Common name: Barrel Cactus (Golden-Ball Cactus).
Description: Several cultivars of slow-growing, ball-shaped, ribbed cacti, to 4 ft. (1.2 m) in diameter, armed with golden yellow becoming white, brown, needlelike spines in flat, radiating clusters, to 1½ in. (38 mm) long, surrounding erect, central spines, to 2 in. (50 mm) long. Offsets form colonies over time.
Blooms/Fruit: Showy, green yellow, open, double-petaled flowers, 1½–2 in. (38–50 mm) wide, in a ringlike cluster circling the top of the plant, in summer, form woolly, red, yellow, round fruit, to ¾ in. (19 mm) wide, in autumn.
Plant hardiness: Zones 7–11. Semi-hardy. Best in arid, mild-winter climates.
Soil: Damp to dry, well-drained, sandy soil. Fertility: Average. 7.0–8.5 pH. Salt tolerant.
Planting: Full sun to partial shade. Space 1–2 ft. (30–60 cm) apart.
Care: Easy. Water deeply in spring–autumn; allow soil to dry between waterings and throughout winter. Fertilize annually in summer. Propagate by offsets, seed.
Features: Good choice for accents, borders, containers in arid, natural, small-space gardens.

Good as houseplant. Pest and disease resistant. Spines can be hazardous; avoid planting in areas frequented by pets and children.

Cactus: *Echinocereus* species. CACTACEAE.
Common name: Hedgehog Cactus (Hedgehog Cereus, Pitaya).
Description: About 35 species of slow-growing, erect or prostrate, round or columnar, ribbed cacti, 1–3 ft. (30–90 cm) tall, usually armed with white becoming brown, red- or black-tipped bristles or needlelike spines in erect, radiating clusters, ½–3 in. (12–75 mm) long, depending on species. Commonly cultivated species include *E. englemanni* and *E. triglochidiatus*.
Blooms/Fruit: Showy, solitary, purple, red, white, yellow, daisylike or tubular, double-petaled flowers, 2–4 in. (50–100 mm) wide, with yellow centers, opening at night, in spring, form fleshy, round, purple red fruit, to 1¾ in. (44 mm) wide, in summer.
Plant hardiness: Zones 4–10. Hardy. Best in arid, cold-winter climates.
Soil: Damp to dry, well-drained, sandy soil. Fertility: Average. 6.0–7.5 pH.
Planting: Full sun. Space 2–3 ft. (60–90 cm) apart.
Care: Easy. Water deeply spring–autumn; allow soil to dry completely between waterings. Drought tolerant. Fertilize annually in summer. Propagate by layering, offsets, seed.
Features: Good choice for accents, barriers, borders, containers in arid, mountain, natural, small-space gardens. Pest resistant. Fungal disease susceptible. Spines can be hazardous; avoid planting in gardens frequented by pets and children.

Cactus: *Ferocactus* species. CACTACEAE.
Common name: Barrel Cactus (Fishhook Cactus, Strawberry Cactus, Visnaga).
Description: About 25 species of slow-growing, erect, stout, ball-shaped becoming columnar, ribbed cacti, to 10 ft. (3 m) tall, armed with flattened, hooked, yellow spines, to 2 in. (50 mm) long, often clothed in woolly, gray, white, hairlike bristles.
Blooms/Fruit: Showy, orange, red, yellow, multicolored, bell- or cup-shaped, double-petaled flowers, to 3 in. (75 mm) wide, in spring–early summer, form fleshy, round, purple, red fruit, to ½ in. (12 mm) wide, in late summer, persisting into winter.
Plant hardiness: Zones 7–10. Semi-hardy. Best in arid, mild-winter climates.
Soil: Damp to dry, well-drained, sandy soil mixed with humus. Fertility: Average. 6.5–8.0 pH. Salt tolerant.
Planting: Full sun. Space 2–3 ft. (60–90 cm) apart.
Care: Easy. Water deeply; allow soil to dry completely between waterings. Drought tolerant. Fertilize annually in summer. Propagate by offsets, seed.
Features: Good choice for accents, containers, edgings in arid, natural, small-space gardens. Good as houseplant. Pest and disease resistant. Spines can be hazardous; avoid planting in gardens frequented by pets and children.

Cactus: *Gymnocalycium saglione (Echinocactus saglionis).* CACTACEAE.
Common name: Chin Cactus.
Description: A few cultivars of slow-growing, erect or prostrate, round becoming columnar, deeply ribbed cacti, 18–36 in. (45–90 cm) tall, armed with black, brown, needlelike spines in flat, radiating clusters, to 1½ in. (38 mm) long, surrounding a few erect central spines, to 2 in. (50 mm) long.
Blooms/Fruit: Showy, pink, white, open, double-petaled flowers, to 1½ in. (38 mm) wide, in summer, form fleshy, broadly oval, red fruit, to 1 in. (25 mm) long, in autumn.
Plant hardiness: Zones 7–10. Semi-hardy. Best in arid, mild-winter climates.
Soil: Damp to dry, well-drained, sandy soil. Fertility: Average. 6.0–7.5 pH.
Planting: Full sun. Space 2–3 ft. (60–90 cm) apart.
Care: Easy. Water deeply; allow soil to dry completely between waterings. Withhold water in winter. Drought tolerant. Fertilize annually in summer. Propagate by layering, offsets, seed.
Features: Good choice for accents, containers, barriers in arid, natural gardens. Good as houseplant. Pest and disease resistant. Spines can be hazardous; avoid planting in gardens frequented by pets and children.

Cactus: *Mammillaria bocasana.* CACTACEAE.
Common name: Snowball Cactus (Powder-Puff Cactus, Puff Cactus).
Description: Many cultivars of slow-growing, mounding, round to columnar, ribbed cacti, to 3 in. (75 mm) tall, armed with cream, white, yellow, needlelike spines in flat, radiating clusters, to ⅜ in. (10 mm) long, surrounding erect, fishhook-shaped, central spines, to ¾ in. (19 mm) long, and clothed in woolly, white, hairlike bristles, to 1 in. (25 mm) long. More than 100 related species of *Mammilaria* with similar care needs are commonly cultivated.
Blooms/Fruit: Showy, pink, purple, red, white, open-faced or fibrous flowers, to ¾ in. (19 mm) wide, in a ringlike cluster circling the top of the plant, in winter, form woolly, round, red fruit, to ¼ in. (6 mm) wide, in autumn.
Plant hardiness: Zones 7–10. Semi-hardy. Best in arid, mild-winter climates.
Soil: Damp to dry, well-drained, sandy soil. Fertility: Average. 7.0–8.0 pH. Salt tolerant.
Planting: Full sun to partial shade. Space 4–6 in. (10–15 cm) apart.
Care: Easy. Keep damp spring–autumn; allow soil to dry completely between waterings. Withhold water in winter. Drought tolerant. Fertilize annually in summer. Propagate by offsets, seed.
Features: Good choice for accents, containers, edgings in arid, natural gardens. Good as houseplant. Pest and disease resistant. Spines can be hazardous; avoid planting in gardens frequented by pets and children.

Cactus: *Opuntia* species. CACTACEAE.

Common name: Prickly Pear (Cholla).

Description: Nearly 300 species of medium- to slow-growing, highly varied, branching cacti, 4–180 in. (10–455 cm) tall, featuring either jointed padlike "tuna" or tubular stems, and usually armed with white, yellow, needlelike, barbed, erect, clustered, often brittle bristles and spines, ¼–1 in. (6–25 mm) long. Commonly cultivated species include *O. basilaris*, beavertail; *O. bigelovii*, teddybear; *O. cholla*, cholla; *O. ficus-indica*, spineless Indian fig; *O. leptocaulis*, Christmas cactus; and *O. vulgaris*, prickly pear.

Blooms/Fruit: Showy, green, pink, purple, red, rose, white, yellow, sometimes multicolored flowers, ½–4 in. (12–100 mm) wide, in winter or spring, form purple, red, yellow, egg-shaped, edible fruit in summer.

Plant hardiness: Zones vary by species; most are hardy zones 8–10, some to zone 4.

Soil: Damp to dry, well-drained, sandy soil. Fertility: Average–low. 6.5–7.0 pH.

Planting: Full sun. Spacing varies depending on species.

Care: Easy. Water deeply; allow soil to dry completely between waterings. Drought tolerant. Fertilize annually in summer. Propagate by cuttings, layering, seed.

Features: Good choice for accents, barriers in arid gardens and landscapes. Fruit, pads of most species are edible. Pest and disease resistant. Spines may be very hazardous; avoid planting in gardens frequented by pets and children.

Cactus: *Schlumbergera bridgesii (S. × buckleyi).* CACTACEAE.

Common name: Christmas Cactus.

Description: A few cultivars of medium- to slow-growing, semi-epiphytic, arching, spreading, wavy, fleshy, jointed cacti, to 2 ft. (60 cm) tall, with silver, white bristles.

Blooms/Fruit: Very showy, cerise, cherry terminal flowers, to 3 in. (75 mm) long, in winter, form dimpled, oblong, red fruit, to 1 in. (25 mm) long, in spring.

Plant hardiness: Zones 8–11. Tender.

Soil: Damp to dry, well-drained humus. Fertility: Rich–average. 5.5–6.5 pH.

Planting: Open to full shade. Space 18–24 in. (45–60 cm) apart.

Care: Moderate–challenging. Keep damp to dry in spring, evenly moist late spring–autumn, damp to dry in autumn until bloom, then evenly moist until blooms fade. Fertilize monthly. Protect from frost. Propagate by cuttings, layering, seed.

Features: Good choice for hanging baskets, containers in tropical and subtropical, woodland gardens and water feature shorelines. Good for holiday decorations, houseplant. Pest and disease resistant.

Cactus: *Stenocereus thurberi (Lemaireocereus thurberi).* CACTACEAE.

Common name: Organ-Pipe Cactus.

Description: Several cultivars of slow-growing, erect, branching, columnar, ribbed cacti, 12–15 ft. (3.7–4.5 m) tall, armed with brown black, needlelike spines, to 2 in. (50 mm) long. Offsets form colonies over time.

Blooms/Fruit: Showy, cream, pink, purple, white, tubular flowers, to 3 in. (75 mm) long, opening at night, in spring, form fleshy, round, red fruit, to 3 in. (75 mm) wide, in summer.

Plant hardiness: Zones 7–11. Semi-hardy. Best in arid, mild-winter climates.

Soil: Damp to dry, well-drained, sandy soil. Fertility: Average–low. 6.5–8.0 pH. Salt tolerant.

Planting: Full sun. Space 6–10 ft. (1.8–3 m) apart.

Care: Easy. Water deeply; allow soil to dry completely between waterings. Withhold water in winter. Drought tolerant. Fertilize annually in spring. Propagate by offsets, seed.

Features: Good choice for accents, containers, fencelines in arid, natural gardens and landscapes. Pest resistant. Fungal disease susceptible. Spines can be hazardous; avoid planting in gardens frequented by pets and children.

FERNS

Fern: *Adiantum capillus-veneris.* POLYPODIACEAE.

Common name: Southern Maidenhair Fern (Dudder Grass, Venus's-Hair).

Description: Many cultivars of slow-growing, mounding, rhizomatous, deciduous ferns, to 18 in. (45 cm) tall and wide, with bright green, fan-shaped, oval or triangular, double-divided, finely cut fronds, 18–24 in. (45–60 cm) long and to 10 in. (25 cm) wide, with oval or round, toothed, alternate leaflets, to ¼ in. (6 mm) wide, on shiny, black, wiry stems. *A. pedatum* fm. *imbricatum*, northern maidenhair; and *A. pedatum* fm. *aleuticum*, Aleutian maidenhair, are closely related species with similar care needs; hardy, zones 2–9.

Plant hardiness: Zones 8–11. Tender. Best in cool, mild, humid climates.

Soil: Moist, well-drained, sandy loam mixed with humus and charcoal or, in water features, shoreline sites. Fertility: Rich. 6.0–7.5 pH.

Planting: Partial to full shade. Space 10–12 in. (25–30 cm) apart.

Care: Easy–moderate. Keep evenly moist. Fertilize monthly during active growth. Deadhead oldest fronds by cutting at base. Protect from sun. Propagate by division, spores.

Features: Good choice for hanging baskets, borders, containers, edgings, ground covers in natural, shade, woodland gardens and water feature shorelines. Good as houseplant. Pest and disease resistant.

Fern: *Asplenium nidus (A. nidus-avis).* POLYPODIACEAE.

Common name: Bird's-Nest Fern (Nest Fern).

Description: A few cultivars of fast-growing, arching, epiphytic, rhizomatous, evergreen, tropical ferns, to 2 ft. (60 cm) tall and 4 ft. (1.2 m) wide, with green, yellow green, paddle-shaped, undivided, wavy-edged fronds, to 4 ft. (1.2 m) long and 6–8 in. (15–20 cm) wide, on stiff, woody, radiating stems.

Plant hardiness: Zones 9–11. Tender. Best in tropical, subtropical climates.

Soil: Moist, well-drained humus mixed with charcoal or, in water features, shallow marginal or shoreline sites. Fertility: Rich. 5.5–6.5 pH.

Planting: Partial to full shade. Space 2–3 ft. (60–90 cm) apart.

Care: Moderate. Keep evenly moist during active growth; reduce watering late autumn–early spring. Fertilize monthly during active growth. Propagate by division, spores.

Features: Good choice for accents, containers in natural, shade, tropical, woodland gardens and water feature margins and shorelines. Good as houseplant. Disease resistant. Slug, snail susceptible.

Fern: *Athyrium filix-femina.* POLYPODIACEAE.

Common name: Lady Fern.

Description: Many cultivars and horticultural varieties of highly varied, medium-growing, erect, arching, rhizomatous, deciduous ferns, to 4 ft. (1.2 m) tall and wide, with deep green, finely cut, divided fronds, 18–36 in. (45–90 cm) long, usually with lance-shaped, toothed or feathery, opposite leaflets, to 1½ in. (38 mm) long. Common cultivars include plants with feathery, irregular, crested, and beaded or pealike foliage, as well as those more typical for the species.

Plant hardiness: Zones 1–11. Hardy.

Soil: Moist, well-drained humus mixed with charcoal or, in water features, shoreline sites. Fertility: Rich. 7.0–7.5 pH.

Planting: Filtered sun to full shade. Space 2–3 ft. (60–90 cm) apart.

Care: Easy. Keep evenly moist during active growth. Fertilize monthly. Allow fronds to mulch rhizome throughout winter; remove when new fiddleheads emerge in spring. Propagate by division, spores.

Features: Good choice for accents, hanging baskets, borders, containers, edgings, ground covers in natural, shade, woodland gardens and water feature shorelines. Good as houseplant. Disease resistant. Slug, snail susceptible.

Fern: *Cibotium glaucum.* DICKSONIACEAE.
Common name: Hawaiian Tree Fern (Hapu'u-ii).
Description: Many culivars of slow-growing, erect, umbrella-crowned, palmlike, evergreen ferns, to 20 ft. (6 m) tall and 12–15 ft. (3.7–4.5 m) wide, with bright becoming deep green, broad, arching, triple-divided, finely cut, lacy fronds, 3–8 ft. (90–240 cm) long, on woolly, brown leafstalks, and with a fibrous, hairy trunk. *C. chamissoi* is a closely related species with similar care needs.
Plant hardiness: Zones 9–11. Tender.
Soil: Moist, well-drained, sandy loam mixed with humus and charcoal or, in water features, shoreline sites. Fertility: Rich. 5.5–7.0 pH.
Planting: Full sun to partial shade. Space 6–10 ft. (1.8–3 m) apart.
Care: Easy. Keep evenly moist. Mist occasionally. Fertilize quarterly. Deadhead old or broken fronds. Protect from wind, drying. Propagate by spores.
Features: Good choice for accents, backgrounds, containers in arid, natural, shade, tropical, woodland gardens and water feature shorelines. Good as houseplant. Pest and disease resistant.

Fern: *Cyathea cooperi (Alsophila australis, Sphaeropteris cooperi).* CYATHEACEAE.
Common name: Australian Tree Fern.
Description: Several cultivars of fast-growing, mounding becoming erect, umbrella-crowned, palmlike, evergreen ferns, to 40 ft. (12 m) tall but seldom more than 15 ft. (4.5 m) tall in landscape use, with shiny, bright becoming deep green, broad, arching, double- or triple-divided, finely cut, leathery fronds, 10–12 ft. (3–3.7 m) long, on woolly, brown leafstalks, and with a fibrous, hairy trunk.
Plant hardiness: Zones 7–11. Semi-hardy.
Soil: Moist, well-drained, sandy loam mixed with humus and charcoal or, in water features, shoreline sites. Fertility: Rich. 5.5–7.0 pH.
Planting: Full to filtered sun. Space 8–12 ft. (2.4–3.7 m) apart.
Care: Easy. Keep evenly moist. Mist occasionally. Fertilize quarterly. Deadhead old or broken fronds. Propagate by cuttings, spores.
Features: Good choice for accents, backgrounds, containers in arid, natural, shade, tropical, woodland gardens and water feature shorelines. Pest and disease resistant.

WARNING
Stalks and fronds of *Cyathea cooperi* may cause skin irritation in sensitive individuals. Wear gloves and protective clothing when pruning or propagating plants.

Fern: *Cyrtomium falcatum.* POLYPODIACEAE.
Common name: Japanese Holly Fern.
Description: Several cultivars and horticultural varieties of erect, open, rhizomatous, semi-evergreen ferns, to 30 in. (75 cm) tall and 4 ft. (1.2 m) wide, with shiny, leathery, deep green, arching, featherlike, divided leaves, to 30 in. (75 cm) long, with lance-shaped, toothed leaflets, to 3 in. (75 mm) long, on fibrous stems. *C. fortunei* and *C. macrophyllum* are closely related species with similar care needs.
Plant hardiness: Zones 7–11. Semi-hardy.
Soil: Moist to damp, well-drained, sandy humus or, in water features, shoreline sites. Fertility: Rich. 6.0–7.0 pH.
Planting: Partial to full shade. Space 18–24 in. (45–60 cm) apart.
Care: Easy. Keep moist; allow soil surface to dry between waterings. Fertilize monthly. Propagate by division.
Features: Good choice for hanging baskets, borders, containers, edgings, fillers in natural, shade, tropical, woodland gardens and water feature shorelines. Good as houseplant. Pest resistant. Fungal disease susceptible.

Fern: *Davallia trichomanoides.* POLYPODIACEAE.
Common name: Squirrel-Foot Fern (Ball Fern).
Description: Many cultivars of slow- to medium-growing, mounding or trailing, spreading, rhizomatous, evergreen ferns, to 1 ft. (30 cm) tall and 30 in. (75 cm) wide, with shiny, bright green, broadly oval, triple-divided, finely cut, lacy fronds, to 18 in. (45 cm) long, and with sprawling, fleshy, brown, tan, white rhizomes covered with hairlike scales. *Humata tyermannii,* bear's-foot fern, is an unrelated species with similar appearance and care needs.
Plant hardiness: Zones 9–11. Tender.
Soil: Moist, well-drained, sandy loam mixed with humus and charcoal or, in water features, shoreline sites. Fertility: Rich–average. 5.5–6.5 pH.
Planting: Open to partial shade. Space 2 ft. (60 cm) apart.
Care: Easy. Keep moist spring–autumn; reduce water in winter. Fertilize every 2 months. Deadhead old or broken fronds. Propagate by division, spores, layering of rhizomes.
Features: Good choice for hanging baskets, borders, containers, edgings, ground covers in natural, shade, tropical, woodland gardens and water feature shorelines. Good as houseplant. Pest and disease resistant.

Fern: *Dennstaedtia punctilobula.* POLYPODIACEAE.
Common name: Hay-Scented Fern (Boulder Fern).
Description: A few cultivars of fast-growing, mounding, spreading, rhizomatous, deciduous ferns, 20–30 in. (50–75 cm) tall and wide, with deep green, lance-shaped, double-divided, feathery, finely cut fronds, to 30 in. (75 cm) long, on hairy, fibrous leafstalks. *D. bipinnata,* glossy cup fern; and *D. davallioides,* lacy ground fern, are closely related species with similar care needs.
Plant hardiness: Zones 3–11. Hardy.
Soil: Damp, well-drained, sandy soil. Fertility: Average–low. 5.5–7.0 pH.
Planting: Partial to full shade. Space 12–16 in. (30–40 cm) apart.
Care: Easy. Keep damp; allow soil surface to dry between waterings. Avoid fertilizing. Propagate by division, spores.
Features: Good choice for hanging baskets, borders, containers, edgings, foregrounds, ground covers in natural, shade, woodland gardens. Good as houseplant. Pest and disease resistant.

Fern: *Dicksonia antarctica.* DICKSONIACEAE.
Common name: Tasmanian Tree Fern.
Description: Several cultivars of slow-growing, erect, umbrella-crowned, palm-like, evergreen ferns, to 50 ft. (15 m) tall but seldom more than 15 ft. (4.5 m) tall in landscape use, with shiny, leathery, deep green, broad, arching, divided, finely cut, toothed fronds, 4–6 ft. (1.2–1.8 m) long, on woolly, red brown leafstalks, and with a fibrous, hairy trunk. *D. squarrosa* is a closely related species with similar care needs. See also *Cibotium glaucum,* Hawaiian tree fern, and *Cyathea cooperi,* Australian tree fern, unrelated species with similar appearances.
Plant hardiness: Zones 8–11. Tender.
Soil: Moist, well-drained, sandy loam mixed with humus and charcoal or, in water features, shoreline sites. Fertility: Rich. 6.0–7.0 pH.
Planting: Full sun to full shade. Space 6 ft. (1.8 m) apart.
Care: Easy. Keep evenly moist; water soil, stalks, and trunks. Fertilize monthly. Deadhead old or broken fronds. Protect from direct sun in arid climates. Propagate by cuttings, spores.
Features: Good choice for accents, backgrounds, containers, entries, paths in natural, shade, tropical, woodland gardens and water feature shorelines. Good as houseplant. Pest and disease resistant.

Fern: *Dryopteris arguta.* POLYPODIACEAE.
Common name: California Wood Fern (Coastal Wood Fern, Shield Fern).
Description: Many cultivars of erect, mounding, arching, open, rhizomatous, semi-evergreen ferns, to 30 in. (75 cm) tall and 4 ft. (1.2 m) wide, with shiny, light green, broadly pyramid-shaped, double-divided, finely cut, toothed fronds, 1–3 ft. (30–90 cm) long, on stiff, fibrous leafstalks. *D. erythrosora,* autumn fern, and *D. expansa,* spreading fern, are closely related species with similar care needs.
Plant hardiness: Zones 5–9. Hardy.
Soil: Moist, well-drained, sandy humus or, in water features, shoreline sites. Fertility: Rich. 5.5–6.5 pH.
Planting: Partial to full shade. Space 18–24 in. (45–60 cm) apart.
Care: Moderate. Keep evenly moist. Mist occasionally. Fertilize every 2 months. Deadhead old, broken fronds. Protect from sun, heat. Propagate by division, spores.
Features: Good choice for accents, backgrounds, borders, containers, edgings, fencelines, ground covers, slopes in natural, shade, small-space, woodland gardens and water feature shorelines. Pest and disease resistant.

Fern: *Matteuccia struthiopteris (M. pensylvanica, Pteretis struthiopteris).* POLYPODIACEAE.
Common name: Ostrich Fern.
Description: A few cultivars of erect, fountain-shaped, arching, rhizomatous, deciduous ferns, 5–10 ft. (1.5–3 m) tall and 3–4 ft. (90–120 cm) wide, with long, deep green, divided sterile leaves, to 10 ft. (3 m) long, and short, green, double-divided fertile leaves, to 4 ft. (1.2 m) long, on stiff, hairy, fibrous stalks.
Plant hardiness: Zones 1–8. Hardy. Best in moist, cool-summer climates.
Soil: Moist, well-drained, sandy humus or, in water features, shoreline sites. Fertility: Rich. 6.5–7.0 pH.
Planting: Full sun to full shade. Space 2–3 ft. (60–90 cm) apart.
Care: Easy. Keep evenly moist. Fertilize monthly. Deadhead old, broken fronds. Protect from heat, wind. Propagate by division, spores.
Features: Good choice for backgrounds, banks, fencelines, slopes in bog, mountain, shade, woodland gardens and water feature shorelines. Sterile-leaf fiddleheads are edible; good for stir-fry or steaming. Pest and disease resistant.

Fern: *Osmunda regalis.* OSMUNDACEAE.
Common name: Royal Fern (Flowering Fern).
Description: A few cultivars and horticultural varieties of erect, fountain-shaped, spreading, rhizomatous, deciduous ferns, 6–8 ft. (1.8–2.4 m) tall and 3 ft. (90 cm) wide, with bronze, purple becoming deep green, double-divided, finely cut sterile leaves, to 6 ft. (1.8 m) long, and green, double-divided fertile leaves, to 4 ft. (1.2 m) long, with bunched and clustered, cream to yellow, flowerlike terminal segments bearing sporangia, or spore bodies.
Plant hardiness: Zones 2–10. Hardy.
Soil: Moist, well-drained, sandy loam or, in water features, shallow-depth marginal or shoreline sites. Fertility: Rich. 6.5–7.0 pH.
Planting: Full to filtered sun. Space 18–24 in. (45–60 cm) apart, or submerge to 4 in. (10 cm) deep in a container.
Care: Easy. Keep very moist. Fertilize monthly. Allow fronds to mulch rhizome through winter; remove when fiddleheads emerge in spring. Propagate by division, spores.
Features: Good choice for accents, backgrounds, containers, fencelines in bog, shade, woodland gardens and water feature margins and shorelines. Sterile-leaf fiddleheads are edible; good for stir-fry or steaming. Pest and disease resistant.

Fern: *Platycerium bifurcatum (P. alcicorne).* POLYPODIACEAE.
Common name: Common Staghorn Fern.
Description: Many cultivars and horticultural varieties of slow-growing, spreading or trailing, epiphytic, rhizomatous, evergreen ferns, to 3 ft. (90 cm) tall and wide, with inconspicuous, green becoming brown, rounded, sterile leaves, to 1 ft. (30 cm) wide, and long, green, elkhorn- or moose-antler-shaped, divided and segmented, fertile leaves, to 3 ft. (90 cm) long, on short, hairy, basal stalks.
Plant hardiness: Zones 8–11. Semi-hardy. Best in moist, subtropical gardens.
Soil: Moist leaf mold mixed with *Osmondia* fiber, finely sifted sphagnum moss, and charcoal, with plant supported by wire on bark, cork, or weathered wood. Fertility: Rich. 6.0–7.0 pH.
Planting: Open to partial shade. Space 18 in. (45 cm) apart.
Care: Moderate. Keep evenly moist. Mist occasionally. Fertilize monthly with liquid fertilizer diluted to one-half its package-recommended strength. Propagate by spores, suckers.
Features: Good choice for hanging on lath, landscape trees, or walls in natural, shade, tropical, woodland gardens or water feature shorelines. Good as houseplant. Pest and disease resistant.

> **WARNING**
> Sphagnum moss may cause skin irritation in sensitive individuals. Wear gloves and protective clothing when mixing or handling potting mix containing sphagnum.

Fern: *Polystichum* species. POLYPODIACEAE.
Common name: Shield Fern (Holly Fern, Sword Fern).
Description: About 120 species of slow- to medium-growing, erect, mounding or arching, rhizomatous, deciduous or evergreen ferns, 1–5 ft. (30–150 cm) tall and wide, with shiny, smooth or leathery, green, lance-shaped, divided fronds, 6–60 in. (15–150 cm) long, with blade-shaped, sharply cut, toothed, opposite leaflets, 1–5 in. (25–125 mm) long, on brown, fibrous stems. Commonly cultivated species include *P. acrostichoides*, Christmas fern; *P. lonchitis,* mountain holly fern; and *P. polyblepharum,* Japanese lace fern.
Plant hardiness: Varies by species. Most species are hardy in zones 5–9, some to zone 2.
Soil: Moist, well-drained, sandy humus. Fertility: Rich. 6.0–7.0 pH.
Planting: Partial to full shade. Space 6–30 in. (15–75 cm) apart, depending on species.
Care: Easy. Keep evenly moist. Fertilize every 2 months. Deadhead old, broken fronds. Propagate by division, spores.
Features: Good choice for accents, hanging baskets, beds, borders, containers, ground covers in natural, shade, small-space, woodland gardens. Good as houseplant. Pest and disease resistant.

Fern: *Polystichum munitum.* POLYPODIACEAE.
Common name: Western Sword Fern (Giant Holly Fern).
Description: Many cultivars of slow-growing, erect, mounding, rhizomatous, evergreen ferns, 3–4 ft. (90–120 cm) tall and wide, with shiny, leathery, yellow green becoming deep green, lance-shaped, divided fronds, to 42 in. (1.1 m) long, with blade-shaped, sharply cut, toothed, opposite leaflets, to 5 in. (13 cm) long, on rough, brown, hairy and fibrous stems. *P. munitum* var. *imbricans,* imbricate sword fern, is a closely related variety with similar care needs.
Plant hardiness: Zones 4–9. Hardy.
Soil: Moist, well-drained, sandy humus. Fertility: Rich. 6.0–7.0 pH.
Planting: Partial to full shade. Space 18–24 in. (45–60 cm) apart.
Care: Easy. Keep evenly moist; drought tolerant when established. Fertilize every 2 months. Deadhead old, broken fronds. Propagate by division, spores.
Features: Good choice for accents, hanging baskets, beds, borders, containers, ground covers in natural, shade, woodland gardens. Pest and disease resistant.

SHRUBS

Shrub: *Abelia* × *grandiflora.* CAPRIFOLIACEAE.
Common name: Glossy Abelia.
Description: Several hybrids of medium-growing, dense, semi-evergreen shrubs, 6–8 ft. (1.8–2.4 m) tall and wide, with shiny, bronze to light green or variegated, oval, pointed leaves, turning purple, red in autumn. Dwarf hybrids available.
Blooms/Berries: Many small, trumpet-shaped, fluted, pink or white flowers, to ¾ in. (19 mm) long, in summer–early autumn, forming upright or dangling clusters with dry, berrylike, seeded fruit in autumn.
Plant hardiness: Zones 5–9; ground hardy, zones 6–9.
Soil: Moist, well-drained humus. Fertility: Rich–average. 5.5–6.5 pH.
Planting: Full sun. Space 4–6 ft. (1.2–1.8 m) apart.
Care: Easy. Keep moist; allow soil surface to dry between waterings until established. Fertilize quarterly spring–autumn. Prune sparingly in autumn. Protect from wind. Propagate by cuttings.
Features: Good choice for accents, backgrounds, hedges in formal, woodland gardens. Humidity tolerant. Pest and disease resistant.

WARNING
Sap and foliage of *Abutilon* × *hybridum* cause eye and skin irritation, stomach upset if eaten. Avoid planting in areas frequented by pets and children.

Shrub: *Abutilon* × *hybridum (A.* hybrids*).* MALVACEAE.
Common name: Chinese-Lantern (Chinese Bellflower, Flowering Maple, Indian Mallow).
Description: Several hybrid cultigens of fast-growing, short-lived, open, arching, deciduous shrubs, 3–5 ft. (90–150 cm) tall and wide, with alternate, smooth, maplelike, green or variegated, simple or lobed, pointed leaves, 2–6 in. (50–150 mm) long, turning yellow in autumn.
Blooms/Seed: Many showy, bell- or cup-shaped, nodding, orange, pink, red, white, yellow flowers, to 2 in. (50 mm) long, in spring–summer, with dry, paired, mapleseed-like fruit in autumn.
Plant hardiness: Zones 7–11; ground hardy, zones 9–11. Tender.
Soil: Moist to damp, well-drained humus. Fertility: Rich–average. 6.0–7.0 pH.
Planting: Full sun to partial shade. Space 3–5 ft. (90–150 cm) apart.
Care: Moderate. Keep moist; allow soil surface to dry between waterings until established. Fertilize monthly. Prune to remove one-half of foliage in autumn. Protect from heat, frost. Propagate by cuttings, seed.
Features: Good choice for accents, containers, edgings in cottage, formal, shade, woodland gardens. Good as houseplant. Mealybug, scale, whitefly and verticillium wilt susceptible.

Shrub: *Aesculus parviflora.* HIPPOCASTANACEAE.
Common name: Buckeye (Bottlebrush Buckeye).
Description: Several cultivars of fast-growing, open, spreading, deciduous shrubs, 8–12 ft. (2.4–3.7 m) tall and wide, with deep green, textured, rounded, 5–7-lobed, pointed leaves, 8–11 in. (20–28 cm) long, turning orange in autumn.
Blooms/Fruit: Many showy, white flowers, in upright, cone-shaped spikes, to 10 in. (25 cm) long, in summer, with leathery, round, scaly fruit, to 2 in. (50 mm) wide, in autumn.
Plant hardiness: Zones 4–10. Hardy. Best in long-season climates.
Soil: Moist to damp, well-drained, sandy loam. Fertility: Rich–average. 6.5–7.5 pH.
Planting: Full sun. Space 4–6 ft. (1.2–1.8 m) apart.
Care: Moderate. Keep moist; allow soil surface to dry between waterings until established. Fertilize quarterly. Prune to shape. Propagate by cuttings, grafting, seed, suckers.
Features: Good choice for accents, backgrounds, screens in cottage, open, turfgrass, woodland gardens. Attracts hummingbirds. Drops flowers, fruit, leaves, requiring maintenance. Japanese beetle, tussock moth and anthracnose susceptible.

WARNING
Seed of *Aesculus parviflora* may cause stomach upset if eaten. Avoid planting in areas frequented by pets and children.

Shrub: *Agave* species. AGAVACEAE.

Common name: Agave (Aloe, Century Plant).

Description: Several cultivars of slow-growing, mounding, succulent, evergreen shrubs, 18–60 in. (45–150 cm) tall and wide, with powdery, gray, blue green, fleshy, arching, lance-shaped, pointed, often toothed and sometimes thready or hairy leaves, 6–60 in. (15–150 cm) long, armed with sharp terminal spines.

Blooms/Fruit: Many fragrant, showy, cream, greenish white, yellow flowers, to 3 in. (75 mm) wide, in upright, branching clusters on a central woody, spiking stalk, 4–18 ft. (1.2–5.5 m) tall, in summer, with leathery, round fruit, to ½ in. (12 mm) wide, in autumn.

Plant hardiness: Zones 8–10. Tender.

Soil: Damp to dry, well-drained soil. Fertility: Average–low. 6.5–7.5 pH. Soil for container plantings should be sterile.

Planting: Full to filtered sun. Spacing varies by species.

> **WARNING**
> Sap of *Agave* species may cause skin and eye irritation in sensitive individuals. Always wear rubber gloves to prune or propagate plants.

Care: Easy. Keep damp; allow soil to dry completely between waterings. Drought tolerant. Avoid fertilizing, pruning. Propagate by budding, bulbils, division, seed, suckers.

Features: Good choice for accents, containers, hedges, screens in arid, desert, seaside gardens. Attracts birds, hummingbirds. Borer, mealybug, scale and fungal disease susceptible.

Shrub: *Aloysia triphylla (Lippia citriodora).* VERBENACEAE.

Common name: Lemon Verbena.

Description: Several cultivars of fast-growing, upright and branching, deciduous shrubs, 8–10 ft. (2.4–3 m) tall and 5–6 ft. (1.5–1.8 m) wide, with bright green, textured, oval, pointed, finely toothed, fragrant leaves, to 3 in. (75 mm) long, in whorls on the branches.

Blooms/Fruit: Inconspicuous cream, white flowers, in spikes or nodding clusters, in summer, with dry, round fruit bearing pairs of nutlike seed in autumn.

Plant hardiness: Zones 8–11. Tender. Best in humid, subtropical climates.

Soil: Moist, well-drained soil. Fertility: Average. 6.0–7.0 pH.

Planting: Full sun. Space 3–4 ft. (90–120 cm) apart.

Care: Easy. Keep evenly moist. Fertilize annually in spring. Prune to shape, promote compact growth. Propagate by cuttings.

Features: Good choice for accents, containers, hedges, screens, walls in arid, seaside, tropical gardens. Good as houseplant. Good for drying, tea. Pest and disease resistant.

Shrub: *Arctostaphylos manzanita.* ERICACEAE

Common name: Common Manzanita.

Description: Several cultivars of slow-growing, upright and branching or spreading, evergreen shrubs, 6–20 ft. (1.8–6 m) tall and wide, with smooth to shiny, deep green, leathery, oval, pointed leaves, to 2 in. (50 mm) long, often with contorted branches and burgundy, red bark.

Blooms/Fruit: Many cream, pink, white flowers, to ¼ in. (6 mm) long, in nodding clusters, to 1¾ in. (44 mm) long, in late spring, with mealy, red, round, berrylike, edible fruit bearing many seed in autumn.

Plant hardiness: Zones 6–9. Semi-hardy. Best in mountains, 3,000–5,000 ft. (920–1,540 m) high.

Soil: Damp to dry, well-drained, sandy soil. Fertility: Average–low. 6.0–7.0 pH.

Planting: Full to filtered sun. Space 4–8 ft. (1.2–2.4 m) apart.

Care: Moderate–challenging. Keep moist until established; drought tolerant thereafter. Deep water monthly; allow soil to dry between waterings. Fertilize annually in spring. Avoid pruning. Propagate by layering, seed.

Features: Good choice for accents, banks, containers, hedges, screens, walls in arid, mountain, woodland, Xeriscape gardens. Branches good for drying. Use berries for jelly. Pest and disease resistant.

Shrub: *Buxus* species. BUXACEAE.

Common name: Boxwood.

Description: About 30 species of slow-growing, compact, dense, evergreen shrubs, to 6 ft. (1.8 m) tall and wide, with shiny, midgreen, round leaves, ½–1 in. (12–25 mm) long. Commonly cultivated species include *B. microphylla* var. *japonica, B. m.* var. *koreana,* and *B. sempervirens.* Dwarf varieties available.

Blooms/Fruit: Tiny, white flowers in spring, in clusters borne at junction of leaf with limb, form berry- or caplike fruit in summer.

Plant hardiness: Zones 5–9; ground hardy, zones 6–9.

Soil: Moist, well-drained humus. Fertility: Rich. 6.0–7.5 pH.

Planting: Full sun to partial shade. Space 1 ft. (30 cm) apart for hedges, 3 ft. (90 cm) apart for landscape plants, depending on species.

Care: Easy. Keep evenly moist. Fertilize quarterly spring–autumn. Avoid cultivating around plants. Mulch, zones 8–9. Prune and shear in spring, autumn. Protect from wind.

Features: Good choice for backgrounds, edgings, hedges, paths, topiary in cottage, formal, natural, small-space gardens and landscapes. Best in mild climates. Scale, spider mite susceptible.

Shrub: *Calluna vulgaris.* ERICACEAE.

Common name: Scotch Heather.

Description: Many cultivars of slow-growing, mounding or spreading, evergreen shrubs, to 3 ft. (90 cm) tall, with small, overlapped, green, maroon, yellow, scaly leaves, tinged bronze or red in autumn. Many named cultivars exist with dwarf habits, distinctive foliage, or varied flower colors.

Blooms/Seed: Tiny, trumpet-shaped, pink, purple, white, double flowers, in upright spikes, to 10 in. (25 cm) long, with caplike seedpods in summer.

Plant hardiness: Zones 5–7.

Soil: Moist, well-drained loam. Fertility: Rich–average. 5.5–6.5 pH.

Planting: Full sun to partial shade. Space 3 ft. (90 cm) apart.

Care: Easy. Keep evenly moist. Fertilize semi-annually, spring and autumn. Mulch. Prune or shear after bloom. Protect from sun, wind in hot climates. Propagate by cuttings, seed.

Features: Good choice for borders, edgings, ground covers, mixed plantings in cottage, rock, small-space, woodland gardens. Best in cool, moist climates. Heat, humidity susceptible.

Shrub: *Calycanthus* species. CALYCANTHACEAE.

Common name: Sweet Shrub (Spice Bush).

Description: Four species of slow-growing, branching, deciduous shrubs, 6–12 ft. (1.8–3.7 m) tall and wide, with shiny, bright to deep green, textured, oval, pointed, veined, fragrant leaves, 5–8 in. (13–20 cm) long, with gray green undersides, turning yellow in autumn. Commonly cultivated species include *C. fertilis,* Carolina allspice; *C. floridus,* Carolina allspice or pineapple shrub; and *C. occidentalis,* spice bush.

Blooms/Fruit: Showy, very fragrant, fountain-shaped, upright, brown, red brown flowers, to 2 in. (50 mm) long, with straplike petals, in summer, form urn-shaped fruit bearing many seed with dry, papery covering, in late autumn.

Plant hardiness: Zones 4–9. Hardy.

Soil: Moist, well-drained humus. Fertility: Rich. 6.5–8.0 pH.

Planting: Full sun to partial shade. Space 4–6 ft. (1.2–1.8 m) apart.

Care: Easy. Keep evenly moist. Fertilize monthly. Prune to keep compact. Propagate by division, layering, seed, suckers.

Features: Good choice for accents, borders, fencelines, paths in cottage, meadow, shade, woodland gardens. Good for drying, sachets. Attracts bees. Pest and disease resistant.

CAMELLIA

About 80 species and many hundreds of named cultivars of showy, bushy, broad-leaved, evergreen shrubs and small trees are included in the *Camellia* genus. They are native to eastern Asia and, while somewhat tender, grow in climates as cold as USDA Plant Hardiness Zone 6 with winter protection.

Camellias are prized for their large, showy flowers with single, double, or very double petals in shades from deep red to white, which appear in late winter in mild regions or spring in cooler areas.

Camellias are slow-growing, usually 6–45 ft. (1.8–13.5 m) tall and sometimes as wide. They are good in containers as well as in the landscape, seldom need heavy pruning, and produce fragrant, long-lasting cut flowers ideal for floating in a bowl or stemmed vase.

While generally resistant to pests, they can be susceptible to mealybugs and scale insects. When weather turns cold and humid, they may contract blight or anthracnose infections.

Many new camellia cultivars, in addition to old favorites, are offered in garden centers each spring. Popular species are listed above, at right.

Camellias deserve a place in the shade garden next to the other beautiful and showy flowering shrubs—azalea, gardenia, and rhododendron. When mature, they are many-branched, densely leaved, glossy green, and lovely. Then their flowers appear, and they fill the shrub border with fragrant, round, pleasing flowers that cloak their limbs for many weeks.

Camellia Species:
C. chrysantha, golden camellia
C. granthamiana, Grantham camellia
C. hiemalis
C. japonica, common camellia
C. lutchuensis
C. oleifera, tea-oil plant
C. reticulata
C. saluenensis
C. sasanqua, Sasanqua camellia
C. sinensis, tea plant
C. x *vernalis*

Most popular cultivars are hybrids of three camellia species, *C. japonica*, *C. reticulata*, and *C. sasanqua*.

Plant camellias in a moist, well-drained, slightly acidic soil rich in organic humus. They perform best in locations with partial shade while young, but mature plants tolerate full-sun locations provided that they receive ample water to keep their soil moist. Plant them with other species of the forest floor, give them regular feedings with an acidic fertilizer, and neaten them after their blooms fade in late spring. Camellias are good container plants for small-space gardens, decks, and patios.

Camellias are at their best when used as understory plants in a woodland garden, mixed with other flowering shrubs and foliage plants. Some species and cultivars have been bred for full shade, others for partial shade or filtered sunlight. You'll find that camellias develop open habits and become lanky when they grow in deep shade, yet become stunted if they receive too much sunlight early in their lives. Plant them under deciduous trees that have open foliage during the summer and lose their leaves in winter for the right mixture of sun and shade.

In ideal climates and growing conditions, camellias are star performers able to turn a woodland garden into a showplace. Highlight a garden path, structure, or wall with their showy color or use them as accents.

Shrub: *Camellia japonica*. THEACEAE.
Common name: Common Camellia.
Description: Over 200 cultivars of slow-growing, bushy, evergreen shrubs or small trees, 6–45 ft. (1.8–13.5 m) tall, with shiny or waxy, deep green, smooth, oval leaves, 2½–4 in. (63–100 mm) long. Popular cultivars include *C. japonica* 'Adolphe Audusson', with red or variegated, semi-double flowers; 'Alba Plena', with white, double flowers; and 'Covina', with pink, red, double flowers. See also *Camellia sasanqua*.
Blooms/Fruit: Fragrant, pink, red, white, or multicolored, single, semi-double, or double flowers, 2–9 in. (50–228 mm) wide, in late winter–spring, form capsule-shaped fruit bearing seed in spring.
Plant hardiness: Zones 6–10; ground hardy, zones 8–10.
Soil: Moist, well-drained soil. Fertility: Rich. 6.0–6.5 pH.
Planting: Partial shade. Space 4–5 ft. (1.2–1.5 m) apart.
Care: Easy. Keep evenly moist. Fertilize every 2 months year-round. Mulch. Prune after bloom. Protect from sun in hot climates, frost in zones 6–7. Propagate by cuttings.
Features: Good choice for accents, borders, containers, hedges, paths, screens, walls in cottage, formal, natural, shade, small-space, woodland gardens. Mealybug, scale and anthracnose, blight susceptible.

Shrub: *Camellia sasanqua.* THEACEAE.

Common name: Sasanqua Camellia (Sasanqua).

Description: Nearly 100 cultivars of slow-growing, erect, branching and open, evergreen shrubs, to 12 ft. (3.7 m) tall and wide, with shiny or waxy, deep green, narrow, oval, pointed leaves, to 2 in. (50 mm) long, with tan green undersides. Common cultivars include *C. sasanqua* 'Flower Girl', 'Jean May', 'Sakae', and 'Tanya'. See also *C. japonica.* Dwarf cultivars available.

Blooms/Fruit: Showy, very fragrant, pink, red, rose, white, and multicolored, single, semi-double, or double flowers, to 2 in. (50 mm) wide, in autumn–winter, form capsule-shaped fruit bearing seed in spring.

Plant hardiness: Zones 8–10. Tender.

Soil: Moist, well-drained soil. Fertility: Rich. 6.5–7.0 pH.

Planting: Partial shade. Space 2–3 ft. (60–90 cm) apart.

Care: Easy. Keep evenly moist. Fertilize every 2 months year-round. Mulch. Prune after bloom. Protect from frost, heat, sun, wind. Propagate by cuttings, grafting.

Features: Good choice for accents, borders, containers, hedges, paths, screens, walls in cottage, formal, natural, shade, small-space, woodland gardens. Mealybug, scale and anthracnose, blight, canker susceptible.

Shrub: *Caragana arborescens.* FABACEAE (LEGUMINOSAE).

Common name: Pea Shrub (Siberian Pea Tree).

Description: Several varieties of fast-growing, bushy, thorny, deciduous small trees, 6–20 ft. (1.8–6 m) tall, depending on variety, with shiny, yellow green leaves, to 3 in. (75 mm) long, with 3–6 paired, oval leaflets.

Blooms/Seed: Showy, sweetpealike, yellow flowers, to 7/8 in. (22 mm) long, in small clusters, form brown, bean- or pealike seedpods in spring.

Plant hardiness: Zones 2–8. Hardy.

Soil: Moist, well-drained, sandy loam. Fertility: Average–poor. 6.5–8.5 pH.

Planting: Full sun. Space 5–6 ft. (1.5–1.8 m) apart.

Care: Easy. Keep moist; allow soil surface to dry between waterings until established. Fertilize annually in spring. Prune after bloom. Propagate by cuttings, division, grafting, layering, seed.

Features: Good choice for accents, barriers, borders, hedges, screens, windbreaks in arid, mountain, woodland gardens and landscapes. Drought tolerant. Deer, rodent and pest, disease resistant.

Shrub: *Caryopteris* species and hybrids. VERBENACEAE.

Common name: Bluebeard (Blue Mist, Blue Spiraea).

Description: About 6 species of fast-growing, erect, deciduous shrubs, 3–4 ft. (90–120 cm) tall, with opposite, textured, blue, gray, or deep green, lance-shaped, often toothed, fragrant leaves, 2–4 in. (50–100 mm) long.

Blooms/Seed: Many tiny, blue, lavender, pink, purple, sometimes hairy flowers, to 1/4 in. (6 mm) long, in whorled clusters, to 4 in. (10 cm) wide, on tall, spiking stems, in late summer, form dry, segmented seedpods in autumn. Commonly cultivated species include *C. x clandonensis,* blue mist; *C. incana,* common bluebeard; and *C. odorata,* Himalayan bluebird.

Plant hardiness: Zones 5–10; ground hardy, zones 7–10.

Soil: Moist, well-drained, sandy humus. Fertility: Rich. 6.5–7.0 pH.

Planting: Full sun. Space 2 ft. (60 cm) apart.

Care: Easy. Keep moist; allow soil surface to dry between waterings. Fertilize every 2 months. Deadhead spent blossoms to prolong bloom. Shear in spring. Propagate by cuttings, seed.

Features: Good choice for accents, backgrounds, borders, containers in cottage, formal gardens. Good for cutting, drying. Pest and disease resistant.

Shrub: *Cestrum nocturnum.* SOLANACEAE.
Common name: Night Jessamine (Night Jasmine).
Description: Several cultivars of bushy, climbing, or spreading, semi-evergreen tropical shrubs, to 12 ft. (3.7 m) tall, with shiny, deep green, oval, narrow leaves, 4–7 in. (10–18 cm) long. *C. aurantiacum, C. elegans,* and *C. fasciculatum* are closely related species with similar care needs.
Blooms/Berries: Many very fragrant, cream, white, green-tinged, flute-shaped flowers, to 1 in. (25 mm) long, in summer, opening in evening, form white berries in autumn.
Plant hardiness: Zones 8–11.
Soil: Moist, well-drained humus. Fertility: Rich. 6.0–7.0 pH.
Planting: Full sun. Space 8–10 ft. (2.4–3 m) apart.
Care: Moderate. Keep moist; allow soil surface to dry between waterings. Fertilize monthly during active growth. Prune after bloom in late summer. Protect from frost, zones 8–9. Propagate by cuttings, seed.
Features: Good choice for accents, arbors, backgrounds, containers, fencelines, trellises in cottage, formal, fragrance gardens. Good for cutting, drying. Attracts birds, hummingbirds. Pest and disease resistant.

Shrub: *Chaenomeles speciosa.* ROSACEAE.
Common name: Japanese Quince (Flowering Quince).
Description: Many cultivars of medium-growing, dense, branching or spreading, mostly spiny, semi-evergreen shrubs, 6–10 ft. (1.8–3 m) tall, with shiny, red turning deep green, oval, toothed leaves, to 3½ in. (90 mm) long, and tinged yellow in autumn.
Blooms/Fruit: Dainty, pink, red, white, single or double, waxy flowers, to 2½ in. (63 mm) wide, in early spring before leaves appear, form showy clusters, sometimes with green, pear-shaped fruit in autumn.
Plant hardiness: Zones 5–9.
Soil: Moist to damp, well-drained soil. Fertility: Average. Add acidic compost or leaf mold. 5.5–6.5 pH.
Planting: Full sun. Space 5–6 ft. (1.5–1.8 m) apart.
Care: Easy. Keep damp; allow soil surface to dry between waterings until established. Fertilize annually in spring. Prune after bloom. Propagate by cuttings, grafting, layering, seed.
Features: Good choice for barriers, bonsai, containers, walls in arid, Asian, cottage, woodland gardens. Good for cutting. Smog tolerant. Chlorosis, leaf spot susceptible.

Shrub: *Choisya ternata.* RUTACEAE.
Common name: Mexican Orange.
Description: A few cultivars of fast-growing, erect, branching or arching, evergreen shrubs, 5–8 ft. (1.5–2.4 m) tall, with opposite, shiny, deep green, oval, divided, pointed leaves, to 6 in. (15 cm) wide, with 3 leaflets, 2–3 in. (50–75 mm) long, in fan-shaped groups.
Blooms/Berries: Showy, cream, white, star-shaped, 4–5-petaled flowers, to 1 in. (50 mm) wide, in profuse, erect, mounding clusters, in early spring, form capsule-like fruit in early summer.
Plant hardiness: Zones 7–11; ground hardy, zones 8–11.
Soil: Damp to dry, well-drained soil. Fertility: Rich. 5.5–7.0 pH.
Planting: Full sun to partial shade. Space 5–8 ft. (1.5–2.4 m) apart.
Care: Moderate. Keep damp; allow soil surface to dry between waterings. Drought tolerant. Fertilize every 2 months. Prune after bloom. Propagate by cuttings.
Features: Good choice for accents, containers, walls in arid, tropical gardens. Attracts bees. Aphid, spider mite and chlorosis, fungal disease susceptible.

Shrub: *Cistus albidus.* CISTACEAE.

Common name: White-Leaved Rock Rose.

Description: Several cultivars of fast-growing, erect, branching and open, evergreen shrubs, to 8 ft. (2.4 m) tall and 4 ft. (1.2 m) wide, with opposite, velvety, gray green or variegated, lance-shaped, pointed, fragrant leaves, to 2½ in. (63 mm) long. *C.* x *cyprius,* spotted rock rose; *C. incanus,* purple rock rose; and *C. laurifolius,* laurel rock rose, are closely related species with similar care needs.

Blooms/Fruit: Showy, flat, open, pink, white, sometimes multicolored flowers, 2–3 in. (50–75 mm) wide, in summer, form nut- or acornlike fruit, to ½ in. (12 mm) wide, with green, leafy bracts in autumn. Single-day blooms, repeating in autumn.

Plant hardiness: Zones 7–10. Semi-hardy.

Soil: Damp to dry, well-drained soil. Fertility: Average–low. 6.5–8.0 pH. Salt tolerant.

Planting: Full sun. Space 2–4 ft. (60–120 cm) apart.

Care: Easy. Keep damp until established; drought tolerant thereafter. Avoid fertilizing. Pinch growth buds to shape. Limit pruning to removing old branches. Propagate by cuttings, layering, seed.

Features: Good choice for accents, banks, borders, containers, edgings, paths in arid, cottage, natural, seaside, small-space, woodland gardens. Disease resistant. Aphid susceptible.

Shrub: *Clethra alnifolia.* CLETHRACEAE.

Common name: Sweet Pepper Bush (Summer-Sweet).

Description: Several cultivars of medium- to slow-growing, erect, branching, spreading, deciduous shrubs, to 8 ft. (2.4 m) tall and wide, with alternate, textured, deep green, oval, pointed, finely toothed leaves, to 4 in. (10 cm) long, turning brown, yellow in autumn.

Blooms/Fruit: Many tiny, fragrant, cream, pink, white, bell-shaped, hairy flowers, to ½ in. (12 mm) long, in dense, whorled, erect or arching, spiking clusters, to 6 in. (15 cm) long, in summer, form small, capsulelike fruit bearing seed in autumn.

Plant hardiness: Zones 3–9. Hardy.

Soil: Moist to damp, well-drained humus. Fertility: Average. 6.0–7.0 pH.

Planting: Full sun to full shade. Space 4–5 ft. (1.2–1.5 m) apart.

Care: Easy. Keep evenly damp. Fertilize quarterly during growth. Prune to thin, shape in spring. Propagate by cuttings, division, layering, seed, suckers.

Features: Good choice for accents, backgrounds, fencelines in bog, seaside, shade, woodland gardens. Disease resistant. Spider mite susceptible.

Shrub: *Cordyline fruticosa (C. terminalis).* AGAVACEAE.

Common name: Ti Plant (Common Dracaena, Good-Luck Plant).

Description: Many cultivars of medium-growing, erect, columnar, palmlike, rhizomatous, evergreen shrubs, to 15 ft. (4.5 m) tall and 5 ft. (1.5 m) wide, with radiating, shiny, green, red, white, yellow or striped, variegated, lance-shaped, narrow, pointed leaves, to 3 ft. (90 cm) long. Sometimes mislabeled as *Dracaena* species.

Blooms/Berries: Many tiny, fragrant, purple, red, white, yellow flowers in winter, in branching clusters, to 1 ft. (30 cm) long, form round, red berries, to ¼ in. (6 mm) wide, in spring.

Plant hardiness: Zones 8–11. Tender.

Soil: Moist, well-drained, sandy humus or, in water features, shoreline sites. Fertility: Rich–average. 6.5–7.0 pH.

Planting: Full to filtered sun. Space 2–3 ft. (60–90 cm) apart.

Care: Easy. Keep evenly moist. Fertilize quarterly. Avoid pruning. Protect from frost. Propagate by cuttings, division, layering.

Features: Good choice for accents, borders, containers in tropical gardens and water feature shorelines. Good as houseplant. Started from "logs" imported from Hawaii. Pest and disease resistant.

Shrub: *Corylopsis* species. HAMAMELIDACEAE.
Common name: Winter Hazel.
Description: About 10 species of graceful, slow-growing, spreading, open, deciduous shrubs, 6–20 ft. (1.8–6 m) tall, depending on species, with red-tinged buds turning to smooth, bright green, broad, oval, pointed, toothed leaves, to 4 in. (10 cm) long, turning yellow in autumn. Commonly cultivated species include *C. glabrescens, C. pauciflora, C. sinensis, C. spicata,* and *C. veitchiana.*
Blooms/Seed: Many bell- or tube-shaped, yellow flowers, to ¾ in. (19 mm) long, in spring, form small, dangling clusters with caplike seedpods in summer. Flowers appear before leaves.
Plant hardiness: Zones 4–9, depending on species; ground hardy, zones 7–9.
Soil: Moist, well-drained soil. Fertility: Rich. Add acidic leaf mold. 5.5–6.5 pH.
Planting: Full sun to partial shade. Space 6–10 ft. (1.8–3 m) apart, depending on species.
Care: Easy. Keep evenly moist. Fertilize annually in spring. Mulch, zones 4–6. Prune after bloom. Protect from sun in hot climates, wind and frost in zones 4–7. Propagate by cuttings, division, layering, seed.
Features: Good choice for backgrounds, borders, walls in cottage, natural, woodland gardens. Pest and disease resistant.

Shrub: *Cotinus coggygria.* ANACARDIACEAE.
Common name: Smoke Tree (Smokebush).
Description: Several cultivars of medium-growing, bushy, open, woody, deciduous shrubs, to 15 ft. (4.5 m) tall, with smooth, blue green or purple, oval, pointed leaves, to 3 in. (75 mm) long, turning purple, red in autumn. Common cultivars include *C. coggygria* 'Daydream', 'Nordine', 'Purpureus', and 'Velvet Cloak'. *C. obovatus,* American smoke tree, is a related native species.
Blooms/Seed: Tiny, yellow flowers in early summer form dangling, branched clusters of lavender or purple, hairy "smoke," with small, berrylike, hard seed.
Plant hardiness: Zones 5–9.
Soil: Dry, well-drained soil. Fertility: Average low. 6.0–8.0 pH.
Planting: Full sun. Space 15–20 ft. (4.5–6 m) apart.
Care: Easy. Allow soil surface to dry between waterings until established. Avoid fertilizing, pruning. Propagate by cuttings, layering, seed.
Features: Good choice for accents in arid, meadow, rock gardens. Drought, smog tolerant. Pest and disease resistant.

Shrub: *Cotoneaster divaricatus.* ROSACEAE.
Common name: Spreading Cotoneaster.
Description: Deciduous shrub, to 6 ft. (1.8 m) tall and 10 ft. (3 m) wide, with shiny, dark green, smooth, oval, pointed leaves, to ¾ in. (19 mm) long. Branches bear thorny spurs. *C. dammeri, C. horizontalis, C. microphyllus, C. multiflorus,* and *C. salicifolius* are closely related species with similar care needs.
Blooms/Berries: Pink or red flowers, to ½ in. (12 mm) wide, in spring, form red berries, ½ in. (12 mm) wide, in autumn–winter.
Plant hardiness: Zones 5–10; ground hardy, zones 7–9.
Soil: Moist, well-drained soil. Fertility: Average–low. 6.5–7.0 pH.
Planting: Partial shade. Space 5 ft. (1.5 m) apart.
Care: Easy. Keep moist; allow soil surface to dry between waterings until established. Fertilize monthly spring–autumn. Prune sparingly. Protect from frost, zones 5–6. Propagate by cuttings, seed.
Features: Good choice for barriers, espaliers, ground covers, hedges, paths in formal, natural, rock gardens. Good ground cover for erosion control on hillsides. Berries attract birds. Drought, salt, wind tolerant.

Shrub: *Daphne* species. THYMELAEACEAE.
Common name: Daphne.
Description: About 50 species of slow-growing, compact or spreading, deciduous or evergreen shrubs, to 4 ft. (1.2 m) tall, with shiny, dark green or variegated, thick, oval, pointed leaves, 1–3 in. (25–75 mm) long.
Blooms/Fruit: Small, very fragrant, funnel-shaped, pink, purple, white, single-petaled, waxy flowers in late winter, form clusters, to 4 in. (10 cm) long, with red fruit in spring.
Plant hardiness: Zones 5–9, depending on species. *D. genkwa*, lilac daphne, and *D. odora*, winter daphne, are ground hardy, zones 7–9; other species are ground hardy, zones 5–9.

WARNING
All parts of *Daphne* species are fatally toxic if eaten. Avoid planting in gardens frequented by children or pets.

Soil: Moist, well-drained humus. Fertility: Rich. 6.5–7.0 pH.
Planting: Partial shade. Space 3–5 ft. (90–150 cm) apart. Set plant 1 in. (25 mm) above surrounding soil.
Care: Moderate–challenging. Keep moist; allow soil surface to dry between waterings until established. Fertilize annually in winter. Mulch. Prune after bloom. Protect from sun, wind in hot climates. Propagate by cuttings, grafting, layering, seed.
Features: Good choice for borders, containers, edgings, paths in cottage, small-space, woodland gardens. Good for corsages, cutting. Aphid susceptible. Disease resistant.

Shrub: *Deutzia* species. SAXIFRAGACEAE.
Common name: Deutzia.
Description: About 40 species of medium- to slow-growing, mounded or arching, usually deciduous shrubs, 6–9 ft. (1.8–2.7 m) tall, with smooth, green, lance-shaped, pointed, finely toothed leaves, 2–5 in. (50–125 mm) long. Dwarf species available. Some species have attractive, reddish brown bark.
Blooms/Seed: Small, star-shaped, pink, purple, white, simple flowers in late spring, to 1 in. (25 mm) wide, in arching clusters, form many small seed.
Plant hardiness: Zones 4–9, depending on species. Most species ground hardy, zones 6–9.
Soil: Moist, well-drained soil. Fertility: Average. 6.0–7.5 pH.
Planting: Full sun to partial shade. Space 5–7 ft. (1.5–2.2 m) apart.
Care: Easy. Keep moist. Fertilize quarterly spring–autumn. Prune after bloom. Protect from frost. Propagate by cuttings, division, layering, seed.
Features: Good choice for backgrounds, borders, hedges, mixed plantings in cottage, natural, woodland gardens. Pest and disease resistant.

Shrub: *Enkianthus campanulatus*. ERICACEAE.
Common name: Redvein Enkianthus.
Description: Several cultivars of slow-growing, dense, spreading, layered, deciduous small trees, to 30 ft. (9 m) tall, with shiny, deep green, oval or lance-shaped, pointed, toothed leaves, to 3 in. (75 mm) long, turning red in autumn.
Blooms/Berries: Small, bell-shaped, orange, yellow, red-veined flowers, in spring, form abundant, hanging clusters with caplike fruit in autumn.
Plant hardiness: Zones 5–9; ground hardy, zones 6–8.
Soil: Moist to dry, well-drained soil. Fertility: Rich. 6.0–6.5 pH.
Planting: Full sun to partial shade. Space 10–12 ft. (3–3.7 m) apart.
Care: Easy. Keep moist; allow soil surface to dry between waterings. Fertilize quarterly spring–autumn. Mulch. Limit pruning. Propagate by cuttings, layering, seed.
Features: Good choice for accents, borders, mixed plantings in natural, shade, woodland gardens. Salt susceptible. Pest and disease resistant.

ERICA (HEATH)

About 500 species of branching and bushy, evergreen shrubs and small trees make up the *Erica* genus. Native to Europe, Mediterranean Africa, and South Africa, they either are hardy or semi-hardy and grow in climates as cold as USDA Plant Hardiness Zone 5.

Heaths bear profuse displays of tiny, dainty, nodding, cup- or bell-shaped, sometimes tubular flowers with pink, red, or white corollas and pink stamens, appearing in summer and persisting until midautumn or even winter.

Heaths are fast-growing shrubs that range in height from 1–6 ft. (30–180 cm) tall and wide, depending on species. Use them as foundation or massed plantings, as borders or edgings, or as seasonal accents in full or filtered sun. Sprays of heath frequently are cut and arranged as delicate floral arrangements.

They generally are resistant to pests and diseases but become lanky if their branches are allowed to grow without pruning or shearing. Prune them after their flowers fade in autumn.

Many new heath cultivars from a variety of species are made available each spring. Most popular species of heath are listed above, at right.

Heath and its close relative, heather, are low- to medium-height shrubs of the essence of English cottage gardens. Growing from a short, woody trunk, they have many branches covered with feathery, needlelike foliage, glossy green or yellow, and are lovely year-round. When their flowers appear, they become carpets or mounds filled with tiny, clustered flowers.

Many hundreds of named cultivars of heath exist, greatly expanding the ranges of flower and foliage colors and times of bloom available in wild species.

Plant heaths in a moist, well-drained, sandy, acidic soil rich in organic humus. Avoid soils high in clay. Heaths grow best in locations with full sun in mild-summer climates and should receive sun protection in hot-summer areas. Apply an acid fertilizer annually in early spring, then repeat after their buds form. Heaths should be sheared after their blooms fade to maintain dense foliage and control their shape.

Heaths are best used at the corners of shrub borders, massed in group plantings that mix color shades and foliage textures, or as anchor plants in a rock garden. They are good companions to other plants that prefer acidic soil conditions, including many spring and summer bulbs, some annual and perennial flowers, as well as deep-forest trees and shrubs.

Heaths and heathers are unmatched foliage plants that can soften your landscape garden with their delicate foliage, yet bring striking color in late summer, when annuals and perennials fade.

Heath Species:
- *E. arborea,* tree heath
- *E. baccans,* berry heath
- *E. canaliculata,* Christmas heather
- *E. carnea,* spring heath
- *E. ciliaris,* fringed heath
- *E. cinerea,* Scots heath
- *E. doliiformis,* everblooming French heather
- *E. hyemalis,* white winter heather
- *E. mediterranea,* Irish heath
- *E. melanthera,* black-eyed heath
- *E. scoparia,* Besom heath
- *E. tetralix,* cross-leaved heath
- *E. vagans,* Cornish heath

Heather Species*:
- *Calluna vulgaris,* Scots heather

*True heather is a closely related species with similar care needs.

Shrub: *Erica* species. ERICACEAE.

Common name: Heath.

Description: Over 500 species of slow-growing, branching or spreading, evergreen shrubs or small trees, usually 1–6 ft. (30–180 cm) tall, with tiny, heatherlike needles or leaves. Dwarf and ground cover species available. *Calluna vulgaris,* Scots heather, is a close relative with similar care needs.

Blooms/Seed: Abundant tiny, green, purple, rose, white, yellow flowers in late winter–early spring or summer–autumn, depending on species, form seedy capsules in summer.

Plant hardiness: Zones 5–10, depending on species.

Soil: Damp, well-drained humus. Fertility: Rich. 5.0–6.0 pH.

Planting: Full sun. Space 3 ft. (90 cm) apart.

Care: Easy. Keep damp; allow soil surface to dry between waterings until established. Fertilize semi-annually in early spring and midsummer. Prune or shear after bloom. Protect from sun in hot climates. Propagate by cuttings, seed.

Features: Good choice for borders, edgings, ground covers, massed plantings in arid, rock gardens. Attracts bees. Pest and disease resistant.

Shrub: *Euonymus atropurpurea.* CELASTRACEAE.

Common name: Burning Bush (Wahoo).

Description: Several cultivars of medium- to slow-growing, mounding, dense, deciduous small trees, to 25 ft. (7.5 m) tall, with shiny, bronze to green or variegated, broad, lance-shaped, pointed, toothed leaves, to 5 in. (13 cm) long, turning red in autumn.

Blooms/Fruit: Inconspicuous, fragrant, pink flowers in spring form red, caplike, woody fruit bearing seed in autumn.

Plant hardiness: Zones 3–10; ground hardy, zones 4–9.

Soil: Damp to dry, well-drained soil. Fertility: Average. 6.0–8.0 pH.

Planting: Full sun. Space 10–12 ft. (3–3.7 m) apart.

Care: Easy. Keep damp; allow soil surface to dry between waterings until established. Drought tolerant. Fertilize quarterly spring–autumn. Mulch, zones 3, 10. Prune sparingly after bloom. Protect from sun in hot climates. Propagate by cuttings, layering, seed.

Features: Good choice for accents, borders, groups in formal, small-space, woodland gardens. Seed attracts birds. Scale and mildew susceptible.

WARNING
Foliage of *Euonymus atropurpurea* may cause digestive upset if eaten. Avoid planting in gardens frequented by pets or children.

Shrub: *Euonymus japonica* varieties and forms. CELASTRACEAE.

Common name: Spindle Tree (Boxleaf Euonymus, Evergreen Euonymus).

Description: Several horticultural varieties and cultivars of medium- to slow-growing, upright, compact, evergreen shrubs, 5–10 ft. (1.5–3 m) tall and 5–6 ft. (1.5–1.8 m) wide, with shiny, bright to deep green, or silver-, white-, yellow-edged or variegated, oval, pointed, finely toothed leaves, 1½–3 in. (38–75 mm) long.

Blooms/Fruit: Many inconspicuous, green white flowers in spring form orange, pink, caplike, woody fruit bearing seed in autumn.

Plant hardiness: Zones 3–10; ground hardy, zones 6–8.

Soil: Damp to dry, well-drained soil. Fertility: Average. 6.0–7.0 pH. Salt tolerant.

Planting: Full sun. Space 3–5 ft. (90–150 cm) apart.

Care: Moderate. Keep damp; allow soil surface to dry between waterings. Drought tolerant. Fertilize quarterly. Prune sparingly after bloom. Protect from sun, frost. Propagate by cuttings, layering, seed.

Features: Good choice for accents, borders, containers, groups in formal, small-space gardens. Attracts birds. Spider mite, scale, thrips and mildew susceptible.

Shrub: *Euphorbia* species. EUPHORBIACEAE.

Common name: Spurge.

Description: Over 1,600 varied species, including many fast- to medium-growing, mounding, bushy, semi-evergreen shrubs and small trees, 4–10 ft. (1.2–3 m) tall and wide, with textured, bright to deep green, often variegated, oval, pointed or rounded leaves, 1–6 in. (25–150 mm) long, turning deep red in autumn. See also *E. pulcherrima*, poinsettia.

Blooms/Fruit: Mostly showy, cream, white, yellow flowers in spring, in clusters at the ends of branches, form capsulelike fruit with seed in summer.

Plant hardiness: Zones vary by species. Hardy or semi-hardy.

Soil: Moist to damp, well-drained soil. Fertility: Average–low. 6.0–7.0 pH. Salt tolerant.

Planting: Full sun to partial shade. Space 1–5 ft. (30–150 cm) apart, depending on species.

Care: Easy. Keep damp until established; allow soil surface to dry between waterings. Fertilize annually in spring. Avoid crowding. Propagate by cuttings, division, seed.

Features: Good choice for accents, borders, containers in formal, seaside, small-space gardens. Avoid planting near water features containing fish. Pest and disease resistant.

WARNING
Sap of *Euphorbia* species causes skin irritation in sensitive individuals, digestive upset if eaten. Avoid planting in areas frequented by pets and children.

Shrub: *Euphorbia pulcherrima.* EUPHORBIACEAE.

Common name: Poinsettia (Mexican Flameleaf).

Description: Many cultivars of medium-growing, upright, branching, semi-evergreen shrubs, 7–10 ft. (2.2–3 m) tall and 4–6 ft. (1.2–1.8 m) wide, with smooth, bright to deep green, white, textured, spoon-shaped, pointed or rounded, veined leaves, 4–7 in. (10–18 cm) long.

Blooms/Fruit: Inconspicuous, yellow flowers in winter at branch ends, surrounded by very showy, pink, red, white, sometimes variegated or marbled clusters of leaflike bracts, to 10 in. (25 cm) wide, form capsulelike fruit with seed in spring.

Plant hardiness: Zones 8–11. Tender.

> **WARNING**
> Sap of *Euphorbia pulcherrima* may cause skin irritation in sensitive individuals. Wear gloves to prune or propagate plants.

Soil: Damp to dry, well-drained soil. Fertility: Average–low. 6.5–8.0 pH. Salt tolerant.

Planting: Full to filtered sun. Space 3–5 ft. (90–150 cm) apart.

Care: Moderate. Keep damp until established; allow soil surface to dry between waterings. Drought tolerant. Fertilize every 2 weeks when leaves begin to color until blooms fade. Prune canes after bloom. Protect from frost, wind. Propagate by cuttings, seed.

Features: Good choice for accents, containers in small-space, tropical gardens. Good holiday color. Pest and disease resistant.

Shrub: *Euryops pectinatus.* ASTERACEAE (COMPOSITAE).

Common name: Gray-Leaved Euryops.

Description: A few cultivars of medium-growing, mounding, bushy, evergreen shrubs, 3–4 ft. (90–120 cm) tall and wide, with alternate, velvety, featherlike, gray green, divided, cut, and pointed leaves, 2–3 in. (50–75 mm) long, each with 8–10 paired leaflets. *E. acraeus* and *E. spathaceus* are closely related species with similar care needs.

Blooms/Seed: Many showy, daisylike, yellow flowers, 1½–2 in. (38–50 mm) wide, in spring–autumn, form dry, wingless seed year-round.

Plant hardiness: Zones 7–11. Tender.

Soil: Damp to dry, well-drained soil. Fertility: Average–low. 6.5–8.0 pH. Salt tolerant.

Planting: Full sun. Space 2–3 ft. (60–90 cm) apart.

Care: Easy. Keep damp until established; allow soil surface to dry between waterings. Drought, wind tolerant. Fertilize annually in spring. Deadhead spent flowers to prolong bloom. Protect from frost, prolonged moisture. Propagate by division, seed.

Features: Good choice for accents, beds, borders, containers, paths in cottage, seaside, small-space gardens. Disease resistant. Aphid susceptible.

Shrub: *Exochorda racemosa (E. grandiflora).* ROSACEAE.

Common name: Common Pearlbush.

Description: A few cultivars of fast-growing, erect, narrow, deciduous shrubs, 10–12 ft. (3–3.7 m) tall and wide, with shiny, green, broadly oval, pointed leaves, 2½–3 in. (63–75 mm) long, and with red brown bark. *E. giraldii,* Wilson pearlbush, is a closely related species with larger blooms and similar care needs.

Blooms/Fruit: Many showy, spirea-like, short-lived, cream, white flowers, 1½–2 in. (38–50 mm) wide, in spring as leaves emerge, in dangling clusters, form dry, divided, capsulelike fruit bearing winged seed in summer.

Plant hardiness: Zones 5–9. Hardy.

Soil: Moist to damp, well-drained soil. Fertility: Average. 5.5–6.5 pH.

Planting: Full sun. Space 4–6 ft. (1.2–1.8 m) apart.

Care: Easy. Keep moist until established; drought tolerant thereafter. Fertilize annually in spring. Mulch in winter. Prune to remove central branches and maintain open form. Propagate by cuttings, layering, seed.

Features: Good choice for accents, borders, containers, screens in cottage, formal, meadow gardens. Pest and oak root fungus resistant. Powdery mildew susceptible.

Shrub: *Fatsia japonica (Aralia sieboldii).* ARALIACEAE.
Common: Japanese Fatsia (Formosa Rice Tree, Japanese Aralia).
Description: Several cultivars of medium-growing, open, tropical-like, evergreen shrubs, to 20 ft. (6 m) high and wide, with shiny, deep green or variegated, 7–11-lobed leaves, to 16 in. (40 cm) wide. Branches and trunk are marked with light, crescent-shaped scars.
Blooms/Fruit: Many tiny, white flowers in autumn, in open, dangling clusters, to 18 in. (45 cm) long, form black, round, berrylike fruit, persisting through winter.
Plant hardiness: Zones 7–10; ground hardy, zones 8–10.
Soil: Moist, well-drained loam. Fertility: Rich–average. 6.0–6.5 pH.
Planting: Partial to full shade. Space 4–6 ft. (1.2–1.8 m) apart.
Care: Moderate. Keep evenly moist. Fertilize monthly spring–autumn. Mulch. Prune to shape in spring. Remove suckers. Protect from sun, wind in hot climates.
Features: Good choice for accents, backgrounds, containers, fencelines, screens in indoor, small-space, tropical gardens. Slug, snail susceptible.

Shrub: *Forsythia* × *intermedia.* OLEACEAE.
Common name: Forsythia.
Description: Many hybrids and cultivars of dainty, fast-growing, arching, open, deciduous shrubs, to 10 ft. (3 m) tall, with bright green, oval, simple, sometimes 3-lobed, pointed leaves, to 5 in. (13 cm) long. Common cultivars include *F.* × *intermedia* 'Fiesta', 'Goldzauber', 'Lynwood', 'Spectabilis', and 'Spring Glory'. *F. ovata, F. suspensa,* and *F. viridissima* are closely related species with similar care needs.
Blooms/Seed: Many yellow flowers in spring, to 1 in. (25 mm) long, in showy clusters along arched branches, form winged seed in autumn. Flowers appear before leave, on second-year wood.
Plant hardiness: Zones 4–8.
Soil: Moist, average loam. Fertility: Average. 6.5–8.0 pH.
Planting: Full sun. Space 8–10 ft. (2.4–3 m) apart.
Care: Easy. Keep moist. Fertilize quarterly spring–autumn. Mulch, zones 4–6. Prune by thinning oldest, canelike stems after bloom. Propagate by cuttings, layering, seed.
Features: Good choice for backgrounds, borders, hedges, mixed plantings in natural, woodland gardens. Good for cutting, indoor floral display.

Shrub: *Fothergilla gardenii.* HAMAMELIDACEAE.
Common name: Dwarf Fothergilla (Witch Alder).
Description: Medium- to slow-growing, bushy, mounding, deciduous shrub, to 4 ft. (1.2 m) tall, with deep or blue green, oval, pointed leaves, 1–2 in. (25–50 mm) long, turning orange, red, yellow, variegated in autumn.
Blooms/Fruit: Tiny, filament-like, white flowers in spring form round, upright, bottle-brush-like clusters, to 2 in. (50 mm) long, with caplike fruit in summer. Flowers usually appear before leaves. Blooms best in full sun.
Plant hardiness: Zones 4–9; ground hardy, zones 5–9.
Soil: Moist, well-drained soil. Fertility: Rich–average. Add acidic compost or leaf mold. 5.5–6.5 pH.
Planting: Full sun to partial shade. Space 3–4 ft. (90–120 cm) apart.
Care: Easy. Keep moist; allow soil surface to dry between waterings until established. Fertilize annually in spring. Mulch, zones 4–6. Prune after bloom. Propagate by cuttings, layering, seed.
Features: Good choice for accents, backgrounds, beds, borders in cottage, woodland gardens. Good for cutting. Pest and disease resistant.

Shrub: *Fuchsia × hybrida.* ONAGRACEAE.
Common name: Fuchsia (Common Fuchsia, Lady's-Eardrops).
Description: Many hybrids of slow-growing, semi-evergreen or evergreen shrubs, to 12 ft. (3.7 m) tall, with shiny, bronze, green, purple, oval to lance-shaped, finely toothed leaves, to 2 in. (50 mm) long. Most hybrid fuchsias derive from *F. fulgens,* and *F. magellanica,* closely related species with similar care needs.
Blooms/Berries: Many showy, nodding, cup- to funnel-shaped, star-pointed, blue, bronze, pink, purple, red, violet flowers, to 3 in. (75 mm) long, with long, pink, red, white sepals in summer, form purple, seedy berries in autumn.
Plant hardiness: Zones 7–10. Tender.
Soil: Moist, well-drained humus. Fertility: Rich. 6.0–7.0 pH.
Planting: Full to filtered sun. Space 3–4 ft. (90–120 cm) apart.
Care: Moderate. Keep evenly moist. Fertilize monthly during active growth. Deadhead spent flowers to prolong bloom. Prune sparingly spring–autumn; cut to main branches in winter. Protect from frost in zones 7–8; sun, zones 9–10. Propagate by cuttings.
Features: Good choice for hanging baskets, borders, containers, walls in cottage, formal, woodland gardens. Good for espaliers, topiaries. Attracts birds, hummingbirds. Aphid, spider mite and chlorosis susceptible.

Shrub: *Gardenia jasminoides.* RUBIACEAE.
Common name: Common Gardenia (Cape Jasmine, Cape Jessamine).
Description: Slow-growing, bushy, evergreen shrub, to 6 ft. (1.8 m) tall, with shiny, dark green, thick, oval, veined leaves, 3–4 in. (75–100 mm) long.
Blooms/Berries: Very fragrant, white, yellow, often double-petaled flowers, 2–3½ in. (50–90 mm) wide, in autumn–winter, form round, seedy berries in spring.
Plant hardiness: Zones 8–11.
Soil: Moist, well-drained soil. Fertility: Average. Add acidic compost or leaf mold. 4.5–5.5 pH.
Planting: Partial shade. Space 2–3 ft. (60–90 cm) apart.
Care: Moderate. Keep evenly moist. Limit watering in summer. Fertilize in spring. Pinch off buds until early autumn. Deadhead blooms and suckers. Prune after bloom. Protect from sun in hot climates, frost in zone 8. Propagate by cuttings.
Features: Good choice for containers, hedges, paths in informal, rock, water gardens. Good for cutting. Aphid, mealybug, spider mite, scale susceptible.

Shrub: *Genista* species *(Cytisus species).* FABACEAE (LEGUMINOSAE).
Common name: Broom.
Description: About 50 species of fast-growing, spreading, deciduous or semi-evergreen shrubs, 8–180 in. (20–460 cm) tall, depending on species, usually with 3-part, divided or sometimes single, green leaves, ½–4 in. (12–100 mm) long.
Blooms/Seed: Fragrant, pealike, brown, red, white, yellow flowers in late spring, to 1 in. (25 mm) long, often in pairs or showy clusters, form beanlike seedpods in summer.
Plant hardiness: Zones 2–9, depending on species; ground hardy, zones 6–8.
Soil: Damp to dry, well-drained soil. Fertility: Average–low. 6.5–7.5 pH. Salt tolerant.
Planting: Full sun. Space 1–8 ft. (30–240 cm) apart, depending on species.
Care: Easy. Keep damp; allow soil surface to dry between waterings until established. Fertilize semi-annually in spring, autumn. Mulch, zones 2–5, 8–9. Prune after bloom. Protect from sun in hot climates. Propagate by cuttings, grafting, layering, seed.
Features: Good choice for accents, borders, hedges, screens in cottage, seaside, small-space gardens. Humidity susceptible. Some species are very invasive.

Shrub: *Hebe* species and hybrids. SCROPHULARIACEAE.

Common name: Hebe Veronica.

Description: More than 70 species and many hybrids of fast- to medium-growing, mounding, evergreen shrubs, 3–6 ft. (90–180 cm) tall and wide, with opposite, shiny, deep or gray green, oval, sometimes finely toothed leaves, to ½–4 in. (12–100 mm) long. Commonly cultivated species include *H. buxifolia*, boxleaf hebe; *H. carnosula; H. elliptica; H. imperialis;* and *H. speciosa*, showy hebe.

Blooms/Fruit: Many tiny, blue, pink, purple, white flowers in showy, spiking clusters, to 3 in. (75 mm) long, often with long, contrasting sepals, in summer, form flat, dry fruit bearing seed in autumn.

Plant hardiness: Zones 8–9. Tender. Best in mild-summer climates.

Soil: Damp to dry, well-drained, sandy loam. Fertility: Rich–average. 6.5–7.5 pH. Somewhat salt tolerant.

Planting: Full sun to partial shade. Space 2–3 ft. (60–90 cm) apart.

Care: Easy. Keep damp; allow soil surface to dry between waterings. Fertilize quarterly. Prune after blooms fade to maintain compact habit. Protect from frost. Propagate by cuttings, layering, seed.

Features: Good choice for backgrounds, beds, borders, containers, paths in cottage, seaside, small-space, woodland gardens. Pest resistant. Mildew susceptible.

Shrub: *Hibiscus mutabilis.* MALVACEAE.

Common name: Confederate Rose (Cotton Rose).

Description: Several cultivars of fast-growing, erect, branching, mounding, deciduous shrubs, to 15 ft. (4.5 m) tall and 6–8 ft. (1.8–2.4 m) wide, with shiny, green, broadly oval, 5–7-lobed leaves, to 6 in. (15 cm) long, often with scalloped lobes. See also *Hibiscus rosa-sinensis*, Chinese hibiscus.

Blooms/Seed: Showy, white becoming pink to red, single or double flowers, 4–6 in. (10–15 cm) wide, in summer, form dry, hairy, capsulelike pods bearing seed in autumn.

Plant hardiness: Zones 7–10. Tender. Best in humid, subtropical gardens.

Soil: Moist, well-drained loam. Fertility: Rich. 6.5–7.5 pH.

Planting: Full sun. Space 3–5 ft. (90–150 cm) apart.

Care: Easy. Keep evenly moist. Fertilize monthly. Prune when dormant to shape. Protect from frost. Propagate by cuttings, grafting, layering; plants grown from seed may revert.

Features: Good choice for backgrounds, beds, borders, containers, paths in seaside, tropical gardens. Disease resistant. Aphid, whitefly susceptible.

Shrub: *Hibiscus rosa-sinensis.* MALVACEAE.

Common name: Chinese Hibiscus (China Rose, Hawaiian Hibiscus).

Description: Several cultivars of fast-growing, erect, branching or spreading, evergreen shrubs, 15–30 ft. (4.5–9 m) tall and 12–18 ft. (3.7–5.5 m) wide, with shiny, bright to deep green, often textured, broadly oval leaves, to 6 in. (15 cm) long. See also *H. mutabilis*, Confederate rose.

Blooms/Seed: Very showy, gold, orange, pink, red, yellow, single or double flowers, 4–8 in. (10–20 cm) wide, often with ruffled petals, in summer, form dry, hairy, capsulelike pods bearing seed in autumn. Single-day blooms.

Plant hardiness: Zones 9–11. Tender. Best in humid, subtropical gardens.

Soil: Moist, well-drained loam. Fertility: Rich. 7.0–7.5 pH.

Planting: Full sun to partial shade. Space 5–10 ft. (1.5–3 m) apart.

Care: Moderate. Keep evenly moist. Fertilize monthly. Prune to shape and control size. Protect from frost, wind. Propagate by cuttings, grafting, layering; plants grown from seed may revert.

Features: Good choice for accents, beds, borders, containers, screens, walls in seaside, tropical, woodland gardens. Disease resistant. Aphid, whitefly susceptible.

HYDRANGEA

The *Hydrangea* genus includes nearly 25 species of midsized, erect, climbing or branching, bushy deciduous shrubs. They are native to both Americas and East Asia, are hardy, and do best in USDA Plant Hardiness Zones 6–10, though a few are hardy to zone 4.

Hydrangeas bear showy pom-pom-like clusters of round-petaled or star-shaped florets ranging in colors from white to blue, pink, and purple. They bud in spring, bloom in summer, and have flowers that are either fertile or sterile, borne in diminutive lace caps or showy clusters.

Hydrangeas are fast-growing shrubs, mostly 4–8 ft. (1.2–2.4 m) tall. Use them as foundation or border plantings, as hedges, or as screens in full or filtered sun or in sites with partial shade. Flower clusters of hydrangea frequently are cut and arranged fresh or dried as showy floral arrangements.

Most hydrangeas are susceptible to aphids and mildew when conditions are too cool and moist. Prune them once their flowers fade in autumn, or in spring before growth begins.

Choose your hydrangeas from the species listed above, at right.

Hydrangeas have long been prized for their showy, clustered flowers, which vary in color depending on the acid-alkaline balance of the soil in which the plant grows, and for their glossy, rich-textured foliage. Their many arching branches create graceful, full-bodied shrubs that complete shrub borders through the entire garden season. Their long-lasting flowers appear in summer, retaining all their charm even after they have dried.

Hydrangea Species:
H. anomala var. petiolaris, climbing hydrangea
H. arborescens, smooth hydrangea
H. aspera, Sargent hydrangea
H. heteromalla, Bretschneider hydrangea
H. macrophylla, big-leaved hydrangea
H. paniculata, panicle hydrangea
H. quercifolia, oak-leaved hydrangea
H. serrata

Plant hydrangeas in a moist, well-drained, acidic soil mixed with rich organic humus. Their flowers are more deeply colored in acidic conditions, and the plants may yellow with chlorosis if their soil turns too alkaline.

Hydrangeas grow best in locations with filtered sun or partial shade and should be protected from the sun in hot-summer climates. Apply an acid fertilizer every two months from early spring until the flowers begin to fade. They tolerate heavy prunings in autumn or spring, when they should be shaped to maintain their compact habit and dense foliage.

Use hydrangeas at the centers of beds, in shrub borders, or as understory plants in shade and woodland gardens. They are good companions for acid-soil plants that bloom in early to midspring, providing annual and perennial flowers a background of rich foliage against which to show their flowers and flowering after azaleas, camellias, and rhododendrons have finished their seasonal bloom.

To dry hydrangea clusters while retaining their form, color, and charm, cut them at their peak bloom, strip their leaves, and hang them upside down in a warm, dry spot. Some gardeners prefer to pack the blossoms in silica gel, a dessicant that quickly removes their moisture. The dried flowers can be used in arrangements year-round.

Shrub: *Hydrangea* species. HYDRANGEACEAE (SAXIFRAGACEAE).

Common name: Hydrangea.

Description: Over 20 species of tall or climbing, bushy, deciduous or evergreen shrubs, 4–8 ft. (1.2–2.4 m) tall, with shiny, dark green, broad, oval, lobed or deeply toothed leaves, to 1 ft. (30 cm) long.

Blooms/Seed: Abundant round or star-shaped, blue, lavender, pink, purple, white, sometimes sterile flowers, to 1 in. (25 mm) wide, in summer–early autumn, form mounding clusters, to 18 in. (45 cm) wide, with seed in autumn.

Plant hardiness: Zones 4–10. Most ground hardy, zones 6–10.

Soil: Moist, well-drained, loose soil. Fertility: Rich. Add compost or leaf mold. 6.5–7.0 pH. For best blue flowers, add aluminum sulfate; reds and pinks, garden lime.

Planting: Full sun to partial shade. Space 6–10 ft. (1.8–3 m) apart.

Care: Moderate. Keep moist; allow soil surface to dry between waterings until established. Fertilize every 2 months spring–summer. Deadhead. Prune severely in autumn or early spring. Propagate by cuttings, division, layering, seed.

Features: Good choice for borders, hedges, screens in cottage, woodland gardens. Cut and dry flower heads for wreaths and floral arrangements. Aphid and chlorosis, mildew susceptible.

Shrub: *Hydrangea quercifolia.* HYDRANGEACEAE (SAXIFRAGACEAE).

Common name: Oak-Leaved Hydrangea.

Description: Several cultivars of rounded, branching, stoloniferous, deciduous shrubs, 4–6 ft. (1.2–1.8 m) tall and 6–8 ft. (1.8–2.4 m) wide, with shiny, oaklike, dark green, broad, broadly oval, 5-lobed leaves, to 8 in. (20 cm) long, turning red in autumn, on woolly-haired branches. Grown primarily for foliage, zones 5–6.

Blooms/Seed: Showy, rose, cream white, 4–5-petaled, mixed fertile and sterile flowers, to ½ in. (12 mm) wide, in late summer–early autumn, form erect, conelike clusters, to 10 in. (25 cm) long, with seed in autumn. Blooms on second-year wood.

Plant hardiness: Zones 5–9. Hardy.

Soil: Moist to damp, well-drained, loose humus. Fertility: Rich. 5.5–7.0 pH.

Planting: Full to filtered sun. Space 3–4 ft. (90–120 cm) apart.

Care: Moderate. Keep moist; allow soil surface to dry between waterings until established. Fertilize every 2 months, spring–summer. Deadhead. Prune after bloom. Propagate by cuttings, division, layering, seed.

Features: Good choice for borders, hedges, screens in cottage, woodland gardens. Cut and dry flower heads for wreaths and floral arrangements. Aphid and chlorosis, mildew susceptible.

Shrub: *Indigofera* species. FABACEAE (LEGUMINOSAE).

Common name: Indigo Bush.

Description: About 750 species of fast-growing, erect, woody, deciduous shrubs, 18–36 in. (45–90 cm) tall and wide, with alternate, smooth, bright green, oval, divided, rounded leaves, to 4 in. (10 cm) long, with 1–5-paired, oval leaflets, to 1½ in. (38 mm) long. Commonly cultivated species include *I. incarnata, I. kirilowii,* and *I. tinctoria.*

Blooms/Seed: Many pink, purple, rose, white, red yellow, pealike flowers, to ¾ in. (19 mm) long, in erect, spiking clusters, 5–8 in. (13–20 cm) long, in summer, form beanlike pods containing seed in autumn.

Plant hardiness: Zones 4–10, depending on species. Hardy.

Soil: Moist, well-drained, sandy loam. Fertility: Rich–average. 6.0–7.0 pH.

Planting: Full sun. Space 10–20 in. (25–50 cm) apart.

Care: Easy. Keep moist; allow soil surface to dry between waterings. Fertilize quarterly. Prune severely in spring, before growth begins. Propagate by cuttings, division, seed.

Features: Good choice for borders, edgings in cottage, meadow gardens. Source of indigo dye. Pest and disease resistant.

Shrub: *Isopogon formosus.* PROTEACEAE.

Common name: Rose Coneflower.

Description: Several cultivars of slow-growing, erect, narrow, evergreen shrubs, 4–8 ft. (1.2–2.4 m) tall and 3–5 ft. (90–150 cm) wide, with shiny, featherlike, deep green, stiff, narrow, flat, deeply divided leaves, to 3 in. (75 mm) long, with branching leaflets, to 1 in. (25 mm) long. *I. anemonifolius* is a closely related species.

Blooms/Fruit: Showy, conelike, pink, purple, rose flowers, to 3 in. (75 mm) wide, on short stalks growing from leaf junctions with stalks, in late winter or early spring, form hairy, nutlike fruit bearing seed in early summer.

Plant hardiness: Zones 8–11. Tender.

Soil: Damp to dry, well-drained, sandy soil. Fertility: Average. 6.5–7.5 pH.

Planting: Full to filtered sun. Space 3–4 ft. (90–120 cm) apart.

Care: Moderate. Keep damp; allow soil surface to dry between waterings. Drought tolerant. Fertilize every 2 months with 5–0–10 formulated fertilizer. Prune growth buds to stimulate flower buds, retain compact form. Protect from heat, sun in hot-summer climates. Propagate by cuttings, seed.

Features: Good choice for accents, beds, borders, containers, screens, walls in arid, seaside gardens. Pest and disease resistant.

Shrub: *Juniperus communis.* CUPRESSACEAE.

Common name: Common Juniper.

Description: Many cultivars of very diverse, medium- to slow-growing, erect, prostrate, or spreading, dense, coniferous, evergreen shrubs and small trees, 2–35 ft. (60–1,100 cm) tall, depending on cultivar, with shiny, green needles that mature to scaly, cedarlike foliage. Columnar, ground cover, shrub, and tree habits are available in various cultivars.

Blooms/Cones: Male, catkinlike, yellow cones and female, aromatic, pulpy, berrylike, blue or black cones appear in spring, ripening in autumn.

Plant hardiness: Zones 2–9. Very hardy.

Soil: Damp to dry, well-drained loam. Fertility: Average. 5.5–8.0 pH.

Planting: Full sun to partial shade. Spacing varies by cultivar.

Care: Easy. Keep damp; allow soil surface to dry between waterings until established. Fertilize annually in spring. Prune only to shape new growth. Propagate by cuttings, grafting, seed.

Features: Good choice for accents, borders, edgings, ground covers, hedges, screens in formal, small-space, woodland gardens. Aphid, borer, spider mite and juniper blight susceptible.

Shrub: *Justicia brandegeana (Beloperone guttata).* ACANTHACEAE.

Common name: Shrimp Plant (False Hop, Shrimp Bush).

Description: Several cultivars of medium-growing, mounding, open, tropical, perennial, evergreen shrubs, to 3 ft. (90 cm) tall, with deep green, textured, soft, hairy, tear-shaped or oval, pointed leaves, to 3 in. (75 mm) long, on weak leaf stalks. *J. californica, J. carnea,* and *J. spicigera* are closely related species.

Blooms/Fruit: Uniquely segmented, tubular, nodding, purple, red, white flowers, surrounded by bronze, green, orange, pink, salmon, yellow bracts, form prawnlike clusters, to 6 in. (15 cm) long, in spring–autumn, and capsulelike fruit bearing seed in autumn.

Plant hardiness: Zones 7–11. Semi-hardy.

Soil: Moist to damp, well-drained soil. Fertility: Rich–average. 6.5–7.5 pH.

Planting: Full to filtered sun. Space 3–4 ft. (90–120 cm) apart.

Care: Easy. Keep damp. Reduce watering in winter. Fertilize monthly during growth. Deadhead spent blooms. Pinch to remove early buds. Prune to half size in spring. Protect from sun. Propagate by stem cuttings, seed.

Features: Good choice for accents, hanging baskets, beds, borders, containers, entries in cottage, shade, woodland gardens. Good for patios. Attracts hummingbirds. Pest and disease resistant.

Shrub: *Kalmia latifolia.* ERICACEAE.

Common name: Mountain Laurel (Calico Bush).

Description: Several cultivars of slow-growing, dense, mounding, evergreen shrubs, to 10 ft. (3 m) tall, with shiny, azalea-like, deep green, leathery, lance-shaped, pointed leaves, to 5 in. (13 cm) long, and tinged orange red in autumn.

Blooms/Seed: Showy, cuplike, star-pointed, chocolate, pink, red, rose, white flowers in late spring, to 1½ in. (38 mm) wide, in mounding clusters, to 8 in. (20 cm) wide, with capsulelike seedpods in late summer. Flowers on second-year wood.

Plant hardiness: Zones 4–9, ground hardy, zones 5–8.

Soil: Moist, well-drained humus. Fertility: Rich. Add acidic compost or leaf mold. 5.5–6.5 pH.

Planting: Full sun to full shade. Space 6–8 ft. (1.8–2.4 m) apart.

Care: Easy. Keep evenly moist. Fertilize quarterly spring–autumn. Mulch. Prune lightly after bloom. Protect from sun in hot climates. Propagate by cuttings, layering, seed.

Features: Good choice for backgrounds, mixed plantings, screens in natural, woodland gardens. Best planted with azalea, camellia, daphne, rhododendron. Rhododendron borer, rhododendron lacebug and fungal disease, leaf spot susceptible.

> **WARNING**
> Foliage of *Kalmia latifolia* may cause severe digestive upset when eaten. Avoid planting in gardens frequented by pets or children.

Shrub: *Kerria japonica.* ROSACEAE.
Common name: Japanese Rose (Kerria).
Description: Several cultivars of medium-growing, upright, bushy, rounded, deciduous shrubs, 4–6 ft. (1.2–1.8 m) tall and to 8 ft. (2.4 m) wide, with alternate, deep green, textured, broadly oval, pointed, toothed, veined leaves, to 2 in. (50 mm) long.
Blooms/Fruit: Many showy, single, gold, yellow, very double flowers, to 2 in. (50 mm) wide, in spring–early summer, form dry, clustered, 1-seeded fruit in late summer.
Plant hardiness: Zones 4–9. Hardy.
Soil: Moist to damp, well-drained soil. Fertility: Average. 6.0–7.0 pH.
Planting: Full sun to partial shade. Space 3–4 ft. (90–120 cm) apart.
Care: Moderate. Keep damp; allow soil surface to dry between waterings. Fertilize quarterly. Prune after bloom to thin. Propagate by cuttings, division, layering, seed.
Features: Good choice for accents, beds, borders in Asian, shade, woodland gardens. Branches good for cutting. Japanese beetle and blight, canker susceptible.

Shrub: *Kolkwitzia amabilis.* CAPRIFOLIACEAE.
Common name: Beautybush.
Description: Fast-growing, arching, deciduous, herbaceous shrub, to 15 ft. (4.5 m) tall and wide, with gray green, oval leaves, to 3 in. (75 mm) long, sometimes turning red in autumn, and with brown, flaking bark.
Blooms/Fruit: Showy, 5-petaled, pink flowers, to ½ in. (12 mm) long, with bristly, yellow centers, in dense clusters, in late spring, form distinctive, bristly, brown fruit in summer. Flowers on second-year wood.
Plant hardiness: Zones 4–9; ground hardy, zones 6–8.
Soil: Moist, well-drained soil. Fertility: Rich–low. 6.0–8.0 pH.
Planting: Full sun to partial shade. Space 12 ft. (3.7 m) apart.
Care: Easy. Keep moist. Fertilize monthly spring–summer. Mulch, zones 4–5. Prune after bloom. Protect from sun in hot climates. Propagate by cuttings.
Features: Good choice for backgrounds, borders, fencelines in woodland gardens. Fruit attracts birds. Pest and disease resistant.

Shrub: *Lagerstroemia indica.* LYTHRACEAE.
Common name: Crape Myrtle.
Description: Many cultivars of medium- to slow-growing, sprawling, branching, dense, deciduous shrubby trees, to 20 ft. (6 m) tall and wide, and often with multiple trunks, with shiny, bronze turning deep green, oval, pointed leaves, to 3 in. (75 mm) long, turning orange, red in autumn, and with flaking, brown, gray bark. Genetic dwarf, bush, and standard forms available, including *L. indica* 'Catawba', 'Centennial', 'Dixie', 'Dwarf Pink', 'Glendora White', 'Peppermint Lace', 'Petite Snow', 'Prairie Lace', and 'Seminole'.
Blooms/Fruit: Many showy, fragrant, red, rose, pink, purple, white, ruffled flowers, to 1 ½ in. (38 mm) wide, in spring, borne in spikelike, pyramid-shaped clusters, 6–12 in. (15–30 cm) long, form brown, round fruit, to ⅓ in. (8 mm) wide, on woody stems in grapelike clusters that dry and persist through winter.
Plant hardiness: Zones 7–10. Best in mild-winter climates.
Soil: Damp, well-drained soil. Fertility: Average. 6.5–7.5 pH.
Planting: Full sun. Space 5–30 ft. (1.5–9 m) apart, depending on cultivar.
Care: Easy. Keep damp; allow soil surface to dry between waterings until established. Fertilize sparingly. Prune in winter. Propagate by cuttings, seed.
Features: Good choice for accents, backgrounds, containers, paths in coastal, cottage, small-space gardens. Deer resistant. Powdery mildew susceptible.

Shrub: *Lantana* hybrids. VERBENACEAE.
Common name: Shrub Verbena (Lantana).
Description: Many hybrids of fast-growing, often thorny, evergreen, tropical shrubs, to 6 ft. (1.8 m) tall and wide, with shiny, deep green, oval, pointed, fragrant leaves, to 5 in. (13 cm) long. Many hybrid cultivars available with spreading or tall habits.
Blooms/Fruit: Many tiny, cream, gold, orange, pink, purple, red, yellow, bicolored flowers, in flat, mounded, or spiking clusters, to 3 in. (75 mm) wide, in summer or continually blooming, form blackberry-like fruit in autumn.
Plant hardiness: Plant as tender annual, zones 6–8; ground hardy, zones 9–10.
Soil: Damp, well-drained, sandy soil. Fertility: Rich–average. 6.5–7.5 pH.
Planting: Full sun. Space 3–4 ft. (90–120 cm) apart.
Care: Easy. Keep damp. Fertilize annually in spring. Prune to promote bushiness. Propagate by cuttings, seed.
Features: Good choice for banks, hanging baskets, borders, containers, ground covers in formal, meadow, wildlife gardens. Attracts butterflies, hummingbirds. Mealybug and orthezia susceptible.

Shrub: *Leonotis leonurus*. LAMIACEAE (LABIATAE).
Common name: Lion's-Ear (Lion's-Tail).
Description: Several cultivars of slow-growing, erect, branching, evergreen shrubs, 5–7 ft. (1.5–2.2 m) tall and 4–6 ft. (1.2–1.8 m) wide, with opposite, green, textured, soft, lance-shaped, pointed, coarsely toothed leaves, 2–4 in. (50–100 mm) long. *L. dysophylla* and *L. nepetifolia* are closely related species with similar care needs.
Blooms/Fruit: Tiers of lipped, blue, orange red, tubular, hairy flowers, to 2½ in. (63 mm) long, in radiating whorls, to 6 in. (15 cm) wide, in summer–autumn, form small, segmented, nutlike fruit bearing seed in autumn.
Plant hardiness: Zones 8–11. Tender.
Soil: Dry, well-drained, sandy soil. Fertility: Average–low. 6.0–7.0 pH.
Planting: Full sun. Space 2–4 ft. (60–120 cm) apart.
Care: Easy. Keep damp; allow soil surface to dry between waterings. Avoid fertilizing. Deadhead spent flower stalks. Shear in late autumn. Protect from frost. Propagate by cuttings, seed.

Features: Good choice for accents, banks, fencelines, paths in cottage, formal, meadow gardens and roadside plantings. Good for cutting. Attracts bees, butterflies, hummingbirds. Pest and disease resistant.

Shrub: *Leucophyllum frutescens*. SCROPHULARIACEAE.
Common name: Texas Sage (Barometer Bush, Ceniza, Texas Ranger).
Description: Several cultivars of slow-growing, compact, evergreen shrubs, 6–8 ft. (1.8–2.4 m) tall and wide, with velvety, mostly gray or silver green, sometimes bright green, oval, pointed, wavy-edged leaves, to 1 in. (25 mm) long, on hairy, arching stalks. Common cultivars include *L. frutescens* 'Compactum' and 'White Cloud'.
Blooms/Fruit: Showy, bell- or flute-shaped, round-lipped, blue, pink, purple, red, rose, white flowers, to 1 in. (25 mm) wide, usually in summer, form capsulelike fruit bearing seed in autumn. Blooms may follow watering after prolonged drought.
Plant hardiness: Zones 7–10. Semi-hardy. Best in arid climates.
Soil: Damp to dry, well-drained, sandy soil. Fertility: Average–low. 6.5–8.0 pH.
Planting: Full sun. Space 3–4 ft. (90–120 cm) apart.
Care: Easy. Keep damp; allow soil to dry between waterings. Drought tolerant. Avoid fertilizing. Prune sparingly. Propagate by cuttings, division, seed.
Features: Good choice for accents, banks, fencelines, ground covers, hedges in arid, cottage, meadow, Xeriscape gardens. Attracts bees, butterflies, hummingbirds. Pest and disease resistant.

Shrub: *Leucothoe* species. ERICACEAE.
Common name: Fetterbush (Doghobble, Sierra Laurel)
Description: About 50 species of medium-growing, upright, arching, evergreen shrubs, to 6 ft. (1.8 m) tall and 4–8 ft. (1.2–2.4 m) wide, with alternate, shiny, green, leathery, oval, pointed leaves, to 7 in. (18 cm) long, turning bronze in autumn. Dwarf cultivars available.
Blooms/Seed: Many tiny, cream, pink, white, heart-shaped flowers, in showy, nodding, clusters, 2–4 in. (50–100 mm) long, in early summer, form capsulelike seedpods in autumn.
Plant hardiness: Zones 4–9, depending on species; most ground hardy, zones 6–9.
Soil: Moist to damp, well-drained, sandy humus. Fertility: Rich. 5.5–6.5 pH.
Planting: Full sun to partial shade. Space 3–4 ft. (90–120 cm) apart.
Care: Easy. Keep evenly moist. Fertilize monthly during growth. Deadhead spent flower stems after bloom. Protect from wind. Propagate by cuttings, division, runners, seed.
Features: Good choice for accents, beds, borders, containers, foregrounds in bog, woodland gardens. Good for cutting. Pest and disease resistant.

Shrub: *Ligustrum* species. OLEACEAE.
Common name: Privet (Hedge Plant).
Description: About 50 species of medium- to slow-growing, dense, bushy, deciduous or evergreen shrubs, 6–40 ft. (1.8–12 m) tall, depending on species, with shiny, green or gold, oval leaves, 1–4 in. (25–100 mm) long, and tinged russet or brown in autumn.
Blooms/Fruit: Abundant tiny, fragrant, white flowers in late spring, in upright, grapelike clusters, to 5 in. (13 cm) long, with black, berrylike, seedy fruit in autumn.
Plant hardiness: Zones 4–10, depending on species.
Soil: Moist to damp, well-drained soil. Fertility: Rich–average. 6.0–8.0 pH.
Planting: Full sun to partial shade. Space according to use.
Care: Moderate. Keep damp. Fertilize quarterly spring–autumn. Mulch, zones 4–8. Prune or shear after bloom. Protect tender species from frost in zones 4–7, sun in hot climates. Propagate by cuttings, division, grafting, seed.
Features: Good choice for borders, containers, hedges, massed plantings, paths, walls in cottage, formal, small-space, woodland gardens and landscapes. Best in mild, cool climates. Fruit attracts birds. Pest and disease resistant.

Shrub: *Lonicera* species. CAPRIFOLIACEAE.
Common name: Honeysuckle.
Description: More than 150 species, cultivars of upright or climbing, deciduous or evergreen shrubs or vines, 3–30 ft. (90–900 cm) tall, with shiny, green or blue green, leathery, oval leaves, 1–6 in. (25–150 mm) long, some turning bronze in autumn–winter.
Blooms/Berries: Many sometimes fragrant, tubular, 2-lipped, coral, pink, white, yellow flowers, ½–2 in. (12–50 mm) long, in spring–autumn, form black, purple, red berries in autumn.
Plant hardiness: Zones 4–9.
Soil: Damp, well-drained soil. Fertility: Rich–average. 6.5–7.5 pH.
Planting: Full sun to partial shade. Spacing varies by species.
Care: Easy. Keep damp; allow soil surface to dry between waterings. Drought tolerant. Fertilize annually in spring. Propagate by cuttings, layering, seed.
Features: Good choice for fencelines, ground covers, hedges, trellises, walls in cottage, formal, small-space gardens. Attracts birds, butterflies, hummingbirds. Invasive. Disease resistant. Aphid susceptible.

Shrub: *Lonicera tatarica.* CAPRIOFOLIACEAE.

Common name: Tatarian Honeysuckle.

Description: Over 12 cultivars of tall and arching, deciduous shrubs, to 10 ft. (3 m) tall, with dull, green to blue green, oval or lance-shaped leaves, to 2½ in. (63 mm) long, turning bronze in autumn. *L. fragrantissima,* winter honeysuckle; *L. japonica,* Japanese honeysuckle; *L. nitida,* box honeysuckle; and *L. sempervirens,* evergreen honeysuckle, are closely related species with similar care needs.

Blooms/Berries: Dainty, fragrant, fuchsialike, tubular, coral, pink, white, yellow, nectar-bearing flowers, to 1 in. (25 mm) wide, in spring, form red berries in late spring–summer.

Plant hardiness: Zones 5–9.

Soil: Moist, well-drained soil. Fertility: Average. 6.0–6.5 pH.

Planting: Full sun to partial shade. Space 7 ft. (2.2 m) apart.

Care: Easy. Keep moist; allow soil surface to dry between waterings until established. Fertilize monthly spring–autumn. Prune after bloom. Propagate by cuttings, layering, seed.

Features: Good choice for fencelines, ground covers, hedges, trellises in cottage, natural gardens. Attracts bees, hummingbirds. Invasive. Ant, aphid susceptible.

Shrub: *Mahonia aquifolium.* BERBERIDACEAE.

Common name: Oregon Grape (Mahonia).

Description: Over 100 species of slow-growing, spreading, broad-leaved, evergreen shrubs, to 12 ft. (3.7 m) tall, depending on species, with shiny, blue green, leathery, toothed, usually spiny leaves, to 3 in. (75 mm) long, arranged along the stem in groups of 5 or 7, and tinged red in autumn. *M. bealei,* leatherleaf mahonia; and *M. repens,* creeping mahonia, are closely related species with similar care needs.

Blooms/Fruit: Tiny, fragrant, bell-shaped, yellow flowers to ½ in. (12 mm) wide, in narrow, spiking clusters, in spring, form blue, blueberry-like, mealy fruit in autumn.

Plant hardiness: Zones 4–8, depending on species.

Soil: Moist, well-drained humus. Fertility: Rich. 5.5–6.5 pH.

Planting: Partial to full shade. Space 5–7 ft. (1.5–2.2 m) apart.

Care: Easy–moderate. Keep evenly moist. Drought tolerant when established. Fertilize quarterly spring–autumn. Mulch, zones 7–8. Avoid pruning. Propagate by cuttings, layering, seed.

Features: Good choice for accents, backgrounds, barriers, fencelines, hedges in natural, woodland, Xeriscape gardens. Fruit attracts birds. Pest and disease resistant.

Shrub: *Murraya paniculata (M. exotica).* RUTACEAE.

Common name: Orange Jasmine (Chinese Box, Orange Jessamine, Satinwood).

Description: Several cultivars of slow-growing, branching, open, woody, tropical, evergreen shrubs, to 15 ft. (4.5 m) tall and wide, with shiny, deep green, oval, divided, nodding leaves, to 1 ft. (30 cm) long, in opposite, 2–4-paired leaflets, to 3 in. (75 mm) long. Dwarf and standard cultivars available.

Blooms/Fruit: Solitary, very fragrant, white, bell-shaped, 4–5-petaled flowers, to ¾ in. (19 mm) wide, in summer, develop red, berrylike fruit, to ½ in. (12 mm) wide, containing seed, often during bloom. Intermittent, year-round blooming.

Plant hardiness: Zones 8–11. Tender. Best in subtropical climates.

Soil: Moist, well-drained humus. Fertility: Rich. 6.0–7.5 pH.

Planting: Filtered sun to partial shade. Space 3–4 ft. (90–120 cm) apart.

Care: Easy–moderate. Keep evenly moist. Fertilize monthly. Prune sparingly. Propagate by layering, seed.

Features: Good choice for accents, containers, hedges in tropical, woodland gardens. Attracts bees. Leaves of *M. koenigii,* a related species, are the source of curry spice. Pest and disease resistant.

Shrub: *Musa* species. MUSACEAE.

Common name: Ornamental Banana (Banana, Plantain).

Description: About 25 species of fast-growing, treelike, spreading, tropical, rhizomatous, ever-green herbs, to over 15 ft. (4.5 m) tall and 10 ft. (3 m) wide, with smooth, shiny, light green, sometimes striped with brown or purple, broad-bladed fronds, to 5 ft. (1.5 m) long, from a trunklike base.

Blooms/Fruit: Showy, yellow flowers, to 5 in. (13 cm) long, with purple, red bracts, on nodding, fleshy stems, from the center of the leafstalks, to 3 ft. (90 cm) long, form edible or inedible fruit in fingerlike clusters. Grown primarily for foliage.

Plant hardiness: Zone 9–11. Very tender.

Soil: Moist, well-drained, sandy humus. Fertility: Very Rich. 6.0–7.0 pH.

Planting: Full to filtered sun. Space 4–6 ft. (1.2–1.8 m) apart.

Care: Moderate–challenging. Keep evenly moist. Fertilize monthly. Prune fruited stalks to soil. Mulch; top dress soil annually with fresh compost, 1–2 in. (25–50 mm) thick. Propagate by division, offsets, seed.

Features: Good choice for backgrounds, fencelines in tropical gardens. Aphid, mealybug, spider mite and brown spot susceptible.

Shrub: *Myrica pensylvanica.* MYRICACEAE.

Common name: Northern Bayberry (Swamp Candleberry).

Description: Medium-growing, dense, spreading, deciduous to semi-evergreen shrub, to 9 ft. (2.7 m) tall, with waxy, yellow green, broad, oval leaves, to 4 in. (10 cm) long, often with conspicuous wax secretions. *M. californica*, Pacific wax myrtle, is a closely related species with similar care needs.

Blooms/Fruit: Inconspicuous, white flowers form small, gray, wax-coated berrylike fruit in autumn, persisting to winter.

Plant hardiness: Zones 2–9; ground hardy, zones 5–8.

Soil: Moist to dry, well-drained soil. Fertility: Average–low. 5.5–7.5 pH.

Planting: Full sun to partial shade. Space 5–7 ft. (1.5–2.2 m) apart.

Care: Easy. Keep moist; allow soil surface to dry between waterings until established. Drought tolerant. Fertilize annually in spring. Prune to maintain size and dense habit. Propagate by layering, seed.

Features: Good choice for borders, hedges, massed plantings in landscapes. Fruit attracts birds. Source of aromatic bayberry wax. Drought, salt, shade, wind tolerant. Pest and disease resistant.

Shrub: *Myrtus communis.* MYRTACEAE.

Common name: Myrtle (Greek Myrtle, Swedish Myrtle).

Description: Many cultivars of medium-growing, rounded, dense, woody, evergreen shrubs, to 15 ft. (4.5 m) tall and wide, with opposite, shiny, deep green, variegated, oval to lance-shaped, fragrant leaves, to 2 in. (50 mm) long. Common cultivars include *M. communis* 'Buxifolia', 'Compacta', 'Microphylla', and 'Variegata'.

Blooms/Fruit: Fragrant, crestlike, white flowers, to ¾ in. (19 mm) wide, with many long stamens, in summer, form black, blue, white, 5-lobed, berrylike fruit, to ½ in. (12 mm) wide, in autumn.

Plant hardiness: Zones 8–11. Tender. Best in subtropical, mild-winter climates.

Soil: Moist to damp, well-drained humus. Fertility: Rich. 6.0–7.5 pH.

Planting: Full to filtered sun. Space 4–5 ft. (1.2–1.5 m) apart.

Care: Easy. Keep evenly moist until established; drought tolerant thereafter. Fertilize monthly. Prune or shear to shape. Protect from wind. Propagate by cuttings, seed.

Features: Good choice for accents, containers, hedges in arid, tropical, woodland gardens. Good for espaliers, topiaries. Pest and disease resistant.

Shrub: *Nandina domestica.* BERBERIDACEAE.

Common name: Heavenly Bamboo.

Description: Bushy, loose, evergreen shrub, to 8 ft. (2.4 m) tall and 4 ft. (1.2 m) wide, with bamboolike, delicate, light green, oval, pointed leaves, 2 in. (50 mm) long, tinted bronze or yellow in some cultivars, turning red in autumn. Dwarf cultivars to 1 ft. (30 cm) tall and 1 ft. (30 cm) wide available.

Blooms/Berries: Small, white flowers in late spring–summer, in lacy clusters, to 1 ft. (30 cm) long, with red berries, to ¼ in. (6 mm) wide, in autumn.

Plant hardiness: Zones 6–10; ground hardy, zones 7–10.

Soil: Moist to dry, well-drained soil. Fertility: Rich–average. 6.5–7.0 pH.

Planting: Full sun to partial shade. Space 2–6 ft. (60–180 cm) apart, depending on cultivar.

Care: Easy. Keep moist; allow soil surface to dry between waterings until established. Fertilize every 2 months spring–autumn. Prune in early spring. Mulch, zones 6–7. Protect from frost in zone 6. Propagate by seed.

Features: Good choice for containers, screens in tropical gardens. Berries more abundant if groups are planted. Drought tolerant. Deer, pest and oak root fungus resistant. Chlorosis susceptible.

Shrub: *Nerium oleander.* APOCYNACEAE.

Common name: Common Oleander.

Description: Many cultivars of fast-growing, dense, bushy and arching, ever-green shrubs, to 20 ft. (6 m) tall and 12 ft. (3.7 m) wide, with dull, green, leathery, narrow leaves, to 1 ft. (30 cm) long.

Blooms/Seed: Mostly fragrant, pink, red, white, yellow, double or single flowers in spring–autumn, 2–3 in. (50–75 mm) wide, in showy clusters, form hairy, tufted seed in autumn.

Plant hardiness: Zones 8–11.

Soil: Moist, well-drained soil. Fertility: Average–low. 6.5–7.0 pH.

> **WARNING**
> All parts and sap of *Nerium oleander* may be fatally toxic if eaten. Avoid planting in gardens frequented by pets or children.

Planting: Full sun. Space 5–10 ft. (1.5 3 m) apart.

Care: Easy. Generally care free. Keep moist; allow soil surface to dry between waterings until established. Fertilize annually in spring. Mulch, zone 8. Prune after bloom. Prune heavily in cold-winter climates. Propagate by cuttings.

Features: Good choice for borders, containers, hedges, screens along driveways. Best in heat. So tough, used as freeway planting. Attractive all seasons. Fire retardant. Drought tolerant. Deer, rodent resistant. Aphid, scale susceptible.

Shrub: *Paxistima* species *(Pachistima* species*).* CELASTRACEAE.

Common name: Cliff-Green (Mountain-Lover).

Description: Two species of slow-growing, low, spreading, evergreen shrubs, to 1 ft. (30 cm) tall and 3 ft. (90 cm) wide, with shiny, deep green, leathery, oval, rounded, finely toothed leaves, ½–¾ in. (12–19 mm) long, turning bronze in autumn.

Blooms/Seed: Many tiny, red brown, white, round, 4-petaled flowers, to ⅛ in. (3 mm) wide, in spring, form dry, segmented capsules containing lobed seed, in summer.

Plant hardiness: Zones 3–9, depending on species; most ground hardy, zones 4–8.

Soil: Moist to damp, well-drained, sandy humus. Fertility: Rich–average. 6.0–7.0 pH.

Planting: Full sun to partial shade. Space 18 in. (45 cm) apart.

Care: Easy. Keep damp; allow soil surface to dry between waterings. Fertilize every 2 months. Prune in spring before growth begins. Protect from sun in hot-summer climates. Propagate by cuttings, division, layering, seed.

Features: Good choice for borders, edgings, foregrounds, ground covers in natural, rock, shade, woodland gardens. Pest and disease resistant.

Shrub: *Philadelphus coronarius.* HYDRANGEACEAE (PHILADELPHACEAE, SAXIFRAGACEAE).
Common name: Sweet Mock Orange.
Description: Many cultivars of fast-growing, dense, spreading, deciduous shrubs, to 10 ft. (3 m) tall and wide, with dull to shiny, green, oval, pointed leaves, 1–3 in. (25–75 mm) long.
Blooms/Seed: Very fragrant, creamy white flowers, to 1½ in. (38 mm) wide, in radiating clusters, in late spring, form abundant seed in late summer.
Plant hardiness: Zones 5–9.
Soil: Moist, well-drained soil. Fertility: Rich–average. Add compost or leaf mold. 6.5–7.5 pH.
Planting: Partial shade. Space 3 ft. (90 cm) apart.
Care: Easy. Generally care free. Keep moist; allow soil surface to dry between waterings until established. Fertilize every 2 months spring–autumn. Prune after bloom. Propagate by cuttings, layering, seed.
Features: Good for borders, edgings, hedges, paths in formal, small-space, woodland gardens. Generally drought tolerant. Pest and disease resistant.

Shrub: *Photinia* species and hybrids. ROSACEAE.
Common name: Photinia.
Description: Many cultivars of fast- to medium-growing, erect, rounded, dense, evergreen shrubs, 5–15 ft. (1.5–4.5 m) tall and wide. Alternate, shiny, bronze, red becoming deep green, oval to lance-shaped leaves, 2–6 in. (50–150 mm) long. Commonly cultivated species and hybrids include *P.* × *fraseri, P. glabra, P. serratifolia,* and *P. villosa.*
Blooms/Fruit: Tiny, fragrant, cup-shaped, cream, green, white flowers, to ⅜ in. (10 mm) wide, with many long stamens, in flat or domed clusters, in early spring, form red, round, berrylike fruit, to ½ in. (12 mm) wide, in summer.
Plant hardiness: Zones 6–9. Semi-hardy.
Soil: Moist to damp, well-drained soil. Fertility: Rich–average. 6.0–7.5 pH.
Planting: Full sun. Space 4–5 ft. (1.2–1.5 m) apart.
Care: Easy. Keep evenly moist until established; drought tolerant thereafter. Fertilize quarterly. Prune or shear to shape. Protect from prolonged freezing. Propagate by cuttings, grafting, layering, seed.
Features: Good choice for accents, backgrounds, hedges, paths, screens, windbreaks in arid, meadow, wildlife, woodland gardens. Good for spring foliage color. Attracts birds. Pest resistant. Chlorosis, fireblight, powdery mildew susceptible.

Shrub: *Pieris japonica (Andromeda japonica).* ERICACEAE.
Common name: Lily-of-the-Valley Bush (Japanese Andromeda).
Description: Many cultivars of slow-growing, rounded, branching, evergreen shrubs, 10–20 ft. (3–6 m) tall and wide, with shiny, rhododendron-like, red becoming deep green, leathery, nodding, oval to lance-shaped, finely toothed leaves, to 3 in. (75 mm) long. Common cultivars include *P. japonica* 'Compacta', 'Crispa', 'Flamingo', 'Spring Snow', 'Variegata', and 'White Cascade'.
Blooms/Fruit: Showy, tiny, bell-shaped, cream, pink, white flowers, ¼–⅜ in. (6–10 mm) wide, in dangling, lily-of-the-valley-like clusters, to 6 in. (15 cm) long, in late winter–spring, form dry, 5-lobed, capsulelike fruit containing seed in summer.
Plant hardiness: Zones 5–9. Hardy. Best in mild-summer climates.
Soil: Moist, well-drained humus. Fertility: Rich–average. 5.0–6.5 pH.
Planting: Filtered sun to partial shade. Space 5–8 ft. (1.5–2.4 m) apart.
Care: Easy. Keep evenly moist until established; drought tolerant thereafter. Fertilize quarterly. Prune after bloom to shape. Propagate by cuttings, layering, seed.
Features: Good choice for accents, backgrounds, fencelines, paths, screens in woodland gardens. Pest resistant. Fungal disease susceptible.

Shrub: *Pinus mugo* var. *mugo*. PINACEAE.
Common name: Mountain Pine (Mugo Pine).
Description: Several varieties and cultivars of slow-growing, usually mounding or spreading, sometimes upright, coniferous, evergreen shrubs or small trees, to 30 ft. (9 m) tall, with upright, bundled pairs of deep green needles, to 2 in. (50 mm) long.
Blooms/Cones: Male, catkinlike, yellow cones and female, brown, woody, clustered, flat-scaled cones appear in spring, ripening in autumn.
Plant hardiness: Zones 2–10. Hardy.
Soil: Damp, well-drained soil. Fertility: Average. 6.0–8.0 pH.
Planting: Full sun. Space 6–8 ft. (1.8–2.4 m) apart.
Care: Easy. Keep damp; allow soil surface to dry between waterings until established. Avoid fertilizing. Shape by partial cutting of new growth "candles" in spring. Propagate by cuttings, grafting, seed.
Features: Good choice for accents, borders, containers in formal, rock, small-space, woodland gardens. Good for bonsai, topiary. Spider mite, scale and chlorosis, rust susceptible.

Shrub: *Pittosporum tobira*. PITTOSPORACEAE.
Common name: Japanese Pittosporum (Mock Orange).
Description: Several cultivars of slow-growing, mounding, evergreen shrubs or small trees, to 18 ft. (5.5 m) tall, with shiny, green, yellow, variegated, leathery, oval leaves, to 4 in. (10 cm) long. Dwarf cultivar 'Wheeler's Dwarf' available.
Blooms/Fruit: Fragrant, bell-shaped, white flowers in spring, to ½ in. (12 mm) wide, in showy, mounded clusters, with attractive, round, orange, berrylike, seed-filled fruit in autumn.
Plant hardiness: Zones 7–10.
Soil: Damp, well-drained soil. Fertility: Average. 6.5–8.0 pH. Salt tolerant.
Planting: Full sun. Space 4–6 ft. (1.2–1.8 m) apart.
Care: Easy. Keep damp; allow soil surface to dry between waterings until established. Drought tolerant. Mulch, zones 8–10. Prune in spring. Propagate by cuttings, grafting, seed.
Features: Good choice for backgrounds, beds, borders, edgings, hedges, paths in arid, Asian, cottage, small-space gardens and landscapes. Humidity tolerant. Aphid, scale susceptible.

Shrub: *Plumeria rubra* forms and cultivars. APOCYNACEAE.
Common name: Plumeria (Frangipani, Nosegay, Temple Tree).
Description: Several horticultural forms of fast- to medium-growing, rounded, woody, tropical, deciduous shrubs, 20–25 ft. (6–7.5 m) tall and 12–18 ft. (3.7–5.5 m) wide, with shiny, green, leathery, oval, pointed, veined leaves, to 20 in. (50 cm) long, often with downy undersides.
Blooms/Seed: Very showy, fragrant, cream, gold, orange, pink, red, white, 5-petaled, waxy, sometimes reflexed flowers, 2–5 in. (50–125 mm) wide, in bunched or flat clusters, in spring–early winter, form dry, winged seed in autumn–winter.
Plant hardiness: Zones 9–11. Tender. Best in subtropical and tropical climates.
Soil: Damp to dry, well-drained humus. Fertility: Average. 6.0–7.0 pH.
Planting: Full to filtered sun. Space 7–10 ft. (2.2–3 m) apart.
Care: Easy. Keep evenly moist until established; drought tolerant

WARNING
Sap of *Plumeria rubra* causes skin irritation in sensitive individuals. Wear rubber gloves when pruning or propagating plants.

thereafter. Fertilize monthly. Prune to maintain shape and promote bushiness or as standard. Propagate by cuttings.
Features: Good choice for accents, backgrounds, containers, hedges, screens in arid, tropical, woodland gardens and water features. Good for Hawaiian leis. Pest and disease resistant.

Shrub: *Polygala* × *dalmaisiana* hybrids. POLYGALACEAE.

Common name: Sweet-Pea Shrub.

Description: Several hybrid cultivars of medium-growing, mounding becoming erect and round-crowned, evergreen shrubs, 4–8 ft. (1.2–2.4 m) tall and wide, with alternate or opposite, smooth, gray green, oval or lance-shaped, pointed leaves, ¾–1 in. (19–25 mm) long. *P. chamaebuxus,* *P. paucifolia, P. polygama, P. ramosa,* and *P. viridescens* are closely related species with similar care needs.

Blooms/Fruit: Very showy, pealike, pink, purple, rose flowers, to 1 in. (25 mm) long, in dangling clusters, in spring–autumn, form capsulelike pods containing seed in autumn.

Plant hardiness: Zones 9–11. Tender. Best in mild-winter, hot-summer climates.

Soil: Moist, well-drained soil. Fertility: Rich–average. 6.5–8.0 pH. Salt tolerant.

Planting: Full to filtered sun. Space 3–4 ft. (90–120 cm) apart.

Care: Easy. Keep moist; allow soil surface to dry between waterings. Fertilize quarterly. Shear in winter. Propagate by seed.

Features: Good choice for accents, backgrounds, fillers in arid, meadow, rock, seaside, tropical gardens. Pest and disease resistant.

Shrub: *Potentilla fruticosa.* ROSACEAE.

Common name: Bush Cinquefoil (Shrubby Cinquefoil).

Description: Many cultivars of medium- to slow-growing, textured, dense, round, deciduous shrubs, 2–4 ft. (60–120 cm) tall, with shiny, light or deep green, oval or lance-shaped, usually 5-lobed, divided leaves, to ¾ in. (19 mm) long. Many flowering perennials, including *P. atrosanguinea, P. neumanniana,* and *P. recta,* are closely related species.

Blooms/Seed: Many open, orange, pink, red, white, or yellow, long-lasting, single flowers, to 1¼ in. (32 mm) wide, in spring–autumn, form brown seed on female shrubs.

Plant hardiness: Zones 2–9. Hardy.

Soil: Moist to damp, well-drained soil. Fertility: Rich–low. 6.0–8.0 pH.

Planting: Full sun to partial shade. Space 3–4 ft. (90–120 cm) apart.

Care: Easy. Keep moist; allow soil surface to dry between waterings until established. Fertilize quarterly spring–autumn. Mulch, zones 2–4. Prune after bloom. Protect from sun in hot climates. Propagate by division, seed.

Features: Good choice for backgrounds, beds, borders, edgings, hedges in cottage, formal, rock, small-space gardens. Drought tolerant. Disease resistant. Spider mite susceptible.

Shrub: *Pyracantha* species. ROSACEAE.

Common name: Pyracantha (Fire Thorn).

Description: About six species of medium-growing, upright or spreading, dense, thorny, evergreen shrubs, 6–20 ft. (1.8–6 m) tall, depending on species, with shiny or leathery, green, lance-shaped leaves, ¾–4 in. (19–100 mm) long. Common species include *P. coccinea, P. crenato-serrata,* and *P. koidzumii.*

Blooms/Berries: Many small, white flowers in dense, mounding clusters, in spring, form bright red berries in autumn, persisting to winter.

Plant hardiness: Zones 4–9, depending on species. All species ground hardy, zones 7–9.

Soil: Moist, well-drained soil. Fertility: Average. 6.0–8.0 pH.

Planting: Full sun. Space 6–8 ft. (1.8–2.4 m) apart.

Care: Moderate. Keep moist; allow soil surface to dry between waterings until established. Fertilize annually in spring. Prune after bloom, using care to avoid sharp thorns. Propagate by cuttings, grafting, layering, seed.

Features: Good choice for accents, barriers, espaliers, ground covers in arid, formal, small-space, wildlife gardens. Best in dry climates. Berries attract birds. Avoid transplanting. Pest resistant. Fireblight, apple scab susceptible.

RHODODENDRON

Azaleas and rhododendrons comprise the nearly 800 varied species and many thousands of named cultivars of bushy, broad-leaved, evergreen and deciduous shrubs and small trees included in the *Rhodendron* genus. They are native to the temperate zone of the northern hemisphere, most commonly to mountainous Asia. Mostly hardy or semi-hardy and suited to climates as cold as USDA Plant Hardiness Zone 4, azaleas and rhododendrons have other climate, soil, and site requirements that limit their growth throughout many areas of central North America.

Azaleas and rhododendrons are prized for their large, showy, clustered flowers in shades of cream, orange, pink, red, white, or yellow, which appear in spring or summer.

They are slow-growing shrubs. The azaleas are mostly under 10 ft. (3 m) tall, while rhododendrons may reach 25 ft. (7.5 m) or more in height. They're good container as well as landscape plants, seldom need pruning, and are best in filtered sun and partial or full shade.

Many new cultivars are offered each spring in garden centers. Some popular hybrids and species are listed at right.

Hybrid Evergreen Azaleas:
  Belgian Indian hybrids
  Belgian–Glen Dale hybrids
  Greenwood hybrids
  Kaempferi hybrids
  Kehr hybrids
  Kurume hybrids
  Linwood hybrids
  Macrantha hybrids
  North Tisbury hybrids
  Satsuki hybrids
  Southern Indian hybrids
Hybrid Deciduous Azaleas:
  Ghent hybrids
  Mollis hybrids
  Occidentale hybrids
  Vicosum hybrids
Species Rhododendrons:
  R. brachycarpum
  R. dauricum
  R. falconeri
  R. fortunei
  R. forrestii var. *forestii*
  R. keiskei
  R. macrophyllum
  R. metternichii
  R. mucronulatum
  R. pemakoense
  R. racemosum
  R. rupicola var. *chryseum*
  R. smirnowii
  R. yakusimanum

Members of the *Rhododendron* genus are outstanding plants for shady gardens in moist climates such as those found in British Columbia and the Maritime Provinces of Canada, and in New England, the Mid-Atlantic, the Great Lakes, the Pacific Northwest, and the South in the United States. Azaleas and rhododendrons are many-branched, densely leaved, and shiny green. When their flowers appear, they become a showcase for beauty that causes passersby to pause and admire.

Plant them in a moist, well-drained, acidic soil rich in organic humus. They do best in sites with filtered sun or partial shade. Plant them as an understory to deciduous or conifer trees, give them regular feedings with an acidic fertilizer, and watch them prosper. Azaleas are good container plants for small-space gardens, decks, and patios, and they can be moved indoors as short-term houseplants during their bloom.

There are technical horticultural differences between azaleas and rhododendrons, and they have been divided into respective show classes by the Azalea Society of America and the American Rhododendron Society. In general, azaleas frequently bloom ahead of the rhododendrons, have hairy undersides on their leaves, and bear flower clusters that are a bit smaller than their larger cousins.

Azaleas and rhododendrons are divas of the landscape garden that can shine in any woodland meadow.

Shrub: *Rhododendron* species. ERICACEAE.

Common name: Azalea.

Description: Over 10 species and many hybrids of slow-growing, spreading, mostly deciduous shrubs or small trees, 3–10 ft. (90–305 cm) tall, with waxy, bright green, oval leaves, to 4 in. (10 cm) long, in radiating clusters, turning yellow in autumn. Commonly cultivated species include *R. japonicum*, *R. luteum*, *R. mucronatum*, *R. occidentale*, *R. schlippenbachii*, and *R. vaseyi*.

Blooms/Fruit: Fragrant, trumpet-shaped, cream, orange, pink, red, white, or yellow flowers, to 2 in. (50 mm) wide, in clusters, in spring–summer, form woody, capsulelike fruit in summer.

Plant hardiness: Zones 4–9; ground hardy, zones 7–9.

Soil: Moist, well-drained soil. Fertility: Rich. 6.0–6.5 pH.

Planting: Filtered sun to full shade. Space 4 ft. (1.2 m) apart.

Care: Moderate. Keep moist until established; reduce watering thereafter. Fertilize monthly spring–autumn. Avoid cultivating around plants. Protect from sun in hot climates. Propagate by cuttings, layering.

Features: Good choice for accents, beds, borders, containers, fencelines, screens in meadow, small-space, woodland gardens. Good autumn color. Root weevil and powdery mildew susceptible.

Shrub: *Rhododendron* species. ERICACEAE.

Common name: Rhododendron.

Description: More than 10 species and over 500 varied hybrid cultivars of slow-growing, spreading, woody, mostly evergreen shrubs or small trees, to 25 ft. (7.5 m) tall and wide, with waxy, deep green, oval to lance-shaped leaves, to 1 ft. (30 cm) long, in radiating clusters. Dwarf and tree-habit cultivars available.

Blooms/Fruit: Very showy, lightly fragrant, trumpet-shaped, cream, lavender, orange, pink, purple, red, white, yellow flowers, to 8 in. (20 cm) long, in spring–summer, in pom pom-like trusses or clusters, to 16 in. (40 cm) wide, at the ends of branches, form woody, capsulelike fruit in summer.

Plant hardiness: Zones 6–10. Hardy or semi-hardy, depending on cultivar.

Soil: Moist, well-drained soil. Fertility: Rich. 5.5–6.5 pH. Best in mild climates.

Planting: Filtered sun to partial shade. Space 6–10 ft. (1.8–3 m) apart.

Care: Moderate. Keep moist until established; reduce watering thereafter. Fertilize monthly spring–autumn. Avoid cultivating around plants. Propagate by cuttings, layering. Protect from sun in hot climates.

Features: Good choice for accents, backgrounds, borders, containers, fencelines, screens in small-space, woodland gardens. Disease resistant. Root weevil susceptible.

Shrub: *Rhododendron* species and hybrids. ERICACEAE.

Common name: Kurume Azalea.

Description: Many hybrid cultivars of slow-growing, compact, mounding, woody, evergreen shrubs, to 6 ft. (1.8 m) tall and wide, with shiny, light green, broadly oval leaves, to 2½ in. (63 mm) long, in radiating clusters. Gable, Girard, and Kaempferi hybrid azaleas are closely related plants with similar care needs.

Blooms/Fruit: Very showy, lightly fragrant, trumpet-shaped, cream, pink, red, scarlet, white flowers, 1–2 in. (25–50 mm) long, in early spring, in loose clusters, to 4 in. (10 cm) wide, at the ends of branches, form capsulelike fruit in summer.

Plant hardiness: Zones 7–9. Semi-hardy.

Soil: Moist, well-drained soil. Fertility: Rich. 6.0–7.0 pH.

Planting: Partial shade. Space 2–3 ft. (60–90 cm) apart.

Care: Moderate. Keep moist until established; reduce watering thereafter. Fertilize monthly spring–autumn. Prune to shape after bloom. Avoid cultivating around plants. Protect from sun in hot climates. Propagate by cuttings, layering.

Features: Good choice for accents, beds, borders, containers, foregrounds in small-space, woodland gardens and patios. Good as houseplant. Disease resistant. Root weevil susceptible.

Shrub: *Rhododendron mucronulatum* and cultivars. ERICACEAE.

Common name: Korean Rhododendron (Snow Azalea).

Description: Many cultivars of slow-growing, open, branching, spreading, woody, deciduous shrubs, to 6 ft. (1.8 m) tall and wide, with shiny or leathery, deep green, oval or lance-shaped, spring leaves, to 2¼ in. (57 mm) long, followed by summer leaves, to 1½ in. (38 mm) long, turning yellow bronze in autumn.

Blooms/Fruit: Very showy, lightly fragrant, bell-shaped, pink, purple, rose flowers, 1½ in. (38 mm) long, in early spring before leaves emerge, form woody, capsulelike fruit in summer.

Plant hardiness: Zones 5–9. Hardy.

Soil: Moist, well-drained soil. Fertility: Rich. 6.0–7.0 pH. Best in mild climates.

Planting: Partial shade. Space 2–3 ft. (60–90 cm) apart.

Care: Moderate. Keep moist until established; reduce watering thereafter. Fertilize monthly spring–autumn. Prune to shape after bloom. Avoid cultivating around plants. Protect from sun in hot climates, frost. Propagate by cuttings, layering.

Features: Good choice for accents, beds, borders, containers, foregrounds, hedges in meadow, small-space, woodland gardens and patios. Root weevil and powdery mildew susceptible.

RHUS (SUMAC)

About 150 species of erect shrubs, trees, and vines make up the *Rhus* genus, a highly varied group of mostly coarse-foliaged shrubs including about a dozen species that commonly are used in landscapes. They are native to temperate and subtropical zones throughout the world, and most species are cold tolerant, hardy to USDA Plant Hardiness Zone 3.

Sumacs are best in large areas. They are fast-growing shrubs that range in height from low and spreading plants 3 ft. (90 cm) tall to large shrubs of 20 ft. (6 m). To control their growth and keep them dense, they should be pruned heavily in winter. Many of the large species make ideal understory foliage plants in natural or woodland gardens, or they can be coppiced to create several trunks, an appealing, many-branched habit, and cloaked, textured foliage.

Autumn is the season during which sumacs reach their greatest appeal. They color brilliantly in every hue of orange and red, a display that sometimes lasts for a month or more.

Though sumacs resist most garden pests, they are susceptible to fungal diseases. Popular sumac species are listed above, at right.

Sumacs are seldom selected for use in landscape gardens, mostly because of their former association with poison oak, ivy, and sumac, as well as for their invasive, freely suckering habits. As outstanding foliage plants noted for their intense autumn color, sumacs deserve a place in sunny or partially shaded gardens in a natural or woodland setting.

Landscape Sumac Species:
R. aromatica, fragrant sumac
R. chinensis, Chinese sumac
R. copallina, dwarf sumac
R. glabra, smooth sumac
R. integrifolia, sourberry
R. lancea, African sumac
R. laurina, laurel sumac
R. microphylla, desert sumac
R. ovata, sugarbush
R. trilobata, skunkbush
R. typhina, staghorn sumac
R. verniciflua, Japanese varnish tree
R. virens, evergreen sumac

(Plants of the *Taxicodendron* genus, including *T. diversiloba, T. radicans, T. toxicodendron,* and *T. vernix,* once were classified as part of *Rhus.* They can cause severe eye irritation and skin rashes in sensitive individuals, and should be avoided.)

Plant them in a damp, well-drained, somewhat acidic, sandy humus, as an understory beneath trees. They rarely need fertilizing, but you should keep their soil from becoming too alkaline; apply an acid fertilizer in early spring if the soil's pH rises above 7.5. Give them good drainage and avoid boggy soils that are saturated; they are subject to fungal diseases when kept constantly moist.

Although they are planted mostly for their foliage, they also produce feathery panicles of tiny, cream or white flowers during the summer months, creating the illusion of wave crests above their deep green, lobed foliage. These mature into colorful clusters of berrylike fruit in autumn. They remain on the plant until winter, attracting many species of birds that feed on the fruit.

Avoid disturbing the roots of sumacs after your plantings mature. When cut, they can sucker and multiply to create new plants. It's best, when planting sumacs near a turfgrass lawn in beds or borders, to install a deep masonry edging to limit their spread.

Sumacs are care-free background plants that add foliage texture to any mixed-shrub border. Choose from evergreen or deciduous species.

Shrub: *Rhus* species. ANACARDIACEAE.
Common name: Sumac.
Description: About 150 species of varied, upright, spreading, deciduous or evergreen shrubs, 3–20 ft. (90–600 cm) tall. Deep green, leathery leaves divided into leaflets, 2–5 in. (50–125 mm) long, turning brilliant red or orange in autumn. Plants of the genus *Toxicodendron,* poison ivy, oak, and sumac are relatives.
Blooms/Fruit: Many tiny, often fragrant, cream, green, yellow flowers, to ¼ in. (6 mm) wide, in upright, spiking clusters, to 2½ in. (63 mm) tall, in summer, form small, round or flat, red, yellow, often woolly fruit containing seed in autumn, persisting into winter.
Plant hardiness: Zones 3–9. Hardy.
Soil: Moist to dry, well-drained soil. Fertility: Average. 6.0–7.0 pH.
Planting: Full sun to partial shade. Spacing varies by species.
Care: Easy. Keep damp; allow soil surface to dry between waterings. Drought tolerant when established. Avoid fertilizing. Prune, coppice in winter. Propagate by cuttings, layering, seed.
Features: Good choice for banks, coppicing, ground covers, hedges, screens in meadow, natural, rock, seaside, woodland gardens. Attracts birds. Invasive. Pest resistant. Fungal disease, verticillium wilt susceptible.

WARNING
Foliage of *Rhus* species causes skin irritation in sensitive individuals. Wear rubber gloves when touching plants.

ROSA (ROSE)

More than 150 species and horticultural varieties of erect, climbing, or rambling shrubs and vines make up the *Rosa* genus, along with many thousands of hybrid cultivars that the American Rose Society has classified into many groups now common to many landscapes and gardens. Though roses are found on every continent except Antarctica, they mostly are native to temperate regions of the northern hemisphere, and all are hardy to USDA Plant Hardiness Zone 5.

Rose cultivars have been hybridized from the native species to create plants with flowers from small to large, and from simple, single blossoms to frilly, very double flowers of every hue except blue. Some have delicious fragrances, while others lack scent. Genetic dwarf and miniature cultivars exist for most popular roses, and grafted standards—tree roses—are a good choice to plant near paths or in fragrance gardens.

Choose roses for your garden that satisfy your specific needs, from low, spreading ground covers to bushes, shrubs, and climbing vines, from the categories and species listed at right.

Rose Classifications:
  Climbing, rambler, and pillar roses
  Floribunda roses
  Grandiflora roses
  Hybrid tea roses
  Miniature roses
  Mini-flora roses
  Polyantha roses
  Shrub roses
Old Garden and Heritage Roses:
  Bourbon roses
  China roses
  Moss roses
  Noisette roses
  Portland roses
Selected Species Roses:
  R. alba, cottage rose
  R. banksiae, Banks rose
  R. centifolia, cabbage rose
  R. chinensis, China rose
  R. gallica, French rose
  R. hugonis, Father Hugo rose
  R. multiflora, Japanese rose
  R. odorata, tea rose
  R. primula, primrose
  R. rugosa, rugosa rose
  R. spinosissima, Scots rose

Roses rightly have been called the queens of the garden. Known for their showy flowers, they fill many different purposes in the landscape, are sturdy plants able to withstand both cold and heat, and are rewarding to grow. With care limited to inspecting them for insect pests and disease symptoms, annual and in-season prunings to ensure health and bloom, and regular fertilizing, they will prosper in most gardens.

Plant them in a moist to damp, well-drained soil with a neutral acid-alkaline balance. Water them regularly, but deeply. Allow the soil surface to dry before a repeat watering. Give them feedings of fertilizer monthly during spring and summer, then limit fertilizer application beginning in early autumn when their growth slows. Allow their final flush of blooms to remain on the plants as the air turns chilly and they begin to lose their leaves.

Roses store most of their nutrients in their canes. As they develop rose hips, the plants prepare for winter.

In the coldest climates, plant *R. rugosa* or one of the many cold-tolerant hybrids and mulch them heavily or prepare them for winter by wrapping and burying the plants. When spring comes and the last frost passes, unwrap your roses and trim off any dead or damaged canes.

Shrub: *Rosa* hybrids. ROSACEAE.
Common name: Floribunda Rose.
Description: Many hybrid cultivars of upright, bushy, deciduous shrubs and standards, 36–42 in. (90–107 cm) tall and 3–4 ft. (90–120 cm) wide, with alternate, shiny, bronze or light green becoming deep green leaves, divided into 3–5-leaflet groups, 1½–2½ in. (38–63 mm) long. *Rosa* 'Brass Band', an All American Rose Selection (1995), is shown at left.
Blooms/Fruit: Many showy, often fragrant, cream, lavender, orange, pink, purple, red, white, yellow and bicolored, blended, striped flowers, to 5 in. (13 cm) wide, in upright, mounding clusters, to 16 in. (40 cm) wide, in spring–autumn, form round, crabapple-like hips containing seed in autumn, persisting into winter. Repeat blooming.
Plant hardiness: Zones 5–10. Hardy. Cold tolerant if protected, to zone 3.
Soil: Moist to damp, well-drained soil. Fertility: Rich. 6.5–7.5 pH.
Planting: Full sun. Space 24–30 in. (60–75 cm) or more apart, depending on cultivar. Space to provide air circulation.
Care: Moderate. Keep damp; allow soil surface to dry between waterings. Drought tolerant when established. Fertilize monthly. Pinch to control growth, promote larger blooms. Prune in late winter. Protect from hard freezes. Vegetative propagation may be restricted. Plants grown from seed hybridize freely.
Features: Good choice for beds, borders, containers, fencelines in cottage, formal, meadow, small-space gardens. Good for cutting. Aphid, midge, spider mite, thrips and mildew, rust, black spot susceptible.

Shrub: *Rosa* hybrids. ROSACEAE.
Common name: Grandiflora Rose.
Description: Many hybrid cultivars of erect, branching, deciduous shrubs and shrub-like standards, 6–9 ft. (1.8–2.7 m) tall and 4–6 ft. (1.2–1.8 m) wide. Alternate, shiny, deep green leaves, divided into 3–5-leaflet groups, 1½–3 in. (38–75 mm) long. *Rosa* 'Queen Elizabeth', an All American Rose Selection (1955), is shown at left.
Blooms/Fruit: Many showy, apricot, cream, pink, red, white, mostly double flowers, to 8 in. (20 cm) wide, solitary or in showy clusters, in spring–autumn, form round, crabapple-like hips containing seed in autumn. Repeat blooming.
Plant hardiness: Zones 3–11. Hardy. May require winter protection, zones 3–4.
Soil: Moist to damp, well-drained soil. Fertility: Rich. 6.5–7.5 pH.
Planting: Full sun. Space 4–5 ft. (1.2–1.5 m) apart. Space to provide air circulation.
Care: Moderate. Keep damp; allow soil surface to dry between waterings. Fertilize monthly. Deadhead. Prune in late winter.
Features: Good choice for backgrounds, beds, screens in cottage, formal gardens. Good for cutting. Aphid, spider mite, thrips and mildew, rust, black spot susceptible.

Shrub: *Rosa* hybrids. ROSACEAE.
Common name: Hybrid Tea Rose.
Description: Many hybrid cultivars of erect and branching, deciduous shrubs and shrub-like standards, 4–6 ft. (1.2–1.8 m) tall and wide, alternate, shiny, sometimes bronze-, red-tinged, deep green leaves, divided into 3–5-leaflet groups, 1½–3 in. (38–75 mm) long. *Rosa* 'Peace', an All American Rose Selection (1946), is shown at right.
Blooms/Fruit: Many showy, apricot, cream, lavender, orange, pink, purple, red, white, yellow and bicolored, blended, striped, single to very double flowers, to 8 in. (20 cm) wide, in spring–autumn, form round hips containing seed in autumn, persisting into winter. Repeat blooming.
Plant hardiness: Zones 2–11. Hardy. May require winter protection, zones 2–4.
Soil: Moist to damp, well-drained soil. Fertility: Rich. 6.5–7.5 pH.
Planting: Full sun. Space 36–42 in. (90–107 cm) apart. Space to provide air circulation.
Care: Moderate. Keep damp; allow soil surface to dry between waterings. Fertilize monthly. Pinch to control growth, promote larger blooms. Prune in late winter.
Features: Good choice for beds, borders, containers, hedges, paths in arid, cottage, formal, small-space gardens and patios. Good for cutting. Aphid, midge, spider mite, thrips and mildew, rust, black spot susceptible.

Shrub: *Rosa* hybrids. ROSACEAE.
Common name: Miniature Rose.
Description: Many hybrid cultivars of low to mounding, bushy, evergreen shrubs and standards, 1–3 ft. (30–90 cm) tall and wide. Alternate, shiny, sometimes bronze-tinged, deep green leaves, divided into 3–5-leaflet groups, ½–1½ in. (12–38 mm) long. *Rosa* 'Child's Play', an All American Rose Selection (1993), is shown at left.
Blooms/Fruit: Many showy, often fragrant, apricot, cream, lavender, orange, pink, purple, red, white, yellow and bicolored, blended, striped flowers, to 2 in. (50 mm) wide, in spring–autumn, form round hips containing seed in autumn.
Plant hardiness: Zones 3–10. Hardy.
Soil: Moist to damp, well-drained soil. Fertility: Rich. 6.5–7.0 pH.
Planting: Full sun. Space 12–18 in. (30–45 cm) apart. Space to provide air circulation.
Care: Moderate. Keep damp; allow soil surface to dry between waterings. Fertilize monthly. Pinch to control growth, promote larger blooms. Prune in late winter. Vegetative propagation may be restricted. Plants grown from seed hybridize freely.
Features: Good choice for hanging baskets, beds, borders, containers, edgings in cottage, formal, small-space gardens and patios. Good for cutting. Aphid, midge, spider mite, thrips and mildew, rust, black spot susceptible.

Shrub: *Rosa* hybrids. ROSACEAE.

Common name: Modern Shrub Rose.

Description: Many hybrid cultivars of erect and bushy, branching, deciduous shrubs and standards, 4–6 ft. (1.2–1.8 m) tall and wide, with alternate, shiny, sometimes bronze-tinged, deep green leaves, divided into 3–5-leaflet groups, 1½–3 in. (38–75 mm) long. *Rosa* 'Mary Rose™', a patented plant hybridized by David Austin, is shown at left.

Blooms/Fruit: Many showy, fragrant, apricot, cream, orange, pink, red, white, yellow and bicolored, blended, striped, single, double, or very double flowers, to 6 in. (15 cm) wide, solitary or in clusters, to 6 in. (15 cm) wide, in spring–autumn, form round hips containing seed in autumn. Single or repeat blooming, depending on cultivar.

Plant hardiness: Zones 3–10. Hardy.

Soil: Moist to damp, well-drained soil. Fertility: Rich. 6.5–7.0 pH.

Planting: Full sun. Space 30–36 in. (75–90 cm) apart. Space to provide air circulation.

Care: Moderate. Keep damp; allow soil surface to dry between waterings. Fertilize monthly. Pinch to control growth. Prune in late winter. Vegetative propagation may be restricted.

Features: Good choice for beds, borders, containers, edgings, paths in cottage, formal, meadow, small-space gardens and patios. Good for cutting. Aphid, midge, spider mite, thrips and mildew, rust, black spot susceptible.

Shrub: *Sambucus* species. CAPRIFOLIACEAE.

Common name: Elderberry (Elder).

Description: About 20 species of fast-growing, open, deciduous shrubs or small trees, 6–30 ft. (1.8–9 m) tall, opposite, shiny, bronze, green, purple, feather-like, 5–7-lobed, toothed leaves, to 1 ft. (30 cm) long.

Blooms/Berries: Many tiny, cream, pink, white, 5-petaled flowers, in flat or domed clusters, to 10 in. (25 cm) wide, in spring, form purple, red, round, sometimes fleshy, edible berries in autumn.

Plant hardiness: Zones 2–10, depending on species.

Soil: Moist, well-drained soil. Fertility: Rich–average. 6.0–7.5 pH.

Planting: Full to filtered sun. Space 10–12 ft. (3–3.7 m) apart.

Care: Easy. Keep moist until established; drought tolerant thereafter. Fertilize annually in spring. Prune to promote bushiness. Propagate by seed, suckers.

Features: Good choice for accents, backgrounds, fencelines in meadow, natural gardens. Good for pies, preserves. Attracts birds. Pest resistant. Powdery mildew susceptible.

Shrub: *Spiraea* x *vanhouttei*. ROSACEAE.

Common name: Vanhoutte Spirea.

Description: Hybrid, fast-growing, arching, dense, deciduous shrub, to 6 ft. (1.8 m) tall, with red-tinged turning to blue green, oval, slightly lobed, veined leaves, to 1½ in. (38 mm) long, turning purple, red in autumn. Many other *Spiraea* species and cultivars available, requiring different care and pruning than does *S.* x *vanhouttei*.

Blooms/Seed: Tiny, fragrant, white flowers in spring form showy, ball-shaped clusters, to 4 in. (10 cm) wide, along arched branches, with inconspicuous seed follicles in summer.

Plant hardiness: Zones 5–9.

Soil: Moist, well-drained soil. Fertility: Average. 6.0–8.0 pH.

Planting: Full sun to partial shade. Space 6–8 ft. (1.8–2.4 m) apart.

Care: Easy. Keep moist. Fertilize semi-annually spring and autumn. Prune after bloom, removing wood that has flowered. Propagate by cuttings, layering, seed.

Features: Good choice for accents, backgrounds, fencelines, hedges, walls in cottage, small-space, woodland gardens. Best in dry climates. Fireblight, powdery mildew susceptible.

Shrub: *Strelitzia reginae.* STRELITZIACEAE.
Common name: Bird-of-Paradise (Crane Flower).
Description: Many cultivars of fast-growing, mounding, tropical, herbaceous, evergreen shrubs, to 4 ft. (1.2 m) tall and wide, with shiny, palmlike, green, broadly lance-shaped, sometimes cut leaves, 18–36 in. (45–90 cm) long, on arching stems.
Blooms/Pods: Unique, showy, birdlike, crested, blue, orange, white flowers, to 1 ft. (30 cm) long, on mature plants 4–6 years old, form woody, capsulelike pods containing seed. Intermittent year-round blooming.
Plant hardiness: Zones 9–11. Tender.
Soil: Moist to damp, well-drained soil. Fertility: Rich. 6.0–7.0 pH.
Planting: Full sun. Space 3–4 ft. (90–120 cm) apart.
Care: Moderate–challenging. Keep damp; allow soil surface to dry between waterings. Reduce watering in winter. Fertilize every 2 weeks. Deadhead spent flowers, yellowed foliage. Top dress in spring with a layer of fresh soil, 1 in. (25 mm) thick. Propagate by division, seed, suckers.
Features: Good choice for accents, beds, containers, paths in arid, formal, small-space, tropical gardens and swimming pool edgings. Good for cutting. Pest and disease resistant.

Shrub: *Symphoricarpos* species. CAPRIFOLIACEAE.
Common name: Snowberry (Coralberry).
Description: About 16 species of fast-growing, upright or spreading, deciduous shrubs, 2–6 ft. (60–180 cm) tall, depending on species, with matte, green, round or oval, slightly lobed leaves, to 2 in. (50 mm) long.
Blooms/Fruit: Many tiny, green, pink, white flowers, in grapelike clusters, in spring–summer, form white, round, mealy, seed-filled fruit, to ¼ in. (6 mm) wide, in autumn.
Plant hardiness: Zones 3–9, depending on species.
Soil: Damp, well-drained soil. Fertility: Average. 6.5–7.5 pH.
Planting: Filtered sun. Space 1–3 ft. (30–90 cm) apart, depending on species.
Care: Easy. Keep damp; allow soil surface to dry between waterings. Fertilize annually in spring. Prune to shape, control growth. Propagate by cuttings, division, seed.
Features: Good choice for backgrounds, ground covers, slopes in shade, woodland gardens. Attracts birds, butterflies, hummingbirds. Aphid, caterpillar, scale and anthracnose susceptible.

Shrub: *Syringa* species. OLEACEAE.
Common name: Lilac.
Description: Over 30 species of fast-growing, spreading, dense, deciduous shrubs, 5–20 ft. (1.5–6 m) tall, with shiny, deep green, smooth, oval, pointed leaves, to 5 in. (13 cm) long.
Blooms/Berries: Fragrant, tiny, lavender, pink, purple, white flowers, in spring, forming large, showy clusters, 3½–10 in. (90–250 mm) long, with leathery seed-filled capsules in summer. First blooms 2–3 years after planting. Requires at least 500 hours of winter chilling to bloom reliably.
Plant hardiness: Zones 3–9. Hardy.
Soil: Moist, well-drained soil. Fertility: Rich. 7.0–7.5 pH.
Planting: Full sun to partial shade. Space 5–10 ft. (1.5–3 m) apart.
Care: Moderate. Keep evenly moist. Fertilize quarterly spring–autumn. Deadhead. Prune sparingly after bloom. Propagate by cuttings, layering.
Features: Good choice for borders in cottage, woodland gardens. Good for cutting. Attracts butterflies. Transplants readily. Invasive. Deer and pest resistant. Powdery mildew susceptible.

TAXUS (YEW)

The *Taxus* genus includes eight species of mostly erect or spreading, coniferous, small trees and shrubs, the cones of which are modified into colorful though tiny, round, fleshy fruit. They are native to the northern hemisphere. Most yew species prefer chilling during winter and will tolerate cold to USDA Plant Hardiness Zone 3.

Yews make excellent border shrubs and hedges. They are slow-growing, ranging in height from 6 ft. (1.8 m) for the shortest species to 50 ft. (15 m) in the tallest. As small trees, they can anchor a mixed-shrub bed, accent a rock garden, or define borders at the corners of structures. Shear or prune them to direct their growth, or use them in bonsai, espalier, and topiary.

Pests and diseases, even persistent deer and rodents, are rare for yews. They are tolerant of drought but become susceptible to chlorosis when their soil turns too alkaline. Mulch with conifer needle compost or apply an acidic fertilizer to reduce chlorotic yellowing.

Choose yews that will thrive in your region and climate, seeking advice from local garden center staff. Popular yew species are listed above, at right.

Yews are the right choice for a slow- to medium-growing, evergreen conifer in the shrub border. The taller species have a fine, dense, pyramid-shaped form, and the low species are good for edgings, borders, and midground plantings.

Yew Species and Hybrids:
T. baccata, English yew
T. brevifolia, western yew
T. canadensis, American yew
T. chinensis, Chinese yew
T. cuspidata, Japanese yew
T. × media

Choose a location with some shade—filtered sun to partial shade is best. Plant yews in a damp tending to dry, well-drained, neutral soil. They need to be fertilized annually. Apply fertilizer each spring and protect them from drying winds, especially during winter when their needles are subject to drying and becoming brown. Prune them in the spring, removing all dead or damaged branches and foliage.

Although they are planted mostly for their foliage, yews also produce highly decorative red or sometimes yellow, berrylike fruit in summer that contrasts nicely with their deep green, feathery foliage.

Yews are good companion plants for perennials, annuals, and other shrubs and trees that prefer neutral soil. They are one of the few needle-bearing evergreens that readily mix with such plants. Take advantage of this trait to create tall, vertical accents to contrast with low-growing shrubs and floral edgings. Place a tall yew in the center of an island bed, at the back of a border, or use them in groups to create a miniature forest in your landscape.

Yew cultivars include plants with bronze, gold, blue green, and yellow foliage, as well as green. Many yew species turn bronze or yellow in autumn, remaining in color through winter.

Remember that the foliage of yew contains alkaloids that cause severe digestive upset if eaten and can be fatally hazardous when large quantities are ingested. Pets and children are at risk for such hazard. Choose another shrub species if your yard is frequented by children or pets, and supervise young visitors while they are in your garden.

Shrub: *Taxus canadensis.* TAXACEAE.
Common name: American Yew (Ground Hemlock).
Description: Several cultivars of slow-growing, long-lived, spreading, open, bushy, needle-bearing, evergreen shrubs, to 6 ft. (1.8 m) tall, with deep green, radiating, slightly flattened needles, to 1 in. (25 mm) long. *T. baccata,* English yew; and *T. cuspidata,* Japanese yew, are related species.
Blooms/Fruit: Red, berrylike fruit, to ½ in. (12 mm) wide, borne by female plants, in summer, form dry seedpods in autumn.
Plant hardiness: Zones 3–8. Best in zones 3–6.
Soil: Damp to dry, well-drained soil. Fertility: Average. 6.5–7.5 pH.
Planting: Partial to full shade. Space 4–6 ft. (1.2–1.8 m) apart.
Care: Easy. Allow soil to dry completely between waterings. Fertilize annually in spring. Mulch. Avoid pruning. Protect from sun in hot climates, wind in cold-winter climates. Propagate by cuttings.
Features: Good choice for containers, hedges, screens in cottage, formal, shade, woodland gardens. Drought tolerant. Pest and disease resistant. Deer susceptible.

Shrub: *Teucrium* x *lucidrys* (*T. chamaedrys, T. lucidum*). LAMIACEAE (LABIATAE).
Common name: Germander.
Description: A few cultivars of medium-growing, mounding, rhizomatous, evergreen shrubs, to 2 ft. (60 cm) tall and wide, with opposite, smooth, deep green, oval, pointed, coarsely toothed leaves, to ⅝ in. (16 mm) long, on hairy stalks. Dwarf cultivars available. *T. cossonii* var. *majoricum; T. fruticans,* bush germander; and *T. marum,* cat thyme, are closely related species with similar care needs.
Blooms/Fruit: Many purple, red, white, 5-petaled flowers, in open, mintlike, spiking clusters, to 3 in. (75 mm) long, in summer, form nutlike fruits in autumn.
Plant hardiness: Zones 4–10. Hardy.
Soil: Damp, well-drained, sandy soil. Fertility: Average–low. 6.5–8.0 pH. Salt tolerant.
Planting: Full sun. Space 6–12 in. (15–30 cm) apart.
Care: Easy. Keep damp; allow soil surface to dry between waterings. Fertilize annually in spring. Shear to shape. Propagate by cuttings, division, seed.
Features: Good choice for containers, edgings, ground covers, hedges, paths in arid, rock, seaside, small-space gardens. Attracts bees. Pest and disease resistant.

Shrub: *Thuja occidentalis.* ARBORVITAE.
Common name: American Arborvitae.
Description: Over 50 cultivars of slow-growing, mounding or narrow, coniferous, evergreen small trees, to 60 ft. (18 m) tall, with cedarlike, deep green needles with lighter undersides, in upright fans, turning russet, yellow in winter. *T. plicata,* western red cedar, is a closely related tree species with similar care needs.
Blooms/Cones: Tiny flowers in spring form ½-in. (12-mm) cones in summer.
Plant hardiness: Zones 3–8.
Soil: Moist, well-drained soil. Fertility: Rich. 6.5–8.0 pH. Best in cool, humid climates.
Planting: Full sun. Space 4–10 ft. (1.2–3 m) apart, depending on use.
Care: Easy. Keep moist. Fertilize quarterly spring–autumn. Train to desired shape while young. Protect from drying wind, zones 3–5. Propagate by cuttings, grafting, seed.
Features: Good choice for accents, beds, containers, edgings, fencelines, hedges, screens in meadow, open, woodland gardens and landscapes. Good for bonsai, topiary. Deer and spider mite susceptible.

Shrub: *Tibouchina urvilleana* (*T. semidecandra*). MELASTOMATACEAE.
Common name: Glory Bush (Lasiandra, Pleroma, Princess Flower).
Description: Several cultivars of fast-growing, open, branching, narrow, evergreen shrubs, 10–15 ft. (3–4.5 m) tall and 5–10 ft. (1.5–3 m) wide, with fuzzy or smooth, deep green, oval, pointed, veined leaves, 2–4 in. (50–100 mm) long, with brown, cream, red edges or variegation, on hairy stalks. *T. bicolor, T. elegans, T. multiflora,* and *T. mutabilis* are closely related species with similar care needs.
Blooms/Fruit: Many cobalt purple, violet, 5-petaled flowers, 1–3 in. (25–75 mm) wide, in spring–autumn, form capsulelike pods, to ½ in. (12 mm) wide, containing seed, in autumn.
Plant hardiness: Zones 8–11. Semi-hardy. May require winter protection, zone 8.
Soil: Moist, well-drained humus. Fertility: Rich. 6.0–7.0 pH.
Planting: Full sun to partial shade. Space 4–5 ft. (1.2–1.5 m) apart.
Care: Easy. Keep evenly moist. Fertilize monthly. Pinch to control growth. Propagate by cuttings.
Features: Good choice for accents, containers, hedges in tropical, woodland gardens. Attracts hummingbirds. Disease resistant. Budworm susceptible.

VIBURNUM (ARROWWOOD)

The diverse *Viburnum* genus numbers 225 species of upright, deciduous and evergreen shrubs, native to the Americas, Europe, and Asia. With many different common names and habits, most are open, attractive plants that bear showy flowers in late spring, followed by bright red or black berries in autumn, a feast for wild birds drawn to them.

Arrowwoods make good foundation shrubs. Their medium- to slow-growth rate and varied species, with a selection of forms and heights that range from 5–40 ft. (1.5–12 m) tall, makes them ideal for many locations and purposes in the home landscape.

Use arrowwoods as specimen and accent shrubs in an island planting. Choose them for backgrounds and borders by fencelines, paths, structures, and walls. Edge your yard with a row of arrowwoods along a drive to screen it from the street.

Arrowwoods are susceptible to aphids, spider mites, and thrips and powdery mildew and leaf spot, fungal diseases caused when spores splash onto the plants' foliage.

Many popularly cultivated species of arrowwood are listed at right.

Arrowwods fill the need for a landscape shrub that will grow slowly, fill an area, bear showy flowers followed by attractive berries, and require minimal care. Evergreen viburnums maintain their charm throughout the year, while the deciduous species show off their sculptural forms and colorful berries in the winter after their leaves fall.

Choose a planting site in full sun or partial shade. Most arrowwoods do best in evenly moist, well-drained, neutral soils with a mix of sand and humus. Mulch them in USDA Plant Hardiness Zones 6–8 to keep their roots cool as the temperature rises in summer. Give them fertilizer in spring as they begin their new growth. Shape them after their flowers fade; they bloom each year on old wood.

Three separate flowers are found on arrowwoods: most are flat clusters, 4–6 in. (10–15 cm) wide; some bear round, compact clusters resembling their namesake snowballs; and others have many flat, tiny, fertile flowers surrounded by large rays, similar to composite flowers such as daisy.

Choose arrowwoods for their foliage, beautiful spring flowers, charming berries that attract foraging birds, or structural branches.

Arrowwood Species:

V. acerifolium, maple-leaved arrowwood
V. awabukii, sweet arrowwood
V. betulifolium, birch arrowwood
V. × burkwoodii, Burkwood viburnum
V. × carlcephalum, fragrant snowball
V. carlesii, fragrant viburnum
V. davidii, David viburnum
V. dentatum, arrowwood
V. dilatatum, linden viburnum
V. edule, highbush cranberry
V. farreri, fragrant arrowwood
V. grandiflorum
V. hybrids, hybrid arrowwood
V. japonicum, Japanese viburnum
V. lantana, rugose wayfaring tree
V. macrocephalum, Chinese snowball
V. opulus, European cranberry bush
V. plicatum, Japanese snowball
V. rhytidophyllum, leather-leaved viburnum
V. rufidulum, southern black haw
V. sargentii, Sargent cranberry bush
V. setigerum, tea viburnum
V. sieboldii, Siebold viburnum
V. suspensum, Sandankwa viburnum
V. tinus, Laurustinus viburnum
V. trilobum, American cranberry bush
V. veitchii, Veitch viburnum
V. wrightii, Wright arrowwood

Shrub: *Viburnum* species. CAPRIFOLIACEAE.

Common name: Arrowwood.

Description: About 225 species of medium-growing, open, deciduous or evergreen shrubs, 5–40 ft. (1.5–12 m) tall, depending on species, with yellow green, textured, oval, toothed leaves, 3–8 in. (75–200 mm) long, turning red in autumn.

Blooms/Berries: Abundant, sometimes fragrant, white, 5-petaled flowers in late spring, 3–5 in. (75–125 mm) wide, form showy, ball-like clusters, with bright red or black berries in autumn.

Plant hardiness: Zones 3–8, depending on species.

Soil: Moist, well-drained soil. Fertility: Rich. 6.0–7.5 pH.

Planting: Full sun to partial shade. Space 4–10 ft. (1.2–3 m) apart, depending on species and use.

Care: Easy. Keep soil moist. Fertilize annually in spring. Mulch, zones 6–8. Prune sparingly after bloom. Propagate by cuttings, layering, seed.

Features: Good choice for accents, borders, edgings, paths in cottage, natural, wildlife, woodland gardens and landscapes. Berries attract birds. Aphid, spider mite, thrips and powdery mildew, leaf spot susceptible.

Shrub: *Viburnum opulus.* CAPRIFOLIACEAE.
Common name: European Cranberry Bush (Whitten Tree).
Description: Several cultivars of graceful, medium-growing, open, deciduous shrubs, to 12 ft. (3.7 m) tall, with maplelike, 3–5-lobed, divided, veined leaves, to 4 in. (10 cm) long, turning bright red in autumn. Common cultivars include *V. opulus* 'Aureum', 'Compactum', 'Nanum', and 'Roseum'.
Blooms/Berries: Many showy, cream, white, single flowers, to ¾ in. (19 mm) wide, in late spring, form mounding clusters, to 4 in. (10 cm) wide, with scarlet berries in autumn, persisting to winter.
Plant hardiness: Zones 3–10; ground hardy, zones 3–8.
Soil: Moist to dry, well-drained soil. Fertility: Rich–average. 6.0–7.5 pH.
Planting: Full sun to partial shade. Space 6–8 ft. (1.8–2.4 m) apart.
Care: Easy. Keep evenly moist. Fertilize quarterly spring–autumn. Mulch, zones 7–10. Prune after bloom. Protect from sun in hot climates. Propagate by cuttings, grafting, layering, seed.
Features: Good choice for accents, borders, margins, screens in cottage, natural, rock, water, woodland gardens. Berries attract birds. Disease resistant. Aphid, spider mite susceptible.

Shrub: *Weigela* species. CAPRIFOLIACEAE.
Common name: Weigela.
Description: Over 10 species and many hybrids of fast-growing, open, spreading, deciduous shrubs, to 10 ft. (3 m) tall, with shiny, deep green, oval, pointed leaves, to 4 in. (10 cm) long. Common species include *W. coraeensis, W. middendorffiana,* and *W. florida,* plus many named hybrids.
Blooms/Seed: Showy, cone-shaped, pink, purple, red, white, yellow flowers, to 1½ in. (38 mm) long, in dense clusters, in late spring, form woody seedpods in summer. Flowers on second-year wood.
Plant hardiness: Zones 5–9. Hardy.
Soil: Moist to damp, well-drained soil. Fertility: Average. 6.5–7.0 pH.
Planting: Full sun to partial shade. Space 8 ft. (2.4 m) apart.
Care: Easy. Keep evenly moist. Fertilize every 2 months spring–autumn. Mulch. Prune after bloom. Propagate by cuttings.
Features: Good choice for accents, borders, hedges in cottage, woodland gardens. Good for cutting. Pest and disease resistant.

Shrub: *Xylosma congestum.* FLACOURTIACEAE.
Common name: Xylosma.
Description: Several cultivars of fast-growing, mounding or spreading, evergreen shrubs, to 15 ft. (4.5 m) tall and wide, armed with sharp, slender spines at the junctions of leaf stalks with nodding branches, and with alternate, shiny, bronze turning yellow green, oval, pointed, finely toothed leaves, 3–4 in. (75–100 mm) long. Dwarf cultivars, multitrunked forms, standards available.
Blooms/Berries: Inconspicuous, white flowers form small, round, seed-filled berries; grown primarily for foliage.
Plant hardiness: Zones 7–10. Semi-hardy.
Soil: Damp to dry, well-drained soil. Fertility: Average. 6.0–7.5 pH.
Planting: Full sun to partial shade. Space 7–10 ft. (2.2–3 m) apart.
Care: Easy. Keep damp until established; drought tolerant thereafter. Fertilize annually in spring. Prune to shape, train. Propagate by cuttings, layering, seed.
Features: Good choice for accents, borders, espaliers, hedges, topiary in formal, woodland gardens. Scale, spider mite and chlorosis susceptible.

YUCCA

About 40 species of mounding, bushy, deciduous shrubs are included in the *Yucca* genus, all lily-family relatives. They are native to the high desert and arid plains of North America. All are cold-tolerant plants, able to survive winters in USDA Plant Hardiness Zone 4.

Yuccas bear basal rosettes of long, sword-shaped leaves in a circular fan. The leaves are thick and leathery. When mature, they produce remarkable, erect flower stalks with branching clusters of purple or white, open or bell-shaped, nodding flowers, to 2 in. (50 mm) wide. After flowering in early summer, the plant may resume its growth or yellow and die, producing many offset plants, depending on the species.

Yuccas are medium-growing shrubs, mostly 2–3 ft. (60–90 cm) tall. Use them as accents in full sun sites, or as windbreaks or natural fences in desert landscapes. In small-space, arid gardens, they make excellent container plants and are a good choice in Xeriscape gardens.

Yuccas are susceptible to aphids and leaf spot.

Choose landscape yuccas from the species listed above, at right.

Yuccas are showy plants that stand alone or in ranked groups in the desert and arid-climate garden. When used as large specimens, they may survive for generations before they bloom. Smaller species are ideal as accent plants in rock gardens or a structural planting on a seaside patio. They are good for cutting and drying for use in arrangements. Yuccas are good companion plants for cacti and succulents in a mixed planting.

Plant yuccas in damp to dry, well-drained, sandy soil of average fertility. They are salt tolerant and require little care. Water them whenever their soil has dried completely, and fertilize them quarterly in spring and summer with liquid nitrogen fertilizer.

Yuccas seldom require pruning. If a leaf discolors or becomes damaged, cut it carefully at its base.

Remember that the leaves of many yuccas are armed with sharp spines at their ends and pose a hazard to passersby on nearby paths and walkways. Cut these spines off with a sharp hand pruner or plant them away from walkways.

Although many yuccas are low, mounding plants, other species are treelike and striking additions to the home landscape. One of these, *Y. brevifolia,* Joshua tree, is a many-branched tree that may reach 30 feet (9 m) or more in height. Its contorted branches with sprays of spiny leaves are especially pleasing when lit from below at night in a site near a deck or other outdoor activity area.

Remember to use yuccas in containers as plants to add visual interest and texture to small-space gardens.

Yucca Species:
Y. aloifolia, Spanish-bayonet
Y. baccata, banana yucca
Y. brevifolia, Joshua tree
Y. carnerosana, Spanish-dagger
Y. elata, soaptree yucca
Y. elephantipes, giant yucca
Y. filamentosa, Adam's-needle
Y. glauca, soapweed
Y. gloriosa, Spanish-dagger
Y. reverchonii, San Angelo yucca
Y. rigida, blue yucca
Y. rupicola, twisted-leaved yucca
Y. schottii, mountain yucca
Y. treculeana, palma pita
Y. whipplei, Our-Lord's-candle

Shrub: *Yucca filamentosa (Y. smalliana).* AGAVACEAE.
Common name: Adam's-Needle (Yucca).
Description: Several cultivars of medium-growing, mounding, evergreen shrubs, 2–3 ft. (60–90 cm) tall and to 5 ft. (1.5 m) wide, with shiny, blue to deep green, stiff, sword-shaped leaves, to 30 in. (75 cm) long, with thready edges and armed with terminal, thorny spines, forming a circular, radiating base. More than 15 closely related species of *Yucca* with similar care needs are commonly cultivated.
Blooms/Seed: Showy, fragrant, saucer-shaped, cream, purple, white flowers, to 2 in. (50 mm) long, in spiking clusters on woody stems, to 8 ft. (2.4 m) tall, in late spring–summer, form winged seed in autumn.
Plant hardiness: Zones 4–10. Hardy.
Soil: Damp to dry, well-drained sandy soil. Fertility: Average. 6.0–7.5 pH.
Planting: Full sun. Space 3–10 ft. (90–305 cm) apart.
Care: Easy. Deep water; allow soil to dry between waterings. Drought tolerant. Fertilize quarterly. Propagate by cuttings, seed.
Features: Good choice for accents, containers in arid, meadow, turfgrass gardens. Good for cutting, drying. Aphid and leaf spot susceptible.

Landscape Trees

Trees give a landscape a sense of permanence and maturity. Their towering presence is more than pleasing to the eye—they enhance the environment in several significant ways. Tree roots aerate and stabilize the soil, while their foliage shields the ground from sun and precipitation. Their foliage gives off moisture, and they breathe in carbon dioxide and exhale oxygen.

Shade and flowering trees are likely to be the dominant element in your landscape or garden. Many trees grow to 80 ft. (24 m) or more in height and have a spread of 50 ft. (15 m) or more. They have many different forms, from conical to round-headed and fountain-shaped to columnar. Select your trees by matching their mature size, form, foliage, and flowers to your site. Keep in mind their habits as well—choose those free of maintenance that will limit the need for care, keep your walkways free of fallen leaves and fruit, and that have deep root systems to prevent cracking pavement. At the same time, remember that some trees may take years to attain great size; plant a fast-growing filler if you desire shade before they can fulfill your needs.

As you select and plant your trees, you'll be creating a lifetime of beauty and enjoyment, both for yourself and for the many generations who will admire you for your planning and foresight.

ABIES (FIR)

About 40 species of large and stately, pyramid-shaped, coniferous trees are included in the *Abies* genus. Native to the northern hemisphere's temperate mountains, they thrive in high-elevation locations and are best in an open landscape where their sturdy trunks and wide-spreading, horizontal branches may be seen from a distance.

Only a few species of fir perform well in landscape settings because they need mild, moist summers and cold winters to thrive. Avoid planting them in areas with hot, dry summers or in urban sites with sustained air pollution.

Firs are fast-growing trees to about 30 ft. (9 m) tall, becoming medium-growing as they reach mature size and begin to produce their upright, clustered cones. If kept rootbound in a planter, they will grow slowly and are ideal for bonsai and shape training. They rarely need pruning; when planted in a site with ample room, they develop into pleasing, conical trees.

While firs generally are resistant to disease, their new growth sometimes attracts aphids. Larval beetles and borers also can infest their bark.

Choose from the landscape and native fir species above, at right.

Firs are large, upright, and conical elements in a landscape garden. When mature, they have massive, single trunks, and their branches begin nearly at the soil's surface.

Landscape Fir Species:
  A. *balsamea*, balsam fir
  A. *concolor*, white fir
  A. *firma*, Momi fir
  A. *fraseri*, Fraser fir
Other Fir Species:
  A. *alba*, silver-tipped fir
  A. *amabilis*, silver fir
  A. *cephalonica*, Greek fir
  A. *grandis*, giant fir
  A. *homolepis*, Nikko fir
  A. *koreana*, Korean fir
  A. *lasiocarpa*, Rocky Mountain fir
  A. *magnifica*, red fir
  A. *nordmanniana*, Nordmann fir
  A. *pinsapo*, Spanish fir
  A. *procera*, noble fir
  A. *sibirica*, Siberian fir
  A. *spectabilis*, Himalayan fir

Plant firs in damp, well-drained soil that is high in acidity. Since all landscape trees perform best when planted in unamended soil, your site should be tested for acid-alkaline balance before planting. If your soil is outside the 5.5–7.0 pH range firs need, pick a tree from another conifer genus. You also should compare your tree's needs to your climate, especially when choosing a native fir species.

Carefully match the depth of the planting hole to the soil line of your tree when planting. Firs need good drainage, and the root crown should be placed underground at the same level as it was growing at the tree nursery. Backfill the planting hole with native soil, surround it with a moat, and give the tree plenty of water through its first summer, watering whenever the soil surface becomes thoroughly dry.

Firs are the right choice for open or woodland gardens. Because they spread quickly at first and later become the dominant feature in the landscape, give them ample room. The recommended spacing of 12–15 ft. (3.7–4.5 m) is the minimum you should consider when planting a conifer near a structure; double or triple that spacing to plant specimen trees.

To use a small fir as an indoor holiday decoration, plant it *and* its container in the soil, applying mulch over its roots. Unearth the tree before the soil freezes, clean its container, and bring it indoors. When the holiday season is over, the tree can be replanted in your garden.

Tree: *Abies concolor*. PINACEAE.
Common Name: White Fir.
Description: Many cultivars of medium- to slow-growing, upright, pyramid-shaped, coniferous, evergreen trees, to 100 ft. (30 m) tall or more, with whorled branches and shiny, blue green or green, flat needles, to 2 in. (50 mm) long, and silver, banded bark with pitch-filled blisters.
Cones/Seed: Female cones are erect, brown, green, purple, cylinder-shaped, to 5 in. (13 cm) long, with woody scales bearing pairs of winged seed.
Plant hardiness: Zones 4–9.
Soil: Damp, well-drained soil. Fertility: Rich–average. 5.5–7.0 pH.
Planting: Full sun. Space 12–15 ft. (3.7–4.5 m) apart.
Care: Easy. Keep damp; allow soil surface to dry between waterings until fully established. Avoid fertilizing and pruning. Protect from heat, smog. Propagate by seed.
Features: Good choice for accents, allées, banks, containers, groups, screens, specimens in meadow, woodland gardens and landscape slopes. Good for bonsai. Seed attracts birds in autumn. Aphid, beetle, borer, spider mite, sawfly susceptible.

ACACIA

As many as 800 species of small and midsized, erect and spreading, broad-leaved, deciduous and evergreen trees make up the *Acacia* genus. They are native to dry tropical and arid regions of the world, and are numerous in both Australia and Central America. They are tender and do best in mild-winter climates with hot, dry summers.

Many different species of acacia have been developed for use in landscape gardens. Choose them as a spectacular accent in your yard because of their autumn and winter blooms, or grow them as a colorful screen along a fence-line or wall to divide and separate areas within your garden.

Acacias are fast-growing but short-lived, compact trees that attain sizes ranging from 6–40 ft. (1.8–12 m) tall. They flower in autumn from their third season, with an increasing display that cloaks their often blue green leaves with copious crestlike flowers.

They generally are resistant to pests and disease, but yellow with chlorosis if their soil becomes too alkaline.

There are acacias in a multitude of forms and flowering habits suited to your landscape. Choose among the popular species above, at right.

Acacias come in many forms depending on their species, from small, shrublike trees to tall and upright, widely spreading, broad-leaved evergreens that will shade an entire backyard. When mature, they have single or multiple trunks with many upturned, much-divided branches.

Popular Acacia Species:
A. baileyana, Bailey acacia
A. boormanii, Snowy River wattle
A. cognata, bower wattle
A. confusa, Formosan koa
A. cultriformis, knife acacia
A. dealbata, silver wattle
A. decora, graceful wattle
A. farnesiana, sweet acacia
A. gregii, catclaw acacia
A. koa, koa tree
A. longifolia, Sydney golden wattle
A. pendula, weeping boree acacia
A. pruinosa, bronze acacia
A. salicina, willow acacia
A. saligna, blue-leaf acacia
A. verticillata, star acacia
A. willardiana, white acacia

Plant acacias in damp to dry, well-drained soil that is slightly acidic or neutral. Since all landscape trees perform best when they are planted in unamended soil, test the acid-alkaline balance of your site before you plant. Acacias need soils that are in the 6.5–7.5 pH range. You also should compare your tree's needs to your climate.

When you plant, carefully match the depth of the planting hole to the soil line of your tree. Backfill around the rootball with native soil and give the tree ample water through its first season, watering whenever the soil surface becomes thoroughly dry.

Acacias are the best choice for late autumn and winter color in mild-winter climates. Many species have bright, fragrant flowers which attract pollen- and seed-foraging birds. Caring for acacias includes regular raking of fallen pollen, flowers, and seed. Note that acacia pollen may cause respiratory congestion in allergic individuals. Acacias are at their best when planted as an accent in an open garden in an arid climate and are especially favored for Xeriscape gardens.

Florists sell as mimosa the flowering branches of *A. dealbata*, silver wattle, which are excellent cut flowers when used in winter arrangements. Many other acacia species have unusual flowers that lend themselves to cutting and arranging with dried grasses and seedpods.

Tree: *Acacia* species. FABACEAE (LEGUMINOSAE).
Common Name: Acacia (Mimosa, Wattle).
Description: Nearly 800 species of fast-growing, short-lived, upright and spreading, deciduous or evergreen shrubs and trees, 6–40 ft. (1.8–12 m) tall, 5–30 ft. (1.5–9 m) wide, depending on species, with dull, leathery, or waxy, blue green, gray green, or green, featherlike, divided, or lance-shaped, pointed leaves, 1–4 in. (25–100 mm) long, some armed with thorny spines.
Blooms/Fruit: Often showy, gold, white, yellow, massed stamens in late autumn–winter, borne in ball-shaped clusters, ¼–2 in. (6–50 mm) wide, form bean- or pealike pods with seed in winter.
Plant hardiness: Zones 8–11. Tender. Best in hot, dry climates.
Soil: Damp to dry, well-drained soil. Fertility: Average. 6.5–7.5 pH.
Planting: Full sun. Space 5–15 ft. (1.5–4.5 m) apart, depending on species.
Care: Easy. Keep damp until established; drought tolerant thereafter. Fertilize annually in spring. Prune to shape and thin interior branches. Propagate by seed.
Features: Good choice for accents, screens, walls in arid, natural, seaside, Xeriscape gardens. Flowers and seedpods attract bees, birds. Pest resistant. Chlorosis susceptible.

ACER (MAPLE)

The *Acer* genus includes about 200 species of highly varied, broad-leaved, deciduous trees, including both small landscape trees and those with great stature. They are native to the northern hemisphere's temperate zone of North America, Europe, and Asia. All are hardy and grow best in cold-winter areas that experience at least 1,000 hours of winter chill at temperatures below 40°F (4°C).

Maples are prized for their narrow or round-crowned form and their foliage, which colors beautifully in autumn in shades of bronze, gold, red, and yellow. Many cultivars also have been developed with foliage that is bronze, purple, or red throughout the season.

Maples generally are slow-growing, long-lived trees with dense foliage that reach sizes ranging from 6 ft. (1.8 m) tall for shrublike species to 100 ft. (30 m) or more for the largest species.

They vary in their resistance to pests and diseases, with aphid, borer, and scale or canker, tar spot, and verticillium wilt being the frequent causes of infestation and infection.

Many different cultivars may be used in a landscape. Choose from among the popular maple species above, at right.

Maples and box elders grow as low ground covers, as shrubs, and as small and large trees, depending on their species. All are broad-leaved and deciduous, with hand-shaped, lobed, and pointed leaves and distinctive, two-winged seeds that carry great distances in the wind. Maples have single and massive or multiple and narrow trunks with many spreading branches.

Plant maples in rich, moist, well-drained soil, either acidic or neutral. Since all landscape trees grow best when planted in unamended soil, test the acid-alkaline balance of your site before you plant. Maples should have soils in the 6.0–7.0 pH range. Choose those species that fit your climate and site.

When planting maples, carefully match the depth of the planting hole to the soil line on the rootball of your tree. Backfill around the rootball with native soil and give the tree ample water for the first few seasons, keeping the soil evenly moist. It may require several seasons for the tree to begin active growth after transplanting.

Maples are the best choice for autumn foliage color in cold-winter climates. Their care needs include regular raking of fallen catkinlike flowers, leaves, and winged seed. Large maples are good shade trees, while those with smaller, more delicate forms are good landscape accents.

Cultivars of the species *A. palmatum*, Japanese maple, have long been the tree of choice for bonsai and for oriental-themed gardens.

Maple Species:

A. buergeranum, trident maple
A. campestre, hedge maple
A. cappadocicum, coliseum maple
A. carpinifolium, hornbeam maple
A. glabrum, Rocky Mountain maple
A. griseum, paperbark maple
A. japonicum, full-moon maple
A. lobelii, Lobel maple
A. macrophyllum, big-leaved maple
A. mandshuricum, Manchurian maple
A. negundo, box elder
A. nigrum, black maple
A. palmatum, Japanese maple
A. pensylvanicum, striped maple
A. platanoides, Norway maple
A. pseudoplatanus, sycamore maple
A. rubrum, red maple
A. saccharinum, silver maple
A. saccharum, sugar maple
A. spicatum, mountain maple
A. tataricum, Tatarian maple
A. tschonoskii, Tschonoski maple

Tree: *Acer griseum*. ACERACEAE.

Common name: Paperbark Maple.

Description: A few cultivars of slow-growing, upright, columnar or spreading, dense, deciduous trees, to 40 ft. (12 m) tall, with smooth, deep green, oval to round, toothed, 3-lobed leaves, to 3 in. (75 mm) wide, with silvery undersides, turning red in autumn, and with red brown, papery, flaking bark.

Blooms/Seed: Few inconspicuous red flowers in early spring, borne in dangling clusters, form showy, red, 2-winged seed in summer.

Plant hardiness: Zones 4–9. Best with winter chill.

Soil: Moist, well-drained soil. Fertility: Rich–average. 6.0–7.0 pH.

Planting: Full to filtered sun. Space 15–20 ft. (4.5–6 m) apart.

Care: Moderate. Keep evenly damp. Fertilize annually in spring until established. Prune sparingly in autumn. Protect from sun, wind. Propagate by grafting, seed.

Features: Good choice for accents, shrub borders in woodland gardens and lawns. Pest and disease resistant.

Tree: *Acer japonicum.* ACERACEAE.
Common name: Full-Moon Maple (Japanese Maple).
Description: Many cultivars of dainty, slow-growing, spreading, deciduous trees, to 30 ft. (9 m) tall, with smooth, light green, oval to round, toothed, 7–13-lobed leaves, to 6 in. (15 cm) long, turning bright red in autumn.
Blooms/Seed: Multiple tiny purple or red flowers in spring, borne in dangling clusters, form typical reddish brown, 2-winged seed in autumn.
Plant hardiness: Zones 5–9. Best with winter chill.
Soil: Moist, well-drained soil. Fertility: Rich–average. 6.0–7.0 pH.
Planting: Partial shade. Space 12–15 ft. (3.7–4.5 m) apart.
Care: Moderate. Keep evenly moist until established; allow soil surface to dry between waterings. Fertilize in spring and autumn. Prune sparingly in autumn. Protect from sun in hot climates, wind. Propagate by cuttings, layering, seed.
Features: Good choice for accents, containers, shrub borders in formal, Japanese-themed, small-space, woodland gardens. Smog tolerant. Shallow rooted. Pest and disease resistant.

Tree: *Acer palmatum.* ACERACEAE.
Common name: Japanese Maple.
Description: Many varieties and cultivars of graceful, slow-growing, open, deciduous shrubby trees, to 50 ft. (15 m) tall, with smooth, light green, red, round or oval, toothed, deeply cut leaves, to 4 in. (10 cm) long, tinged red in spring and turning scarlet or yellow in autumn. Beautiful branching habit. Common cultivars include *A. palmatum* 'Atro-purpureum,' 'Bloodgood', 'Dissectum', 'Garnet', 'Ornatum', and 'Red Dragon.'
Blooms/Seed: Many tiny, yellow green, red, purple, variegated flowers in early spring, borne in dangling clusters, form typical 2-winged seed in autumn.
Plant hardiness: Zones 5–10.
Soil: Moist, well-drained soil. Fertility: Rich–average. 5.5–7.0 pH.
Planting: Full sun to partial shade. Space according to desired effect.
Care: Moderate. Keep evenly damp. Fertilize in spring and autumn. Mulch. Prune sparingly in autumn. Protect from sun, wind. Propagate by cuttings, layering, seed.
Features: Good choice for accents, shrub borders, containers, walls in cottage, small-space, woodland gardens. Subject to leaf-fringe drying. Chlorosis susceptible.

Tree: *Acer platanoides.* ACERACEAE.
Common name: Norway Maple.
Description: Many cultivars of fast- to medium-growing, round-crowned, dense, deciduous trees, 70–90 ft. (21–27 m) tall, with smooth, deep green, purple, oval to round, toothed, 5-lobed leaves, to 6 in. (15 cm) wide, turning yellow in autumn. Cultivars include *A. platanoides* 'Cleveland II', with compact form; 'Crimson King' and 'Royal Red', with deep red to purple leaves; and 'Variegatum', with white-fringed leaves.
Blooms/Seed: Multiple tiny, yellow green flowers in spring, borne in dangling clusters, form typical reddish brown, 2-winged seed in autumn.
Plant hardiness: Zones 3–9. Best with winter chill.
Soil: Moist, well-drained soil. Fertility: Rich–average. 6.0–7.0 pH.
Planting: Partial shade. Space 20–30 ft. (6–9 m) apart.
Care: Moderate. Keep evenly moist until established; water when soil dries thereafter. Fertilize in spring until established. Prune in autumn. Propagate by cuttings, layering, seed.
Features: Good choice for accents, allées, screens, specimens in open, woodland gardens and lawns. Drops flowers, seed, requiring maintenance. Invasive. Shallow rooted. Smog tolerant. Pest and disease resistant. Chlorosis susceptible.

Tree: *Acer rubrum.* ACERACEAE.

Common name: Red Maple (Scarlet Maple, Swamp Maple).

Description: Many cultivars of fast- to medium-growing, upright, round-crowned, dense, deciduous trees, to 120 ft. (37 m) tall, with shiny, deep green, oval to round, deeply toothed, 3–5-lobed leaves, to 6 in. (15 cm) wide, with pale green undersides, turning bright red in autumn, and with red turning brown, smooth bark. Common cultivars include *A. rubrum* 'Autumn Blaze', 'Columnare', 'Northwood', 'Shade King', and 'V. J. Drake'.

Blooms/Seed: Many showy, red, yellow flowers, borne in dangling clusters, to 1 in. (25 mm) long, in early spring before leaves emerge, form showy, red, 2-winged seed in late spring.

Plant hardiness: Zones 2–9. Best with winter chill.

Soil: Moist, well-drained soil. Fertility: Rich–average. 6.0–7.0 pH.

Planting: Full to filtered sun. Space 15–20 ft. (4.5–6 m) apart.

Care: Moderate. Keep evenly damp. Fertilize annually in spring until established. Prune sparingly in autumn. Propagate by cuttings, layering, seed.

Features: Good choice for accents, allées, borders, screens in woodland gardens, lawns, roadside plantings. Shallow rooted. Pest and disease resistant. Smog susceptible.

Tree: *Acer saccharinum.* ACERACEAE.

Common name: Silver Maple (Soft Maple, White Maple).

Description: Many cultivars of fast-growing, upright, spreading, open, deciduous trees, 90–120 ft. (27–37 m) tall, with shiny, deep green, round, deeply toothed, 5-lobed leaves, to 6 in. (15 cm) wide, with silver white undersides, turning orange, red, yellow in autumn, and with silver gray, flaking bark. Common cultivars include *A. saccharinum* 'Laciniatum', 'Lutescens', 'Pendulum', 'Pyramidale', and 'Silver Queen'.

Blooms/Seed: Many pinkish green flowers, borne in dangling clusters, to ½ in. (12 mm) long, in early spring before leaves emerge, form showy, red, 2-winged seed in late spring.

Plant hardiness: Zones 2–9. Best with winter chill.

Soil: Moist, well-drained soil. Fertility: Rich–average. 5.5–7.0 pH.

Planting: Full to filtered sun. Space 15–20 ft. (4.5–6 m) apart.

Care: Moderate. Keep evenly damp. Fertilize annually in spring until established. Prune sparingly in autumn. Propagate by cuttings, layering, seed.

Features: Good choice for accents, allées, borders, screens in woodland gardens, lawns, roadside plantings. Weak-crotched branches are susceptible to breakage. Shallow rooted. Invasive. Aphid, scale and chlorosis, smog susceptible.

Tree: *Acer tataricum* var. *ginnala.* ACERACEAE.

Common name: Amur Maple (Tatarian Maple).

Description: Several varieties and cultivars of medium-growing, round-crowned, dense, deciduous trees, to 30 ft. (9 m) tall and wide, with shiny, green, elongated, toothed, 3-lobed leaves, to 3½ in. (90 mm) long, turning yellow, then scarlet in autumn. Dwarf cultivars available. Other *A. tataricum* species are closely related, with similar care needs.

Blooms/Seed: Many tiny, yellow green flowers in early spring, borne in dangling clusters, to 2 in. (50 mm) long, form typical red, 2-winged seed in summer.

Plant hardiness: Zones 2–9.

Soil: Moist, well-drained soil. Fertility: Rich–average. 6.5–7.5 pH.

Planting: Full sun to partial shade. Space 15–20 ft. (4.5–6 m) apart.

Care: Moderate. Keep evenly damp. Fertilize annually in spring until established. Prune sparingly in autumn. Protect from sun, wind. Propagate by cuttings, layering, seed.

Features: Good choice for accents, shrub borders, containers in small-space, woodland gardens and lawns. Pest and disease resistant.

Tree: *Aesculus* species. HIPPOCASTANACEAE.
Common name: Horse Chestnut (Buckeye).
Description: About 13 species of medium-growing, upright, round-crowned, deciduous shrubs or trees, 15–100 ft. (4.5–30 m) tall, depending on species, with light to deep green, textured, pointed, toothed leaves, divided into 5- or 7-lobed fanlike leaflets, 8–12 in. (20–30 cm) long, on long leafstalks.
Blooms/Fruit: Abundant, fragrant, spikelike pink, red, white, yellow flowers, to 14 in. (36 cm) long, in spring, form ball-like, leathery fruit, to 3 in. (75 mm) wide, enclosing smooth seed and persisting into winter.
Plant hardiness: Zones 3–9, depending on species.
Soil: Damp, well-drained soil. Fertility: Rich–average. 6.5–7.5 pH.
Planting: Full sun. Space as recommended for species.
Care: Easy–moderate. Allow soil surface to dry between waterings until established. Fertilize and prune sparingly. Protect from sun in hot climates. Propagate by budding, grafting, layering, seed.
Features: Good choice for accents, shade in open landscapes, lawn. Flowers attract hummingbirds. Drops flowers, fruit, leaves, requiring maintenance. Invasive. Shallow rooted. Spider mite susceptible.

Tree: *Albizia julibrissin.* FABACEAE (LEGUMINOSAE).
Common Name: Silk Tree (Albizia, Albizzia, Mimosa Tree, Strawberry Tree).
Description: Several cultivars of fast-growing, spreading, deciduous or semi-evergreen trees, 20–40 ft. (6–12 m) tall, 15–30 ft. (4.5–9 m) wide, with fine-textured, deep green, yellow green, feathery, divided leaves, 9–12 in. (23–30 cm) long, and often multitrunked. Cultivated species include *A. distachya,* plume albizia; *A. julibrissin,* silk tree; and *A. lebbeck,* woman's-tongue tree.
Blooms/Fruit: Showy, yellow green, pink, white, plume- or tassle-like flowers, in late summer, borne in ball- or cone-shaped clusters, 1–2 in. (25–50 mm) wide, form beanlike pods with seed in winter.
Plant hardiness: Zones 7–10. Tender. Best in mild-winter, warm-summer climates.
Soil: Damp to dry, well-drained, sandy soil. Fertility: Average–low. 6.5–8.0 pH.
Planting: Full sun to partial shade. Space 5–10 ft. (1.5–3 m) apart, depending on species.
Care: Easy. Keep damp until established; drought tolerant thereafter. Avoid fertilizing. Pinch growth sprouts on trunk to prevent bushiness. Propagate by seed.
Features: Good choice for accents, screens, walls in arid, natural, seaside, small-space gardens and patios. Good for color. Flowers and seedpods attract bees, birds. Drops flowers, leaves, seedpods, requiring maintenance. Pest and disease resistant.

Tree: *Alnus* species. BETULACEAE.
Common name: Alder.
Description: About 30 species of fast-growing, upright, open, deciduous trees, usually 60–80 ft. (18–24 m) tall, with shiny, deep green, heart-shaped or oval, finely toothed leaves, to 4 in. (10 cm) long, turning yellow in autumn. Cultivated species include *A. cordata,* Italian alder; *A. crispa,* American green alder; *A. glutinosa,* black alder; and *A. rhombifolia,* white alder. Dwarf species available.
Catkins/Cones: Willowlike catkins, to 3 in. (75 mm) long, in spring before leaves emerge, with brown, clustered cones, ½–1 in. (12–25 mm) long in autumn.
Plant hardiness: Zones 4–10, depending on species.
Soil: Moist, well-drained soil. Fertility: Average. 5.5–6.5 pH.
Planting: Full sun to full shade. Space 15–20 ft. (4.5–6 m) apart. Transplant in spring.
Care: Easy. Keep soil evenly moist. Prune to thin. Propagate by cuttings, seed.
Features: Good choice for margins, moist areas, understory in landscapes and water features. Very invasive. Shallow rooted. Borer, tent caterpillar, leaf miner and fungal disease susceptible.

Tree: *Amelanchier* species. ROSACEAE.

Common name: Serviceberry (Juneberry, Shadblow).

Description: About 25 species of medium-growing, upright, round-crowned, open, deciduous shrubby trees, 20–40 ft. (6–12 m) tall, depending on species, often with multiple trunks, and with shiny, deep green, oval, pointed, toothed leaves, to 3 in. (75 mm) long, turning orange, yellow in autumn, and with silver gray, white bark.

Blooms/Fruit: Many ribbonlike, white flowers, to 2 in. (50 mm) long, borne in clusters in spring as leaves emerge, form edible, deep blue, berrylike fruit, to ⅓ in. (8 mm) wide, in summer.

Plant hardiness: Zones 1–8, depending on species. Best with winter chill.

Soil: Moist, well-drained soil. Fertility: Rich–average. 6.0–7.0 pH.

Planting: Full sun. Space 8–15 ft. (2.4–4.5 m) apart.

Care: Moderate. Keep evenly moist. Fertilize annually in spring until established. Prune in autumn; remove suckers to maintain treelike appearance. Propagate by seed, suckers.

Features: Good choice for accents, containers, margins, paths, screens in cottage, small-space, woodland gardens and water features. Fruit attracts birds. Drops flowers, fruit, requiring maintenance. Lacewing, spider mite, scale and fireblight susceptible.

Tree: *Araucaria heterophylla (A. excelsa).* ARAUCARIACEAE.

Common name: Norfolk Island Pine.

Description: Single cultivar of medium-growing, conical, erect, open and branching, coniferous, evergreen trees, to 200 ft. (61 m) tall, 60 ft. (18 m) wide, with shiny, deep green, awl-shaped becoming narrow and lance-shaped, overlapping leaves, 1½–2 in. (38–50 mm) long, on broad, symmetrical, radiating branches. *A. araucana,* monkey-puzzle tree, is a closely related species with similar care needs.

Cones/Seed: Female cones are green, brown, oval-shaped, 3–6 in. (75–150 mm) long, with woody scales, each bearing a single, winged seed. Male cones are narrow and oval, 1½–2 in. (38–50 mm) long.

Plant hardiness: Zones 7–11. Semi-hardy. Best in subtropical climates.

Soil: Moist to dry, well-drained soil. Fertility: Rich–average. 6.5–7.5 pH.

Planting: Full sun. Space 25–40 ft. (7.5–12 m) apart.

Care: Easy. Keep moist until established. Fertilize annually. Avoid pruning. Propagate by cuttings.

Features: Good choice for accents, containers, screens, walls in seaside, small-space, turfgrass gardens and patios. Good for holiday decoration. Drops cones, requiring maintenance. Pest and disease resistant.

Tree: *Arbutus unedo.* ERICACEAE.

Common name: Strawberry Tree.

Description: Several cultivars of medium-growing, spreading, round, broad-leaved, evergreen trees, to 30 ft. (9 m) tall and wide, with shiny, deep green, oval, pointed, toothed leaves, to 2 in. (50 mm) long, with matte undersides. Deep red, brown, exfoliating bark.

Blooms/Fruit: Many tiny, pink, white flowers, ¼–½ in. (6–12 mm) long, borne in dangling clusters in autumn–winter, form edible, red, yellow, mealy, berrylike fruit, to ¾ in. (19 mm) wide, in winter.

Plant hardiness: Zones 7–10. Semi-hardy. Best in mild-winter, hot-summer climates.

Soil: Moist to dry, well-drained soil. Fertility: Average–low. 6.5–8.0 pH.

Planting: Full sun to partial shade. Space 12–15 ft. (3.7–4.5 m) apart.

Care: Easy. Keep damp; allow soil to dry between waterings. Drought tolerant when established. Avoid fertilizing. Prune to thin or shape. Propagate by buds, cuttings, layers, seed.

Features: Good choice for accents, containers, screens in arid, seaside, turfgrass gardens. Drops bark, cones, flowers, requiring maintenance. Pest and disease resistant.

BETULA (BIRCH)

The *Betula* genus includes nearly 60 species of graceful, open, broad-leaved, deciduous trees, many with narrow, erect habits and often thin, nodding or weeping branches. They are native to the northern hemisphere's temperate zones and are found throughout North America, Europe, and Asia. All are hardy and grow best in cold-winter climates.

Birches are prized for their dainty foliage and showy bark. Their leaves emerge bronze, light green, or maroon, become deep green above and silver gray beneath, and turn golden yellow in autumn. Marked and patterned, birch bark is attractively colored in hues from reddish brown to icy silver. Cultivars have been developed with dramatic foliage colors.

Birches are fast-growing, short-lived trees that reach 25–90 ft. (7.5–27 m) tall. A species or cultivar exists for nearly every garden need throughout their climate range.

They are susceptible to birch leaf miner, a pest that causes leaves to turn yellow and prematurely drop, as well as aphid, borers, sawfly, and gypsy moth. Nectaria canker can infect their bark.

Choose from among the popularly cultivated species above, at right.

Birches are popular in landscape gardens as ornamental trees that rapidly fill small-space areas, create island plantings in a turfgrass lawn, or provide a seasonal screen. They are broad-leaved, deciduous, and appear constantly in motion due to their long-stemmed leaves which wave and quiver in any breeze. Birches grow in a variety of forms, from those with single, narrow trunks to multi-trunked, nearly vining species that retain a shrublike character. They are good trees for coppicing in natural landscapes along streams.

Plant birches in moderately rich, moist, well-drained soil that is slightly acidic. Since all landscape trees grow best when planted in unamended soil, test the acid-alkaline balance of your site before you plant. Birches should have soils in the 6.0–7.0 pH range. Choose from those species that fit your climate and site.

When planting a birch, carefully match the depth of the hole to the soil line on the rootball of your tree, taking care to avoid too-deep planting. Backfill around the rootball with native soil and keep the tree well watered until it becomes established and begins to spurt new growth.

Birches are a good choice for seasonal shade and bright autumn foliage color in cold-winter climates, though many species perform well in a variety of conditions. Their care needs include regular raking of fallen catkinlike flowers in spring and leaves in autumn. Birds find their seed attractive during winter.

Small birches are good container trees suited to use on balconies, decks, and patios. Keep birches grown in planters or large containers evenly moist, fertilize them regularly to replace leached nutrients, and protect their roots from sun exposure.

Birch Species and Varieties:
B. albo-sinensis, Chinese paper birch
B. alleghaniensis, yellow birch
B. davurica, Dahurian birch
B. jacquemontii, Indian birch
B. lenta, sweet birch
B. maximowicziana, monarch birch
B. nana, dwarf arctic birch
B. nigra, river birch
B. occidentalis, water birch
B. papyrifera, canoe birch
B. pendula, European birch
B. platyphylla japonica, Japanese birch
B. platyphylla szechuanica, Chinese birch
B. populifolia, gray birch

Tree: *Betula alleghaniensis.* BETULACEAE.

Common name: Yellow Birch (Gray Birch).

Description: Several cultivars of graceful, fast-growing, short-lived, upright, deciduous trees, to 90 ft. (27 m) tall, with matte, light green, oval, pointed, finely toothed, veined leaves, to 5 in. (13 cm) long, with gray green undersides, turning yellow in autumn. Patterned, red brown, gray, silver gray, yellow bark peels in narrow, thin strips.

Catkins/Cones: Insignificant green flowers in spring, borne in catkins, to 2 in. (50 mm) long, form oval cones containing seed, to 1 in. (25 mm) long, in late summer, persisting to winter.

Plant hardiness: Zones 4–7. Hardy.

Soil: Moist, well-drained soil. Fertility: Rich–average. 6.0–7.0 pH.

Planting: Full sun. Space 10–15 ft. (3–4.5 m) apart.

Care: Easy. Keep evenly moist. Fertilize annually in spring. Prune sparingly in late spring. Propagate by cuttings, layering, seed.

Features: Good choice for accents, borders in cottage, meadow, woodland gardens. Seed attracts birds in winter. Borer, leaf miner susceptible.

Tree: *Betula nigra.* BETULACEAE.
Common name: River Birch (Black Birch, Red Birch).
Description: Many cultivars of graceful, fast-growing, upright, open, deciduous trees, to 100 ft. (30 m) tall, with light green, oval or diamond-shaped, toothed leaves, to 3 in. (75 mm) long, with white undersides, turning gold in autumn, and with red, white, flaking, paperlike bark. *B. nigra* 'Heritage', Heritage River birch, is a popular cultivar with pink-tinted bark.
Catkins/Cones: Willowlike male and female catkins, to 1½ in. (38 mm) long, in autumn, form brown cones on female trees, to 1 in. (25 mm) long, the following summer.
Plant hardiness: Zones 4–7.
Soil: Moist, well-drained, sandy soil. Fertility: Rich–average. 5.5–6.5 pH.
Planting: Full to filtered sun. Space 20–25 ft. (6–7.5 m) apart.
Care: Easy. Keep moist. Prune in late spring. Propagate by cuttings, layering, seed.
Features: Good choice for margins, moist areas in landscapes and water features. Tolerates occasional drought. Seed attracts birds in winter. Somewhat invasive. Shallow rooted. Aphid, birch leaf miner susceptible.

Tree: *Betula papyrifera.* BETULACEAE.
Common name: Canoe Birch (Paper Birch, White Birch).
Description: Over 10 cultivars of graceful, fast-growing, short-lived, upright, deciduous trees, to 100 ft. (30 m) tall with matte, light green, oval, pointed, finely toothed leaves, to 4 in. (10 cm) long, turning yellow in autumn. Patterned gray and silver bark peels in paperlike strips. Sometimes multitrunked.
Catkins/Cones: Insignificant green flowers borne in catkins in spring, to 4 in. (10 cm) long, form scaly seed clusters, to 2 in. (50 mm) long, in late summer, persisting to winter.
Plant hardiness: Zones 2–9. Hardy.
Soil: Moist, well-drained soil. Fertility: Rich–average. 6.0–7.0 pH.
Planting: Full sun. Space 10–15 ft. (3–4.5 m) apart.
Care: Easy. Keep evenly moist; some cultivars are drought tolerant. Fertilize annually in spring. Prune sparingly in late spring. Propagate by cuttings, layering, seed.
Features: Good choice for accents, borders in cottage, meadow, woodland gardens. Seed attracts birds in winter. Borer, leaf miner susceptible.

Tree: *Betula pendula.* BETULACEAE.
Common name: Weeping Birch (European White Birch).
Description: Several cultivars of graceful, fast-growing, pyramid-shaped, open, deciduous trees, to 60 ft. (18 m) tall, with green, oval or diamond-shaped, toothed, veined leaves, to 2½ in. (63 mm) long, turning gold in autumn, and with white, flaking bark. Common cultivars include *B. pendula* 'Dalecarlica', with nodding or weeping branches; 'Fastigata', with upright, columnar form; 'Purpurea', with purple becoming bronze green leaves; 'Whitespire', a borer-resistant variety; and 'Youngii', Young's weeping birch, a graceful, pendulous tree. Single and multi-trunked cultivars available.
Catkins/Cones: Willowlike male and female catkins, to 2 in. (50 mm) long, in winter, with brown cones to 1 in. (25 mm) long, on female trees, in autumn.
Plant hardiness: Zones 3–7.
Soil: Moist, well-drained humus. Fertility: Rich–average. 5.5–6.5 pH.
Planting: Full to filtered sun. Space 12–15 ft. (3.7–4.5 m) apart.
Care: Easy. Keep moist. Prune in late spring. Propagate by cuttings, seed.
Features: Good choice for accents, borders, containers, paths, planters, screens in cottage, natural, small-space, woodland gardens and water feature shorelines. Good for coppicing. Seed attracts birds in winter. Tolerates occasional drought. Shallow rooted. Aphid, birch leaf miner susceptible.

Tree: *Callistemon* species. MYRTACEAE.
Common name: Bottlebrush.
Description: About 20 species of fast-growing, arching, erect, or spreading, dense or open, broad-leaved, evergreen shrubs or small trees, 20–30 ft. (6–9 m) tall and to 15 ft. (4.5 m) wide, with shiny, bronze becoming bright green, lance-shaped, folded leaves, 2–6 in. (50–150 mm) long. Commonly cultivated species include *C. citrinus,* crimson bottlebrush; *C. salignus,* white bottlebrush; and *C. viminalis,* weeping bottlebrush.
Blooms/Fruit: Showy brushlike, cream, pink, red, white, upright or nodding, columnar, hairy flowers, 2–6 in. (50–150 mm) long, in spring–summer, form woody, brown, nutlike fruit, to ¾ in. (19 mm) wide, filled with seed, in autumn.
Plant hardiness: Zones 7–11. Tender. Best in mild-winter, hot-summer climates.
Soil: Moist to dry, well-drained, sandy soil. Fertility: Average–low. 7.0–8.0 pH.
Planting: Full sun. Space 5–7 ft. (1.5–2.2 m) apart.
Care: Easy. Keep moist; allow soil to dry between waterings. Drought tolerant. Avoid fertilizing. Prune to espalier or promote treelike growth. Stake to support. Propagate by cuttings, seed.
Features: Good choice for accents, containers, hedges, screens in arid, seaside gardens. Attracts bees, hummingbirds. Drops flowers, pollen, requiring maintenance. Pest and disease resistant. Chlorosis susceptible.

Tree: *Carpinus caroliniana.* BETULACEAE.
Common name: American Hornbeam (Blue Beech).
Description: A few cultivars of medium- to slow-growing, upright, round-crowned, open, deciduous trees, to 40 ft. (12 m) tall, often with multiple trunks, with deep green, oval, pointed, sharp-toothed, veined leaves, to 4 in. (10 cm) long, turning deep red in autumn, and with smooth, gray bark.
Catkins/Nuts: Willowlike catkins, to 4 in. (10 cm) long, in spring, form brown, 3-lobed nuts with leafy bracts, in clusters to 5 in. (13 cm) long, in summer.

Plant hardiness: Zones 3–9. Choose *C. caroliniana* var. *virginiana,* zones 3–5.
Soil: Moist, well-drained soil. Fertility: Average. 6.0–7.0 pH.
Planting: Full sun to full shade. Space 15–20 ft. (4.5–6 m) apart.
Care: Easy. Keep moist. Fertilize and prune sparingly. Protect from sun, wind in hot climates. Propagate by grafting, seed.
Features: Good choice for accents, paths, screens in landscapes, lawns, roadside plantings. Good for seasonal shade. Disease resistant. Scale susceptible.

Tree: *Catalpa bignonioides.* BIGNONIACEAE.
Common name: Common Catalpa (Catawba, Indian Bean).
Description: Several cultivars of fast-growing, short-lived, round, deciduous trees, to 60 ft. (18 m) tall and wide, with opposite, smooth, light green, heart-shaped or oval, broadly pointed, whorled, acridly fragrant leaves, 4–12 in. (10–30 cm) long.
Blooms/Fruit: Showy, white, flared, deep-throated flowers, to 2 in. (50 mm) long, with yellow stripes and brown spots, in spring–summer, form beanpodlike fruit, to 10 in. (25 cm) long, in late summer.
Plant hardiness: Zones 4–10. Hardy.
Soil: Moist to dry, well-drained soil. Fertility: Average. 5.5–7.0 pH.
Planting: Full or filtered sun. Space 8–12 ft. (2.4–3.7 m) apart.
Care: Easy. Keep moist until established; drought tolerant thereafter. Fertilize annually in spring. Prune to promote treelike form, remove low branches in autumn. Propagate by cuttings, layering, seed.
Features: Good choice for accents, screens, shade in turfgrass, woodland gardens. Good for tropical effects. Oak leaf fungus resistant. Mealybug, midge, catalpa sphinx moth and chlorosis susceptible.

Tree: *Cedrus* species. PINACEAE.

Common name: True Cedar.

Description: About 4 species of medium-growing, long-lived, sometimes spreading or drooping, pyramid-shaped, open, coniferous, evergreen trees, 100–150 ft. (30–45 m) tall, with deep blue green or green, stiff, clustered needles, 1–2 in. (25–50 mm) long. Species include *C. atlantica*, Atlas cedar; *C. brevifolia*, Cyprus cedar; *C. deodara*, deodar cedar; and *C. libani*, cedar-of-Lebanon. Dwarf, pendulous cultivars available

Cones/Seed: Male cones are egg-shaped, 3–5 in. (75–125 mm) long; female cones are small and pointed with woody scales and winged seed.

Plant hardiness: Zones 7–10. Best in areas with limited winter snow.

Soil: Damp to dry, well-drained soil. Fertility: Rich–average. 5.5–6.5 pH.

Planting: Full to filtered sun. Space 10–15 ft. (3–4.5 m) apart.

Care: Easy. Allow soil surface to dry between waterings until established. Prune in spring. Protect from snow in cold-winter climates. Propagate by cuttings, seed.

Features: Good choice for accents, screens, specimen in formal, woodland gardens. Male catkins release staining, allergen-bearing pollen in spring. Smog tolerant. Drought tolerant when established. Pest and disease resistant.

Tree: *Celtis* species. ULMACEAE.

Common name: Hackberry (Nettle Tree, Sugarberry).

Description: About 70 species of fast- to medium-growing, upright, round-crowned, deciduous trees, 70–120 ft. (21–37 m) tall, with elmlike, green, textured, droplet-shaped, pointed, sharp-toothed leaves, 3–6 in. (75–150 mm) long, turning yellow in autumn, and with corklike, textured, cinnamon-colored bark.

Blooms/Fruit: Inconspicuous flowers form many edible, round, orange purple, red, fruit, to ¼ in. (6 mm) wide, in summer.

Plant hardiness: Zones 6–8. Choose *C. occidentalis*, zones 3–8. Best with winter chill.

Soil: Moist to dry, sandy to clayey soil. Fertility: Average–low. 6.0–8.0 pH.

Planting: Full sun. Space large species 15–20 ft. (4.5–6 m) apart, small species and dwarf cultivars 10 ft. (3 m) apart.

Care: Easy. Keep damp until established. Drought tolerant. Avoid fertilizing and pruning. Stake until established. Propagate by cuttings, grafting, layering, seed.

Features: Good choice for allées, edgings, screens in natural, open, prairie gardens and roadside plantings. Good for seasonal shade. Fruit attracts birds. Very deep rooted. Wind tolerant. PSYLLIDAE, or harmless leaf gall, may disfigure foliage.

Tree: *Cercidiphyllum japonicum.* CERCIDIPHYLLACEAE.

Common name: Katsura Tree.

Description: Several cultivars of graceful, medium- to slow-growing, upright and branching becoming open and layered, deciduous trees, usually to 50 ft. (15 m) tall and with multiple trunks, with shiny, bronze purple turning blue green, round or heart-shaped, pointed, finely toothed, veined leaves, to 4 in. (10 cm) long, turning red, yellow in autumn.

Blooms/Seed: Many brushlike, red flowers, to ¾ in. (19 mm) long, in early spring before leaves emerge, form beanlike pods containing many seed.

Plant hardiness: Zones 4–8. Best with winter chill.

Soil: Moist, well-drained soil. Fertility: Rich–average. 6.5–7.0 pH.

Planting: Full to filtered sun. Space 20–30 ft. (6–9 m) apart.

Care: Easy. Keep evenly moist; reduce watering in late summer. Fertilize until established. Prune sparingly. Protect from sun, wind in hot climates. Propagate by cuttings, layering, seed.

Features: Good choice for accents, containers in Asian, small-space gardens and landscapes. Good for seasonal foliage color and shade. Pest and disease resistant.

Tree: *Cercis canadensis.* FABACEAE (LEGUMINOSAE).
Common name: Eastern Redbud.
Description: Several cultivars of fast-growing, spreading, deciduous trees, to 40 ft. (12 m) tall, with glossy, bronze to purple, heart-shaped leaves, to 4 in. (10 cm) long, turning yellow in autumn. *C. chinensis,* Chinese redbud; *C. occidentalis,* western redbud; and *C. siliquastrum,* Judas tree, are closely related species with similar care needs.
Blooms/Fruit: Many rose pink, purple, white flowers, ½ in. (12 mm) wide, borne in clusters in early spring, form pealike, clustered fruit, to 3½ in. (90 mm) long, in late spring. First blooms 4–5 years after planting.
Plant hardiness: Zones 5–9. Best in cold-winter climates.
Soil: Moist, well-drained soil. Fertility: Rich. 6.5–7.5 pH.
Planting: Open to partial shade. Space 20 ft. (6 m) apart.
Care: Easy. Allow soil surface to dry between waterings until established. Fertilize every 2 months spring–autumn. Mulch. Prune in autumn. Protect from sun in hot climates. Propagate by cuttings, layering, seed.
Features: Good choice for backgrounds in cottage, woodland gardens. Good companion for dogwood. Disease resistant.

Tree: *Chamaecyparis* species. CUPRESSACEAE.
Common name: False Cypress.
Description: Eight species of slow-growing, upright, pyramid-shaped, dense, coniferous, evergreen trees, 20–100 ft. (6–30 m) tall, depending on species, with blue, green, yellow, variegated, needle- or scalelike foliage, in spreading sprays, and matted, red brown bark. Commonly cultivated species include *C. lawsoniana,* Port Orford cedar; *C. nootkatensis,* Nootka cypress; *C. obtusa,* Hinoki false cypress; *C. pisifera,* Sawara false cypress; and *C. thyoides,* white cedar.
Cones/Seed: Male cones are pink, red, yellow, egg-shaped, ¾ in. (19 mm) long; female cones are woody, ⅜ in. (10 mm) long, with scales and winged seed.
Plant hardiness: Zones 5–9, depending on species.
Soil: Damp, well-drained soil. Fertility: Average. 5.5–6.5 pH.
Planting: Full sun. Space 10–20 ft. (3–6 m) apart, depending on species.
Care: Easy. Allow soil surface to dry between waterings until established. Fertilize annually in spring until established. Protect from wind. Propagate by seed.

Features: Good choice for accents, allées, containers, hedges, screens in lawns, woodland gardens. Drops leaves, requiring maintenance. Spider mite susceptible.

Tree: *Chamaerops humilis.* ARECACEAE (PALMAE).
Common name: Mediterranean Fan Palm.
Description: Several cultivars of slow-growing, round-headed, evergreen palms, to 10–20 ft. (3–6 m) tall and wide, with shiny, fanlike, radiating, blue green, stiff leaves, 2–3 ft. (60–90 cm) wide, on woody stalks armed with sharp spines. Develops offsets. Common cultivars include *C. humilis* 'Canariensis' and 'Robusta'.
Blooms/Fruit: Inconspicuous to small white flowers, in spring–summer, form fleshy, round, datelike fruit in autumn–winter, varying in size.
Plant hardiness: Zones 6–11. Hardy.
Soil: Moist to dry, well-drained soil. Fertility: Average–low. 6.5–8.0 pH.
Planting: Full sun to partial shade. Space 8–12 ft. (2.4–3.7 m) apart.
Care: Easy. Keep damp until established; drought tolerant thereafter. Avoid fertilizing to slow growth. Prune to remove dried leafstalks at trunk. Heat, wind tolerant. Propagate by seed, suckers.
Features: Good choice for accents, barriers, containers, fencelines, groups, screens in arid, seaside, turfgrass gardens. Good for desert, tropical effects. Pest and disease resistant.

Tree: *Chilopsis linearis.* BIGNONIACEAE.
Common name: Desert Willow (Desert Catalpa).
Description: Many cultivars of fast-growing, open, shrubby, semi-evergreen trees, to 15–25 ft. (4.5–7.5 m) tall and wide, with willowlike, green, fine-textured, narrow leaves, to 1 ft. (30 cm) long. Smooth gray bark becoming rough, on twisted, branching trunks. Common cultivars include *C. linearis* 'Burgundy', 'Hope', and 'Regal'.
Blooms/Seed: Showy, pink, purple, red, white, or multicolored, catalpa-like, deep-throated flowers, to 2 in. (50 mm) long, in spring and autumn, borne in clusters, form long, narrow, woody, seed-filled pods, to 1 ft. (30 cm) long, in autumn–winter.
Plant hardiness: Zones 6–10. Hardy. Best in arid, hot-summer climates.
Soil: Dry, well-drained, sandy soil. Fertility: Average–low. 6.0–7.5 pH.
Planting: Full sun. Space 7–10 ft. (2.2–3 m) apart.
Care: Moderate. Keep damp until established; drought tolerant thereafter. Avoid fertilizing. Prune to shape, promote treelike form. Remove seedpods. Heat, wind tolerant. Propagate by cuttings, seed.
Features: Good choice for accents, backgrounds, hedges, screens in arid gardens. Good for sculpted foliage, form. Attracts hummingbirds. Drops flowers, leaves, seedpods, requiring maintenance. Pest and disease resistant.

Tree: *Chionanthus virginicus.* OLEACEAE.
Common name: Fringe Tree (Old-Man's-Beard).
Description: Several cultivars of slow-growing, wide and spreading, dense, branching, deciduous shrubby trees, to 30 ft. (9 m) tall and wide, with deep green, textured, lance-shaped, broad, folded, pointed leaves, to 8 in. (20 cm) long, turning yellow in autumn, and with brown, tan bark. Late leafing in spring. *C. retusus,* Chinese fringe tree, is a related species with similar care needs.
Blooms/Fruit: Many feathery, cream, white flowers, to 1 in. (25 mm) wide, in early summer, borne in dangling, lacy clusters, to 8 in. (20 cm) long, form oval, blue, purple, mealy fruit in autumn, to ⅝ in. (16 mm) long, in clusters.
Plant hardiness: Zones 4–9. Best with winter chill.
Soil: Damp, well-drained soil. Fertility: Rich–average. 6.0–7.0 pH.
Planting: Full sun. Space 15–20 ft. (4.5–6 m) apart.
Care: Easy. Allow soil surface to dry between waterings until established. Fertilize annually in spring until established. Avoid pruning. Propagate by cuttings, grafting, layering, seed.

Features: Good choice for accents, backgrounds, containers, edgings, paths, walls in cottage, small-space gardens. Fruit attracts birds. Drops staining fruit, requiring maintenance. Smog tolerant. Disease resistant. Scale susceptible.

Tree: *Cinnamomum camphora.* LAURACEAE.
Common name: Camphor tree.
Description: Slow-growing, upright, spreading, dense, broad-leaved, evergreen tree, 50–70 ft. (15–21 m) tall and wide though usually smaller, with bronze or pink turning light green, paddle-shaped, pointed, fragrant leaves, to 5 in. (13 cm) long. Leaves simultaneously drop and are replaced in spring.
Blooms/Fruit: Inconspicuous, very fragrant, yellow flowers in spring, form round, black fruit in summer.
Plant hardiness: Zones 9–11.
Soil: Well-drained, sandy soil. Fertility: Average. 6.5–7.5 pH.
Planting: Full sun. Space 10–15 ft. (3–4.5 m) apart.
Care: Moderate. Allow soil surface to dry between waterings until established. Prune sparingly. Propagate by cuttings, seed.
Features: Good choice for edgings, lawns in open landscapes. Source of camphor oil. Drops flowers, fruit, leaves, twigs, requiring maintenance. Shallow rooted; avoid planting near pavement. Salt burn, verticillium wilt susceptible.

CITRUS AND FORTUNELLA

Sixteen species of small or midsized, round-crowned, broad-leaved, evergreen trees are included in the *Citrus* genus and its close relative, *Fortunella*. They are native to Southeast Asia but have become naturalized in other regions. They are tender and do best in mild-winter climates with hot, dry summers.

Calamondin, citron, grapefruit, kumquat, sweet and sour lemon, lime, loquat, mandarin, blood orange, both sweet and sour orange, pomelo, tangor, tangelo, and tangerine make up the many citrus. In addition, many cross-hybrid forms exist.

Citrus are slow-growing, long-lived, compact trees that range in size from 6 ft. (1.8 m) tall for dwarf varieties to 30 ft. (9 m) or more for full-sized cultivars. They flower year-round and set fruit that mostly ripens in autumn or early winter.

They are susceptible to many pests and diseases, which affect their flowers, foliage, and fruit, and to manganese, iron, and zinc deficiencies.

Choose from the species, at right.

Citrus and kumquats are upright or shrublike, broad-leaved evergreens that make great landscape trees with a bonus of tasty fruit. When mature, they have single trunks with a round crown filled with clusters of white, star-shaped, very fragrant flowers and colorful fruit. They need sustained high temperatures to set and ripen edible fruit.

Citrus Species:
C. aurantium, sour orange
C. baurantifolia, lime
C. limon, lemon
C. × *limona*, lemandarin
C. maxima, pomelo
C. medica, citron
C. × *nobilis*, tangor
C. × *paradisi*, grapefruit
C. reticulata, Mandarin orange
C. sinensis, sweet orange
C. tachibana, Tachibana orange
C. × *tangelo*, tangelo
Fortunella Species:
F. crassifolia, Meiwa kumquat*F. japonica*, Marumi kumquat
F. naqgami, Spanish kumquat

Plant citrus in moist, well-drained, humus-rich soil that is acidic. Since all trees perform best when they are planted in unamended soil, test the balance of your site prior to planting. Citrus require soils that are in the 6.0–6.5 pH range.

When you plant, note the soil line on your tree's trunk and dig the hole 1–2 in. (25–50 mm) shallower. Citrus do best with good drainage. Backfill around the rootball with native soil, mound soil to make a basin, and give the tree ample water through its first season, watering whenever the soil surface becomes dry.

Citrus provide color and visual interest for those with gardens in mild-winter or subtropical climates. If you garden in a mild-summer climate, use citrus as landscape trees. Caring for them includes feeding every other month with a fertilizer formulated specifically for citrus. Such fertilizers contain buffering agents to increase acidity and trace nutrients needed to avoid chlorosis and other mineral deficiencies. Always water deeply after you apply fertilizer to your citrus or kumquat trees.

Tree: *Citrus* species. RUTACEAE.

Common name: Citrus (Calamondin, Citron, Grapefruit, Kumquat, Lemon, Lime, Mandarin, Orange, Pomelo).

Description: Sixteen species of slow-growing, branching, round-headed, fruiting, evergreen shrubs and trees, to over 30 ft. (9 m) tall, often armed with sharp spines, and with smooth, shiny, deep green, oval, pointed leaves, to 4 in. (10 cm) long. Dwarf cultivars available.

Blooms/Seed: Many very fragrant, pink, purple, white, star-shaped flowers, 1–2 in. (25–50 mm) wide, in spring or year-round, depending on species and cultivar, form edible and inedible segmented, juicy fruit, in late autumn–winter.

Plant hardiness: Zones 8–11. Tender. Best in mild-winter, hot-summer climates. Sweet-fruited citrus require high summer temperatures, mild or warm winters.

Soil: Moist, well-drained humus. Fertility: Rich. 6.0–6.5 pH.

Planting: Full sun. Space full-sized cultivars 8–15 ft. (2.4–4.5 m) apart, dwarf cultivars 3–6 ft. (90–180 cm) apart.

Care: Moderate. Keep moist; allow soil surface to dry between waterings. Reduce waterings in winter. Fertilize every 2 months with acid organic fertilizer containing micronutrients: calcium, iron, manganese, zinc. Pollinate using an artist's brush. Mulch. Avoid pruning, thinning. Pinch blooms and remove fruit to increase vigor, fruit size. Propagate by cuttings, grafting, seed.

Features: Good choice for accents, barriers, containers, hedges, screens in arid, Mediterranean, orchard gardens. Good for fruit. Attracts bees. Aphid, mealybug, spider mite, scale and chlorosis susceptible.

Tree: *Cladrastis kentukea (C. lutea)*. FABACEAE (LEGUMINOSAE).

Common name: Yellowwood.

Description: A few cultivars of slow-growing, upright, round-crowned, open, deciduous trees, to 50 ft. (15 m) tall, with frondlike, yellow turning green leaves, to 1 ft. (30 cm) long, divided into dangling, 1–7-offset, walnutlike, oval leaflets, to 4 in. (10 cm) long, turning yellow in autumn, and with charcoal gray, smooth becoming furrowed bark.

Blooms/Fruit: Many showy, fragrant, wisteria-like, pink, white flowers, to 1 in. (25 mm) long, borne in dangling clusters, to 16 in. (40 cm) long, in early summer on mature trees, form brown, beanlike pods, 4 in. (10 cm) long, containing smooth seed, in autumn.

Plant hardiness: Zones 4–8. Best with winter chill, summer heat.

Soil: Moist, well-drained soil. Fertility: Average–low. 6.5–7.5 pH.

Planting: Full to filtered sun. Space 15–20 ft. (4.5–6 m) apart.

Care: Moderate. Allow soil surface to dry between waterings until established. Prune in summer. Propagate by cuttings, seed.

Features: Good choice for accents, containers in small-space gardens. Pest and disease resistant.

Tree: *Cornus* species. CORNACEAE.

Common name: Flowering Dogwood.

Description: About 45 species of fast-growing, spreading, shrublike deciduous trees, 10–60 ft. (3–18 m) tall, with shiny, bronze becoming deep green, oval leaves, 3–6 in. (75–150 mm) long, turning purple, deep red in autumn. Commonly cultivated species include *C. alba,* Tartarian dogwood; *C. alternifolia,* alternate-leaved dogwood; *C. amomum,* silky dogwood; *C. canadensis,* bunchberry; *C. capitata,* evergreen dogwood; *C. controversa,* giant dogwood; *C. florida,* flowering dogwood; and *C. stolonifera,* red dogwood.

Blooms/Fruit: Profuse, flowerlike, green, pink, white, 4-petaled bracts, 3–4 in. (75–100 mm) wide, in spring, form small, scarlet, berrylike fruit in autumn.

Plant hardiness: Zones 4–10.

Soil: Moist, well-drained soil. Fertility: Rich. 6.0–7.0 pH.

Planting: Full sun to partial shade. Space 20–35 ft. (6–11 m) apart.

Care: Easy. Keep evenly moist. Fertilize in spring. Prune, thin in autumn to shape, control growth. Protect from heat in hot climates. Propagate by budding, cuttings.

Features: Good choice for accents, backgrounds in cottage, natural, woodland gardens. Fruit attracts birds. Borer and anthracnose, smog susceptible.

Tree: *Corylus* species. BETULACEAE.

Common name: Hazelnut (Filbert, Hazel).

Description: About 10 species of slow-growing, spreading, deciduous shrubs or trees, 10–120 ft. (3–37 m) tall, depending on species, with smooth, alderlike, yellow green, fuzzy, oval, pointed, toothed leaves, usually 4–6 in. (10–15 cm) long, turning yellow in autumn. *C. avellana* 'Contorta', Harry Lauder's Walking Stick, has distinctive twisted trunk and limbs.

Blooms/Nuts: Inconspicuous female flowers and long, dangling, willowlike male catkins borne on same tree in spring, form edible nuts in autumn.

Plant hardiness: Zones 5–9. Ground hardy, zones 6–8.

Soil: Damp, well-drained soil. Fertility: Average. 6.0–8.0 pH.

Planting: Full sun to partial shade. Space 8–12 ft. (2.4–3.7 m) apart.

Care: Easy. Allow soil surface to dry between waterings until established. Fertilize quarterly spring–autumn. Remove all suckers. Prune in autumn. Propagate by cuttings, grafting, nuts.

Features: Good choice for accents, backgrounds, edgings, screens in cottage, woodland gardens. Some species regulated to prevent eastern filbert blight.

Tree: *Craetaegus* species. ROSACEAE.

Common name: Hawthorn.

Description: Many species and hybrid cultivars of medium-growing, spreading, thorny, deciduous shrubby trees, 15–35 ft. (4.5–11 m) tall and wide and often with multiple trunks, with shiny, deep green, lobed or toothed leaves, 2–4 in. (50–100 mm) long, turning red, yellow in autumn.

Blooms/Fruit: Many cream, white, flat flower clusters, to ½ in. (12 mm) wide, in spring, form abundant, edible, shiny, red fruit, to ⅓ in. (8 mm) wide, in summer, in showy clusters that persist into winter.

Plant hardiness: Zones 4–9.

Soil: Damp, well-drained soil. Fertility: Average–low. 6.0–7.0 pH.

Planting: Full to filtered sun. Space 10–12 ft. (3–3.7 m) apart.

Care: Moderate. Keep damp until established. Avoid fertilizing. Prune in autumn to remove suckers, twiggy growth. Propagate by grafting, seed.

Features: Good choice for accents, borders, hedges in natural, wildlife gardens. Fruit attracts birds. Aphid, scale and fireblight susceptible.

Tree: *Cycas* species. CYCADACEAE.

Common name: Sago Palm (Bread Palm, Cycad, Funeral Palm).

Description: About 20 species of slow-growing, upright, columnar, round-headed, primitive, palmlike, evergreen cycads, 10–20 ft. (3–6 m) tall. Smooth, shiny, deep green, feathery, stiff, divided, palmlike leaves, to 8 ft. (2.4 m) long, in opposite, lance-shaped leaflets, to 1 ft. (30 cm) long, radiate from a central crown. Horticulturally related to conifers.

Cones/Seed: Dense, upright, conelike fruiting bodies, 4–12 in. (10–30 cm) long, form many cream, white, plumelike, sporophylls, 8–12 in. (20–30 cm) long, on female trees, in branching clusters, in autumn, with round to oval, orange, red, pith-covered, fertile or infertile seed, in winter.

Plant hardiness: Zones 8–11. Tender. Best in subtropical climates.

Soil: Moist, well drained humus. Fertility: Rich. 5.5–7.0 pH.

Planting: Full sun to partial shade. Space 5 ft. (1.5 m) apart.

Care: Easy. Keep evenly moist. Fertilize monthly. Mulch. Deadhead spent leaves by cutting at trunk. Protect from frost. Propagate by seed, suckers.

Features: Good choice for accents, barriers, containers in arid, seaside gardens. Good for bonsai, tropical effects. Pest and disease resistant.

Tree: *Elaeagnus angustifolia.* ELAEAGNACEAE.

Common name: Oleaster (Russian Olive, Silver Berry, Wild Olive).

Description: Several varieties of fast-growing, spreading, often spiny, deciduous small trees, to 20 ft. (6 m) tall, with dull, olivelike, green, oval, pointed leaves, to 2 in. (50 mm) long, with silver undersides, and with brown, flaking bark.

Blooms/Fruit: Fragrant, yellow green, fluted, bell-shaped flowers, to ½ in. (12 mm) long, in early spring, borne in clusters at leaf axils, with olivelike, mealy, red, silver, yellow fruit on short stalks in autumn.

Plant hardiness: Zones 3–8. Hardy.

Soil: Damp, well-drained soil. Fertility: Average–low. 5.5–8.0 pH.

Planting: Full sun to partial shade. Space 12–14 ft. (3.7–4.3 m) apart.

Care: Easy. Allow soil surface to dry between waterings until established. Fertilize annually in spring. Prune after bloom. Propagate by cuttings, grafting, layering, seed.

Features: Good choice for accents, barriers, espaliers, hedges in landscapes. Drought tolerant.

EUCALYPTUS (GUM)

The *Eucalyptus* genus contains more than 750 species and varieties of highly varied, round- or narrow-crowned, broad-leaved, evergreen trees. They are native to Australia, New Zealand, and Polynesia. They're tender, performing best in mild-winter climates with hot, dry summers.

Gums are fast-growing, long-lived, open and branching or spreading trees or large shrubs that range in size from 10–100 ft. (3–30 m) tall and 6–40 ft. (1.8–12 m) wide. Many gums bear juvenile leaves that are different from their mature leaves, and most have showy inflorescences of caplike flowers with plume, brush, or crestlike, hairy stamens, in colors that range from light yellow to deep purple and red. They also have beautiful, mottled, often exfoliating bark that sheds in long, stringy patches.

They are resistant to most insects and diseases, except for the Eucalyptus longhorn beetle and gum psyllid, two introduced pests, and to iron chlorosis.

Large gums make bold statements when specimens are planted in open landscapes. Smaller gums are the right choice for accents, hedges, and screens. Choose from the species above, at right.

Gum trees, whether true gums, bloodwoods, boxes, peppermints, stringbarks, or ironbarks, are striking additions to the home landscape. Their foliage exudes a pungent scent—many are the source of essential oils—and they have crested or plumelike, fragrant flowers in late spring to early summer.

Eucalyptus Species:
- *E. camaldulensis,* red gum
- *E. cinerea,* silver-dollar tree
- *E. citriodora,* lemon-scented gum
- *E. ficifolia,* red flowering gum
- *E. globulus,* blue gum
- *E. gunnii,* cider gum
- *E. leucoxylon,* white ironbark
- *E. microtheca,* coolibah
- *E. moluccana,* gray box eucalyptus
- *E. perriniana,* spinning gum
- *E. polyanthemos,* redbox gum
- *E. pulverulenta,* dollar-leaved eucalyptus
- *E. punctata,* gray gum
- *E. regnans,* giant gum
- *E. resinifera,* red mahogony
- *E. salubris,* gimlet gum
- *E. sideroxylon,* red ironbark
- *E. torquata,* coral gum
- *E. viminalis,* white gum

Plant eucalypti in average, damp, well-drained, sandy soil with neutral acidity. Since all trees perform best when they are planted in unamended soil, test the acid-alkaline balance of your site prior to planting. Gums are best in soils of 6.5–7.5 pH.

When you plant, carefully match the depth of the planting hole to the soil line of your tree. Backfill around the rootball with native soil and give the tree ample water through its first season, watering whenever the soil becomes thoroughly dry. Gums are very drought tolerant once they have become established and should be planted in sites where they will avoid receiving water from irrigation of turfgrass lawns or shrub borders.

Gums provide tall elements with strong form for those with gardens in mild-winter or arid climates. They require seasonal maintenance and care: their branches are brittle and subject to breaking in strong winds, and they drop bark, seed caps, flowers, and leaves that require raking. To balance these traits, they seldom require fertilizing, although leaf yellowing may signal the need for application of a fertilizer that contains buffering agents to increase soil acidity and trace nutrients needed to avoid chlorosis. Water deeply after you apply such fertilizer to your gum trees.

Tree: *Eucalyptus* species. MYRTACEAE.

Common name: Australian Gum (Eucalypt, Ironbark).

Description: About 700 species of fast-growing, often aromatic, usually upright and spreading, sometimes shrublike, brittle, broad-leaved, evergreen trees, varying in height depending on the species, with juvenile leaves of varied shapes and blue green or green, leathery, round, oval, or dagger-shaped mature leaves and papery, persistent or deciduous bark. The genus is divided into the bloodwoods, boxes, gums, peppermints, stringybarks, and ironbarks.

Blooms/Fruit: Distinctive green, pink, red, white, yellow, feathery and plumelike flowers in a woody bud cap, 1–4 in. (25–100 mm) long, in spring, form fragrant, blue green, leathery, oily, caplike fruit with many seed in summer.

Plant hardiness: Zones 7–10. Semi-hardy or tender.

Soil: Damp, well-drained, sandy soil. Fertility: Average. 6.5–7.5 pH.

Planting: Full sun. Space as recommended for species.

Care: Easy–moderate. Keep damp until established; drought tolerant thereafter. Prune to shape and remove dead branches. Propagate by cuttings, seed.

Features: Good choice for accents, screens, walls, windbreaks in landscapes. Pest and disease resistant. Eucalyptus longhorn beetle and chlorosis susceptible in alkaline soils.

Tree: *Eucalyptus cinerea.* MYRTACEAE.

Common name: Silver-Dollar Tree (Spiral Eucalyptus).

Description: A few cultivars of fast-growing, aromatic, upright, round-headed, brittle, broad-leaved, evergreen trees, 20–50 ft. (6–15 m) tall and wide, with alternate or opposite, gray green, round, coinlike juvenile leaves and blue green or green, leathery, lance-shaped, narrow mature leaves, and with fibrous, deciduous and peeling, red brown bark. A stringybark eucalyptus.

Blooms/Fruit: Inconspicuous white plumelike flowers in a woody bud cap, ¼ in. (6 mm) long, in spring, form oily, caplike fruit, in summer; grown primarily for unique, coin-shaped foliage.

Plant hardiness: Zones 7–11. Semi-hardy.

Soil: Damp to dry, well-drained, sandy soil. Fertility: Average. 6.0–7.5 pH.

Planting: Full sun. Space 10–15 ft. (3–4.5 m) apart.

Care: Easy. Keep damp; drought tolerant when established. Prune to shape and remove dead branches. Propagate by cuttings, seed.

Features: Good choice for accents in landscapes. Good for cut foliage. Eucalyptus longhorn beetle, borer, gum psyllid and chlorosis susceptible.

Tree: *Eucalyptus ficifolia (Corymbia ficifolia)* and hybrids. MYRTACEAE.

Common name: Red-Flowering Gum (Scarlet-Flowering Gum).

Description: Several cultivars of medium-growing, aromatic, upright, spreading, flat-crowned, brittle, broad-leaved, evergreen trees, 20–30 ft. (6–9 m) tall and 15–45 ft. (4.5–13.5 m) wide, with leathery, oval to lance-shaped leaves, 3–6 in. (75–150 mm) long, and rough, gray, persistent bark. A gum eucalyptus.

Blooms/Fruit: Showy, pink, red, yellow, plumelike flowers, in a woody cap, in clusters in spring, form fragrant, leathery, caplike fruit, to ¼ in. (6 mm) wide, containing seed.

Plant hardiness: Zones 9–10. Tender.

Soil: Damp to dry, well-drained, sandy soil. Fertility: Average. 6.0–7.5 pH. Best in mild-summer climates.

Planting: Full sun. Space 15–20 ft. (4.5–6 m) apart.

Care: Easy–moderate. Keep damp until established; drought tolerant thereafter. Prune to shape and remove dead branches. Deadhead fruit. Propagate by cuttings, seed.

Features: Good choice for accents, fencelines, paths in seaside, small-space gardens. Root secretions limit plantings beneath canopy. Eucalyptus longhorn beetle, borer, gum psyllid and chlorosis susceptible.

Tree: *Eucalyptus perriniana.* MYRTACEAE.

Common name: Spinning Gum (Round-Leaved Snow Gum).

Description: Several cultivars of medium-growing, aromatic, upright, round-crowned, brittle, broad-leaved, evergreen trees, 10–30 ft. (3–9 m) tall and wide, with alternate, silver gray, gray green, round juvenile leaves becoming leathery, round or dagger-shaped mature leaves, and white becoming red brown, gray, mottled, syacamore-like, persistent bark. A gum eucalyptus. Dried leaves rotate on their leaf stems in wind.

Blooms/Fruit: Inconspicuous, cream, white, plumelike flowers, in a woody bud cap, to ¼ in. (6 mm) wide, in spring, form fragrant, leathery, oily, caplike fruit, to ¼ in. (6 mm) wide.

Plant hardiness: Zones 9–11. Tender.

Soil: Damp, well-drained, sandy soil. Fertility: Average. 6.0–7.5 pH.

Planting: Full sun. Space 8–15 ft. (2.4–4.5 m) apart.

Care: Easy. Keep damp until established; drought tolerant thereafter. Prune to maintain abundant juvenile foliage. Propagate by cuttings, seed.

Features: Good choice for accents, paths in arid, seaside, small-space gardens. Good for cut foliage, drying. Root secretions limit plantings beneath canopy. Attracts bees. Eucalyptus longhorn beetle, borer, gum psyllid and chlorosis susceptible.

Tree: *Fagus* species. FAGACEAE.

Common name: Beech.

Description: About 10 species of slow-growing, spreading or round-crowned, deciduous trees, to 100 ft. (30 m) tall, with shiny, green, oval, toothed, deeply veined leaves, 4–6 in. (10–15 cm) long, turning brown, yellow in autumn, and with smooth gray bark. Cultivated species include *F. crenata*, Japanese beech; *F. grandifolia*, American beech; and *F. sylvatica*, European beech.

Blooms/Seed: Inconspicuous flowers borne separately on male and female trees in spring. Bristle-covered seedpods bear beechnuts in autumn.

Plant hardiness: Zones 4–9. Best in cold-winter climates.

Soil: Well-drained soil. Fertility: Rich–average. 6.0–7.0 pH.

Planting: Full sun to partial shade. Space 15–20 ft. (4.5–6 m) apart.

Care: Moderate. Allow soil surface to dry between waterings until established. Prune to remove pendulous branches and maintain high crown. Avoid transplanting. Propagate by seed.

Features: Good choice for accents, allées in shade, woodland gardens and roadside plantings. Pest and disease resistant. Leafburn susceptible in hot, dry climates.

Tree: *Franklinia alatamaha (Gordonia alatamaha)*. THEACEAE.

Common name: Franklin Tree.

Description: Several cultivars from a single-species genus of medium-growing, upright, round-crowned, deciduous shrubby trees, 10–30 ft. (3–9 m) tall and sometimes as wide, single or multitrunked, with shiny, green, narrow, oval, pointed, veined leaves, to 6 in. (15 cm) long, turning orange, purple, red in autumn, and gray, ridged bark.

Blooms/Fruit: Showy, fleshy, cream, white, camellia-like, fragrant flowers, to 3 in. (75 mm) wide, with gold, clustered stamens, in summer–autumn, form dry, woody, capsulelike fruit the following spring.

Plant hardiness: Zones 5–9. Semi-hardy. Best in humid-summer climates.

Soil: Moist, well-drained humus. Fertility: Rich. 5.0–6.0 pH. Avoid planting near cotton.

Planting: Full to filtered sun. Space 8–12 ft. (2.4–3.7 m) apart.

Care: Easy. Keep moist; allow soil surface to dry between waterings. Fertilize quarterly. Mulch. Prune to promote treelike growth. Propagate by cuttings, seed.

Features: Good choice for accents, backgrounds, borders, paths in cottage, formal, Japanese-themed, meadow, turfgrass gardens. Pest resistant. Chlorosis, fungal disease susceptible.

Tree: *Fraxinus* species. OLEACEAE.

Common name: Ash.

Description: About 65 species of fast-growing, spreading, mostly deciduous trees, 25–80 ft. (7.5–24 m) tall, with shiny, deep green to bronze, divided leaves, to 16 in. (40 cm) long, as 5–11 leaflets, turning purple, red in autumn. Cultivated species include *F. americana*, white ash; *F. excelsior*, European ash; *F. ornus*, flowering ash; *F. oxycarpa*, 'Raywood'; *F. pennsylvanica*, red ash; and *F. texensis*, Texas ash.

Blooms/Seed: Inconspicuous, panicled flowers borne separately on male and female trees in spring. Maplelike seed in autumn. Seedless male cultivars available.

Plant hardiness: Varies by species; most are hardy in zones 7–10, some to zone 4.

Soil: Damp, well-drained soil. Fertility: Average–low. 6.5–8.0 pH.

Planting: Full sun. Space 15–20 ft. (4.5–6 m) apart. Transplant in spring.

Care: Easy. Keep soil damp. Prune to thin. Propagate by seed.

Features: Good choice for screens in arid, shade, woodland gardens and roadside plantings. Reduce maintenance by planting seedless cultivars. Drought tolerant. Borer, ash whitefly and anthracnose susceptible.

Tree: *Ginkgo biloba.* GINKGOACEAE.

Common name: Ginkgo Tree (Maidenhair Tree).

Description: Several cultivars of slow-growing, pyramid-shaped to round-crowned, resinous, deciduous trees, rarely to 120 ft. (37 m) tall but usually 30–50 ft. (9–15 m), with fanlike, light green, leathery, fringed leaves, 2–3 in. (50–75 mm) long, turning gold and dropping together in autumn.

Blooms/Fruit: Inconspicuous flowers on female trees form round, kernel-pitted fruit, to 2 in. (50 mm) wide, with a foul, rancid scent. Choose fruitless male cultivars.

Plant hardiness: Zones 4–9.

Soil: Moist, well-drained sandy loam. Fertility: Rich. 6.0–7.0 pH.

Planting: Full sun. Space 15–20 ft. (4.5–6 m) apart.

Care: Easy. Keep evenly moist. Fertilize annually in spring until established. Prune sparingly in autumn. Propagate by cuttings, grafting, layering, seed.

Features: Good choice for accents, containers, groups, paths in Asian, small-space gardens and lawns. Pest and disease resistant. Some cultivars smog susceptible.

WARNING
Fruit of *Ginkgo biloba* may cause skin or eye irritation in sensitive individuals. Always wear rubber gloves when handling fruit.

Tree: *Gleditsia triacanthos* var. *inermis.* FABACEAE (LEGUMINOSAE).

Common name: Honey Locust.

Description: Thornless variety of fast- to medium-growing, upright, spreading, deciduous trees, 50–75 ft. (15–23 m) tall, with acacia- and frondlike fans of light green or yellow turning midgreen leaves, 8–10 in. (20–25 cm) long, divided into 10–15-paired, lance-shaped leaflets, turning gold in autumn.

Blooms/Fruit: Choose fruitless male cultivars with insignificant flowers.

Plant hardiness: Zones 3–8.

Soil: Moist, well-drained soil. Fertility: Average–low. 6.0–8.0 pH.

Planting: Full sun. Space 15–20 ft. (4.5–6 m) apart.

Care: Easy. Keep moist until established. Avoid fertilizing. Prune to thin, remove crossing branches. Propagate by budding, seed.

Features: Good choice for accents, backgrounds, edgings, paths in open gardens, landscapes, lawns. Drought tolerant when established. Invasive. Shallow rooted. Honey locust borer, locust pod gall, gypsy moth, mimosa webworm and nectria canker susceptible.

Tree: *Grevillea* species and hybrids. PROTEACEAE.

Common name: Grevillea (Firewheel, Silky Oak, Spider Flower).

Description: More than 250 species of medium-growing, mostly upright, highly varied, brittle, evergreen shrubs and trees, 6–150 ft. (1.8–45 m) tall, with alternate or opposite, bronze becoming deep green, cedar- and needlelike, textured, often scaly, deeply lobed and cut leaves, 1–10 in. (25–254 mm) long. Cultivated species include *G. aquafolium, G. robusta, G. thelemanniana,* and *G. wilsonii.*

Blooms/Seed: Showy, fragrant, tuftlike, cream, red, white, yellow flowers, 1–6 in. (25–150 mm) long, as hairy clusters at leaf stem junctions, in autumn–spring, form dry, feathery seed in spring–summer.

Plant hardiness: Zones 8–11. Tender.

Soil: Moist, well-drained humus. Fertility: Rich. 5.5–7.0 pH.

Planting: Full sun to partial shade. Space as recommended for species.

Care: Moderate. Keep moist; reduce watering in summer. Fertilize with 10–0–5 fertilizer. Protect from frost. Propagate by seed.

Features: Good choice for accents, backgrounds, containers, paths in cottage, formal, meadow, woodland gardens and roadside plantings. Attracts birds, hummingbirds. Drops flowers, foliage, seed, requiring maintenance. Pest and disease resistant.

Tree: *Halesia carolina.* STYRACACEAE.
Common name: Silver-Bell Tree (Wild Olive).
Description: Several cultivars of slow-growing, narrow, dense, deciduous trees, to 40 ft. (12 m) tall and 20 ft. (6 m) wide, with smooth, light green, oval leaves, to 4 in. (10 cm) long, turning yellow in autumn, with black, brown, gray, roughly furrowed bark.
Blooms/Fruit: Abundant, white to pink, bell-shaped, drooping flowers, ¾ in. (19 mm) long, in spring, form winged fruit in autumn.
Plant hardiness: Zones 5–11. Hardy.
Soil: Moist, well-drained humus. Fertility: Rich. 5.0–6.5 pH.
Planting: Partial shade. Space 15–20 ft. (4.5–6 m) apart.
Care: Easy. Generally care free. Keep moist. Fertilize annually in spring. Limit pruning. Protect from drying wind. Propagate by cuttings, layering, seed.
Features: Good choice for spring flower accent and attractive addition near azaleas or rhododendrons. Transplants readily. Pest and disease resistant.

Tree: *Hamamelis virginiana.* HAMAMELIDACEAE.
Common name: Common Witch Hazel.
Description: Several cultivars of medium- to slow-growing, mostly upright, open, spreading, irregular or vase-shaped, deciduous trees, 15–25 ft. (4.5–7.5 m) tall and wide, with alternate, deep green, textured, round leaves, 4–6 in. (10–15 cm) long, with light green, smooth undersides, turning gold, orange, yellow in autumn.

Blooms/Seed: Many yellow, wavy-rayed, fragrant, ribbonlike flowers, to 1½ in. (38 mm) wide, with yellow brown centers, borne in clusters on spurs, in autumn as leaves turn color and fall, form dry, capsulelike pods in early autumn that crack open suddenly, throwing seed.
Plant hardiness: Zones 4–9. Hardy. Best in cold-winter climates.
Soil: Moist, well-drained humus. Fertility: Rich. 6.0–6.5 pH.
Planting: Full sun to partial shade. Space 8–10 ft. (2.4–3 m) apart.
Care: Easy. Keep moist. Fertilize quarterly. Prune sparingly to promote bushy growth. Propagate by grafting, layering, seed.
Features: Good choice for accents, containers, edgings, fencelines, paths in cottage, formal, meadow, small-space, woodland gardens. Bark is source of astringent medicinal tincture. Pest and disease resistant.

Tree: *Hedyscepe canterburyana.* ARECACEAE (PALMAE).
Common name: Canterbury Palm.
Description: Sole member of a single-species genus of slow-growing, erect, round-crowned, evergreen palms, to 30 ft. (9 m) tall, with shiny, light green, stiff leaves, to 14 in. (36 cm) long, radiating from both sides of long, woody, arched, raylike stalks, 20–24 in. (50–60 cm) long. Develops offsets. *Howea forsterana*, sentry or kentia palm, is a closely related species with similar care needs.
Blooms/Seed: Showy, small white flowers on clustered bracts in the foliage crown, in spring–summer, form fleshy, datelike fruit containing, oval, hard-shelled seed, 1½ in. (38 mm) long, in autumn.
Plant hardiness: Zones 9–11. Tender. Best in subtropical and tropical climates.
Soil: Moist, well-drained humus. Fertility: Rich–average. 7.0–8.0 pH.
Planting: Full to filtered sun. Space 8–10 ft. (2.4–3 m) apart.
Care: Moderate. Keep evenly moist. Fertilize quarterly. Prune to remove dried leafstalks at trunk. Wind tolerant. Propagate by seed, suckers.
Features: Good choice for accents, containers, fencelines, groups, screens in seaside, turfgrass gardens. Good for tropical effects. Pest and disease resistant.

Tree: *Ilex* species. AQUIFOLIACEAE.

Common name: Holly.

Description: Nearly 400 species of medium- to slow-growing, rounded, dense, mostly evergreen shrubs or small trees, 10–50 ft. (3–15 m) tall, depending on species, with shiny, leathery, deep green, toothed, usually spiny leaves, to 4 in. (10 cm) long. Commonly cultivated species include *I. aquifolium, I. cornuta, I. crenata,* and *I. opaca.*

Blooms/Berries: Inconspicuous white or green flowers form round, black or red berries on female trees, in clusters, to 6 in. (15 cm) long, in autumn. Plant a pollinating male tree with one or more female trees.

Plant hardiness: Zones 4–8, depending on species; ground hardy, zones 7–8.

Soil: Moist, well-drained soil. Fertility: Average. 6.0–7.0 pH.

Planting: Full sun to partial shade. Space 8–12 ft. (2.4–3.7 m) apart, depending on species.

Care: Moderate. Keep moist. Fertilize annually in spring. Mulch. Prune in spring. Protect from sun, wind in hot climates. Propagate by cuttings, grafting, seed.

Features: Good choice for accents, backgrounds, borders, hedges in cottage, formal, small-space gardens. Berries attract birds. Mealybug, leaf miner and scale susceptible.

Tree: *Ilex opaca.* AQUIFOLIACEAE.

Common name: American Holly.

Description: Over 1,000 cultivars of slow-growing, upright, pyramid-shaped to round-crowned, broad-leaved, evergreen trees, to 50 ft. (15 m) tall, with shiny or leathery, dark green, oval, pointed, mostly spine-toothed leaves, to 4 in. (10 cm) long.

Blooms/Berries: Insignificant white flowers in spring form round, red or yellow berries, to 1/3 in. (8 mm) wide, in winter, in clusters on female trees. Requires both male and female trees to bear fruit.

Plant hardiness: Zones 6–9.

Soil: Moist, well-drained soil. Fertility: Rich. 6.0–6.5 pH.

Planting: Full sun to partial shade. Space 10 ft. (3 m) apart. Add acidic compost.

Care: Easy. Allow soil surface to dry between waterings until established. Fertilize in spring and autumn. Mulch. Prune sparingly in early spring. Protect from wind. Propagate by cuttings, grafting.

Features: Good choice for backgrounds, barriers, specimens in cottage gardens. Good for cutting. Berries attract birds. Mealybug, leaf miner, holly bud moth and scale susceptible.

Tree: *Jacaranda mimosifolia (J. acutifolia).* BIGNONIACEAE.

Common name: Green Ebony Jacaranda (Sharp-Leaved Jacaranda).

Description: Several cultivars of fast-growing, erect, round-crowned, brittle, deciduous trees, to 50 ft. (15 m) tall, with shiny or smooth, light green, soft, deeply cut and divided leaves, to 8 in. (20 cm) long, each with many feather- or fernlike, oblong leaflets, to 3/4 in. (19 mm) long, usually appearing after bloom.

Blooms/Fruit: Showy, blue, purple, white, tube-shaped flowers, to 2 in. (50 mm) long, mostly in spring, repeat blooming in summer–autumn, form rounded, flattened, dry fruit, 2 1/4 in. (57 mm) wide, each with 2 seed, in autumn.

Plant hardiness: Zones 7–11. Semi-hardy. Best in hot-summer, tropical and subtropical climates.

Soil: Damp to dry, well-drained, sandy soil. Fertility: Average. 7.0–8.0 pH.

Planting: Full sun. Space 8–15 ft. (2.4–4.5 m) apart.

Care: Easy. Keep damp; allow soil to dry between waterings. Fertilize quarterly. Prune young trees to direct growth. Propagate by cuttings, seed.

Features: Good choice for accents, containers, screens in arid, meadow, turfgrass gardens and roadside plantings. Good for tropical effects. Pest, oak root fungus, and disease resistant.

JUNIPERUS (JUNIPER)

More than 70 species of highly varied, coniferous shrubs and trees are found in the *Juniperus* genus. They are native to the northern hemisphere, from the tropics to the arctic. Because species vary from low, prostrate ground covers to stately, pyramid-shaped trees, they are widely used as landscape plants.

Most junipers are small conifers that are clothed either in needles or scalelike foliage and which have berrylike cones. They are tolerant of harsh conditions and perform well in urban sites with salt exposure or smoggy air.

Depending on their species, junipers grow fast, medium, or slowly. They range in size from 4–6 in. (10–15 cm) tall for the low shrub species to trees as tall as 100 ft. (30 m). In a planter that constricts their roots, they grow slowly, making them ideal for bonsai and shape training. They rarely need pruning yet tolerate severe cutting of their limbs and new foliage.

Junipers are susceptible to several tree pests, including aphids, bagworms, borers, spruce mites, and webworms. They can be infected by blight and several forms of rust.

Choose from the species at right.

Juniper Ground Cover Species*:
J. chinensis procumbens, Chinese juniper
J. conferta, shore juniper
J. horizontalis, creeping juniper
J. sabina, Savin juniper
J. scopulorum, western red cedar

Juniper Shrub Species*:
J. chinensis, Chinese juniper
J. communis, common juniper
J. sabina, Savin juniper
J. scopulorum, western red cedar
J. squamata, single-seed cedar

Juniper Columnar Species*:
J. chinensis, Chinese juniper
J. scopulorum, western red cedar
J. virginiana, eastern red cedar

Juniper Tree Species*:
J. californica, California juniper
J. deppeana, alligator juniper
J. excelsa, spiny Greek juniper
J. lucayana, West Indies juniper
J. monsperma, cherrystone juniper
J. occidentalis, western juniper
J. osteosperma, Utah juniper
J. recurva, Cox juniper
J. reigida, needle juniper
J. scopulorum, western red cedar
J. virginiana, eastern red cedar

*Many cultivars of several commonly cultivated juniper species have been developed with varied growth traits, appearance, and habits.

Junipers perform yeomen's labor in the landscape garden. When a bank or slope is subject to erosion, they will stabilize the hillside with their spreading roots and dense foliage. When a border needs a green, yellow, or variegated shrub for a background planting, the interesting texture of junipers fills the bill. When seeking a stately tree with conical form and beautiful texture in a hot-summer, mountain area, red cedars—more juniper species—are fine specimens.

Plant your juniper in damp, well-drained loam, one that can range from acid to alkaline. Junipers need soils from 6.0–8.0 pH, a wide range that permits their use in most garden soils. Closely compare the tree's needs to your climate conditions to choose the best species for your area.

Carefully match the depth of the planting hole to the soil line on your tree's rootball. Junipers do best when planted with their shallow, surface roots 6–12 in. (15–30 cm) below the surface. Give the tree ample water through its first summer, irrigating whenever the soil surface dries.

Check the spacing needs of the juniper species and cultivar you select. Small ground covers may be planted as closely as 3 ft. (90 cm) apart, while large trees may need spacing as great as 20 ft. (6 m) apart.

Tree: *Juniperus* species. CUPRESSACEAE.

Common name: Juniper (Red Cedar).

Description: More than 70 species of fast- to slow-growing, highly varied, coniferous, evergreens, from low, spreading shrubs, 4–6 in. (10–15 cm) high, to tall, pyramid-shaped trees, 50–100 ft. (15–30 m) tall, with shiny, deep green, sometimes blue green, yellow, scaly or needlelike, fragrant foliage with overlapped plates, and with reddish brown, furrowed bark.

Blooms/Cones: Yellow, catkinlike, male cones and light blue, aromatic, pulpy, berrylike female cones appear in spring, ripening in autumn.

Plant hardiness: Zones 2–9. Hardy.

Soil: Damp, well-drained loam. Fertility: Average. 6.0–8.0 pH.

Planting: Full to filtered sun. Space as recommended for species.

Care: Easy. Allow soil surface to dry between waterings. Fertilize annually in spring until established. Propagate by cuttings, grafting, seed.

Features: Good choice for accents, barriers, beds, borders, containers, fencelines, hedges, screens, specimens in natural, open, woodland gardens and landscapes. Aphid, borer, spruce mite, webworm and juniper blight, rust susceptible.

Tree: *Laburnum* x *watereri* hybrids. FABACEAE (LEGUMINOSAE).
Common name: Golden-Chain Tree.
Description: Several cultivars of fast-growing, short-lived, erect, round-crowned, deciduous trees, 15–25 ft. (4.5–7.5 m) tall, with shiny, cloverlike, bright green, 3-lobed, divided leaves, to 4 in. (10 cm) long. *L. alpinum* and *L. anagyroides* are related species.
Blooms/Seed: Showy, sweet-pea-like, gold, yellow flowers, to ¾ in. (19 mm) long, in nodding, wisteria- or lilaclike clusters, to 20 in. (50 cm) long, in late spring–early summer, form flattened, beanlike pods, to 3 in. (75 mm) long, containing seed, in autumn.
Plant hardiness: Zones 5–9. Hardy. Best in dry-summer, mild-winter climates.
Soil: Moist to damp, well-drained soil. Fertility: Average. 6.5–8.0 pH. Salt tolerant.
Planting: Full to filtered sun. Space 8–10 ft. (2.4–3 m) apart.
Care: Easy. Keep damp; allow soil to dry between waterings. Drought tolerant. Fertilize annually in spring. Prune after bloom; deadhead seedpods to maintain vigor. Propagate by budding, grafting, layering, seed.
Features: Good choice for accents, containers, paths, screens in arid, meadow, seaside, turfgrass gardens. Drops flowers, leaves, seedpods, requiring maintenance. Pest and disease resistant.

> **WARNING**
> Seedpods and seed of *Laburnum* x *watereri* are hazardous if eaten. Avoid planting them in areas frequented by pets or children.

Tree: *Larix* species. PINACEAE.
Common name: Larch (Tamarack).
Description: About 10 species of fast-growing, long-lived, pyramid-shaped, coniferous, deciduous trees, 20–100 ft. (6–30 m) tall, depending on species, with shiny, deep green, needle-shaped, whorled leaves, to 1½ in. (38 mm) long, turning brilliant yellow in autumn. Common species include *L. decidua, L. kaempferi,* and *L. occidentalis.*
Cones/Seed: Male cones are single, to ¾ in. (19 mm) long; female cones are erect, blue, brown, green, yellow, egg-shaped, to 1½ in. (38 mm) long, with woody scales and winged seed, arranged in lines along the top of branches.
Plant hardiness: Zones 1–7. Hardy. Best in cold-winter climates, high elevations.
Soil: Moist, well-drained loam. Fertility: Average. 5.5–7.0 pH.
Planting: Full sun. Space 10–20 ft. (3–6 m) apart.
Care: Moderate. Keep evenly moist; allow soil surface to dry between waterings. Drought tolerant when established. Avoid fertilizing. Prune sparingly in winter. Propagate by seed.
Features: Good choice for accents, shade, specimens in bog, meadow, natural gardens. Drops needles, requiring maintenance. Larch casebearer caterpillar and canker susceptible.

Tree: *Laurus nobilis.* LAURACEAE.
Common name: Laurel (Bay, Grecian Laurel, Sweet Bay, Willow-Leaved Bay).
Description: A few cultivars of slow-growing, long-lived, erect, columnar, dense, evergreen trees, 15–40 ft. (4.5–12 m) tall, with shiny, leathery, deep green, oval, pointed, finely toothed, fragrant leaves, 2–4 in. (50–100 mm) long, with lighter, gray green undersides.
Blooms/Berries: Insignificant cream, white, yellow flowers, to ¼ in. (6 mm) wide, borne in clusters, in spring, form black, purple, round berries, to ¾ in. (19 mm) wide, in summer.
Plant hardiness: Zones 7–10. Semi-hardy. Best in dry-summer, mild-winter climates.
Soil: Moist to damp, well-drained humus. Fertility: Average. 6.5–8.0 pH.
Planting: Full to filtered sun. Space 7–10 ft. (2.2–3 m) apart.
Care: Easy. Keep moist; allow soil surface to dry between waterings. Drought tolerant. Fertilize annually in spring. Prune to harvest leaves, shape, remove suckers. Propagate by cuttings, seed.
Features: Good choice for accents, containers, hedges in arid, seaside gardens. Good as culinary herb. Drops flowers, requiring maintenance. Disease resistant. Laurel psyllid, scale susceptible.

Tree: *Leucodendron argenteum.* PROTEACEAE.
Common name: Silver Tree (Silver Leucodendron).
Description: Several cultivars of medium-growing, short-lived, erect and columnar becoming rounded and branching, dense, evergreen trees, 30–40 ft. (9–12 m) tall and wide, with opposite, silver gray, hairy, leathery, needlelike, lance-shaped, narrow, pointed leaves, 4–6 in. (10–15 cm) long, and gray bark on contorted trunks. *L. adscendens, L. discolor, L. stokoei, L. tinctum,* and *L. venosum* are closely related species with similar care needs.
Blooms/Berries: Insignificant grasslike or conelike flowers borne separately on male and female trees, in spring, form nutlike fruit, in autumn. Grown for foliage.
Plant hardiness: Zones 8–11. Tender. Best in humid, subtropical or seaside climates.
Soil: Moist to damp, well-drained, sandy soil. Fertility: Average–low. 6.0–7.0 pH.
Planting: Full sun. Space 15–20 ft. (4.5–6 m) apart.
Care: Challenging. Keep moist; allow soil surface to dry between waterings. Avoid fertilizing. Prune, pinch to shape. Propagate by seed.
Features: Good choice for accents, banks, containers, groups, slopes in rock, seaside, tropical gardens. Good for cutting. Pest and disease resistant.

Tree: *Liquidambar styraciflua.* HAMAMELIDACEAE.
Common name: Sweet-Gum.
Description: Slow-growing, broad, symmetrical, open, deciduous tree, to 120 ft. (37 m) tall and 50 ft. (15 m) wide, with glossy, maplelike, deep green, deeply toothed leaves, 4–7 in. (10–18 cm) wide, turning purple, red, yellow in autumn, and with furrowed bark. *L. formosana,* Chinese sweet-gum; and *L. orientalis,* Oriental sweet-gum, are closely related species with similar care needs.
Blooms/Seed: Inconspicuous small flowers, in spring, borne in dangling clusters, form round, spiny, dangling seed clusters, in autumn.
Plant hardiness: Zones 5–9; ground hardy, zones 6–9.
Soil: Moist, well-drained soil. Fertility: Rich. 6.5–7.0 pH.
Planting: Full sun to partial shade. Space 25–30 ft. (7.5–9 m) apart, after soil warms. Transplant in spring.

Care: Easy. Allow soil surface to dry between waterings until established. Fertilize semi-annually spring–autumn. Prune sparingly in autumn. Transplants readily. Propagate by seed.
Features: Good choice for accents, specimens in most gardens. Shallow rooted. Chlorosis susceptible.

Tree: *Liriodendron tulipifera.* MAGNOLIACEAE.
Common name: Tulip Tree (Tulip Poplar).
Description: Several cultivars of fast- to medium-growing, open, deciduous trees, to 120 ft. (37 m) tall, with maplelike, dark green, toothed, 5- or 7-lobed leaves, to 7 in. (18 cm) long, turning yellow gold tinged with rose in autumn. Common cultivars include *L. tulipifera* 'Arnold', 'Aureo-marginatum', and 'Integrifolium'.
Blooms/Seed: Fragrant, apricot yellow–tinged green, cup-shaped flowers, to 2 in. (50 mm) wide, in late spring on mature trees, form leathery seed clusters, to 3 in. (75 mm) long, in autumn.
Plant hardiness: Zones 4–9.
Soil: Moist, well-drained soil. Fertility: Rich. Add acidic compost. 6.0–6.5 pH.
Planting: Full sun. Space 15–25 ft. (4.5–7.5 m) apart.
Care: Easy. Allow soil surface to dry between waterings until established. Fertilize annually in spring until established. Prune in autumn. Propagate by cuttings, layering, seed.
Features: Good choice for accents, paths, screens in cottage, woodland gardens, lawns. Drops flowers, leaves, dry pods, requiring maintenance. Shallow rooted. Smog tolerant. Pest and disease resistant. Chlorosis susceptible.

MAGNOLIA

About 85 species of medium to large, round-crowned, broad-leaved, deciduous and evergreen trees are comprised by the ancient *Magnolia* genus. Native to North and Central America and East Asia, they are semi-hardy trees; most will tolerate temperatures as low as 5°F (−15°C), thriving in areas with mild winters and warm, humid summers.

Magnolias are very showy trees with large, cream, pink, or white, cup- or star-shaped flowers that appear before the leaves on deciduous species and in late spring and early summer on evergreen species. They are good choices for urban sites and are often used as street trees.

They are slow- to medium-growing trees, with species that range in size from 20–100 ft. (6–30 m) tall. Four divisions segregate the magnolias into evergreen, deciduous cup-flowered, deciduous star-flowered, and the other, miscellaneous species.

Magnolias are susceptible to scale insects and fungal diseases that cause leaf spot; both are preventable and easily treated.

The landscape magnolia species listed above, at right, are widely planted in landscape gardens.

Magnolia species include both the large, upright, round-crowned landscape trees and many delicate, shrublike accents ideal for a small-space garden or container. Choose from evergreen or deciduous magnolias; evergreens bear their flowers in late spring, while most deciduous magnolias bloom in early spring, some before leaves emerge.

Plant magnolias in a moist, well-drained, acidic humus. Since all landscape trees perform best when planted in unamended soil, test your site for acid-alkaline balance before planting. Magnolias require soils in the 6.0–6.5 pH range. Choose species with your climate in mind, especially when you plant magnolias in USDA Plant Hardiness Zones 7 or 8.

Carefully match the depth of your planting hole to the mark of the soil line on your tree's rootball. Magnolias do best when you position the root crown at the same depth as it was grown in the tree nursery. Backfill the planting hole with native soil, surround it with a moat, and water the tree during its first season, whenever the soil surface dries.

Evergreen Magnolias:
- *M. delavayi*
- *M. grandiflora*, southern magnolia
- *M. × thompsoniana*, Thompson magnolia
- *M. virginiana*, sweet bay

Deciduous Cup-Flowered Magnolias:
- *M. campbellii*, Campbell magnolia
- *M. dawsoniana*, Dawson magnolia
- *M. fraseri*, Fraser magnolia
- *M. hetapeta*, yulan
- *M. sargentiana*, Sargent magnolia
- *M. × soulangeana*, saucer magnolia
- *M. sprengeri*, Sprenger magnolia
- *M. × veitchii*, Veitch magnolia

Deciduous Star-Flowered Magnolias:
- *M. kobus*, Kobus magnolia
- *M. × loebneri*, Loebner magnolia
- *M. nitida*, shiny-leaved magnolia
- *M. salicifolia*, anise magnolia
- *M. stellata*, star magnolia

Miscellaneous Magnolia Species:
- *M. acuminata*, cucumber tree
- *M. hypoleuca*, white-leaved magnolia
- *M. macrophylla*, big-leaved magnolia
- *M. rostrata*
- *M. sieboldii*, Oyama magnolia
- *M. tripetala*, umbrella magnolia
- *M. wilsonii*, Wilson magnolia

Magnolias are the right choice for open or turfgrass landscapes. Keep the spread of large species in mind, spacing your plantings 20–30 ft. (6–9 m) apart—or more if they're near a structure. Magnolias look best with space to allow you to appreciate their beautiful form.

Tree: *Magnolia grandiflora.* MAGNOLIACEAE.
Common name: Southern Magnolia (Bull Bay Magnolia).
Description: Many cultivars of medium-growing, dense, broad-leaved, evergreen trees, to 100 ft. (30 m) tall, with succulent, waxy, dark green, oval, pointed leaves, to 8 in. (20 cm) long, with rust tan undersides and smooth, brown, gray bark.
Blooms/Seed: Fragrant, cream white, cup-shaped flowers, to 10 in. (25 cm) wide, in late spring and early summer, sometimes repeating bloom in autumn, form orange, red, leathery, cone-shaped, segmented seed clusters, to 4 in. (10 cm) long, in autumn–winter.
Plant hardiness: Zones 7–11.
Soil: Moist, well-drained soil. Fertility: Rich. Add acidic compost. 6.0–6.5 pH.
Planting: Full to filtered sun. Space 20–30 ft. (6–9 m) apart.
Care: Moderate. Allow soil surface to dry between waterings until established. Fertilize annually in spring until established. Prune in autumn. Protect from wind. Propagate by cuttings, layering, seed.
Features: Good choice for accents, allées in open gardens, landscapes, lawns. Good for shade. Drops flowers, leaves, dry pods, requiring maintenance. Shallow rooted. Magnolia scale and chlorosis, leaf spot susceptible.

Tree: *Magnolia stellata.* MAGNOLIACEAE.

Common name: Star Magnolia.

Description: Many cultivars of slow-growing, long-lived, erect, spreading, open, deciduous, shrubby trees, 20–25 ft. (6–7.5 m) tall and to 30 ft. (9 m) wide, with smooth, deep green, leathery, broad, oval leaves, 4–5 in. (10–13 cm) long, with tan undersides, turning yellow bronze, rose in autumn, and with smooth, gray bark.

Blooms/Cones: Showy, fragrant, pink, purple, red becoming white, star-shaped flowers, to 3 in. (75 mm) wide, with 12–15 narrow, lance-shaped petals, in early spring before leaves emerge, form scaly seed cones in autumn.

Plant hardiness: Zones 5–9. Hardy. Best in mild-summer climates.

Soil: Moist, well-drained humus. Fertility: Rich. 5.5–6.5 pH.

Planting: Filtered sun to partial shade. Space 6–15 ft. (1.8–4.5 m) apart.

Care: Moderate. Keep evenly moist. Fertilize quarterly with acidic liquid fertilizer diluted to one-half its package-recommended rate. Prune, remove suckers to direct growth, maintain treelike form. Stake. Avoid plantings beneath canopy. Propagate by cuttings; plants grown from seed may revert.

Features: Good choice for borders, containers, edgings, entries in formal, meadow, woodland gardens. Good for cutting; winter branch form. Shallow rooted. Disease resistant. Scale, spider mite and chlorosis susceptible.

Tree: *Malus floribunda.* ROSACEAE.

Common name: Flowering Crabapple (Showy Crabapple).

Description: Many hybrids of slow-growing, spreading, dense, deciduous trees, to 25 ft. (7.5 m) tall, with deep green to purple, fuzzy, oval, pointed, toothed leaves, 2–3 in. (50–75 mm) long, turning brown or red in autumn.

Blooms/Fruit: Profuse, fragrant, carmine to pink or white flowers, to 1 1/4 in. (32 mm) wide, borne in dangling clusters, in spring, form yellow or orange, round fruit, to 5/16 in. (8 mm) wide, in summer–autumn.

Plant hardiness: Zones 5–9.

Soil: Damp, well-drained soil. Fertility: Average. 6.5–7.5 pH.

Planting: Full sun. Space 15 ft. (4.5 m) apart.

Care: Easy. Allow soil surface to dry between waterings until established. Fertilize quarterly spring–autumn. Prune in autumn. Protect from sun in hot climates. Propagate by budding, seed.

Features: Good choice for accents, backgrounds, containers, fencelines, screens in cottage gardens. Fruit attracts birds in winter. Blight, mildew, rust, scab susceptible. Choose disease-resistant hybrids.

Tree: *Metasequoia glyptostroboides.* TAXODIACEAE.

Common name: Dawn Redwood.

Description: Single ancient species of fast-growing, pyramid-shaped, coniferous, deciduous tree, to 100 ft. (30 m) tall, with shiny, flat, deep green needles, 1/2–1 1/2 in. (12–38 mm) long, with silvery undersides, turning golden red in autumn, with fibrous, red, fissured bark, and with trunks to 9 ft. (2.7 m) wide. Classified first by fossil record, then rediscovered in 1945 in Sichuan, China. Related trees, coast redwood, *Sequoia sempervirens;* and giant sequoia, *Sequoiadendron giganteum,* with great size and similar general appearance, are evergreens.

Blooms/Cones: Stemless, drooping, spikelike, male cones and round, green, stemmed, female, cones appear in spring, ripening in summer, containing scaly, winged seed.

Plant hardiness: Zones 5–9. Best with winter chill.

Soil: Moist, well-drained soil. Fertility: Rich–average. 6.0–7.0 pH.

Planting: Full sun. Space 20–30 ft. (6–9 m) apart.

Care: Easy. Keep evenly moist. Fertilize annually. Prune suckers. Protect from salt, sun in hot, coastal climates. Propagate by cuttings, seed, suckers.

Features: Good choice for accents, seasonal screens in open landscapes. Shallow rooted. Pest and disease resistant.

Tree: *Michelia doltsopa* and hybrids. MAGNOLIACEAE.
Common name: False Magnolia.
Description: Several cultivars of slow-growing, long-lived, erect, narrow, evergreen trees, usually to 30 ft. (9 m) tall and 20–30 ft. (6–9 m) wide, with shiny, deep green, leathery, oval, pointed leaves, 4–8 in. (10–20 cm) long, and with smooth, gray brown bark. A commonly cultivated cultivar hybrid is *M. doltsopa* × *figo* 'Jack Fogg'. *M. figo*, banana shrub, is a closely related tropical species with similar care needs.
Blooms/Cones: Showy, fragrant, magnolia-like, cream, white, segmented flowers, 3–4 in. (75–100 mm) wide, in early spring before leaves emerge, form scaly seed cones in autumn.
Plant hardiness: Zones 5–11. Hardy.
Soil: Moist, well-drained soil. Fertility: Rich–average. 6.0–7.0 pH.
Planting: Full to filtered sun. Space 5–10 ft. (1.5–3 m) apart.
Care: Moderate. Keep evenly moist. Fertilize annually in spring. Prune to shape. Propagate by cuttings, seed.
Features: Good choice for accents, borders, containers in formal, small-space, woodland gardens. Pest and disease resistant.

Tree: *Nyssa sylvatica*. NYSSACEAE.
Common name: Tupelo (Black Gum, Pepperidge, Sour Gum).
Description: Medium- to slow-growing, upright, pyramid-shaped then irregular, open, deciduous tree, to 100 ft. (30 m) tall, with shiny, deep green, oval leaves, to 5 in. (13 cm) long, turning purple, red in autumn, and with contorted branches and reddish bark. Related to cotton gum, *N. aquatica*, a wetland species.
Blooms/Fruit: Inconspicuous male and female flowers in spring form many deep blue, round, blueberry-like fruit, to ½ in. (12 mm) wide, in summer.
Plant hardiness: Zones 4–9.
Soil: Moist, well-drained soil. Fertility: Rich. 5.5–6.5 pH.
Planting: Full sun. Space 20–25 ft. (6–7.5 m) apart.
Care: Easy. Keep evenly moist. Fertilize annually in spring until established. Prune to direct growth in autumn. Protect from wind. Avoid transplanting. Propagate by layering, seed.

Features: Good choice for accents, backgrounds, paths in natural, woodland gardens. Good for seasonal color, shade. Fruit attracts birds. Drops staining fruit, requiring maintenance. Smog susceptible.

Tree: *Olea europaea*. OLEACEAE.
Common name: Olive (Common Olive).
Description: Many cultivars of slow-growing, long-lived, fruiting or fruitless, erect, round-crowned, evergreen trees, to 30 ft. (9 m) tall and 20–30 ft. (6–9 m) wide, with opposite, gray green, leathery, oval, often narrow, pointed leaves, to 3 in. (75 mm) long, with silver undersides, and with smooth, silver gray bark. Produces numerous suckers. Common cultivars include *O. europaea* 'Bonita', 'Majestic Beauty', 'Mission', 'Sevillano', and 'Wilsoni', among others.
Blooms/Fruit: Many inconspicuous, cream, white, dangling flowers formed in the junctions of leaf stems and branches, in spring, form edible, blue black, fleshy, pitted, staining fruit in autumn. Requires winter chilling to set fruit. Fruitless cultivars may produce sparse fruit.
Plant hardiness: Zones 7–11. Semi-hardy. Best in arid, hot-summer climates.
Soil: Dry, well-drained, sandy soil. Fertility: Rich–low. 6.5–8.0 pH. Best in rich soils.
Planting: Full sun. Space 10–15 ft. (3–4.5 m) apart.
Care: Easy. Keep moist until established; drought tolerant thereafter. Avoid fertilizing. Prune to shape, thin. Propagate by cuttings, grafting, seed, suckers.
Features: Good choice for accents, containers in formal, orchard, small-space gardens. Fresh olives are inedible; preserve them by soaking in lye, a caustic compound requiring caution for use. Nematode, scale and olive knot, verticillium wilt susceptible.

Tree: *Oxydendrum arboreum.* ERICACEAE.
Common name: Sourwood (Sorrel Tree, Titi).
Description: Single species of medium-growing, upright, pyramid-shaped, deciduous tree, eventually 50–80 ft. (15–24 m) tall but usually less than 30 ft. (9 m), with alternate, shiny, bronze turning deep green, lance-shaped, pointed, finely toothed leaves, to 8 in. (20 cm) long, turning orange, purple, red, yellow in autumn, and with brown gray bark.
Blooms/Fruit: Many fragrant, lily-of-the-valley–like, creamy white, bell-shaped flowers, to 5/16 in. (8 mm) long, in dangling clusters, in summer, form leathery green fruit caps containing seed, in branched, spreading clusters, in autumn.
Plant hardiness: Zones 5–9. Hardy. Best with winter chill, mild summers.
Soil: Moist, well-drained soil. Fertility: Rich. 5.5–6.5 pH.
Planting: Full sun to partial shade. Space 8–12 ft. (2.4–3.7 m) apart.
Care: Easy. Keep moist; allow soil surface to dry between waterings until established. Avoid cultivating beneath tree. Prune in autumn. Propagate by seed.
Features: Good choice for accents, beds, borders, containers, edgings in formal, small-space gardens and patios. Good for seasonal shade. Attracts bees. Pest, disease resistant.

Tree: *Parrotia persica.* HAMAMELIDACEAE.
Common name: Persian Ironwood (Persian Parrotia).
Description: A slow-growing, upright, round-crowned, deciduous shrubby tree, rarely 50 ft. (15 m) tall but usually smaller and often with multiple trunks, with witch-hazel-like, purple turning deep green, oval, wavy-edged, pointed, faintly toothed, veined leaves, to 4 in. (10 cm) long, turning orange, red, yellow in autumn, and with smooth, flaking gray bark patterned with white.
Blooms/Fruit: Inconspicuous, brown and red flowers, in early spring before leaves emerge, form tiny, caplike, seedy fruit in summer.
Plant hardiness: Zones 5–8. Best with winter chill.
Soil: Damp, well-drained soil. Fertility: Rich–average. 5.5–7.0 pH.
Planting: Full to filtered sun. Space 10–15 ft. (3–4.5 m) apart.
Care: Easy. Allow soil surface to dry between waterings until established. Fertilize annually until established. Prune sparingly. Propagate by cuttings, layering, seed.
Features: Good choice for accents, borders, containers, paths in open and mixed-shrub gardens. Deep rooted. Pest and disease resistant.

Tree: *Phoenix* species. ARECACEAE (PALMAE).
Common name: Date Palm.
Description: About 17 species of slow-growing, erect, round-crowned, evergreen palms, 6–60 ft. (1.8–18 m) tall, 6–50 ft. (1.8–15 m) wide, with shiny, blue or gray green, stiff leaflets, to 2 ft. (60 cm) long, radiating from both sides of long, woody, arched, leafstalks, 2–10 ft. (60–305 cm) long. Develops suckers.
Blooms/Dates: Many small, white flowers on clustered bracts in the foliage crown, in spring–summer, form fleshy, egg-shaped, seed-filled, edible and inedible dates, ¾–3 in. (19–75 mm) long, in autumn.
Plant hardiness: Zones 7–11. Semi-hardy. Best in mild-winter, seaside climates.
Soil: Moist to damp, well-drained, sandy soil. Fertility: Average. 6.5–8.0 pH. Best in rich soils.
Planting: Full sun; some species tolerate partial shade. Space as recommended for species.
Care: Easy. Keep moist until established; drought tolerant thereafter. Fertilize annually in spring. Prune to remove dried leafstalks at trunk. Propagate by seed, suckers.
Features: Good choice for accents, barriers, groups, hedges in meadow, seaside gardens and roadside plantings. Drops fronds, fruit, requiring maintenance. Smog tolerant. Pest and disease resistant.

PICEA (SPRUCE)

The *Picea* genus, with its 45 species of firlike, large and stately, pyramid-shaped conifers, is native to the cool, temperate mountains of the northern hemisphere. Spruces can be distinguished from the firs by their large, dangling cones and stiff needles. They are excellent trees for use in full-sun, open landscapes where their tall form and upraised branches may be appreciated.

Spruces need mild, moist summers and cold winters to thrive. Avoid planting them in lowland gardens with hot, dry summers and mild winters.

All are medium- to slow-growing trees, eventually reaching 75–150 ft. (23–45 m) tall. Many dwarf cultivars have been hybridized, making them ideal for growing in containers in small-space gardens. When kept rootbound in a planter, they grow slowly and are ideal for bonsai and shape training. They otherwise rarely need pruning.

Spruces are sometimes susceptible to aphids, spider mites, and the larvae of gypsy and tussock moth. They also can contract cytosperma canker, which kills their inner, lower branches.

Choose from among the popular spruce species listed above, at right.

Spruces are easily recognized in the garden because of their arrow-straight, conical form; whorled branches; rigidly stiff needles; and large, dangling cones. When mature, they have straight, limbless trunks and open crowns, traits that made them the tree of choice for wood used for sailing ship masts throughout the 19th century.

Spruce Species:
- *P. abies,* Norway spruce
- *P. brewerana,* Brewer weeping spruce
- *P. engelmanii,* Engelmann spruce
- *P. fraserii,* Fraser spruce
- *P. glauca,* white spruce
- *P. mariana,* black spruce
- *P. pungens,* Colorado spruce
- *P. sitchensis,* Sitka spruce

Popular Cultivars:
- *P. abies* 'Nidiformis', bird's-nest spruce
- *P. glauca* var. *albertiana,* Alberta spruce
- *P. glauca* var. *densata,* Black Hills spruce
- *P. pungens* 'Glauca', blue spruce
- *P. pungens* 'Pendula', weeping blue spruce

Plant all spruces in moist, well-drained, acidic soil. Since all landscape trees do best when they are planted in unamended soil, your site should be tested for acid-alkaline balance before planting. Spruces need soils in the 5.0–7.0 pH range; you should choose another conifer if your soil is too alkaline. You also should compare your tree's needs to your USDA Plant Hardiness Zone.

Carefully match your planting hole's depth to the soil line on the rootball of your tree when you plant. Spruces are shallow-rooted trees that need good drainage. Their root crowns should be positioned at the same level as they were grown at the tree nursery. Backfill the planting hole with native soil, surround it with a moat, and water the tree often through its first two seasons, whenever the soil surface becomes dry. Water established trees in times of drought.

Choose spruces for open or woodland gardens. They grow slowly to become the dominant feature in the landscape, so plant them with ample space, especially near structures or paving.

To use a spruce as an indoor holiday decoration, plant it *and* its container in the soil, applying mulch over its roots. Unearth the tree before the soil freezes, clean its container, and bring it indoors. When the holiday season is over, the tree can be replanted in your garden.

Tree: *Picea* species. PINACEAE.

Common name: Spruce.

Description: About 45 species of medium- to slow-growing, upright, pyramid-shaped, coniferous, evergreen trees, 75–150 ft. (23–45 m) tall, depending on species, often with whorled branches and radiating, shiny, deep blue green, stiff, round needles, to ¾ in. (19 mm) long, and with blue gray, resinous bark.

Blooms/Cones: Male cones resemble feathery catkins, 1–3 in. (25–75 mm) long; female cones are dangling, elongated, and pointed, 2–6 in. (50–150 mm) long, with woody scales and pairs of single-winged seed.

Plant hardiness: Zones 1–8, depending on species. All hardy to zone 6.

Soil: Moist, well-drained soil. Fertility: Rich–average. 5.5–7.0 pH.

Planting: Full to filtered sun. Space as recommended for species.

Care: Easy–moderate. Allow soil surface to dry between waterings until established. Avoid fertilizing. Prune only to shape in spring, removing half of new growth "candles." Propagate by cuttings, seed.

Features: Good choice for accents in containers, open landscapes. Maturing trees shade underfoliage, causing needle loss. Shallow rooted. Aphid, spider mite, gypsy moth, tussock moth and canker susceptible.

Tree: *Picea abies (P. excelsa).* PINACEAE.

Common name: Norway Spruce.

Description: Several cultivars of fast-growing, upright, pyramid-shaped, coniferous, evergreen trees, to 150 ft. (45 m) tall, with whorled, nodding branches, and radiating, shiny, deep blue green, stiff, sharp, round needles, to ¾ in. (19 mm) long, and with blue gray, resinous bark blistered with pitch pockets. Dwarf cultivars are available, some with low, ground cover habits.

Blooms/Cones: Male cones resemble feathery catkins, to 2 in. (50 mm) long; female cones are dangling, elongated, and pointed, to 7 in. (18 cm) long, with woody scales containing pairs of single-winged seed.

Plant hardiness: Zones 1–9. Hardy.

Soil: Damp to dry, well-drained soil. Fertility: Rich–average. 5.0–6.5 pH.

Planting: Full to filtered sun. Space 12–16 ft. (3.7–4.9 m) apart.

Care: Easy–moderate. Allow soil surface to dry between waterings. Avoid fertilizing. Prune only to shape in spring, removing half of new growth "candles." Propagate by cuttings, seed.

Features: Good choice for ground covers, screens, windbreaks in meadow, woodland gardens. Maturing trees shade underfoliage, causing needle loss. Aphid, spider mite, gypsy moth, tussock moth and canker susceptible.

Tree: *Picea glauca.* PINACEAE.

Common name: White Spruce (Alberta Spruce, Black Hills Spruce, Cat Spruce).

Description: Many cultivars of fast-growing, upright, pyramid-shaped, coniferous, evergreen trees, to 100 ft. (30 m) tall, with whorled, nodding branches, and radiating, shiny, deep blue green, stiff, sharp needles, to ¾ in. (19 mm) long, and with blue green bark.

Blooms/Cones: Male cones resemble feathery catkins, 1–3 in. (25–75 mm) long; female cones are dangling, oval, and pointed, to 2 in. (50 mm) long, with scales and winged seed.

Plant hardiness: Zones 1–9. Hardy. Somewhat heat tolerant.

Soil: Damp to dry, well-drained soil. Fertility: Rich–average. 5.0–6.5 pH.

Planting: Full to filtered sun. Space 10–15 ft. (3–4.5 m) apart.

Care: Easy–moderate. Allow soil surface to dry between waterings until established. Avoid fertilizing. Prune only to shape in spring, removing half of new growth "candles." Propagate by cuttings, seed.

Features: Good choice for accents, screens, specimens, windbreaks in meadow, woodland gardens. Maturing trees shade underfoliage, causing needle loss. Aphid, spider mite, gypsy moth, tussock moth and canker susceptible.

Tree: *Picea pungens.* PINACEAE.

Common name: Colorado Spruce (Blue Spruce).

Description: Several cultivars of medium-growing, upright, pyramid-shaped, coniferous, evergreen trees, to 100 ft. (30 m) tall and 25 ft. (7.5 m) wide, with whorled, nodding branches, and radiating, shiny, silver gray, blue silver, stiff, sharp, round needles, to ¾ in. (19 mm) long, and with smooth becoming rough, blue gray, resinous bark.

Blooms/Cones: Male cones resemble feathery catkins, to 2 in. (50 mm) long; female cones are blue green, dangling, elongated, and pointed, 3–4 in. (75–100 mm) long, with scales and winged seed.

Plant hardiness: Zones 3–8. Hardy. Best in cold-winter climates.

Soil: Moist to damp, well-drained soil. Fertility: Rich–average. 5.0–6.5 pH.

Planting: Full sun. Space 12–16 ft. (3.7–4.9 m) apart.

Care: Easy–moderate. Keep moist; allow soil surface to dry between waterings. Avoid fertilizing. Prune to shape in spring, removing half of new growth "candles." Propagate by cuttings, seed.

Features: Good choice for accents, screens, windbreaks in meadow, woodland gardens and open landscapes. Maturing trees shade underfoliage, causing needle loss and branch death. Aphid, spider mite, gypsy moth, tussock moth and canker susceptible.

PINUS (PINE)

About 90 species of varied, rounded, pyramid-shaped, coniferous trees are included in the *Pinus* genus. They're native to the northern hemisphere, from seacoasts to the mountains. They are fast-growing, short-lived trees best used as container plants, temporary fillers, screens, or windbreaks.

Pines include both low and spreading as well as erect, pyramid-shaped, stately trees, from 10–200 ft. (3–61 m) tall. Because of this variation, choose species and cultivars carefully with their growth habits and mature size in mind. If kept rootbound in a planter, they will grow slowly and are good for use as bonsai and shape training. They are popular subjects for use in Asian gardens.

Pines require frequent raking of their fallen needles. They are susceptible to numerous pests and diseases, including some that may cause weakening of the tree's makeup. Keep these factors in mind as you plant pines near structures.

Because the *Pinus* genus is so varied, consider options beyond the popular pine species above, at right, consulting your garden center for advice.

Pines are important landscape trees prized for their rapid growth and versatility, from erect, conical elements in a landscape garden to plantings of many other purposes. They can have single or branching trunks with nodding branches that begin low on the tree, and easily are recognized by their bundles of mostly long, soft needles.

Plant pine trees in well-drained, acidic soil. Since all landscape trees perform best when they are planted in unamended soil, your site should be tested for acid-alkaline balance before planting. Pines need soils in the 5.0–6.5 pH range. Choose trees with characteristics that match your climate, USDA Plant Hardiness Zone, and local conditions.

Carefully match the depth of the planting hole to the soil line of your tree when planting. Backfill the hole with native soil, and water the tree whenever the soil surface becomes dry until it is well established.

To use pines as indoor holiday decorations, plant them in their containers, then unearth them, clean their containers, and bring them indoors. When use is finished, replant the trees in your garden.

Pine Species:

P. albicaulis, white-bark pine
P. attenuata, knob-cone pine
P. balfouriana, foxtail pine
P. banksiana, jack pine
P. bungeana, lace-bark pine
P. canariensis, Canary Island pine
P. cembra, Swiss stone pine
P. cembroides, Mexican piñon pine
P. contorta, shore pine
P. contorta var. *murrayana,* lodgepole pine
P. coulteri, big-cone pine
P. densiflora, Japanese red pine
P. eduluis, piñon pine
P. eldarica, Afghan pine
P. flexilis, limber pine
P. halepensis, aleppo pine
P. jeffreyi, Jeffrey pine
P. lambertiana, sugar pine
P. monticola, western white pine
P. mugo, mountain pine
P. muricata, Bishop pine
P. nigra, Austrian pine
P. parviflora, Japanese white pine
P. patula, Mexican yellow pine
P. pinea, Italian stone pine
P. pondersosa, ponderosa pine
P. radiata, Monterey pine
P. strobus, white pine
P. sylvestris, Scots pine
P. torreyana, Torrey pine

Tree: *Pinus* species. PINACEAE.

Common name: Pine.

Description: Over 90 species and many hybrids of fast-growing, short-lived, mostly upright, narrow, and conical, coniferous evergreen trees, to 200 ft. (61 m) tall, with both small, scale-like, deciduous and smooth, green, needlelike, evergreen leaves, 2–9 in. (50–229 mm) long, borne in 2-, 3-, or 5–needle, bundled clusters. Commonly cultivated landscape species include *P. aristata,* bristle-cone pine; *P. cembra,* Swiss stone pine; *P. contorta,* shore pine; *P. koraiensis,* Korean pine; *P. mugo,* mountain pine; and *P. peuce,* Balkan pine, among many others.

Catkins/Cones: Male cone resemble feathery catkins, 1–4 in. (25–100 mm) long; female cones are globular and pointed, 2–6 in. (50–150 mm) long, with woody seed and winged cone scales.

Plant hardiness: Zones 2–9. Mostly hardy; some semi-hardy or tender species.

Soil: Moist to dry, well-drained soil. Fertility: Rich–low. 5.0–6.5 pH.

Planting: Full sun. Space as recommended for species or hybrid.

Care: Easy. Allow soil surface to dry between waterings until established. Avoid fertilizing. Prune to shape in spring, removing half of new growth "candles." Propagate by cuttings, seed.

Features: Good choice for accents, shrub borders, containers, fencelines, screens, windbreaks in meadow, woodland gardens, lawns, and open landscapes. Drops needles, requiring maintenance. Susceptible to pine and pine-bark aphid, various beetles and moths, pine sawfly, scale, weevil, webworm and blister rust.

Tree: *Pinus densiflora* 'Umbraculifera'. PINACEAE.

Common name: Japanese Umbrella Pine (Japanese Red Pine, Tanyosho Pine).

Description: Cultivar of slow-growing, short-lived, upright, flat-crowned, coniferous, evergreen trees, to 12 ft. (3.7 m) tall, with both small, scalelike, deciduous and smooth, blue green, needlelike, evergreen leaves, 3–5 in. (75–125 mm) long, borne in 2-needle, bundled clusters, and orange red bark. *P. densiflora* 'Globosa' and 'Oculis-draconis', dragon's-eye pine, are closely related cultivars with similar care needs.

Catkins/Cones: Male cones, to 1–2 in. (25–50 mm) long, resemble feathery catkins; female cones are egg-shaped and pointed, 2 in. (50 mm) long, with woody seed and winged cone scales.

Plant hardiness: Zones 5–11. Semi-hardy.

Soil: Moist to dry, well-drained soil. Fertility: Rich–low. 5.0–6.5 pH.

Planting: Full sun. Space 10 ft. (3 m) apart.

Care: Easy. Allow soil surface to dry between waterings until established. Avoid fertilizing. Prune to shape in spring, removing half of new growth "candles." Propagate by cuttings, seed.

Features: Good choice for accents, containers, espaliers, screens in Chinese, Japanese, woodland gardens. Good for bonsai. Susceptible to pine and pine-bark aphid, various beetles and moths, scale and blister rust.

Tree: *Pinus strobus*. PINACEAE.

Common name: White Pine.

Description: Many cultivars of fast-growing, conical to rounded, coniferous, evergreen trees, to 120 ft. (37 m) tall, with smooth, blue or gray green, round, slender needles, to 6 in. (15 cm) long, borne in basal, 5-needle clusters. Common cultivars include *P. strobus* 'Brevifolia', 'Fastigata', 'Nana', and 'Pendula'.

Catkins/Cones: Male cones resemble feathery catkins, to 3 in. (75 mm) long; female cones are globular and pointed, to 6 in. (15 cm) long, with woody scales and winged seed.

Plant hardiness: Zones 3–9.

Soil: Damp to dry, well-drained soil. Fertility: Average–low. 6.0–7.0 pH.

Planting: Full sun. Space 15 ft. (4.5 m) apart.

Care: Easy. Allow soil surface to dry between waterings until established. Avoid fertilizing. Prune to shape in spring, removing half of new growth "candles." Propagate by cuttings, seed.

Features: Good choice for accents, shrub borders, containers, screens in woodland gardens and lawns. Susceptible to pine and pine-bark aphid, various beetles and moths, scale and blister rust.

Tree: *Pinus sylvestris*. PINACEAE.

Common name: Scots Pine (Scotch Pine).

Description: Many cultivars of medium-growing, upright, pyramid-shaped becoming irregular, open, coniferous, evergreen trees, 75–100 ft. (23–30 m) tall, with smooth, blue green, stiff, round, contorted needles, to 3 in. (75 mm) long, borne in basal, paired clusters, and with reddish gray bark. Common cultivars include *P. sylvestris* 'Argentea', 'Fastigata', 'French Blue', 'Nana', and 'Watereri'.

Catkins/Cones: Male cones resemble feathery catkins, to 3 in. (75 mm) long; female cones are blue to yellow green, oval and pointed, to 2½ in. (63 mm) long, with woody scales and winged seed.

Plant hardiness: Zones 2–9.

Soil: Damp, well-drained soil. Fertility: Average–low. 6.0–7.0 pH.

Planting: Full sun. Space 15–20 ft. (4.5–6 m) apart.

Care: Easy. Allow soil surface to dry between waterings until established, and water deeply during drought. Avoid fertilizing. Prune to shape in spring, removing half of new growth "candles." Propagate by cuttings, seed.

Features: Good choice for accents, screens in woodland gardens. Popular as cut, sheared tree for holiday decorations. Aphid, beetle, European pine shoot moth, scale and rust susceptible.

Tree: *Pistacia chinensis.* ANACARDIACEAE.

Common name: Chinese Pistache (Chinese Pistachio).

Description: A few cultivars of medium- to slow-growing, upright, round-crowned, open becoming dense, deciduous trees, to 60 ft. (18 m) tall, with shiny, frondlike, deep green leaves, 1 ft. (30 cm) long, divided into 6–10-paired, lance-shaped leaflets, to 2½ in. (63 mm) long, turning orange, red in autumn, and with pinkish gray, flaking bark.

Blooms/Fruit: Insignificant flowers in spring form round, red turning black, leathery, clustered fruit on female trees in summer, to 1½ in. (38 mm) wide, containing seed. Choose fruitless male cultivars.

Plant hardiness: Zones 6–9.

Soil: Damp, well-drained soil. Fertility: Average. 6.0–7.5 pH.

Planting: Full sun. Space 20–25 ft. (6–7.5 m) apart.

Care: Easy. Allow soil surface to dry between waterings until established. Avoid fertilizing. Prune to head and shape in autumn. Stake to support. Propagate by budding, grafting, seed.

Features: Good choice for accents, allées, backgrounds, containers, fencelines, screens in landscapes, roadside plantings and on sloped sites. Pest resistant. Verticillium wilt susceptible.

Tree: *Platanus* × *acerifolia.* PLATANACEAE.

Common name: London Plane Tree (Sycamore).

Description: Hybrids and cultivars of fast-growing, upright, branching or round-crowned, open to dense, deciduous trees, to 120 ft. (37 m) tall, with textured, maplelike, green, toothed, 3–5-lobed, veined leaves, to 8 in. (20 cm) long and wide, turning brown, yellow in autumn, and with patchy, brown, older bark, flaking to reveal irregular, light gray, younger bark.

Blooms/Seed: Insignificant hairy flowers in spring form dangling, round, brown seed clusters, to 1½ in. (38 mm) wide, in autumn, persisting through winter.

Plant hardiness: Zones 5–9. Best with winter chill.

Soil: Moist to damp, well-drained soil. Fertility: Rich–average. 6.5–7.5 pH.

Planting: Full sun. Space 20–30 ft. (6–9 m) apart.

Care: Easy. Allow soil surface to dry between waterings until established. Fertilize annually in spring until established. Prune in autumn to shape, pollard. Propagate by cuttings, grafting, layering, seed.

Features: Good choice for accents, allées, backgrounds, canopies, paths, screens, walls in open landscapes, lawns, roadside plantings. Drops fruit, leaves, twigs, requiring maintenance. Oak root fungus resistant. Sycamore lace bug, scale and anthracnose susceptible.

Tree: *Podocarpus* species. PODOCARPACEAE.

Common name: Yew Pine (Fern Pine, Southern Yew, Yellowwood).

Description: About 75 species of medium-growing, shrubby or upright and conical, either broad- or narrow-leaved, evergreen trees, 15–70 ft. (4.5–21 m) tall, depending on species, with mostly opposite, shiny or smooth, yewlike, deep green, divided leaves, ¼–7 in. (6–180 mm) long, in flat, nodding, feathery leaflets. Commonly cultivated species include *P. gracilior, P. latifolius, P. macrophyllus,* and *P. totara.*

Blooms/Fruit: Inconspicuous flowers on female trees form red, yellow, fleshy, berry-like fruit. Grown for foliage.

Plant hardiness: Zones 7–11. Semi-hardy.

Soil: Moist to damp, well-drained soil. Fertility: Average–low. 6.0–7.5 pH.

Planting: Full sun to partial shade. Spacing varies depending on species.

Care: Very easy. Keep damp; allow soil surface to dry between waterings. Avoid fertilizing. Prune to shape as for coniferous evergreens. Propagate by cuttings, seed.

Features: Good choice for accents, backgrounds, containers, hedges, screens in small-space, woodland gardens. Pest and disease resistant. Chlorosis susceptible.

POPULUS (POPLAR)

The *Populus* genus includes between 30 and 40 species of erect, slim, broad-leaved, deciduous trees, from as small as 15–20 ft. (4.5–6 m) tall and to as large as 100 ft. (30 m). They are native to the northern hemisphere. All are hardy and grow best in cold-winter, mild-summer areas that experience winter chill below 20°F (–7°C) for several months.

Poplars are prized for their narrow or round-crowned form and their graceful foliage, which colors to gold, red, and yellow in autumn. Because they are fast-growing and short-lived, their best use is as a temporary filler or accent.

Keep in mind that aspen and poplar are shallow-rooted trees that tend to be invasive. While they are moderately pest and disease resistant while young, they quickly become susceptible to beetle, poplar curculio, and scale as they mature and their growth slows. Also plan for frequent rakings to remove their fallen catkins, leaves, seed, and twigs.

Because poplar species are so varied, consider choices beyond the ones listed above, at right, and consult your garden center's staff for advice on the best tree species to plant in your region.

Aspens, cottonwoods, and poplars are often featured in landscapes found in cold-winter climates, along creeks and rivers, or where soils are naturally moist. All three trees are broad-leaved and deciduous, with attractive, heart-shaped leaves and open crowns. Because their wood is weak and branches sometimes fail at the crotch, they should be planted away from structures.

Poplar Species:
P. × *acuminata*, lance-leaved cottonwood
P. alba, white poplar
P. angustifolia, narrow-leaved poplar
P. balsamafera, balsam poplar
P. × *berolinensis*, Berlin poplar
P. × *canadensis*, Carolina poplar
P. canescens, big-leaved poplar
P. deltoides, eastern poplar
P. fremontii, western cottonwood
P. grandidentata, large-toothed aspen
P. lasiocarpa, Chinese poplar
P. maximowiczii, Japanese poplar
P. nigra 'Italica', Lombardy poplar
P. simonii, Simon poplar
P. tremuloides, quaking aspen
P. trichocarpa, black cottonwood

Plant poplars in moderately rich, moist, well-drained, acidic soil. All landscape trees grow best if planted in unamended soil; test the acid-alkaline balance of your site before you plant. Poplars should have soils in the 5.5–7.0 pH range. Choose those species that fit your climate and site.

When planting poplars, carefully match the depth of the planting hole to the soil line on the rootball of your tree. They do best when planted with their roots at the same depth below ground as they were grown at the nursery. Backfill around the rootball with native soil and give the tree ample water, keeping the soil evenly moist until the tree becomes established. Avoid applying fertilizer as you plant poplars.

Care needs for poplars include regular raking of fallen catkin-like flowers, leaves, twigs, and winged seed. Large poplars are good for seasonal shade above mixed-shrub borders, while those with smaller, more delicate forms are good landscape accents. In small-space gardens, the smaller species also make good container plants for use on balconies, decks, and patios. Be sure to regularly water all container trees.

Tree: *Populus* species. SALICACEAE.
Common name: Poplar (Aspen, Cottonwood).
Description: Nearly 40 species of fast-growing, short-lived, upright, columnar or branching, open, deciduous trees, varying in height depending on the species, with shiny, light green, heart-shaped, pointed, toothed leaves, 2–5 in. (50–125 mm) long, sometimes with light green, silver undersides, turning gold, red, yellow in autumn, and with gray, gray green, white, rough, furrowed bark.
Catkins/Seed: Willowlike catkins, to 2 in. (50 mm) long, in early spring before leaves emerge, form brown, clustered, hairy seed, ½–1 in. (12–25 mm) long, in spring.
Plant hardiness: Zones 2–9, depending on species.
Soil: Moist, well-drained soil. Fertility: Rich–average. 5.5–7.0 pH.
Planting: Full sun. Space as recommended for species.
Care: Moderate. Keep evenly moist. Avoid fertilizing. Prune in autumn to shape, remove suckers. Propagate by cuttings, grafting, seed, suckers.
Features: Good choice for borders, fencelines, groups, screens in cold-climate, mountain gardens. Good for temporary plantings. Drops leaves, seed, twigs, requiring maintenance. Very invasive. Shallow rooted. Generally disease resistant. Cottonwood leaf beetle, poplar curculio, scale susceptible.

Tree: *Populus nigra* 'Italica'. SALICACEAE.

Common name: Lombardy Poplar.

Description: Several cultivars of fast-growing, short-lived, upright, columnar or conical, branching, open, deciduous trees, to 90 ft. (27 m) tall and 30 ft. (9 m) wide, with shiny, light green, heart-shaped, pointed, toothed leaves, to 4 in. (10 cm) long, turning gold, yellow in autumn, and with gray, gray green, white, smooth becoming rough and furrowed bark.

Catkins/Seed: Willowlike catkins, to 2 in. (50 mm) long, in early spring before leaves emerge, form brown, clustered, hairy seed, ½–1 in. (12–25 mm) long, in spring.

Plant hardiness: Zones 2–9. Hardy. Best in cold-winter climates.

Soil: Moist, well-drained soil. Fertility: Rich–average. 5.5–7.0 pH.

Planting: Full sun. Space 7–10 ft. (2.2–3 m) apart.

Care: Moderate. Keep evenly moist. Avoid fertilizing. Prune in autumn to shape, remove suckers. Propagate by cuttings, grafting, seed, suckers.

Features: Good choice for borders, fencelines, groups, screens in cold-climate, mountain gardens. Good for temporary plantings. Drops leaves, seed, twigs, requiring maintenance. Very invasive. Shallow rooted. Cottonwood leaf beetle, poplar curculio, scale and canker susceptible.

Tree: *Populus tremuloides.* SALICACEAE.

Common name: Quaking Aspen.

Description: Several cultivars of fast-growing, short-lived, upright, branching, open, deciduous trees, to 60 ft. (18 m) tall and 30 ft. (9 m) wide, with shiny, light green, heart-shaped, pointed, toothed leaves, 1–3 in. (25–75 mm) long, turning gold, yellow in autumn, and with gray green, white, smooth becoming rough bark.

Catkins/Seed: Willowlike catkins, to 1 in. (25 mm) long, in early spring before leaves emerge, form brown, clustered, hairy seed, ½–1 in. (12–25 mm) long, in spring.

Plant hardiness: Zones 2–8. Hardy. Best in cold-winter climates, high elevations.

Soil: Moist, well-drained soil. Fertility: Rich–average. 5.5–7.0 pH.

Planting: Full sun. Space 8–12 ft. (2.4–3.7 m) apart.

Care: Moderate. Keep evenly moist. Avoid fertilizing. Prune in autumn to shape, remove suckers. Propagate by cuttings, grafting, seed, suckers.

Features: Good choice for borders, fencelines, groups, screens in cold-climate, mountain, woodland gardens. Drops leaves, seed, twigs, requiring maintenance. Very invasive. Shallow rooted. Generally disease resistant. Cottonwood leaf beetle, poplar curculio, scale susceptible.

Tree: *Prunus* species, hybrids, and cultivars. ROSACEAE.

Common name: Flowering Plum.

Description: Many hybrid cultivars and several species of medium-growing, short-lived, upright, branching, deciduous trees, 20–25 ft. (6–7.5 m) tall and 12–15 ft. (3.7–4.5 m) wide, with shiny, bronze becoming deep green, purple, oval, pointed, toothed leaves, 3–4 in. (75–100 mm) long, turning gold, purple, red, yellow in autumn, and with gray, tan, smooth bark.

Blooms/Fruit: Many showy, pink, rose, white, mostly single, sometimes wavy-petaled flowers, 1–2 in. (25–50 mm) long, borne in profuse clusters, in early spring, may form edible, round, purple, yellow, fleshy, pitted fruit, ½–1 in. (12–25 mm) wide, in summer. Best with winter chill.

Plant hardiness: Zones 5–9. Hardy.

Soil: Damp, well-drained, sandy loam. Fertility: Rich. 6.0–7.0 pH.

Planting: Full sun. Space 6–8 ft. (1.8–2.4 m) apart.

Care: Moderate. Keep moist until established; drought tolerant thereafter. Fertilize quarterly. Prune after bloom to shape. Propagate by budding, cuttings, grafting, seed.

Features: Good choice for accents, groups, screens in formal, woodland gardens. Good for Chinese-, Japanese-themed gardens. Shallow rooted. Aphid, spider mite and black spot, fungal disease susceptible.

Tree: *Prunus* species and hybrids. ROSACEAE.
Common name: Flowering Cherry.
Description: About 5 species and hundreds of hybrids of medium-growing, short-lived, upright, spreading, deciduous ornamental trees, 25–35 ft. (7.5–11 m) tall and wide, with smooth, green, veined leaves, to 5 in. (13 cm) long, turning yellow in autumn.
Blooms/Fruit: Many showy, crepelike, pink, rose, white, clustered flowers, 1–2 in. (25–50 mm) wide, in spring, form cherries in late spring or are fruitless.
Plant hardiness: Zones 4–9, depending on species or cultivar. Best with winter chill, in cool, low-humidity climates.
Soil: Damp, well-drained soil. Fertility: Rich. 6.5–7.5 pH.
Planting: Full to filtered sun. Space 15–20 ft. (4.5–6 m) apart.
Care: Moderate. Allow soil surface to dry between waterings until established. Fertilize annually in spring until established. Prune after flowering; remove root suckers on grafted stock. Propagate by cuttings, grafting, seed.
Features: Good choice for accents, containers, paths in Asian gardens. Drops flowers, foliage, requiring maintenance. Smog, pest and fungal disease susceptible.

Tree: *Pseudolarix amabilis (P. kaempferi)*. PINACEAE.
Common name: Golden Larch.
Description: Single species of medium-growing, upright, branching and layered, cone-shaped, coniferous, deciduous trees closely related to true larch, usually 20–50 ft. (6–15 m) tall and wide, with smooth, feathery, blue green needles, to 2½ in. (63 mm) long, borne singly or in whorled clusters along the branchlets, turning gold and dropping in autumn.
Blooms/Seed: Cones are green turning brown, rose-shaped, to 3 in. (75 mm) long, borne in dangling clusters, with woody scales and 2-winged seed.
Plant hardiness: Zones 6–7. Best with winter chill.
Soil: Moist, well-drained soil. Fertility: Average. 5.5–7.0 pH.
Planting: Full sun. Space 12–25 ft. (3.7–7.5 m) apart. Avoid crowding to prevent disease.

Care: Moderate. Keep evenly moist. Fertilize annually until established. Prune sparingly in winter. Propagate by seed.
Features: Good choice for accents, backgrounds, foliage color, screens in open landscapes and lawns. Good for seasonal shade. Drops cones, foliage, requiring maintenance. Pest and disease resistant.

Tree: *Pseudotsuga menziesii (P. douglasii, P. taxifolia)*. PINACEAE.
Common name: Douglas Fir.
Description: Several cultivars of fast-growing, long-lived, erect, narrow, conical, coniferous evergreen trees, occasionally to 275 ft. (85 m) tall though rarely over 150 ft. (45 m) tall in landscape use, with smooth, light green becoming deep blue green, soft needles, 1–1½ in. (25–38 mm) long, with scaly growth tips and chocolate brown, gray, rough bark. Common cultivars and varieties include *P. menziesii* 'Fastigiata' and 'Pendula', and *P. menziesii* var. 'Glauca'.
Catkins/Cones: Male cones, to 1 in. (25 mm) long; female cones are narrow, oval, and pointed, 4–5 in. (10–13 cm) long, with paired woody seed and long, winged cone scales. Differs from *Abies* species, fir, by bearing nodding rather than erect cones.
Plant hardiness: Zones 2–9. Hardy. Best in mild-summer climates.
Soil: Moist, well-drained humus. Fertility: Rich–average. 5.5–7.5 pH.
Planting: Full sun to partial shade. Space 15–20 ft. (4.5–6 m) apart.
Care: Easy. Keep moist until established; allow soil to dry between waterings. Avoid fertilizing. Prune in spring, removing half of new growth "candles". Propagate by grafting, seed.
Features: Good choice for accents, shrub borders, screens, windbreaks in meadow, turfgrass, woodland gardens and open landscapes. Good for holiday decorations. Aphid, borer, budworm, Douglas-fir pitch moth, pine moth and scale susceptible.

Tree: *Psorothamnus spinosus (Dalea spinosa).* FABACEAE (LEGUMINOSAE).

Common name: Smoke Tree.

Description: Several cultivars of slow-growing, long-lived, bushy, deciduous trees, to 20 ft. (6 m) tall, with smooth, silver gray, light green, hairy, lance-shaped, pointed leaves, to ½ in. (12 mm) long, and gray, smooth or furrowed bark armed with sharp spines.

Blooms/Seed: Many showy, pealike, pink, purple, violet flowers, in late spring, borne in dangling clusters, 1½–2 in. (38–50 mm) long, form kidney-shaped, hairy, beanlike pods, 1–2 in. (25–50 mm) long, each bearing a single seed, in late summer.

Plant hardiness: Zones 7–9. Hardy. Best in hot-summer, arid climates.

Soil: Dry, well-drained, sandy soil. Fertility: Average–low. 6.5–8.0 pH.

Planting: Full sun. Space 7–10 ft. (2.2–3 m) apart.

Care: Easy. Keep damp until established; allow soil to dry between waterings. Avoid fertilizing and pruning. Propagate by seed.

Features: Good choice for accents, backgrounds, screens, shade in arid gardens. Good for cutting. Pest and disease resistent.

Tree: *Punica granatum.* PUNICACEAE.

Common name: Pomegranate.

Description: Many cultivars of slow-growing, fruiting, upright, branching, deciduous, shrubby trees, 3–10 ft. (90–305 cm) tall and wide, with shiny, deep green, oval or lance-shaped, pointed leaves, 2–3 in. (50–75 mm) long, turning gold, yellow in autumn, and with gray brown, smooth bark, sometimes armed with spines.

Blooms/Fruit: Many showy, carnation-like, cream, orange, red, white, yellow, single or double flowers, 1–2 in. (25–50 mm) wide, in spring–summer, form edible, round, yellow becoming ruby red, leather-husked, seedy fruit, 3–5 in. (75–125 mm) wide, in late autumn.

Plant hardiness: Zones 8–11. Semi-hardy.

Soil: Moist, well-drained loam. Fertility: Rich–average. 6.0–7.0 pH.

Planting: Full sun. Space 4–6 ft. (1.2–1.8 m) apart.

Care: Easy. Keep moist until established; drought tolerant thereafter. Fertilize quarterly. Prune in early spring to shape, remove spent branches. Propagate by cuttings, layering, seed.

Features: Good choice for accents, backgrounds, borders, containers, edgings, hedges in formal, natural, small-space gardens. Good for edible fruit. Attracts birds, hummingbirds. Pest and disease resistant.

Tree: *Pyrus calleryana.* ROSACEAE.

Common name: Callery Pear.

Description: Many cultivars of fast-growing, upright, round-crowned or columnar, open, thorny, semi-evergreen trees, to 50 ft. (15 m) tall, with shiny, green, broadly oval, pointed leaves, to 3 in. (75 mm) long, turning red, yellow in autumn, and with gray green, smooth bark. Avoid brittle, disease-susceptible, short-lived 'Bradford' cultivar; choose instead 'Aristocrat', 'Chanticleer', 'Redspire', or 'Whitehouse'.

Blooms/Fruit: Many showy, white, simple flowers, to 1 in. (25 mm) wide, in early spring, borne in stemmed clusters, form brown, pearlike, inedible fruit or are fruitless, depending on cultivar.

Plant hardiness: Zones 5–9. Best with winter chill.

Soil: Damp, well-drained soil. Fertility: Average. 6.5–7.5 pH.

Planting: Full sun. Space 8–12 ft. (2.4–3.7 m) apart.

Care: Easy. Allow soil surface to dry between waterings until established. Fertilize annually in spring. Prune in autumn. Propagate by budding, grafting.

Features: Good choice for accents, backgrounds, borders, containers, edgings, paths, walls in formal, small-space gardens. Smog tolerant. Pest, disease, and fireblight resistant.

QUERCUS (OAK)

About 450 species of mostly large, long-lived, round-crowned, many-branched, deciduous and evergreen trees belong to the important *Quercus* genus. All are native to the temperate zones and tropical mountains of the northern hemisphere. They also are commercially important trees grown for their hard, durable lumber used for furniture.

Oaks perform best in regions with winter chill. If you garden in an area of mostly hot, dry summers and mild winters, choose native species adapted to your region.

Ornamental oak species usually are medium-growing trees. Most reach 60–80 ft. (18–24 m) tall, becoming slow-growing as they become mature.

Pests of oaks include gall insects, gypsy moth larva, leaf miner, oak twig pruner, scale, as well as canker and oak worms. They also are susceptible to diseases such as anthracnose, sudden oak death, shoe-string rot, and oak wilt.

Oaks can take many years to mature. Consult with your garden center staff for recommendations before planting one of the popular landscape and native oak species above, at right.

Oaks are prized, major elements of any landscape. When mature, they have massive, single trunks with radiating, thick, sweeping branches that are uplifted and spreading. Those found in warm-summer climates often are evergreen or semi-evergreen, but the deciduous species found in cold-winter areas frequently have spectacular displays of red or yellow autumn color.

Plant oaks in rich, moist, well-drained, acidic soil. While all trees perform best when planted in native soil, it is especially important for oaks. Your site should be tested for an acid-alkaline balance measuring 5.5–7.0 pH before planting. Also match your tree's needs to your climate, especially when choosing a native oak species.

When you plant, carefully measure so that the depth of the planting hole is equal to the soil line of your tree's rootball. The roots of the planting should be at the same depth in its new location as when it was grown at the tree nursery. Backfill the planting hole with native soil, surround it with a moat, and water the tree whenever the soil surface becomes dry.

Oak Species:

Q. acutissima, sawtooth oak
Q. agrifolia, coast live oak
Q. alba, white oak
Q. berberidifolia, scrub oak
Q. bicolor, swamp white oak
Q. buckleyi, Spanish oak
Q. chrysolepis, canyon live oak
Q. coccinea, scarlet oak
Q. douglasii, blue oak
Q. durata, leather oak
Q. emoryi, Emory oak
Q. englemanni, Englemann oak
Q. frainetto, Italian oak
Q. gambellii, Gambel oak
Q. ilex, holly oak
Q. kelloggii, California black oak
Q. lobata, California white oak
Q. macrocarpa, bur oak
Q. muehlenbergii, chinquapin
Q. myrsinifolia, Japanese live oak
Q. palustris, pin oak
Q. phellos, willow oak
Q. robur, English oak
Q. rubra, red oak
Q. suber, cork oak
Q. virginiana, live oak
Q. wislizenii, interior live oak

Give your oaks ample room. The recommended spacing of 15–25 ft. (4.5–7.5 m) is the minimum to consider when planting oaks near a structure; double or triple that spacing to plant specimen trees.

Tree: *Quercus coccinea*. FAGACEAE.

Common name: Scarlet Oak.

Description: Several cultivars of medium-growing, upright, pyramid-shaped or round-crowned, open, deciduous trees, to 80 ft. (24 m) tall, with shiny, deep green, lance-shaped, pointed, 7–9-lobed, very deeply cut leaves, to 6 in. (15 cm) long, turning red in autumn, persisting into winter, and with gray brown, platelike bark.

Catkins/Nuts: Many inconspicuous, willowlike, pale green, dangling or spiking catkins, in spring, form round acorns in autumn, to 1 in. (25 mm) long, with cup-shaped caps half surrounding each nutshell.

Plant hardiness: Zones 4–9. Best with winter chill.

Soil: Moist, well-drained soil. Fertility: Rich. 5.5–7.0 pH.

Planting: Full sun. Space 15–25 ft. (4.5–7.5 m) apart.

Care: Moderate. Allow soil surface to dry between waterings. Fertilize annually in spring until established. Prune in autumn. Propagate by cuttings, grafting, seed.

Features: Good choice for accents, allées, paths, screens in open landscapes, lawns, and road-side plantings. Drops acorns, leaves, requiring maintenance. Gall, gypsy moth, oak-leaf pruner, scale and anthracnose, canker, chlorosis, oak wilt susceptible.

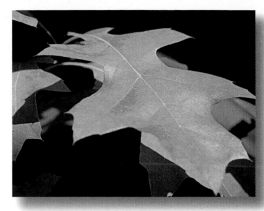

Tree: *Quercus palustris.* FAGACEAE.

Common name: Pin Oak (Spanish Oak, Swamp Oak).

Description: Several cultivars of medium-growing, upright, pyramid-shaped, open, deciduous trees, to 80 ft. (24 m) tall, with shiny, deep green, lance-shaped, pointed, 5–7-lobed, deeply cut leaves, to 5 in. (13 cm) long, turning brown, red, yellow in autumn, persisting into winter, and with gray brown, furrowed bark.

Blooms/Nuts: Many inconspicuous, willowlike, pale green, dangling or spiking catkins, in spring, form round acorns, to ¾ in. (19 mm) long, in autumn, with cup-shaped caps partially surrounding each nutshell.

Plant hardiness: Zones 2–10.

Soil: Moist, well-drained soil. Fertility: Rich. 6.0–7.0 pH.

Planting: Full sun. Space 15–25 ft. (4.5–7.5 m) apart.

Care: Moderate. Keep evenly moist. Fertilize annually in spring until established. Propagate by cuttings, grafting, seed.

Features: Good choice for accents, paths, screens in open landscapes and lawns. Drops acorns, leaves, requiring maintenance. Gall, gypsy moth, oak-leaf pruner, scale and anthracnose, canker, chlorosis, oak wilt susceptible.

Tree: *Quercus rubra (Q. borealis).* FAGACEAE.

Common name: Red Oak (Northern Red Oak).

Description: Several cultivars of fast-growing, upright, pyramid-shaped turning round-crowned and branching, open, deciduous trees, to 80 ft. (24 m) tall, with shiny, red turning deep green, oval, pointed, 7–11-lobed, deeply cut leaves, turning red in autumn, and with deep gray to chocolate brown, roughly furrowed bark.

Catkins/Nuts: Many inconspicuous, willowlike, pale green, dangling or spiking catkins, in spring, form acorns to 1 in. (25 mm) long, in autumn, with cup-shaped caps partially surrounding each nutshell.

Plant hardiness: Zones 2–9. Best with winter chill.

Soil: Moist, well-drained soil. Fertility: Rich. 5.5–7.0 pH.

Planting: Full sun. Space 15–25 ft. (4.5–7.5 m) apart.

Care: Moderate. Keep moist. Pinch to train, prune in autumn. Transplants easily in spring. Propagate by cuttings, grafting, seed.

Features: Good choice for accents, screens in open landscapes. Drops acorns, leaves, requiring maintenance. Gall, gypsy moth and canker, oak wilt susceptible.

Tree: *Robinia pseudoacacia.* FABACEAE (LEGUMINOSAE).

Common name: Black Locust (False Acacia).

Description: Many cultivars of fast- to medium-growing, upright, round-crowned, open, thorny, deciduous trees, to 75 ft. (23 m) tall, with frondlike, green leaves, 8–12 in. (20–30 cm) long, divided into 9-paired oval leaflets, turning yellow in autumn, and with black or deep brown, roughly furrowed bark.

Blooms/Fruit: Depending on the species, many or few, fragrant, pealike, white flowers, borne in dangling clusters, 3–4 in. (75–100 mm) long, in late spring, form reddish brown, podlike fruit, to 4 in. (10 cm) long, containing a row of seed and persisting into winter.

Plant hardiness: Zones 3–10. Best with some winter chill.

Soil: Damp to dry, well-drained soil. Fertility: Average–low. 6.0–7.5 pH. Salt tolerant.

Planting: Full sun. Space 10–20 ft. (3–6 m) apart, depending on species.

Care: Easy. Allow soil surface to dry between waterings until established. Drought tolerant. Avoid fertilizing. Prune to thin, remove suckers in summer. Propagate by cuttings, division, grafting, seed, suckers.

Features: Good choice for low-fertility soil in arid, open gardens. Drops flowers, pods, requiring maintenance. Invasive. Shallow rooted. Locust borer, leaf miner, scale susceptible.

SALIX (WILLOW)

While the *Salix* genus numbers nearly 300 species of diverse trees, shrubs, and ground covers, most are noted for habits that limit their use in the landscape. They are native to cold and temperate zones throughout most of the world except Australia. All are hardy and grow best in cold-winter climates.

Willows have narrow, lance-shaped leaves hung from their limber, often nodding or pendulous branches made of weak, brittle wood. They turn various shades of brown or yellow in autumn, before beginning a year-round cycle of dropped leaves, woody capsules, catkins, twigs, and seed.

The large landscape willows—*S. alba*, white willow; and *S. babylonica*, weeping willow—are trees worthy of use in many landscape settings.

Willows are fast-growing trees that vary from 6–100 ft. (1.8–30 m) tall. A species or cultivar exists for nearly every garden purpose.

They are susceptible to a host of pests and many different fungal and viral diseases.

If you choose to plant willows, select a tree from the list above, at right.

The glamour of a weeping willow swaying gently over the water's edge belies the constant care they require to maintain their attractive appearance. Still, in the right setting, willows can create a lush and beautiful effect worthy of estuarine, meadow, natural, and woodland gardens. As coppiced shrubs, they grow copious branches full of delightful pussy willows in spring, and some cultivars have contorted branches ideal for cutting and arranging.

Willow Species:
- *S. alba*, white willow
- *S. babylonica*, weeping willow
- *S. caprea*, French pussy willow
- *S. discolor*, pussy willow
- *S. gracilistyla*, rose gold pussy willow
- *S. integra*, dappled willow
- *S. matsudana*, Hankow willow
- *S. pentandra*, laurel willow
- *S. purpurea*, purple osier
- *S. reticulata*, neat-leaved willow
- *S. udensis*, Japanese fantail willow

Plant willows in average, moist, well-drained, sandy, acidic to neutral soil. All landscape trees grow best in undisturbed native soil. It's best to test the acid-alkaline balance of your site before you plant; willows should have soils in the 5.5–7.5 pH range. Choose species that fit your USDA Plant Hardiness Zone, climate, and site.

When planting a willow, match the depth of the hole to the soil line on the rootball of your tree, taking care to avoid too-deep planting. Backfill around the rootball with native soil and keep the tree well watered until it becomes established and begins to spurt upwards with new growth.

Willows are ideal companions to garden water features. Their dense foliage shades and cools the water, helping to prevent growth of algae. They are good companions to other acid-loving plants, including azaleas, camellias, ferns, and rhododendrons . Their care needs include regular raking of fallen catkinlike flowers in spring and leaves, seed, and seed-pods in autumn. They attract birds drawn to their supple limbs for their nest building, egg laying, and young rearing.

Small willows are good container trees for use on balconies, patios, and decks. Keep them evenly moist and protect their roots from sun.

Tree: *Salix* species. SALICACEAE.

Common name: Willow.

Description: About 300 species of fast-growing, usually upright and spreading, open, branching, brittle, deciduous trees, 6–100 ft. (1.8–30 m) tall, depending on species, with smooth, light green to yellow green, usually lance-shaped, pointed leaves, ¾–6 in. (19–150 mm) long, depending on species, turning yellow in autumn, and with pink or red turning gray, smooth becoming fissured bark.

Catkins/Fruit: Small catkins, ½–3 in. (12–75 mm) long, in spring before leaves emerge or with leaf buds, form brown, woody capsules, ½–1 in. (12–25 mm) long, bearing hairy, tuftlike seed, in early summer.

Plant hardiness: Zones 1–10, depending on species.

Soil: Moist, well-drained soil. Fertility: Rich–low. 6.0–7.5 pH.

Planting: Full sun. Space as recommended for species.

Care: Easy–moderate. Keep evenly moist. Avoid fertilizing. Prune in autumn to shape, limit spread. Propagate by cuttings, seed.

Features: Good choice for accents, screens in landscapes and water gardens. Good for erosion control, temporary plantings. Very invasive. Shallow rooted. Susceptible to more than 120 insect pests and numerous diseases.

Tree: *Salix babylonica.* SALICACEAE.

Common name: Weeping Willow (Babylon Weeping Willow).

Description: Several cultivars of fast-growing, usually upright, spreading, arching and dangling, dense, deciduous trees, 40–50 ft. (12–15 m) tall and wide, with smooth, light green to green, lance-shaped, narrow, pointed leaves, to 6 in. (15 cm) long, on long, nodding branches, turning yellow in autumn.

Catkins/Fruit: Small catkins, ½–1 in. (12–25 mm) long, in spring with emerging leaves, form brown, woody capsules, ½–1 in. (12–25 mm) long, bearing hairy, tuft-like seed, in early summer.

Plant hardiness: Zones 5–11, depending on species.

Soil: Moist, well-drained soil. Fertility: Rich–low. 5.5–7.5 pH.

Planting: Full sun. Space 15–20 ft. (4.5–6 m) apart.

Care: Easy. Keep evenly moist until established. Fertilize quarterly. Prune in autumn to open, shape. Propagate by cuttings, grafting, seed.

Features: Good choice for accents, screens, specimens in bog, meadow, woodland gardens, landscapes and water feature shorelines. Good for basket weaving. Shallow rooted. Pest and disease resistant.

Tree: *Sassafras albidum.* LAURACEAE.

Common name: Sassafras.

Description: A few cultivars of fast- to medium-growing, upright, irregular, open, deciduous trees, to 60 ft. (18 m) tall, with fragrant bark, often with multiple trunks, and with shiny, green, oval or mitten-shaped, broad, often lobed, fragrant leaves, to 5 in. (13 cm) long and wide, turning gold, red in autumn, and with red brown bark.

Blooms/Fruit: Many fragrant, ribbonlike, yellow flowers, to 2 in. (50 mm) long, borne in clusters in spring, form deep blue, purple, clustered, berrylike fruit, to ½ in. (12 mm) wide, on red stalks in autumn.

Plant hardiness: Zones 4–9.

Soil: Damp, well-drained soil. Fertility: Average–poor. 6.0–7.0 pH.

Planting: Full sun. Space 15–20 ft. (4.5–6 m) apart.

Care: Easy. Allow soil surface to dry between waterings. Avoid fertilizing and transplanting. Prune suckers in autumn to maintain treelike appearance. Propagate by cuttings, seed.

Features: Good choice for allées, screens in open landscapes. Disease resistant. Japanese beetle, borer, gypsy moth susceptible.

Tree: *Schinus molle.* ANACARDIACEAE.

Common name: California Pepper Tree (Australian Pepper).

Description: Several cultivars of fast-growing, upright, spreading, deciduous trees, 20–50 ft. (6–15 m) tall and wide, with smooth, frondlike, light green, fragrant leaves, to 9 in. (23 cm) long, as 15–41-paired, lance-shaped leaflets along each nodding branch, and with rough, cinnamon, gnarled, flaking bark. *S. terebinthifolius* is a closely related species.

Blooms/Fruit: Many fragrant, spikelike, dangling, white, yellow, clustered flowers, to 6 in. (15 cm) long, in spring, form small, edible, red, clustered, berrylike fruit in autumn–winter.

Plant hardiness: Zones 6–11. Best in hot-summer climates.

Soil: Damp, well-drained soil. Fertility: Average–low. 6.5–7.5 pH.

Planting: Full sun. Space 5 ft. (1.5 m) apart, zones 6–8; 8–12 ft. (2.4–3.7 m) apart, zones 9–11.

Care: Easy. Allow soil surface to dry between waterings until established. Prune in autumn. Propagate by cuttings, seed.

Features: Good choice for accents, walls in arid climates, open gardens, lawns. Drought tolerant when established. Drops flowers, fruit, leaves, twigs, requiring maintenance. Invasive. Shallow rooted. Disease resistant. Black scale susceptible.

Tree: *Sequoia sempervirens.* TAXODIACEAE.

Common name: Coast Redwood (Sequoia).

Description: Single species of fast-growing, pyramid-shaped, narrow, coniferous, ever-green tree, sometimes to 360 ft. (110 m) tall but seldom more than 100 ft. (30 m) tall in landscape use, and with trunks to 50 ft. (15 m) in diameter but usually less than 5 ft. (1.5 m) wide, with shiny, flat, blue green, deep green needles, ¾–1 in. (19–25 mm) long, with silvery undersides, and with thick, fibrous, red, fissured bark.

Blooms/Cones: Stemless, drooping, spikelike male cones and tiny, round, chocolate brown, stemmed female cones, to ¾ in. (19 mm) long, appear in spring, ripening in summer, containing scaly, winged, seldom fertile seed.

Plant hardiness: Zones 7–10. Best in mild year-round climates with ample humidity.

Soil: Moist, well-drained soil. Fertility: Rich–average. 5.5–7.0 pH.

Planting: Full to filtered sun. Space 7–12 ft. (2.2–3.7 m) apart.

Care: Easy. Keep evenly moist. Fertilize annually. Prune suckers. Protect from heat. Propagate by burls, cuttings, seed, suckers.

Features: Good choice for accents, groups, screens in meadow, seaside, turfgrass, woodland gardens. Drops cones, needles, requiring maintenance. Shallow rooted. Pest and disease resistant. Chlorosis susceptible.

Tree: *Sequoiadendron giganteum (S. gigantea).* TAXODIACEAE.

Common name: Giant Sequoia (Big Tree Redwood)

Description: Single species of medium-growth, conical becoming broad, coniferous, ever-green tree, sometimes to 250 ft. (79 m) tall but seldom more than 100 ft. (30 m) tall in landscape use, with trunks to 37 ft. (11.3 m) in diameter but usually less than 5 ft. (1.5 m) wide, with shiny, cypresslike, gray green, lance-shaped needles, ½–¾ in. (12–19 mm) long, with silvery undersides, and with thick, fibrous, red, fissured bark.

Blooms/Cones: Stemless, drooping, spikelike male cones and tiny, oval, green, stemmed, female cones, to 3 in. (75 mm) long, appear in spring, ripening in autumn, containing seed, and remaining on the tree for many seasons.

Plant hardiness: Zones 2–9. Best in cold-winter climates with ample snowfall.

Soil: Moist to damp, well-drained, sandy soil. Fertility: Average–low. 5.5–7.5 pH.

Planting: Full sun. Space 7–12 ft. (2.2–3.7 m) apart.

Care: Easy. Keep moist until established; drought tolerant therafter. Avoid fertilizing. Prune to remove dangling branches. Propagate by seed.

Features: Good choice for accents, groups, screens in alpine, meadow, turfgrass, woodland gardens. Shallow rooted. Pest resistant. Fungal disease susceptible.

Tree: *Sophora japonica.* FABACEAE (LEGUMINOSAE).

Common name: Japanese Pagoda Tree.

Description: Several cultivars of medium-growing, upright, vase-shaped becoming round-crowned, open, deciduous trees, to 80 ft. (24 m) tall, with frondlike green leaves, 7–10 in. (18–25 cm) long, divided into 3–8-paired, oval or lance-shaped leaflets, to 2 in. (50 mm) long, with light green undersides, turning yellow in autumn.

Blooms/Fruit: Many showy, pealike, white, yellow flowers, to ½ in. (12 mm) long, in summer when mature, borne in spiking clusters, to 1 ft. (30 cm) long, form brown, beanlike pods in autumn, to 3 in. (75 mm) long, containing smooth seed.

Plant hardiness: Zones 4–10. Best with summer heat.

Soil: Damp, well-drained soil. Fertility: Average–low. 6.5–7.5 pH.

Planting: Full sun. Space 15–20 ft. (4.5–6 m) apart.

Care: Moderate. Allow soil surface to dry between waterings. Prune sparingly. Protect from ice. Propagate by cuttings, grafting, layering, seed.

Features: Good choice for accents, containers in small-space gardens. Drops staining flowers, seedpods, requiring maintenance. Smog tolerant. Pest and disease resistant.

Tree: *Sorbus aucuparia.* ROSACEAE.

Common name: European Mountain Ash (Rowan Tree).

Description: Several cultivars of medium-growing, upright, oval- or round-crowned, dense, deciduous trees, to 60 ft. (18 m) tall, with frondlike, green leaves, 4–10 in. (10–25 cm) long, divided into 13- or 15-paired, blade-shaped, sharp-toothed leaflets, to 2½ in. (63 mm) long, turning red in autumn, and with gray brown bark.

Blooms/Fruit: Many showy, white flowers, to ¼ in. (6 mm) wide, borne in flat clusters in spring, form round, orange, red, mealy, berrylike, clustered fruit, to ¼ in. (6 mm) wide, in late summer.

Plant hardiness: Zones 1–9. Best with winter chill and mild summers.

Soil: Moist, well-drained soil. Fertility: Rich–average. 6.0–7.0 pH.

Planting: Full sun. Space 10–15 ft. (3–4.5 m) apart.

Care: Easy. Allow soil surface to dry between waterings until established. Fertilize annually in spring until established. Prune to shape in autumn. Protect from sun, wind in hot climates. Propagate by budding, layering, seed.

Features: Good choice for accents, containers, espaliers in small-space gardens and landscape beds. Drops staining fruit, requiring maintenance. Sawfly, scale and canker, fireblight susceptible.

Tree: *Stewartia* species. THEACEAE.

Common name: Stewartia.

Description: A few species of slow-growing, spreading, pyramid-shaped becoming round-crowned, open, deciduous, shrubby trees, 10–25 ft. (3–7.5 m) tall, with shiny, deep green, oval, pointed, toothed leaves, 2–4 in. (50–100 mm) long, turning orange, red, yellow in autumn, and with flaking, red brown turning white bark.

Blooms/Fruit: Single, camellia-like, white, wavy-edged, orange-centered flowers, 2–3 in. (50–75 mm) wide, in summer, form woody, brown, oval capsules containing wingless seed, in autumn.

Plant hardiness: Zones 6–9, depending on species.

Soil: Moist, well-drained humus. Fertility: Rich. 5.5–6.5 pH.

Planting: Full to filtered sun. Space 6–10 ft. (1.8–3 m) apart.

Care: Easy. Keep evenly moist. Fertilize annually in spring. Prune to shape in autumn. Avoid transplanting. Propagate by cuttings, layering, seed.

Features: Good choice for accents, beds, borders, foregrounds, mixed plantings in cottage, shade, woodland gardens. Pest and disease resistant.

Tree: *Styrax japonicus.* STYRACACEAE.

Common name: Japanese Snowbell (Snowdrop, Storax).

Description: Several cultivars of medium- to slow-growing, upright, spreading, deciduous shrubby trees, to 30 ft. (9 m) tall, often with multiple trunks, with shiny, deep green, lance-shaped, pointed, veined leaves, to 3 in. (75 mm) long, turning red, yellow in autumn, and with smooth, gray, fissured bark. *S. obassia* is a closely related species with similar care needs.

Blooms/Fruit: Many showy, sometimes fragrant, yellow, bell-shaped flowers, to ¾ in. (19 mm) long, in early summer, borne in dangling clusters, to 8 in. (20 cm) long, form mealy, berrylike fruit, to ½ in. (12 mm) long, containing seed, in autumn.

Plant hardiness: Zones 5–9. Protect from cold until established, zones 5–7.

Soil: Moist, well-drained soil. Fertility: Rich–average. 5.5–7.0 pH.

Planting: Full to filtered sun. Space 15–20 ft. (4.5–6 m) apart.

Care: Moderate. Allow soil surface to dry between waterings until established. Fertilize annually in spring until established. Prune to shape after bloom, remove suckers. Avoid transplanting. Propagate by grafting, layering, seed.

Features: Good choice for accents, backgrounds, beds, containers, paths, walls in Asian, formal, small-space gardens and lawns. Pest and disease resistant.

Tree: *Syringa reticulata.* OLEACEAE.
Common name: Japanese Tree Lilac.
Description: Several cultivars and varieties of medium-growing, pyramid-shaped, dense, deciduous trees, to 30 ft. (9 m) tall, with shiny, dark green, smooth, oval leaves, to 5 in. (13 cm) long, and with smooth, reddish bark.
Blooms/Berries: Tiny, fragrant, cream, lavender flowers in spring, forming large, showy, dangling clusters, to 1 ft. (30 cm) long. First blooms 2–3 years after planting. Requires chilling to bloom.
Plant hardiness: Zones 4–8.
Soil: Moist, well-drained soil. Fertility: Rich. 7.0–7.5 pH.
Planting: Full sun to partial shade. Space 10–15 ft. (3–4.5 m) apart.
Care: Moderate. Keep evenly moist. Fertilize annually in spring until established. Deadhead. Prune sparingly after bloom. Propagate by cuttings, layering.
Features: Good choice for accents, borders in cottage, woodland gardens. Good for cutting. Attracts butterflies. Invasive. Deer resistant. Powdery mildew susceptible.

Tree: *Taxodium distichum.* TAXODIACEAE.
Common name: Bald Cypress (Pond Cypress).
Description: Medium-growing, upright, pyramid-shaped, open, coniferous, deciduous tree, 100–150 ft. (30–45 m) tall, with green, stiff, oval or flattened needles, to ½ in. (12 mm) long, in fingerlike sprays, turning bronze in autumn, and fibrous, red brown bark. Root projections, or "knees," buttress the trunk, protruding from the water in swampy sites. Growth slows in cold-winter climates.
Cones/Seed: Egg-shaped and knobby cones, 1 in. (25 mm) wide, in autumn, bearing tiny, flattened seed.
Plant hardiness: Zones 5–11.
Soil: Wet to damp, well-drained soil. Fertility: Rich–average. 5.0–7.0 pH.
Planting: Full sun. Space 15–20 ft. (4.5–6 m) apart.
Care: Easy. Keep damp. Fertilize annually in spring until established. Prune sparingly. Propagate by cuttings, seed.
Features: Good choice for accents, aquatic plantings, margins in water features, woodland gardens. Pest and disease resistant. Chlorosis susceptible.

Tree: *Tilea* species. TILIACEAE.
Common name: Linden (Basswood, Lime Tree, Whitewood).
Description: About 30 species of slow-growing, long-lived, erect, narrow or pyramid-shaped, deciduous trees, 15–60 ft. (4.5–18 m) tall, with alternate, round or heart-shaped, pointed, veined leaves, 3–6 in. (75–150 mm) long, with pale undersides, turning brown, yellow in autumn. Commonly cultivated species include *T. americana*, American linden; *T. chinensis*, Chinese linden; *T. cordata*, little-leaved linden; and *T. tomentosa*, silver linden.
Blooms/Fruit: Many tiny, fragrant, green, white, yellow, 5-petaled flowers, in showy, branching, nodding clusters, to 4 in. (10 cm) long, in early summer, form nutlike, seedy fruit, to ¼ in. (6 mm) wide, in autumn.
Plant hardiness: Zones 3–9.
Soil: Moist, well-drained humus. Fertility: Rich. 6.0–7.0 pH.
Planting: Full sun. Space 10–15 ft. (3–4.5 m) apart.
Care: Easy. Keep moist. Fertilize annually in spring. Prune to thin, shape, coppice, shear in autumn. Propagate by cuttings, grafting, layering, seed.
Features: Good choice for accents, allées, containers, hedges, shade in cottage, meadow, natural, small-space gardens and roadside plantings. Attracts bees. Smog tolerant. Aphid, Japanese beetle, borer, tussock moth, whitefly and anthracnose, fungal disease susceptible.

Tree: *Tsuga canadensis*. PINACEAE.

Common name: Canadian Hemlock (Weeping Hemlock).

Description: Many cultivars of medium-growing, upright, pyramid-shaped, dense, coniferous, evergreen trees, to 80 ft. (24 m) tall and often with multiple trunks, with shiny, flat, dark green needles, to ¾ in. (19 mm) long, with white undersides, on graceful, nodding branchlets.

Cones/Seed: Female cones are tan and oblong, ¾ in. (19 mm) long, with woody scales and winged seed.

Plant hardiness: Zones 4–9. Best with cool, humid summers, winter chill.

Soil: Moist, well-drained soil. Fertility: Rich–average. 5.5–6.5 pH.

Planting: Full to filtered sun. Space 10–15 ft. (3–4.5 m) apart as specimens, 5–7 ft. (1.5–2.2 m) as sheared and hedge plantings.

Care: Easy. Keep evenly moist. Drought susceptible. Fertilize annually until established. Prune new growth in spring to shape, shear. Protect from sun, wind in hot climates. Propagate by seed.

Features: Good choice for accents, backgrounds, hedges, screens in landscapes, lawns. Shallow rooted. Salt susceptible. Hemlock woolly aphid susceptible.

Tree: *Ulmus parvifolia*. ULMACEAE.

Common name: Lacebark Elm (Chinese Elm).

Description: Several cultivars of fast-growing, upright and spreading, deciduous or semi-evergreen trees, to 60 ft. (18 m) tall and wide, with willowlike, nodding branchlets and deep green, oval, pointed, finely toothed leaves, to 3 in. (75 mm) long, turning bronze, yellow in autumn, and with sycamore-like, flaking, reddish to gray bark.

Blooms/Seed: Inconspicuous, clustered flowers in early spring form numerous winged seed, to ⁵⁄₁₆ in. (8 mm) wide, in late spring.

Plant hardiness: Zones 5–10.

Soil: Moist to damp, well-drained soil. Fertility: Average. 5.5–7.0 pH.

Planting: Full sun. Space 15–20 ft. (4.5–6 m) apart.

Care: Moderate. Allow soil surface to dry between waterings until established. Fertilize annually in spring until established. Prune to thin after bloom. Propagate by cuttings, layering, seed.

Features: Good choice for allées, containers, shade in bonsai, patio, roadside plantings. Drops flowers, seed, leaves, requiring maintenance. Somewhat resistant to elm leaf beetle, Dutch elm disease. Aphid, leafhopper, scale and fireblight susceptible.

Tree: *Vitex agnus-castus*. VERBENACEAE.

Common name: Chaste Tree (Hemp Tree, Wild Pepper).

Description: Several cultivars of fast- to medium-growing, broad, spreading, deciduous, frequently multitrunked, shrubby trees, 20–25 ft. (6–7.5 m) tall and wide, with deep green, lobed, fragrant leaves, to 4 in. (10 cm) long, as 5–7 fan-shaped leaflets, with gray undersides. Cultivars include *V. agnus-castus* 'Alba', 'Latifolia', 'Rosea', and 'Silver Spire'.

Blooms/Fruit: Many fragrant, spikelike, blue, pink, purple, red, clustered flowers, to 1 ft. (30 cm) long, in summer, form small, berrylike fruit in autumn.

Plant hardiness: Zones 6–11, depending on cultivar.

Soil: Damp, well-drained soil. Fertility: Rich–average. 6.5–7.5 pH. Best in hot-summer climates.

Planting: Full sun. Space 5 ft. (1.5 m) apart, zones 6–8; 8–12 ft. (2.4–3.7 m) apart, zones 9–11.

Care: Easy. Allow soil surface to dry between waterings until established; drought tolerant thereafter. Mulch in cold-winter climates. Prune severely to shrublike form in zones 6–8, moderately in zones 9–11. Propagate by cuttings, seed.

Features: Good choice for accents, beds, borders, containers, fencelines, walls in arid, Asian, small-space gardens, tropical. Good for cutting, drying, sachets, and potpourris. Pest and disease resistant.

Planting and Care Techniques

An Overview
of Essential
Preparation,
Planting,
Pruning, and
Care Techniques
for Landscape
Plants

Regular waterings are essential to plant health, but keep in mind that too much water, as well as too little, can make them struggle to survive. A good rule of thumb is to apply water when the soil's surface has dried for those plants that thrive in damp conditions. You'll learn more tips on how to water and care for your plants in this chapter.

WHEN YOU'VE SELECTED ALL YOUR LANDSCAPE PLANTS, it's a good idea to take a few minutes to review the things you'll need to do to help get them off to a good start in your garden. In the pages that follow, you'll find information about testing your soil and planting seed and bulbs, bedding plants, and larger landscape plants grown in nursery containers, such as trees and shrubs. You'll then be shown how to make watering easier by installing in-ground irrigation, and the proper techniques for applying water to your plants, fertilizing them, and pruning care. Finally, complete information is given to help you recognize and treat common garden pests and diseases before they harm your plants.

The best landscapes are those grown with plants that will thrive naturally in your plant hardiness zone [see USDA Plant Hardiness, pgs. 10–11]. After you have determined your zone, consider local conditions, including microclimates, which may make your site different than other gardens in your region. These may make conditions in your yard milder or harsher than those found in your surroundings. Seek help from the staff of local garden centers and nurseries when selecting your plant stock. Handle the new plants with care prior to planting, giving them ample water and protecting them from sun or frost. For best results, acquire your plants at the proper time for planting and install them right away, following the techniques shown in this chapter. Space your plants at the distances recommended for each species. A new landscape may look sparse for a time, but it quickly will fill in; consider planting annual flowers as fillers for the first season or two.

That's the basics…let's start by first evaluating your soil.

SOIL ANALYSIS

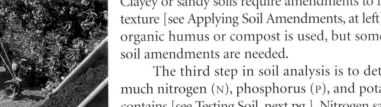

Start your soil evaluation by identifying those plants that are already growing in your landscape and which seem to be thriving. Look them up in the plant encyclopedia [see Encyclopedia of Landscape Plants, pgs. 23–279]. Note their soil needs; it's likely that they are good indicators of your garden soil's conditions.

The second step is to perform a so-called percolation test to determine how well your soil drains. Simply dig holes in your planting bed 2 ft. (60 cm) deep, then fill them with water and note the time. The length of time that the water takes to drain shows the density of your soil—how much sand or clay it contains. The water level in well-drained garden soil should decrease at a rate of 1–2 in. (25–50 mm) per hour. Slower rates indicate poor drainage. Also note if it drains too fast, say in 15 minutes or less. That means your soil is too sandy. Clayey or sandy soils require amendments to improve their texture [see Applying Soil Amendments, at left]. Most often, organic humus or compost is used, but sometimes other soil amendments are needed.

The third step in soil analysis is to determine how much nitrogen (N), phosphorus (P), and potassium (K) it contains [see Testing Soil, next pg.]. Nitrogen salts are water-soluble and tend to leach from the soil over time. The other two macronutrients bind chemically to the soil and are more likely to remain in place. If more nutrients are needed, add an appropriate organic or chemical fertilizer, choosing one with a formulation that matches your soil's needs. Fertilizer labels show the amount of each nutrient by percentage of weight as three numbers—say 0–10–10—for the NPK they contain.

Finally, test your soil's acid and alkaline balance and correct it as necessary.

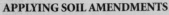

APPLYING SOIL AMENDMENTS

Soil amendments include fertilizer, compost, humus, and additives such as sand and gypsum—to improve drainage—or garden lime and sulfur —to raise or lower pH, respectively.

To apply amendments, clear all weeds, rake and remove any rocks or debris, then turn the soil to loosen it. Spread the additives on the soil's surface, in a layer about 4 in. (10 cm) thick.

Use a shovel or a garden fork to turn the amendment layer into the top 9–12 in. (23–30 cm) of soil.

SOIL TESTING

You can perform soil tests for texture, nutrients, and pH yourself. Many nurseries and garden centers provide testing services to assess soil and recommend necessary amendments as well as offer reliable home test kits. If you use a laboratory, follow their staff's instructions to gather your soil sample. To perform soil tests at home, follow these steps:

1 Collect a small amount of moist soil 3–4 in. (75–100 mm) below the surface. If you are testing several sites within your garden, be sure to track each location carefully.

2 Determine its texture by squeezing the moist soil sample in your fist, then open your hand. If it feels gritty and falls apart when lightly poked, it contains excess sand. If it holds together, push it between thumb and forefinger to make a ribbon of soil. If the ribbon cracks apart before it is ½ in. (12 mm) long, the sample is silty or loamy. If the ribbon holds together for 1 in. (25 mm), the soil is mostly clay.

3 Determine your soil's acid and alkaline balance using a pH test kit available at most garden centers. Follow the package instructions which vary according to the specific kit used, and use distilled water for accuracy.

4 Check amounts of the three soil macronutrients —nitrogen, phosphorus, and potassium — in your soil samples using a home soil test kit available at most garden retailers.

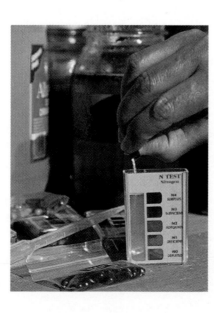

5 Electronic meters check soil pH, too. Check accuracy by testing cow's milk, which has a 6.5–7.0 pH, then thoroughly clean the probe before testing the soil sample.

PLANTING

Choices abound when it comes time to plant your garden. Besides nursery starts and bedding plants, you can choose from plants in containers, bulbs, and seed. Each type of plant—sometimes each species—may require slightly different approaches.

(Right) After the first true leaves of seedlings have emerged, begin the hardening process by taking off their protective cover.

(Below, top) Transplant larger seedlings into containers until the soil warms.

(Bottom) Nursery starts are usually available in various sizes. Young plants are most adaptable and quickly grow.

Start your planting by choosing quality seed, bedding plants, and nursery-grown stock. Pick plants that are in good condition, free of broken or diseased foliage, and which seem to be thriving. Avoid plants that bear flowers or buds about to open, plus those that are rootbound. Turn over their leaves to look for chewed foliage or insect pests that may be hiding. Finally, select those plants that are dense and stocky, rather than lanky and sparse.

Carefully transport your plants from the nursery, put them in a sheltered location, and water them. If the weather is uncertain, hold them in your garden for a few days to help them adjust before planting—it's always best to acquire plants after danger of frost has passed and plant them immediately, but sometimes it's necessary to hold your stock. Give them protection from direct sun and drying winds, water them regularly, and, if frost threatens, cover them at night.

Water your plants again the night before planting so that they are fully hydrated and ready for the change that transplanting brings. Young plants—and smaller shrubs and trees—adjust to this change more easily than do larger, older plants. Move the plants to your yard, then pause for a moment to consider their spacing.

Each species has a specific habit of growth. It may be low and prostrate, as for ground covers. It may be tall, narrow, and columnar. Or, it may be round, spreading, trailing, or vining, among many other possibilities. Note the width and spacing that is recommended for each plant. While they are still in their nursery containers or flats, arrange them in the bed or border so that you can gauge their effect.

When creating groups with shrubs, trees, or perennial plants, you'll find that odd-numbered groups of three, five, or seven have a natural symmetry that makes them appealing. Sometimes, drifts or waves of a single species help to unite your plantings; set the plants in arcs or offset rows to determine which look best. Groups made of two species, each triangular in shape and interlocking, fill an area better than do massed plantings of a single species.

Before you pick up your spade and begin to plant, step back from the arranged plants and look at them from different viewing angles such as from your walk, the street, or from inside your house. Make any final adjustments—it's a lot easier to move a plant at this point than it will be after they have been installed. Be sure to consider how the plant will look when it is mature, envisioning its height, spread, and the shadows it will cast. When you have finalized your groups, you'll be ready to plant.

In the pages that follow, you'll be shown many common techniques used for planting seed, bulbs, plants, ornamental grasses, ground covers, shrubs, and trees. Follow each technique, step by step, for best results.

PLANTING SEED

Planting Seed in Trays Indoors

1 Clean tray and tools with a mixture of 1 part household bleach to 9 parts water. Fill tray with potting soil. Open furrows in parallel rows.

Whether to seed indoors or in the garden is a choice to make when planting most annual and some biennial and perennial flowers. Indoor starts extend the growing season, but seeding in the garden is an option in areas with a long growing season, especially for those plants that grow best without transplanting. Gather your seed and materials, then plant when air and soil temperatures have peaked, following these easy steps:

2 Carefully tap seed from the seed package into each of the prepared rows, spacing the seed as recommended by the seed supplier.

3 Close the furrow over each seed, burying it to the recommended depth shown on the package. Press the soil with your palms until it is firm. Good soil contact is essential to germination.

4 Seedlings are ready for transplant after they have developed two true leaves.

Planting Seed in Garden Beds

1 Scatter your seed over the prepared bed at the recommended spacing. Sift soil over them, pressing firmly to ensure good soil contact.

2 In a few days, seed will sprout. The first leaves to emerge are called seed leaves. Wait until two true leaves develop before you thin, to avoid confusing the seedlings with weeds.

3 If some plants are too crowded, thin by removing the weakest members of the planting. If there are bare spots, transplant some of the thinned plants into them to fill out the bed.

TRANSPLANTING BEDDING PLANTS

Most perennial plants are sold in 1-gallon (4-l) or 5-gallon (20-l) nursery containers. Choose plants that have developed roots that fill their pots, but avoid those that are rootbound. Plants should be healthy and free of obvious insect infestation. Water transplants the day before placing them into the garden, then follow these easy steps to plant your perennials:

1 Dig a hole half again as wide and twice as deep as the nursery container of your perennial plant. Mix balanced fertilizer into the removed soil along with abundant organic compost.

2 Invert the nursery container and gently tap on its bottom and sides to remove the plant. Let it slide gently into your outstretched hand.

3 With a hand fork, gently break up any encircling roots to ensure that the plant quickly establishes itself and will grow into the surrounding soil rather than remain in the planting hole.

4 Place the plant in the hole so that its container soil line is level with the surrounding soil. Backfill around the sides of the rootball and press the soil firmly against it.

5 Water the transplant to settle the soil and refresh the plant. Water frequently for the first 10 days, then slowly extend the time between waterings to once a week or whenever the soil becomes dry.

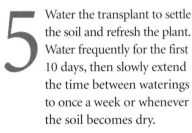

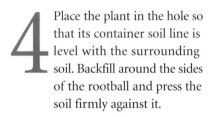

PLANTING GROUND COVERS

Ground covers are planted in much the same way as are bedding plants. Spacing the plants properly is important to achieve a good result; consult the greengoods supplier or refer to the plant tag that comes in the ground cover flat. Gather your plants, tools, and materials, and follow these steps to plant a spreading ground cover:

1 Rake and remove any mulch, rocks, and debris from the planting site, then turn the soil and add any amendments and fertilizer. The soil should be smooth and level when you are ready to plant.

2 Space the plants evenly across the bed as recommended for your species. Avoid spacing plants either too far apart or closer than recommended.

3 After the plants have been spaced, set each aside and dig a planting hole. Set the plant into the hole.

4 Press the plant's roots down with both hands to ensure good contact with the soil. This is essential if the plant is to root quickly.

5 Water gently as you complete each planting. Keep the soil evenly moist for a week, then reduce frequency.

BULBS

Spring and summer bulbous plants add bright color to landscape beds and borders. Gardeners generally refer to those plants that have enlarged roots as bulbs, whether they are true bulbs, corms, rhizomes, or tubers. In practice, all are planted the same way.

Start by choosing healthy bulbs, using size, firmness, and freshness as your keys. Bulbs that are large for their type have more room to store nutrients and moisture. They will produce the largest flowers. Those that are solid and heavy for their size are preferable to bulbs that are soft and light. Make sure that they are fresh—choose bulbs soon after they arrive in your garden center or nursery—and free of premature sprouts. Avoid any that show obvious signs of fungal disease, cuts, or other damage.

Persian Buttercup

If some time will pass before they are planted, store them in a cool, dark place with good air circulation. Some bulbs, such as lilies, may dry out easily and should be planted soon after you obtain them.

Planting bulbs in containers is a popular pastime, whether to grow pots of colorful plants for an entryway or patio, or to bring indoors. Be sure to choose containers that have ample drain holes, and sterilize them prior to planting by soaking them for several minutes in a mild solution of 1 part household bleach mixed with 9 parts of water. Remember that bleach contains sodium hypochlorite, a powerful skin and eye irritant, so you always should wear protective clothing and gloves when handling it. Pick containers deep enough to allow at least 6 in. (15 cm) of soil beneath the bulbs when they're planted at the recommended depth for their species.

Tuberous Begonia

Tulip

Windflower

Bulbs in containers should be crowded into the pot; you'll discard them after their blooms fade, or you can plant them in your garden where they'll take a few seasons to recover.

Planting bulbs outdoors is usually done in autumn for spring-blooming species and in spring for those that bloom in summer or autumn. As a consequence, including bulbs in your landscape requires some planning, both to plant and to choose companions for them. Most bulb species are native to climates that experience periods of drought. The plants survive dry periods by becoming semi-dormant; these conditions must be duplicated in your garden or the bulbs should be lifted and stored once their foliage withers and fades. Bulbous plants can grow successfully beneath turfgrass or ground covers, but the grass or plants should accommodate the bulbs' watering needs throughout the year.

Florist's Amaryllis

When planting an accent, bed, or border with bulbs, prepare the soil deeply—some bulbs are planted as much as 8–10 in. (20–25 cm) deep and extend their roots down a foot (30 cm) or more—and keep its texture loose by adding ample humus or organic compost and digging it in. Recently prepared beds will be full of air and should be allowed to settle for about a week before you plant [see Planting Bulbs, opposite pg.].

For naturalized beds, choose species that will multiply naturally, retain their vigor, and are hardy in your USDA Plant Hardiness Zone. The best naturalizing bulbs are crocus, grape hyacinth, hyacinth, narcissus, and tulip.

Crocus

PLANTING BULBS

Most bulbs are planted individually. It's the right approach for planting small areas, or for as many as 30 bulbs. Planting single bulbs is ideal when you want to create sinuous drifts in a naturalized garden or for making bulb accents in your borders. Gather a bulb planting tool, hand fork, your bulbs, and planting depth information for each species, then follow these easy steps:

1 Note the planting depth for the bulb species and check that each bulb is free of decay, mildew, or cuts. Discard any bulbs that have become dehydrated.

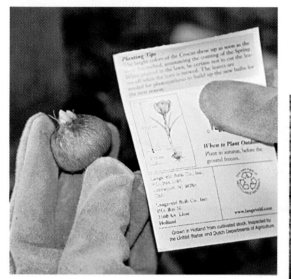

2 At the site, use a bulb planting tool to excavate a hole 2 in. (50 mm) deeper than the recommended depth. Add 10–10–5 fertilizer and cover it with 2 in. (50 mm) of soil.

3 Determine the top of the bulb. Turn it so its pointed end is up and its platelike base or the roots are down. For tubers, or if orientation is unclear, plant the bulb on its side. Place the bulb in its hole.

4 Check your final planting arrangement after all of the bulbs have been placed. Relocate bulbs to fill any sparse or skipped spots, adding more bulbs if needed.

5 Fill the holes with soil. Gently press the soil over each bulb to ensure good soil contact and to eliminate any air pockets. Then water the planting area until the water begins to run off. Repeat in half an hour until the soil is moist to the depth of the deepest bulbs.

GRASSES

Grasses differ from broad-leaved plants. When their seeds sprout, the young grass has a single leaf in contrast with the two leaves found on other plants. In the landscape, grasses are divided into the clump-forming, ornamental grasses and the sod-building turfgrasses usually used for lawns. Each requires its own planting technique. The most popular method of installing a turfgrass lawn is using rolled sod for cool-season grasses such as bentgrass, bluegrass, fescue, and perennial ryegrass [see Planting Sod Lawns, at right]. Other choices include seed, sprigs, and plugs.

Grass lawns require regular care, ample water, and frequent fertilizing to look their best. Because of the effort required to maintain them, many homeowners prefer to install ground covers or plant their yards with shrubs and ornamental grasses, which are more carefree to grow.

When choosing grasses for your landscape, carefully match their requirements with your climate, soil, and site. This is true for both turfgrasses and ornamental species. Another consideration is the appearance of the planting. You may wish to contrast the graceful, feathery plumes of an ornamental grass species with the green foliage and flowers of perennials and shrubs in other parts of the bed or border.

Grasses are adaptable to soil conditions found in many different sites. Many species are drought tolerant and able to take prolonged sun and heat. Ornamental grasses' erect, flowing, constantly moving form is pleasing when they're used for accents, and they'll also make good massed plantings if an erosion-controlling cover is needed for a slope or bank.

Most turfgrasses extend their roots down 18–30 in. (45–75 cm) deep and spread through underground stolons or above-ground runners. Ornamental grasses, by contrast, may have deep or shallow roots, and some of the species are slow to spread.

Most ornamental grasses are offered as nursery container plants. Choose those in good condition, with active new blades, and plant them in the spring to allow them to become established before summer heat begins.

When planting grasses, prepare the soil as you would for perennial flowers or shrubs. Good drainage is important for all grasses, and many species require average to low fertility. Check and observe the recommended spacing between plants to ensure sufficient room exists to grow. Check their placement and spacing before you plant [See Planting Ornamental Grasses, opposite pg.].

Ornamental grasses are perfect companions for a home water garden. Some species are true aquatics that should be planted in the shallow margins of the water feature. Most others are terrestrial and perform best on the pond's shoreline with their roots in damp soil.

PLANTING SOD LAWNS

Planting rolled sod lawns requires considerable effort but is simple to accomplish. Arrange for delivery of the sod to your site on the morning of the day it will be installed.

The starter row—the first one placed—is the most important. Lay the row parallel to an edge to avoid excess cutting on the rows to follow. Overlap the ends and sides of the sod at least 1 in. (25 mm) where they touch, pressing them down to make a tight joint. Trim excess sod using a sharp knife, fitting the grass as is needed. Roll the sod, then water it daily for the first 10 days.

PLANTING ORNAMENTAL GRASSES

Ornamental grasses are among the easiest plants to grow. Verify the spacing requirements of individual plants—many grow quite large. Cut grasses annually to enjoy their graceful beauty year after year. Spring is the best time to plant most grasses; it takes a whole growing season for the plants to become established. To plant ornamental grasses from nursery containers, follow these easy steps:

1 Prepare the planting area. Mark each planting point based on your garden plan. Dig holes as deep as the containers and slightly wider.

2 Remove the plant from its nursery container. Set the plant in the hole so that its root crown is level with the surrounding soil surface and matches the soil level of the container. Add or remove soil as necessary to create proper depth.

3 Fill the hole, using your hands to gently firm the soil around the crown. Water thoroughly at the time of planting and keep the soil moist until the plant is established. Water thereafter whenever the soil dries.

4 In late winter or early spring, use hedge clippers to trim delicate grasses; use hedge shears for species with woody stems. Trim old grass foliage 2–3 in. (50–75 mm) above any new growth from the crown.

SHRUBS AND TREES

Tree- and shrub-planting techniques vary slightly, depending on whether your plant is balled-and-burlapped, bare root, boxed, or in a nursery container.

When planting a containerized plant, dig a planting hole the same depth as the rootball, and 2–4 in. (25–50 mm) wider. Using a garden fork or other tined tool, poke holes into the bottom and sides of the hole, penetrating the surrounding soil. These holes will help the plant's roots to grow into the surrounding soil. Carefully remove the plant from its container, loosen and fan out the roots, and prune any that are damaged or which encircle the rootball. Place the plant into the prepared hole, making sure that the roots are relatively straight and fanned down. Be sure the top of the rootball is level with or slightly higher than the soil. Backfill with native soil that has been loosened and is free of rocks or other debris. Tamp the soil as you go, removing any air pockets, while retaining the soil's loose and breathable texture.

Trees do best when transplanted directly into native soil. If you are planting a tree grown in potting medium different than your yard's soil, gently wash away about half of it from the rootball with a garden hose, then set the tree into the prepared hole.

For balled-and-burlapped plants, prepare the hole as for a container plant. Leave natural-fiber burlap around the rootball, but pull the top fabric away from the stem or trunk, tucking it alongside the rootball; completely remove synthetic burlap. Use a sharp knife to make vertical cuts in the fabric, backfill the hole with soil, and water well.

When you plant a bare-root plant, soak the roots in water for 4–5 hours before the intended time of planting, then plant it [See Planting Bare-Root Shrubs and Trees, opposite pg.].

Boxed trees are usually large specimens. They are planted in a manner similar to that used for containerized plants but, because of their great size and considerable weight, require assistance at the time of planting by a landscaping professional with heavy-lifting equipment.

Caring for your recently planted trees includes regular waterings during their first several months until new growth begins, and feeding in spring the following year.

(Above) Those seeking an easy-care yard could consider planting a mixed shrub bed mulched with a stone mulch. The stones help hold moisture and slow temperature changes in the soil, a perfect fit with Xeriscape shrubs.

(Below) Plant evergreen conifers in native soil, but mulch their roots with an acidic compost to keep them moist as it slowly decomposes, releasing nutrients for the growing tree.

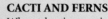

CACTI AND FERNS

When planting cacti, avoid hazard by protecting yourself from spines. Cacti do best in a fast-draining, sandy soil. They are planted in the same manner as containerized shrubs. Some species require delayed watering while damaged roots form protective calluses.

Ferns need a shady site and sandy humus-rich soil with granular charcoal. Plant them as you would other shrubs. Water them immediately after planting, then keep them evenly moist.

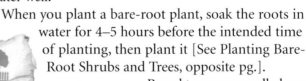

PLANTING BARE-ROOT SHRUBS AND TREES

Bare-root trees and shrubs are available each spring. Usually vigorous species, they quickly develop roots when planted in unamended garden soil. Gather a ruler or measuring tape, gloves, shovel, and your tree, then follow these easy steps:

1 Notice the discolored point on the trunk marking the tree's previous soil level. Measure the depth from that point to the center of the root crown's base.

2 Dig a planting hole 4–6 in. (10–15 cm) deeper than the tree's root crown depth and half again the distance of its roots' spread. Create a cone-shaped mound in the center, 4–6 in. (10–15 cm) high.

3 Place the tree in the planting hole straddling the mound and spreading the roots evenly around it. Use a shovel handle across the hole to check that the new planting depth is the same as it originally was.

4 Enlist a helper to hold the tree securely and straight as you backfill the hole with soil and firm it around the tree's roots.

5 Raise a soil moat around the outer perimeter of the planting hole, 3–4 in. (75–100 mm) high. Use it as a watering basin for the newly planted tree.

6 Thoroughly water the tree after planting, adding more soil if uneven settling occurs. Repeat when the soil surface dries until new growth appears.

WATERING

How much and how often plants should be watered are key questions. To answer them, first refer to the information in the plant encyclopedia regarding the specific plant's soil and care preferences [see Encyclopedia of Landscape Plants, pgs. 23–279]. Next, evaluate the moisture in your soil—surprisingly, this step is more complicated than it first seems, for the soil under discussion rarely is the soil surface that you see; rather, it is the soil around the plants' roots.

It works like this. Water applied to the soil—by nature, as rain, or by a gardener—penetrates slowly depending on the texture of the soil [see Soil Analysis, pg. 282]. If the soil contains much clay, the water percolates slowly downward. If the application of water is brief, little water may reach the root zone of the plants. By contrast, in a sandy soil, the water may flow down and out of the root zone in a matter of minutes. To be effective for your plants, the texture of the soil and its make-up are equally important. The very best garden soils consist of equal parts of sand, silt, and clay mixed with decomposed organic matter, or humus. Such soils hold most of the moisture applied to them, yet drain freely. Most plants thrive in these balanced soils.

A few plants such as cacti and some grasses are very drought tolerant. Others such as ferns and rushes prefer moist conditions—indeed, some of these grow best when submerged in water. Most landscape plants, however, thrive when the soil is moist for a time, is allowed to drain becoming damp or dry, then receives another watering. This usually is the situation in your garden.

So, when do you water, and how much? Water when the surface of the soil is dry and the soil around the roots has become damp. Avoid evenly moist conditions that may make your plants susceptible to fungal disease and eventual suffocation.

Check the subsurface soil for its moisture, either with a probe attached to a moisture meter or by the simpler act of digging down a bit and feeling the soil. A good rule of thumb for the amount of water to apply is the axiom "an inch of water, until it runs off," which suggests that you water the soil until its surface is thoroughly saturated, stopping before the water stands and pools or runs off.

A final recommendation is to water in the morning after air temperatures have risen and avoid wetting any foliage during watering. This permits the plant's roots to receive the water they need and gives the foliage a chance to dry before evening's cool temperatures.

(Above) Simple rain gauges tell how much moisture fell, and the amount of water your plants still will need.

(Below) Use overhead sprays only on warm days, allowing sufficient time for the foliage to dry before evening.

MULCHING
Mulch protects soil from the direct heat of the sun, keeps plant roots cool, and helps hold soil moisture by limiting the amount of water lost by evaporation.

Organic materials and minerals both are good mulches; choose from such mulches as bark and wood chips, pine needles, salt hay, and stones or decomposed granite. The advantage of the organic materials is their contribution to your soil as they slowly decompose. Renew your mulches every few seasons for best results.

INSTALLING IN-GROUND IRRIGATION

1 Trench from the control valve site to the starting point of each watering circuit, and to create each irrigation circuit. Turn off water at the main, then install a gate valve and a backflow prevention valve to isolate the water supply for the irrigation system.

Design your system to match your soil, water pressure, and slope. Choose approved backflow prevention valves, and comply with all local code requirements. Locate control valves in an accessible spot near the control timer. In cold-winter areas, use an insulated subsurface enclosure or install it indoors. Locate any spray heads to avoid damage to foliage. Follow these steps:

2 Lay schedule 40 PVC pipe from the backflow prevention valve to the control valve for each circuit. Use a step-down bushing to reduce the line gauge, then install lateral lines to create the irrigation circuit.

3 Join each pipe section with couplers, using PVC primer and solvent for slip fittings, Teflon® tape for threaded fittings.

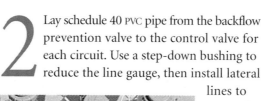

4 Install swing joints or risers at the site of each sprinkler head or drip emitter hose coupler.

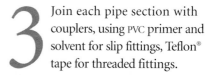

5 Flush the system by turning on each valve until the water runs clear, then turning it off again. Install all sprinkler heads or emitter couplers.

6 Install an automatic control timer. Connect it with direct-buried control cable to the manifold valves. Program the controller and test the system; adjust spray heads as needed. Refill trenches.

FERTILIZING

To be fertile, soil must contain mineral and organic compounds in a form that plants can use to grow. When we test our soil and fertilize our landscape plants, most often we concentrate on supplying them the three macronutrients, nitrogen (N), phosphorus (P), and potassium (K). While all plants need these elements to grow, they also need a host of other micronutrients and trace minerals in order to stay healthy, maintain vigor, produce dense foliage, develop flowers, and reproduce.

These essential compounds must be available to the plants' root systems as either water-soluble salts or in another form that readily can be absorbed and converted within the plants' cells. For this to happen, the soil must contain moisture, and it also must have an acid-alkaline balance—pH—that allows the complex chemical process of absorption to take place.

Testing your soil is a good starting point [see Soil Analysis, pg. 282]. A soil test will reveal the amount of macronutrients and the pH of your soil. Laboratory tests often include analysis information about micronutrients as well. If your soil is deficient in one of the nutrients or has an acid-alkaline balance that is too low or too high, you can fertilize and amend it to make it more hospitable to your plants.

Start by reading the fertilizer label. It contains a trio of numbers such as 5–10–20 to indicate by percentage of total weight the amount of NPK that the formula contains. In other words, the fertilizer in the example given will contain 5 percent nitrate, 10 percent phosphorus, and 20 percent potassium. Fertilizers in which the amounts of NPK are equal are said to be "balanced" formulations, while a mixture that has different amounts of all three is "complete." Specialty fertilizers may have only one or two of the three macronutrients. Other mixes may increase acidity or provide iron, a key component in avoiding the yellowing disease, chlorosis.

Besides containing various amounts of nutrients, fertilizers come in many forms. There are liquids, liquid-soluble powders, granular and powdered dry fertilizers, and naturally occurring fertilizers, including guano, manure, and mineral phosphate [see Organic Fertilizers, this pg.]. All are guaranteed to provide nutrients to your plants at the quantity and efficacy stated on their labels.

As a general rule, it's best to avoid fertilizing large shrubs and trees once they become established, unless they show signs of nutrient deficiency or chlorosis—they grow best in native soil. For other garden plants, fertilize when they are actively growing and producing their flower buds, reducing the amount and frequency when autumn's chill begins. Always fertilize each plant in the amount and frequency recommended for the species [see Applying Fertilizers, opposite pg.].

It's always best to work your fertilizers into the soil soon after application. A hand fork spreads the granules out, mixing them with the soil, and helping prevent burning their leaves with too much nitrogen. Follow up by giving your plants a thorough watering to further dilute the fertilizer and carry it deeply into the soil.

ORGANIC FERTILIZERS

Organic fertilizer has many benefits. It is naturally occurring, containing organic and mineral ingredients that were produced as waste from plants or animals, or which were mined from ancient deposits. It often has trace elements and micronutrients besides NPK. Finally, it decomposes and slowly releases its nutrients over time, avoiding the foliage burning that can happen with synthetics.

Organic fertilizers are gentle to the environment. They often contain smaller amounts of nutrients, so application may have to be made more frequently in order to keep plants green and growing. Still, they are the best choice for your yard.

APPLYING FERTILIZERS

Fertilize new plantings when growth begins in spring, then fertilize halfway through the growing season. Avoid fertilizing at the end of the growing season. It promotes new growth which can be damaged easily by frost. Measure amounts—too much nitrogen will burn foliage. Apply granular and encapsulated fertilizers at the plant's drip line, the circle following the edge of the plant's foliage. Water well after fertilizing. Wear protective gloves when handling fertilizers, then follow the steps shown for each fertilizer type:

Granular Fertilizer

1 Measure carefully and apply granular fertilizer according to package directions. Spread or scatter it evenly on the soil above the root zone of your plants.

2 Sprinkle granules on the soil, in a circular pattern beneath the edge of the plant's drip line. Use a hand fork or cultivator to mix fertilizer into the top 2 in. (50 mm) of soil. Water thoroughly to dilute it immediately after application.

Liquid Fertilizer

Dilute liquid fertilizer as its package directs, then apply over the plant's root zone. Water-soluble foliar fertilizers are absorbed directly by the leaves. Apply the liquid fertilizer with a hose-end sprayer. Fertilize on wind-free days cooler than 85° F (29°C).

Solid Fertilizer

To apply solid organic fertilizers, spread a layer of fertilizer ½ in. (13 mm) deep around the base of the plants. Work the fertilizer into the soil.

Encapsulated Fertilizer

1 Read and closely follow all package directions when applying granules of encapsulated fertilizer. Always carefully measure.

2 Sprinkle encapsulated fertilizer on the soil surface at the plant's drip line. Use a trowel or hand fork to mix the fertilizer into the top 2 in. (50 mm) of soil. Water thoroughly immediately after application.

PRUNING

Essential pruning tools include (counterclockwise from left) a pole pruner, a reciprocating saw, a hedge trimmer, various pruning saws, a pair of hand bypass pruners, long-handled lopping shears, and a foldable pruning saw.

Pruning is necessary to shape and control the growth of your plants, maintain dense foliage, remove spent flowering stems, cull dead or broken branches, eliminate diseased wood, and keep your plants healthy. It is appropriate for both deciduous and evergreen trees and shrubs, and may sometimes be needed on conifers as well. The major goal of most pruning is to open a shrub or tree's canopy and allow sunlight to penetrate to its inner branches and trunk.

Different techniques are needed for young and old plants. When working with a young tree or shrub, the goal is to provide it with a good framework for future growth. For a shade tree, for example, the ideal structure is a strong central trunk with five to eight branches that radiate from it at different levels. On shrubs, you may make the plant narrower, help it fit into a corner space, or train it into a specific form, such as for a hedge, topiary, or espalier.

Before trimming, examine the stem or trunk to identify the branch collar—the ring of rough bark that encircles the area where a limb attaches to the trunk. When pruning, cut just outside the branch collar. Leave the cut open to the air—avoid wound-dressing compounds, which once were common but now are considered unnecessary.

On mature plants, you should prune out decaying branches, since they can affect the overall health of the plant. Also remove any crossed limbs—those that grow back toward the center of the plant—to help the remaining branches stay strong and allow light to reach its center.

If you must remove a large branch, use the three-cut method. Make the first cut on the underside of the limb, about 1 ft. (30 cm) from the main trunk. This cut, which should extend about one-quarter of the way through the limb, will keep the bark from tearing as the other cuts are made. Make the second cut from the top, about 1 in. (25 mm) outside of the first cut, away from the trunk. Cut all of the way through the limb, leaving a stub. With the weight of the branch relieved, make the third cut flush with the tree's branch collar, removing the stub.

Pruning evergreen conifers should be done in spring, when their new growth "candles" have sprouted. When shaping a conifer, make cuts within the new growth so that the tree will develop new sprouts and needles to fill in the cut. When you remove a branch from a conifer, remove it entirely down to the branch collar. Arborvitae, hemlock, juniper, yew, and other trees with branching habits can take heavier pruning than other conifers.

DEADHEADING

Many annual and perennial flowers that stop flowering once their seed develops will prolong their bloom if you pinch off, or deadhead, spent blossoms between your fingernails.

Deadhead weekly from late spring through autumn. For woody perennials and shrubs such as roses, use sharp hand pruners designed for small plants.

Pinch or cut the stalk just below its flower. For species that have new shoots, cut off the old flower stalks near the ground as new sprouts begin to emerge.

Your efforts will be richly rewarded with a prolonged, continual bloom of flowers.

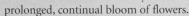

PRUNING OPTIONS

Thinning

Select three to five laterals from each main branch to retain, then remove the remainder.

Pruning can be performed to thin, shape, or maintain your shrubs and trees, or it can be used to create a foliage espalier or topiary. For large plants, you'll need sharp lopping shears; for smaller ones, use hand bypass pruners or hedge trimmers. Gather your materials and a cart to hold the trimmed foliage, choose the technique to use, and follow these easy steps:

Shaping

1 When shrubs grow together, prune them to create a new symmetrical outline and separate the plants.

2 Note the central stem or trunk of each plant, then remove foliage equally from each side, opening space between them.

Annual Pruning

1 Remove branches and laterals that cross the centerline of the tree. Trim off suckers and sprouts from the main trunk.

2 Make the tree more compact by pruning terminal branches at their ends, or at the forks of any divided branches.

Espalier

Gradually train espaliered branches to a sturdy lattice frame by binding them with tape and selectively pruning.

PESTS AND DISEASES

Once you have installed your landscape, many creatures—birds, insects, mollusks, arachnids, and amphibians—will move in to enjoy it with you. The vast majority of these creatures are harmless to your plants, and many dine on those that chew plant foliage and flowers. As the gardener, you are the manager, the referee, and the host of this open-air society that is your landscape's ecologic balance.

Pest and disease control begins with choosing plants that are suited to your climate [see USDA Plant Hardiness, pgs. 10–11]. They also should match your growing conditions, site, and soil. Whenever possible, select disease-resistant cultivars, and plant them in soil enriched with manure or compost to boost the population of helpful microorganisms. Healthy plants shrug off most insect attacks, bugs, and diseases.

Reduce the likelihood of significant disease infections, including many mildews, molds, and other fungi, by limiting overhead watering late in the day. Inspect your plants frequently, noting any damage from pests or diseases. Look everywhere as you walk through your yard—at the soil, stems, trunks, branches, and tops and undersides of leaves. When disease or infestation strikes, immediately remove the damaged foliage and discard it. This step helps avoid spreading spores and other disease organisms to healthy plants and it removes insect eggs and larvae from the garden.

Become acquainted with the most common insect pests and their predators, what they eat, and when to expect them. Even beneficial insects can look ferocious—one example is the orange-and-black lady beetle larva, a voracious predator of aphids and friend of gardeners.

As a good host, offer beneficial creatures shelter in rocks and leaf litter, a water source, and nectar and pollen plants to sip and eat. Many helpful insects are tiny and inhabit such flowers as cosmos, yarrow, and daisy. Birds are drawn to the garden and eat their weight in insects each week. Give flycatchers a place to nest and you'll be amply rewarded.

When you first notice plants with signs of insect or disease damage, wait before quick use of a pesticide or fungicide. Remember that there are other, preferred approaches. Many gardeners rely on a four-step method called Integrated Pest Management (IPM):

1. Identify the organism causing the problem. When unsure, bag the pest or affected foliage in clear plastic and take it to your garden center or a local extension office for identification.

2. Monitor the damage. How severe is it? Is it increasing or decreasing? Sometimes, letting nature take its course results in natural control.

3. Consider your expectations for levels of tolerable foliage and flower damage.

4. Take action, beginning with the lowest-impact treatment. Try the following in turn: hand picking, biological control with predator insects, plain soap solutions, insecticidal soaps, naturally occurring pesticides such as pyrethrin, and lastly, synthetic pesticides applied in a limited, focused manner.

(Top right) Grasshopper.

(Top) Aphids.

(Upper middle) Spider mites.

(Lower middle) Mosaic virus.

(Above) Black spot.

(Right) Beetles.

(Bottom right) Snail.

APPLYING GARDEN CHEMICALS

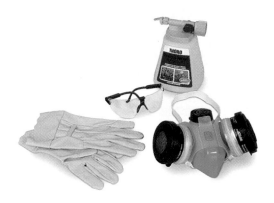

Most plant diseases are caused by fungus. Once established, they can be difficult to cure. Treat black spot, powdery mildew, and rust when they first appear. The same is true for many garden pests. Infections and infestations should be treated as a last resort with garden fungicides and pesticides that specifically list the problem on their labels. Always read completely and follow exactly the label directions. Wear protective clothing and a respirator when applying garden chemicals, and follow these steps to apply control agents directly to the affected area:

1 Read completely and follow exactly all directions on the package label, including warnings. Only apply control agents that specifically list the disease or insect and the plant that is affected. Wear protective clothing. Measure carefully and mix solutions in disposable containers.

2 Water thoroughly the day before application, taking care to avoid splashing the foliage. On a warm, wind-free day, apply the control to the affected area by spraying it directly on the pest or diseased areas; avoid broadcast spraying. Be sure to treat every foliage area, including the undersides of leaves, stems, and canes. Spray early in the day to allow the plant's foliage to completely dry.

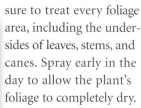

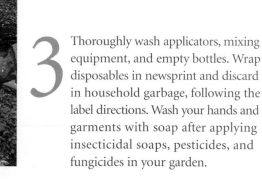

3 Thoroughly wash applicators, mixing equipment, and empty bottles. Wrap disposables in newsprint and discard in household garbage, following the label directions. Wash your hands and garments with soap after applying insecticidal soaps, pesticides, and fungicides in your garden.

PEST SYMPTOMS, CAUSES, AND CURES

Symptom	Cause	Cure
Leaves curled and twisted, often with a black sooty appearance. Stunted or deformed blooms on new growth.	Aphids. Look for soft-bodied, round, black, gray, green, or yellow insects, 1⁄16–1⁄4 inch (1.5–6 mm) long. Found on many plants. Frequently found in association with ants.	Wash off light infestations with a strong stream of water. If ineffective, spray with superior oil. Spray with botanical neem or pyrethrin as a last resort.
Foliage chewed, sometimes entire plants eaten, beginning at the edges of the garden and moving toward its center.	Armyworms. Look for smooth, brown, light green, sometimes striped caterpillars, 1¼ in. (32 mm) long, or green white eggs on leaf undersides.	Hand pick caterpillars from center leaves of plant. Release parasitic wasps and flies. Spray with *Bacillus thuringiensis* (BT). Apply horticultural oil in summer.
Weakened and defoliated trees and shrubs. Small, silken bags, about 1–2 in. (25–50 mm) long, hanging from branches.	Bagworms. Caterpillars hidden by silky bag. In North America, east of the Rocky Mountains. Found on deciduous plants and conifers; worst damage on arborvitae and cedars.	For small infestations, hand pick and destroy bags. For large infestations, spray with *Bacillus thuringiensis* (BT) as soon as young bagworms are noticed.
Green parts of leaves are removed and veins remain. Later, leaves are dry and skeletonized.	Beetles, including elm leaf beetles, Japanese beetles, and willow leaf beetles. Hard-shelled beetles are most active in the heat of the day.	Hand pick beetles on small shrubs in early morning while they are inactive. Apply milky spore (*Bacillus popilliae*) to lawns to give long-term control for Japanese beetle grubs.
Larvae tunnels found in fruit of trees such as apple, crabapple, peach, pear, plum.	Coddling moths. Look for cream, pink caterpillars with brown heads, to ¾ in. (19 mm) long, in fruit, or white, flat eggs on fruit spurs, twigs.	Set pheromone traps and release parasitic wasps. Spray parasitic nematodes on branches and trunks of fruit trees. Spray with ryania after flower petals fall every 2 weeks for 3 cycles.
Many chewed, eaten leaves, especially on petunias, other SOLANACEAE (nightshade) family plants.	Colorado potato beetles. Look for nearly round, striped, yellow orange adult beetles, ¼ in. (6 mm) long, or plump, black-spotted grubs, in spring.	Hand pick after shaking plant. Apply *Bacillus thuringiensis* (BT) directly to pest. Spray with botanical neem, pyrethrin, or rotenone as a last resort.
Seedlings cut off at ground level.	Cutworms. Look for smooth gray brown worm-like moth larvae under plant debris or just below soil surface.	Install cardboard collars, e.g., toilet-paper rolls, around plant stems, and sink 2 in. (50 mm) into the soil.
Chewed blossoms and petals, especially those with soft, fleshy parts.	Earwigs. Look for brown to black pests with sharp pincers extending from the rear part of their bodies.	Set out crumpled or rolled newspaper—earwigs will hide inside for later collection and destruction. Apply bait or spray with solutions containing sevin.
Silvery spots on upper surfaces of leaves; black spots on undersides of leaves.	Lacebugs. Bugs are 1⁄8–1⁄4 inch (3–6 mm) in length. Common during the growing season on elms, hawthorns, laurels, rhododendrons.	Wash off light infestations with a strong stream of water. If necessary, spray with superior oil. Spray with botanical neem or pyrethrin as a last resort.
Mottled white leaves; edges brown or yellow.	Leafhoppers. Look for small, green wedge-shaped insects.	Spray with insecticidal soap; many natural enemies will quickly control infestation.
White trails on or inside leaves; papery yellow or brown blotches on foliage.	Leaf miners. Look for small, pale larvae and 1⁄6-in. (4.2-mm) tiny, green or black, flying insects.	Remove infested leaves. Move plant to sheltered outdoor spot and spray foliage with neem oil extract solution.
Branches have curled leaves wrapped in a silky web.	Leaf rollers. Look in rolled leaves for green, hairy caterpillars, 1 in. (25 mm) long, or light brown, yellow egg clusters on tree branches.	Hand pick and destroy. Spray dormant oil in early spring before leaves emerge. Apply *Bacillus thuringiensis* (BT) directly to pest. Spray with pyrethrin or rotenone as a last resort.

PEST SYMPTOMS, CAUSES, AND CURES

Symptom	Cause	Cure
Stunted plants; white, cottony clusters in leaf axils (junction of leaf stem with branch).	Mealybugs. Look in the junctions between leaves and stems or at the base of leaf clusters for gray or white, waxy bugs, ⅛ in. (3 mm) long.	Dab or spray with rubbing alcohol diluted 3:1; spray with insecticidal soap; spray with horticultural oil.
Stunted, discolored, spotted plants with deformed roots, sometimes bearing swollen galls; loss of vigor.	Nematodes, microscopic wormlike creatures that live in soil and feed on plant roots.	Release beneficial nematodes. Remove and destroy affected plants. Replant with unrelated species. Solarize bed for 3–4 weeks prior to planting by covering soil with clear plastic and allowing sunlight to raise soil temperature to 140°F (60°C).
Leaves with brown or black spots. Roots and shoots may be deformed.	Plant bugs. Look for greenish yellow insects ¼ in. (6 mm) long.	Hand pick. Spray with insecticidal soap. If infestation is severe, spray affected areas with pyrethrin or rotenone.
Stunted, yellow plants lacking vigor; leaves may drop.	Scales. Look for ⅟₂₀-in. (1.2-mm) flylike insects accompanying soft or hard ⅟₅₀-in. (0.5-mm) mounded bumps on stems and leaves.	Remove infested foliage. Swab scales with soapy water or dilute denatured alcohol solution; rinse well after solution dries. Apply horticutural oil. Spray with pyrethrin, rotenone.
Leaves are bronzed or yellowed, curled, and dried; may fall off. Plants stunted. Webs may be present.	Spider mites and other mites. Microscopic size and therefore difficult to see. Prevalent in hot, dry areas on both conifers and deciduous plants.	Wash off light infestations with a strong stream of water. If necessary, spray with insecticidal soap. Spray with a miticide as a last resort.
In spring and summer, silky webs, or tents, appear in the forks of small limbs, and leaves are eaten. In winter, masses of eggs encircle stems, appearing as a band.	Tent caterpillars. Adult caterpillars are 1–2 in. (25–50 mm) long with short, fuzzy bodies. Common only on deciduous trees and shrubs.	In winter, remove egg masses from bare branches. In spring, prune branches with small tents and destroy clippings. If necessary, spray with insecticidal soap or *Bacillus thuringiensis* (BT).
Brown-, silver-, or white-speckled leaves; may be gummy or deformed. Blooms are deformed and fail to open.	Thrips. Shake foliage and blossoms over white paper and look for moving, winged specks. Thrive in hot, dry conditions.	Release lady beetles. Spray with water; spray with insecticidal soap; avoid use of sprays that kill natural predators. Remove and destroy infested foliage.
Spotted, sometimes semi-transluscent leaves, frequently accompanied by fungal disease.	Stem borers. Look on foliage, roots for segmented larvae and caterpillars, ½–1 in. (12–25 mm) long. In corn-farming regions, corn borer may infest dahlia, gladiolus.	Hand pick; apply *Bacillus thuringiensis* (BT) to affected foliage. Remove and destroy infested foliage.
In summer and autumn, silky webs appear at the tip end of branches, with larvae visible inside. Leaves are chewed.	Webworms. Adult fall webworms are about 1 in. (25 mm) long, with a dark stripe down their backs. Common on deciduous trees and shrubs.	Prune and destroy branches infected with webs. If necessary, spray with *Bacillus thuringiensis* (BT) after breaking open web with a stick.
Yellow leaves and stunted, sticky plants. When foliage is shaken, a cloud of white insects may fly up.	Whiteflies. Shake foliage and look for ⅟₂₀-in. (1.2-mm) mothlike, flying insects. Inspect leaf undersides for scalelike, gray or yellow eggs.	Catch with sticky traps. Spray with soap solution. Spray infested foliage with insecticidal soap. Move plant to sheltered outdoor spot and spray foliage with horticultural oil or neem oil extract solution. Spray with pyrethrin.
Uprooted plants; foliage eaten to ground level; bulbs and roots eaten, leaving dying foliage stalks and leaves.	Deer and rodents. Look for hoof and paw prints, burrows, mounds, tunnels.	Plant resistant plants. Install fence barriers or cages when planting, including beneath-soil barriers. Trap and remove. Avoid bone-meal use.
Chewed leaves and blossoms; silvery mucus trails.	Slugs and snails. Look after dark for shelled and unshelled mollusks on foliage or soil.	Remove leaf litter, which is used as a hiding place. Hand pick after dark; use copper foil barriers around beds or containers; dust with diatomaceous earth; use non-toxic baits containing iron phosphate; use bait gel.

DISEASE SYMPTOMS, CAUSES, AND CURES

Symptom	Cause	Remedies
Black, tan, or red spots on leaves; leaves yellow and drop. Black cankers on stems, with a general wilt of branch tips.	Anthracnose. A fungal disease sometimes called black spot or twig blight. Occurs in late spring and summer, typically after humid conditions.	Remove infected leaves and branch tips. Collect and destroy infected fallen leaves. Thin excessive growth to promote air circulation. Spray with a fungicide as a last resort.
White, yellow splotches appear on surface of leaves; leaves yellow and drop. Plants appear stunted, turn green yellow. Some flower petals may be green.	Aster yellows. Incurable viral disease of asters and other plants spread by aphids, leafhoppers.	Remove and destroy infected plants. Spray remaining plants with insecticidal soap weekly for 3 cycles.
Leaves are mottled with black spots, eventually yellow and die.	Black spot. A fungal disease, found on many plants but widespread on roses. Spreads by spores blown onto moist plant leaves.	Space plantings to allow good air circulation. Apply water at base of plant. Strip and destroy infected leaves. Spray with a solution of 1 part household bleach mixed with 9 parts water.
Flowers collapse under heavy fuzz of brown or gray fungal spores.	Botrytis rot, also known as gray mold.	Remove affected blossoms, foliage, or entire plant; space plants for more air circulation; reduce nitrogen fertilizer.
Brown stains and softened tissue near base of stem or crown of plant; leaves may yellow, drop.	Crown or stem rot. Look for decaying stems. Usually associated with keeping soil overly moist.	Rarely curable; remove infected foliage, dipping pruning shears in isopropyl alcohol solution between cuts. Reduce watering. Repot to soil-free, well-drained mix. Root cuttings of healthy growth.
Young twigs and branches die back, starting at tip ends. Leaves shrivel and turn brown. Tips of twigs curl to resemble a hook.	Fireblight. A bacterial disease common on crab-apples, ornamental pears, and quinces. Infection occurs in early spring and is favored by cool, wet conditions.	Prune out branches 6 in. (15 cm) below signs of damage. Dip pruning tool in isopropyl alcohol after each cut to sterilize and prevent spreading infection. Avoid heavy nitrogen fertilization.
Leaves turn light green and are puffy, swollen, and distorted.	Leaf gall. A fungal disease found on azaleas, camellias, and rhododendrons.	Pick off and destroy affected leaves as soon as galls are noticed.
Powdery black or brown dusting on foliage and blossoms; leaves may drop.	Leaf spot. A fungal disease. Common in shady, massed plantings.	Remove shading foliage. Increase air circulation. Spray with sulfur fungicide.
Streaked and mottled foliage, deformed blooms; stunting; loss of vigor.	Mosaic virus. An incurable plant disease.	Remove and destroy affected plants. Promptly control aphid, spider mite, thrips infestations, which can spread viral infection. Plant resistant bulb types.
Leaves have white to grayish, powdery patches, as though they have been dusted with flour.	Powdery mildew. A fungal disease prevalent when days are hot and nights are cool. Mostly attacks new leaves.	Thin branches to improve air circulation. Spray with a 0.5% solution of baking soda (sodium bicarbonate): 1 tsp. (5 ml) baking soda per quart [1 l] of water.
Blades of grass and leaves are marked with pale spots above, brown, red, round spots on their undersides; leaves may brown and drop.	Rust. Wipe grass or leaf on white cloth, which stains orange, pink. Common on bluegrass, ryegrass, some ornamental grasses.	Plant resistant cultivars. Fertilize with nitrogen monthly until symptoms subside. Mow turfgrass to height recommended for the species.
Center of plant becomes soft and turns brown. Strong odor is present in diseased plant tissue.	Soft rot. A bacterial disease, usually begun on bruised plant tissue. Usually incurable.	Remove and destroy infected plants. Avoid replanting species in same soil for 2–3 years.

INDEX OF PLANTS

GENERAL INDEX